HEALTH AND INEQUALITY

RESEARCH ON ECONOMIC INEQUALITY

Series Editors: John Bishop and
 Juan Gabriel Rodríguez

RESEARCH ON ECONOMIC INEQUALITY VOLUME 21

HEALTH AND INEQUALITY

EDITED BY

PEDRO ROSA DIAS
Department of Economics, University of Sussex, UK

OWEN O'DONNELL
*Erasmus School of Economics,
Erasmus University Rotterdam, the Netherlands;
University of Macedonia, Greece*

Emerald

United Kingdom – North America – Japan
India – Malaysia – China

Emerald Group Publishing Limited
Howard House, Wagon Lane, Bingley BD16 1WA, UK

First edition 2013

Copyright © 2013 Emerald Group Publishing Limited

Reprints and permission service
Contact: permissions@emeraldinsight.com

No part of this book may be reproduced, stored in a retrieval system, transmitted in any form or by any means electronic, mechanical, photocopying, recording or otherwise without either the prior written permission of the publisher or a licence permitting restricted copying issued in the UK by The Copyright Licensing Agency and in the USA by The Copyright Clearance Center. Any opinions expressed in the chapters are those of the authors. Whilst Emerald makes every effort to ensure the quality and accuracy of its content, Emerald makes no representation implied or otherwise, as to the chapters' suitability and application and disclaims any warranties, express or implied, to their use.

British Library Cataloguing in Publication Data
A catalogue record for this book is available from the British Library

ISBN: 978-1-78190-553-1
ISSN: 1049-2585 (Series)

ISOQAR certified Management System, awarded to Emerald for adherence to Environmental standard ISO 14001:2004.

Certificate Number 1985
ISO 14001

INVESTOR IN PEOPLE

CONTENTS

LIST OF CONTRIBUTORS   ix

INTRODUCTION   xiii

PART I: MEASUREMENT OF HEALTH INEQUALITY

LOST IN TRANSLATION: RETHINKING THE INEQUALITY EQUIVALENCE CRITERIA FOR BOUNDED HEALTH VARIABLES
Gustav Kjellsson and Ulf-G. Gerdtham   3

MEASURING THE INEQUALITY OF BOUNDED DISTRIBUTIONS: A JOINT ANALYSIS OF ATTAINMENTS AND SHORTFALLS
Oihana Aristondo and Casilda Lasso de la Vega   33

MEASURING HEALTH INEQUALITY WITH CATEGORICAL DATA: SOME REGIONAL PATTERNS
Joan Costa Font and Frank Cowell   53

INEQUALITY AND BI-POLARIZATION IN SOCIOECONOMIC STATUS AND HEALTH: ORDINAL APPROACHES
Bénédicte Apouey and Jacques Silber   77

ON THE MEASUREMENT OF THE (MULTIDIMENSIONAL) INEQUALITY OF HEALTH DISTRIBUTIONS
Jens Leth Hougaard, Juan D. Moreno-Ternero and Lars Peter Østerdal   111

EQUITY IN HEALTH AND EQUIVALENT INCOMES
Erik Schokkaert, Carine Van de Voorde, Brigitte Dormont, Marc Fleurbaey, Stéphane Luchini, Anne-Laure Samson and Clémence Thébaut   *131*

REFERENCE VALUE SENSITIVITY OF MEASURES OF UNFAIR HEALTH INEQUALITY
Pilar García-Gómez, Erik Schokkaert and Tom Van Ourti   *157*

ACCOUNTING FOR POPULATION CHANGE IN THE LONGITUDINAL ANALYSIS OF INCOME-RELATED HEALTH INEQUALITIES
Paul Allanson and Dennis Petrie   *193*

REGRESSION-BASED DECOMPOSITIONS OF RANK-DEPENDENT INDICATORS OF SOCIOECONOMIC INEQUALITY OF HEALTH
Guido Erreygers and Roselinde Kessels   *227*

PART II: DETERMINANTS OF HEALTH INEQUALITY

HEALTH INEQUALITIES THROUGH THE LENS OF HEALTH-CAPITAL THEORY: ISSUES, SOLUTIONS, AND FUTURE DIRECTIONS
Titus J. Galama and Hans van Kippersluis   *263*

THE DEVELOPMENTAL ORIGINS OF HEALTH INEQUALITY
Gabriella Conti   *285*

THE CONTRIBUTION OF OCCUPATION TO HEALTH INEQUALITY
Bastian Ravesteijn, Hans van Kippersluis and Eddy van Doorslaer   *311*

PART III: INEQUALITY OF OPPORTUNITY IN HEALTH

INEQUALITY OF OPPORTUNITIES IN HEALTH AND THE PRINCIPLE OF NATURAL REWARD: EVIDENCE FROM EUROPEAN COUNTRIES
Damien Bricard, Florence Jusot, Alain Trannoy and Sandy Tubeuf   335

EX-ANTE AND *EX-POST* MEASUREMENT OF INEQUALITY OF OPPORTUNITY IN HEALTH: EVIDENCE FROM ISRAEL
Adi Lazar   371

PART IV: EMPIRICAL STUDIES OF HEALTH INEQUALITY

EARLY LIFE CONDITIONS AND LATER LIFE INEQUALITY IN HEALTH
Maarten Lindeboom and Reyn van Ewijk   399

WEALTH, HEALTH, AND THE MEASUREMENT OF MULTIDIMENSIONAL INEQUALITY: EVIDENCE FROM THE MIDDLE EAST AND NORTH AFRICA
Mohammad Abu-Zaineh and Ramses H. Abul Naga   421

INCOME INEQUALITY, HEALTH AND DEVELOPMENT – IN SEARCH OF A PATTERN
Therese Nilsson and Andreas Bergh   441

PART V: EQUITY IN HEALTH CARE

EQUITY IN HEALTH CARE DELIVERY: SOME THOUGHTS AND AN EXAMPLE
John E. Roemer   471

MEASURING HEALTH INEQUALITY IN THE CONTEXT OF COST-EFFECTIVENESS ANALYSIS
Miqdad Asaria, Susan Griffin and Richard Cookson   491

LIST OF CONTRIBUTORS

Mohammad Abu-Zaineh	INSERM-IRD-University of Aix-Marseille, Aix-Marseille School of Economics (AMSE), Economics & Social Sciences, Health and Medical Information Processing (SESSTIM-UMR 912), Marseille, France
Ramses H. Abul Naga	Business School, Health Economics Research Unit & Centre for European Labor Market Research, University of Aberdeen, Aberdeen, UK
Paul Allanson	University of Dundee Perth Road, Dundee, UK
Bénédicte Apouey	Paris School of Economics – CNRS, Paris, France
Oihana Aristondo	BRiDGE Research Group, University of the Basque Country, UPV-EHU, Spain
Miqdad Asaria	Centre for Health Economics, University of York, Heslington, York, UK
Andreas Bergh	The Research Institute for Industrial Economics (IFN), Sweden; Department of Economics, Lund University, Sweden
Damien Bricard	PSL, Université Paris-Dauphine, Leda-Legos, France
Richard Cookson	Centre for Health Economics, University of York, Heslington, York, UK
Gabriella Conti	Department of Applied Health Research, University College London, London, UK
Joan Costa Font	London School of Economics, London, UK

LIST OF CONTRIBUTORS

Frank Cowell	London School of Economics, London, UK
Eddy van Doorslaer	Erasmus School of Economics; Tinbergen Institute, The Netherlands
Brigitte Dormont	PSL, Université Paris-Dauphine, Leda-Legos, France
Guido Erreygers	Department of Economics, University of Antwerp, Antwerp, Belgium
Reyn van Ewijk	IMBEI, University Medical Centre Mainz; Department of Economics, University of Mainz, Germany; Department of Economics, VU University Amsterdam, The Netherlands
Marc Fleurbaey	Princeton University, Princeton, NJ, USA
Titus J. Galama	Dornsife College Center for Economic and Social Research, University of Southern California, Los Angeles; RAND Corporation, Santa Monica, CA, USA
Pilar García-Gómez	Erasmus School of Economics, Erasmus University Rotterdam; Tinbergen Institute, The Netherlands
Ulf-G. Gerdtham	Department of Economics, Health Economics & Management, Institute of Economic Research; Center for Primary Health Care Research, Malmö University Hospital, Lund University, Sweden
Susan Griffin	Centre for Health Economics, University of York, Heslington, York, UK
Jens Leth Hougaard	Department of Food and Resource Economics, University of Copenhagen, Denmark
Florence Jusot	Université de Rouen CREAM & PSL, Université Paris-Dauphine, Leda-Legos, France

List of Contributors

Roselinde Kessels	Department of Economics & StatUa Center for Statistics, University of Antwerp, Antwerp, Belgium
Gustav Kjellsson	Department of Economics, Lund University; Health Economics & Management Institute of Economic Research, Lund University, Sweden
Casilda Lasso de la Vega	BRiDGE Research Group, University of the Basque Country, UPV-EHU, Spain
Adi Lazar	Department of Economics, Bar-Ilan University, Ramat-Gan, Israel
Maarten Lindeboom	Department of Economics, VU University, Amsterdam, The Netherlands
Stéphane Luchini	Aix-Marseille University (Aix-Marseille School of Economics) & CNRS & EHESS, Paris, France
Juan D. Moreno-Ternero	Department of Economics, Universidad Pablo de Olavide, Seville, Spain; CORE, Université catholique de Louvain, Louvain-la-Neuve, Belgium
Therese Nilsson	Department of Economics and Center for Economic Demography, Lund University, Sweden; The Research Institute for Industrial Economics (IFN), Sweden
Dennis Petrie	Centre for Health Policy Programs & Economics, Melbourne School of Population Health, University of Melbourne, Melbourne, Australia
Bastian Ravesteijn	Erasmus School of Economics, Erasmus University Rotterdam; Tinbergen Institute, The Netherlands
John E. Roemer	Departments of Political Science and Economics, Yale University, New Haven, CT, USA

Anne-Laure Samson	PSL, Université Paris-Dauphine, Leda-Legos, France
Erik Schokkaert	Department of Economics, University of Leuven; CORE, Université catholique de Louvain, Leuven, Belgium
Jacques Silber	Department of Economics, Bar-Ilan University, Ramat-Gan, Israel; CEPS/INSTEAD, Esch-sur-Alzette, Luxembourg
Clémence Thébaut	Haute Autorité Santé, France
Alain Trannoy	Aix-Marseille University (Aix-Marseille School of Economics), EHESS & CNRS, Paris, France
Sandy Tubeuf	Academic Unit of Health Economics, University of Leeds, West Yorkshire, UK
Carine Van de Voorde	Department of Economics, University of Leuven, Leuven, Belgium
Hans van Kippersluis	Erasmus School of Economics, Erasmus University Rotterdam; Tinbergen Institute, The Netherlands
Tom Van Ourti	Erasmus School of Economics, Erasmus University Rotterdam; Tinbergen Institute, The Netherlands
Lars Peter Østerdal	Department of Business and Economics, Centre of Health Economics Research, University of Southern Denmark, Odense, Denmark

INTRODUCTION

Research on economic inequality is concerned with differences in incomes and wealth. Economic research on inequality casts its net more widely and is increasingly turning attention to differences in health. Google Scholar turns up 1,380 articles with 'health' and 'inequality' in the title, and a further 290 with 'mortality' and 'inequality', compared with 4,480 with 'income' and 'inequality'. Most research on inequality focusses on the economic dimension but there is a very substantial body of work that looks at health.

Inequality in health (often referred to as health disparity) is a core topic of the discipline of public health. But what motivates economists to sharpen their tools in readiness for putting them to use on a subject matter — differences in health — that might be considered beyond their domain of expertise? It may be realisation that ill-health is a constraint on earnings power. Economic inequality is, to an extent, a reflection of health inequality. While this realisation may motivate some, and it is a strong stimulus for economic analysis of population health in low-income countries, it is unlikely to explain the growing interest in health inequality among economists in recent years. A more probable explanation is the trend away from the more narrow focus on inequality in income to the more encompassing analysis of inequality in well-being, along with recognition that health, like economic resources, is a core determinant of welfare. Researchers interested in establishing the extent to which well-being differs across individuals, why it differs and whether the differences are narrowing or widening cannot but turn their analytical gaze on health inequalities.

This 21st volume of Research on Economic Inequality series is devoted to the topic of *Health and Inequality*. Interpretation of the subject is sufficiently wide to embrace analysis of inequality in health, income-related inequality in health, inequality of opportunity in health, multi-dimensional inequality in income and health, economic inequality as a determinant of health and equity in the distribution of health care. The volume contains 19 chapters divided into five parts. Part I, which includes around two-fifths of the chapters, deals with methods for the measurement of health inequality, income-related health inequality and multi-dimensional inequality in income and health. Part II is concerned not with measurement but with development of an understanding of the determinants of health inequalities using the tools of the economist's trade. Part III contains two analyses of inequality of opportunity in health, which is rapidly becoming one of the main outcomes examined with this approach. Part IV of the volume contains three other empirical studies. The final part switches attention from health to health care. It includes one chapter that considers the appropriate definition of equity in the distribution of health care resources, drawing on the equality of opportunity apparatus, and another that explores how concerns for health inequality may be taken into account in analysis of the efficient allocation of health care.

The economic literature on health inequality and equity began by borrowing techniques developed for the measurement of income inequality and tax progression and applying them to health, health care and health finance variables (Wagstaff, Paci, & van Doorslaer, 1991; Wagstaff & van Doorslaer, 2000). In the last 10 years, the literature has moved on from the passive adoption of indices designed to satisfy axioms that are appealing within the context of income inequality to consideration of whether these indices have the same properties, and indeed whether the properties are equally desirable, in relation to inequality in health outcomes that typically have substantially different measurement characteristics to income. A number of the chapters in Part I continue with this reappraisal, considering whether the measurement tools being applied are suitable for the job at hand and honing those that are not.

The measurement issue that has probably received most attention in the literature is the bounding of many health outcomes from above. The most extreme case is when the health outcome is binary, for example dead or alive, disabled or not, immunised or not. With such phenomena one can measure inequality in either *attainments* towards the state of perfect health, or *shortfalls* from that state. Hitherto it has generally been thought desirable that comparison across populations is not sensitive to whether one measures inequality in attainments or inequality in shortfalls. The literature has largely concentrated on identifying indices that do not have this property and proposing alternatives that do.

Two chapters make enlightening contributions to the reasoning on this issue. Gustav Kjellsson and Ulf-G. Gerdtham provide a compass for the analyst who has lost his bearings concerning the type of inequality measured by a variety of indices that have been proposed. They uncover the value judgements implicit in common rank-dependent inequality measures for bounded health outcomes. The surplus sharing approach – how an

Introduction

infinitesimal additional amount of health must be distributed in order to keep the measured degree of inequality constant – is used to reveal Inequality Equivalence Criteria (IEC) for such outcomes. The IEC encapsulates the value judgement concerning the distributional change that represents an increase/decrease in inequality. The authors suggest their own IEC that lies between those that are implicit in the two most popular inequality indices for bounded health measures – those of Wagstaff (2005) and Erreygers (2009).

The subtle message is that adoption of an inequality index consistent with a particular value judgement when applied to income is imprudent since the index may imply a different ethical position when applied to a bounded health measure. What we mean by inequality gets lost in translation in moving from the income to the health domain. In fact, the meaning can even be distorted in applying the same index across different measures of the same underlying health phenomenon. The value judgement implicit in the index can depend on whether one measures inequality in attainments or shortfalls.

Oihana Aristondo and Casilda Lasso de la Vega, partially aided by Kjellsson and Gerdtham's compass, propose a route out of the quagmire. They propose indices that reflect inequality in both attainments and shortfalls each of which is invariant with respect to a particular transformation of the joint distribution of the two measures of health. The transformations are defined by expressing deviations of both attainments and shortfalls from the respective means as differences (absolute invariance), ratios (relative invariance) or a combination of the two (intermediate invariance). Any standard (univariate) inequality measure can then be applied to the respectively defined deviations. The resulting index inherits the basic properties of the standard inequality measure. Within the class of indices that arises, the authors identify a family of those that are decomposable and which are consistent with the IEC proposed by Kjellsson and Gerdtham. Applied researchers may be relieved to learn that, within this family, the inequality index of the joint distribution is simply the arithmetic mean of the standard index applied to both attainments and shortfalls.

The measurement of health is frequently even more constrained than that offered by bounded, and yet still cardinal, outcomes. The health information available from surveys is often restricted to identifying ordinal levels of health with no cardinal interpretation of the differences between those levels. The most commonly used health measure from survey data – self-assessed health (SAH) – identifies a label out of four or five (e.g. excellent, ..., poor) selected by the respondent as the best description of his overall health.

Approaches to the measurement of inequality, or polarization, in the distribution of ordinal health variables, such as SAH, have been suggested (Allison & Foster, 2004; Abul Naga & Yalcin, 2007; Apouey, 2007). Joan Costa Font and Frank Cowell propose adoption of the approach of Cowell and Flachaire (2012), which unlike that of Abul Naga and Yalcin (2007) does not require definition of quantiles of the health outcome. Instead, it simply aggregates across the population a transformation of the number of individuals with either better or worse health than each person. This approach is illustrated using data from the World Health Survey. The results establish some regional patters and indicate that international inequality rankings may change considerably according to whether health status of each individual is defined with respect to better or worse states of health.

Previously proposed methods for measuring inequality in ordinal health outcomes have been restricted to capturing dispersion in the marginal distribution of health. Often interest lies in the degree to which differences in health are related to differences in some measure of socio-economic status (SES). Bénédicte Apouey and Jacques Silber propose two approaches to the measurement of inequality and bi-polarization in health and SES when both of these outcomes are measured on ordinal scales only. The first measures the degree of dependence between health and SES. The second is sensitive to inequality in the marginal distributions of health and SES, as well as the association between the two. The measures are used to compare inequality and bi-polarization in SAH and income categories through time and across 24 European countries.

Fleurbaey and Schokkaert (2012, p. 1008) emphasise that health is inherently multi-dimensional and so health inequality measures should quantify the joint disparities in its relevant dimensions. Jens Leth Hougaard, Juan D. Moreno-Ternero, and Lars Peter Østerdal respond to this challenge and propose a measure that captures inequality in two fundamental dimensions: quality of life and longevity. They impose standard assumptions on social preferences over health profiles, incorporating quantity and quality of life. Grounded on these assumptions, a family of population health evaluation functions can be derived, which ranks health profiles according to social preferences over the distribution of healthy year equivalents. This procedure is reminiscent of the approach proposed by Maasoumi (1986) to deal with multi-attribute social evaluation: first, for each individual, a utility function is used to aggregate his allocation of the several attributes into a (unidimensional) summary measure of well-being; second, a univariate inequality index is applied to the distribution of this summary measure.

Introduction

While health itself is multi-dimensional, it is also one domain of individual well-being. Most of the bourgeoning research in recent years on the measurement of inequality in well-being has cited health as the main dimension of welfare, along with income. The most popular approach taken in this literature, followed by Apouey and Silber (2013), is to construct an index that is sensitive to the marginal distribution of each dimension, as well as the association between them. Erik Schokkaert, Carine Van de Voorde, Brigitte Dormont, Marc Fleurbaey, Stéphane Luchini, Anne-Laure Samson, and Clémence Thébaut take a different approach that has been proposed by Fleurbaey (2005) together with François Maniquet (Fleurbaey & Maniquet, 2011). Rather than evaluate an index over the joint distribution of dimensions of well-being, as with Maasoumi (1986), the dimensions are collapsed to one and standard unidimensional inequality measures (Gini in this case) are applied to this. This is analogous to approach adopted by Moreno-Ternero, Houthgard and Østerdal in the preceding chapter. Whereas the latter transform information on quality of life into the scale of the length of life to produce *healthy years equivalents*, Schokkaert et al. transform health information to the income scale to get *healthy equivalent income*. That is, the income in combination with a state of perfect health that would generate the same welfare, given the individual's own preferences, as the actual income and health possessed. The main contribution of the paper is to demonstrate that empirical implementation of the concept of equivalent income is feasible using reported willingness-to-pay for health from a representative survey in France.

Progressing from the measurement of health inequality to that of health equity requires narrowing the focus from the total variation in health to that which is considered to arise from injustice of some kind or another. This might be done by holding ethically legitimate determinants of health constant (however those are defined) and evaluating the variation driven by the illegitimate determinants. Alternatively, one might examine inequality across individuals in the divergence of the health of each from the health he would enjoy given characteristics considered to be ethically legitimate determinants of health. Implementation of these approaches requires obtaining predictions from an estimated model of health in which the values of either legitimate or illegitimate determinants of health are fixed (across the sample) at some vector of values. The measured degree of absolute health inequity will depend on the values chosen unless the model of health is additively separable in the legitimate and illegitimate determinants (Fleurbaey & Schokkaert, 2009). Relative measures will depend on these reference values even with additive separability.

Erik Schokkaert, Pilar García-Gómez, and Tom Van Ourti demonstrate that the sensitivity extends beyond the magnitude of an inequality index to the direction of change in unfair health inequality arising from comparison of simulated distributions under alternative policy scenarios. Far from being innocuous, the choice of reference values might result in predicting a fall, rather than a rise, in health inequity. This is an unsettling message for empirical researchers. The authors recognise that it calls for the development of theory to guide what has hitherto been a rather *ad hoc* choice. In the interim, they outline a statistical approach to the selection of reference values that can be implemented by analysts.

A particularly widespread practical use of health inequality measures is for monitoring purposes. A ministry of health may compare the degree of health inequality across regions within a country. The WHO (2013a) monitors health equity across 90 low- and middle-income countries. Besides geographic comparisons, an integral part of monitoring is to assess progress through time. Has health inequality in country X fallen over the last ten years? Has it fallen by more, or at a greater rate, than in country Y? It is answers to these questions that can immediately grab the attention senior policy makers. Methods are required that identify changes in health inequality over time that arise from substantive changes in the distribution of the disease burden, the structure of society, the economy or policy, rather than being mere artefacts of change in the population composition.

Paul Allanson and Dennis Petrie develop a general framework to identify the impact of multiple sources of (adult) population entry (immigration, ageing) and exit (emigration, death), as well as sample attrition or intermittent survey response, on the change in the concentration index measure of income-related health inequality. While some of these population changes may be considered to be confounding factors, mortality clearly is not. Treating death as a form of attrition and re-weighting the sample such that it remains representative of the population as it was in the first period is to ignore the most dramatic health changes that have occurred over time. Instead, Allanson and Petrie treat death as the minimum point on a cardinal scale of health. Applying their method to British panel data covering 1999 to 2004, the authors reveal that not taking proper account of mortality and of the rate of entry of youths into adulthood (at which point they report health) results in a substantial underestimation of the rise in income-related health inequality in Britain over the period.

The analytical tools for health inequality monitoring are currently being established (WHO, 2013b). Methods such as that proposed by Allanson and Petrie need to be incorporated into the toolkit in order to minimise the

Introduction xix

risk of breaking unduly pessimistic, or optimistic, news to the minister responsible for public health.

A popular method of 'explaining' socio-economic-related health inequality measured by a rank-dependent index, such as the concentration index, has been to write the index as a sum of contributions of factors that are correlated with both health and socio-economic rank. The typical method has been derived from a regression model for health, such that each contribution is the product of the factor's health regression parameter and its concentration index, measuring association with SES rank. Guido Erreygers and Roselinde Kessels point out that alternative decompositions of the same index are possible by using regressions for (a) SES rank, (b) both health and SES rank and (c) the product of health and SES rank. They also show that depending upon the (mathematically equivalent) formula for the rank-dependent index from which the decomposition is derived, it will or will not include a constant term. The alternative ways of decomposing the same inequality index produce very different results. The same factor can contribute to either pro-poor or pro-rich inequality in health depending on the method. Inclusion of a constant or not in the decomposition makes a big difference. When included, the contribution of the constant is large (often multiples of the index itself) and, consequently, greatly changes the contributions of the other factors.

On the basis of these results, the authors warn that researchers should be cautious of reading too much into decomposition results that may be very sensitive to the formula and regression from which the decomposition is derived. They note that techniques introduced for the explanation of univariate income inequality are not necessarily suited to the explanation of bivariate SES-related health inequality and call for an axiomatic approach to provide a stronger foundation to the understanding of health inequality.

The basic question addressed in Part II is, 'Why do health inequalities exist'? Titus J. Galama and Hans van Kippersluis argue that with extensions to accommodate decreasing returns to scale in health technology, a health cost of work, distinction between healthy and unhealthy consumption, the Grossman (1972) health capital model provides a useful conceptual framework for understanding a number of empirical phenomena regarding socio-economic inequalities in health, including the widening of inequalities until around retirement age and subsequent narrowing. However, further extensions are required to better understand stylised facts that, as yet, are largely unexplained. First, they recommend development of a joint model of human and health capital in order to provide insight into the mechanisms driving what appears to be a causal impact of education on health. Second, recognising the growing importance being attached to early life and childhood conditions for later life economic circumstances and health, they advocate the addition of a childhood phase during which investments in both health and human capital are undertaken.

Gabriella Conti also addresses the causes of health inequalities. She reviews the most recent evidence on the developmental origins of health inequalities and shows that these tend to open up early in life and to be amplified through biologic and behavioural channels. While disadvantaged early life conditions may harm individuals permanently, remedial action is often possible. She thus argues that, from a policy perspective, a key challenge is to design interventions that allow nurturing human development at times when biology is still amenable to change. Recent evidence from biology, neuroscience, psychology and the use of animal models is essential to identify the correct timing and the nature of such interventions.

While most descriptive economic research on socio-economic-related health inequality focusses on the health-income relationship (at least in Europe), evidence that income exerts a substantial causal effect on health in high-income countries is actually rather weak (O'Donnell, van Doorslaer, & Van Ourti, 2014). Some third factor, possibly another dimension of SES, appears to be mainly responsible for the strongly positive health-income correlation. Some fingers point to occupation. The low paid may be confined to physically demanding jobs that take a toll on health. Bastian Ravesteijn, Eddy van Doorslaer and Hans van Kippersluis weigh the evidence with the aid of the Galama and van Kippersluis model to identify the mechanisms that may be responsible for the extremely large differences in health and mortality rates by occupation. They argue that selection effects are likely to be strong. The most physically and mentally frail will be constrained with respect both to entrance jobs and career opportunities. They also emphasise behavioural responses to occupational health hazards. These could go either way. Unhealthy working conditions may be compensated by a healthy lifestyle. But health hazards at work may reduce the expected returns to investments in health through exercise, diet etc. The potential selection and behavioural effects, along with the scarcity of truly exogenous variation in occupation, make it extremely difficult to obtain convincing evidence on the causal effect of work on health. Work may well be one of the strongest socio-economic determinants of health but we are unlikely to know this for sure for some time yet.

Among the normative criteria proposed to ascertain the fairness of health distributions, equality of opportunity has attracted growing attention from applied researchers, policy makers and international organisations such as

Introduction xxi

the World Bank (Paes de Barros, Ferreira, Molinas Vega, & Saavedra Chanduvi, 2008; World Bank, 2005). In general, health outcomes are caused both by circumstances beyond individual control, such as parental background and by factors that reflect individual effort, such as lifestyle. According to the inequality of opportunity approach, only inequalities caused by the first set of factors lead to unfair inequalities. Adi Lazar measures inequality of opportunity in health in Israel. Her analysis reveals that nearly 80% of inequalities in health outcomes are explained by circumstances beyond individual control (such as parental background, ethnicity, religion and place of birth).Damien Bricard, Florence Jusot, Alain Trannoy and Sandy Tubeuf find that the equivalent figure is 50—60% in 13 European countries. These authors addresses an important methodological question. If inequalities due to circumstances are considered unfair and those due to individual effort are justified, how should the applied researcher deal with the correlation between circumstances and effort? They examine the consequences of adopting conflicting normative views about these correlations on the measurement of inequality of opportunity and show that this affects the measured degree of health inequity in some countries. This is an issue that needs to be taken into account by applied researchers.

Childhood circumstances have been shown to have long-lasting effects on health and human development, thereby contributing to the perpetuation of inequalities of opportunity in health. Maarten Lindeboom and Reyn Van Ewijk examine the effect of *in utero* exposure to the Great Depression (in the decade preceding World War II) on health disparities in a sample of individuals aged 71—91 from eight European countries. They find that early-life macro-economic circumstances do not affect health, and health inequalities, at advanced ages. This result, which is partially inconsistent with previous evidence, is attributed to the effect of selective mortality, which is likely to mask the impact of early-life circumstances on health inequalities amongst older individuals.

The literature on the measurement of health inequalities when health is treated as multi-dimensional, or part of a multi-dimensional concept of wellbeing, is recent and has remained largely theoretical. Mohammad Abu-Zaineh and Ramses H. Abul Naga innovate by applying the method proposed by Abul Naga and Geoffard (2006) to data from the World Health Survey on health and income in a set of Middle Eastern and North African countries. They uncover interesting regional patterns in bivariate inequality in health and income. Moreover, decomposition reveals that the measure of bivariate inequality can be particularly sensitive to the correlation between inequalities in health and income, as opposed to inequality in the marginal distributions.

The idea that economic inequality poses a threat to population health has attracted a great deal of attention across a number of disciplines over the last two decades. The claim that inequality imposes a health cost on all individuals living in an unequal society has been made mostly vociferously by researchers in the field of public health (Kawachi & Kennedy, 1997; Wilkinson, 1996; Wilkinson and Pickett, 2009). Economists have tended to be sceptical, arguing that the observed negative correlation between average population health and income inequality can be spurious, arising from a concave relationship between health and income, and questioning the mechanisms that could possibly underlie a causal effect (Deaton, 2001, 2003; Gravelle, 1998).

Lacking in the literature has been evidence on the relationship between health and economic inequality across and within developing countries. Addressing this gap, Therese Nilsson and Andreas Bergh uncover some intriguing relationships that pose further puzzles for a research field already in a state of flux. Unlike in middle- and high-income countries, child ill-health (measured by malnutrition) is actually negatively correlated with income inequality across low-income countries. Recognising the limitations of cross-country analysis, the authors examine individual level data from Zambia, one of the poorest countries in the world with extremely low levels of population health. Controlling for the economic circumstances of the household, as well as many other covariates, child malnutrition continues to be *lower* in areas (defined at a variety of levels) with higher income inequality. The authors propose that the different directions of the relationship between health and economic inequality in rich and poor countries reflect inequality being correlated with different types of unobserved factors in the two contexts.

Despite the growing interest in the inequality of opportunity framework in health economics, the literature has focused on the distribution of health, not healthcare. John E. Roemer shows that horizontal inequality in healthcare is insufficient as a characterization of what constitutes a just distribution of resources in this sector. Provocatively, he argues that it does not even constitute a necessary condition for distributive justice. He characterises the just allocation of health care resources according to equality of opportunity ethics and illustrates its potential practical implications using a stylised example. This makes clear that the allocation of resources required to satisfy equality of opportunity is generally more egalitarian than a utilitarian one, but less egalitarian than a *Rawlsian* allocation of health care.

Introduction

Cost-effectiveness analysis of healthcare interventions is widely used to inform the allocation of resources to and within health care. Health inequality concerns have not yet made their way into this type of analysis and, as a result, are in danger of being overlooked. Miqdad Asaria, Susan Griffin and Richard Cookson propose a new method to take account of health inequality within cost-effectiveness analysis. They demonstrate that the most widely used cost-effectiveness methods can be combined with standard inequality measures, grounded on welfare foundations. They illustrate their proposed approach using a stylised example of health policy evaluation.

This volume of Research on Economic Inequality series contains methodological and empirical contributions to research on health inequality that will add further momentum to a field that has rightly attracted a good deal of interest in the last 10 years. The contributors include experts both in health economics and in income distribution. With increasing collaboration across these two fields on a topic of major societal importance, research on health and inequality seems set to continue to blossom over the next 10 years.

Pedro Rosa Dias
Owen O'Donnell
Editors

REFERENCES

Abul Naga, R. H., & Geoffard, P. (2006). Decomposition of bivariate inequality indices by attributes. *Economics Letters*, *90*, 362–367.
Abul Naga, R. H., & Yalcin, T. (2007). Inequality measurement for ordered response health data. *Journal of Health Economics*, *27*(6), 1614–1625.
Allison, R. A., & Foster, J. E. (2004). Measuring health inequality using qualitative data. *Journal of Health Economics*, *23*, 505–524.
Apouey, B. (2007). Measuring health polarization with self-assessed health data. *Health Economics*, *16*(9), 875–894.
Apouey, B., & Silber, J. (2013). Inequality and bi-polarization in socioeconomic status and health: Ordinal approaches. In P. R. Dias & O. O'Donnell (Eds.), *Health and inequality* (Vol. 21). Research on Economic Inequality. Bingley, UK: Emerald Group Publishing Limited.
Cowell, F. A., & Flachaire, E. (2012). *Inequality with ordinal data*. Public Economics Programme Discussion Paper 16. London School of Economics, London.
Deaton, A. (2001). Inequalities in income and inequalities in health. In F. Welch (Ed.), *The causes and consequences of increasing inequality* (pp. 129–170). Chicago, IL: Chicago University Press.

Deaton, A. (2003). Health, inequality and economic development. *Journal of Economic Literature*, *41*, 113–158.

Erreygers, G. (2009). Correcting the concentration index. *Journal of Health Economics*, *28*, 504–515.

Fleurbaey, M. (2005). Health, wealth, and fairness. *Journal of Public Economic Theory*, *7*, 253–284.

Fleurbaey, M., & Maniquet, F. (2011). *A theory of fairness and social welfare*. Cambridge: Cambridge University Press.

Fleurbaey, M., & Schokkaert, E. (2009). Unfair inequalities in health and health care. *Journal of Health Economics*, *28*, 73–90.

Gravelle, H. (1998). How much of the relation between population mortality and unequal distribution of income is a statistical artefact? *British Medical Journal*, *316*, 382–385.

Grossman, M. (1972). On the concept of health capital and the demand for health. *The Journal of Political Economy*, *80*, 223–255.

Kawachi, I., & Kennedy, B. P. (1997). The relationship of income inequality to mortality: does the choice of indicator matter? *Social Science Medicine*, *45*, 1121–1127.

Maasoumi, E. (1986). The measurement and decomposition of multi-dimensional inequality. *Econometrica*, *54*, 991–997.

O'Donnell, O., van Doorslaer, E., & van Ourti, T. (2014). Health and inequality. In A. B. Atkinson & F. J. Bourguignon (Eds.), *Handbook of Income Distribution volume* (2B), Amsterdam: Elsevier.

Paes de Barros, R., Ferreira, F., Molinas Vega, J., & Saavedra Chanduvi, J. (2008). *Measuring inequality of opportunities in Latin America and the Caribbean*. The World Bank.

Wagstaff, A. (2005). The bounds of the concentration index when the variable of interest is binary, with an application to immunization inequality. *Health Economics*, *14*, 429–432.

Wagstaff, A., Paci, P., & van Doorslaer, E. (1991). On the measurement of inequalities in health. *Social Science and Medicine*, *33*, 545–557.

Wagstaff, A., & van Doorslaer, E. (2000). Equity in health care finance and delivery. In A. J. Culyer & J. P. Newhouse (Eds.), *Handbook of health economics* (Vol. 1), Amsterdam: Elsevier.

Wilkinson, R. G. (1996). *Unhealthy societies: The afflictions of inequality*. London: Routledge.

Wilkinson, R. G., & Pickett, K. (2009). *The spirit level: Why equality is better for everyone*. London: Allen Lane.

World Bank. (2005). *World development report 2006: Equity and development*. Washington, DC.

World Health Organization (WHO). (2013a). *Global health observatory: Health equity monitor*. Geneva: WHO. http://www.who.int/gho/health_equity/en/index.html. Accessed on 22 July 2013.

World Health Organization (WHO). (2013b). *Handbook on health inequality monitoring: with a special focus on low- and middle-income countries*. Geneva: WHO.

PART I
MEASUREMENT OF HEALTH INEQUALITY

LOST IN TRANSLATION: RETHINKING THE INEQUALITY EQUIVALENCE CRITERIA FOR BOUNDED HEALTH VARIABLES

Gustav Kjellsson and Ulf-G. Gerdtham

ABSTRACT

What change in the distribution of a population's health preserves the level of inequality? The answer to this analogous question in the context of income inequality lies somewhere between a uniform and a proportional change. These polar positions represent the absolute and relative inequality equivalence criterion (IEC), respectively. A bounded health variable may be presented in terms of both health attainments and shortfalls. As a distributional change cannot simultaneously be proportional to attainments and to shortfalls, relative inequality measures may rank populations differently from the two perspectives. In contrast to the literature that stresses the importance of measuring inequality in attainments and shortfalls consistently using an absolute IEC, this chapter formalizes a new compromise concept for a bounded variable by explicitly considering the two relative IECs, defined with respect to attainments and shortfalls, to represent the polar cases of defensible positions.

We use a surplus-sharing approach to provide new insights on commonly used inequality indices by evaluating the underpinning IECs in terms of how infinitesimal surpluses of health must be successively distributed to preserve the level of inequality. We derive a one-parameter IEC that, unlike those implicit in commonly used indices, assigns constant weights to the polar cases independent of the health distribution.

Keywords: Health inequality; bounded variable; inequality equivalence criteria

JEL Classifications: D63; I14

INTRODUCTION

Despite decades of enhancing average health status and egalitarian public policies, inequality in health persists in many countries (e.g., Kunst et al., 2004a, 2004b; Marmot et al., 2012). To evaluate levels of and changes in health inequality over time, it is vital to have a measurement framework which captures the distribution of health in an index value. Health economics research frequently uses the (univariate) Gini coefficient to evaluate total health inequalities and the (bivariate) concentration index to measure health inequalities related to a socioeconomic variable (e.g., income). The recent literature intensively discusses how to adjust these rank-dependent inequality indices for health variables that, unlike income, are bounded from above (Erreygers, 2009a, 2009b, 2009c; Erreygers & van Ourti, 2011a, 2011b; Kjellsson & Gerdtham, forthcoming; Wagstaff, 2009, 2011a, 2011b; see also Aristondo & Lasso de la Vega, 2013). This discussion boils down to the more general issue of the vertical value judgments inherent in an index's inequality equivalence criterion (IEC); the distributional change to which an inequality measure should be invariant (cf. Allanson & Petrie, 2013a). Choosing an IEC is controversial in the income inequality literature and becomes even more delicate in relation to inequality in a health variable that is bounded and may arbitrarily be coded in terms of either health attainments or shortfalls.

To provide further understanding of the implicit value judgments the different rank-dependent indices embody, we scrutinize the IECs using a surplus-sharing approach, that is, evaluating how an additional infinitesimal surplus should be distributed to keep inequality constant. In particular, we extend the flexible IEC suggested by Zoli (2003) and Yoshida (2005) to bounded health measures. Beyond providing insights into the IECs underpinning commonly used rank-dependent indices such as Wagstaff's (2005) and the univariate and bivariate version of Erreygers' index (2009a, 2009b, respectively), we suggest our own intermediate IEC. In the next section, before formalizing a new compromise concept in the third section and deriving a new nonlinear IEC in the fourth, we draw upon the inequality literature to illustrate why it is necessary to rethink existing IECs for bounded health variables.

RETHINKING THE IECS FOR A BOUNDED VARIABLE

Income Inequality

The income inequality literature has hosted a long-lasting discussion of whether it is appropriate to adopt an absolute or a relative IEC. That is, using an inequality measure that is invariant to either equiproportionate or uniform changes of the variable of interest. In a seminal article, Kolm (1976) introduces the vocabulary of *rightist* and *leftist* to represent the implicit vertical value judgment that underpins the choice between relative and absolute measures, respectively. Kolm further claims that these two IECs represent the natural polar cases of positions that are generally considered to be ethically defensible, although they do not necessarily represent all ethically defensible positions. Referring to Dalton (1920), among others, Kolm (1976, p. 433) further claims that "many people feel that an equal augmentation in everyone's income decreases inequality, whereas an equiproportional increase in everyone's income increases it," which indicates that both absolute and relative perspectives are important. Consequently, he also introduces an intermediate view of inequalities as a compromise between the rightist (relative) and the leftist (absolute) views.[1] One may find it hard to defend positions outside these boundaries; for example, a vertical value judgment that implies that inequality increases in response to a uniform increment of income or, alternatively, a vertical value judgment that implies that inequality decreases in response to an equiproportionate increase of income. Zheng (2007) refers to IECs representing such positions outside the boundaries as *extreme leftist* and *extreme rightist*, respectively (Table 1).

Several intermediate IECs that yield the rightist (relative) and the leftist (absolute) positions as polar cases have since been suggested

Table 1. Vocabularies of Inequality Equivalence Criteria.

Income Inequality Vocabulary	Erreygers and van Ourti (2011a)	Definition
Extreme rightist	Inverse absolute	Inequality decreases in response to equiproportionate improvements
Rightist	Quasirelative	Inequality is invariant to equiproportional changes
Intermediate	Mixed	Inequality decreases (increases) in response to uniform (equiproportional) improvements
Leftist	Quasiabsolute	Inequality is invariant to uniform changes
Extreme leftist	Inverse relative	Inequality increases in response to uniform improvements

Note: Erreygers and van Ourti (2011a) use the prefix *quasi-* to acknowledge that, for a bounded variable, equiproportional and uniform changes are not feasible for all distributions.

(e.g., Bossert & Pfingsten, 1990; Krtscha, 1994; Yoshida, 2005; Zheng, 2007; Zoli, 2003). Bossert and Pfingsten (1990) suggest a linear compromise between the two polar cases, but Zheng (2004), Zoli (2003), and Yoshida (2005) all point out that this is overly restrictive, that is, a linear IEC fails to represent all intermediate vertical value judgments individuals may have. This argument also gains support from experiments (e.g., Amiel & Cowell, 1999). As linearity implies that the *level of intermediateness* depends on the initial income distribution, a surplus of $1 must be distributed in the same way as a surplus of $1 million. Consequently, a procedure of distributing a surplus of $1 million by repeatedly distributing smaller surpluses of $1 would imply that the distribution of each and every surplus would depend on the initial income distribution.

An alternative approach, promoted by Krtscha (1994), Yoshida (2005), and Zoli (2003), suggests that each infinitesimal amount of extra income must be distributed as a convex combination of the relative and the absolute IEC with respect to the presently prevailing income distribution in order to keep inequality constant. The important difference from the linear IECs is that the next infinitesimal amount of extra income should be distributed according to the present, rather than the initial, distribution. Krtscha (1994) suggests a *fair compromise* between the relative and absolute views, implying that the portions of the surplus that must be distributed proportionally and uniformly to the income distribution are of equal size. Yoshida (2005) generalizes this fair compromise so that the size of the portions depends on a parameter. Zoli (2003) further shows how to use this surplus-sharing approach to identify the local vertical value judgment, or the level of intermediateness, for a given income distribution for any well-behaved IEC.

From Income to Health

As most health inequality measures originate from the income inequality literature, the discussion of IECs is directly relevant also for health inequality researchers. In addition, the boundedness of health variables further complicates matters. Nevertheless, the discussion of IECs underpinning inequality indices tends to get lost in translation when moving from income to a bounded health variable.

For bounded health variables that may be coded in terms of either attainments or shortfalls, an index can be invariant to equiproportionate changes of either attainments or shortfalls of health, but not to both perspectives at the same time (Erreygers & van Ourti, 2011a). Clarke, Gerdtham, Johannesson, Bingefors, and Smith (2002) show that a relative inequality index may rank populations differently according to attainments and shortfalls. This did not cause the health inequality literature to acknowledge that these are two different IECs representing two different vertical value judgments. Instead, the finding has rather started a quest for a *consistent* inequality measure (e.g., Lambert & Zheng, 2011; Lasso de la Vega & Aristondo, 2012) and has been used as an argument in favor of an absolute IEC as it ranks populations consistently (e.g., Erreygers, 2009a, 2009b, 2009c; Erreygers & van Ourti, 2011a; Lambert & Zheng, 2011). The only exception in the literature, as far as we know, is Allanson and Petrie (2013a, 2013b). Using a two-dimensional inequality map borrowed from the income inequality literature and applied to a bounded variable standardized in the unit interval, Allanson and Petrie (2013b) illustrate that the vertical value judgment is fundamentally different if the relative IEC is defined with respect to attainments or shortfalls. The inequality map in Fig. 1, adapted from Allanson and Petrie (2013b), represents an economy of two individuals, where the attainment and the shortfall of the richer/healthier (poorer/less-healthy) individual are represented on the first and the second horizontal axis (vertical axis). For coherence between the interpretation for total and income-related health inequality, assume that the richer individual also possesses more health. All equal (egalitarian) distributions constitute a 45-degree line departing from the origin; distributions further from the line of equality are generally considered as more unequal.

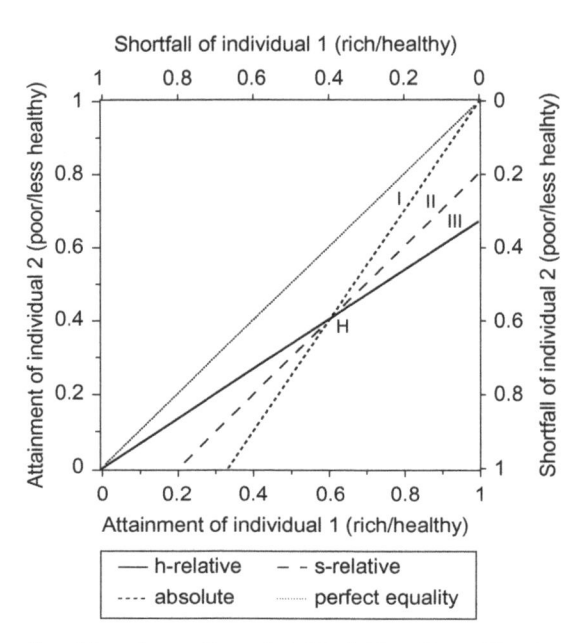

Fig. 1. Inequality Map for a Bounded Variable. *Note*: The inequality map is adapted from Allanson and Petrie (2013b), who present a more comprehensive explanation of the map.

Any IEC defines a set of health distributions that are equivalent in terms of inequality. These sets constitute iso-inequality contours, which can be represented in the inequality map. Thus, for an arbitrary initial distribution H, all points on a line that passes point H represent a linear iso-inequality contour of distributions that is equivalent to H. All points in the set below the contour represent distributions that are considered more unequal, while all points in the set above the contour and below the 45-degree line represent distributions that are considered less unequal. All distributions obtained by uniform changes of either attainments or shortfalls constitute the absolute IEC as represented by line II. In contrast, lines III and I consist of distributions obtained by proportional changes of attainments and of shortfalls, respectively. Thus, the graph convincingly illustrates that while the absolute IEC of the two perspectives coincide, the relative IECs with respect to attainments and shortfalls represent two distinct vertical value judgments. To explicitly distinguish between the two, we label a relative IEC with respect to attainments as h-relative and a relative IEC with respect to shortfalls as s-relative.

The previous literature has tended to disregard the boundedness by referring to both the h-relative and the s-relative IEC as either rightist or (quasi) relative. That is, using the income inequality vocabulary or a related version[2] without acknowledging that one — implicitly or explicitly — needs to choose either attainments or shortfalls as a reference point. The exception is again Allanson and Petrie (2013a, 2013b) who explicitly argue for attainments as the natural reference point "as health is generally considered as a *good* like income" and, therefore, define all IECs in terms of attainments. However, labeling the h-relative IEC as rightist implies that the s-relative IEC is only a subset of the extreme leftist IECs, which are represented in the inequality map by any iso-inequality contour that is above (below) the absolute line to the right (left) of H. That is, inequality increases when health increases uniformly and the IEC is outside the range that Kolm (1976) considers as ethically defensible. Choosing attainments as the reference point further implies that an IEC is intermediate if it is a compromise between the h-relative and the absolute IEC (i.e., represented by an iso-inequality contour between lines II and III), while an IEC is extreme leftist if it is a compromise between the s-relative and the absolute (i.e., represented by an iso-inequality contour in the area between lines I and II). However, reversing the perspective implies that an IEC that was intermediate with respect to attainments is now extreme leftist with respect to shortfalls. Table 2 summarizes the correspondence between the IECs defined with respect to attainments and shortfalls. These issues may be considered semantic. We claim they are not. Rather, they are a symptom of the problem of transferring inequality measures from income to a bounded health variable without considering that the natural polar cases of the ethically defensible positions have changed.

Table 2. IECs of a Bounded Health Variable.

	Attainments	Shortfalls
	Extreme rightist	Extreme leftist
H-relative	Rightist	Extreme leftist
	Intermediate	Extreme leftist
Absolute	Leftist	Leftist
	Extreme leftist	Intermediate
S-relative	Extreme leftist	Rightist
	Extreme leftist	Rightist

For an unbounded variable such as income, it may be difficult to argue in favor of an extreme leftist IEC (i.e., for most people it appears counterintuitive that inequality increases when both absolute and relative differences decrease). For a bounded health variable, such a position excludes any compromise between the s-relative and the absolute IEC. However, that an equiproportional decrease of the shortfall distribution preserves (or at least does not increase) the inequality may appear as an intuitive concept and be compatible, at least in some contexts, with people's perception of inequality. For example, Allanson and Petrie (2013a) stress that this view is consistent with the principle of proportional universalism presented in the Marmot Review: "To reduce the steepness of the social gradient in health, action must be universal, but with a scale and intensity that is proportionate to the level of disadvantage" (Marmot, 2010, p. 15). That is, to reduce (income-related) health inequality, interventions must reduce both relative and absolute inequality in attainments, which is consistent with an extreme leftist IEC. Drawing upon Allanson and Petrie's (2013a) argument, we suggest that for a bounded health variable we shall not rule out that individuals may have inequality perceptions that are either (a) in line with an IEC that intermediates the h-relative and the absolute IEC, (b) in line with an extreme leftist IEC that intermediates the absolute and the s-relative IEC, or compatible with a combination of (a) and (b). Thus, the natural polar cases of the ethically defensible positions are no longer the (h-)relative and absolute, but rather the h-relative and s-relative IECs.

Contribution of the Chapter

We formalize this new compromise concept for bounded health variables using the s-relative and the h-relative IEC as the more appropriate polar cases. We show that the surplus-sharing rule of any IEC that satisfies this compromise can be interpreted as a weighted sum of the sharing rules of the two polar cases with weights in the unit interval. Thus, for the level of inequality to remain constant, one portion of an infinitesimal extra amount of health should be distributed proportionally to the distribution of attainments and one portion proportionally to the distribution of shortfalls. Analogous to Erreygers and van Ourti's (2011a) measure of a rank-dependent index's sensitivity to relative inequality in relation to absolute inequality, the weights of the surplus-sharing rules may be interpreted as a measure of an inequality index's sensitivity to relative inequality in attainments in relation to relative inequality in shortfalls. Using these weights, we may evaluate the level of intermediateness of any rank-dependent index, including the indices suggested by Erreygers (2009a, 2009b) and Wagstaff (2005), each of which satisfies our suggested compromise concept. We also derive a nonlinear IEC that, in contrast to the IECs underpinning Erreygers' and Wagstaff's indices, weights the relevant polar cases constantly and independently of the health distribution. That is, we translate Yoshida's (2005) generalization of Krtscha's (1994) fair compromise to a bounded health variable.

In another chapter of this volume, Aristondo and Lasso de la Vega (2013) approach the problem of measuring inequality of a bounded health variable from an alternative perspective. Without explicitly considering the underlying IECs, they acknowledge our compromise concept suggesting measuring inequality of the joint distribution of shortfalls and attainments. For a univariate index that is decomposable (cf. Shorrocks, 1980), analyzing relative inequality of the joint distribution is equivalent to evaluating inequality of the distribution of either attainments or shortfalls using a subset of the indices suggested in a previous paper by Lasso de la Vega and Aristondo (2012). This class of indices is underpinned by the same IEC as Wagstaff's (2005) index (cf. Kjellsson & Gerdtham, forthcoming). Note, however, that the rank-dependent indices considered in our chapter are not included in the class of decomposable indices.

INEQUALITY EQUIVALENCE CRITERIA FOR BOUNDED VARIABLES

Preliminaries

Let the vector $h = (h_1, h_2, ..., h_n)$ represent the health distribution of a given population of n individuals or groups of individuals, where each h_i ($i = 1, 2, ..., n$) is a standardized cardinal health variable in the unit interval. The boundedness implies that we can construct a vector $s = (s_1, s_2, ..., s_n)$ that represents the ill-health situation of the whole population defined as shortfalls of health $s_i = 1 - h_i$. By defining the IECs in terms of a standardized (cardinal) health variable, we will, in line with Erreygers and van Ourti (2011a), only consider real differences in health that are not due to changes in the unit of measurement. For technical convenience, we let individual i's position in the vector h be decided by the individual rank based on the position in the distribution of health and income, denoted as ρ_i and ϕ_i for total- and income-related inequalities, respectively.[3] The average attainment and shortfall of the population is denoted as $\mu_h = \frac{1}{n}\sum_{i=1}^{n} h_i$ and $\mu_s = \frac{1}{n}\sum_{i=1}^{n} s_i$.

We denote that distribution h is considered at least as equal as distribution $\tilde{h}$ by $\hat{h} \geqslant \tilde{h}$. To denote that two distributions are considered to be equivalent in terms of inequality we use $h \sim \tilde{h}$. For income-related health inequality, we further assume that, on average, richer individuals have better health. *More equal*, then, means that health is less concentrated among the rich. We define an IEC in terms of a normalized distance between the health vector and the mean; two health distributions are considered equal in terms of inequality if the normalized distances are equal.

Definition 1. (General IEC) $\forall h, \tilde{h}; h \sim \tilde{h}$ if

$$\frac{h - \mu_h \mathbf{1}}{g(\mu_h)} = \frac{\tilde{h} - \mu_{\tilde{h}} \mathbf{1}}{g(\mu_{\tilde{h}})} \quad (1)$$

where $\mathbf{1}$ is the unit vector and $g(\mu_h)$ is a positive, continuous, and (piecewise) differentiable function with the derivative denoted as $g'(\mu_h)$.

Rank-Dependent Indices

Later in the chapter, we will relate the IECs to the families of univariate and bivariate rank-dependent indices defined for a standardized health variable. Following Erreygers (2009a, 2009b), we express the two families as normalized sums of weighted health levels.

Definition 2. (Rank-Dependent Index)

(a) A univariate rank-dependent index takes the form

$$G(h) = f(\mu_h, n) \sum_{i}^{n} w_i h_i \quad (2)$$

(b) A bivariate rank-dependent index takes the form

$$I(h) = f(\mu_h, n) \sum_{i}^{n} z_i h_i \quad (3)$$

Here, $w_i = (n+1)/2 - \rho_i$, $z_i = (n+1)/2 - \phi_i$ and the normalization function $f(\mu_h, n) > 0$.

A rank-dependent index represents a General IEC if it is invariant to the distributional change from h to $\tilde{h}$ represented in Eq. (1). This relationship is specified in Proposition 1. (*All proofs in the appendix.*)

Proposition 1. A rank-dependent index, $I(h)$ or $G(h)$, represents a General IEC if the normalization function $f(\mu_h, n) = v(n)/g(\mu_h)$, where $v(n)$ is a positive scalar function.

The Absolute, h-Relative, and s-Relative IECs

We formally define the absolute, h-relative, and s-relative IECs in terms of a General IEC by varying $g(\mu_h)$ in Eq. (1). For an absolute IEC, the level of inequality is constant if health changes uniformly across the distribution.

Definition 3. (Absolute IEC) $\forall h, \tilde{h}$; $h \sim \tilde{h}$ if

$$h - \mu_h \mathbf{1} = \tilde{h} - \mu_{\tilde{h}} \mathbf{1} \tag{4}$$

As we deal with a bounded health variable, we distinguish between an IEC that implies invariance to equiproportionate changes in attainments and an IEC that implies invariance to equiproportionate changes in shortfalls by labeling them as h-relative and s-relative, respectively.

Definition 4. (h-Relative IEC) $\forall h, \tilde{h}$; $h \sim \tilde{h}$ if

$$\frac{h - \mu_h \mathbf{1}}{\mu_h} = \frac{\tilde{h} - \mu_{\tilde{h}} \mathbf{1}}{\mu_{\tilde{h}}} \tag{5}$$

Definition 5. (s-Relative IEC) $\forall s, \tilde{s}$; $s \sim \tilde{s}$ if

$$\frac{s - \mu_s \mathbf{1}}{\mu_s} = \frac{\tilde{s} - \mu_{\tilde{s}} \mathbf{1}}{\mu_{\tilde{s}}} \tag{6}$$

To formally illustrate that these two IECs capture two distinct vertical value judgments, it is illuminating to define the s-relative IEC in terms of attainments.

Definition 6. (s-Relative IEC) $\forall h, \tilde{h}; h \sim \tilde{h}$ if

$$\frac{h - \mu_h \mathbf{1}}{1 - \mu_h} = \frac{\tilde{h} - \mu_{\tilde{h}} \mathbf{1}}{1 - \mu_{\tilde{h}}} \tag{7}$$

Note that Eqs. (4), (5), and (7) are equivalent to Eq. (1) using $g(\mu_h) = 1$, $g(\mu_h) = \mu_h$, and $g(\mu_h) = 1 - \mu_h$, respectively.

The New Compromise Concept

In line with Kolm's (1976) intermediate view of inequality, Bossert and Pfingsten (1990) define a compromise concept that intermediates the two polar cases for income inequality, absolute and relative. For a bounded variable, we may define this concept both as a compromise between the h-relative and absolute IEC and as a compromise between the s-relative and absolute IEC.

Definition 7. (h-Relative–Absolute Compromise) An IEC is a compromise between the h-relative and the absolute IEC if $\forall h, \tilde{h}$ such that $\mu_h \leq \mu_{\tilde{h}}$

$$h \geqslant \tilde{h} \quad \text{if} \quad \frac{h - \mu_h \mathbf{1}}{\mu_h} = \frac{\tilde{h} - \mu_{\tilde{h}} \mathbf{1}}{\mu_{\tilde{h}}} \tag{8}$$

$$\tilde{h} \geqslant h \quad \text{if} \quad h - \mu_h \mathbf{1} = \tilde{h} - \mu_{\tilde{h}} \mathbf{1} \tag{9}$$

and if $\forall h, \tilde{h}$ such that $\mu_h \geq \mu_{\tilde{h}}$, the opposite applies.

Definition 8. (s-Relative–Absolute Compromise) An IEC is a compromise between the absolute and the s-relative IEC if $\forall h, \tilde{h}$ such that $\mu_h \leq \mu_{\tilde{h}}$

$$h \geqslant \tilde{h} \quad \text{if} \quad h - \mu_h \mathbf{1} = \tilde{h} - \mu_{\tilde{h}} \mathbf{1} \tag{10}$$

$$\tilde{h} \geqslant h \quad \text{if} \quad \frac{h - \mu_h \mathbf{1}}{1 - \mu_h} = \frac{\tilde{h} - \mu_{\tilde{h}} \mathbf{1}}{1 - \mu_{\tilde{h}}} \tag{11}$$

and if $\forall h, \tilde{h}$ such that $\mu_h \geq \mu_{\tilde{h}}$, the opposite applies.

In short, these compromise concepts require that an equiproportional increase in attainments (shortfalls) does not decrease inequality, and a uniform increase in attainments (shortfalls) does not increase inequality. Relating back to Allanson and Petrie's (2013a) inequality map, a compromise between the h-relative and the absolute IECs is graphically represented by any contour in the area between lines III and II, whereas a compromise between the s-relative and the absolute IECs is represented by any contour in the area between lines I and II. If we consider both these compromise concepts to represent ethically defensible positions, it is natural to define a new compromise concept that is graphically represented by the union of the two areas. That is, a compromise concept adapted to a bounded variable with the h-relative and the s-relative IECs as the polar cases.

Definition 9. (hs-Relative Compromise) An IEC is a compromise between the h-relative and s-relative IECs if $\forall h, \tilde{h}$ such that $\mu_h \leq \mu_{\tilde{h}}$

$$h \geqslant \tilde{h} \quad \text{if} \quad \frac{h - \mu_h \mathbf{1}}{\mu_h} = \frac{\tilde{h} - \mu_{\tilde{h}} \mathbf{1}}{\mu_{\tilde{h}}} \tag{12}$$

$$\tilde{h} \geqslant h \quad \text{if} \quad \frac{h - \mu_h \mathbf{1}}{(1 - \mu_h)} = \frac{\tilde{h} - \mu_{\tilde{h}} \mathbf{1}}{(1 - \mu_{\tilde{h}})} \tag{13}$$

and if $\forall h, \tilde{h}$ such that $\mu_h \geq \mu_{\tilde{h}}$, the opposite applies.

In words, an equiproportional increase in attainments must not decrease the inequality and an equiproportional decrease in shortfalls must not increase the inequality. All linear contours in the space that represent the compromise concept constitute Bossert and Pfingsten's (1990) linear intermediate IEC adapted to bounded health variables — that is, a General IEC with $g(\mu_h) = \mu_h \kappa + (1 - \kappa)(1 - \mu_h)$, where $0 \leq \kappa \leq 1$. The perfect linear compromise, $\kappa = 0.5$, equals the absolute IEC. The compromise concept is however not limited to linear IECs. In the following section, we will use a surplus-sharing approach to derive nonlinear IECs that are represented by iso-inequality contours within this space where the set of inequality equivalent distributions is represented by a curve instead of a line.

A SURPLUS-SHARING APPROACH

As the vertical value judgment behind an IEC tells us what kind of distributional change leaves inequality unchanged, any IEC also entails a rule for how an additional surplus of health must be distributed. In this section, we follow Zoli's (2003) introduction of a vector function that identifies how an additional surplus ε must be distributed to not alter the inequality with respect to distribution h

$$h + d(h, \varepsilon) \sim h \qquad (14)$$

We refer to this vector $d(h, \varepsilon)$ as an inequality equivalent distributional vector (IEDV). Eq. (14) represents the set of all distributions that compile an inequality contour in an inequality map. That is, $d(h, \varepsilon)$ tells us how the surplus is distributed along the path from the initial health distribution h to the new distribution $\tilde{h}$. For a General IEC, the corresponding IEDV is[4]

$$d(h, \varepsilon) = \frac{\varepsilon}{n}\mathbf{1} + (h - \mu_h \mathbf{1})\left(\frac{g(\mu_h + \frac{\varepsilon}{n})}{g(\mu_h)} - 1\right) \qquad (15)$$

As we assume $g(\mu_h)$ to be continuous and (piecewise) differentiable, Eq. (15) is continuous and has a piecewise continuous partial derivative with respect to ε.[5] The IEDV in Eq. (15) also satisfies what Zoli (2003) refers to as *path independence* (and is represented by a continuous iso-inequality contour). That is, a surplus $\varepsilon + \varepsilon'$ is identically distributed across the population irrespective of being distributed all at once or successively distributed as two surpluses.[6] These properties restrict an IEDV to not change dramatically due to marginal changes in ε, assuring that it is possible to evaluate how the surplus-sharing rules are affected by marginal changes in the health distribution.

Dividing each element of the IEDV by the total surplus ε yields a vector $d(h, \varepsilon)/\varepsilon$ that equals the shares of the surplus distributed to each of the individuals in the population. Following Zoli (2003), we claim that, for a given distribution h, this vector, $d(h, \varepsilon)/\varepsilon$, can be interpreted as representing the vertical value judgment of an IEC for a given change between the initial and the new distribution. However, the vertical value judgment represented by the vector $d(h, \varepsilon)/\varepsilon$ generally depends not only on the initial distribution, h, but also on the surplus size ε. To isolate the effect of the initial distribution, we follow Zoli's (2003) suggestion of using the vector $\delta(h) = \lim_{\varepsilon \to 0+} [d(h, \varepsilon)/\varepsilon]$. As this vector, for a given distribution h, identifies how an *infinitesimal* positive surplus of health must be distributed to leave inequality unchanged, it represents the *local* vertical value judgment of the IEC for a given distribution h. Thus, by using $\delta(h)$, we may compare the surplus-sharing rules, or the local vertical value judgment, for a given distribution for any General IECs.

Local Vertical Value Judgment

To relate the local vertical value judgment represented by an IEC to the surplus-sharing rules of the absolute, h-relative, and s-relative IECs, we express the IEDV representing the three IECs as, respectively

$$d(h, \varepsilon) = \frac{\varepsilon}{n} \mathbf{1} \qquad (16)$$

$$d(h, \varepsilon) = \frac{\varepsilon}{n} \frac{h}{\mu_h} \qquad (17)$$

and

$$d(h, \varepsilon) = \frac{\varepsilon}{n} \left(\mathbf{1} - \frac{h - \mu_h \mathbf{1}}{(1 - \mu_h)} \right) \qquad (18)$$

Calculating the limit of the function that identifies the shares distributed to each individual, that is, $\delta(h) = \lim_{\varepsilon \to 0+} [d(h, \varepsilon)/\varepsilon]$, for each of the three IECs yields

$$\delta(h) = \frac{1}{n} \mathbf{1} \qquad (19)$$

$$\delta(h) = \frac{h}{n\mu_h} \qquad (20)$$

and

$$\delta(h) = \left(\frac{1}{n} \mathbf{1} - \frac{h - \mu_h \mathbf{1}}{n(1 - \mu_h)} \right) \qquad (21)$$

For any General IEC, the local sharing rules — the corresponding $\delta(h)$ — may be expressed as a weighted sum of the local sharing rules of both the h-relative and the absolute IEC and, more importantly, the s-relative and the h-relative IEC.

Proposition 2. For any General IEC, we may express $\delta(h)$ as

$$\delta(h) = \frac{1}{n}\mathbf{1}(1 - \omega_{\text{ra}}(\mu_h)) + \frac{1}{n}\frac{h}{\mu_h}\omega_{\text{ra}}(\mu_h) \quad (22)$$

and

$$\delta(h) = \omega_{\text{hs}}(\mu_h)\frac{h}{n\mu_h} + (1 - \omega_{\text{hs}}(\mu_h))\left(\frac{1}{n}\mathbf{1} - \frac{h - \mu_h\mathbf{1}}{n(1 - \mu_h)}\right) \quad (23)$$

where the weights are

$$\omega_{\text{ra}}(\mu_h) = \frac{g'(\mu_h)\mu_h}{g(\mu_h)}$$

and

$$\omega_{\text{hs}}(\mu_h) = \mu_h + \frac{g'(\mu_h)\mu_h}{g(\mu_h)}(1 - \mu_h)$$

Thus, Eqs. (22) and (23) represent the h-relative $\delta(h)$ for $\omega_{\text{ra}} = 1$ and $\omega_{\text{hs}} = 1$ and the absolute and the s-relative for $\omega_{\text{ra}} = 0$ and $\omega_{\text{hs}} = 0$, respectively. For an IEC that satisfies the hs-relative compromise concepts, the corresponding weights, $\omega_{\text{hs}}(\mu_h)$, will be bounded in the unit interval and, thus, the local surplus-sharing rules will be a convex combination of the polar cases. That is, for the level of inequality to remain constant $100 \times \omega_{\text{hs}}(\mu_h)\%$ of the surplus must be distributed proportionally to the attainment distribution h and $100 \times (1 - \omega_{\text{hs}}(\mu_h))\%$ must be distributed proportionally to the shortfall distribution $s = 1 - h$. Analogously, for an IEC that satisfies the h-relative–absolute compromise, $\omega_{\text{ra}}(\mu_h)$ is in the unit interval implying that $100 \times \omega_{\text{ra}}(\mu_h)\%$ of the surplus must be distributed proportionally and $100 \times (1 - \omega_{\text{ra}}(\mu_h))\%$ must be distributed uniformly to the attainment distribution.

Proposition 3. A General IEC satisfies

(a) the h-relative–absolute compromise concept if and only if the weights in Eq. (22) are in the unit interval, that is, $\omega_{\text{ra}}(\mu_h) \in [0,1]$.
(b) the hs-relative compromise concept if and only if the weights in Eq. (23) are in the unit interval, that is, $\omega_{\text{hs}}(\mu_h) \in [0,1]$.

Relation to Erreygers and van Ourti's (2011a) Inequality Weights

For relevancy and interpretation of the surplus-sharing rules, it is noteworthy that the weights in Eq. (22), $\omega_{ra}(\mu_h)$ and $1-\omega_{ra}(\mu_h)$, coincide with Erreygers and van Ourti's (2011a) measures of how sensitive a rank-dependent index is to (h-)relative and absolute inequalities, or more precisely how sensitive an index is to relative differences in relation to absolute differences and vice versa. Using the elasticity of the normalization function of a rank-dependent index

$$\eta(\mu_h) = \frac{\partial f(\mu_h, n)}{\partial \mu_h} \frac{\mu_h}{f(\mu_h, n)} \qquad (24)$$

Erreygers and van Ourti (2011a) define the weight that an index gives to (h-)relative inequality as $-\eta(\mu_h)$ and the weight it gives to absolute inequality as $1 + \eta(\mu_h)$.

As we consider the two relative IECs to be the relevant polar cases for bounded variables, we adapt Erreygers and van Ourti's (2011a) measures to our new hs-relative compromise concept. By normalizing the distance in terms of elasticity to one of the polar cases, we obtain analogous inequality weights that coincide with the weights in Eq. (23). Thus

$$\omega_{hs}(\mu_h) = \frac{\mu_h/(1-\mu_h) - \eta(\mu_h)}{1 + \mu_h/(1-\mu_h)} \qquad (25)$$

indicates how much of an additional surplus must be distributed according to the sharing rules of the two relative IECs and may be interpreted as a measure of how sensitive the corresponding rank-dependent index is to relative differences in attainments in relation to relative differences in shortfalls. We express this formally in Proposition 4.

Proposition 4. Let a rank-dependent inequality index, that is, $I(\mathbf{h})$ or $G(\mathbf{h})$, represent a General IEC, then the h-relative weight in Eq. (22) equals $\omega_{ra}(\mu_h) = -\eta(\mu_h)$ and the h-relative weight in Eq. (23) equals

$$\omega_{hs}(\mu_h) = \frac{\mu_h/(1-\mu_h) - \eta(\mu_h)}{1 + \mu_h/(1-\mu_h)} \qquad (26)$$

A New θ-Inequality Concept

As the inequality weights in Eqs. (22) and (23), $\omega_{ra}(\mu_h)$ and $\omega_{hs}(\mu_h)$, are functions of the average health in the population, the local vertical value judgment — or level of intermediateness defined by the fractions being distributed according to the surplus-sharing rules of the two polar cases — is generally dependent on the health distribution h. For the (h-) relative–absolute compromise concept, the only IEC that weights the polar cases constantly and independently of the mean is Yoshida's (2005) generalization of Krtscha's (1994) fair compromise.[7] For the new hs-relative compromise concept, we adapt Yoshida's (2005) inequality concept to a bounded health variable so that each infinitesimal surplus of health, ε, should be distributed as a convex combination of the h-relative and s-relative sharing rules with weights equal to the parameter θ.

Definition 10. (A θ-IEC) $\forall h, \tilde{h}; h \sim \tilde{h}$ if

$$\frac{h - \mu_h \mathbf{1}}{\mu_h^\theta (1-\mu_h)^{1-\theta}} = \frac{\tilde{h} - \mu_{\tilde{h}} \mathbf{1}}{\mu_{\tilde{h}}^\theta (1-\mu_{\tilde{h}})^{1-\theta}} \qquad (27)$$

with parameter $\theta \in [0,1]$.

Proposition 5. For any General IEC, the corresponding $\delta(h)$ equals

$$\delta(h) = (1-\theta)\left(\frac{1}{n}\mathbf{1} - \frac{h - \mu_h \mathbf{1}}{n(1-\mu_h)}\right) + \theta\left(\frac{h}{n\mu_h}\right) \qquad (28)$$

if and only if $g(\mu_h) = \mu_h^\theta (1-\mu_h)^{(1-\theta)}$ where $0 \leq \theta \leq 1$.

Thus, analogously to Yoshida's (2005) suggested IEC, the nonlinear θ-IEC implies that for inequality to remain constant, $100 \times \theta\%$ of the infinitesimal surplus must be distributed proportionally to the attainment distribution and $100 \times (1-\theta)\%$ must be distributed proportionally to the shortfall distribution. The inequality map in Fig. 2 illustrates the nonlinear iso-inequality contour representing the θ-IEC for different values of θ. The solid line, $\theta = 0.5$, represents the only IEC that is a perfect compromise between the polar cases. That is, it weights the relative inequality in attainments and relative inequality in shortfalls equally for any health distribution.

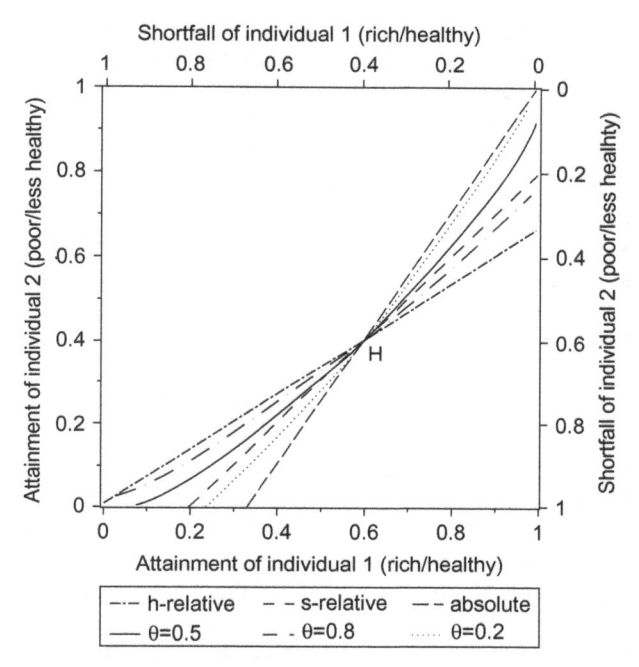

Fig. 2. A θ-IEC. *Note*: The h-relative (i.e., $\theta = 1$) and the s-relative (i.e., $\theta = 0$) cases are the extrema for the θ-IEC. The absolute line is included in the figure for reference. The inequality map is adapted from Allanson and Petrie (2013b).

Extending the θ-IEC

It is further illuminating to use these inequality weights to evaluate the level of intermediateness (for a given health distribution) of a rank-dependent index: how the vertical value judgment relates to the relevant polar cases for bounded variables. For that purpose, we extend the θ-IEC to a more general two-parameter IEC that underpins several of the intensively discussed rank-dependent indices.

Definition 11. (Extended θ-IEC) $\forall h, \tilde{h}; h \sim \tilde{h}$ if

$$\frac{h - \mu_h \mathbf{1}}{\mu_h^{\theta_1}(1-\mu_h)^{\theta_2}} = \frac{\tilde{h} - \mu_{\tilde{h}} \mathbf{1}}{\mu_{\tilde{h}}^{\theta_1}(1-\mu_{\tilde{h}})^{\theta_2}} \tag{29}$$

with parameters $\theta_1 \in [0,1]$ and $\theta_2 \in [0,1]$.

Note that Eq. (29) equals Eq. (27) for all θ_1 and θ_2 such that $\theta_2 = 1 - \theta_1$. The Extended θ-IEC includes Yoshida's (2005) generalization of the fair compromise (with respect to attainments, $\theta_2 = 0$, or shortfalls, $\theta_1 = 0$) and the IECs represented by the rank-dependent indices suggested by Wagstaff (2005), $\theta_1 = \theta_2 = 1$, and Erreygers (2009a, 2009b), $\theta_1 = \theta_2 = 0$ (i.e., the absolute IEC). For any index representing an Extended θ-IEC, the inequality weights $\omega_{hs}(\mu_h)$ — that is, the measure of sensitivity to relative inequality in attainments in relation to relative inequality in shortfalls — may be expressed as a linear function of μ_h and the two parameters, θ_1 and θ_2. Formally, we substitute $g'(\mu_h)\mu_h/g(\mu_h) = -\eta(\mu_h) = \theta_1 - \theta_2(\mu_h/(1 - \mu_h))$ into $\omega_{hs}(\mu_h)$ and rearrange into

$$\omega_{hs}(\mu_h) = \theta_1 + \mu_h(1 - \theta_1 - \theta_2) \tag{30}$$

Thus, for any rank-dependent index corresponding to the Extended θ-IEC, the level of intermediateness for a given level of μ_h is represented by a line from θ_1 to $(1 - \theta_2)$ for $0 < \mu_h < 1$. For Erreygers' index, the line goes from $\omega_{hs} = 0$ to $\omega_{hs} = 1$. That is, being close to an s-relative IEC in the lower limit of μ_h and approaching the h-relative IEC in the upper limit of μ_h by linearly increasing the weight on relative inequality in attainments (in relation to shortfalls). As Wagstaff's index goes from being h-relative to s-relative, these two indices are each other's opposites in terms of the level of intermediateness.

DISCUSSION AND CONCLUSIONS

Implications of the New Compromise Concept

There has recently been an intense discussion of the problems of using measures of income inequality to measure health inequality when health is represented by a bounded variable, which is often the case. Although Clarke et al. (2002) showed that relative inequality measures may order populations differently for attainments and shortfalls, the idea that the two relative IECs representing different, but potentially ethically defensible, vertical value judgments did not occur in the literature until Allanson and Petrie (2013a, 2013b). In line with this idea, we have formalized a general compromise concept with the h-relative IEC (relative inequality with respect to attainments) and the s-relative IEC (relative inequality with respect to shortfalls) as endpoints. Such a compromise concept implies — and we believe most people would not oppose — that an equiproportional increase in attainments does not decrease inequality and an equiproportional decrease in shortfalls does not increase inequality. In addition to all IECs that satisfy the absolute–relative compromise in terms of either attainments or shortfalls, this hs-relative compromise also includes IECs that partly intermediate the absolute and the h-relative (i.e., intermediate with respect to attainments) and partly intermediate the absolute and the s-relative (i.e., extreme leftist with respect to attainments). Unlike for an unbounded variable, we do not necessarily rule out an IEC just because it is extreme leftist for some health distributions.

This position is different from what is presented by Erreygers (2009a, 2009b), Erreygers and van Ourti (2011a), and Lambert and Zheng (2011), who all argue in favor of an absolute IEC and dismiss any relative or intermediate IEC as they do not rank populations consistently. For example, Lambert and Zheng (2011) use the relative–absolute-compromise concept, which is relevant for income inequality,[8] to show that the absolute IEC is the only one for which an inequality ranking is consistent for both shortfalls and attainments. However, the inequality map in Fig. 1 illustrates that this result is a direct consequence of implicitly allowing for both intermediate and extreme leftist IECs without acknowledging that they represents different vertical value judgments. Every IEC with respect to attainments that is represented by an iso-inequality contour in the area between the h-relative and absolute line is mirrored by a contour representing the corresponding IEC with respect to shortfalls in the area between the s-relative and absolute line (i.e., extreme leftist IEC with respect to attainments). For any distribution between the two contours, the ranking in comparison to the initial distribution will vary with the chosen perspective. That means implicitly comparing the ranking of an intermediate IEC with an extreme leftist IEC. As the absolute iso-inequality contour defines the intersection of the areas representing the two relative–absolute compromises, the corresponding inequality measure is the only one that ranks distributions consistently for attainments and shortfalls. If we instead explicitly allow an IEC to be extreme leftist for some values of μ_h by acknowledging the new hs-relative compromise concept, there also exist IECs represented by nonlinear iso-inequality contours that rank distributions consistently. Among these are any Extended θ-IEC such that $\theta_1 = \theta_2$, including the IEC underpinning the index suggested by Wagstaff (2005).[9]

However, if one truly considers it important to jointly measure the distributions of attainments and shortfalls, which is the main rationale behind the quest for a consistent inequality measure (compare Erreygers, 2009a, 2009b; Lasso de la Vega & Aristondo, 2012; Lambert & Zheng, 2011), would one not call for an IEC that in addition to ranking populations consistently also weights relative differences in attainments and shortfalls equally for any health distribution? Even though the absolute IEC that underpins Erreygers' (2009a, 2009c) index is the perfect linear combination between the two polar cases of the hs-relative compromise concept, it does not weight the polar cases equally (or independent of the mean). Neither does the IEC underpinning Wagstaff's index.

Our surplus-sharing approach characterizes an IEC by how it requires successive infinitesimal surpluses of health to be distributed to leave inequality unchanged. An IEC satisfying the hs-compromise concept implies that, for a given health distribution, an infinitesimal surplus must be distributed as a convex combination of the surplus-sharing rules of the two polar cases. The proportion being distributed according to the h-relative sharing rule is a measure of the level of intermediateness and may be interpreted as how sensitive the corresponding rank-dependent index is to relative differences in attainments in relation to shortfalls. The intermediateness of Erreygers' and Wagstaff's indices are linear functions of the average health in the population. Erreygers' goes from being s-relative to h-relative, while Wagstaff's goes in the opposite direction. This relationship explains the ranking pattern often seen in empirical applications (e.g., Erreygers, 2009b; Fleurbaey & Schokkaert, 2011; Kjellsson & Gerdtham, 2013a). For $\mu_h > 0.5$, the absolute and the s-relative indices, on the one hand, and Wagstaff's and the h-relative indices, on the other hand, tend to rank populations similarly. For $\mu_h < 0.5$, the opposite pairs apply. Consequently, choosing one of the two indices, Erreygers' or Wagstaff's, will for some values of μ_h implicitly imply one of the two relative IECs. In contrast, we show that the only IEC that weights the two polar cases equally and independently of the health distribution is our adaptation of Krtscha's (1994) fair compromise to a bounded health variable: the θ-IEC with $\theta = 0.5$.

However, by formalizing the new compromise concept, we acknowledge that IECs defined with respect to attainments and shortfalls may represent different vertical value judgment (just as the relative and absolute) and thereby question the focus on consistent inequality measures. Consequently, the chapter broadens rather than narrows the set of ethically defensible IECs.

Where to Go from Here

Our reasoning suggests a very general IEC without giving any guidance on the choice of the parameter values. We stress the importance of considering the value judgments implicit in the health inequality measure. But we recognize that the question of how to choose an appropriate measure will be asked by applied researchers. One way forward is to run experiments to find the parameters that represent the views held in the general population. However, rather than focusing on finding an optimal IEC, the main implication of the chapter, in order to guide policy, is to use a range of inequality measures bounded by the two relative IECs — preferably complemented by the Extended θ-IEC with various parameter values. Note, however, that before applying this new abundance of inequality concepts, one needs to, in line with Erreygers (2009a, 2009b), derive corresponding indices with desirable properties.

NOTES

1. Although Kolm (1976) refers to this intermediate view as centralist, we will consistently use the term intermediate to avoid using multiple terms for the same concept.
2. Erreygers and van Ourti (2011a) label the leftist, rightist, intermediate, extreme leftist, and extreme rightist IEC as quasiabsolute, quasirelative, mixed, inverse relative, and inverse absolute, respectively. See Table 1 for the correspondence between the two vocabularies.
3. The individual with the highest value is ranked first. Any tied individuals are assigned the average rank within the tied subgroup, leaving gaps in the ranking both above and below their rank.
4. See the proof of Proposition 2 in the appendix.
5. We assume that the whole surplus ε must be distributed.
6. For a formal definition see proof of Proposition 3 in the appendix.
7. That is, a General IEC with $g(\mu_h) = \mu_h^\lambda$, where $0 \leq \lambda \leq 1$.
8. Formally, any IEC that may be represented by Zoli's (2003) flexible two-parameter IEC: $g(\mu_h) = (\kappa\mu_h - (1-\kappa))^\lambda$, where $\lambda \in [0, 1]$ and $\kappa \in [0, 1]$.
9. See Lasso de la Vega and Aristondo (2012) for other consistent indices.
10. For some values of ε, some h_i may exceed its upper bound.
11. Observe that the left-hand side of Eq. (A.16) reduces to $-E(h_i - h_j)/(n(1 - \mu_h))$.

ACKNOWLEDGMENT

We acknowledge financial support from the Swedish Council for Working Life and Social Research (FAS) (dnr 2012-0419). The Health Economics

Program (HEP) at Lund University also receives core funding from FAS (dnr. 2006-1660), the Government Grant for Clinical Research ("ALF"), and Region Skåne (Gerdtham). We would like to thank Dennis Petrie for inspiring and fruitful discussions on the topic. We are also grateful to Jens Gudmundsson, Jens Dietrichson, Åsa Ljungvall, and the editors of this volume for providing valuable feedback and suggestions. We are responsible for all remaining errors.

REFERENCES

Allanson, P., & Petrie, D. (2013a). On the choice of health inequality measure for the longitudinal analysis of income-related health inequalities. *Health Economics, 22*, 353–365. doi:10.1002/hec.2803

Allanson, P., & Petrie, D. (2013b). Understanding the vertical equity judgements underpinning health inequality measures. *Health Economics*.

Amiel, Y., & Cowell, F. A. (1999). *Thinking about inequality: Personal judgment and income distributions*. Cambridge, UK: Cambridge University Press.

Aristondo, O., & Lasso de la Vega, C. (2013). Measuring the inequality of bounded distributions: A joint analysis of attainments and shortfalls. In P. Rosa Dias & O. O'Donnell (Eds.), *Health and inequality* (Vol. 21). Research on Economic Inequality. Bingley, UK: Emerald Group Publishing.

Bossert, W., & Pfingsten, A. (1990). Intermediate inequality: Concepts, indices, and welfare implications. *Mathematical Social Sciences, 19*, 117–134. doi:10.1016/0165-4896(90)90055-C

Clarke, P. M., Gerdtham, U.-G., Johannesson, M., Bingefors, K., & Smith, L. (2002). On the measurement of relative and absolute income-related health inequality. *Social Science and Medicine, 55*, 1923–1928. doi:10.1016/S0277-9536(01)00321-5

Dalton, H. (1920). The measurement of the inequality of incomes. *The Economic Journal, 30*, 348–361. doi:10.1016/j.jhealeco.2008.02.003

Erreygers, G. (2009a). Can a single indicator measure both attainment and shortfall inequality? *Journal of Health Economics, 28*, 885–893. doi:10.1016/j.jhealeco.2009.03.005

Erreygers, G. (2009b). Correcting the concentration index. *Journal of Health Economics, 28*, 504–515. doi:10.1016/j.jhealeco.2008.02.003

Erreygers, G. (2009c). Correcting the concentration index: A reply to Wagstaff. *Journal of Health Economics, 28*, 521–524. doi:10.1016/j.jhealeco.2008.12.001

Erreygers, G., & van Ourti, T. (2011a). Measuring socioeconomic inequality in health, health care and health financing by means of rank-dependent indices: A recipe for good practice. *Journal of Health Economics, 30*, 685–694. doi:10.1016/j.jhealeco.2011.04.004

Erreygers, G., & van Ourti, T. (2011b). Putting the cart before the horse. A comment on Wagstaff on inequality measurement in the presence of binary variables. *Health Economics, 20*, 1161–1165. doi:10.1002/hec.1754

Fleurbaey, M., & Schokkaert, E. (2011). Equity in health and health care. In M. V. Pauly, T. G. Mcguire, & P. P. Barros (Eds.), *Handbook of health economics* (Vol. 2, pp. 1003–1092). Amsterdam: Elsevier. doi:10.1016/B978-0-444-53592-4.00016-5

Kjellsson, G., & Gerdtham, U.-G. (2013a). Measuring health inequalities using the concentration index approach. In A. Culyer (Ed.), *Encyclopedia of health economics*. Amsterdam: Elsevier.

Kjellsson, G., & Gerdtham, U.-G. (forthcoming). On correcting the concentration index for binary variables. *Journal of Health Economics, 32*, 659–670. doi:10.1016/j.jhealeco.2012.10.012

Kolm, S.-C. (1976). Unequal inequalities. I. *Journal of Economic Theory, 12*, 416–442. doi:10.1016/0022-0531(76)90037-5

Krtscha, M. (1994). A new compromise of inequality. In W. Eichhorn (Ed.), *Models and measurement of welfare and inequality* (pp. 111–120). Heidelberg: Springer-Verlag.

Kunst, A., Bos, V., Andersen, O., Cardano, M., Costa, G., Harding, S., & Hemström, S. (2004a). Monitoring of trends in socioeconomic inequalities in mortality: Experiences from a European project. *Demographic Research, S2*, 229–254. doi: 10.4054/DemRes.2004.S2.9

Kunst, A., Bos, V., Lahelma, E., Bartley, M., Lissau, I., Regidor, E., ... Mackenbach, J. (2004b). Trends in socioeconomic inequalities in self-assessed health in 10 European countries. *International Journal of Epidemiology, 34*, 295–305. doi:10.1093/ije/dyh342

Lambert, P., & Zheng, B. (2011). On the consistent measurement of attainment and shortfall inequality. *Journal of Health Economics, 30*, 214–219. doi:10.1016/j.jhealeco.2010.10.008

Lasso de la Vega, C., & Aristondo, O. (2012). Proposing indicators to measure achievement and shortfall inequality consistently. *Journal of Health Economics, 31*, 578–583. doi:10.1016/j.jhealeco.2012.02.006

Marmot, M. (2010). *Fair society, healthy lives: Strategic review of health inequalities in England Post 2010*. London: Marmot Review.

Marmot, M., Allen, J., Bell, R., Bloomer, E., Goldblatt, P., & the Consortium for the European Review of Social Determinants of Health and the Health Divide (2012). WHO European review of social determinants of health and the health divide. *The Lancet, 380*, 1011–1029. doi:10.1016/S0140-6736(12)61228-8

Shorrocks, A. F. (1980). The class of additively decomposable inequality measures. *Econometrica, 48*, 613–625. Retrieved from http://www.jstor.org/stable/1913126

Wagstaff, A. (2005). The bounds of the concentration index when the variable of interest is binary, with an application to immunization inequality. *Health Economics, 14*, 429–432. doi:10.1002/hec.953

Wagstaff, A. (2009). Correcting the concentration index: A comment. *Journal of Health Economics, 28*, 516–520. doi: 10.1016/j.jhealeco.2008.12.003

Wagstaff, A. (2011a). The concentration index of a binary outcome revisited. *Health Economics, 20*, 11552–1160. doi:10.1002/hec.1752

Wagstaff, A. (2011b). Reply to Guido Erreygers and Tom van Ourti's comment on "The concentration index of a binary outcome revisited". *Health Economics, 20*, 1166–1168. doi:10.1002/hec.1753

Yoshida, T. (2005). Social welfare rankings of income distributions. A new parametric concept of intermediate inequality. *Social Choice and Welfare, 24*, 557–574. doi:10.1007/s00355-004-0318-2

Zheng, B. (2004). On intermediate measures of inequality. *Research on Economic Inequality, 12*, 135–157. doi:10.1016/S1049-2585(04)12005-X

Zheng, B. (2007). Unit-consistent decomposable inequality measures. *Economica, 74*, 97–111. doi:10.1111/j.1468-0335.2006.00524.x

Zoli, C. (2003). *Characterizing inequality equivalence criteria*. Mimeo, School of Economics, University of Nottingham. Retrieved from http://web.econ.unito.it/gma/sem/zoli.pdf

APPENDIX

Proof of Proposition 1. For a univariate rank-dependent index, $G(h)$, to represent a General IEC

$$\frac{h - \mu_h \mathbf{1}}{g(\mu_h)} = \frac{\tilde{h} - \mu_{\tilde{h}} \mathbf{1}}{g(\mu_{\tilde{h}})} \tag{A.1}$$

must be a sufficient condition for

$$G(h) = f(\mu_h, n) \sum h_i w_i = f(\mu_{\tilde{h}}, n) \sum \tilde{h}_i w_i = G(\tilde{h}) \tag{A.2}$$

Let w_i $(n+1)/2 - \rho_i$ represent the ith element in the vector $\mathbf{w} = (w_1, w_2, \ldots, w_n)$ and let $v(n)$ be a positive scalar function of n. Multiplying both sides of Eq. (A.1) by $v(n)$ and the vector $\mathbf{w}$ yields

$$v(n) \sum_i^n \frac{h_i - \mu_h}{g(\mu_h)} w_i = v(n) \sum_i^n \frac{\tilde{h}_i - \mu_{\tilde{h}}}{g(\mu_{\tilde{h}})} w_i \tag{A.3}$$

As $\sum_{i=1}^n w_i = 0$, $\sum_{i=1}^n (h_i - \mu_h) w_i = \sum_{i=1}^n h_i w_i$ and Eq. (A.3) becomes

$$\frac{v(n)}{g(\mu_h)} \sum_i^n h_i w_i = \frac{v(n)}{g(\mu_{\tilde{h}})} \sum_i^n \tilde{h}_i w_i \tag{A.4}$$

implying that $G(h) = G(\tilde{h})$ if $f(\mu_h, n) = v(n)/g(\mu_h)$. For an analogous proof for a bivariate index, such as $I(h) = I(\tilde{h})$, substitute z_i for w_i. ∎

Proof of Proposition 2. For a General IEC, $h \sim \tilde{h}$ and $h + d(h, \varepsilon) \sim h$ imply $d(h, \varepsilon) = \tilde{h} - h$ and $\mu_{\tilde{h}} - \mu_h = \frac{\varepsilon}{n}$. Substituting $\tilde{h} = h + d(h, \varepsilon)$ and $\mu_{\tilde{h}} = \mu_h + \frac{\varepsilon}{n}$ into Eq. (1) and solving for $d(h, \varepsilon)$ yields the corresponding IEDV

$$d(h, \varepsilon) = \frac{\varepsilon}{n} \mathbf{1} + (h - \mu_h \mathbf{1}) \left(\frac{g(\mu_h + \frac{\varepsilon}{n})}{g(\mu_h)} - 1 \right) \tag{A.5}$$

As we assume $g(\mu_h)$ to be continuous and (piecewise) differentiable, Eq. (A.5) is continuous and has a piecewise continuous partial derivative with respect to ε. For simplicity, rearrange Eq. (A.5) into $d(h,\varepsilon) = \frac{\varepsilon}{n}\mathbf{1} - \mu_h\mathbf{1}\left(\frac{g(\mu_h+\frac{\varepsilon}{n})-g(\mu_h)}{g(\mu_h)}\right) + h\left(\frac{g(\mu_h+\frac{\varepsilon}{n})-g(\mu_h)}{g(\mu_h)}\right)$. Let the vector $\boldsymbol{\delta}(h) = \lim_{\varepsilon\to 0+}[d(h,\varepsilon)/\varepsilon]$ represent the local vertical value judgment and calculate the limits as

$$\boldsymbol{\delta}(h) = \lim_{\varepsilon\to 0+}\frac{\varepsilon}{n\varepsilon}\mathbf{1} - \lim_{\varepsilon\to 0+}\mu_h\mathbf{1}\left(\frac{1}{\varepsilon}\frac{g(\mu_h+\frac{\varepsilon}{n})-g(\mu_h)}{g(\mu_h)}\right) + \lim_{\varepsilon\to 0+}h\left(\frac{1}{\varepsilon}\frac{g(\mu_h+\frac{\varepsilon}{n})-g(\mu_h)}{g(\mu_h)}\right) \tag{A.6}$$

As $\lim_{\varepsilon\to 0+}\frac{1}{\varepsilon}\frac{g(\mu_h+\frac{\varepsilon}{n})-g(\mu_h)}{g(\mu_h)} = \frac{1}{n}\frac{g'(\mu_h)}{g(\mu_h)}$, for instance by L'Hôpital's rule, Eq. (A.6) becomes

$$\boldsymbol{\delta}(h) = \frac{1}{n}\left(1 - \frac{g'(\mu_h)\mu_h}{g(\mu_h)}\right) + \frac{1}{n}\frac{h}{\mu_h}\left(\frac{g'(\mu_h)\mu_h}{g(\mu_h)}\right) \tag{A.7}$$

Let $\omega_{\mathrm{ra}}(\mu_h) = g'(\mu_h)\mu_h/g(\mu_h)$, then Eq. (A.7) becomes $\boldsymbol{\delta}(h) = \frac{1}{n}(1-\omega_{\mathrm{ra}}(\mu_h)) + \frac{1}{n}\frac{h}{\mu_h}\omega_{\mathrm{ra}}(\mu_h)$. To show the second part of the proposition, that is, Eq. (23), add

$$\frac{1}{n}\left((h-h) + \mathbf{1}(\mu_h - \mu_h) + \left(\frac{g'(\mu_h)\mu_h}{g(\mu_h)}\right)(h - h + \mathbf{1}(\mu_h - \mu_h))\right) = 0 \tag{A.8}$$

to the right-hand side of Eq. (A.7) and rearrange to

$$\boldsymbol{\delta}(h) = \frac{1}{n}\left(h + \frac{g'(\mu_h)\mu_h}{g(\mu_h)}\frac{h}{\mu_h} - \frac{g'(\mu_h)\mu_h}{g(\mu_h)}h\right)$$
$$+ \mathbf{1}\frac{1}{n}\left(1 - \mu_h - \frac{g'(\mu_h)\mu_h}{g(\mu_h)} + \frac{g'(\mu_h)\mu_h}{g(\mu_h)}\mu_h\right)$$
$$- \frac{1}{n}\left(h - \mu_h\mathbf{1} - \frac{g'(\mu_h)\mu_h}{g(\mu_h)}h + \frac{g'(\mu_h)\mu_h}{g(\mu_h)}\mu_h\mathbf{1}\right) \tag{A.9}$$

which simplifies to

$$\boldsymbol{\delta}(h) = \left(\mu_h + \frac{g'(\mu_h)\mu_h}{g(\mu_h)}(1-\mu_h)\right)\frac{h}{n\mu_h} + \left(1 - \left(\mu_h + \frac{g'(\mu_h)\mu_h}{g(\mu_h)}(1-\mu_h)\right)\right)\left(\frac{1}{n} - \frac{h - \mu_h\mathbf{1}}{n(1-\mu_h)}\right) \tag{A.10}$$

Let $\omega_{\text{hs}}(\mu_h) = \left(\mu_h + \frac{g'(\mu_h)\mu_h}{g(\mu_h)}(1-\mu_h)\right)$ and Eq. (A.10) becomes

$$\delta(h) = \omega_{\text{hs}}(\mu_h)\frac{h}{n\mu_h} + (1-\omega_{\text{hs}}(\mu_h))\left(\frac{1}{n}\mathbf{1} - \frac{h-\mu_h}{n(1-\mu_h)}\right) \quad \text{(A.11)}$$

∎

Proof of Proposition 3. First, note that we may rearrange $0 \leq \omega_{\text{ra}}(\mu_h) \leq 1$ and $0 \leq \omega_{\text{hs}}(\mu_h) \leq 1$ into

$$0 \leq \frac{g'(\mu_h)\mu_h}{g(\mu_h)} \leq 1 \quad \text{(A.12)}$$

and

$$\frac{-\mu_h}{1-\mu_h} \leq \frac{g'(\mu_h)\mu_h}{g(\mu_h)} \leq 1 \quad \text{(A.13)}$$

respectively. Note also that, for any feasible[10] pair of h and ε, the definition of a compromise between h-relative and absolute is equivalent to

$$h + 1\frac{\varepsilon}{n} \geq h + d(h,\varepsilon) \geq h + \frac{\varepsilon h}{n\mu_h} \quad \text{(A.14)}$$

and the definition of a compromise between h-relative and s-relative is equivalent to

$$h + \frac{\varepsilon}{n}\left(1 - \frac{h-\mu_h\mathbf{1}}{1-\mu_h}\right) \geq h + d(h,\varepsilon) \geq h + \frac{\varepsilon h}{n\mu_h} \quad \text{(A.15)}$$

As the IEDV corresponding to a General IEC is continuous and path independent (formally defined as $d(h, \varepsilon) + d[h + d(h, \varepsilon), \varepsilon'] = d(h, \varepsilon + \varepsilon')$ $\forall h$, $\forall \varepsilon, \varepsilon' > 0$), it is sufficient for proving Proposition 3 to only consider an infinitesimal surplus for any h by showing that Eqs. (A.12) and (A.13) are necessary and sufficient conditions for an IEC to satisfy the relative–absolute compromise and the hs-relative compromise, respectively. The proof is set out for income-related health inequality, but extends to total health inequality.

Sufficiency: Let an IEC be a compromise between (a) the h-relative and the s-relative IECs and (b) the h-relative and the absolute IECs. Consider any two individuals (i, j) such that $\phi_i < \phi_j$. The assumption of a pro-rich health distribution implies that the expected value of the difference of h_i and h_j is positive: $E(h_i - h_j) > 0$. (For total inequality, consider instead two individuals such that $\rho_i < \rho_j$, then $h_i - h_j > 0$ holds by definition.) Note that the ith element in $\boldsymbol{\delta}(\boldsymbol{h})$ corresponding to the absolute, h-relative, and s-relative IECs are $\delta_i = 1/n$, $\delta_i = h_i/n\mu_h$, and $\delta_i = 1/n - (h_i - \mu_h)/(n(1 - \mu_h))$, respectively. Path independency implies that Eqs. (A.14) and (A.15) hold if and only if the expected value of the difference between the shares of an infinitesimal surplus distributed to i and j lies in the range between the expected values of the differences between the surplus shares of the polar cases. That is, (a) for a hs-relative compromise

$$E\left(\frac{1}{n} - \frac{h_i - \mu_h}{n(1-\mu_h)} - \left(\frac{1}{n} - \frac{h_j - \mu_h}{n(1-\mu_h)}\right)\right) \leq E(\delta_i - \delta_j) \leq E\left(\frac{h_i}{n\mu_h} - \frac{h_j}{n\mu_h}\right) \quad (A.16)$$

and (b) for a relative–absolute compromise

$$E\left(\frac{1}{n} - \frac{1}{n}\right) \leq E(\delta_i - \delta_j) \leq E\left(\frac{h_i}{n\mu_h} - \frac{h_j}{n\mu_h}\right) \quad (A.17)$$

where

$$E(\delta_i - \delta_j) = E\left(\frac{1}{n} + \frac{g'(\mu_h)\mu_h}{g(\mu_h)} \frac{(h_i - \mu_h)}{n\mu_h} - \left(\frac{1}{n} + \frac{g'(\mu_h)\mu_h}{g(\mu_h)} \frac{(h_j - \mu_h)}{n\mu_h}\right)\right)$$
$$= \frac{g'(\mu_h)\mu_h}{g(\mu_h)} \left(\frac{E(h_i - h_j)}{n\mu_h}\right) \quad (A.18)$$

Multiplying each term in Eqs. (A.17) and (A.16) by $n\mu_h/E(h_i - h_j)$ yields Eqs. (A.12) and (A.13),[11] which completes this part of the proof.

Necessity: Let, instead, (a) $-\mu_h/(1-\mu_h) \leq g'(\mu_h)\mu_h/g(\mu_h) \leq 1$ and (b) $0 \leq g'(\mu_h)\mu_h/g(\mu_h) \leq 1$ and reverse the exercise above. ∎

Proof of Proposition 4. A rank-dependent index represents a General IEC if $f(\mu_h, n) = v(n)/g(\mu_h)$ (Proposition 1). Then the elasticity of the normalization function is

$$\eta(\mu_h) = f'(\mu_h)\frac{\mu_h}{f(\mu_h)} = -v(n)\frac{g'(\mu_h)}{g(\mu_h)^2}\frac{\mu_h}{\frac{v(n)}{g(\mu_h)}} = -g'(\mu_h)\frac{\mu_h}{g(\mu_h)} \quad (A.19)$$

To complete the proof, using Proposition 2, substitute Eq. (A.19) into Eqs. (22) and (23) to obtain $\omega_{ra} = -\eta(\mu_h)$ and

$$\omega_{hs}(\mu_h) = \mu_h - \eta(\mu_h)(1 - \mu_h) = \frac{\frac{\mu_h}{1-\mu_h} - \eta(\mu_h)}{1 + \frac{\mu_h}{1-\mu_h}}$$

respectively. ∎

Proof of Proposition 5. Sufficiency: Represent a General IEC as $\forall h, \tilde{h}; h \sim \tilde{h}$ if

$$\frac{h - \mu_h \mathbf{1}}{\mu_h^\theta (1 - \mu_h)^{1-\theta}} = \frac{\tilde{h} - \mu_{\tilde{h}} \mathbf{1}}{\mu_{\tilde{h}}^\theta (1 - \mu_{\tilde{h}})^{1-\theta}} \quad (A.20)$$

that is, $g(\mu_h) = \mu_h^\theta (1 - \mu_h)^{1-\theta}$, then $g'(\mu_h)\mu_h/g(\mu_h) = \theta - (1-\theta)\mu_h/(1-\mu_h)$. Solving for θ yields $\theta = \mu_h + \frac{g'(\mu_h)\mu_h}{g(\mu_h)}(1 - \mu_h)$. Proposition 2 implies

$$\delta(h) = (1 - \omega_{hs}(\mu_h))\left(\frac{1}{n} - \frac{h - \mu_h \mathbf{1}}{n(1 - \mu_h)}\right) + \omega_{hs}(\mu_h)\frac{h}{n\mu_h} \quad (A.21)$$

where $\omega_{hs}(\mu_h) = \mu_h + \frac{g'(\mu_h)\mu_h}{g(\mu_h)}(1 - \mu_h) = \theta$. Thus, Eq. (28) holds.

Necessity: Let the local surplus-sharing rules of a General IEC be represented by the vector in Eq. (28). Proposition 2 implies $\omega_{hs}(\mu_h) = \theta = \mu_h + \frac{g'(\mu_h)\mu_h}{g(\mu_h)}(1 - \mu_h)$. Solve for $g'(\mu_h)\mu_h/g(\mu_h)$ to obtain a differential equation

$$\frac{g'(\mu_h)\mu_h}{g(\mu_h)} = \theta - (1-\theta)\frac{\mu_h}{1 - \mu_h} \quad (A.22)$$

that has the single solution: $g(\mu_h) = C\mu_h^\theta (1 - \mu_h)^{1-\theta}$, where C is a constant that may be normalized to one as it appears on both sides of Eq. (1). ∎

MEASURING THE INEQUALITY OF BOUNDED DISTRIBUTIONS: A JOINT ANALYSIS OF ATTAINMENTS AND SHORTFALLS

Oihana Aristondo and Casilda Lasso de la Vega

ABSTRACT

When health is measured by a bounded variable, differences in health can be presented as levels of attainment or shortfall. Measurement of heath inequality then usually involves the choice of either the attainment or the shortfall distribution, and this choice may affect comparisons of inequality across populations. A number of indices have been introduced to overcome this problem. This chapter proposes a framework in which attainment and shortfall distributions can be jointly analyzed. Joint distributions of attainments and shortfalls are defined from points of view consistent with concerns for relative, absolute or intermediate inequality. Inequality measures invariant according to the corresponding ethical criterion are then applied. A dominance criterion that guarantees unanimous rankings of the joint distributions is also proposed.

Keywords: Inequality measurement; health inequality; bounded variables; Lorenz curves

JEL classifications: I30; D63

INTRODUCTION

Health distributions are usually defined for bounded variables, which can be described in terms of either health attainments or shortfalls. Inequality comparisons across populations may not coincide for attainments and shortfalls. In fact, the inequality rankings will usually be reversed. A number of papers have drawn attention to the issue and proposed solutions (among them Clarke, Gerdtham, Johannesson, Bingefors & Smith, 2002; Erreygers, 2009c; Lambert & Zheng, 2011; Lasso de la Vega & Aristondo, 2012).

Where does this problem come from? As long as we compare populations with the same means, the standard dominance criteria guarantee that comparison of inequality in the distribution of attainments coincides with that in the distribution of shortfalls (see Lambert & Zheng, 2011). But when the means differ, even in the simplest case with only two individuals, the inequality rankings may be reversed. Consider the following two-person distributions $\mathbf{x} = (10, 40)$ and $\mathbf{y} = (35, 65)$. The respective means are $\mu(\mathbf{x}) = 25$ and $\mu(\mathbf{y}) = 50$. In order to compare the inequality levels of these distributions, some invariance condition needs to be invoked. Assume a relative point of view. Then distribution $\mathbf{x}$ is relative-equivalent to distribution $\mathbf{x}^* = (20, 80)$. In a nonambiguous way $\mathbf{x}^*$ in more unequal than $\mathbf{y}$. Then the relative inequality level is higher in the first population than in the second. Now imagine that the bound is $\alpha = 100$ and focus on the shortfall side. The corresponding shortfall distributions are $\alpha - \mathbf{x} = (90, 60)$ and $\alpha - \mathbf{y} = (65, 35)$. Again, from a relative point of view the first situation is equivalent to $(\alpha - \mathbf{x})^* = (60, 40)$ which displays unambiguously less inequality than $\alpha - \mathbf{y}$. The conclusion is now that the inequality level is lower in the first population than in the second. Focusing either on attainments or on shortfalls leads to contradictory conclusions.

Should there be any connection between the inequality of attainments and the inequality of shortfalls? Clarke et al. (2002) argue that attainments and shortfalls are "different sides of the same coin" and inequality in one should be the mirror of that in the other. Erreygers (2009c) proposes the "strongest form" of the mirror property, referred to as *complementary*, demanding that the magnitude of inequality of the attainments coincides with that of shortfalls. He characterizes two indicators, appropriate normalizations of the absolute Gini index and the coefficient of variation respectively, both depending on the distribution bounds, which measure attainment and shortfall inequality identically.

Lambert and Zheng (2011) introduce a weaker property requiring that only the inequality rankings remain unchanged when we focus either on the attainment side or on the shortfall side. They show that all the relative and the intermediate (between relative and absolute) standard inequality indices fail this requirement. They identify two classes of *complementary* absolute inequality measures, according to which the level of inequality of attainments and shortfalls is identical, and show that, among them, only the variance can be decomposed by population subgroups.

Lasso de la Vega and Aristondo (2012) propose a unified framework in which attainment and shortfall distributions can be jointly analyzed. One simple way to do this, given any inequality measure, is to aggregate the respective attainment and shortfall inequality levels in a single indicator. Specifically, taking a generalized mean of the inequality of attainments and of the inequality of shortfalls allows us to transform any inequality measure into a *complementary* indicator.

This chapter introduces an alternative procedure to measure the inequality of attainments and shortfalls. An inequality measure is supposed to capture the divergences between the current distribution and the hypothetical situation in which all the individuals enjoy the mean. Assessing these divergences imposes a value judgment since it is crucial to determine what distributional changes guarantee that the divergences do not vary and, consequently, the inequality level remains unaltered. The relative and the absolute point of views assume that the divergences are invariant to equiproportional and uniform distribution changes, respectively. These are usually considered the two extreme criteria. Invariance under changes in between are referred to as intermediate points of view (Kolm, 1976).

In a first step, this chapter proposes to compute the divergences between the joint distribution of attainments and shortfalls and the hypothetical egalitarian situation. We allow these divergences to be relative, absolute, or intermediate. Thus the respective relative, absolute, and intermediate joint distributions are proposed. In a second step, inequality measures consistent with the respective criteria are applied. The indicators obtained take into consideration jointly the attainment and shortfall distributions. We also show the relationship between the indicators proposed in this chapter and the measures derived by Lasso de la Vega and Aristondo (2012). A family of decomposable measures is identified and a dominance criterion based on the Lorenz curves of the joint distributions is also proposed.

In this same volume, Kjellsson and Gerdtham (2013) also propose to jointly analyze the distributions of attainments and shortfalls. Whereas we introduce indicators for doing so, they focus on the criteria of invariance that should be satisfied. Specifically they formalize a new criterion of invariance considering the two equiproportional distribution changes, with respect to attainments and to shortfalls respectively, as the extreme cases. Following their suggestion, we examine the behavior of the joint indicators under these kinds of distributional changes. In particular, we find that the joint indicators associated with decomposable measures fulfill the requirement.

In recent years, there has been a growing interest in analyzing health distribution. The literature on this issue has two main branches. One of them is concerned only with total health inequality across individuals in a population and is closely related to the measurement of income inequality. Our contribution fits this area.

A second branch of the literature tries to incorporate a socioeconomic dimension in the measurement to asses to what extent the inequality in health is related to socioeconomic status (see Wagstaff & van Doorslaer, 2000, van Doorslaer & van Ourti, 2011; Fleurbaey & Schokkaert, 2012, for survey chapters). In the last section we will discuss some possible extensions of our approach to this field.

The rest of the chapter is organized as follows. Notation and basic definitions are presented in the next section. The third section introduces the attainment and shortfall joint distributions from points of view consistent with relative, absolute or intermediate concerns. The following two sections make the proposal to measure the inequality of the joint distributions and provide some examples. The penultimate section is devoted to analyzing dominance criteria for ranking the joint distributions. Finally, we conclude. The proofs are presented in the appendix.

NOTATION AND BASIC DEFINITIONS

We consider a population consisting of $n \geq 2$ individuals. An *attainment distribution* is represented by a vector $\mathbf{x} = (x_1, x_2, \ldots, x_n) \in \mathbb{R}^n_{++}$, where x_i

Measuring the Inequality of Bounded Distributions

represents individual i's attainment. We assume that the variables are ratio-scale and are lower bounded by 0. We denote by $D = \cup_{n \geq 2} D^n$ the set of all finite dimensional distributions. For any $\mathbf{x} \in D$, $\mu_\mathbf{x} = \mu(\mathbf{x})$ and $n_x = n(\mathbf{x})$ stand, respectively, for the mean and population size of the distribution $\mathbf{x}$.

We denote by α the maximum level of attainments. We assume that α is given and fixed. We let D^α represent the set of distributions for which α is an upper bound, that is, $D^\alpha = \{\mathbf{x} \in D / x_i < \alpha \text{ for all } i\}$. The *shortfall distribution* associated with $x \in D^\alpha$ is denoted as $\alpha \mathbf{1} - \mathbf{x}$, where $\alpha - x_i$ represents individual i's shortfall. We use the notation $\mathbf{1} = (1, ..., 1)$ and $\lambda \mathbf{1} = (\lambda, ..., \lambda)$.

Given two distributions $\mathbf{x}, \mathbf{x}' \in D$, we say that $\mathbf{x}'$ is obtained from $\mathbf{x}$ by a *progressive transfer* if there exist two individuals i, $j \in \{1, ..., n\}$ and $h > 0$ such that $x'_i = x_i + h \leq x_j - h = x'_j$ and $x'_k = x_k$ for every $k \in \{1, ..., n\} \setminus \{i, j\}$.

A standard inequality index I is a real valued continuous function $I : D \to \mathbb{R}$ which fulfills the following properties.

Pigou-Dalton Transfer Principle (TP). $I(\mathbf{x}') < I(\mathbf{x})$ whenever $\mathbf{x}'$ is obtained from $\mathbf{x}$ by a progressive transfer.

Symmetry (SYM). $I(\mathbf{x}) = I(\mathbf{x}')$ whenever $\mathbf{x} = \mathbf{x}' \Pi$ for some permutation matrix Π.

Replication Invariance (RI). $I(\mathbf{x}) = I(\mathbf{x}')$ whenever $\mathbf{x}' = (\mathbf{x}, \mathbf{x}, ..., \mathbf{x})$ with $n_{\mathbf{x}'} = m n_\mathbf{x}$ for some positive integer m.

Normalization (NOR). $I(\lambda \mathbf{1}) = 0$ for all $\lambda > 0$.

The crucial axiom in inequality measurement is the *Pigou-Dalton transfer principle* which requires, in the context of income inequality, that a transfer from a richer person to a poorer one decreases inequality. *Symmetry* establishes that the inequality index should be insensitive to a reordering of the individuals, whereas *replication invariance* allows populations of different sizes to be compared. Finally, in this field, it is usually assumed that the indices are *normalized* with the inequality level equal to 0 when everybody enjoys the same value. These four properties are considered to be inherent to the concept of inequality and have come to be accepted as basic properties for an inequality index.

Comparing distributions with different means requires making an assumption concerning the conditions under which inequality remains unchanged when an increment of the attribute is distributed among the population. Adoption of such an invariance condition involves the imposition of value judgments (see Kolm, 1976). One of the most popular conditions is ratio-scale invariance, which demands that the inequality level remains unchanged under proportional changes in all the values. This property guarantees that the inequality level is insensitive to changes in the unit of measurement.

Ratio-Scale Invariance. $I(\lambda \mathbf{x}) = I(\mathbf{x})$ for all $\lambda > 0$.

Relative indices are those that are ratio-scale invariant.

Translation invariance requires that the same increase in all the values does not change the inequality level.

Translation Invariance. $I(\mathbf{x} + \eta \mathbf{1}) = I(\mathbf{x})$ for all η whenever $\mathbf{x} + \eta \mathbf{1} \in D$.

Absolute indices are those that are translation invariant.

An intermediate viewpoint is also possible. Bossert and Pfingsten (1990) introduced the following no-change-in-inequality path, defining some intermediate inequality measures:

β Intermediate Invariance. $I((1 + \eta\beta)\mathbf{x} + \eta(1 - \beta)\mathbf{1}) = I(\mathbf{x})$ for some $\beta \in (0, 1)$ and all $\eta \in \mathbb{R}$, whenever $(1 + \eta\beta)\mathbf{x} + \eta(1 - \beta)\mathbf{1} \in D$.

Given $\beta \in (0, 1)$, this transformation can be viewed as an equal proportion increase $(1 + \eta\beta)$ followed by an equal amount addition $\eta(1 - \beta)$ to all incomes. Note that the two extreme cases, that is, when $\beta = 1$ and $\beta = 0$, coincide, respectively, with the relative and absolute viewpoints. Thus, the β parameter can be interpreted as the degree of intermediateness. When necessary we will denote by I_β any inequality measure β intermediate invariant.

In empirical applications, the population is often classified into groups according to characteristics such as area of residence, social status, age, gender, race, and so on. Then it is interesting to relate the overall inequality to the inequality in each group. Shorrocks (1980) introduces the *decomposability property* that requires the overall inequality may be decomposed as the sum of the between-group and the within-group components. The between-group component is defined as the inequality level of a hypothetical distribution in which each person's value is replaced by the mean of his/her subgroup. The within-group component is a weighted sum of the subgroup inequality levels.

To formalize this property, assume that a population of n individuals is split into $K \geq 2$ mutually exclusive subgroups with distribution $\mathbf{x}^j = (x_1^j, ..., x_{n_j}^j)$, where $\mu_j = \mu(\mathbf{x}^j)$ denotes the mean of the jth subgroup and $n_j = n(\mathbf{x}^j)$ represents its size for all $j = 1, ..., K$. Let inequality in group j be written $I_j = I(\mathbf{x}^j)$. Let us denote by $\mathbf{x}^B = (\mu_1 \mathbf{1}_{n_1}, ..., \mu_K \mathbf{1}_{n_K})$ the distribution in which each person's value is replaced by the respective subgroup mean.

Decomposability. An index I is *decomposable* if the following relationship holds

$$I(\mathbf{x}^1, ..., \mathbf{x}^K) = I(\mathbf{x}^W) + I(\mathbf{x}^B) = \sum_{j=1}^{K} w^j(\mu_1, ..., \mu_K; n_1, ..., n_K) I(\mathbf{x}^j) + I(\mu_1 \mathbf{1}_{n_1}, ..., \mu_K \mathbf{1}_{n_K})$$

(1)

where $w^j(\mu_1, ..., \mu_K; n_1, ..., n_K) \geq 0$ is the weight on subgroup j's inequality level $I_j = I(\mathbf{x}^j)$ in the within-group term $j = 1, ..., K$.

Shorrocks (1980) showed that the only family of relative decomposable inequality measures is the Generalized Entropy (GE) family. It is defined as follows:

$$GE_\theta(\mathbf{x}) = \begin{cases} \left(\sum_{i=1}^{n}(x_i/\mu(\mathbf{x}))^\theta - 1\right)/n\theta(\theta-1) & \theta \neq 0, 1 \\ \sum_{i=1}^{n}\ln(\mu(\mathbf{x})/x_i)/n & \theta = 0 \\ \sum_{i=1}^{n}(x_i/\mu(\mathbf{x}))\ln(x_i/\mu(\mathbf{x}))/n & \theta = 1 \end{cases} \quad (2)$$

where GE_1 is the first Theil measure and GE_0, is the second Theil measure.

The weights for which Eq. (1) is fulfilled are given by

$$w_\theta^j = (n_j/n)(\mu_j/\mu)^\theta \quad \text{with} \quad j = 1, ..., K \quad (3)$$

Note that when $\theta = 0$ the weights are the population shares.

Assuming an absolute viewpoint, Chakravarty and Tyagarupananda (1998) in a differentiable framework, and Bosmans and Cowell (2010) in a continuous one, prove that the family of absolute decomposable inequality measures is the following:

$$KV_\delta(\mathbf{x}) = \begin{cases} \frac{1}{n}\left(\sum_{i=1}^{n}(e^{\delta(x_i - \mu(\mathbf{x}))} - 1)\right) & \delta \neq 0 \\ \frac{1}{n}\sum_{i=1}^{n}(x_i - \mu(\mathbf{x}))^2 & \delta = 0 \end{cases} \quad (4)$$

When $\delta \neq 0$, KV_δ is the well-known Kolm's family (1976) and when $\delta = 0$ we find the variance. We will refer to this family as the Kolm-Variance family.

The decomposable weights are given by

$$w_\delta^j = (n_j/n)e^{\delta(\mu_j - \mu)} \quad \text{with} \quad j = 1, ..., K \quad (5)$$

The variance weights are the population shares.

Finally, Chakravarty and Tyagarupananda (2009) prove that the unique decomposable Bossert-Pfingsten type of intermediate inequality measures is the following transformed GE family:

$$BP_{\beta,\theta}(\mathbf{x}) = \begin{cases} \dfrac{1}{n\theta(\theta-1)}\left(\sum_{i=1}^{n}\left(\dfrac{x_i+c}{\mu(\mathbf{x})+c}\right)^{\theta}-1\right) & \theta \neq 0,1 \\ \dfrac{1}{n}\sum_{i=1}^{n}\ln\left(\dfrac{\mu(\mathbf{x})+c}{x_i+c}\right) & \theta = 0 \\ \dfrac{1}{n}\sum_{i=1}^{n}\dfrac{x_i+c}{\mu(\mathbf{x})+c}\ln\left(\dfrac{x_i+c}{\mu(\mathbf{x})+c}\right) & \theta = 1 \end{cases} \quad (6)$$

where $\theta = r(1+\beta)/\beta$, $c = (1-\beta)/\beta$, and $0 < \beta < 1$ and r is a constant. We will refer to this family as the Bossert-Pfingsten (BP) family.

And Eq. (1) is satisfied for the following weights:

$$w_{\beta\theta}^{j} = (n_j/n)(\beta\mu_j + 1 - \beta/\beta\mu + 1 - \beta)^{\theta} \quad \text{with} \quad j = 1,...,K \quad (7)$$

Also in this case, we find that the weights coincide with the population shares when $\theta = 0$.

The GE family corresponds to the extreme case when the β parameter value is equal to 1. Similarly, it is easy to show that the weights given in Eq. (3) are the particular values of those in Eq. (7) when $\beta = 1$.

THE ATTAINMENT AND THE SHORTFALL JOINT DISTRIBUTION

From now on we focus on distributions of bounded characteristics. Thus we can consider attainment or shortfall distributions, such as the percentage of survival or alternatively the percentage of mortality. We will consider the same upper bound for all the distributions involved, denoted by α, whereas 0 is always the lower bound.

Dominance analysis using Lorenz curves allows distributions to be compared in terms of inequality in a nonambiguous way. Lambert and Zheng (2011) show that as long as the distributions have equal means, the inequality rankings provided by the Lorenz curves remain unchanged when we focus either on attainments or on shortfalls. When the distributions have unequal means, only the absolute Lorenz curves rank the attainment and the shortfall distributions in a consistent way.

Measuring the Inequality of Bounded Distributions

Basically the difficulty stems from the need to invoke invariance conditions that impose quite different behaviors when applied to attainments or to shortfalls. To make this clearer, imagine that we assume a relative point of view. When an additional unit has to be distributed keeping inequality unchanged, the more one individual has the more he has to receive. But the criterion leads to different results when looking at attainments or at shortfalls. Indeed, from the attainment side, the more one individual has, the healthier he is. However, from the shortfall side, the more one individual has, the greater the gap is. From the attainment side, the healthier individual will receive the higher amount, whereas from the shortfall side, the less healthy individual will receive more. Then there is no way to make a consistent relative distribution to either side. The same happens with all the intermediate points of view. As regards the absolute criterion, as everybody receives the same amount regardless of what they have, no inconsistency appears.

In a nutshell, the aim is to evaluate the inequality of a characteristic distribution that can be described equivalently in terms of attainments or in terms of shortfalls. Depending on the side we focus on, the conclusions differ. Our proposal is to consider jointly the distributions of attainments and shortfalls and evaluate the inequality as the divergence between the joint distribution and the hypothetical situation, where everybody enjoys the mean. In other words, we would like to evaluate the divergence between the distribution $(\mathbf{x}, \alpha\mathbf{1} - \mathbf{x})$ and the reference distribution $(\mu(\mathbf{x})\mathbf{1}, (\alpha - \mu(\mathbf{x}))\mathbf{1})$.

When a relative point of view is assumed, the divergence is measured in terms of ratios. We define the *relative joint distribution* as follows.

$$\mathbf{x}_R = \left(\frac{\mathbf{x} - \mu(\mathbf{x})\mathbf{1}}{\mu(\mathbf{x})} + \mathbf{1}, \frac{(\alpha\mathbf{1} - \mathbf{x}) - (\alpha - \mu(\mathbf{x}))\mathbf{1}}{\alpha - \mu(\mathbf{x})} + \mathbf{1} \right) \qquad (8)$$

Note that the mean of this relative joint distribution is always equal to 1.

As regards the absolute viewpoint, the divergence is now understood in terms of differences. Consequently, we define the *absolute joint distribution* as follows:

$$\mathbf{x}_A = (\mathbf{x} - \mu(\mathbf{x})\mathbf{1} + \mathbf{1}, \ \mu(\mathbf{x})\mathbf{1} - \mathbf{x} + \mathbf{1}) \qquad (9)$$

The mean of this absolute joint distribution is also equal to $\mathbf{1}$.

Finally, under the β intermediate invariance condition, inequality measures remain unchanged if $\mathbf{x}$ becomes $(1 + \eta\beta)\mathbf{x} + \eta(1 - \beta)\mathbf{1}$ for some $\beta \in (0, 1)$ and all feasible $\eta \in \mathbb{R}$. Then distribution $\mathbf{x}$ is β intermediate-equivalent to the distribution $\frac{x+(1-\beta)(1-\mu(x))1}{\beta\mu(x)+(1-\beta)} = \frac{x-\mu(x)1}{\beta\mu(x)+(1-\beta)} + 1$. We define the β *intermediate joint distribution* as follows:

$$x_{BP} = \left(\frac{x-\mu(x)1}{\beta\mu(x)+(1-\beta)} + 1, \frac{(\alpha 1 - x) - (\alpha - \mu(x))1}{\beta(\alpha-\mu(x))+(1-\beta)} + 1 \right) \qquad (10)$$

All these intermediate distributions have a mean equal to 1. Note that x_R and x_A in Eqs. (8) and (9) are no more than the x_{BP} extreme distributions when $\beta = 1$ and $\beta = 0$ respectively. Then we will denote the β joint distributions as follows:

$$x_\beta = \begin{cases} x_R & \text{if } \beta = 1 \\ x_A & \text{if } \beta = 0 \\ x_{BP} & \text{if } 0 < \beta < 1 \end{cases} \qquad (11)$$

where the β-parameter represents the invariance viewpoint assumed.

MEASURING INEQUALITY OF THE JOINT DISTRIBUTION

Once the divergence between the joint and the reference mean distributions is introduced, the standard inequality measures will evaluate this divergence. Consider an inequality measure I_β invariant according to the β invariance condition, and, for any given $x \in D^\alpha$, the joint distribution x_β. If we are interested in analyzing simultaneously the attainment and the shortfall inequality from a β-invariant point of view, we may think of applying the inequality measure I_β to the joint distribution x_β.

Specifically, given $\alpha > 0$ we propose to consider the *joint indicator associated with* I_β, denoted by I_β^J, as the indicator that, for each distribution $x \in D^\alpha$, takes the following value

$$I_\beta^J(x) = I_\beta(x_\beta) \qquad (12)$$

The proposition below states that some properties fulfilled by I_β are inherited by the joint indicators.

Proposition 1. If I_β is a β-invariant inequality measure satisfying continuity, the transfer principle, symmetry, replication invariance, and normalization the joint indicator associated, I_β^J, also satisfies continuity, the transfer principle, symmetry, replication invariance and normalization.

In addition $I_\beta^J(\mathbf{x}) = I_\beta^J(\alpha\mathbf{1} - \mathbf{x})$ for any distribution $\mathbf{x} \in D^\alpha$.

Proof: In the appendix. □

The joint indicator I_β^J satisfies all the properties usually assumed for an inequality measure and so it captures the joint distribution inequality.

Since $I_\beta^J(\mathbf{x}) = I_\beta^J(\alpha\mathbf{1} - \mathbf{x})$, Proposition 1 allows the derivation of *perfect complementary* indices according to Erreygers' designation, both rank-dependent and rank-independent.

Lasso de la Vega and Aristondo (2012) propose *perfect complementary* indicators taking the generalized mean of the inequality of attainments and inequality of shortfalls. Specifically, *the arithmetic mean indicator associated with an inequality index* has the following form:

$$I^1(\mathbf{x}) = \frac{I(\mathbf{x}) + I(\alpha\mathbf{1} - \mathbf{x})}{2} \tag{13}$$

Proposition 2 shows that the joint indicator I_β^J associated with a decomposable index I_β is exactly the *arithmetic mean indicator associated with* I_β.

Proposition 2. If I_β is a β-invariant decomposable inequality measure then,

$$I_\beta^J(\mathbf{x}) = I_\beta^1(\mathbf{x}) = \frac{I_\beta(\mathbf{x}) + I_\beta(\alpha\mathbf{1} - \mathbf{x})}{2} \tag{14}$$

for any distribution $\mathbf{x} \in D^\alpha$.

Proof: In the appendix. □

We focus on these specific joint indicators associated with decomposable measures. Following Kjellsson and Gerdtham (2013) we now analyze their behavior under equiproportionate changes in attainments and in shortfalls. Consider an equiproportional increase in attainments. For any $\lambda > 0$ such that $\mathbf{x} + \lambda\mathbf{x} \in D^\alpha$ we find

$$I_\beta^J(\mathbf{x} + \lambda\mathbf{x}) = \frac{I_\beta(\mathbf{x} + \lambda\mathbf{x}) + I_\beta(\alpha\mathbf{1} - (\mathbf{x} + \lambda\mathbf{x}))}{2} \tag{15}$$

Equiproportional decreases in shortfalls lead to

$$I_\beta^J(\mathbf{x} + \lambda(\alpha\mathbf{1} - \mathbf{x})) = \frac{I_\beta(\mathbf{x} + \lambda(\alpha\mathbf{1} - \mathbf{x})) + I_\beta((\alpha\mathbf{1} - \mathbf{x}) - \lambda(\alpha\mathbf{1} - \mathbf{x}))}{2} \tag{16}$$

for all $\lambda > 0$ such that $\mathbf{x} + \lambda(\alpha\mathbf{1} - \mathbf{x}) \in D^\alpha$.

The following proposition holds.

Proposition 3. If I_β is a β-invariant decomposable inequality measure then for any distribution $\mathbf{x} \in D^\alpha$

(i) $I_\beta^J(\mathbf{x}) \leq I_\beta^J(\mathbf{x} + \lambda \mathbf{x})$ for all $\lambda > 0$ with $\mathbf{x} + \lambda \mathbf{x} \in D^\alpha$, and
(ii) $I_\beta^J(\mathbf{x}) \geq I_\beta^J(\mathbf{x} + \lambda(\alpha \mathbf{1} - \mathbf{x}))$ for all $\lambda > 0$ with $\mathbf{x} + \lambda(\alpha \mathbf{1} - \mathbf{x}) \in D^\alpha$.

Proof: In the appendix. □

In words, the joint indicators associated with β-invariant decomposable measures do not decrease under equiproportional increases in attainments and do not increase under equiproportional decreases in shortfalls. They are *hs-relative* indicators according to Kjellsson-Gerdtham's designation.[1]

As mentioned before, decomposability is quite useful since it allows policy makers to target the subgroups in which inequality is higher. The following proposition shows that for any point of view assumed, it is always possible to find joint indicators that are decomposable. All of them are *hs-relative*.

Proposition 4. The joint indicators associated with the second Theil measure, GE_0, variance and the members of the BP family $BP_{\beta,0}$ are decomposable measures.

In all cases the weights on subgroup j's inequality level for which the respective decomposable decompositions hold are $w_j = n_j/n$.

Proof: In the appendix. □

As proved in the proposition, the weights in the within-group component depend only on the subgroup population shares. Then the decomposition satisfies the path independence property (Foster & Shneyerov, 2000). This means that the variations in between-group inequality as measured by these indices do not affect the within-group term, contrary to what happens with most of the decompositions.

SOME EXAMPLES

The joint indicators associated with the GE family (Eq. (2)), the Kolm-Variance family (Eq. (4)) and the BP family (Eq. (6)) are presented below. Some of them are decomposable and all of them are *hs-relative*.

The *joint indicator* associated with the GE family is the following.

Measuring the Inequality of Bounded Distributions

$$(GE_\theta)^J(\mathbf{x}) = \begin{cases} \dfrac{1}{2n\theta(\theta-1)}\left[\left(\sum_{i=1}^n\left(\dfrac{x_i}{\mu(\mathbf{x})}\right)^\theta - 1\right) + \left(\sum_{i=1}^n\left(\dfrac{\alpha-x_i}{\alpha-\mu(\mathbf{x})}\right)^\theta - 1\right)\right] & \theta \neq 0, 1 \\[1em] \dfrac{1}{2n}\sum_{i=1}^n \ln\left[\dfrac{\mu(\mathbf{x})(\alpha-\mu(\mathbf{x}))}{x_i(\alpha-x_i)}\right] & \theta = 0 \\[1em] \dfrac{1}{2n}\sum_{i=1}^n\left[\dfrac{x_i}{\mu(\mathbf{x})}\ln\left(\dfrac{x_i}{\mu(\mathbf{x})}\right) + \dfrac{\alpha-x_i}{\alpha-\mu(\mathbf{x})}\ln\left(\dfrac{\alpha-x_i}{\alpha-\mu(\mathbf{x})}\right)\right] & \theta = 1 \end{cases}$$

(17)

According to proposition 4 $(GE_0)^J$ is a decomposable index that satisfies

$$(GE_0)^J(\mathbf{x}^1, ..., \mathbf{x}^K) = \sum_{j=1}^K \dfrac{n_j}{n}(GE_0)^J(\mathbf{x}^j) + (GE_0)^J(\mu_1\mathbf{1}_{n_1}, ..., \mu_K\mathbf{1}_{n_K})$$

Taking as a basis the Kolm-Variance family, the associated *joint indicators* are written as follows:

$$(KV_\delta)^J(\mathbf{x}) = \begin{cases} \dfrac{1}{2n}\left(\sum_{i=1}^n(e^{\delta(x_i-\mu(\mathbf{x}))} - 1) + \sum_{i=1}^n(e^{\delta(\mu(\mathbf{x})-x_i)} - 1)\right) & \delta \neq 0 \\[1em] \dfrac{1}{n}\sum_{i=1}^n(x_i-\mu(\mathbf{x}))^2 & \delta = 0 \end{cases}$$

(18)

It is well known that the variance is a decomposable measure.
With respect to the BP family, we get

$$(BP_{\beta,\theta})^J(\mathbf{x}) = \begin{cases} \dfrac{\left(\sum_{i=1}^n\left(\dfrac{x_i+c}{\mu(\mathbf{x})+c}\right)^\theta + \left(\dfrac{\alpha-x_i+c}{\alpha-\mu(\mathbf{x})+c}\right)^\theta - 2\right)}{2n\theta(\theta-1)} & \theta \neq 0, 1 \\[1em] \dfrac{\sum_{i=1}^n \ln\dfrac{(\mu(\mathbf{x})+c)(\alpha-\mu(\mathbf{x})+c)}{(x_i+c)(\alpha-x_i+c)}}{2n} & \theta = 0 \\[1em] \dfrac{\sum_{i=1}^n\left[\dfrac{x_i+c}{\mu(\mathbf{x})+c}\ln\left(\dfrac{x_i+c}{\mu(\mathbf{x})+c}\right) + \dfrac{\alpha-x_i+c}{\alpha-\mu(\mathbf{x})+c}\ln\left(\dfrac{\alpha-x_i+c}{\alpha-\mu(\mathbf{x})+c}\right)\right]}{2n} & \theta = 1 \end{cases}$$

(19)

where $\theta = r(1+\beta)/\beta$, $c = (1-\beta)/\beta$, and $0 < \beta \leq 1$ and r is a constant. Proposition 3 establishes that $BP_{\beta,0}$ is a decomposable measure that fulfills

$$(BP_{\beta,0})^J(\mathbf{x}^1, ..., \mathbf{x}^K) = \sum_{j=1}^{K} \frac{n_j}{n}(BP_{\beta,0})^J(\mathbf{x}^j) + (BP_{\beta,0})^J(\mu_1 \mathbf{1}_{n_1}, ..., \mu_K \mathbf{1}_{n_K})$$

RANKING THE JOINT DISTRIBUTIONS

The joint distributions proposed in the third section achieve two goals. On the one hand, the attainments and the shortfalls are incorporated after having been previously transformed according to the invariance criterion chosen. Consequently, the same invariant viewpoint can be assumed on both sides. Once the point of view has been selected, we propose to analyze the inequality of a bounded distribution by applying a standard inequality measure to the joint distribution.

However, as usual, different inequality measures can lead to different conclusions. In order to obtain unanimous rankings Lorenz dominance criteria can be applied. The second interesting feature of the β joint distributions is that all of them enjoy the same mean equal to one. Then the Lorenz curves of the joint distributions can be constructed without assuming an invariance condition.

Consider $\mathbf{x} \in D^\alpha$ and the β-joint distribution $\mathbf{x}_\beta$. Denote by $\overline{\mathbf{x}_\beta} = (\bar{x}_1, ..., \bar{x}_{2n})$ the permutation of $\mathbf{x}_\beta$ such that $\bar{x}_1 \leq ... \leq \bar{x}_{2n}$. Let $\pi_0 = \omega_0 = 0$. Define, for all $l = 1, ..., 2n$, $\pi_l = 1/2n$ and $\omega_l = \sum_{1 \leq i \leq l} \bar{x}_i / 2n$. Clearly, $\pi_{2n} = \omega_{2n} = 1$.

The *Lorenz curve* of $\mathbf{x}_\beta$ is the graph that is obtained by plotting the points $(\pi_l, \omega_l)_{l=0,...,2n}$ and connecting the dots. We will refer to this curve as the *β-joint Lorenz curve* of $\mathbf{x}$.

We propose the following Lorenz dominance condition to order the bounded distributions.

Joint Lorenz dominance. Given $\mathbf{x}, \mathbf{y} \in D^\alpha$ we will say that $\mathbf{x}$ *β-joint Lorenz dominates* $\mathbf{y}$, denoted as $\mathbf{x} L_\beta \mathbf{y}$, if the β-joint Lorenz curve of $\mathbf{x}$ is nowhere below the β-joint Lorenz curve of $\mathbf{y}$.

Corresponding to the three invariance conditions, three types of Lorenz curves have been proposed in the literature, namely relative, absolute, and intermediate Lorenz curves. The respective Lorenz dominance conditions have been established. Note that when $\beta = 1$, the β joint Lorenz curve of $\mathbf{x}$ is the relative Lorenz curve of the relative joint distribution. Similarly, when $\beta = 0$, the β joint Lorenz curves coincide, up to a translation of 1, with the absolute Lorenz curves of the absolute joint distributions. Finally, the Lorenz curves of the β intermediate joint distributions are, up to the constant translation of $(1-\beta)$, simply the intermediate joint Lorenz curves proposed by Pfingsten (1986). The corresponding Lorenz dominance conditions can be established. When applied to the joint distributions we obtain the following result.

Proposition 5. For any two distributions $\mathbf{x}, \mathbf{y} \in D^\alpha$, and any $\beta \in [0, 1]$

$$\text{if } \mathbf{x} L_\beta \mathbf{y} \text{ then } I_\beta^J(\mathbf{x}) \leq I_\beta^J(\mathbf{y})$$

for any joint indicator I_β^J associated with a β invariant inequality measure I_β.

Proof: In the appendix. □

We consider again the previous example with $\mathbf{x} = (10, 40)$ and $\mathbf{y} = (35, 65)$ and $\alpha = 100$. The relative joint distributions are $\mathbf{x}_1 = (0.4, 1.6, 1.2, 0.8)$ and $\mathbf{y}_1 = (0.7, 1.3, 1.3, 0.7)$. It is easy to verify $\mathbf{y}_1$ Lorenz dominates $\mathbf{x}_1$. Then according to our proposal, from a relative point of view, inequality is greater in the first situation than in the second.

DISCUSSION AND CONCLUSIONS

This chapter focuses on total health inequality. In contrast to income distributions, health distributions are usually bounded. Traditional inequality measures should not be blindly applied to the distribution of health attainments or shortfalls. We propose indices to measure inequality in the joint distribution of attainments and shortfalls.

As mentioned in the introduction, another branch of the literature on the distribution of health is concerned with socioeconomic inequality. Researchers often attempt to assess to what extent the inequality in health is related to socioeconomic status. Wagstaff, van Doorslaer, and Paci (1989) propose the use of the concentration curve and the concentration index for this purpose. Variations of the concentration index are proposed by Wagstaff, Paci and van Doorslaer (1991), Wagstaff (2002), Erreygers (2009a, 2009b), Wagstaff (2009), and Erreygers, Clarke and van Ourti (2012). When the health measure is bounded, application of the concentration index to attainments or shortfalls is problematic. Erreygers (2009b, 2009c) and Erreygers et al. (2012) introduce variations of the concentration index to overcome this problem. Our proposal to analyze jointly the attainment and the shortfall distributions may be of use for future research in the measurement of socioeconomic related inequality in health.

NOTE

1. As stressed by Kjellsson and Gerdtham (2013), the hs-relative by represents "a new compromise concept for a bounded variable by explicitly considering the two relative invariance equivalent criteria, defined with respect to attainments and shortfalls, to represent the polar cases of defensible positions."

ACKNOWLEDGMENTS

This research has been partially supported by the Spanish Ministerio de Educación y Ciencia under project ECO2012-31346, cofounded by FEDER and by Departamento de Educación, Política Lingüística y Cultura del Gobierno Vasco, under the project IT568-13.

We are very grateful to the editors of this issue for useful comments and suggestions that have helped us to improve the chapter.

REFERENCES

Bosmans, K., & Cowell, F. (2010). The class of absolute decomposable inequality measures. *Economics Letters*, *109*, 154–156.

Bossert, W., & Pfingsten, A. (1990). Intermediate inequality: Concepts, indices and welfare implications. *Mathematical Social Sciences*, *19*, 117–134.

Chakravarty, S., & Tyagarupananda, S. (1998). The subgroup decomposable absolute indices of inequality. In S. R. Chakravarty, D. Coondoo, & R. Mukherjee (Eds.), *Quantitative economics: Theory and practice, essays in honor of professor N. Bhattacharya* (pp. 247–257). New Delhi: Allied Publishers Limited.

Chakravarty, S., & Tyagarupananda, S. (2009). The subgroup decomposable intermediate indices of inequality. *Spanish Economic Review*, *11*, 83–97.

Clarke, P. M., Gerdtham, U. G., Johannesson, M., Bingefors, K., & Smith, L. (2002). On the measurement of relative and absolute income-related health inequality. *Social Science and Medicine*, *55*, 1923–1928.

Erreygers, G. (2009a). Correcting the concentration index. *Journal of Health Economics*, *28*, 504–515.

Erreygers, G. (2009b). Correcting the concentration index: A reply to Wagstaff. *Journal of Health Economics*, *28*, 521–524.

Erreygers, G. (2009c). Can a single indicator measure both attainment and shortfall inequality? *Journal of Health Economics*, *28*, 885–893.

Erreygers, G., Clarke, P., & Van Ourti, T. (2012). "Mirror, mirror, on the wall, who in this land is fairest of all?" – Distributional sensitivity in the measurement of socioeconomic inequality of health. *Journal of Health Economics*, *31*, 257–270.

Fleurbaey, M., & Schokkaert, E. (2012). Equity in health and health care. In M. V. Pauly, T. G. Mcguire & P. P. Barros (Eds.), *Handbook of health economics* (Vol. 2, pp. 1003–1092). Elsevier B. V.

Foster, J. E. (1985). Inequality measurement. In W. P. Young (Ed.), *Fair allocation, proceedings of symposia in applied mathematics* (pp. 31–68). Providence, RI: American Mathematical Society.

Foster, J., & Shneyerov, A. (2000). Path independent inequality measures. *Journal of Economic Theory, 91*, 199–222.

Kjellsson, G., & Gerdtham, U.-G. (2013). Lost in translation: Rethinking the inequality equivalence criteria for bounded health variables. In P. R. Dias & O. O'Donnell (Eds.), *Health and inequality*, (Vol. 21). Research on Economic Inequality, Bingly, UK: Emerald Group Publishing Limited.

Kolm, S. (1976). Unequal inequalities: I. *Journal of Economic Theory, 12*, 416–442.

Lambert, P., & Zheng, B. (2011). On the consistent measurement of attainment and shortfall inequality. *Journal of Health Economics, 30*, 214–219.

Lasso de la Vega, C., & Aristondo, O. (2012). Proposing indicators to measure achievement and shortfall inequality consistently. *Journal of Health Economics, 31*, 578–583.

Pfingsten, A. (1986). *New concepts of Lorenz domination and risk aversion*. Discussion Paper 278, Karlsruhe.

Shorrocks, A. F. (1980). The class of additively decomposable inequality measures. *Econometrica, 48*, 613–625.

van Doorslaer, E., & van Ourti, T. (2011). Chapter 35: Measuring inequality and inequity in health and health care. In P. Smith & S. Glied (Eds.), *The Oxford handbook of health economics* (pp. 837–869). Oxford: Oxford University Press.

Wagstaff, A. (2002). Inequality aversion, health inequalities, and health achievement. *Journal of Health Economics, 21*, 627–641.

Wagstaff, A. (2009). Correcting the concentration index: A comment. *Journal of Health Economics, 28*, 516–520.

Wagstaff, A., Paci, P., & van Doorslaer, E. (1991). On the measurement of inequalities in health. *Social Science and Medicine, 33*, 545–557.

Wagstaff, A., & van Doorslaer, E. (2000). Equity in health care finance and delivery. In A. J. Culyer & J. P. Newhouse (Eds.), *Handbook of health economics*. Amsterdam: Elsevier.

Wagstaff, A., van Doorslaer, E., & Paci, P. (1989). Equity in the finance and delivery of health care: Some tentative cross-country comparisons. *Oxford Review of Economic Policy, 5*, 89–112.

APPENDIX

Proof of Proposition 1. It is clear that I_β^J satisfies continuity, replication invariance and symmetry if I_β does. As regards the normalization axiom we get

$$I_\beta^J(\lambda \mathbf{1}) = I_\beta(\lambda \mathbf{1}_\beta) \text{ by definition Eq. (12)}$$

$$= I_\beta\left(\frac{\lambda\mathbf{1} - \lambda\mathbf{1}}{\beta\lambda + (1-\beta)} + \mathbf{1}, \frac{(\alpha\mathbf{1} - \lambda\mathbf{1}) - (\alpha - \lambda)\mathbf{1}}{\beta(\alpha - \lambda) + (1-\beta)} + \mathbf{1}\right) \text{ from Eq. (10)}$$

$$= I_\beta(\mathbf{1}, \mathbf{1}) = 0 \text{ operating and by normalization}$$

To show that the *transfer principle* is satisfied, assume that $\mathbf{x}'$ is obtained from $\mathbf{x}$ by a progressive transfer. Then, note that for any $\beta \in [0,1]$, $\frac{\mathbf{x}' - \mu(\mathbf{x}')\mathbf{1}}{\beta\mu(\mathbf{x}') + (1-\beta)} + \mathbf{1}$ and $\frac{(\alpha\mathbf{1} - \mathbf{x}') - (\alpha - \mu(\mathbf{x}'))\mathbf{1}}{\beta(\alpha - \mu(\mathbf{x}')) + (1-\beta)} + \mathbf{1}$ are obtained from $\frac{\mathbf{x} - \mu(\mathbf{x})\mathbf{1}}{\beta\mu(\mathbf{x}) + (1-\beta)} + \mathbf{1}$ and $\frac{(\alpha\mathbf{1} - \mathbf{x}) - (\alpha - \mu(\mathbf{x}))\mathbf{1}}{\beta(\alpha - \mu(\mathbf{x})) + (1-\beta)} + \mathbf{1}$ respectively by the same progressive transfer. Therefore, $\mathbf{x}'_\beta = \left(\frac{\mathbf{x} - \mu(\mathbf{x}')\mathbf{1}}{\beta\mu(\mathbf{x}') + (1-\beta)} + \mathbf{1}, \frac{(\alpha\mathbf{1} - \mathbf{x}') - (\alpha - \mu(\mathbf{x}'))\mathbf{1}}{\beta(\alpha - \mu(\mathbf{x}')) + (1-\beta)} + \mathbf{1}\right)$ can be obtained from $\mathbf{x}_\beta = \left(\frac{\mathbf{x} - \mu(\mathbf{x})\mathbf{1}}{\beta\mu(\mathbf{x}) + (1-\beta)} + \mathbf{1}, \frac{(\alpha\mathbf{1} - \mathbf{x}) - (\alpha - \mu(\mathbf{x}))\mathbf{1}}{\beta(\alpha - \mu(\mathbf{x})) + (1-\beta)} + \mathbf{1}\right)$ by two progressive transfers.

Since I_β satisfies the *transfer principle* so does I_β^J.

Finally, as I_β fulfils symmetry from the definitions it is straightforward that $I_\beta^J(\alpha\mathbf{1} - \mathbf{x}) = I_\beta^J(\mathbf{x})$. □

Proof of Proposition 2. Let be I_β a decomposable measure. Then I_β belongs to one of the families given in Eqs (2), (4), or (6). For any $\beta \in [0,1]$ and $\mathbf{x} \in D^\alpha$, from Eqs. (11) and (12), we have

$$I_\beta^J(\mathbf{x}) = I_\beta(\mathbf{x}_\beta) = I_\beta\left(\frac{\mathbf{x} - \mu(\mathbf{x})\mathbf{1}}{\beta\mu(\mathbf{x}) + (1-\beta)} + \mathbf{1}, \frac{(\alpha\mathbf{1} - \mathbf{x}) - (\alpha - \mu(\mathbf{x}))\mathbf{1}}{\beta(\alpha - \mu(\mathbf{x})) + (1-\beta)} + \mathbf{1}\right)$$

Split the distribution $\mathbf{x}_\beta$ into two distributions $\mathbf{x}_\beta = (\mathbf{x}^1, \mathbf{x}^2)$, such that $\mathbf{x}^1 = \frac{\mathbf{x} - \mu(\mathbf{x})\mathbf{1}}{\beta\mu(\mathbf{x}) + (1-\beta)} + \mathbf{1}$ and $\mathbf{x}^2 = \frac{(\alpha\mathbf{1} - \mathbf{x}) - (\alpha - \mu(\mathbf{x}))\mathbf{1}}{\beta(\alpha - \mu(\mathbf{x})) + (1-\beta)} + \mathbf{1}$.

Note that $\mu_1 = \mu_2 = 1 = \mu(\mathbf{x}_\beta)$. Then $I_\beta\left(\mathbf{x}_\beta^B\right) = 0$ and $\frac{\beta\mu_j + 1 - \beta}{\beta\mu + 1 - \beta} = 1$.

Since $n_1 = n_2$ according to Eqs. (5) or (7), we get that the decomposable weights are $w_\beta^j = 1/2$. From Eqs. (12) and (1), we find

$$I_\beta^J(\mathbf{x}) = I_\beta(\mathbf{x}_\beta) = I_\beta(\mathbf{x}^1, \mathbf{x}^2) = \frac{I_\beta(\mathbf{x}^1) + I_\beta(\mathbf{x}^2)}{2} = \frac{I_\beta(\mathbf{x}) + I_\beta(\alpha\mathbf{1} - \mathbf{x})}{2} = I_\beta^1(\mathbf{x}) \quad \square$$

Proof of Proposition 3. For Proposition 2 we have that $I_\beta^J(\mathbf{x}) = I_\beta^1(\mathbf{x})$. For any $\beta \in [0, 1]$, given any β-intermediate invariant measure I_β, the following expressions hold.

$$I_\beta(\mathbf{x} + \bar{\lambda}(\alpha\mathbf{1} - \mathbf{x})) \leq I_\beta(\mathbf{x} + \eta\mathbf{1}) \leq I_\beta(\mathbf{x}) \leq I_\beta(\mathbf{x} + \lambda\mathbf{x}) \tag{20}$$

$$I_\beta((\alpha\mathbf{1} - \mathbf{x}) - \bar{\lambda}(\alpha\mathbf{1} - \mathbf{x})) \leq I_\beta(\alpha\mathbf{1} - \mathbf{x}) \leq I_\beta((\alpha\mathbf{1} - \mathbf{x}) - \eta\mathbf{1}) \leq I_\beta((\alpha\mathbf{1} - \mathbf{x}) - \lambda\mathbf{x})$$
$$= I_\beta(\alpha\mathbf{1} - (\mathbf{x} + \lambda\mathbf{x})) \tag{21}$$

for any $\mathbf{x} \in D^\alpha$ and for any $\lambda, \eta > 0$ whenever $\mathbf{x} + \lambda\mathbf{x}$, $\mathbf{x} + \eta\mathbf{1}$, $\mathbf{x} + \bar{\lambda}(\alpha\mathbf{1} - \mathbf{x}) \in D^\alpha$ and $n\eta = \lambda \sum_{1 \leq i \leq n} x_i = \bar{\lambda} \sum_{1 \leq i \leq n}(\alpha - x_i)$.

From Eqs. (20) and (21), and taking into account Eqs. (15) and (16), Proposition 3 holds. □

Proof of Proposition 4. First of all note that the decomposable weights of GE_0, variance and $BP_{\beta,0}$, given in Eqs (5) and (7), are the population shares. As regards variance, KV_0, since $(KV_0)^J(\mathbf{x}) = KV_0(\mathbf{x})$, the result is clear.

For the second Theil measure GE_0, we get

$$(GE_0)^J(\mathbf{x}^1, ..., \mathbf{x}^K) = \frac{GE_0(\mathbf{x}^1, ..., \mathbf{x}^K) + GE_0(\alpha\mathbf{1} - \mathbf{x}^1, ..., \alpha\mathbf{1} - \mathbf{x}^K)}{2} \text{ by Proposition 2}$$

$$= \frac{1}{2} \left(\sum_{j=1}^K \frac{n_j}{n} GE_0(\mathbf{x}^j) + GE_0(\mathbf{x}^B) \right.$$

$$\left. + \sum_{j=1}^K \frac{n_j}{n} GE_0(\alpha\mathbf{1} - \mathbf{x}^j) + GE_0((\alpha\mathbf{1} - \mathbf{x})^B) \right) \text{ since } GE_0 \text{ is decomposable}$$

$$= \frac{1}{2} \left(\sum_{j=1}^K \frac{n_j}{n} (GE_0(\mathbf{x}^j) + GE_0(\alpha\mathbf{1} - \mathbf{x}^j)) + GE_0(\mathbf{x}^B) + GE_0((\alpha\mathbf{1} - \mathbf{x})^B) \right) \text{ operating}$$

$$= \sum_{j=1}^K \frac{n_j}{n} \left(\frac{GE_0(\mathbf{x}^j) + GE_0(\alpha\mathbf{1} - \mathbf{x}^j)}{2} \right) + \frac{GE_0(\mathbf{x}^B) + GE_0((\alpha\mathbf{1} - \mathbf{x})^B)}{2} \text{ operating}$$

$$= \sum_{j=1}^{K} \frac{n_j}{n} (GE_0)^J(\mathbf{x}^j) + (GE_0)^J(\mathbf{x}^B) \text{ by Proposition 2}$$

$$= (GE_0)^J(\mathbf{x}^W) + (GE_0)^J(\mathbf{x}^B) \text{ operating}$$

The proof is analogous for the $BP_{\beta,0}$ indices and is left to the reader. □

Proof of Proposition 5. If $\mathbf{x} \, L_\beta \, \mathbf{y}$ then, by definition, the Lorenz curve of the distribution $\mathbf{x}_\beta$ lies above the curve of the distribution $\mathbf{y}_\beta$. As any inequality measure is Lorenz consistent (Foster, 1985), for any inequality measure I: $I(\mathbf{x}_\beta) \leq I(\mathbf{y}_\beta)$. Specifically, for any inequality measure β-invariant I_β:

$$I_\beta(\mathbf{x}_\beta) = I_\beta^J(\mathbf{x}) \leq I_\beta(\mathbf{y}_\beta) = I_\beta^J(\mathbf{y}) \qquad \square$$

MEASURING HEALTH INEQUALITY WITH CATEGORICAL DATA: SOME REGIONAL PATTERNS

Joan Costa Font and Frank Cowell

ABSTRACT

Much of the theoretical literature on inequality assumes that the equalisand is a cardinal variable like income or wealth. However, health status is generally measured as a categorical variable expressing a qualitative order. Traditional solutions involve reclassifying the variable by means of qualitative models and relying on inequality measures that are mean independent. We argue that the way status is conceptualised has important theoretical implications for measurement as well as for policy analysis. We also bring to the data a recently proposed approach to measuring self-reported health inequality that meets both rigorous and practical considerations. We draw upon the World Health Survey data to examine alternative pragmatic methods for making health-inequality comparisons. Findings suggest significant differences in health-inequality measurement and that regional and country patterns of inequality orderings do not coincide with any reasonable categorisation of countries by health system organisation.

Keywords: Health inequality; categorical data; health surveys; upward status; downward status

JEL classifications: D63; H23; I18

INTRODUCTION

The measurement of inequality typically has three components: an equalisand (the thing that may be unequally distributed), the unit of analysis (the social or economic entities among whom the distribution takes place) and an aggregation method (the mathematical formula that assembles the information in the distribution). The first and third of these components can be tricky. If the equalisand is something that has an unambiguous cardinal representation and is intrinsically non-negative (consumption expenditure? hectares of land?) then the rest of the measurement problem is comparatively straightforward: you specify carefully whether the unit of analysis is the individual person, the household or something else, you choose the particular aggregation method that appropriately represents the inequality principles that you consider reasonable (an Atkinson index? the Gini coefficient?) and the problem is solved. If the equalisand is cardinally measurable but can take negative values (personal net worth?) then matters become trickier — not all inequality measures are well defined in such cases and so you will be restricted in your choice of aggregation method. However, there may be a deeper problem: the equalisand itself may be a concept that is not naturally susceptible to representation on a cardinal scale. This is often the case when considering inequality of health status (Van Doorslaer & Jones, 2003) or satisfaction (Oswald & Wu, 2011; Stevenson & Wolfers, 2008; Yang 2008). This measurability problem raises serious theoretical and practical difficulties when one wants to discuss the inequality in health status, which we will address in this chapter, namely cardinalisation strategies and dealing with self-reported health correlation with other relevant covariates.

'Health inequality' suggests an approach to inequality that incorporates some concept of the hierarchy or status that covaries with health measures. Most of the world in epidemiology and health economics take a 'materialistic approach' to inequality measurement whereby individual status refers to the individual position in the hierarchy of consumption or income (Marmot, 2005; Wagstaff & van Doorslaer, 2000). Therefore, policies that improve the distribution of material conditions are assumed to translate into fairer distribution of health status. The latter comes with some important caveats. First, health inequalities might not be the result of the status variable, and income as a status variable is itself a matter of choice and its use is problematic. Second, we ignore the proportion of social inequalities in health that are essentially 'avoidable' or perhaps 'ethically legitimate' (Fleurbaey & Schokkaert, 2011; LeGrand, 1987). For instance, inequalities resulting from the pure depreciation of health capital over time are arguably not avoidable; the same could apply to biologically or generically driven gender differences in health (Wagstaff, Paci, & van Doorslaer, 1991).

The response to these difficulties has mainly been pragmatic. For example, the current mainstream literature on health inequality relies heavily on concentration indices (Costa-Font & Hernández-Quevedo, 2012) and the use of categorical variables, but there is really very little in the literature that examines the assumptions that underpin the techniques that are commonly used. There are various types of cardinalisation methods that have been proposed in the literature − such as imputation, interval regression and so on − but there is insufficient discussion of the economic rationale for these methods or the practical implications of using one method rather than another. Furthermore, such cardinalisation has been found to be the main source of bias: in a paper running a meta-regression of health-inequality studies in the economics literature Costa-Font and Hernández-Quevedo (2013) find that the main reason for estimate heterogeneity is the way studies cardinalise the health status. As a consequence, one should treat the existing literature with some caution.

There is also a theoretical literature on the problem of making inequality comparisons when the underlying equalisand is ordinal, but it has mainly resulted in a number of rather limited propositions that are difficult to interpret or apply. However, recent work on the analysis of distributions of categorical variables has shown how natural interpretations of individual *status* can be used to provide a robust approach to the inequality-measurement problem in this context without resort to arbitrary cardinalisation of ordinal concepts (Cowell & Flachaire, 2012). The status concept is similar to concepts used in poverty and relative deprivation and in recent approaches to the inequality of opportunity (de Barros, Ferreira, Chanduvi, & Vega, 2008). This gives rise to a new set of inequality indices that incorporate conventional distributional views such as degrees of inequality aversion and that can be applied to commonly used measures of well-being.

The results from this chapter are the first outcomes of an attempt to identify a more precise definition of measures of health status. We expect our findings to provide researchers with a means of testing alternative ways of measuring inequalities of non-cardinal outcomes that may have significant policy implications. This is particularly important taking into account that measures of health inequality are used to rank health systems, and increasingly measures of well-being are used by the United Nations to evaluate institutions and public policies. Here we undertake the following:

1. We examine the extent to which health-inequality rankings are affected by alternative analytical approaches to the categorical-data problem, including the conventional cardinalisation methods and the Cowell–Flachaire status-inequality approach.
2. We provide a first estimate of well-being inequality rankings of world countries using the status-inequality approach.
3. We then examine whether patterns of inequalities in categorical measures health vary across different world regions. Do poor countries look different from medium/rich in terms of health-inequality rankings? Is there a regional consistency in inequality patterns?

The rest of the chapter is organised as follows. The second section contains some necessary theoretical background, the third section introduces the data set and explains our empirical strategy, the fourth section contains our results and the fifth section concludes.

APPROACHES TO INEQUALITY MEASUREMENT WITH ORDINAL DATA

There are two main approaches to the measurement of inequality using ordinal data. One could impute some artificial index of individual health status as a function of the categories. In some cases the imputation is achieved through subjective evaluation by individuals (e.g. on a Likert scale) and in some cases by making use of quality of life indices (e.g. the Quality-Adjusted Life Year). The same procedure can be applied to entities that do not have a natural ordering, such as vectors of attributes or endowments; one uses a utility function to force an ordering of the data. This is similar to one of the standard theoretical approaches to the measurement of multi-dimensional inequality – one computes the 'utility' of factors and then computes inequality of utility, where the utility function is an appropriate aggregator (Maasoumi, 1986; Tsui, 1995). However the approach faces serious objections such as the arbitrariness of the cardinalisation, the arbitrariness of aggregating apples and oranges and the arbitrariness of attempting to include measures of dispersion into the index as well. Even if the resulting well-being index appears reasonable over a wide subset of categories one might still be concerned about the way extreme values are represented in the index and their consequences for inequality comparisons.

A second approach to inequality developed within the health literature involves a reworking of traditional inequality-ranking approaches focusing on first-order dominance criteria – see Abul Naga and Yalcin (2008), Allison and Foster (2004) and Zheng (2011).[1] It is commonly suggested that the median could be used as an equality concept corresponding to the use of the mean in conventional inequality analysis, although it has been noted that comparing distributions with different medians raises special issues (Abul Naga & Yalcin, 2010). But the approach runs into difficulty if quantiles are not well-defined, as may happen in the case of categorical variables – see Cowell and Flachaire (2012).

An alternative way forward introduced by Cowell and Flachaire (2012) tackles the problem by separating out carefully the two tricky components of inequality measurement mentioned in the introduction, the equalisand and the aggregation method, each of these is underpinned by an axiomatic argument that goes back to first principles. In short the resulting Cowell and Flachaire method amounts to an aggregation of the discrepancies between each person's actual status and some status reference point. In such an approach clearly a lot rests on the precise definition of status. In the case of applications where the equalisandum has a natural cardinalisation (income or wealth for example) then it makes sense to define status as income or wealth. However, where only ordinal information is available – as with categorical data on health status – then we have to do more. Suppose that information is purely categorical, in that we only know how many people are in each category $k = 1, 2, \ldots K$, but that the categories can be arranged in increasing order of their desirability. Then a simple argument shows that, if there are n_k persons in category $k = 1, 2, 3, \ldots K$, then the status of person i who is currently in category $k(i)$ must be a function of either $\sum_{l=1}^{k(i)} n_l$, or $\sum_{l=k(i)}^{K} n_l$.[2] The first of these is a 'downward-looking' concept and the second is its 'upward-looking' counterpart. It may be appropriate to normalise by the size of the total population $n := \sum_{k=1}^{K} n_k$ so that person i's status is given by either the downward-looking version

$$s_i = \frac{1}{n} \sum_{l=1}^{k(i)} n_l \qquad (1)$$

or by the 'upward-looking' counterpart of Eq. (1)

$$s'_i = \frac{1}{n} \sum_{l=k(i)}^{K} n_l \qquad (2)$$

On either definition status must lie between zero and one. If there were perfect equality (everyone in the same category) then it is clear that both Eqs. (1) and (2) take the value 1. It turns out that this, the maximum-status value, is the only thing that makes sense as the reference point.[3]

So the inequality-measurement problem then amounts to aggregating the information in the vector $\mathbf{s} := (s_1, s_2, \ldots, s_n)$ in relation to the equality vector $(1, 1, \ldots, 1)$. On the basis of some elementary axioms Cowell and Flachaire show that inequality must take the form of an index in the following family, indexed by α

$$I_\alpha(\mathbf{s}) = \begin{cases} \frac{1}{\alpha(\alpha-1)} \left[\frac{1}{n} \sum_{i=1}^{n} s_i^\alpha - 1 \right], & \text{if } \alpha \neq 0 \\ -\frac{1}{n} \sum_{i=1}^{n} \log s_i, & \text{if } \alpha = 0 \end{cases} \qquad (3)$$

where α is a parameter less than 1. The family (3) is very similar to the well-known generalised entropy class of inequality indices. The parameter α specifies the desired sensitivity of the index to a particular part of the income distribution: for low values of α the index $I_\alpha(\mathbf{s})$ is particularly sensitive to values of s_i close to zero.

So we have a *family* of indices that is suitable for making comparisons of inequality in terms of health status. In what follows we shall suggest a way of using this to make health-inequality comparisons internationally.

DATA AND METHODS

The core of the analysis involves three main components: (1) extraction of suitable categorical variables on which to construct well-being indices; (2) computation of cardinal imputations, status measures and associated inequality indices and rankings; (3) an analysis of cross-country inequality comparisons.

Data

Our approach requires quantitative analysis of internationally comparable data that contain measures of health status. Accordingly the main data source to be used is the World Health Survey (WHS) which contains data from 70 countries; it collects comparable multidimensional micro-data on income, employment education and health. There are two reasons for the choice of this data base: first, its great advantage for comparative work; second, its standardised worldwide stricture can assist in examining cross country patterns across heterogeneous world regions that exhibits different levels of economic and social development.

The WHS is a general population survey, developed by WHO to address the need for reliable information and to cater to the increased attention to the role of health in economic and human development. The survey contains data from randomly selected adults (i.e. older than 18 years of age) who reside in 70 countries who implemented household face-to-face surveys, computer-assisted telephone interview, or computer-assisted personal interview in 2002. Sample sizes vary from 1,000 to 10,000.

Our measure of health status is the standard measure of self-reported health widely used in the literature as described in Table A1. As a measure, it suffers from cultural adaptation problems that make cross country comparison challenging, but it appears to be an adequate measure for computing within-country inequalities.

Background

It is possible to estimate a health production h_i function for individual i in the following kind of specification

$$h_i = \Phi(x_i) + \varepsilon_i$$

where x_i represents known determinants of health and ε_i a random component. Estimating such a function is more challenging than one might imagine because health status is a latent variable that cannot be observed in full. Instead, we can only rely on proxy estimates. A growing literature that takes as it point of departure Idler and Benyamini (1997) typically employs self-reported measures of health as proxies for individuals' health status. However, more recently a literature has developed to show that perception and observation might not necessarily match Sen (2002). The relevant variable, namely health status, can take the form of a censored (when quality of life measures are used), binary, ordered scale and interval variable depending on the underlying assumptions maintained by researchers.

In some exceptional circumstances, health status is measured using a censored continuous variable approach (e.g. when visual analogue scales are employed). If, instead of this, a binary approach is followed (e.g. measuring morbidity of a certain condition), inequalities can be measured using a standard limited-dependent model such as a logistic regression techniques (Kunst & Mackenbach, 1994). As a result, it might be argued, the odds ratio of the underlying social position variable could say something about the extent to which social position influences health status. In the first place, if the health variable allows an unambiguous ordering, then ordered probit models will take into account the structure of the data. So, by assuming an order and that it is possible to observe the variable health (a latent health variable) and the cut-off points, the probability of respondents' classifying themselves on a specific scale can be modelled in the standard fashion. However, even where this is an improvement with respect to binary measures of health for the purposes of measuring health inequality, it is still difficult to interpret the meaning of a change in the order between scales of self-reported health status. An alternative way has been to obtain a linear index based on rescaling the ordered variable to obtain a normalised health index, such as in Cutler and Richardson (1997). However, this still implies accepting some arbitrary assumptions on the value and distribution of a person's health status. Furthermore, the underlying reasons for an individual's categorisation into a specific health scale are still not accounted for. Therefore, some research claims that self-reported health status can be interpreted instead as individual's categorisation into an interval, which can be ascertained by finding a link between self-reported measures of health and some health utility indices (Van Doorslaer & Jones, 2003). This allows the use of interval regression to convert categories into continuous indexes (by running the predictions of a model with an acceptable goodness of the fit) which can then be used to compute measures of inequality. However, all the strategies followed in the literature are liable to be problematic.

Empirical Strategies

The first step is to select categorical variables for measuring health. It is usual for both national and international surveys to contain information on measures of self-reported health in categorical form. The literature adopts different strategies to measure such a latent variable from categorical responses, but there is no consensus nor theoretically sound strategy to deal with that specific feature. For example, in the data set used here, the WHS, the categorical measure of health is based on the responses to the question 'how would you rate your health today?'. This yields a personal evaluation of overall health with potential responses in five categories ranging from 'very good' to 'very bad' – see the appendix for more detail.

In this chapter we draw upon the Cowell and Flachaire (2012) methodology to undertake international comparisons of inequality of self-reported health status. This is an alternative to cardinalisation proposals include the imputation of values from the Health-Related Quality of Life scales as in Van Doorslaer and Jones (2003) and Fonseca and Jones (2003). Following Van Doorslaer and Jones (2003), the equivalent cardinal value of the cut-off point of each response to the ordinal question was obtained so as to estimate the cardinal value of self-reported health using an interval-regression approach. Alternatively, the common cardinalisation strategy includes using either ordinal or interval regression (Wagstaff & Van Doorslaer, 1994). However, even when methods are statistically valid, they impose non-neutral assumptions that are not theoretically grounded. Indeed, some studies estimate cardinal health status measures using a linear index based on rescaling the ordered variable to obtain a normalised health index, as in Cutler and Richardson (1997). This still implies accepting some arbitrary assumptions on the value and distribution of individual health status. In order to carry out our methodological comparison we will also employ those techniques.

In the case of categorical data a simple way to process the data is to rank the values underlying the latent variable health. But in doing so the real distance between categories is unknown. Furthermore, given the multiplicity of survey data, scales tend to be arbitrary. Ordinal regression is used with ordinal dependent variables, and uses the logit/probit link function. However, ordinal regression requires the assumption that the effect of the independent variables is the same for each level of the dependent variable. Then model outcomes can be interpreted to exhibit an interval censoring. In other words, we observe the ordered category into which each observation falls, but not the exact value of the observation. Interval regression is a generalisation of censored regression. Both ordered and interval regressions models can be used to then transform a categorical outcome into a continuous variable based on the parameters of the regression. However, the transformation is highly dependent on the covariates of the regression and on the arbitrary nature of different variable categories. The strategy we pursue here addresses this latter point and provides an alternative cardinalisation method that we argue is more suitable to measure inequalities in health. The Cowell and Flachaire (2012) paper includes the derivation of the statistical properties of the class of inequality indices that emerge from the status-inequality approach.

Our Approach

Our approach in this chapter is to identify patterns arising from the WHS international data set using a robust methodology that takes account of the categorical nature of the data and the problems of making comparisons between countries. This involves two steps:

1. We use the Cowell and Flachaire (2012) class of measures for a variety of values of the sensitivity parameter α. In this way we avoid problems associated with arbitrary cardinalisation of the underlying categorical variables and allow some flexibility in the choice of inequality measure.
2. Bearing in mind that the data are based on subjective evaluation it is important to avoid problems that may arise from systematic response bias between countries (some progress has been made in using anchoring vignettes that is increasingly used to correct for this type of bias – see Kapteyn, Smith, & Van Soest (2007) and Rice, Robone, & Smith (2012)). Specifically, median categories are regarded as not informative given that some countries habitually over-report. The term 'moderate health' means different things across countries because people's expectations are different. For this reason we focus on inequality orderings within the WHS sample as well as inequality levels.
3. Furthermore we examine possible patterns of health inequality by looking at the way in which (i) $I_\alpha(\mathbf{s})$ for each country varies and (ii) the way country orderings change as the parameter α varies.

4. Finally, we use rank correlation analysis to examine the association of country orderings when we vary the way status is computed, alongside changes in the values of the sensitivity parameter α. A high association between different ordering and measures of status would be indicative of a limited effect of those two variables. In addition, identifying the values of α and status that yield higher correlation coefficients is of some interest as a sensitivity analysis.

RESULTS

So, let us apply the status-based inequality measure (3) to the WHS data using the two definitions of status given in Eqs. (1) and (2). Figs. 1 and 2 show the relationship between $I_\alpha(\mathbf{s})$ and α for downward-looking and upward-looking status respectively for eight OECD countries; a close-up version of the these figures (for $-½ \leq \alpha \leq +½$) is shown in Figs. 3 and 4.

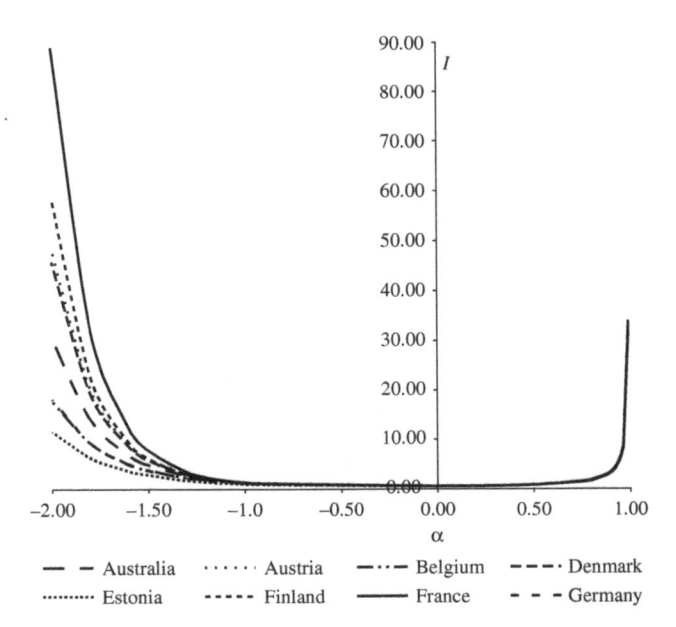

Fig. 1. OECD Inequality and α. Downward-Looking Status.

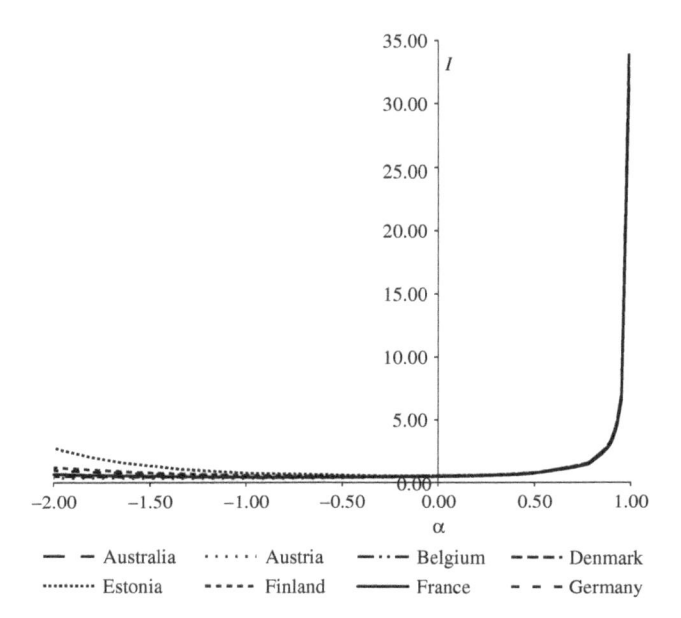

Fig. 2. OECD Inequality and α. Upward-Looking Status.

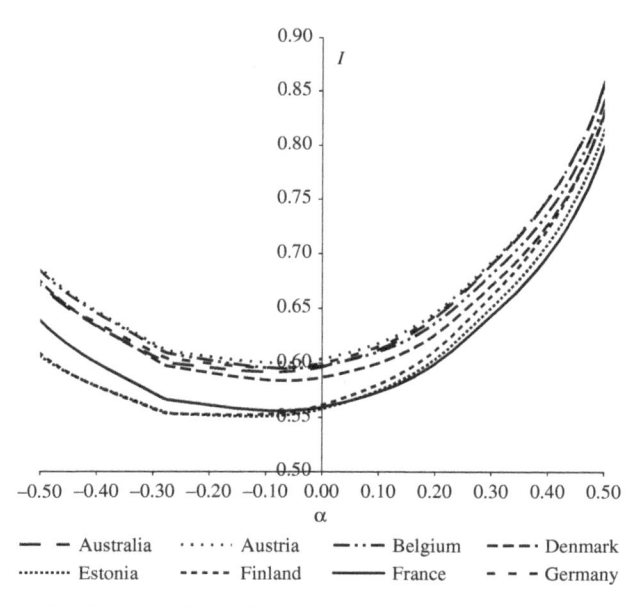

Fig. 3. OECD Inequality and α. Downward-Looking Status (Close-Up).

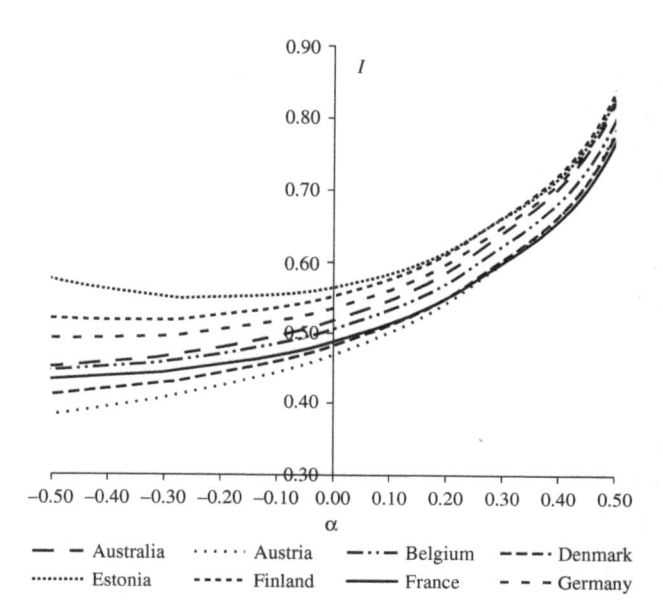

Measuring Health Inequality with Categorical Data 65

Fig. 4. OECD Inequality and α. Upward-Looking Status (Close-Up).

The patterns illustrated in Figs. 1–4 are typical. At a first pass it is clear that if we restrict attention to moderate values of the sensitivity parameter ($-½ \leq \alpha \leq +½$) some of the conventional wisdom about OECD countries is confirmed: in the downward-looking case we can see that both Finland and France enjoy low health-status inequality. It is also clear that there is a difference between downward- and upward-looking measures of status: compare the charts for neighbours Austria and Germany. However, if we allow versions of the inequality measure that are very sensitive to low status ($\alpha < -½$) it is clear that the inequality profiles fan out dramatically and the conventional wisdom breaks down: within the OECD countries of WHS Finland and France are no longer low-inequality countries for this range of α.

Differences in Upward- and Downward-Looking Status

As explained in section 'Our Approach', we are interested in examining how rank order correlation vary when upward and downward status measures are used. To do so, we make use of graphical methods and correlation analysis.

So now let us rank the 70 countries by inequality (such that 1 = 'most equal', 70 = 'most unequal') and plot Figs. 5 and 6, which are snapshots of the orderings generated by the inequality estimates for each value of α. In the case of downward-looking status Fig. 5 shows a typical pattern for developed countries: the profile is usually downward-sloping[4] so that as one uses an inequality measure that is progressively less sensitive to observations at the bottom of the status distribution these OECD countries appear lower in the hierarchy. To some extent this is manifest in the case of upward-looking status (Fig. 6): but notice that for the range $\alpha < \frac{1}{2}$, the profiles are almost flat. However it is important to note that countries' positions in the health-inequality hierarchy depends crucially on whether a downward-looking or upward-looking status concept is adopted: contrast the ranking positions of Australia and Estonia within the six-country grouping depicted in Figs. 5 and 6.

To throw further light on this in Table 1 we provide the association between upward and downward status. As expected, we find that correlations are dramatically different when values of α vary. Findings are suggestive that the highest correlation between rank orders between upward and downwards status takes place at a value of $\alpha = 0.99$ and the highest inverse correlation for $\alpha = -1$. As expected, we find a positive correlation for positive α, and a negative correlation for negative α. For an $\alpha = 0$ we find a modest but significant correlation of 0.33, which suggests that the adoption of a downward or upward status perspective does indeed exert a rather significant difference in ranking estimates.

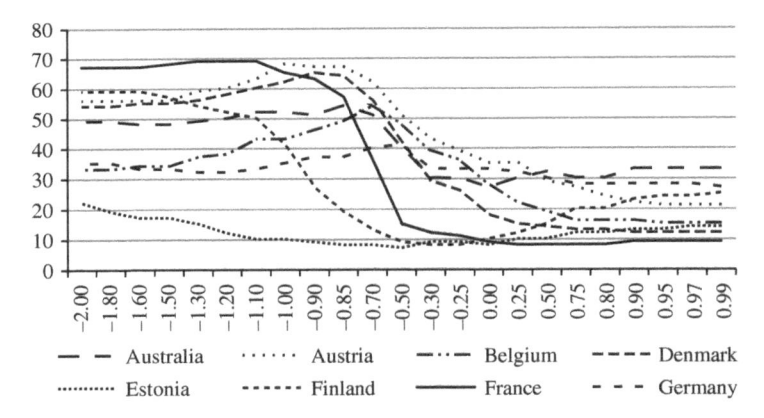

Fig. 5. OECD Country Ranking and α. Downward-Looking Status.

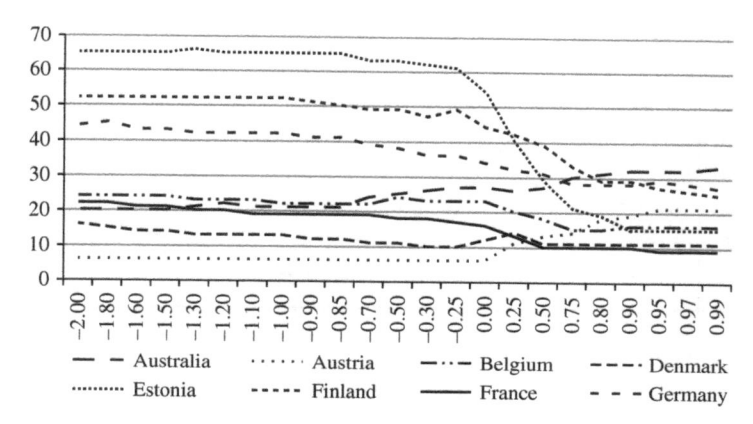

Fig. 6. OECD Country Ranking and α. Upward-Looking Status.

Table 1. Rank-Order Correlation between Upward and Downward Status Inequality for Different Values of α.

Sensitivity parameter α	Correlation ρ
−2	−0.3436
−1	−0.7997
−0.5	−0.5265
0	0.3354
0.5	0.8334
0.99	0.9718

Note: Significant at 5% level.

The Role of Inequality Sensitivity

We now turn to a closer examination of the effect of the choice of the inequality-sensitivity parameter, keeping the status concept fixed. In some cases the reranking with α is remarkable; indeed we have seen this in the case of downward-looking status for the six OECD countries depicted in Fig. 5. A further nice example is shown in Fig. 7: consider the question, for downward-looking status which is the most unequal Nordic country? Fig. 7 shows that it depends crucially on the sensitivity index: for large and negative values of α Finland is the most unequal, for positive values of α it is Sweden, and for intermediate values it is Norway.

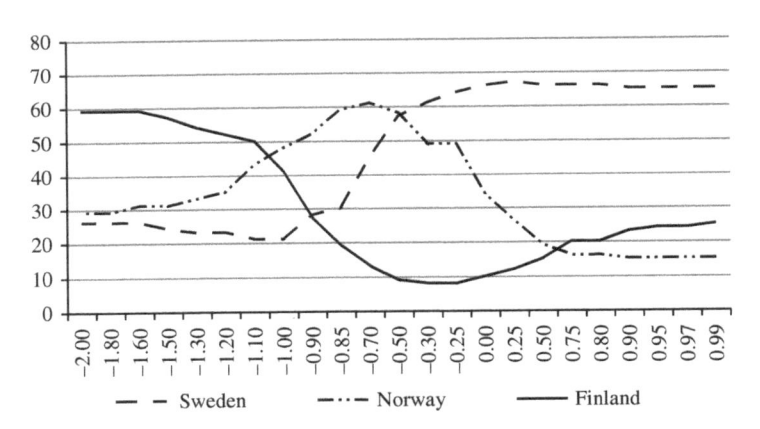

Fig. 7. Rerankings of Nordic Countries: Downward-Looking Status.

Table 2. Rank Order Correlation between Order from Different Values of α: Downward-Looking Status.

		α					
		−2	−1	−0.5	0	0.5	0.99
α	−2	1					
	−1	0.8484	1				
	−0.5	−0.2803	0.1388	1			
	0	−0.6475	−0.4059	0.7478	1		
	0.5	−0.6566	−0.5569	0.5196	0.9365	1	
	0.99	−0.6420	−0.6031	0.4223	0.8860	0.9886	1

Note: Significant at 5% level.

A more formal method of investigating whether the association of country health-inequality rank orders varies with α would be simply to use a measure of rank order correlation. Table 2 presents the Spearman correlation coefficient for downward-looking status. As expected, changes in the values of α induce changes in the ranking of countries based on their health inequalities. In Table 2 we find high correlations when α is positive. As expected turning from a positive α to a negative α flips the sign of the correlation coefficient with the exception of values close to $\alpha = 0$, where we still find positive correlations.

In Table 3 we follow the same strategy as before for upward-looking status, yet in this case we find positive correlation coefficients irrespective

Table 3. Rank Order Correlation between Order from Different Values of α: Upward-Looking Status.

		α					
		-2	-1	-0.5	0	0.5	0.99
	-2	1					
	-1	0.9865	1				
α	-0.5	0.9239	0.9692	1			
	0	0.7302	0.8187	0.9238	1		
	0.5	0.4388	0.5579	0.7111	0.9066	1	
	0.99	0.2380	0.3651	0.5351	0.787	0.9651	1

Note: Significant at 5% level.

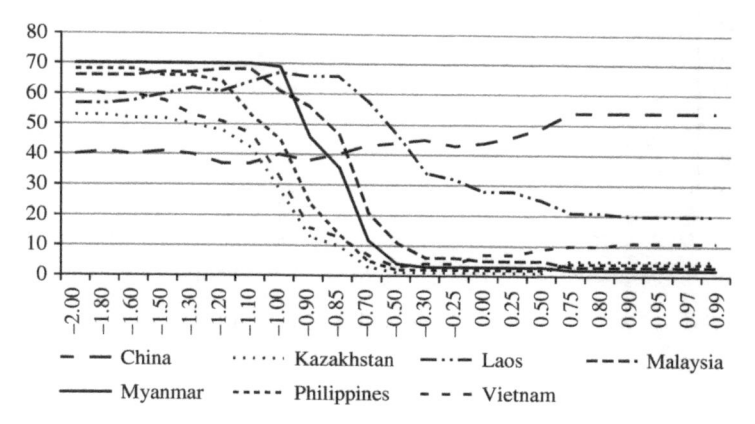

Fig. 8. Central and East Asian Rankings and α Downward-Looking Status.

of α, and generally we find high correlation coefficients except when rankings for extreme values of α are correlated. Based on this data, we can conclude that upward measures of status appear to be less sensitive to changes in α that downward measures of status.

Regional Patterns

In addition, we find that inequality-based rankings do exhibit a specific regional mappings, although they do not reflect clear cut or appreciable differences in how health systems are funded and organised. Instead, rankings are sensitive to other unobserved effects that merit additional empirical analysis. For example consider the Asian profiles in Figs. 8 and 9: the majority of the profiles are similar to the typical OECD pattern; the major exceptions are the two Asian giants, China and India, where the ranking increases with α. These countries' profiles are similar to those typical of North and Central Africa (Fig. 10) where as α increases towards 1 the position in the health-inequality ranking also increases.

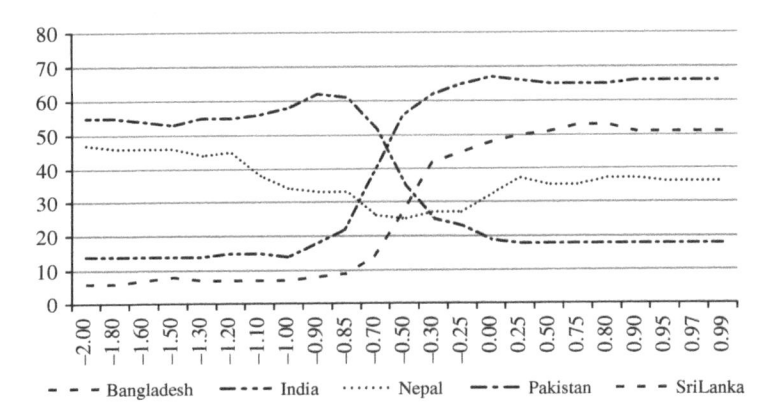

Fig. 9. South Asian Rankings and α. Downward-Looking Status.

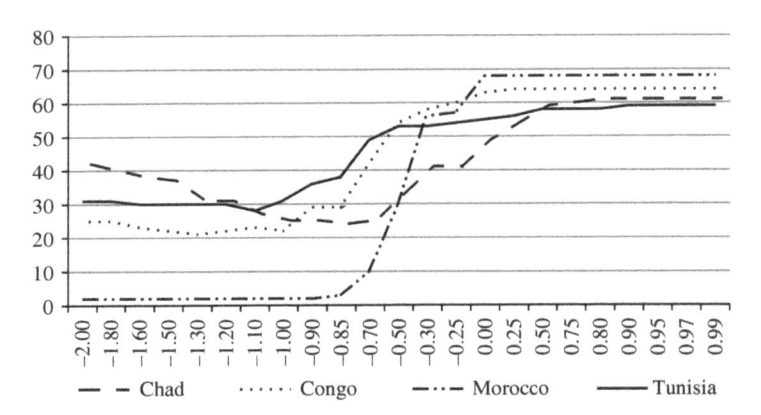

Fig. 10. North and Central African Rankings and α. Downward-Looking Status.

CONCLUSION

This chapter has shown the applicability of a new method that can be used to undertake international comparisons of health inequality, in line with the aims of the WHO (2000) goals of comparing health systems. We have shown that the methodology can be simply and reliably implemented with categorical data for the purpose of making comparisons of health inequality. From inequality analysis applied in other fields that use cardinal data we know that inequality rankings of different societies can be sensitive to the 'inequality aversion' parameter that is used; that applies here too in that changes in the inequality-sensitivity parameter α may have a substantial effect on health-inequality estimates and country rankings. Furthermore, in our case, where categorical data are used, there is an additional consideration: there are two natural methods of quantifying status — downward-looking and upward-looking — and it is possible that the choice of status concept may also affect country rankings along with choice of α.

Our results provide empirical confirmation of the importance of the status concept and the parameter α in ranking health systems (based on health inequalities). We have shown that the downward or upward status perspective does indeed exert an important difference in ranking estimates. However, whilst changes up the parameter α can invert the country inequality rank-order for downward-looking status, we do not find a flip in the coefficients for upward-looking status. Hence, based on this evidence our tentative recommendation for applied and policy work would be to adopt an upward-looking status perspective.

Finally, we have provided some insights on the regional patterns of self-reported health inequality that will form the basis for further research.

NOTES

1. See also the similar polarisation approach developed by Apouey (2007).
2. This is in line with recent proposal for a cardinalisation of Self-reported Health Status (SRHS) by applying an imputation of the values of Health-Related Quality of Life (HRQoL) values employed by Van Doorslaer and Jones (2003) and Fonseca and Jones (2003). See section 'Empirical Strategies'.
3. If you try to use the mean (of status) this does not remain constant under changes in the distribution and, as a consequence, produces counterintuitive behaviour of the index. The median is ambiguous in the case of categorical data. But the zero-inequality distribution just described is well-defined and always produces a well-behaved index.
4. Not all OECD profiles follow this pattern — see the discussion of Fig. 7 below.

REFERENCES

Abul Naga, R. H., & Yalcin, T. (2008). Inequality measurement for ordered response health data. *Journal of Health Economics, 27*, 1614–1625.

Abul Naga, R. H., & Yalcin, T. (2010). *Median independent inequality orderings*. Technical report, University of Aberdeen Business School.

Allison, R. A., & Foster, J. E. (2004). Measuring health inequality using qualitative data. *Journal of Health Economics, 23*, 505–552.

Apouey, B. (2007). Measuring health polarization with self-assessed health data. *Health Economics, 16*(9), 875–894.

Costa-Font, J., & Hernández-Quevedo, C. (2012). Measuring inequalities in health: What do we know? What do we need to know? *Health Policy, 106*, 195–206.

Costa-Font, J., & Hernández-Quevedo, C. (2013). *Inequalities in self-reported health: A meta-regression analysis*. LSE Health working paper series in health policy and economics 32/2013, LSE Health and Social Care, London School of Economics and Political Science, London.

Cowell, F. A., & Flachaire, E. (2012). *Inequality with ordinal data*. Public Economics Programme Discussion Paper No. 16, London School of Economics. Retrieved from http://darp.lse.ac.uk/pdf/IneqOrdinal.pdf

Cutler, D., & Richardson, E. (1997). Measuring the health of the United States population. *Brookings Papers on Economic Activity, 2*, 217–271.

de Barros, R. P., Ferreira, F., Chanduvi, J., & Vega, J. (2008). *Measuring inequality of opportunities in Latin America and the Caribbean*. Bakinstore: Palgrave Macmillan.

Fleurbaey, M., & Schokkaert., E. (2011). Health and health care. In M. Pauly, T. McGuire, & P. Pita-Barros (Eds.), *Handbook of health economics (Vol. 2)*. Oxford, UK: North-Holland.

Fonseca, L., & Jones, A. M. (2003). *Inequalities in self-assessed health in the health survey of England*. Equity Working Paper No. 11, University of York.

Idler, E., & Benyamini, Y. (1997). Self-rated health and mortality: A review of 27 community studies. *Journal of Health and Social Behaviour, 38*, 21–37.

Kapteyn, A., Smith, J. P., & Van Soest, A. (2007). Vignettes and self-reports of work disability in the United States and the Netherlands. *The American Economic Review, 97*(1), 461–473.

Kunst, A. E., & Mackenbach, J. P. (1994). International variation in the size of mortality differences associated with occupational status. *International Journal of Epidemiology, 23*, 1–9.

LeGrand, J. (1987). Inequalities in health: Some international comparisons. *European Economic Review, 31*, 182–191.

Maasoumi, E. (1986). The measurement and decomposition of multidimensional inequality. *Econometrica, 54*, 991–997.

Marmot, M. (2005). Social determinants of health inequalities. *Lancet, 365*(9464), 1099–104.

Oswald, A. J., & Wu, S. (2011). Well-being across America. *The Review of Economics and Statistics, 93*(4), 1118–1134.

Rice, N., Robone, S., & Smith, P. C. (2012). Vignettes and health systems responsiveness in cross-country comparative analyses. *Journal of the Royal Statistical Society: Series A (Statistics in Society), 175*(2), 337–369.

Sen, A. (2002). Health: Perception vs. observation. *British Medical Journal, 324*, 860–861.

Stevenson, B., & Wolfers, J. (2008). Happiness inequality in the United States. *The Journal of Legal Studies, 37*, S33–S79.

Tsui, K.-Y. (1995). Multidimensional generalizations of the relative and absolute inequality indices: the Atkinson-Kolm-Sen approach. *Journal of Economic Theory, 67,* 251–265.

Van Doorslaer, E., & Jones, A. M. (2003). Inequalities in self-reported health: Validation of a new approach to measurement. *Journal of Health Economics, 22,* 61–87.

Wagstaff, A., Paci, P., & van Doorslaer, E. (1991). On the measurement of inequalities in health. *Social Science and Medicine, 33,* 545–557.

Wagstaff, A., & Van Doorslaer, E. (1994). Measuring inequalities in health in the presence of multiple-category morbidity indicators. *Health Economics, 3,* 281–291.

Wagstaff, A., & van Doorslaer, E. (2000). Equity in health care financing and delivery. In A. J. Culyer & J. P. Newhouse (Eds.), *Handbook of health economics* (pp. 1803–1806). Oxford, UK: North-Holland.

WHO. (2000). *The World Health Report 2000 – Health systems: Improving performance.* Geneva, Switzerland: The World Health Organization.

Yang, Y. (2008). Social inequalities in happiness in the United States, 1972 to 2004: An age-period-cohort analysis. *American Sociological Review, 73,* 204–226.

Zheng, B. (2011). A new approach to measure socioeconomic inequality in health. *Journal of Economic Inequality, 9,* 555–577.

APPENDIX

The data are taken from the World Health Organization's *World Health Survey*, which is described in http://www.who.int/healthinfo/survey/instruments/en/index.html

In particular, for our categorical variable, we use the responses to one specific question in this survey's collection of individual questions about overall health.

'Q2000: In general, how would you rate your health today? The respondent should answer according to how he/she considers his/her health to be and give his/her best estimate. Both physical and mental health must be taken into consideration.'

Table A1 reports the answers to this question across 70 countries. The titles of columns (1)–(5) give the categories used in the survey: we follow the natural order taking (1) as the best category and (5) as the worst. The total number of respondents is in column (6): if in any row this total exceeds the sum of columns (1)–(5), the difference is attributable to non-response.

Table A1. Responses in WHS to Self-Rated Health Question.

	Country	(1) Very good	(2) Good	(3) Moderate	(4) Bad	(5) Very bad	(6) Total
1.	Australia	487	775	446	74	11	1,793
2.	Austria	423	390	200	36	4	1,053
3.	Bangladesh	494	1,949	2,132	741	228	5,544
4.	Belgium	252	487	197	48	11	995
5.	Bosnia	271	328	279	127	23	1,028
6.	Brazil	715	1,934	1,881	348	119	4,997
7.	Burkina Faso	1,254	2,104	1,137	288	36	4,819
8.	Chad	889	1,767	1,371	549	37	4,613
9.	China	982	1,485	1,215	277	34	3,993
10.	Cosmoros	312	631	523	261	30	1,757
11.	Congo	693	550	693	252	33	2,221
12.	Côte d'Ivoire	661	1,215	955	266	21	3,118
13.	Croatia	200	302	312	132	43	989
14.	Czech	160	350	311	90	19	930
15.	Denmark	320	472	166	40	4	1,002
16.	Dominican	722	1,806	1,560	397	34	4,519
17.	Ecuador	650	1,945	1,569	378	53	4,595
18.	Estonia	70	293	499	134	16	1,012
19.	Ethiopia	2,138	1,549	972	220	47	4,926
20.	Finland	158	395	391	64	3	1,011

Table A1. (Continued)

	Country	(1) Very good	(2) Good	(3) Moderate	(4) Bad	(5) Very bad	(6) Total
21.	France	255	525	192	34	2	1,008
22.	Georgia	265	778	1,111	476	125	2,755
23.	Germany	229	582	343	85	13	1,252
24.	Ghana	1,379	1,433	830	234	46	3,922
25.	Greece	347	325	246	63	19	1,000
26.	Guatemala	730	1,790	1,747	472	24	4,763
27.	Hungary	139	579	503	155	34	1,410
28.	India	2,159	3,577	2,616	1,311	202	9,865
29.	Ireland	366	257	101	29	5	758
30.	Israel	519	405	234	40	23	1,221
31.	Italy	182	449	305	46	15	997
32.	Kazakhstan	265	1,894	2,088	231	18	4,496
33.	Kenya	1,115	1,798	1144	309	40	4,406
34.	Lao	1,787	2,005	906	168	17	4,883
35.	Latvia	35	244	390	155	32	856
36.	Luxembourg	164	346	155	33	2	700
37.	Malawi	2,855	1,334	838	231	33	5,291
38.	Malaysia	1,194	3,495	1,111	204	12	6,016
39.	Mali	1,334	1,526	895	266	11	4,032
40.	Mauritania	941	1,672	1,024	154	9	3,800
41.	Mauritius	850	1,677	827	427	104	3,885
42.	Mexico	7,193	1,8112	11,221	2,002	218	38,746
43.	Morocco	598	1,454	1,754	821	372	4,999
44.	Myanmar	1,215	3,412	1,100	157	2	5,886
45.	Namibia	1,622	1,249	863	204	45	3,983
46.	Nepal	1,455	3,908	2,505	767	53	8,688
47.	Netherlands	189	640	214	41	2	1,086
48.	Norway	314	456	140	46	13	969
49.	Pakistan	1,770	2,996	1,315	263	25	6,369
50.	Paraguay	1,700	1,920	1,370	133	16	5,139
51.	Philippines	817	5,127	3,759	354	19	10,076
52.	Portugal	62	342	390	180	55	1,029
53.	Russia	261	1,102	2,192	770	91	4,416
54.	Senegal	646	1,028	984	217	24	2,899
55.	Slovakia	400	798	506	94	17	1,815
56.	Slovenia	90	238	193	53	9	583
57.	South Africa	837	865	467	129	42	2,340
58.	Spain	1,051	2,984	1,689	502	117	6,343
59.	Sri Lanka	1,844	3,019	1,535	298	22	6,718
60.	Swaziland	198	451	508	676	236	2,069
61.	Sweden	262	354	235	133	14	998
62.	Tunisia	1,236	1,850	1,476	411	58	5,031
63.	Turkey	1,301	4,809	4,035	869	189	11,203

Table A1. (*Continued*)

	Country	(1) Very good	(2) Good	(3) Moderate	(4) Bad	(5) Very bad	(6) Total
64.	UAE	536	472	146	18	6	1,178
65.	UK	318	498	278	82	17	1,193
66.	Ukraine	129	659	1,364	594	103	2,849
67.	Uruguay	725	1,632	547	63	9	2,976
68.	Vietnam	398	1,368	1,489	225	10	3,490
69.	Zambia	1,436	1,292	816	228	39	3,811
70.	Zimbabwe	837	1,263	1,501	385	65	4,051

INEQUALITY AND BI-POLARIZATION IN SOCIOECONOMIC STATUS AND HEALTH: ORDINAL APPROACHES

Bénédicte Apouey and Jacques Silber

ABSTRACT

Traditional indices of bi-dimensional inequality and polarization were developed for cardinal variables and cannot be used to quantify dispersion in ordinal measures of socioeconomic status and health. This chapter develops two approaches to the measurement of inequality and bi-polarization using only ordinal information. An empirical illustration is given for 24 European Union countries in 2004–2006 and 2011. Results suggest that inequalities and bi-polarization in income and health are especially large in Estonia and Portugal, and that inequalities have significantly increased in recent years in Austria, Belgium, Finland, Germany, and the Netherlands, whereas bi-polarization significantly decreased in France, Portugal, and the United Kingdom.

Keywords: Inequality; bi-polarization; ordinal variables; self-assessed health

JEL classifications: I1; I3

INTRODUCTION

Evaluation of policy reform in the health sector sometimes requires assessment of effects on the dispersion of health — its inequality or polarization — within a population. However, the traditional approach to measuring dispersion requires cardinality of the variable whose dispersion is studied, while the most widely used comprehensive health measure — self-assessed health — is ordinal. This measure is generated by asking respondents to evaluate their health, in general, in response categories ranging from "1: very good" to "5: very poor," in the World Health Organization recommended version, and from "1: excellent" to "5: poor" in the US version.[1] Self-rating has several advantages. First, it offers a summary of an individual's general state of health. Second, a person's own appraisal of his or her health is a very good predictor of future mortality and morbidity. The correlation between self-assessed health and mortality remains strong even when controlling for other health variables and for socioeconomic status (Idler & Benyamini, 1997).

Because self-assessed health is ordinal rather than cardinal, some dispersion measures, like the Gini coefficient, cannot be applied to it. In a seminal paper, Blair and Lacy (1996) suggested developing specific dispersion measures for ordinal variables, using the cumulative distribution function of the variable of interest. Some studies followed this suggestion and derived uni-dimensional inequality and bi-polarization measures for health (Abul Naga & Yalcin, 2007; Apouey, 2007; Kobus & Miłoś, 2012; Lazar & Silber, 2013).

These univariate measures of dispersion in health alone are arguably less relevant than a bivariate approach that would consider dispersion in a socioeconomic dimension (like income) as well as in health. In this chapter, we present indices of inequality and bi-polarization in income and health, which can be used when only ordinal information on individuals' income and health is available. Typically, income is ordinal when it is given in brackets. The distribution of the exact amount of income between the brackets is unknown and thus it seems natural to assume that the income variable is ordinal.

We develop two approaches to quantify inequality and bi-polarization in income and health. The difference between the two approaches lies in the definition of the absence of inequality and bi-polarization. In the first approach, we make the hypothesis that there is no inequality and bi-polarization when the actual share (h, y) of individuals reporting a health category h and an income category y is equal to the product of the marginal shares of individuals in health category h and of individuals in income category y. This approach implies that inequality and bi-polarization will be minimal when health and income are independent. In the second approach, we assume that there is no inequality and bi-polarization when all individuals report the exact same health and income categories.

We provide an empirical illustration of our methods using data on 24 countries from the European Union Statistics on Income and Living Conditions (EU-SILC) for 2004–2006 and 2011. Results suggest that inequalities and bi-polarization are especially large in Estonia and Portugal, and that inequalities have significantly increased in recent years in Austria, Belgium, Finland, Germany, and the Netherlands, whereas bi-polarization significantly decreased in France, Portugal, and the United Kingdom.

The chapter is organized as follows. In the next section, we review the existing literature and identify the contribution of our chapter. We then present the notations and general approach. Subsequent sections develop the two specific approaches to the measurement of inequality and bi-polarization. The penultimate section presents the empirical illustration and the final section makes some concluding remarks.

PREVIOUS LITERATURE

Dispersion in Health When Health Is a Cardinal Variable

One approach to quantifying dispersion in self-assessed health consists of two steps. In the first stage, the ordinal self-rated health is transformed into a cardinal variable. Each individual is assigned a cardinal health score depending on his/her answer to the self-assessed health question and his/her observable characteristics (Groot, 2000; Van Doorslaer & Jones, 2003). The underlying assumption is that it is possible to consistently transform the ordinal self-assessed health variable into a cardinal variable. In the second stage, an index of dispersion is computed on the basis of this cardinal health variable.

One strand of this literature quantifies total dispersion in health, irrespective of the socioeconomic characteristics of the individuals (Wolfson & Rowe, 2001). A second strand only looks at a subset of dispersion and quantifies the health dispersion that occurs across the distribution of a socioeconomic variable. Socioeconomic inequality in health is generally assessed using the concentration index (Kakwani, Wagstaff, & Van Doorslaer, 1997; Koolman & Van Doorslaer, 2004; Van Doorslaer & Jones, 2003), whereas social bi-polarization in health can be quantified using the index developed by Apouey (2010).

Dispersion in Health When Health Is an Ordinal Variable

Allison and Foster (2004) made it clear that the two-step procedure — transforming the ordinal health variable into a cardinal variable and then quantifying health dispersion using a dispersion index for cardinal variables — is fundamentally flawed. Small variations in the scale that is used to transform the ordinal health variable into a cardinal one may reverse the ordering of the distributions that are compared. Allison and Foster (2004) provide an example of a reversal using the variance, whereas Lazar and Silber (2013) provide a second example using the coefficient of variation.

To overcome this limitation, several authors have developed dispersion measures for ordinal health variables that are scale invariant or independent (Abul Naga & Yalcin, 2007; Apouey, 2007; Lazar & Silber, 2013). These authors adopt a univariate approach and quantify overall health dispersion within a population, irrespective of the income levels of the individuals.

The next step is to develop tools to quantify multi-dimensional dispersion in several ordinal variables. This seems critical to describe the evolution of dispersion in the many dimensions of well-being (health, socioeconomic status, life satisfaction, education, among other). The literature on the measurement of bi- or multi-dimensional dispersion for ordinal variables is small. Silber and Yalonetzky (2011) present several measures of multi-dimensional dispersion that can be used when the variable of interest is ordinal and the other variables are nominal/unordered. As far as we know, there is only one paper that examines bi-dimensional inequality in two ordinal variables (Kobus, 2012).

Our Approach

Our chapter also focuses on the measurement of dispersion in two ordinal variables, namely income and health. Our approach is different from that of Kobus (2012) in two respects. First, our definitions of minimal and maximal dispersion are different. She assumes that dispersion in income and health is minimal when all individuals are in the same income and health category, and that it is maximal when three criteria are met: first, bi-polarization in income is maximal, second, bi-polarization in health is maximal, and third, the medial correlation coefficient between income and health equals 1. In the case where there are three income and health categories, this implies that dispersion is maximal when half of the individuals report the highest health level and the poorest income level, and the other half report the poorest health level and the highest income level. In contrast, in our first approach, we assume that inequality and bi-polarization are minimal when the actual share of individuals reporting a certain combination of income and health levels is equal to the expected share of individuals reporting that combination given the marginal distributions of income and health. In our second approach, we use the same definition of minimal bi-polarization as Kobus (2012), but we consider that bi-polarization in income and health is maximal when half individuals report the lowest income and health levels, whereas the second half report the highest income and health levels. A second difference between our approach and that of Kobus (2012) is that we examine the measurement of both inequality and bi-polarization in ordinal variables, whereas Kobus (2012) focuses on only one type of dispersion measures.

PRELIMINARIES

In what follows, we consider two ordinal variable, health and income. We denote H and Y the numbers of health and income categories. Category 1 corresponds to the lowest health and income categories, and categories H and Y to the highest health and income levels. We denote $m(h)$ and $m(y)$ the median categories of the two variables.

We consider a matrix of probabilities p and a matrix of cumulative distribution functions F. p is a $H \times Y$-dimensional matrix with element $p_{h,y}$ indicating the share of the population who reports being in health category h and income category y. By definition, the sum of the elements of matrix p equals 1.

$p_{h.}$ denotes the share of the whole population having health level h, $p_{.y}$ is the share of the population belonging to income class y.

$F_{h,y}$ is the share of individuals who are in a health category smaller than or equal to h and in an income category smaller than or equal to y:

$$F_{h,y} = \sum_{i=1}^{h} \sum_{j=1}^{y} p_{i,j}.$$

Two Approaches to Measuring Bi-Dimensional Inequality and Bi-Polarization in Income and Health

In this subsection, we briefly present our two approaches regarding inequality and bi-polarization in income and health. The goal here is to give some intuition about different ways of conceiving of inequality and bi-polarization in a bi-dimensional context.

The first conception assumes that the marginal distribution of income and health is given, and does not quantify dispersion in these marginal distributions. It also assumes that there is no inequality and bi-polarization if conditional on their income category, individuals have the same probability of reporting a certain health category, *and* conditional on their health category, individuals have the same probability of reporting a certain income category. The probability matrix for the case of no inequality and bi-polarization corresponds then to the product of the margins

$$p = \begin{pmatrix} p_{1.}p_{.1} & p_{1.}p_{.2} & \cdots & p_{1.}p_{.Y} \\ p_{2.}p_{.1} & p_{2.}p_{.2} & \cdots & p_{2.}p_{.Y} \\ \cdots & \cdots & \cdots & \cdots \\ p_{H.}p_{.1} & p_{H.}p_{.2} & \cdots & p_{H.}p_{.Y} \end{pmatrix}$$

In our second approach, we quantify overall dispersion in income and health. In contrast with the first approach, we do not assume that the absence of association between income and health means an absence of dispersion. In addition, we consider that there is no inequality and bi-polarization in income and health if there is both perfect equality in income and perfect equality in health. In that case, all individuals report exactly the same income and the same health level. For example:

$$p = \begin{pmatrix} 0 & 0 & 0 & 0 & \cdots & 0 \\ 0 & 0 & 0 & 0 & \cdots & 0 \\ 0 & 0 & 1 & 0 & \cdots & 0 \\ 0 & 0 & 0 & 0 & \cdots & 0 \\ \cdots & \cdots & \cdots & \cdots & \cdots & \cdots \\ 0 & 0 & 0 & 0 & \cdots & 0 \end{pmatrix} \text{ and } F = \begin{pmatrix} 0 & 0 & 0 & 0 & \cdots & 0 \\ 0 & 0 & 0 & 0 & \cdots & 0 \\ 0 & 0 & 1 & 1 & \cdots & 1 \\ 0 & 0 & 1 & 1 & \cdots & 1 \\ \cdots & \cdots & \cdots & \cdots & \cdots & \cdots \\ 0 & 0 & 1 & 1 & \cdots & 1 \end{pmatrix}$$

More generally, the probability matrices p with no inequality and bi-polarization contain $((H \times Y) - 1)$ zeros and a single one. In total, there are $H \times Y$ such matrices.

Inequality is maximal if all individuals except one are in the lowest health and income cell, whereas one individual is in the highest health and income cell. We suppose that there are n individuals, so the individual in the greatest income and health categories represent a share $\frac{1}{n}$ of the population. Then the corresponding matrices for maximal inequality are written as

$$p = \begin{pmatrix} 1-\frac{1}{n} & 0 & \cdots & 0 & 0 \\ 0 & 0 & \cdots & 0 & 0 \\ \cdots & \cdots & \cdots & \cdots & \cdots \\ 0 & 0 & \cdots & 0 & 0 \\ 0 & 0 & \cdots & 0 & \frac{1}{n} \end{pmatrix} \text{ and } F = \begin{pmatrix} 1-\frac{1}{n} & 1-\frac{1}{n} & \cdots & 1-\frac{1}{n} & 1-\frac{1}{n} \\ 1-\frac{1}{n} & 1-\frac{1}{n} & \cdots & 1-\frac{1}{n} & 1-\frac{1}{n} \\ \cdots & \cdots & \cdots & \cdots & \cdots \\ 1-\frac{1}{n} & 1-\frac{1}{n} & \cdots & 1-\frac{1}{n} & 1-\frac{1}{n} \\ 1-\frac{1}{n} & 1-\frac{1}{n} & \cdots & 1-\frac{1}{n} & 1 \end{pmatrix}$$

This definition is very similar to the definition of maximal inequality in a uni-dimensional context: indeed, uni-dimensional inequality in income is assumed to be maximal when all individuals except one have no income and one individual has all the available income. In the bi-dimensional context, all individuals except one have the poorest health and income status, and one individual has both excellent health and the highest possible income.

Finally, bi-polarization is maximal if half of the individuals are in the poorest health and income cell, whereas the other half are in the highest health and income cell so that

$$p = \begin{pmatrix} 0.5 & 0 & \cdots & 0 & 0 \\ 0 & 0 & \cdots & 0 & 0 \\ \cdots & \cdots & \cdots & \cdots & \cdots \\ 0 & 0 & \cdots & 0 & 0 \\ 0 & 0 & \cdots & 0 & 0.5 \end{pmatrix} \text{ and } F = \begin{pmatrix} 0.5 & 0.5 & \cdots & 0.5 & 0.5 \\ 0.5 & 0.5 & \cdots & 0.5 & 0.5 \\ \cdots & \cdots & \cdots & \cdots & \cdots \\ 0.5 & 0.5 & \cdots & 0.5 & 0.5 \\ 0.5 & 0.5 & \cdots & 0.5 & 1 \end{pmatrix}$$

This is similar to the definition of maximal bi-polarization in the univariate context: uni-dimensional bi-polarization in health is maximal if half individuals report the poorest health status whereas the other half reports the highest health status (Apouey, 2007).

General Properties of the Measures

In what follows, we present the continuity and scale independence properties that are satisfied by our indices.

Property of continuity: The inequality and bi-polarization indices are continuous in p (or F).

The property of continuity guarantees that small errors in the values taken by the variables will not lead to big variations in the indices proposed.

Definition of health and income scales: Each health and income category can be attributed a cardinal value according to the scales $s^{health} = (s_1^{health}, ..., s_H^{health})$ and $s^{income} = (s_1^{income}, ..., s_Y^{income})$. The scales are arbitrary with the restrictions $0 < s_1^{health} < ... < s_H^{health}$ and $0 < s_1^{income} < ... < s_Y^{income}$.

We denote S the set of scales.

Let D be a bivariate dispersion (i.e., inequality or bi-polarization) index.

Property of scale independence: $D(p^1, s^{health1}, s^{income1}) = D(p^1, s^{health2}, s^{income2})$ (or $D(F^1, s^{health1}, s^{income1}) = D(F^1, s^{health2}, s^{income2})$) for any $s^{health1}$, $s^{health2}$, $s^{income1}$, and $s^{income2}$ elements of S.

The property means that changing the numerical values of the scales has no influence on the value of the dispersion index.

All the inequality and bi-polarization measures presented in the next two sections satisfy the continuity and the scale independence properties.

A FIRST APPROACH TO MEASURING INEQUALITY AND BI-POLARIZATION IN INCOME AND HEALTH: DEFINING CONDITIONAL INDICES

Property of minimal inequality and bi-polarization: There is no inequality and bi-polarization if the actual distribution of income and health is identical to the expected distribution (product of the margins).

All the inequality and bi-polarization indices presented in this section satisfy this property, which implies that the measures will be zero if there is no association between income and health.

Measures of Inequality

In what follows, we present a theoretical derivation of a number of dispersion indices. A numerical example can be found in Appendix A. We consider the H by Y matrix p of population shares, whose rows and columns correspond, respectively, to the various health and income categories. Using Theil's approach to the measurement of inequality, we may derive the following measure of health inequality within income category y:

$$T_y = \sum_{h=1}^{H} \{(p_{h.})\ln[(p_{h.})/(p_{h,y}/p_{.y})]\} \tag{1}$$

where $p_{h.}$ is the share in the whole population (whatever the income category is) of individuals having health level h, $p_{.y}$ the share in the whole population (whatever the health level) of individuals belonging to income class y, and $p_{h,y}$ the share in the whole population of individuals belonging to income class y and having health level h. The intuitive idea is that a priori the probability for people belonging to income class y of having health level h should be identical to the share in the whole population of individuals with health level h ($p_{h.}$). It turns out however that a posteriori this probability is different and equal to $(p_{h,y}/p_{.y})$.

Eq. (1) can then be extended to a measure T of overall inequality in income and health for the whole population [2]:

$$T(p) = \sum_{y=1}^{Y}(p_{.y})T_y = \sum_{y=1}^{Y}(p_{.y})\sum_{h=1}^{H}\{(p_{h.})\ln[(p_{h.})/(p_{h,y}/p_{.y})]\} \tag{2}$$

It is also possible to measure health inequality on the basis of the Gini index. Here again we first measure health inequality within a given income class by comparing the distribution of the "actual shares" $(p_{h,y})/(p_{.y})$ for each income class y with what could be considered as the "expected shares" $(p_{h.}/1) = p_{h.}$. Using the concept of G-matrix[3] (Silber, 1989) we then derive the following measure G_y of health inequality within income class y with

$$G_y = [...(p_{h.})...]'G[...(p_{h,y}/p_{.y})..] = (1/p_{.y})[...(p_{h.})...]'G[...(p_{h,y})...] \tag{3}$$

where the two vectors (of length H) on both sides of the G-matrix in Eq. (3) are ranked by decreasing values of the ratios $(p_{h,y})/(p_{h.})$.

To derive a Gini index I_G of health inequality for the whole population, we weight the indices given in Eq. (3) by the weights of the income classes y. We should, however, remember that in defining such an overall within groups Gini inequality index, the sum of the weights will not be equal to 1, because each weight will in fact be equal to $(p_{.y})^2$, in the same way as in the traditional within groups Gini index, the weights are equal to the product of the population and income shares. We therefore end up with

$$I_G = \sum_{y=1}^{Y}(p_{.y})^2(1/p_{.y})[...(p_{h.})...]' G[...(p_{h,y})...]$$

$$\Leftrightarrow I_G = \sum_{y=1}^{Y}(p_{.y})[...(p_{h.})...]' G[...(p_{h,y})...] = \sum_{j=1}^{Y}[...((p_{h.})(p_{.y}))...]' G[...(p_{h,y})...] \quad (4)$$

Note that the last expression on the right hand side of Eq. (4) shows clearly that one compares "a priori" shares which are equal to the product $((p_{h.})(p_{.y}))$ of the margins (and hence assumes independence between health and income) with "a posteriori" shares $(p_{h,y})$, which correspond to the actual shares of cells (h,y) in the total population. It should be stressed here that in computing I_G we consider first the lowest income class, then the second lowest, etc. ... since the elements of the row vector $[...((p_{h.})(p_{.y}))...]'$ and of the column vector $[...(p_{h,y})...]$ on the extreme right of Eq. (3) are ranked by decreasing ratios $(p_{h,y})/(p_{h.})$, this ranking being implemented separately for each income class y.

We can also compute an expression

$$\tilde{I}_G = [...((p_{h.})(p_{.y}))...]' G[...(p_{h,y})...] \quad (5)$$

for the population as a whole, where the elements of the row vector $[...((p_{h.})(p_{.y}))...]'$ and of the column vector $[...(p_{h,y})...]$ would have been ranked by decreasing ratios $(p_{h,y})/((p_{h.})(p_{.y}))$.

To see the difference between the indices I_G and $\tilde{I}_G$ the following graphical interpretation is given.

A Graphical Illustration of the Bivariate Approach to Health Inequality

In Fig. 1, we put respectively on the horizontal and vertical axes the cumulative values of the expected shares $(p_{h.})(p_{.y})$ and the cumulative value of the actual shares $(p_{h,y})$, starting with income class 1 and ranking both sets of shares by increasing ratios $(p_{h,y})/((p_{h.})(p_{.y}))$, that is, by increasing ratios $(p_{h,1})/((p_{h.})(p_{.1}))$. Since we start by working only with the individuals belonging to the first income class, $p_{.1}$ will be common to all these individuals so that the order of ranking of the individuals will be a function of the ratios $(p_{h,1})/(p_{h.})$. Then we do the same for income class 2 and continue with the other classes until we end up with income class Y. We obtain a "within income classes inequality curve" (dotted curve in Fig. 1) that is made of Y sections, one for each income class. Clearly the slope of this curve is not always non-decreasing. It is non-decreasing within each income class but the curve reaches the diagonal each time we end with an income class.

If now we want to derive the curve that corresponds to Eq. (5) (dashed curve in Fig. 1), we will have to rank both sets of shares (the cumulative shares $(p_{h.})(p_{.y})$ on the one hand and the cumulative shares $(p_{h,y})$ on the other hand) by increasing values of the ratios $(p_{h,y})/((p_{h.})(p_{.y}))$ working from the onset with all the H by Y cells (and not, as we did previously, working first with the shares corresponding to the first (poorest) income class and ranking them by increasing ratios $(p_{h,1})/((p_{h.})(p_{.1}))$ and then doing the same successively for all the other income classes).

An illustration of the difference between the two approaches is given in Fig. 1, where the index I_G is equal to twice the area lying between the

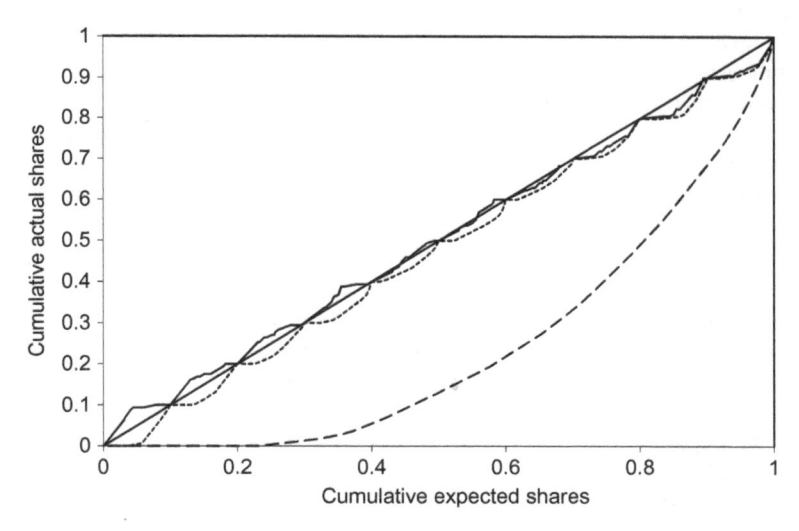

Fig. 1. Two Inequality Curves and One Distributional Change Curve. *Note*: On the basis of the dotted curve, we can compute the "within income classes Gini index" I_G. The dashed curved is the basis for the derivation of the "overall Gini index" $\breve{I}_G$. The solid curve finally is what we call a "distributional change curve." It enables us to compute the index of bi-polarization.

dotted curve and the diagonal, while the index $\tilde{I}_G$ is equal to twice the area lying between the dashed curve and the diagonal. The area lying between these two curves may then be considered as a measure of the degree of overlap between the various income classes in terms of the gaps between the "expected" and "actual" shares.

Measures of Social "Pro-Poorness" in Health

In Eq. (3), we estimated a within income group y Gini index G_y which was computed by comparing, for each cell (h,y), its expected share $(p_{h.})$ in column y with its actual share $(p_{h,y}/p_{.y})$ (see the first expression on the R.H.S. of Eq. (3)). This comparison of expected and actual shares was based on the use of the G-matrix, the operator we have been using to compute the Gini index. Moreover, the elements of the row vector $[...(p_{h.})...]'$ and of the column vector $[...(p_{h,y}/p_{.y})..]$, which appear on the first expression on the R. H.S. of Eq. (3), were both classified by decreasing ratios $(p_{h,y}/p_{h.})$.

Let us, however, assume now that, within each income class, we classify these elements (of the vectors $[...(p_{h.})..]'$ and $[...(p_{h,y}/p_{.y})..])$ by decreasing health level h. It can then be shown that what we would compute would be another kind of relative concentration ratio, one that would measure the link between the ratios $(p_{h,y}/p_{.y})$ and the health level of the individuals. If these ratios grow in a monotonic way with the level of health then we will get in fact, for each income class, the Gini indices G_y ratios we previously derived (see Eq. (3)). The corresponding curve obtained for a given income class by plotting points corresponding on the horizontal axis to the cumulative shares $((p_{h.})(p_{.y}))$ and on the vertical axis to the cumulative shares $(p_{h,y})$, both sets of shares being ranked by increasing health level, would be identical to that depicting the inequality measured by G_y.

If however, for a given income class, there is an inverse relationship between the ratios $(p_{h,y}/p_{.y})$ and the level of health of the individuals, the index we propose to compute in this section will be a kind of Pseudo-Gini.[4] It will be negative and equal in absolute value to the Gini index measuring the inequality given by G_y. In such a case, the curve will lie above the diagonal (in the range of the corresponding income class) and its slope will be decreasing.[5]

In the more general case, we may observe a curve (the solid curve in Fig. 1) that can cross one or several times the diagonal but it will still be an increasing curve. If the sum of the areas lying below the diagonal is close to the sum of the areas lying above the diagonal, this Pseudo-Gini will be close to zero. This kind of relative concentration curve was previously suggested to measure the income elasticity of the consumption of a specific good (Kakwani, 1980) and more recently spatial segregation (Dawkins, 2006).

In our case, one may observe that if this curve lies mostly below (respectively above) the diagonal, it means that cases where the actual number of individuals in a given cell is higher than the expected number will be observed mainly among individuals with a high (respectively low) level of health.

The overall measure of "health concentration" in the population, taking such a bivariate approach, would then be equal of the sum of the areas defined for each income class, these areas taking the sign defined previously. If the overall measure of "health concentration" is positive, this would mean that on average it is more common to see a positive link between health and income among richer people than among poorer people. If, however, we find that it is more common to observe an individual with a low health level among people with an income lower than the median income and individuals with a high health level among people with an income higher than the median income, then the overall measure of concentration may well be close to zero (despite the fact that we clearly have a positive correlation between income and health). We may therefore want to derive a better measure of such a correlation.

Measures of Bi-Polarization

Assume now that the areas defined previously and corresponding to the indices G_y given in Eq. (3) are attributed the following signs. For individuals belonging to an income class which is below the median income, the area will be positive, for a given income class, if it is above the diagonal and negative otherwise, while for individuals belonging to an income class above the median income, the area will be given a positive sign if it is below the diagonal and a negative sign otherwise. The sum of the income class specific areas, assuming the correct sign (as it was just defined) has been attributed to each area, will be a measure of the degree of bi-polarization of the distribution of health.[6] It is indeed easy to check that if for income classes below the median income the areas are mostly above the diagonal and for those income classes above the median income, the areas are mostly below the diagonal (the case of the solid curve in Fig. 1), we would have here a clear case of bi-polarization, individuals with a high income having usually a high health level and individuals with a low income a low health level. The sum of the areas would then have a positive sign.

If, on the contrary, for income classes below the median income, the areas defined previously are mostly below the diagonal while for those income classes above the median income, the areas are mostly above the diagonal, it would mean that individuals with a low income have a high level of health and those with a high income a low health level. The sum of the areas would then be clearly negative, another extreme case of bi-polarization, one corresponding to a negative correlation between health and income.

Finally, it is possible that, attributing again to each area the sign defined previously, we end up with a sum of areas whose value would be close to zero. This would indicate that there is no clear correlation between income and health. A zero value for the sum of areas would also be obtained when for each income class the expected number of individuals at each health level is equal to the actual number. This would mean that the conditional probabilities (the probability of having a given health level h, given the income class to which the individual belongs) would be the same whatever the income class — the distributions of health levels would be the same for each income class.

A simple numerical illustration of all the concepts which have just been defined is given in Appendix A.

A SECOND APPROACH TO MEASURING INEQUALITY AND BI-POLARIZATION IN INCOME AND HEALTH: OVERALL INDICES

In this section, we quantify overall bi-polarization in the joint distribution of health and income. This approach differs from that presented in the previous section, because it quantifies the dispersion in the marginal distributions in income and health, and makes a different assumption regarding minimal bi-polarization. $B(F)$ denotes the overall bi-polarization in health and income associated with the matrix of joint cumulative probabilities F.

Properties

Property of minimal bi-polarization: The bi-polarization index is minimal and equals zero when all individuals report the same income and health category.

Inequality and Bi-Polarization in Socioeconomic Status and Health

Property of maximal bi-polarization: The bi-polarization index is maximum and equals one when half of the individuals report the smallest income and health status whereas the other half of the individuals report the greatest income and health status.

Definition of a bi-polarization decreasing transfer: Let p^1 and p^2 be any two matrices (with the same dimensions) representing the probability distributions, and let F^1 and F^2 be the corresponding matrices representing the cumulative distribution functions. F^2 is derived from F^1 using a bi-polarization decreasing transfer if

- F^1 and F^2 have the same median health and income categories.
- In the cells (h,y) for which $h<m(h)$ and $y<m(y)$, $F^2_{h,y} \leq F^1_{h,y}$.
- In the cells (h,y) for which $h>m(h)$ and $y>m(y)$, $F^2_{h,y} \geq F^1_{h,y}$.
- For the other cells (h, y), $p^2_{h,y} = p^1_{h,y}$.

Note that the cells (h,y) for which $h<m(h)$ and $y<m(y)$ are the cells where both health and income are below the median health and income categories, whereas the cells for which $h>m(h)$ and $y>m(y)$ are the cells, where both health and income are greater than the median health and income categories.

Property of bi-polarization decreasing transfers: If F^2 is derived from F^1 using this type of transfers, F^2 exhibits less bi-polarization than F^1: $B(F^2) \leq B(F^1)$.

This property implies that overall bi-polarization decreases when a greater proportion of people is concentrated around the median health and income categories, rather than segregated in the two poles of "healthy and wealthy people" (bottom right of the p- and F-matrices) on the one hand and "unhealthy and poor people" (upper left of the matrices) on the other hand. For instance, let us consider a health variable with five categories and an income variable with five categories as well:

$$p^1 = \begin{pmatrix} .05 & 0 & 0 & 0 & 0 \\ .05 & .05 & 0 & 0 & .025 \\ .05 & .15 & .1 & .05 & 0 \\ .05 & 0 & .05 & .05 & .05 \\ 0 & .05 & .1 & .025 & .1 \end{pmatrix} \text{ and } F^1 = \begin{pmatrix} .05 & .05 & .05 & .05 & .05 \\ .1 & .15 & .15 & .15 & .175 \\ .15 & .35 & .45 & .5 & .525 \\ .2 & .4 & .55 & .65 & .725 \\ .2 & .45 & .7 & .825 & 1 \end{pmatrix}$$

The median health category is 3 and the median income category is also 3. We consider a transfer of people from a cell below the medians to another cell below the medians that is "closer" to the medians: for instance, a transfer of a .05 share of the population from cell (1,1) to cell (2,2).

Similarly, we also consider a transfer of people from a cell above the medians to another cell above the medians that is "closer" to the medians: for instance, a transfer of a .025 share of the population from cell (5,4) to cell (4,4). The new matrices are as follows:

$$p^2 = \begin{pmatrix} 0 & 0 & 0 & 0 & 0 \\ .05 & .1 & 0 & 0 & .025 \\ .05 & .15 & .1 & .05 & 0 \\ .05 & 0 & .05 & .075 & .05 \\ 0 & .05 & .1 & 0 & .1 \end{pmatrix} \text{ and } F^2 = \begin{pmatrix} 0 & 0 & 0 & 0 & 0 \\ .05 & .15 & .15 & .15 & .175 \\ .1 & .35 & .45 & .5 & .525 \\ .15 & .4 & .55 & .675 & .75 \\ .15 & .45 & .7 & .825 & 1 \end{pmatrix}$$

The new distribution of health and income is more concentrated around the median health and income categories. According to the property, bi-polarization for F^2 is smaller than bi-polarization for F^1.

Measures of Overall Bi-Polarization

We generalize the existing measures of bi-polarization for ordinal data in the uni-dimensional approach to the bi-dimensional perspective.

First, we extend the univariate measure of Abul Naga and Yalcin (2007), Apouey (2007), and Reardon (2009) to the bivariate case. Our overall index is a function of the absolute distance between the observed cumulative probabilities F, whose elements are $F_{h,y}$, and the maximal bi-polarization F-matrix, whose elements equal 0.5:

$$B_1 = 1 - \frac{\left(2 \sum_{h=1}^{H} \sum_{y=1}^{Y} |F_{h,y} - 0.5|\right) - 1}{HY - 1}$$

Second, we consider an extension to the bivariate case of an index proposed by Reardon (2009):

$$B_2 = \frac{1}{HY - 1} \sum_{h=1}^{H} \sum_{y=1}^{Y} 4F_{h,y}(1 - F_{h,y})$$

It is easy to prove that the overall bi-polarization indices B_1 and B_2 satisfy the continuity, scale independence, minimal bi-polarization, maximal bi-polarization, and bi-polarization decreasing transfer properties.

EMPIRICAL ILLUSTRATION

In this section, we provide an empirical illustration of the use of the indices developed above, focusing on dispersion in income and health in 2004–2006 and 2011, in 24 European countries.

Our data come from the EU – Statistics on Income and Living Condition (EU-SILC) surveys, whose summary statistics are available from the Eurostat website.[7] The EU-SILC project was launched in 2003 on the basis of a "gentleman's agreement" in six member states of the European Union, as well as in Norway. The starting date for the EU-SILC instrument (under the framework regulation) was 2004 for the EU-15 (with the exception of Germany, the Netherlands and the United Kingdom, which had derogations until 2005), as well as for Estonia, Norway and Iceland. The 10 new member states with the exception of Estonia started in 2005. Bulgaria started in 2006.

The goal of the surveys is to collect timely and comparable data on income, poverty, social exclusion, and living conditions, across European countries. Each EU-SILC surveys is based on a nationally representative probability sample of the population residing in private households and aged 16 years old or over in the respective target country.

We use countries for which information on health and income is available in 2011. Our analysis sample is thus made of Austria, Belgium, Bulgaria, Cyprus, Denmark, Estonia, Finland, France, Germany, Greece, Hungary, Iceland, Italy, Lithuania, Luxembourg, the Netherlands, Norway, Portugal, Romania, Slovakia, Slovenia, Spain, Sweden, and the United Kingdom.

We use data for the years 2004–2006 and 2011, which are respectively the first and the most recently available waves. Focusing on these years enables us to get a precise picture of the recent evolution of dispersion in health and income in Europe. As explained above, the first year of data is either 2004, or 2005, or 2006, depending on countries.

The health variable is ordinal self-reported health with five categories: "very bad," "bad," "fair," "good," and "very good." Income is also ordinal, since it is given in quintiles. It is computed on the basis of the total equalized disposable income during the year preceding the interview, that is, total disposable household income divided by the household equalized size, using the modified OECD equivalence scale. This scale gives a weight of 1.0 to the first adult, 0.5 to any other household member aged 14 and over, and 0.3 to each child below age 14.

Note that this section is intended as merely illustrative, as the underlying income variable is continuous rather than ordinal, and the continuous income measure could be obtained if we were to use the original EU-SILC data instead of the published tables. In addition, our income variable is a particular one — quintiles. Consequently, the sample is evenly distributed across categories of income. This implies that in the second approach, our bi-polarization measures are necessarily bounded away from the minimum and maximum.

An interesting feature of the EU-SILC datasets compared to other datasets that are generally used to study inequalities in Europe (such as SHARE or the ESPS) is that they contain information on Eastern European countries. This enables us to get a global picture of income/health inequalities in Europe.

Fig. 2 gives the distribution of self-assessed health in the sample. We observe that for both waves the median health category is "Good" in most countries. However there are some exceptions. First, Greece appears as a healthier country than its neighbors, since for both waves the median health category is "Very good." In contrast, Lithuania and Portugal systematically report poorer health than the rest of Europe. The median health category of these countries is "Fair" for both waves. Finally, Estonia and Hungary may have experienced an improvement of the general health status of the population, since the median health category increased from "Fair" in 2004—2006 to "Good" in 2011.

Some other countries also show some signs of an improvement in health. In particular, this is the case in Germany, Portugal, Sweden, Spain, and the United Kingdom, since the proportion of individuals in the two top health categories increased whereas those in the three lowest health categories decreased.

In Bulgaria and France, the shares of individuals in the middle categories ("Fair" and "Good") increased between 2004—2006 and 2011, whereas the shares of individuals in the extreme categories ("Very bad," "Bad," and "Very good") decreased. This means that there is a decrease in (uni-dimensional) bi-polarization in health over time, since the distribution of health was more concentrated around the median health category in 2011.

In what follows, we present two tables giving the indices of the bi-polarization and inequality indices developed in the chapter.

To derive the inequality and bi-polarization indices based on the first approach, we build for each country and year two matrices whose rows correspond to health and whose columns correspond to income: the first matrix contains the actual shares, whereas the second matrix contains the expected shares. These matrices enable us to draw the "within income

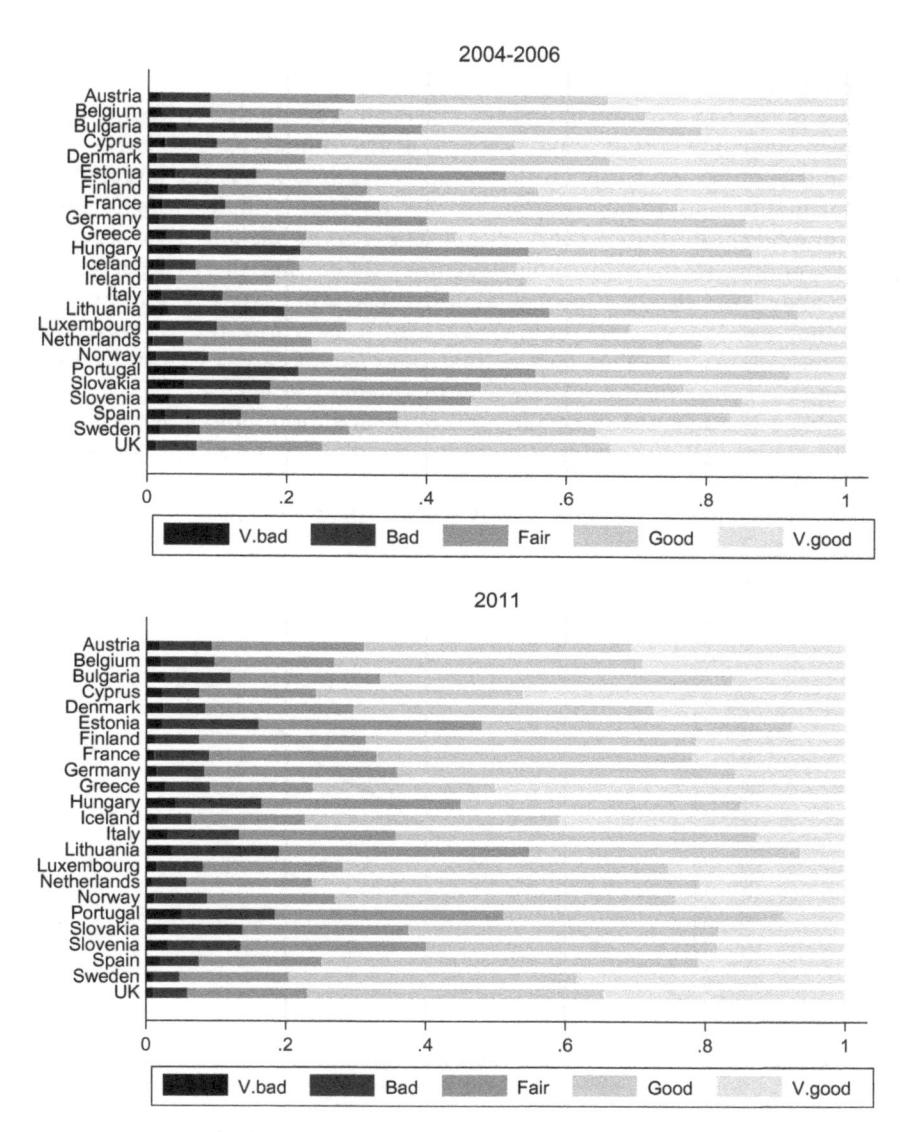

Fig. 2. Distribution of Self-Assessed Health by Country and Year.

classes inequality curve" and the "distributional change curve" and to compute the indices.

We present in Fig. 3 a graphical representation of the "within income classes inequality curve" and of the "distributional change curve" for Estonia in 2011. We focus on that country because it has the largest level of inequality and bi-polarization in our analysis sample, which makes the graphical illustration very clear. The curves include five sections, corresponding to the five income quintiles. Note that the two curves are confounded for the top income quintile. The solid curve lies above the diagonal for low-income groups, whereas it is below the diagonal for high-income groups. This implies that poor people are less healthy than expected, whereas rich people are healthier than expected.

Table 1 contains the inequality and bi-polarization indices derived from the first approach. The technique that we use to compute the confidence intervals for the indices is presented in Appendix B. Inequality and bi-polarization indices are significantly greater than zero in all countries, in both 2004–2006 and 2011.

Our results do not necessarily imply that policies should try to reduce dispersion in health, since not all dispersion can and should be avoided.

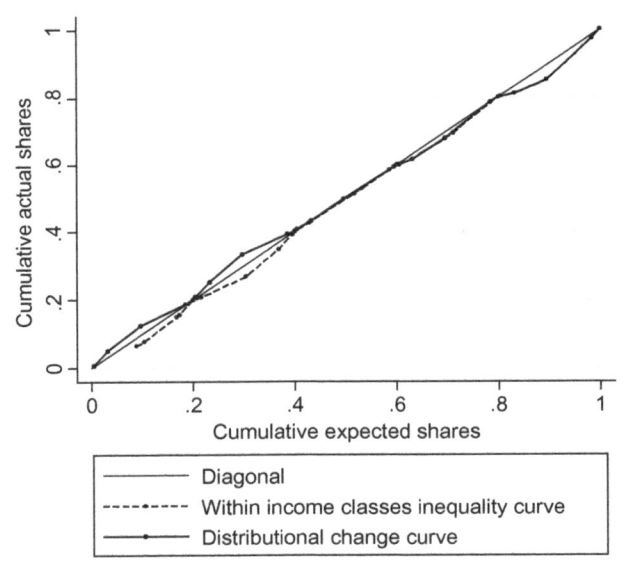

Fig. 3. "Within Income Classes Inequality" and "Distributional Change" Curves for Estonia in 2011.

Table 1. Conditional Indices, for European Countries, in 2004–2006 and 2011 (First Approach).

	First Year of Data	Within Income Classes Gini Index First year of data (1)	Within Income Classes Gini Index 2011 (2)	Gini Index First year of data (3)	Gini Index 2011 (4)	Bi-Polarization Index First year of data (5)	Bi-Polarization Index 2011 (6)
Austria	2004	**.014** [.011; .016]	**.021** [.019; .023]	**.084** [.070; .093]	**.128** [.116; .138]	**.013** [.011; .015]	**.020** [.018; .022]
Belgium	2004	**.021** [.018; .023]	**.027** [.025; .029]	**.129** [.117; .139]	**.157** [.145; .167]	**.021** [.019; .023]	**.027** [.024; .029]
Bulgaria	2006	.020 [.018; .022]	.023 [.020; .025]	.120 [.109; .129]	.134 [.122; .144]	.019 [.017; .021]	.022 [.020; .023]
Cyprus	2005	.026 [.024; .028]	.023 [.020; .025]	.168 [.154; .178]	.140 [.127; .151]	.026 [.023; .029]	.023 [.020; .025]
Denmark	2004	.016 [.013; .017]	.018 [.015; .020]	.096 [.082; .106]	.112 [.098; .123]	.015 [.013; .018]	.016 [.013; .018]
Estonia	2004	.027 [.024; .029]	.030 [.028; .033]	.162 [.148; .173]	.185 [.172; .196]	.025 [.023; .028]	.028 [.026; .031]
Finland	2004	**.016** [.014; .018]	**.022** [.019; .024]	**.093** [.079; .103]	**.130** [.116; .142]	**.016** [.013; .018]	**.021** [.018; .023]
France	2004	.014 [.011; .015]	.010 [.008; .011]	.085 [.075; .093]	.063 [.053; .070]	.013 [.011; .015]	.009 [.007; .011]
Germany	2005	**.014** [.012; .015]	**.019** [.017; .020]	**.085** [.074; .093]	**.115** [.106; .123]	**.012** [.011; .014]	**.017** [.016; .019]
Greece	2004	.019 [.016; .020]	.016 [.013; .017]	.117 [.105; .127]	.094 [.082; .103]	.018 [.016; .020]	.012 [.010; .014]
Hungary	2005	.016 [.013; .017]	.016 [.014; .017]	.093 [.080; .100]	.098 [.085; .106]	.011 [.009; .013]	.012 [.010; .014]
Iceland	2004	.012 [.009; .013]	.011 [.008; .012]	.080 [.062; .092]	.071 [.053; .081]	.010 [.007; .014]	.009 [.005; .012]
Italy	2004	.012 [.010; .013]	.014 [.012; .015]	.071 [.061; .078]	.082 [.072; .088]	.010 [.008; .012]	.008 [.007; .010]
Lithuania	2005	.023 [.021; .025]	.018 [.016; .020]	.135 [.122; .144]	.106 [.092; .114]	.017 [.015; .019]	.011 [.009; .013]

Table 1. (Continued)

	First Year of Data	Within Income Classes Gini Index First year of data (1)	Within Income Classes Gini Index 2011 (2)	Gini Index First year of data (3)	Gini Index 2011 (4)	Bi-Polarization Index First year of data (5)	Bi-Polarization Index 2011 (6)
Luxembourg	2004	.017 [.013; .019]	.015 [.012; .017]	.097 [.079; .108]	.092 [.076; .102]	.015 [.012; .017]	.013 [.011; .016]
Netherlands	2005	**.013** [**.011; .015**]	**.018** [**.015; .019**]	**.084** [**.071; .093**]	**.107** [**.096; .116**]	**.012** [**.010; .014**]	**.016** [**.014; .018**]
Norway	2004	.018 [.014; .020]	.019 [.016; .021]	.104 [.086; .115]	.114 [.098; .125]	.016 [.013; .019]	.016 [.014; .019]
Portugal	2004	.025 [.022; .026]	.023 [.021; .025]	.144 [.132; .153]	.133 [.121; .142]	.024 [.022; .026]	.020 [.018; .022]
Slovakia	2005	.016 [.014; .017]	.017 [.014; .018]	.097 [.085; .104]	.104 [.091; .112]	**.008** [**.006; .011**]	**.014** [**.012; .016**]
Slovenia	2005	.022 [.020; .024]	.021 [.019; .023]	.134 [.121; .145]	.126 [.114; .137]	.020 [.018; .023]	.020 [.017; .022]
Spain	2004	.016 [.014; .017]	.016 [.014; .017]	.098 [.088; .106]	.098 [.089; .106]	.015 [.014; .017]	.014 [.012; .016]
Sweden	2004	.019 [.016; .021]	.019 [.016; .021]	.109 [.095; .119]	.113 [.100; .124]	.017 [.015; .020]	.019 [.016; .021]
UK	2005	.022 [.020; .024]	.018 [.017; .020]	.130 [.120; .138]	.108 [.099; .116]	.020 [.018; .022]	.015 [.013; .017]

Notes: Indices in columns (1) and (2) are computed from Eq. (3) and those in columns (3) and (4) from Eq. (4). Indices in columns (5) and (6) are computed following the technique explained in the last subsection in the first approach to the measurement of inequality and bi-polarization. We indicate with bold letters the countries in which the index has significantly increased over time, and we underline the indices for the countries in which the index has significantly decreased over time.

It would be worth understanding the reasons why dispersion arises in Europe. In particular, future research could investigate a decomposition of the indices by factors, to identify the reasons underlying inequality and bi-polarization. Following the literature on inequality of opportunities in health, these factors could be classified as either circumstances or efforts variables (Rosa Dias, 2009; Trannoy, Tubeuf, Jusot, & Devaux, 2010). If our findings on the positive levels of inequality and bi-polarization reflect differences in circumstances between individuals, this would mean that there are opportunities for reducing inequalities and bi-polarization in health in Europe.

We now turn to the comparison of the levels of dispersion between countries. Note that caution is required when doing this comparison exercise, since differential health reporting might render the indices not comparable between countries (Bago d'Uva, O'Donnell, & Van Doorslaer, 2008). Having this limitation in mind, we rank the countries according to the values of the inequality and bi-polarization indices given in the table. We find that Cyprus, Estonia, and Portugal exhibit a great level of inequality and bi-polarization, in both waves of the data. The very large level of inequality in Estonia in 2004 and 2011 is in line with the substantial level of inequalities in mortality in that country at the end of the 1980s, that was followed by a "tremendous rise of inequalities in mortality" between 1989 and 2000 (Mackenbach, 2006). Our result for Portugal is consistent with the previous literature, which shows that among 13 European countries, Portugal is the most unequal (Van Doorslaer & Koolman, 2004). In contrast, we observe that Iceland and Italy have low levels of health/income dispersion. Our data also suggest that in 2005 the Netherlands had a relatively small level of inequality and bi-polarization, which is consistent with the literature (Van Doorslaer & Koolman, 2004). However, the level of dispersion increased significantly between 2005 and 2011, so that the Netherlands have today a European average level of inequality and bi-polarization.

Looking more closely at the evolution of dispersion over time, we observe that inequality and bi-polarization remained stable in most countries between 2004−2006 and 2011. However, some countries went through important changes. There is strong evidence that inequality and bi-polarization decreased over time in France, Greece, Lithuania, and the United Kingdom. In contrast, inequality and bi-polarization rose in Austria, Belgium, Finland, Germany, and the Netherlands.

We then turn to the results for our second approach, which is based on a different definition of minimal dispersion. Table 2 contains the bi-polarization indices B_1 and B_2 for 2004−2006 and 2011.

Table 2. Overall Bi-Polarization Indices for European Countries, in 2004–2006 and 2011 (Second Approach).

	First Year of Data	Bi-Polarization Index B_1 First year of data	Bi-Polarization Index B_1 2011	Bi-Polarization Index B_2 First year of data	Bi-Polarization Index B_2 2011
Austria	2004	.178 [.171; .185]	.192 [.184; .199]	**.491** **[.483; .498]**	**.507** **[.500; .516]**
Belgium	2004	.176 [.169; .183]	.187 [.180; .195]	.493 [.486; .501]	.507 [.500; .515]
Bulgaria	2006	.245 [.237; .253]	.197 [.190; .204]	.564 [.557; .572]	.520 [.512; .527]
Cyprus	2005	.189 [.180; .200]	.172 [.163; .182]	.507 [.497; .518]	.486 [.477; .497]
Denmark	2004	**.151** **[.144; .159]**	**.176** **[.168; .184]**	**.464** **[.455; .473]**	**.493** **[.485; .502]**
Estonia	2004	.252 [.245; .260]	.247 [.239; .255]	.556 [.549; .564]	.552 [.545; .559]
Finland	2004	.193 [.183; .203]	.176 [.168; .184]	.506 [.496; .516]	.489 [.481; .497]
France	2004	.192 [.185; .198]	.175 [.169; .180]	.510 [.504; .517]	.489 [.483; .495]
Germany	2005	.192 [.186; .198]	.183 [.178; .189]	.503 [.498; .508]	.497 [.492; .503]
Greece	2004	.143 [.135; .153]	.158 [.150; .166]	.468 [.459; .477]	.472 [.464; .481]
Hungary	2005	.279 [.273; .285]	.244 [.237; .251]	.586 [.580; .592]	.557 [.551; .564]
Iceland	2004	.141 [.130; .152]	.143 [.131; .154]	.453 [.441; .466]	.451 [.439; .463]
Italy	2004	.205 [.200; .210]	.192 [.187; .196]	.513 [.508; .518]	.513 [.508; .518]
Lithuania	2005	.263 [.257; .270]	.253 [.247; .259]	.567 [.561; .573]	.559 [.553; .565]
Luxembourg	2004	.179 [.171; .188]	.165 [.157; .172]	.497 [.487; .506]	.481 [.472; .489]
Netherlands	2005	.131 [.125; .137]	.139 [.133; .145]	.442 [.436; .450]	.451 [.444; .458]
Norway	2004	.163 [.155; .172]	.164 [.155; .172]	.480 [.472; .489]	.481 [.473; .489]
Portugal	2004	.290 [.283; .297]	.267 [.261; .274]	.600 [.593; .608]	.576 [.569; .583]
Slovakia	2005	.266 [.258; .273]	.213 [.207; .220]	.575 [.569; .582]	.531 [.524; .538]

Table 2. (*Continued*)

	First Year of Data	Bi-Polarization Index B_1 First year of data	Bi-Polarization Index B_1 2011	Bi-Polarization Index B_2 First year of data	Bi-Polarization Index B_2 2011
Slovenia	2005	.252 [.244; .260]	.229 [.221; .237]	.563 [.555; .570]	.545 [.537; .552]
Spain	2004	.204 [.199; .209]	.151 [.146; .156]	.525 [.520; .530]	.467 [.462; .472]
Sweden	2004	.178 [.171; .186]	.141 [.134; .148]	.489 [.482; .498]	.446 [.438; .454]
UK	2005	.165 [.159; .171]	.147 [.142; .152]	.477 [.471; .484]	.456 [.451; .461]

Notes. The 95% confidence intervals are in brackets. We indicate with bold letters the countries in which the index has significantly increased over time, and we underline the indices for the countries in which the index has significantly decreased over time.

The table shows a significant level of bi-polarization in all countries both in 2004–2006 and 2011. The two indices indicate that bi-polarization significantly increased in Denmark between 2004 and 2011, whereas it significantly decreased in France, Hungary, Portugal, Slovakia, Slovenia, Spain, Sweden, and the United Kingdom. One index also indicates an increase of bi-polarization in Austria and a decrease in Italy.

Comparing the results of Table 2 with the last two columns of Table 1, we find that the evolution of bi-polarization between 2004–2006 and 2011 are often consistent across tables. For instance, both tables show an increase of bi-polarization in Austria and Belgium, and a decrease in Cyprus (these changes can be significant or insignificant). Both tables suggest a significant decrease in bi-polarization in France, Portugal, and the United Kingdom between 2004–2005 and 2011.

CONCLUSION

This chapter develops original methods to quantify the level of inequality and bi-polarization in socioeconomic status and health, when both variables are ordinal. We present two distinct approaches that are embedded in different definitions of minimal inequality and bi-polarization. The empirical illustration is based on data from the EU-SILC surveys for 24 countries between 2004–2006 and 2011.

Our study suggests several routes for future research. A first avenue could be to provide an axiomatic derivation of bivariate indices, in order to derive the family of dispersion measures that have the most interesting properties. Second, one could develop a decomposition technique for bivariate indices enabling researchers to decompose the total observed income/health disparity into the contribution of several factors. By extension, one could also identify the factors that explain the changes in the level of disparity over time. This is all the more relevant as we find that inequality increased in Austria, Belgium, Finland, Germany, and the Netherlands (see the first four columns of Table 1), and that bi-polarization decreased in France, Portugal, and the United Kingdom (see the last two columns of Table 1, and Table 2), over the past decade. A first factor that could explain the rise of inequalities and that could be tested is access to health care services. Indeed, the financial crisis, which started in Europe in 2007, put a strain on health-care systems in some countries. Another relevant factor that could potentially explain the rise in inequality in Germany in particular is the ageing of the population. Indeed, income/health inequality tend to be larger among older generations in that country (Van Kippersluis, Van Ourti, O'Donnell, & Van Doorslaer, 2009).

NOTES

1. Some questionnaires add "compared to other people your age."
2. The Theil index is not defined when some probability $p_{h,y}$ is equal to zero.
3. The G-matrix is a square matrix with zeros on the diagonal, −1 above the diagonal, and +1 below.
4. See Silber (1989) for more details on the concept of Pseudo-Gini.
5. The area between the diagonal and this curve will be equal to half the absolute value of this Pseudo-Gini.
6. We borrow here some ideas from Deutsch, Silber, and Yalonetzky (2013).
7. See http://appsso.eurostat.ec.europa.eu/nui/show.do?wai=true&dataset=hlth_silc_10.
8. We use the minimal number of observations (per country) as a proxy for the number of observations (per country). See the Eurostat website: http://epp.eurostat.ec.europa.eu/portal/page/portal/income_social_inclusion_living_conditions/documents/tab/Tab/EU-SILC%20sample%20size.pdf

ACKNOWLEDGEMENTS

The authors would like to thank Owen O'Donnell for his helpful comments on this chapter.

REFERENCES

Abul Naga, R. H., & Yalcin, T. (2007). Inequality measurement for ordered response health data. *Journal of Health Economics, 27*(6), 1614–1625.

Allison, R. A., & Foster, J. E. (2004). Measuring health inequality using qualitative data. *Journal of Health Economics, 23*, 505–524.

Apouey, B. (2007). Measuring health polarization with self-assessed health data. *Health Economics, 16*(9), 875–894.

Apouey, B. (2010). On measuring and explaining socioeconomic polarization in health with an application to French data. *Review of Income and Wealth, 56*(1), 141–170.

Bago d'Uva, T., O'Donnell, O., & Van Doorslaer, E. (2008). Differential health reporting by education level and its impact on the measurement of health inequalities among older Europeans. *International Journal of Epidemiology, 37*(6), 1375–1383.

Blair, J., & Lacy, M. G. (1996). Measures of variation for ordinal data as functions of the cumulative distribution. *Perceptual & Motor Skills, 82*(2), 411–418.

Dawkins, C. (2006). The spatial pattern of black–white segregation in US metropolitan areas: An exploratory analysis. *Urban Studies, 43*(11), 1943–1969.

Deutsch, J., Silber, J., & Yalonetzky, G. (2013). *On relative bi-polarization and the middle class in Latin America. A look at the first decade of the 21st century*. Paper presented at the XX Encuentro de Economía Pública, Sevilla, Spain.

Groot, W. (2000). Adaptation and scale of reference bias in self-assessments of quality of life. *Journal of Health Economics, 19*(3), 403–420.

Idler, E. L., & Benyamini, Y. (1997). Self-rated health and mortality: A review of twenty-seven community studies. *Journal of Health and Social Behavior, 38*(1), 21–37.

Kakwani, N. C. (1980). *Income inequality and poverty: Methods of estimation and policy applications*. New York, NY: Oxford University Press.

Kakwani, N., Wagstaff, A., & Van Doorslaer, E. (1997). Socioeconomic inequalities in health: Measurement, computation, and statistical inference. *Journal of Econometrics, 77*(1), 87–103.

Kobus, M. (2012). *Multidimensional inequality for ordinal data*. Retrieved from http://coin.wne.uw.edu.pl/mkobus/Multi_1_two_dimensions_final.pdf

Kobus, M., & Miłoś, P. (2012). Inequality decomposition by population subgroups for ordinal data. *Journal of Health Economics, 31*(1), 15–21.

Lazar, A., & Silber, J. (2013). On the cardinal measurement of health inequality when only ordinal information is available on individual health status. *Health Economics, 22*(1), 106–113.

Mackenbach, J. P. (2006). *Health inequalities: Europe in profile. An independent expert report commissioned by the UK presidency of the EU*. London: Department of Health.

Reardon, S. F. (2009). Measures of ordinal segregation. *Research on Economic Inequality, 17*, 129–155.

Rosa Dias, P. (2009). Inequality of opportunity in health: Evidence from a UK cohort study. *Health Economics, 18*(9), 1057–1074.

Silber, J. (1989). Factors components, population subgroups and the computation of the Gini index of inequality. *Review of Economics and Statistics, LXXI*, 107–115.

Silber, J., & Yalonetzky, G. (2011). Measuring inequality in life chances with ordinal variables. *Research on Economic Inequality, 19*, 77–98.

Trannoy, A., Tubeuf, S., Jusot, F., & Devaux, M. (2010). Inequality of opportunities in health in France: A first pass. *Health Economics, 19*(8), 921–938.

Van Doorslaer, E., & Jones, A. (2003). Inequalities in self-reported health: Validation of a new approach to measurement. *Journal of Health Economics*, *22*, 61–87.

Van Doorslaer, E., & Koolman, X. (2004). Explaining the differences in income-related health inequalities across European countries. *Health Economics*, *13*(7), 609–628.

Van Kippersluis, H., Van Ourti, T., O'Donnell, O., & Van Doorslaer, E. (2009). Health and income across the life cycle and generations in Europe. *Journal of Health Economics*, *28*(4), 818–830.

Wolfson, M., & Rowe, G. (2001). On measuring inequalities in health. *Bulletin of the World Health Organization*, *79*(6), 553–560.

APPENDIX A: NUMERICAL EXAMPLE FOR THE FIRST APPROACH TO INEQUALITY/BI-POLARIZATION

Assume two income levels ($y=1$ and $y=2$, with $y=2$ the highest income level) and three health levels ($h=A$, $h=B$ and $h=C$, with $h=C$ the highest health level).

Table A1 gives the distribution of the individuals among the six potential cells.

Table A2 gives the actual share of each cell in the total population.

Table A3 gives the expected shares (product of the margins).

Finally, Table A4 gives the ratio of the actual over the expected shares and in parenthesis the rank of each cell, as far as this ratio is concerned (cells ranked by increasing values of the ratios).

Table A1. Original Data.

	$y=1$	$y=2$	Horizontal Margins
$h=A$	50	20	70
$h=B$	20	10	30
$h=C$	30	70	100
Vertical margins	100	100	200

Table A2. Actual Shares.

	$y=1$	$y=2$	Horizontal Margins
$h=A$	0.25	0.10	0.35
$h=B$	0.10	0.05	0.15
$h=C$	0.15	0.35	0.50
Vertical margins	0.50	0.50	1

Table A3. Expected Shares.

	$y=1$	$y=2$	Horizontal Margins
$h=A$	0.175	0.175	0.35
$h=B$	0.075	0.075	0.15
$h=C$	0.250	0.25	0.50
Vertical margins	0.50	0.50	1

Table A4. Ratio of Actual Over Expected Shares.

	$y=1$	$y=2$
$h=A$	1.42 (6)	0.57 (1)
$h=B$	1.33 (4)	0.66 (3)
$h=C$	0.60 (2)	1.40 (5)

Within Income Classes Gini Curve and Within Income Classes Gini Index

For the graphical representation we first plot the cumulative values of the expected and actual shares for the lower income class ($y=1$), on the horizontal and vertical axes, these shares being again ranked by increasing values of the corresponding ratios of the actual over the expected shares. Note that when we complete the plot for this lower income class we will have reached the point (0.5; 0.5) on the graph. We then do the same thing for the higher income class ($y=2$) and end up at the point (1; 1). This graph then represents the inequality of health opportunity within the income classes.

We can then compute the corresponding within income classes Gini index.

The contribution C_1 of the within income class 1 inequality of health opportunities will be written as

$$C_1 = [0.175\ 0.075\ 0.250]'G[0.25\ 0.10\ 0.15]$$

and it is easy to find out that $C_1 = 0.05125$.

Similarly the contribution C_2 of the within income class 2 inequality of health opportunities will be written as

$$C_2 = [0.25\ 0.075\ 0.175]'G[0.35\ 0.05\ 0.10]$$

and it is easy to find out that $C_2 = 0.05125$.

The overall within income classes inequality of health opportunities is then equal to

$$C_1 + C_2 = 0.1025$$

Gini Curve and the Gini Index

Here we draw a graph where on the horizontal axis we plot the cumulative values of the expected shares and on the vertical axis the cumulative values of the actual shares but here all the shares are ranked by increasing ratios of the actual over the expected shares.

We can also compute the corresponding Gini index comparing the expected values (row vector) with the actual values (column vector), the shares in this vector being classified this time by decreasing values (Silber, 1989).

In other words we compute the product $e'Ga$, where e' is a row vector of the expected shares, a column vector of the actual shares and G is the G-matrix, a matrix whose typical cell g_{ij} is equal to 0 if $i=j$, to -1 if $j > i$ and to $+1$ if $i > j$. Note again that in both e' and a all the shares have to be ranked by decreasing values of the ratios of the actual over the expected shares.

In other words, we get
$e'Ga = [0.175\ 0.25\ 0.075\ 0.075\ 0.25\ 0.175]'G[0.25\ 0.35\ 0.10\ 0.05\ 0.15\ 0.10]$.
It is then easy to find out that $e'Ga = 0.2075$

This is then a measure of the overall inequality of health opportunities.

Measuring Distributional Change

But we can also compute an alternative measure. Let us again plot first the cumulative expected and actual shares for the lower income level, but we would rank both sets of cumulative shares by increasing health level. If the higher the actual health level, the higher the ratio of actual over expected shares, then we would get the previous graph.

We could then give an alternative interpretation to this graph and say that it measures the "distributional change" obtained when comparing actual and expected shares. Since by construction this curve will be completely below the diagonal (and have in fact a non-decreasing slope) we could consider this distributional change as positive since the higher the health level, the higher the ratio of the actual over the expected shares.

If on the contrary, when ranking the cumulative shares, within income class 1, by increasing health level, we find that the lower the health level, the higher the ratio of actual over expected shares, we could consider this distributional change as negative, because, as was just stressed, it indicates that within income class 1, individuals with a low health level are in greater numbers than we would have a priori expected.

Naturally such a distributional curve (for income class 1) can be partly above, partly below the diagonal (especially when we consider more than three health levels) and in computing the total distributional change we will have to give a positive sign to any area below the diagonal and a negative sign to any area above the diagonal. However, it turns out that a simple algorithm that takes into account this sign constraint can be implemented to compute the sum of these signed areas. We just have to define a row vector $\tilde{e}'$ of the expected shares and a column vector $\tilde{a}$ of the actual shares, both shares being ranked by decreasing health level, and compute the product $\tilde{e}'G\tilde{a}$. It then turns out that for income level 1

$$\tilde{e}'G\tilde{a} = [0.250 \quad 0.075 \quad 0.175]'G[0.15 \quad 0.10 \quad 0.25]$$

and it is easy to find that $\alpha = \tilde{e}'G\tilde{a} = -0.05125$

We can similarly compute the corresponding product $\tilde{e}'G\tilde{a}$ for income level 2 and find out that

$$\tilde{e}'G\tilde{a} = [0.25 \quad 0.075 \quad 0.175]'G[0.35 \quad 0.05 \quad 0.10]$$

and it is easy to find that, for income level 2, $\beta = \tilde{e}'G\tilde{a} = 0.05125$.

The overall distributional change DC will then be expressed as $DC = \alpha + \beta = 0$.

Measuring Bi-Polarization

If however our goal is to look at the bi-polarization of the inequality of opportunities, assuming two income levels of equal population size, we should give a positive sign to any area above the diagonal for the lower income level 1 and a positive sign for any area below the diagonal for the higher income class 2, because we would then check whether, among the poor, the lower the health level, the higher the ratio of actual over expected shares and whether, among the rich, on the contrary, the higher the health level, the higher the ratio of actual over expected shares.

In other words, a simple measure of bi-polarization B would be written as $-\alpha + \beta$ and it is then easy to check that in our simple empirical illustration we get

$$B = -(-0.05125) + 0.05125 = 0.1025$$

APPENDIX B: METHOD TO COMPUTE THE CONFIDENCE INTERVALS

Assume that there are Y income groups and H health levels. Let us call $p_{h,y}$ the probability of being in income category y and of having health level h. The table which was the basis for drawing the distributional change curves is such that

$$\sum_{h=1}^{H}\sum_{y=1}^{Y} p_{h,y} = 1$$

Let us now define $n_{h,y}$ as $n_{h,y} = (N \times p_{h,y})$ with N the number of observations per country.[8] Assume we have a box with N balls of different colors, the number of colors being $(H \times Y)$. In other words, we have $n_{1,1}$ balls of color "11," ..., $n_{h,y}$ balls of color "hy," ..., and $n_{H,Y}$ balls of color "HY."

Let us draw *with repetition* 1,000 balls from this box and call $m_{h,y}$ the number of balls of color "hy." Obviously in general $m_{h,y}$ is likely to be different from $n_{h,y}$, although it may happen that, for some "hy," $m_{h,y} = n_{h,y}$. Call now $q_{h,y}$ the ratio $q_{hy} = \left(\frac{m_{h,y}}{1000}\right)$. We can use these proportions $q_{h,y}$ to compute the indices originally computed (inequality, distributional change, bi-polarization...).

Let us repeat 500 to 1,000 times this procedure where we draw 1,000 balls with repetition, the number of balls of color "hy" in the box being as before $n_{h,y}$ and compute each time the indices of distributional change, inequality and bi-polarization mentioned previously.

We will then obtain a distribution of each of the indices mentioned previously and can then derive a 5–95% or a 10–90% confidence interval for each index. By comparing the confidence interval of an index for a given year with the corresponding confidence interval in another year, we can then test whether the index in one year differs significantly from the estimate of the index in another year.

ON THE MEASUREMENT OF THE (MULTIDIMENSIONAL) INEQUALITY OF HEALTH DISTRIBUTIONS

Jens Leth Hougaard, Juan D. Moreno-Ternero and Lars Peter Østerdal

ABSTRACT

Health outcomes are often described according to two dimensions: quality of life and quantity of life. We analyze the measurement of inequality of health distributions referring to these two dimensions. Our analysis relies on a novel treatment of the quality-of-life dimension, which might not have a standard mathematical structure. We single out two families of (absolute and relative) multidimensional health inequality indices, inspired by the classical normative approach to income inequality measurement. We also discuss how to extend the analysis to deal with the related problem of health deprivation measurement in this setting.

Keywords: Inequality; health; quantity of life; quality of life; QALYs; HYEs

JEL classifications: D63; I14

INTRODUCTION

Equity is typically recognized as a relevant policy objective in the health care field, as witnessed by the chapters devoted to this topic in the two volumes of the *Handbook of Health Economics* (e.g., Fleurbaey & Schokkaert, 2012; Wagstaff & van Doorslaer, 2000; Williams & Cookson, 2000). Most of the literature on health inequality is inspired by the standard economic approach to the measurement of income inequality (e.g., Bleichrodt & van Doorslaer, 2006).[1] However, such standard framework is unidimensional and, as such, not sufficiently rich to analyze relevant aspects in the health care field. More precisely, it is frequently argued that the benefit a patient derives from a particular health care intervention is defined according to two dimensions: quality of life and quantity of life (e.g., Pliskin, Shepard, Weinstein, 1980). Therefore, it seems that an appropriate approach to the measurement of health inequality should take into account the multidimensionality of the problem.

Research on multidimensional economic inequality has played an important role since the seminal articles by Kolm (1977) and Atkinson & Bourguignon (1982).[2] The recent awake of interest in multidimensional inequality is driven by the recognition that univariate indices of income inequality provide an inadequate basis for comparing the inequality of well-being within and between populations. Multivariate generalizations of the procedures used to construct univariate inequality indices from social evaluation abound in the literature.[3] Nevertheless, all these procedures rely on a common assumption stating that all dimensions have an Euclidean structure (i.e., they lie within the space of real numbers), which eases their formulation. This may, however, not be totally justified in the context of health; in particular, if we endorse the view that the benefit a patient derives from a particular health care intervention is defined according to the two dimensions mentioned above. To wit, whereas the "quantity of life" is naturally represented by a real number (years), objections might be raised concerning the "quality of life," which needs a richer description than what can be represented by a single number (or even by vectors of numbers).

The model we analyze here builds onto the models of Østerdal (2005) and Hougaard, Moreno-Ternero, and Østerdal (2013), in which we assume that each individual in the population is described by a duplet indicating the level achieved in quality of life and quantity of life. The set of possible "quality of life" states is defined generally enough so that no specific mathematical structure is imposed on it. We only assume that such a set contains a superior element, referred to as *perfect health*. In doing so, our model is able to accommodate, not only standard modeling assumptions endorsing an Euclidean structure in each dimension, but also recent approaches assuming that health data is reported categorically (e.g., Abu-Naga & Yalcin, 2008; Allison & Foster, 2004).[4]

The aim of this chapter is then to develop a normative foundation to the measurement of (multidimensional) health inequality in such a general context. In particular, following the analysis in Hougaard et al. (2013), we impose a number of basic assumptions on social preferences over health profiles. Thanks to these assumptions, we derive a family of population health evaluation functions (PHEFs), which rank health profiles according to social desirability, that depend on the distribution of healthy years equivalents (HYEs).

Adding an invariance property with respect to re-scaling of life years, the above family of PHEFs is restricted to impose a power concave function of HYEs. Based on the resulting family, we derive the so-called *Atkinson family of multidimensional indices of health inequalities*, which inherit the property of being invariant to arbitrary re-scaling of life years (i.e., they all are relative indices of inequality).

Instead of the previous invariance property, we can add an axiom stating that if all agents have perfect health then the evaluation of the profile will be invariant to positive translation of the distribution of life spans. If so, we would obtain a PHEF which is exponentially concave in HYEs. Based on this, we derive the so-called *Kolm-Pollak family of multidimensional indices of health inequalities*, which inherit the property of being invariant to adding a common constant to all life years (i.e., they all are absolute indices of inequality).

As the above PHEFs are obtained in a fixed-population setting, we also extend the framework in Hougaard et al. (2013) to deal with a variable-population setting. The resulting families of inequality indices in this setting coincide with those derived in the fixed-population setting mentioned above.

Finally, we also explore how to extend the previous normative analysis of inequality measurement to deal with the related problem of health deprivation measurement.

The rest of the chapter is organized as follows. In the second section, we set up the preliminaries, mostly summarizing the model and basic notions in Hougaard et al. (2013). In the third section, we present our contribution to deal with the measurement of multidimensional health inequality, and further extensions to the model are elaborated in the fourth section. We conclude in the fifth section. For a smooth passage, we defer the proofs to an appendix.

THE PRELIMINARIES

Let us identify the population (society) with a fixed finite set of individuals $N = \{1, ..., n\}$, $n \geq 3$. The health of each individual in the population is described by a duplet indicating the level achieved in two parameters: quality of life and quantity of life.[5] Assume that there exists a set of possible health states, A, defined generally enough to encompass all possible health states for everybody in the population. Quantity of life is simply described by a set of nonnegative real numbers, $T \subset \mathbb{R}$. In what follows, we assume that $T = [0, +\infty)$. Formally, let $h_i = (a_i, t_i) \in A \times T$ denote the health duplet of individual i.[6] A population health distribution (or, simply, a health profile) $h = [h_1, ..., h_n] = [(a_1, t_1), ..., (a_n, t_n)]$ specifies the health duplet of each individual in society. Denote the set of all possible health profiles by H, that is, H is the n-Cartesian product of the set $A \times T$. Even though we do not impose a specific mathematical structure on the set A, we assume that it contains a specific element, a_*, referred to as *perfect health* (typically understood as absence of abnormal conditions) and which is identified by the policy maker, as a "superior" state.

The policy maker's preferences (or social preferences) over health profiles are expressed by a preference relation $\succsim$, to be read as "at least as preferred as." As usual, $\succ$ denotes strict preference and $\sim$ denotes indifference. Assume the relation $\succsim$ is a weak order, that is, it is complete (for each pair of health profiles h, h', either $h \succsim h'$, or $h' \succsim h$, or both) and transitive (if $h \succsim h'$ and $h' \succsim h''$ then $h \succsim h''$).

A *population health evaluation function* (PHEF) is a real-valued function $P : H \to \mathbb{R}$.

We say that P represents $\succsim$ if

$$P(h) \geq P(h') \Leftrightarrow h \succsim h'$$

for each h, $h' \in H$. Note that if P represents $\succsim$ then any strictly increasing transformation of P will also do so.

We now list a set of basic axioms for social preferences that we shall endorse in this chapter.[7] *Anonymity* (in short, ANON) says that the evaluation of the population health should depend only on the list of quality-quantity duplets, not on who holds them. *Separability* (in short, SEP) says that if the distribution of health in a population changes only for a subgroup of agents in the population, the relative evaluation of the two distributions should only depend on that subgroup. *Continuity* (in short, CONT) says that, for fixed distributions of health states, small changes in lifetimes should not lead to large changes in the evaluation of the population health distribution. *Perfect health superiority* (in short, PHS) says that replacing the health status of an agent by that of perfect health, ceteris paribus, cannot worsen the evaluation of the population health. *Time monotonicity at perfect health* (TMPH) says that if each agent is at perfect health, increasing the time dimension is strictly better for society. *Positive lifetime desirability* (PLD) says that society improves if any agent moves from zero lifetime to positive lifetime (for a given health state). Finally, the *social zero condition* (in short, ZERO) says that if an agent gets zero lifetime, then her health state does not influence the social desirability of the health distribution. Formally,

ANON: $h \sim h_\pi$ for each $h \in H$, and each $\pi \in \Pi^N$.
SEP: $[h_S, h_{N\setminus S}] \succsim [h'_S, h_{N\setminus S}] \Leftrightarrow [h_S, h'_{N\setminus S}] \succsim [h'_S, h'_{N\setminus S}]$, for each $S \subseteq N$, and $h, h' \in H$.
CONT: Let $h, h' \in H$, and $h^{(k)}$ be a sequence in H such that, for each $i \in N$, $h_i^{(k)} = (a_i, t_i^{(k)}) \to (a_i, t_i) = h_i$. If $h^{(k)} \succsim h'$ for each k then $h \succsim h'$, and if $h' \succsim h^{(k)}$ for each k then $h' \succsim h$.
PHS: $[(a_*, t_i), h_{N\setminus\{i\}}] \succsim h$, for each $h = [h_1, ..., h_n] \in H$ and $i \in N$.
TMPH: If $t_i \geq t'_i$, for each $i \in N$, with at least one strict inequality, then $[(a_*, t_1), ..., (a_*, t_n)] \succ [(a_*, t'_1), ..., (a_*, t'_n)]$.
PLD: $h \succsim [h_{N\setminus\{i\}}, (a_i, 0)]$, for each $h = [h_1, ..., h_n] \in H$ and $i \in N$.
ZERO: For each $h \in H$ and $i \in N$ such that $t_i = 0$, and $a'_i \in A, h \sim [h_{N\setminus\{i\}}, (a'_i, 0)]$.

In what follows, we refer to the set of axioms introduced above as our *basic structural axioms*; in short, **BASIC**.

In Hougaard et al. (2013) it is demonstrated that BASIC implies the existence of a PHEF that depends on the healthy years equivalents (HYEs) only. In what follows, we show how this fact can be used to establish indices of multidimensional health inequality.

INDICES OF MULTIDIMENSIONAL HEALTH INEQUALITY

The Atkinson-Kolm-Sen Approach

We first explore the application to our setting of the so-called "Atkinson-Kolm-Sen approach." This approach, originated in the seminal articles of

Atkinson (1970) and Kolm (1969) on univariate inequality measurement, and later popularized by Sen (1973), basically amounts to constructing an inequality index from a social evaluation ordering. Now, in contrast with those seminal contributions in the unidimensional case, we shall derive first such a social welfare function (or social evaluation ordering) axiomatically, rather than proposing it exogenously. In order to do that, let us add two more axioms to the basic structural axioms from the previous section.

The first one, *time scale independence at perfect health* (TSIPH), is a specific form of homotheticity, a notion with a long tradition in the literature on income inequality measurement, and particularly embedded in the Atkinson-Kolm-Sen approach. It says that if all agents in society are enjoying the perfect health status, then the evaluation of this society will be invariant to a proportional scaling of the distribution of lifespans. Formally,

TSIPH: For each $c > 0$, and $h = [(a_*, t_i)_{i \in N}]$, $h' = [(a_*, t'_i)_{i \in N}]$,

$$h \succsim h' \Rightarrow [(a_*, ct_i)_{i \in N}] \succsim [(a_*, ct'_i)_{i \in N}]$$

The second one, *Pigou-Dalton transfer at perfect health* (PDTPH), is a specific form of the Pigou (1912)-Dalton (1920) transfer principle, which is also deeply rooted in the literature on income inequality measurement, that hence refers to the distributional sensitivity of the social evaluation. It states that a hypothetical progressive transfer of lifespans between two agents at perfect health would be welcomed.

Formally,

PDTPH: For each $h = [(a_*, t_k)_{k \in N}]$, and $i, j \in N$, such that $t_i \neq t_j$,

$$\left[\left(a_*, \frac{t_i + t_j}{2}\right), \left(a_*, \frac{t_i + t_j}{2}\right), h_{N \setminus \{i,j\}}\right] \succ h$$

It turns out, as the next result shows, that the so-called *power (concave) HYE* PHEFs, formally defined next, are characterized by the axioms described above. To wit,

$$P^{ph}[h_1, \ldots, h_n] = P^{ph}[(a_1, t_1), \ldots, (a_n, t_n)] = \sum_{i=1}^{n} f(a_i, t_i)^{\gamma} \quad (1)$$

where $\gamma \in (0, 1)$, and $f : A \times T \to T$ is a (continuous with respect to its second variable) function indicating the HYEs for each individual, that is, for each $h = [h_1, \ldots, h_n] = [(a_1, t_1), \ldots, (a_n, t_n)] \in H$, and each $i \in N$,

$$h \sim [(a_*, f(a_i, t_i))_{i \in N}]$$

On the Measurement of the Inequality of Health Distributions 117

Theorem 1. (Hougaard et al. 2013) The following statements are equivalent:

1. $\succsim$ is represented by a PHEF satisfying Eq. (1).
2. $\succsim$ satisfies BASIC, TSIPH, and PDTPH.

We then assume that the social welfare associated to a given health profile is evaluated by Eq. (1). It is worth mentioning that the representation for the social ordering we obtain is of the separable form. As such, it could be interpreted as being the value assigned to a health profile by a utilitarian social welfare function that uses the HYE function (which might look like a utility function) to convert individual health duplets into an interpersonally comparable measure of health. That is indeed the starting motivation in the Atkinson-Kolm-Sen approach. Pursuing such approach from this point, we define the *equally-distributed-equivalent HYE*, $E(h)$, associated with a given health profile h, as the per capita HYE which, if distributed equally, would be indifferent to the actual health profile according to the social preference relation $\succsim$. Formally, $E^{ph}(h)$ is defined implicitly by

$$[(a_*, E^{ph}(h)), \ldots, (a_*, E^{ph}(h))] \sim h \sim [(a_*, f(a_i, t_i))_{i \in N}] \qquad (2)$$

for each $h \in H$. By Eq. (1), it follows that

$$E^{ph}(h) = \left(\frac{1}{n}\sum_{i=1}^{n} f(a_i, t_i)^{\gamma}\right)^{1/\gamma}$$

for each $h \in H$.

Therefore, letting $\mu^f(h)$ denote the mean of the distribution of HYEs associated with h, the *Atkinson family of multidimensional health inequality indices*, associated to any social ordering $\succsim$ satisfying BASIC, TSIPH, and PDTPH, would be given by

$$I^A(h) = 1 - \frac{E^{ph}(h)}{\mu^f(h)} = 1 - \frac{\left(\frac{1}{n}\sum_{i=1}^{n} f(a_i, t_i)^{\gamma}\right)^{1/\gamma}}{\frac{1}{n}\sum_{i=1}^{n} f(a_i, t_i)} = 1 - \left(\frac{1}{n}\sum_{i=1}^{n}\left(\frac{n \cdot f(a_i, t_i)}{\sum_{i=1}^{n} f(a_i, t_i)}\right)^{\gamma}\right)^{1/\gamma} \qquad (3)$$

The previous family is defined by means of the parameter $\gamma \in (0, 1)$, which can be interpreted as the degree of inequality aversion, or the relative sensitivity to transfers at different HYE levels, reflected by the index. As γ

rises, more weight is given to transfers at the lower end of the distribution (of HYEs), and less weight to transfers at the top. Note that the index (Eq. (3)) is a relative inequality index in the sense that it is invariant to proportional changes in life years when all agents enjoy perfect health.

It is worth mentioning that a more specific expression for the Atkinson family could be given in the so-called *Quality-Adjusted-Life-Years* (QALYs) case, that is, the case in which $f(a_i, t_i) = q(a_i)t_i$, for each $(a_i, t_i) \in A \times T$, where $q : A \to [0, 1]$ is a function satisfying $0 \leq q(a_i) \leq q(a_*) = 1$, for each $a_i \in A$.[8]

The Kolm-Pollak Approach

As mentioned above, the Atkinson family of multidimensional health inequality indices, just presented, is a family of relative indices of inequality. In other words, each index within the family is invariant to a scaling of HYEs. This is a consequence of the TSIPH axiom we have imposed on the underlying social ordering. One might wonder if an alternative family could be constructed so that each index within the family would be invariant instead to an increase or decrease of all of its variables by a common amount. We pursue such an aim in the next lines, by following the seminal route proposed by Kolm (1969) and Pollak (1971). To do so, we need to formalize first the following counterpart to the TSIPH axiom. In words, *time translatability at perfect health* (TTRPH), says that if all agents in society are enjoying the perfect health status, then the evaluation of this society will be invariant to a positive translation of the distribution of lifespans. Formally,

TTRPH: For each $c > 0$, and $h = [(a_*, t_i)_{i \in N}]$, $h' = [(a_*, t'_i)_{i \in N}]$,

$$h \succsim h' \Rightarrow [(a_*, t_i + c)_{i \in N}] \succsim [(a_*, t'_i + c)_{i \in N}]$$

It turns out, as the next result shows, that the so-called *exponential (concave) HYE* PHEFs, formally defined next, are characterized when we replace the TSIPH axiom by this one in the statement of Theorem 1. To wit,

$$P^{eh}[h_1, \ldots, h_n] = P^{eh}[(a_1, t_1), \ldots, (a_n, t_n)] = -\sum_{i=1}^{n} e^{\gamma f(a_i, t_i)} \quad (4)$$

where $\gamma \in \mathbb{R}_{--}$, and $f : A \times T \to T$ is a function indicating the HYEs for each individual, as described above.

Theorem 2. The following statements are equivalent:

1. $\succsim$ is represented by a PHEF satisfying Eq. (4).
2. $\succsim$ satisfies BASIC, TTRPH and PDTPH.

Consequently, we now assume that the social welfare associated to a given health profile is evaluated by Eq. (4). Thus, it follows that the equally-distributed-equivalent HYE function is now given by

$$E^{eh}(h) = \frac{1}{\gamma} \ln\left[\frac{1}{n}\sum_{i=1}^{n} e^{\gamma f(a_i, t_i)}\right]$$

Therefore, the *Kolm-Pollak family of multidimensional health inequality indices*, associated to any social ordering $\succsim$ satisfying BASIC, TTRPH, and PDTPH, would be given by[9]

$$I^{KP} = \mu^f(h) - E^{eh}(h) = -\frac{1}{\gamma}\ln\left[\frac{1}{n}\sum_{i=1}^{n}e^{\gamma\left(f(a_i,t_i) - \frac{\sum_{k=1}^{n}f(a_k,t_k)}{n}\right)}\right] \quad (5)$$

As in the case of the Atkinson family, the Kolm-Pollak family of multidimensional health inequality indices is defined by means of the parameter $\gamma \in \mathbb{R}_{--}$, which can also be interpreted as the degree of inequality aversion. Now, in contrast with the Atkinson family, each index (Eq. (5)) is an absolute inequality index in the sense that it is invariant to adding the same number of life years to all agents, in situations where they all enjoy perfect health.

Finally, as in the case of the Atkinson family, it is worth mentioning that a more specific expression for the Kolm-Pollak family could be given in the QALY case, that is, the case in which $f(a_i, t_i) = q(a_i)t_i$, for each $(a_i, t_i) \in A \times T$, where $q : A \rightarrow [0, 1]$ is a function satisfying $0 \leq q(a_i) \leq q(a_*) = 1$, for each $a_i \in A$.

FURTHER INSIGHTS

Variable Population

The analysis in the previous section has been made in a fixed-population setting. There are many instances in which a variable-population setting is more suitable. An obvious point in case is that in which one is interested in comparisons across countries or regions. Because population size and individual identities may be different, this is not a straightforward issue. Nevertheless, the next lines convey a plausible way to move from the fixed-population setting described in the previous sections to a variable-population setting.[10]

Let $\mathcal{N}$ be the family of finite subsets of $\mathbb{N}$, the set of positive integer numbers, with generic elements N and M. A population health distribution is now described by a population $N \in \mathcal{N}$, and the corresponding health profile $h = [h_i]_{i \in N} = [(a_i, t_i)]_{i \in N}$ specifying the health duplet of each individual in society. Let $\mathcal{H}^N$ be the set of (health) distributions with population N and $\mathcal{H} \equiv \cup_{N \in \mathcal{N}} \mathcal{H}^N$. With a slight abuse of notation, we still denote by $\succsim$ the policy maker's preferences over health distributions of different populations (that might have different sizes).

We now consider the following standard axiom in the literature, which involves a replication operation that is often considered in economic modeling. Let $N \in \mathcal{N}$ and k be a positive integer. By a k-replica of a health distribution with population set N we mean a distribution in which each member of N has $k - 1$ clones, each of whom is endowed with a health duplet equal to his. Formally, given $h \in \mathcal{H}^N$, and if M designates the set of agents in the replica problem and $h' \in \mathcal{H}^M$ the replica problem, we have $N \subset M$, $|M| = k|N|$, and there is a partition of M into $|N|$ groups of k agents indexed by $i \in N$, $(N^i)_{i \in N}$, such that for each $i \in N$ and each $j \in N^i$, $h'_j = h_i$. The requirement of *replication invariance* (in short, RI) says that a k-replica of a distribution is indifferent to such distribution.

RI: For each $N \in \mathcal{N}$, each $h = [(a_i, t_i)_{i \in N}] \in \mathcal{H}^N$, each $M \supset N$, and each $h' \in \mathcal{H}^M$, if h' is a k-replica of h then $h \sim h'$.

It turns out, as the next results show, that the *average* versions of the (power and exponential) concave HYE PHEFs considered in the third section, and formally defined next, can be characterized thanks to this axiom, building onto the analysis of the third section. To wit,

$$P^{aph}[h] = P^{aph}[(a_i, t_i)_{i \in N}] = \frac{1}{|N|} \sum_{i \in N} f(a_i, t_i)^\gamma \tag{6}$$

where $\gamma \in (0, 1)$, and f is constructed as in Eq. (1).

$$P^{aeh}[h] = P^{aeh}[(a_i, t_i)_{i \in N}] = -\frac{1}{|N|} \sum_{i \in N} e^{\gamma f(a_i, t_i)} \tag{7}$$

where $\gamma \in \mathbb{R}_{--}$, and f is constructed as in Eq. (1).

The following results are obtained:

Theorem 3. In the variable-population setting, the following statements are equivalent:

1. $\succsim$ is represented by a PHEF satisfying Eq. (6), for each $h \in \mathcal{H}$.
2. $\succsim$ satisfies BASIC, TSIPH and PDTPH, for each population N, and RI.

Theorem 4. In the variable-population setting, the following statements are equivalent:

1. $\succsim$ is represented by a PHEF satisfying Eq. (7), for each $h \in \mathcal{H}$.
2. $\succsim$ satisfies BASIC, TTRPH and PDTPH, for each population N, and RI.

If we now assume that the social welfare associated to a given health profile is evaluated by Eq. (6), then the equally-distributed-equivalent HYE would be exactly defined as in Eq. (2). Therefore, the corresponding Atkinson family of multidimensional health inequality indices, in this variable population setting, would be exactly defined as in Eq. (3). Likewise, if we assume that the social welfare associated to a given health profile is evaluated by Eq. (7), then the corresponding Kolm-Pollak family of multidimensional health inequality indices, in this variable population setting, would be exactly defined as in Eq. (5). It is worth mentioning that each index within both families would inherit the property of replication invariance from the underlying (variable-population) PHEFs.

Health Deprivation Measurement

The concept of deprivation can be traced back to Runciman (1966), who formulated the idea that a person's feeling of deprivation in a society arises out of comparing its situation with those who are better off. This intuition was early used by Sen (1976) and Yitzhaki (1979), among others, in order to obtain a measure of deprivation in the uni-dimensional space of income. Now, as pointed out by philosophers (e.g., Rawls, 1971) and economists (e.g., Ravallion, 1996) alike, income is often not a perfect indicator of deprivation. Consequently, attention has recently shifted to study poverty (deprivation) in a multidimensional framework (e.g., Decancq, Fleurbaey & Maniquet, 2013). The concern for cumulative deprivation, with the poorest being at the same time less healthy, might constitute one of the main motivations for the sizable scientific literature and the rapidly increasing policy interest in socio-economic inequities in health (e.g., Fleurbaey & Shokkaert, 2012). Our main aim in this section is, precisely, to extend our analysis from the previous sections to deal with health deprivation measurement in the multidimensional framework we consider in this work.

It is well known that the normative approach to inequality measurement can be extended to poverty measurement, as pioneered by Sen (1976) and Blackorby and Donaldson (1980). Therefore, we can build onto the analysis of the third section to derive ethical indices for the measurement of health deprivation (poverty) in our setting.

More precisely, suppose that the deprivation threshold is a pre-specified level of HYEs z, and that the set of the *deprived* (those people for whom the healthy years equivalents are at or below the deprivation threshold) is $Z(z)$.[11] Let $n(z)$ denote the cardinality of $Z(z)$.

A general relative health deprivation index may be defined as

$$Q = \frac{n(z)}{n} \frac{z - E(h_p)}{z} \tag{8}$$

where $E(h_p)$ is the representative HYE of the deprived, as measured by an arbitrary (homothetic) social evaluation function. Similarly, a general absolute deprivation index may be defined as

$$Q = n(z)(z - E(h_p)) \tag{9}$$

The previous deprivation indices are defined with respect to social evaluation functions defined over the deprived. Nevertheless, as shown by Blackorby and Donaldson (1980), they become ethically significant (i.e., they reflect ethical judgments for the whole society) when $E(\cdot)$ is completely (additively) separable. That is precisely the case of the functions $E^{ph}(\cdot)$ and $E^{eh}(\cdot)$ considered in the third section. Consequently, the *Atkinson family of multidimensional health deprivation indices*, associated to any social ordering $\succsim$ satisfying BASIC, TSIPH and PDTPH, given by

$$Q^A = \frac{n(z)}{n}\frac{z - E^{ph}(h_p)}{z} = \frac{n(z)z - \left(\sum_{i \in Z(z)} f(a_i, t_i)^\gamma\right)^{1/\gamma}}{nz} \tag{10}$$

and the *Kolm-Pollak family of multidimensional health deprivation indices*, associated to any social ordering $\gtrsim$ satisfying BASIC, TTRPH, and PDTPH, given by

$$Q^{KP} = n(z)(z - E^{eh}(h_p)) = n(z)\left(z - \frac{1}{\gamma}\ln\left[\frac{1}{n(z)}\sum_{i \in Z(z)} e^{\gamma f(a_i, t_i)}\right]\right) \qquad (11)$$

are (relative and absolute, respectively) deprivation indices with ethical content.

DISCUSSION

We have explored in this chapter the measurement of inequality of health distributions referring to two dimensions: quality of life and quantity of life. Our analysis relies on a novel treatment of the quality-of-life dimension, which might not have a standard mathematical structure. We have mostly concentrated on the normative approach to the problem, adapting to our setting the classical formulation in the literature on income inequality measurement credited to Atkinson, Kolm and Sen. As a result, we have singled out several proposals for inequality indices to evaluate health distributions in our setting. They all share the feature of relying on the so-called HYE functions to move from our multidimensional setting of health to a unique dimension over which we could use standard indices that are so popular in the literature on income inequality measurement.[12] As such, our contribution is reminiscent of the two-stage aggregation procedure proposed by Maasoumi (1986) to deal with multi-attribute social evaluation and, in particular, to construct multi-attribute inequality indices. More precisely, in the first stage of such procedure, and for each individual, a utility function is used to aggregate the individual's allocation of the several attributes into a summary measure of well-being. This initial aggregation results in a unidimensional distribution of utilities. In the second stage, a univariate inequality index is applied to this distribution to obtain a measure of the inequality in the distribution matrix.[13]

Our contribution is also reminiscent of Tsui's (1995) multi-attribute (Euclidean) generalization of the Atkinson class of (univariate) indices. As in our case, Tsui's (1995) generalization is also identified axiomatically. In contrast, his axioms are formulated in terms of a social evaluation function, rather than in terms of the underlying binary relation. In any case, our differentiating aspect is to generalize the Atkinson (and the Kolm-Pollak) family to a multidimensional, but not necessarily Euclidean, space.

To conclude, it is worth mentioning that our analysis throughout this chapter has been framed without making assumptions about individual preferences over length and quality of life. This is in contrast with the more standard approach in the health economics literature, where a given relationship is assumed between quality and quantity of life at the individual level, entailing the existence of possibly asymmetric individual utility functions (e.g., Østerdal, 2005). Nevertheless, information over such individual preferences is sometimes not available, either for practical or ethical reasons. Furthermore, even though there is a vast literature on assessing individual preferences over health profiles (see, for instance, Dolan (2000) and the literature cited therein) recurrent criticisms are made to each of the approaches in that literature. Therefore, in situations where solid information concerning individual preference is absent, but social preferences are more easily available, our approach offers a viable alternative for inequality measurement.

NOTES

1. The literature has also paid considerable attention to socioeconomic health inequalities focusing on the association between income and health (e.g., Wagstaff, Paci, & van Doorslaer, 1991). We do not deal with this issue here.

2. See Weymark (2006) for an excellent survey.

3. Again, see Weymark (2006) for further details.

4. They deal with non-Euclidean spaces but with more mathematical structure than ours, as they assume the existence of an ordering of health states.

5. Here, as in much of the literature on inequality measurement, it is assumed that the population is homogeneous in the sense that individuals do not differ in welfare-relevant characteristics other than the attributes that are the focus of the analysis.

6. For ease of exposition, we establish the notational convention that $h_S \equiv (h_i)_{i \in S}$, for each $S \subset N$.

7. The reader is referred to Hougaard et al. (2013) for further discussion of the axioms.

8. It turns out that the corresponding social ordering could be characterized by replacing TSIPH in Theorem 1 with a stronger axiom requiring time scale invariance at any health state. QALYs constitute the standard currency in the methodology of cost-utility analyses, probably the most widely accepted methodology in the economic evaluation of health care nowadays (e.g., Drummond Sculpher, Torrance, O'Brien, & Stoddart, 2005).

9. This class of inequality indices was introduced by Kolm (1969) in the univariate case. In consumer theory, the same functional form was shown by Pollak (1971) to characterize the additive utility functions that have linear Engel curves. Hence the name of the family.

10. The reader is referred to Blackorby, Bossert and Donaldson (2005) for a thorough account of population issues in welfare economics and related areas.

11. Note that z might arise from different combinations of quality and quantity of life. In other words, agents can also be considered deprived for a deficit in only one of the two dimensions of health, and not necessarily both.

12. This was not an arbitrary choice, but rather a consequence of imposing some basic structural assumptions on the social welfare ordering over health distributions.

13. Maasoumi (1986) also proposed functional forms for these aggregators. For the second-stage aggregator, he suggested using a member of the class of generalized entropy inequality indices. This class of indices contains the Atkinson class and all of the indices that are ordinally equivalent to some member of the Atkinson class.

14. The proof of Theorem 4 is analogous to this one and, thus, we omit it.

15. For ease of notation, we refer to h' in the definition of the RI axiom as $k \cdot h$.

ACKNOWLEDGEMENTS

We thank Pedro Rosa Dias, as well as conference participants at the PET13 Meeting (Lisbon) and the Conference on Economic Design 2013 (Lund) for helpful comments and suggestions. Financial support from the Spanish Ministry of Economy and Competitiveness (ECO2011-22919), as well as from the Andalusian Department of Economy, Innovation and Science (SEJ-4154, SEJ-5980) via the "FEDER operational program for Andalusia 2007–2013" is gratefully acknowledged.

REFERENCES

Abu-Naga, R., & Yalcin, T. (2008). Inequality measurement for ordered response health data. *Journal of Health Economics, 27*, 1614–25.

Allison, R., & Foster, J. (2004). Measuring health inequalities using qualitative data. *Journal of Health Economics, 23*, 505–524.

Atkinson, A. (1970). On the measurement of inequality. *Journal of Economic Theory, 2*, 244–263.

Atkinson, A., & Bourguignon, F. (1982). The comparison of multi-dimensioned distributions of economic status. *Review of Economic Studies, 49*, 183–201.

Blackorby, C., Bossert, W., & Donaldson, D. (2005). Population issues in social choice theory, welfare economics, and ethics. *Econometric society monograph*. Cambridge University Press.

Blackorby, C., & Donaldson, D. (1980). Ethical indices for the measurement of poverty. *Econometrica, 48*, 1053–1060.

Bleichrodt, H., & van Doorslaer, E. (2006). A Welfare economics foundation for health inequality measurement. *Journal of Health Economics, 25*, 945–957.

Burk, A. (1936). Real income, expenditure proportionality, and Frisch's new methods of measuring marginal utility. *Review of Economic Studies, 4*, 33–52.

Dalton, H. (1920). The measurement of the inequality of incomes. *Economic Journal, 30*, 348–361.

Decancq, K., Fleurbaey, M., Maniquet, F., (2013). *Multidimensional poverty measurement: Shouldn't we take preferences into account?* CORE Discussion Paper.

Dolan, P. (2000). The measurement of health-related quality of life. In A. J. Culyer & J. P. Newhouse (Eds.), *Handbook of health economics*. Elsevier science. Amsterdam: North-Holland.

Drummond, M., Sculpher, M. J., Torrance, G. W., O'Brien, B. J., & Stoddart, G. L. (2005). *Methods for the economic evaluation of health care programmes* (3rd ed.), Oxford: Oxford University Press.

Fleurbaey, M., & Schokkaert, E. (2012). Equity in health and health care. In M. Pauly, T. McGuire, & P. Pita Barros (Eds.), *Handbook of health economics (Vol. 2)*, Amsterdam: North-Holland.

Hougaard, J., Moreno-Ternero, J. D., & Østerdal, L. P. (2013). A new axiomatic approach to the evaluation of population health. *Journal of Health Economics, 32*, 515–523.

Kolm, S.-C. (1969). The optimal production of social justice. In J. Margolis & H. Guitton (Eds.), *Public economics* (pp. 145–200). London: Macmillan.

Kolm, S.-C. (1977). Multidimensional egalitarianisms. *Quarterly Journal of Economics, 91*, 1–13.

Maasoumi, E. (1986). The measurement and decomposition of multi-dimensional inequality. *Econometrica, 54*, 991–997.

Moulin, H. (1988). *Axioms of cooperative decision making*. Cambridge: Cambridge University Press.

Pigou, A. C. (1912). *Wealth and welfare*. London: Macmillan.

Pliskin, J., Shepard, D., Weinstein, M. (1980). Utility functions for life years and health status. *Operations Research, 28*, 206–224.

Pollak, R. A. (1971). Additive utility functions and linear Engel curves. *Review of Economic Studies, 38*, 401–414.

Ravallion, M. (1996). Issues in measuring and modeling poverty. *The Economic Journal, 106*, 1328–1343.

Rawls, J. (1971). *A theory of justice*. Cambridge, MA: Harvard University Press.

Runciman, W. G. (1966). *Relative deprivation and social justice*. London: Routledge.

Samuelson, P. A. (1965). Using full duality to show that simultaneously additive direct and indirect utilities implies unitary price elasticity of demand. *Econometrica, 33*, 781–796.

Sen, A. K. (1973). *On economic inequality*. Oxford: Clarendon Press.

Sen, A. K. (1976). Poverty: An ordinal approach to measurement. *Econometrica, 44*, 219–232.

Tsui, K.-Y. (1995). Multidimensional generalizations of the relative and absolute inequality indices: The Atkinson-Kolm-Sen approach. *Journal of Economic Theory, 67*, 251–265.

Wagstaff, A., Paci, P., & van Doorslaer, E. (1991). On the measurement of inequalities in health. *Social Science & Medicine, 33*, 545–557.

Wagstaff, A., & van Doorslaer, E. (2000). Equity in health care delivery and finance. In A. J. Culyer & J. P. Newhouse (Eds.), *Handbook of health economics*. *Elsevier science*. Amsterdam: North-Holland.

Weymark, J. (2006). The Normative approach to the measurement of multidimensional inequality. In F. Farina & E. Savaglio (Eds.), *Inequality and economic integration*. London: Routledge.

Williams, A., & Cookson, R (2000). Equity in health. In A. J. Culyer & J. P. Newhouse (Eds.), *Handbook of health economics*. Amsterdam: Elsevier science, North-Holland.

Yitzhaki, S. (1979). Relative deprivation and the Gini coefficient. *Quarterly Journal of Economics*, *93*, 321–324.

Østerdal, L. P. (2005). Axioms for health care resource allocation. *Journal of Health Economics*, *24*, 679–702.

APPENDIX: PROOFS OF THE THEOREMS

For the proof of Theorem 2, we focus on its non-trivial implication, that is, $2 \to 1$. Formally, assume $\succsim$ satisfies BASIC, TTRPH, and PDTPH.

Consider the following family:

$$P^S[h_1, ..., h_n] = P^S[(a_1, t_1), ..., (a_n, t_n)] = \sum_{i=1}^{n} g(f(a_i, t_i)) \qquad (12)$$

where $f: A \times T \to \mathbb{R}_+$ and $g: \mathbb{R}_+ \to \mathbb{R}$ are such that:

- f is continuous with respect to its second variable,
- $0 \leq f(a_i, t_i) \leq t_i$, for each $(a_i, t_i) \in A \times T$,
- $h \sim [(a_*, f(a_i, t_i))_{i \in N}]$, for each $h = [(a_1, t_1), ..., (a_n, t_n)] \in H$, and
- g is a strictly increasing and continuous function.

By BASIC, $\succsim$ can be represented by a PHEF, P, satisfying Eq. (12) (see Theorem 1 in Hougaard et al. 2013). By TTRPH,

$$\sum_{i=1}^{n} g(f(a_i, t_i)) \geq \sum_{i=1}^{n} g(f(a'_i, t'_i)) \Leftrightarrow \sum_{i=1}^{n} g(f(a_i, t_i) + c) \geq \sum_{i=1}^{n} g(f(a'_i, t'_i) + c)$$

for each $h = [(a_1, t_1), ..., (a_n, t_n)] \in H$, $h' = [(a'_1, t'_1), ..., (a'_n, t'_n)] \in H$ and $c > 0$.

By a classical result (e.g., Moulin, 1988) whose inspiration can be traced back to Bergson and Samuelson (e.g., Burk, 1936; Samuelson, 1965), there are only three possible functional forms for P:

- $P[h_1, ..., h_n] = P[(a_1, t_1), ..., (a_n, t_n)] = \sum_{i=1}^{n} e^{\gamma f(a_i, t_i)}$, for some $\gamma > 0$
- $P[h_1, ..., h_n] = P[(a_1, t_1), ..., (a_n, t_n)] = -\sum_{i=1}^{n} e^{\gamma f(a_i, t_i)}$, for some $\gamma < 0$
- $P[h_1, ..., h_n] = P[(a_1, t_1), ..., (a_n, t_n)] = \sum_{i=1}^{n} f(a_i, t_i)$

for each $i \in N$.

It is straightforward to show that the first and last functional forms cannot satisfy PDTPH. Altogether, we have that $P = P^{eh}$, as desired.

We now move to the proof of the remaining theorems. We focus on the proof of Theorem 3, where, again, we only present its nontrivial implication, that is, $2 \to 1$.[14] Formally, assume $\succsim$ satisfies BASIC, TSIPH, and PDTPH, for each population N, and RI.[15] By Theorem 1, when restricted to $\mathcal{H}^N$, $\succsim$ is represented by a PHEF satisfying Eq. (1). Now, let $h = [(a_i, t_i)_{i \in N}]$ and $h' = [(a'_i, t'_i)_{i \in N}]$ be two arbitrary distributions, and denote by n and n',

On the Measurement of the Inequality of Health Distributions

respectively, the cardinalities of their corresponding populations. Then, by RI, transitivity, and the previous statement,

$$h \succsim h' \Leftrightarrow n' \cdot h \succsim n \cdot h'$$
$$\Leftrightarrow P^{ph}[n' \cdot h] \geq P^{ph}[n \cdot h']$$
$$\Leftrightarrow n' \cdot \sum_{i \in N} f(a_i, t_i)^\gamma \geq n \cdot \sum_{i \in N'} f(a'_i, t'_i)^\gamma$$
$$\Leftrightarrow \frac{\sum_{i \in N} f(a_i, t_i)^\gamma}{n} \geq \frac{\sum_{i \in N'} f(a'_i, t'_i)^\gamma}{n'}$$

as desired.

EQUITY IN HEALTH AND EQUIVALENT INCOMES

Erik Schokkaert, Carine Van de Voorde, Brigitte Dormont, Marc Fleurbaey, Stéphane Luchini, Anne-Laure Samson and Clémence Thébaut

ABSTRACT

We compare two approaches to measuring inequity in the health distribution. The first is the concentration index. The second is the calculation of the inequality in an overall measure of individual well-being, capturing both the income and health dimensions. We introduce the concept of equivalent income as a measure of well-being that respects preferences with respect to the trade-off between income and health, but is not subjectively welfarist since it does not rely on the direct measurement of happiness. Using data from a representative survey in France, we show that equivalent incomes can be measured using a contingent valuation method. We present counterfactual simulations to illustrate the different perspectives of the approaches with respect to distributive justice.

Keywords: Healthy-equivalent income; concentration index; inequity in health; contingent valuation

JEL classifications: D63; H51; I18

INTRODUCTION

Health is generally considered one of the main dimensions of individual well-being. The distribution of health therefore features prominently in all attempts to measure inequity as soon as these go beyond simple unidimensional income measures. There is near complete consensus, however, that "pure health inequalities" are only one component of equity, and that health inequalities have to be integrated into some broader view on justice. In this respect there are different approaches possible, implying different value judgments and therefore possibly leading to different evaluations of policies and situations (Fleurbaey & Schokkaert, 2012). In this chapter we discuss and compare two of these approaches and we show their empirical implications with data that are obtained from a representative survey in France.

By far the most popular approach in the recent health economic literature has been the use of concentration curves and concentration indices (see, e.g., van Doorslaer & Van Ourti, 2011). Their use is justified by the argument that only those inequalities that are caused by the social environment and can therefore be influenced by policy are a cause of concern from the point of view of justice. Some health inequalities, for example, those related to age and gender, are unavoidable. One may deplore these inequalities, so the reasoning goes, but they are just a fact of life. What is relevant from an equity perspective is the link between health and socioeconomic characteristics. In principle, there are many aspects of the social environment that may be relevant — social class, education, region, race — but most of the literature has focused on one dimension, albeit that the focus is different on either side of the Atlantic. In the United States it is on racial disparities in health. In Europe, at least within the economic literature, the focus is more on income-related inequality in health. While there may be pragmatic reasons for such an exclusive interest in one variable, there does not seem to be a convincing moral justification for it (see the discussion in Fleurbaey & Schokkaert, 2009, 2012). However, in order to focus on other aspects of the problem, we leave this question aside in this chapter and we assume that the situation of each individual can be described by her health and by her income. The first measure that we will analyze is therefore the concentration index, with income as the ranking variable.

A second approach starts from the observation that health is only important to individuals in so far as it contributes to overall individual well-being. Yet, health is only one of the many dimensions of well-being and these dimensions may be strongly correlated. Only looking at inequality in health may therefore be very misleading. To quote Hausman: "A state of affairs in which those who are otherwise worse off are healthier than those who are otherwise more fortunate is more just rather than less just than a state of affairs which is exactly the same except that health is equally distributed" (Hausman, 2007). The most direct way to tackle this issue is the construction of an overall measure of individual well-being. Economists have thought for a long time that the measurement of individual well-being was hopelessly difficult or even impossible. We will show that this is too pessimistic and we will propose and implement one specific measure of individual well-being: the equivalent income. As we will explain, equivalent incomes take into account the variation in individual preferences. Our second measure of inequity will therefore be the inequality in equivalent incomes, as measured by the Gini.

Opting for equivalent incomes is one choice. In recent years the literature on subjective happiness, or life satisfaction, is booming and this is also a candidate measure of individual well-being. We will argue that this measure is too subjective and does not give enough weight to the objective features of the life situation of individuals. Another possible track that we will not explore is the use of multidimensional inequality measures. We feel that these measures have an essential shortcoming, in that they implicitly impose an "objective" concept of well-being on all individuals without taking into account in any way interindividual differences in preferences. In this chapter we do not discuss in great detail the normative arguments underlying our choice of equivalent income as a measure of well-being. More on this can be found in Fleurbaey and Schokkaert (2012) and in Fleurbaey and Blanchet (2013).

The structure of the chapter is as follows. The next section summarizes the value judgments underlying the concentration index. We then introduce the equivalent income as a measure of well-being and discuss the normative foundations of measuring inequity as the inequality in these equivalent incomes. In the fourth section we introduce our data and we show how the concept of equivalent income can be operationalized. We then calculate the concentration index of health in France and the inequality in equivalent incomes. We simulate counterfactual situations to illustrate the equity implications of both measures. The final section concludes.

VALUE JUDGMENTS UNDERLYING THE CONCENTRATION INDEX

As mentioned in the introduction, we simplify the analysis by assuming that there are only two relevant dimensions in the well-being of individuals:

their income y_i and their health level h_i. The concentration curve then is a plot of the cumulative proportion of h_i against the cumulative proportion of y_i. The concentration index is twice the area between the concentration curve and the diagonal. Both concepts are well known and explained in great detail, for example, in the World Bank monograph by O'Donnell, van Doorslaer, Wagstaff, and Lindelow (2008). Mathematically, the concentration index can be written in many equivalent ways. For our purposes, it is useful to consider the following formulation that has been proposed by Koolman and van Doorslaer (2004)

$$\text{CI}(h) = \frac{\sigma_h}{\bar{h}} \times \rho(h_i, R_i^y) \times 2\sigma_R \qquad (1)$$

where $\bar{h}$ is average health, σ_h is the standard deviation of h, $\rho(h_i, R_i^y)$ is the correlation coefficient between health and the fractional rank R_i^y of i in the income distribution, and σ_R is the standard deviation of R_i^y (which is close to a constant). Eq. (1) shows that the concentration index (CI) will increase if the correlation between health and the fractional rank increases (and if the coefficient of variation of health increases).

A coherent welfare economic interpretation of the concentration index has been derived by Bleichrodt and Van Doorslaer (2006) and Fleurbaey (2006). In the former paper it is shown that one of the axioms characterizing it is the "principle of income-related health transfers," which is defined as follows:

> Transferring health from someone who is better-off in terms of socioeconomic status to someone who is worse-off in terms of socioeconomic status does not lead to a reduction in social welfare provided the transfer does not change the ranking of the individuals in terms of socioeconomic status.

It is obvious that the principle should be interpreted as a comparison between two possible situations, not as the evaluation of an actual transfer of health from one person to another. The latter interpretation is not only unrealistic, it may also be provocative from an ethical point of view.

That the concentration index satisfies the principle of income-related health transfers is immediately obvious from the way it is constructed. If one reasons within a broad concept of well-being (our second approach to equity in health), the plausibility of the principle is contestable. Indeed, if the richer person in the formulation of the principle is already at a (possibly much) lower health level than the poorer person, it is very well possible that his overall level of well-being is lower than that of the poorer person. A further decrease in his health should then increase (rather than decrease) inequity. Bleichrodt and van Doorslaer argue that the principle of income-related health transfers is more acceptable "the stronger the correlation between health and other attributes such as income" (2006, p. 955). Indeed, the phenomenon of cumulative deprivation is a feature of most real world situations and is probably one of the main explanations for the relative popularity of the concentration index. If socioeconomic inequality in health comes on top of inequality in socioeconomic status, this is especially worrying. However, it is not adequate to justify a general feature of a measure of inequity on the basis of contingent empirical observations. Moreover, if there is cumulative deprivation, that is, if there is a strong positive correlation between health and income, this can be captured at least as well by the inequality in a synthetic measure of individual well-being. All this clearly shows that the concentration index is not an adequate measure of the inequity in the overall distribution of income and health. Its ambition is more limited, in that it just focuses on the correlation between the two.

A second feature of the concentration index, or for that matter, of most measures of socioeconomic inequality in health, is put forward by Brekke and Kverndokk (2012). They want to explain the somewhat surprising finding that the egalitarian Scandinavian countries perform rather poorly in terms of the concentration index and they suggest that this can best be seen as a methodological artifact. To show this, they start from the assumption that there is a causal effect of health on income and they represent this by a simple linear model

$$y_i = \phi a_i + \mu h_i + e_i \tag{2}$$

where a_i represents other variables influencing income (such as education or social background of the parents), e_i is an error term, and ϕ and μ are coefficients to be estimated. They then define a more egalitarian society as one where ϕ is smaller, that is, where variables such as education and social background play a less important role in the explanation of income. It is immediately clear that the relative effect of health on income will become more important in that case, that is, the income ranking will resemble more closely the health ranking. Therefore the correlation $\rho(h_i, R_i^y)$ in Eq. (1) will increase and for the same health distribution, the concentration index will be larger in the more egalitarian society. This leads to the conclusion that it is possible that "the index finds larger inequalities in the egalitarian country than are found in the less egalitarian country, even if health is equally distributed and the egalitarian country has less income inequality" (Brekke & Kverndokk, 2012, p. 329). The interpretation of the concentration index as a measure of overall inequity then becomes rather ambiguous: "If measured health inequality in Nordic countries is higher than in the rest of Europe, it could well be because there is more illegitimate health inequality because of income differences or fewer illegitimate differences in income because of, for example, the parents' socioeconomic class. This could be bad news or good news, although the measures cannot tell us which" (Brekke & Kverndokk, 2012, p. 331).

The two features of the concentration index that we described illustrate very well its partial and conditional nature. Of course, its proponents deliberately opt for a measure with a partial and conditional nature. Yet, if one takes the perspective that inequity in the first place has to be related to individual well-being, the focus on socioeconomic inequality is too narrow. Rather than the principle of income-related transfers, one would prefer a more traditional Pigou–Dalton principle stating that a redistribution of income (or health) is welfare-improving if it goes from someone at a higher level of well-being to someone at a lower level of well-being. In the same vein, it is very likely that the more income egalitarian Scandinavian countries would indeed be seen as more egalitarian in terms of well-being. As a matter of fact, both Bleichrodt and van Doorslaer (2006) and Brekke and Kverndokk (2012) advocate at the end of their paper that the analysis of the concentration index should be complemented with the use of multidimensional inequality measures or with the measurement of inequality in some measure of overall well-being. In this chapter we explore the second track. Of course, to make this broader approach operational, one needs a measure of well-being which encompasses both income and health. Many authors are skeptical about the possibility of constructing such a measure. Let us therefore now turn to this issue.

THE EQUIVALENT INCOME AS A MEASURE OF INDIVIDUAL WELL-BEING

The recent popularity of research on the measurement of happiness or life satisfaction suggests that a growing number of economists accepts that happiness can be measured in a robust and reliable way. At first sight it seems but a small step from this empirical finding to the normative position that maximizing happiness should also be the ultimate goal of economic policy. However, the fact that happiness (perhaps) can be measured, is not, as such, an answer to the ethical criticism of using subjective satisfaction as a measure of individual well-being for policy analysis. We will not go into this philosophical debate (see, e.g., Sen, 1985), but simply point out one important finding: happiness measures, when used for interpersonal comparisons, do not respect individual preferences (see, e.g., Fleurbaey, Schokkaert, & Decancq, 2012). Take two individuals, Ernest and Peter. Ernest is rich, has some minor health problems but not a serious disease. Peter is poor and suffers from a heart problem that makes it impossible for him to do sports. Ernest and Peter have identical preferences over all possible bundles. Ernest definitely prefers his own (income, health) combination over that of Peter, while Peter would prefer to be in Ernest's situation. Respecting preferences would then imply that we take the well-being level of Ernest to be higher than that of Peter. However, there is no guarantee at all that Ernest is also happier or more satisfied with life than Peter. It is very well possible that he is dissatisfied and complaining about his situation, because he has been brought up in an extremely rich family and is very sensitive to his minor health problems. At the same time, Peter can be reasonably satisfied, if, for example, he comes from a deprived social background and has learnt to adapt his aspirations to his unfortunate situation. Taking happiness as our metric of well-being would mean that an egalitarian has to favor an income transfer from poor Peter to rich Ernest. This recommendation sounds provocative.

Does rejection of happiness measures lead ineluctably to the construction of objective indices in which the weights for the different dimensions are set by the analyst? In a democratic society with widely diverging opinions about what is a good life, it seems essential to try to respect people's own ideas about what is important for them, that is, to respect their own preferences. In this vein, Richard Layard (2005, p. 121) defends the use of happiness measures, as the alternatives for him imply that "we play God and decide what is good for others, even if they will never feel it to be so." We argue that it is possible to formulate a concept of individual well-being that does respect individual preferences, that is, individual marginal rates of substitution between income and health, without falling in the subjectivistic happiness trap.

Let us illustrate this concept of well-being with the example in Fig. 1. Suppose we want to compare the well-being of Ann in A with that of Bob in B. We pick for the non-income dimension (health in our setting) a reference value. We will argue later in this section that "perfect health" is the obvious choice. Given that we respect preferences, we have to accept that Ann reaches an identical level of well-being in situations A and A′, since these two situations are both on the same indifference curve for her.

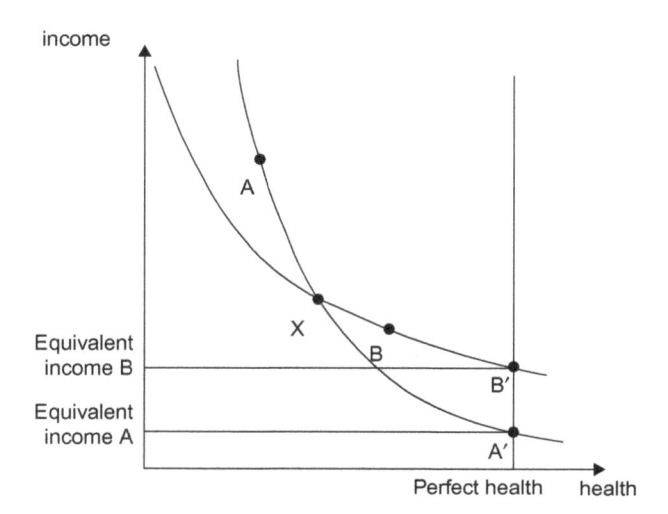

Fig. 1. Equivalent Income.

The same is true for Bob and for situations B and B'. We now make the crucial assumption that, when two individuals are in the reference situation of perfect health, we can compare their well-being levels on the basis of their incomes only. We then take as a measure of the well-being of A her so-called equivalent income y_A^*, that is, the income that would bring her in the hypothetical situation A', that is, the (income, perfect health) bundle that is on the same indifference curve as her actual bundle A. Analogously, the well-being of Bob is measured with his equivalent income y_B^*.

More formally, let us define R_i as the individual preference ordering of individual i over bundles (y_i, h_i), with P_i and I_i denoting strict preference and indifference respectively. The (healthy) equivalent income y_i^* is then defined implicitly by

$$(y_i, h_i) I_i (y_i^*, \bar{h}) \tag{3}$$

where $\bar{h}$ denotes the "normal" health level. It is important to see that the equivalent income function $y_i^*(y_i, h_i)$ is a representation of the preference ordering. Indeed, if preferences are monotonic in income, it follows immediately from Eq. (3) that

$$(y_i, h_i) R_i (y'_i, h'_i) \Leftrightarrow y_i^*(y_i, h_i) \geq y_i^*(y'_i, h'_i) \tag{4}$$

The equivalent income is one possible "utility" function from the set of all positive monotonic transformations representing the same preference ordering. The equivalent income uses only information about the (ordinal) indifference curves themselves and is not sensitive to differences in aspirations or expectations. This is the essential difference with measures of subjective life satisfaction. In the example given previously, the equivalent income of Ernest will always be larger than that of Peter, even if Ernest is less happy.

The notion of equivalent income is not new, as it is a variant of the concept of money-metric utility that was already introduced as a representation of preferences by Samuelson (1974) and Samuelson and Swamy (1974). After having lost its popularity, it experienced a surprising revival from within the so-called theory of fair allocation (Fleurbaey & Maniquet, 2011).[1] One of the main insights from the latter theory is that the choice of the reference value is not necessarily arbitrary (as was suggested, e.g., by Donaldson, 1992), but can be founded on a coherent normative reasoning. Compare the situation of two individuals that are equally ill. Would it then be meaningful in general to compare their well-being levels on the basis of their incomes only, since they reach the same health level? Not necessarily, since the individual that cares more about her health, may legitimately claim to suffer more than the other individual from being ill. However, let us now (realistically) suppose that there is a large degree of interindividual consensus about what is a normal, unproblematic health level, and let us focus on the specific situation where the two individuals both reach that "normal" level of health. In this case (returning to the figure, consider Alice in A' and Bert in B'), it seems natural to say that differences in preferences should not matter for the comparison of well-being levels. Whatever the relative preferences of the individuals for health, they are in the best possible situation anyway. In that specific situation, it is possible to compare well-being levels on the basis of incomes only. This is precisely the intuition that is underlying the concept of equivalent income. It is therefore natural to take "perfect health" as the reference value h. With this choice of reference, the difference between actual and equivalent income is given by the welfare loss that results from deviations from the "normal" level, and this loss is dependent on preferences. This seems an attractive way to proceed.

We can now measure inequity as the inequality in these equivalent incomes. The equivalent income is a convenient measure for that purpose: it is expressed in monetary terms and can easily be used in all traditional inequality measures. Despite the fact that it is expressed in monetary terms, it is an encompassing measure of well-being, taking into account the welfare effects of being ill. As Fig. 1 shows, the difference between actual and equivalent income, that is, the welfare loss resulting from not achieving a situation of perfect health, is measured by the individual willingness-to-pay to be in that hypothetical situation, that is

$$y_i^* = y_i - \text{WTP}_i(y_i, h_i \to \bar{h}) \tag{5}$$

where $\text{WTP}_i(y_i, h_i \to \bar{h})$ is a short hand notation for the willingness-to-pay of individual i with an income y_i for a move from h_i to $\bar{h}$. It is clear from Eq. (5) that the ranking of individuals on the basis of their incomes can be very different from their ranking on the basis of equivalent incomes. This is also illustrated in the figure, where Bob obtains a larger equivalent income than Ann, despite the fact that his income is smaller.

As a matter of fact, Eq. (5) suggests that making the equivalent income operational is not at all a hopeless task. Economists in general (and health economists in particular) have by now acquired a lot of experience in the collection of information about willingness-to-pay. Of course, the willingness-to-pay to be in a situation of perfect health, as referred to in Eq. (5), does not refer to a marginal change, but there is no reason why common techniques could not be implemented in this context.

Let us finally mention an important ethical difference between the concentration index approach and the approach in terms of equivalent income. Contrary to the former, the latter considers differences in health that follow from differences in age or gender as illegitimate. This can be justified on the basis that individuals cannot be held responsible for these differences. It can even be argued that the social environment does have an influence on the health differences between different age groups and, a fortiori, between men and women. However, this remains a point of ethical debate. Moreover, there is one important qualification to be made. If different age groups, or men and women, have different preferences with respect to health, these preference differences will be respected in the equivalent income approach. Individuals that suffer relatively more from being ill (in ordinal terms, i.e., in terms of their marginal rate of substitution between income and health), will reach a lower level of well-being.

THE MEASUREMENT OF EQUIVALENT INCOMES THROUGH CONTINGENT VALUATION

To calculate equivalent incomes, we need information about the willingness-to-pay for being in perfect health (see Eq. (5)). We will use the estimates obtained from a contingent valuation study of a representative sample of the French population.[2] In the first subsection we describe the questionnaire method and show some descriptive statistics. For evaluating the effects of policy changes, we need to predict what will be the effect of changes in the environment on the equivalent incomes of the individuals. To do that, we need information on their preferences. The estimation of preferences is discussed in the second subsection.

Estimating Equivalent Incomes: Description of the Survey Results

Data are obtained from face-to-face interviews. In total, 3,331 questionnaires have been administered in the course of November and December 2009. After a series of questions on demographic and socioeconomic characteristics of the individual and his/her household (including income and education), the questionnaire continued with a series of detailed questions on specific diseases and health problems that the respondent might have experienced in the previous 12 months. The list of diseases was taken from the Enquête Santé et Protection Sociale (Health and Social Protection Survey) of IRDES (Institute for Research and Information in Health Economics). At the end of that section came a question on overall self-assessed health (SAH), where use was made of a visual 0–100 scale:

> In the previous questions, you have indicated the health problems you have suffered from during the last twelve months. Taking this into account, can you now evaluate your health during the last twelve months on a scale from 0 to 100 (where 100 is the best possible health state and 0 is death).

The SAH question was followed by a series of questions on health care use in the past 12 months, including non-reimbursed out-of-pocket payments. The questionnaire then turned to the evaluation of the willingness-to-pay for perfect health[3]:

> Imagine now that you would not have had any health problem during the last twelve months. In that case you would have been in perfect health and your quality of life would have improved. (We talk here only about the last twelve months and not about the potential improvement of your future health). Compared to your actual life experience during the last twelve months, would you have preferred not to have had the health problems that you had but with a reduction of your income (on top of the €x that you now have paid already as non-reimbursed care expenditures).

Respondents could answer "yes," "no," or "do not know." Those who answered "no" were asked for further information about their reasons for not answering. Some of them were ready to answer after some additional explanation. All those who were willing to answer, then were asked:

> What is the maximal amount of monthly income you would have accepted to give up under these conditions (i.e. in exchange for being in a state of perfect health during the last twelve months)?

As a help, the respondents were shown payment cards (ranging from "less than €15" to "more than €1,500"), but after having been shown the cards, they were asked an open question about the exact amount of income they were willing to give up.

For each respondent that answered these questions, we have all the information needed to calculate his/her equivalent income. Descriptive information about the most important variables is given in Table 1. To be able to compare with the French population, all numbers are weighted with sample weights.[4] For income y_i we use the household income, divided by

Table 1. Descriptive Statistics.

Variable	Weighted Sample	French Population
Income		
Mean	€1,414	€1,873
Median	€1,238	€1,603
Sex		
Female	52.27%	52.26%
Education		
None	10.96%	13.61%
Primary education	14.83%	10.95%
Lower secondary education	8.44%	6.93%
Vocational education	27.71%	25.64%
Secondary education	14.14%	15.40%
University degree (first cycle)	10.66%	9.98%
University degree (second and third cycle)	12.88%	14.73%
Other	0.39%	2.75%
Age		
18–24	11.26%	12.25%
25–34	15.92%	16.83%
35–49	26.94%	24.84%
50–64	24.61%	26.41%
65–74	10.19%	10.27%
75+	11.08%	9.41%

The data for the French population are taken from INSEE (2009) for income and from ESPS (Enquête Santé et Protection Sociale 2008) for sex, age, and education.

the modified OECD-scale (with weights 1 for a single, 0.5 for each additional adult in the household, and 0.3 for each child below the age of 14). When we use the term "income" later in this chapter, we refer to this "OECD-equivalized income." It is, of course, crucial to avoid confusion between "income" and "equivalent income." The mean and the median of the incomes in our sample are respectively €1,414 and €1,238.[5] We use self-assessed health SAH, divided by 100, as our measure of h_i.[6] Perfect health (SAH = 100) will then be denoted $\bar{h} = 1$. Mean SAH is 73.5, while the median is 80.0. Only 8.6% of the sample report a SAH < 50 (with 9.9% reporting SAH = 50), and only 2.9% declare a SAH < 20. At the other side of the scale 14.0% have a SAH > 90 and 6.7% of the respondents state that they are in perfect health.

After removing in a first stage clearly wrong or incomplete answers (e.g., respondents that did not report their income or refused to give a reason for not answering the willingness-to-pay question), we keep a sample of 2,836 respondents, of which 328 could be interpreted as protest voters.[7] The identification of protest voters was based on the reasons given for not answering the willingness-to-pay questions. It is indeed perfectly possible for a rational respondent to have a zero willingness-to-pay. Respondents who answered that they did not want to give up any income because "my living standard is already so low that I cannot imagine to have less, even with perfect health" or that answered "other aspects of my life are more important for me than my health" are included in our analysis as having a true willingness-to-pay equal to zero. True protest voters are those who answered that the question was too difficult or who, even after further explanation, kept to the position "it is not my duty to pay for a better health." Because the protest voters differed from the rest of the sample in terms of observable variables (e.g., they have higher incomes and a higher proportion of females), we introduced a selection equation for the estimation of the preferences (see the following subsection).

The mean willingness-to-pay for perfect health (WTP) is €75.1, but there is a large spread (standard deviation of €180.9, with many zeros and a maximum of €1,500).[8] Fig. 2 shows a nonparametric estimate of the relationship between WTP and health (estimated by a local polynomial approximation, with the gray area denoting the 95% confidence interval) and a kernel estimate of the density of health (with the scale at the right hand side of the graph). Fig. 3 gives the analogous information for WTP and income. Since income and health are positively correlated and WTP to be in perfect health can be assumed to be increasing with income and decreasing with health, the bivariate relationships between WTP and health

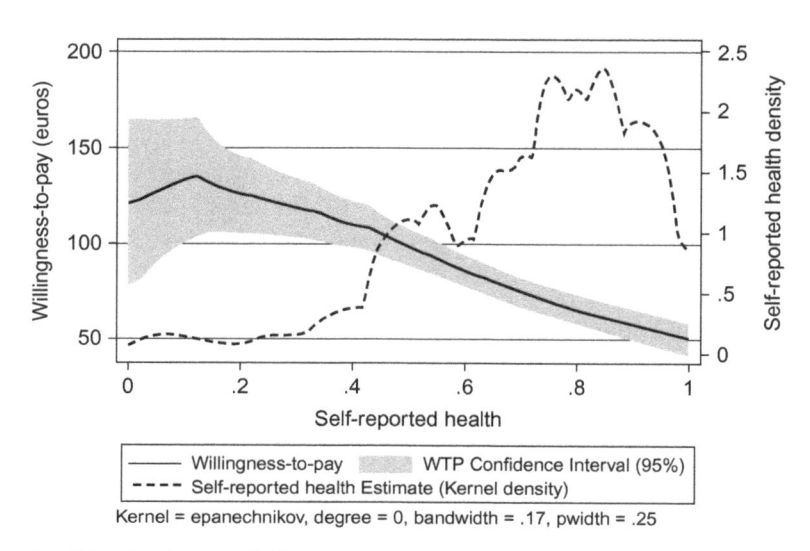

Fig. 2. Distribution of Self-Reported Health and Relationship with WTP for Perfect Health.

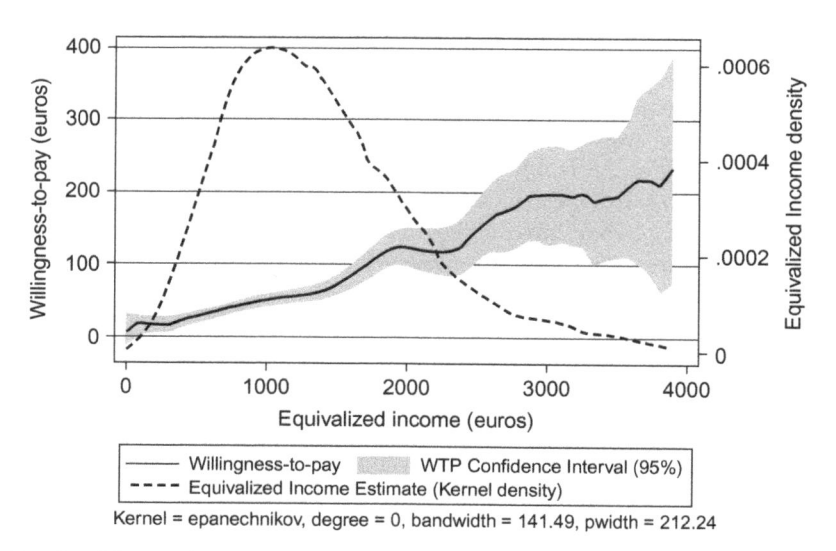

Fig. 3. Distribution of Income and Relationship with WTP for Perfect Health.

(income) need not be monotonic. Fig. 2 shows that respondents in lower health are in general willing to pay more to get to perfect health, with the exception of those with a very low value of SAH. The relationship between income and WTP (Fig. 3) is generally positive, but contains some flat or even slightly decreasing segments.

Using Eq. (5) we can now calculate equivalent incomes immediately. The resulting distribution is shown in Fig. 4. The mean and median equivalent incomes are €1,380.4 and €1,200.0, respectively. We also can immediately calculate the inequality in these equivalent incomes: the Gini is 0.28419189 (see the results in Table 3). This can be compared to the Gini of incomes, which is 0.27832805. Since low income and poor health are correlated, it is not surprising that the Gini of equivalent incomes is larger than the income Gini. This is not necessary, however, because the preferences of different groups in the population can be different and, as is clear from Fig. 3, the rich generally have a higher WTP. For comparison, the concentration index in our data is 0.020203, also suggesting some pro-rich health inequalities.[9] As such, these numbers are not comparable. To get a better insight into the features of both measures, we will run some illustrative simulations in the next section. For these simulations, we need information about individual preferences.

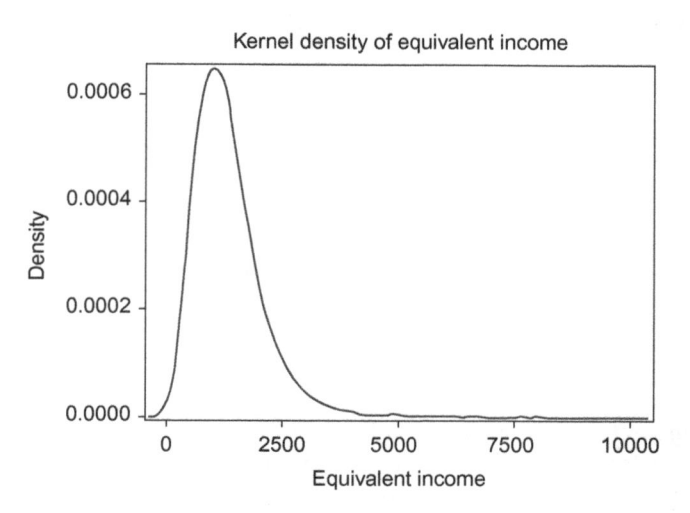

Fig. 4. Distribution of Equivalent Income.

Recovering Preferences in the Income-Health Space

We have shown in the previous section that the equivalent income can be seen as one possible representation of the individual preference ordering (see Eq. (4)). The utility of individual i can indeed be written as $y_i^*(y_i, h_i) = y_i - \text{WTP}_i(y_i, h_i \to \bar{h})$, where WTP_i is the answer given to the valuation question. Since interindividual differences in preferences play an important role in the approach, in principle, one would like to estimate for each individual a specific utility function $y_i^*(y_i, h_i)$. This is impossible with our data, since the only information we have at the level of the individual is that his/her actual situation (y_i, h_i) and the hypothetical situation $(y_i - \text{WTP}, \bar{h})$ are on the same indifference curve. To make progress we have to specify a functional form and assume some degree of preference homogeneity. There is a trade-off here. If we opt for a very flexible form of the utility function, we will not be able to introduce at the same time a large degree of preference heterogeneity. On the other hand, imposing a restrictive functional form means that we push the data into a straitjacket. Our compromise is to opt for a reasonably flexible functional form, allowing for coefficients that differ according to age and gender.

More specifically, we specify the willingness-to-pay of individual i to be in perfect health, that is, $\text{WTP}_i(y_i, h_i \to \bar{h})$, as

$$\text{WTP}_i = \alpha_i(1-h_i) + \beta_i(1-h_i)^2 + \gamma_i y_i(1-h_i) + \delta_i y_i^2(1-h_i) + \mu_i y_i(1-h_i)^2 + \varepsilon_i \tag{6}$$

where ε_i is an idiosyncratic disturbance term with mean zero. Interindividual differences in the marginal rate of substitution between income and health are modeled by varying the coefficients

$$\begin{aligned}
\alpha_i &= \alpha_0 + \alpha_A \text{age}_i + \alpha_M \text{male}_i \\
\beta_i &= \beta_0 + \beta_A \text{age}_i + \beta_M \text{male}_i \\
\gamma_i &= \gamma_0 + \gamma_A \text{age}_i + \gamma_M \text{male}_i \\
\delta_i &= \delta_0 + \delta_A \text{age}_i + \delta_M \text{male}_i \\
\mu_i &= \mu_0 + \mu_A \text{age}_i + \mu_M \text{male}_i
\end{aligned} \tag{7}$$

where age_i refers to the age of individual i and male_i is a dummy, taking the value 1 for males. The functional form (6) is flexible, in that it does not impose monotonicity or quasi-concavity of the utility function. What it does impose, however, is that the expected willingness-to-pay for an individual in perfect health (i.e., with $h_i = \bar{h} = 1$) is equal to zero. This is a minimal theoretical constraint that we do have to impose to make our specification consistent with the theoretical framework sketched in the previous section.[10]

As described in the previous subsection, the protest voters have different observable characteristics than the other respondents. It is very likely that they also differ on unobservable characteristics. We therefore estimated the parameters of Eqs. (6)–(7) with a two-step procedure. The first step is a probit selection equation for refusing to give a WTP answer as a function of health, income, age, and gender.[11] In the second step we estimated Eqs. (6)–(7) with OLS with the inverse Mill's ratio derived from the probit equation as an additional regressor.[12] We have only very few observations with SAH < 20 or with an income > €4,000. Not surprisingly, our flexible functional form gives strange results for this range of observations (see also the sharply growing confidence intervals in Figs. 2 and 3). We therefore removed these 98 observations, leaving us with 2,738 observations, of which 316 did not provide WTP responses.

The estimation results are given in Table 2. Given the highly nonlinear specification of Eq. (6) and the large degree of multicollinearity between

Table 2. Estimates of Willingness-to-Pay Function (Heckman Selection Model).

Variable		Parameter Estimate	Standard Error
$(1-h)$	α_0	−194.179	259.264
	α_A	0.729	4.410
	α_M	75.509	168.868
$(1-h)^2$	β_0	513.699	418.829
	β_A	−6.904	7.165
	β_M	−365.753	286.271
$y(1-h)$	γ_0	0.353	0.265
	γ_A	−0.002	0.004
	γ_M	−0.020	0.155
$y^2(1-h)$	δ_0	−0.00010	0.00006
	δ_A	0.0000019	0.0000010
	δ_M	−0.0000216	0.0000324
$y(1-h)^2$	μ_0	−0.197	0.319
	μ_A	0.003	0.005
	μ_M	0.314	0.198
Inverse Mill's ratio		71.860	31.334
	N		2,422
	R^2		0.2878
	F-value		60.77

the right-hand side variables, it is impossible to interpret the coefficients in Table 2 directly. Yet the F-test shows that the overall fit of the equation is satisfactory ($p < 0.0001$). Of course, the whole procedure cannot be seen as the testing of any theory, it is rather a curve-fitting exercise. It is therefore

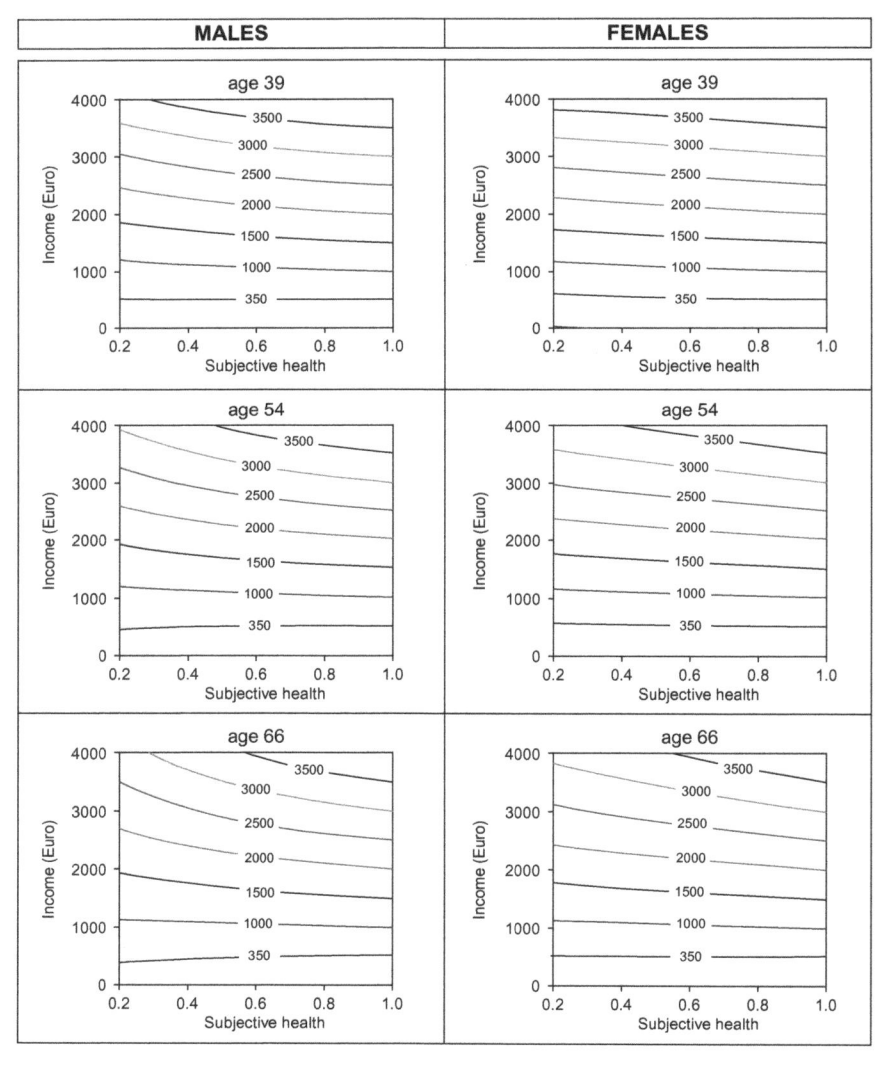

Fig. 5. Indifference Curves.

more informative to look at the indifference curves that follow from it. These can be computed on the basis of the estimated parameters from Table 2, and knowing that utility is given by $y_i^*(y_i, h_i) = y_i - \text{WTP}_i(y_i, h_i \to \bar{h})$. The resulting indifference curves are shown in Fig. 5 for three age levels. Overall, they look reasonably good, certainly for income levels above €1,000 (remember that the median income in the full sample is €1,238). They are rather flat, however, especially at very low incomes. This can be partly due to the fact that the WTP question referred to the health situation in the previous 12 months. Mortality issues were excluded and so was the anxiety related to uncertainty about future health. A bit more worrying is the lack of monotonicity of the preferences for elderly males with a low income and in poor health. However, as mentioned before, in this range of the variables, we have only a very limited number of observations and they have a strong influence on the curvature that is implied by the flexible specification. While our results must be interpreted with caution, they are nevertheless good enough to proceed with some simulations.

COMPARING THE CONCENTRATION INDEX OF HEALTH AND THE INEQUALITY IN EQUIVALENT INCOMES

Now that we have shown that equivalent incomes can be calculated and that it is possible to derive information about preferences in a meaningful way, we can come back to the comparison between on the one hand the concentration index approach and on the other hand the measurement of inequality in equivalent incomes. The results for the base situation are summarized in the first row of Table 3. We mentioned already that the Gini for equivalent incomes is larger than that for incomes. The small difference between the two is in line with the small value we find for the concentration index (last column): the correlation between health and income turns out to be rather low in our sample. This might be due to the fact that we use SAH as our health measure, and that we did not correct for possible reporting bias in SAH. If the rich have stronger health aspirations, using SAH may lead to a lower concentration index than using more objective health measures. This hypothesis is more or less supported if we look at more objective (but still self-reported) indicators of disease, suggesting a strong concentration among the poor (see examples in the last rows of Table 3). However, it is not obvious that the low CI for SAH is only due to reporting bias. All objective health indices are partial, and it may be argued that

Table 3. Simulation Results.

	Gini Income	Gini Equivalent Income	Concentration Index
Base situation	0.27832805	0.28419189	0.02204203
Mean health for all	0.27832805	0.28150891	0
Mean income for all	0	0.04673083	/
Incomes net of OOP	0.27913427	0.28509985	0.02236913
OOP financed with proportional contributions	0.27832805	0.28451679	0.02204203
	CI disease		
Diabetes (6.64%)	−0.10544247 0.27832805	0.28447336	0.01643896
Depression (9.55%)	−0.21234586 0.27832805	0.28325333	0.00786087
Prostate adenoma (0.95%)	0.26382086 0.27832805	0.28445162	0.02301186
Angina pectoris (1.73%)	−0.16082041 0.27832805	0.28416603	0.01988076

SAH captures important health elements, that are missing when one only uses objective measures. Subjective feelings of mental health are an obvious example. It is therefore not clear if it would be an improvement to turn from SAH to partial indicators.[13] In any case, for the mainly methodological purposes of this chapter, we opted not to go for more sophisticated corrections and we decided to stick to the easily interpretable approach with uncorrected SAH as the health indicator.

To understand better the implications of the different approaches to inequity, we ran some simulations of counterfactual situations. When the incomes or the SAH values change, it is straightforward to calculate the new values for the Gini of incomes or for the concentration index. Equivalent incomes have to be simulated, however. For that purpose, we use Eq. (6) with the estimated coefficients from Table 2 to calculate the new equivalent incomes of all the individuals in the sample. In this simulation we keep the residual and the term involving the inverse Mill's ratio constant, so that the difference between the actual and the simulated equivalent income reflects only the differences in the income and health variables of the two simulated situations.

The first set of simulations confirms the dominant role played by the income in the explanation of the inequality in equivalent incomes. If we give all individuals in our sample the mean health level, the Gini of equivalent incomes goes down, but only very little. It remains larger than the Gini of incomes: this is perfectly possible since different groups have different preferences. As shown in Fig. 1, even two individuals with exactly the same income-health bundle (like X in the figure) may end up with different equivalent incomes if their preferences differ. While equalizing health has a minor effect on the Gini of equivalent incomes, equalizing incomes reduces the Gini of equivalent incomes to 0.0467. Apparently, income differences dominate the evaluation of distributional inequity.

As mentioned in the previous section, we obtained information about the actual out-of-pocket (OOP) payments of the respondents in our sample during the previous year. These OOP payments consist of two components: official copayments on the one hand and price supplements on the other hand. It could be argued that such OOP payments are an economic burden on individuals and should therefore be subtracted from the incomes to get a better indicator of their economic possibilities. The resulting inequity measures are shown in the fourth row of Table 3. Since OOP payments are more concentrated among the poor, subtracting them from incomes leads to an increase in the inequality, both for incomes and for equivalent incomes. The income that is used to calculate the CI is meant to measure socioeconomic status "before" health problems, and therefore the traditional CI would not capture the negative welfare implications of the OOP payments. However, if we use the corrected incomes as the ranking variable, we observe also an increase in the CI (see the last column). Indeed, because of the negative correlation between health and OOP payments, subtracting the latter from incomes leads to a ranking where bad health is more concentrated among lower incomes.

Let us now assume that we abolish OOP payments and finance them with a proportional reduction in all incomes. The results are shown in the fifth row. Comparing the fourth and the fifth row shows that abolishing OOP-payments leads to a reduction in measured inequity with all the measures. It is also interesting to compare rows 5 and 1 in the table. The incomes in row 5 coincide again with our original definition of incomes, but with all incomes proportionally reduced. Such a proportional reduction does not change the Gini of incomes and the concentration index. However, a proportional change in the incomes does not coincide with a proportional change in equivalent incomes. As Table 3 shows, the Gini of equivalent incomes increases, suggesting that a proportional reduction in incomes has a relatively larger negative effect on individuals with a smaller equivalent income. This is an interesting finding from the broader perspective of inequality measurement.

The next set of simulations shows the features of some counterfactual situations in which specific health problems have been removed. For these specific diseases we give in the first column the prevalence in our sample and in the second column their specific concentration index: diabetes, depression, and angina pectoris are more concentrated among the poor, prostate adenoma occurs more among the rich. Each of the simulations consists of putting all individuals with the specific disease at SAH = 100. This is, of course, not realistic, but it offers an illustration of how the different measures react to health policies. The CI reacts as one would predict. Removing illnesses that are concentrated among the poor (diabetes, depression, and angina pectoris) lowers the CI, removing a disease that is concentrated among the rich (prostate adenoma) leads to an increase in the CI. In a loose sense, these results just illustrate the theoretical findings of Bleichrodt and van Doorslaer (2006). More interesting are the effects on the inequality in equivalent incomes. These cannot be predicted on pure theoretical grounds, because they will depend on the overall distribution of equivalent incomes – and this distribution in its turn will depend on the pattern of preferences. As a matter of fact, while the Gini of equivalent incomes moves in the same direction as the CI for depression, angina pectoris, and prostate adenoma, this is not true in the case of diabetes. Putting all individuals with diabetes at SAH = 100 increases the Gini of equivalent incomes.

CONCLUSION

In this chapter we compared two possible approaches to measuring inequity in the overall distribution of income and health. The first is to focus on the correlation between the two. This leads to measures of income-related health inequality, the most famous being the concentration index. The second approach is the calculation of the inequality in an overall measure of individual well-being, capturing both the income and health dimensions. It can be argued that such a broader approach is better suited to measure cumulative deprivation and is more in line with common intuitions about overall distributive justice in society. However, it has until now hardly been applied, mainly because most analysts have been very skeptical about the possibility to make it operational. Moreover, many health economists are deeply suspicious of welfarist approaches. The main purpose of this chapter was to show that there is room for some optimism in this regard. It is possible to devise a measure of well-being that does respect preferences, but is not subjectively welfarist: equivalent incomes definitely do not coincide with subjective feelings of personal happiness. Moreover, using data from a representative survey in France, we have shown that the concept of equivalent income can be made operational. Counterfactual simulations have shown that it yields interesting insights, which could not have been obtained within the traditional concentration index approach.

The main purpose of this chapter is methodological. The equivalent income methodology is still in an experimental stage and it has to be further refined before it can be applied at a large scale. From a theoretical point of view, the choice of the reference values for the non-income dimensions remains a moot point. More work is needed to strengthen the understanding of the ethical foundations of different choices (see, e.g., Fleurbaey & Blanchet, 2013). From the empirical point of view, we have to build up more experience with the measurement of individual preferences for income-health bundles. In this chapter we implemented a contingent valuation methodology to measure the willingness-to-pay to be in perfect self-assessed health. The consequences of using other, more objective, health measures should be explored (see, e.g., Fleurbaey et al., 2013).

Moreover, the contingent valuation method is only one of the many possibilities to measure preferences. Other stated preference techniques (e.g., discrete choice models) can also be informative. Or one can derive estimates of marginal rates of substitution from the answers on questions about life satisfaction (as in Fleurbaey, Schokkaert et al., 2012).[14] Many questions remain open, but the direction in which we could try to move is clearly defined.

NOTES

1. The equivalence approach, as it has been introduced in the recent welfare economic literature, is broader than the concept of equivalent income, on which we focus in this chapter. See Fleurbaey and Maniquet (2011) and Fleurbaey and Blanchet (2013) for a more general treatment.

2. More information about the survey (including the original formulation of the questions in French) can be found in Fleurbaey, Luchini, Schokkaert, and Van de Voorde (2012). Empirical results with a similar pilot study are reported in Fleurbaey, Luchini, Muller, and Schokkaert (2013).

3. This formulation of the question was used for single respondents. For individuals living in a household, the formulation was slightly different. For the "x Euros of non-reimbursed care" mentioned in the question, the interviewer filled in the amount of out-of-pocket payments that the respondents themselves had declared before. The questionnaire did not mention explicitly the possibility of earnings losses and gains as a result of changes in the health situation. It is possible that some of the respondents who have experienced an income (or earnings) loss due to ill-health had difficulties in answering the question given they would expect to gain

income from being in perfect health. However, at this stage, we were afraid that mentioning earnings losses/gains explicitly would be even more confusing for some respondents. Different formulations of the willingness-to-pay question should be tested and compared in future work.

4. Sample weights were based on age and gender, with the population shares derived from the French population statistics for 2009, available at insee.fr.

5. This can be compared with a median income for France of €1,613 in 2009, as reported by INSEE (French National Institute for Statistics and Economics Studies).

6. In Fleurbaey et al. (2013) the calculation of equivalent incomes was based on a list of specific diseases.

7. The number of observations is larger in this chapter than in Fleurbaey, Luchini et al. (2012), because we now have coded the open-ended answers to the question about the reasons for not answering the willingness-to-pay question. We therefore have included a larger number of respondents with "true zeros" (and a larger number of protest voters).

8. The values we report on willingness-to-pay and on equivalent incomes are based on the sample of 2,508 respondents, that is, disregarding the protest voters.

9. We restrict ourselves to the standard concentration index. Recent work (e.g., Erreygers & Van Ourti, 2011) has shown that this is not fully appropriate with bounded health variables, such as the SAH. Equivalent incomes are measured on a ratio scale and therefore all standard inequality indices can be applied.

10. In Fleurbaey, Luchini et al. (2012) a different functional form was estimated in which this theoretical restriction had to be imposed in a less natural way. This was the main reason why we moved in this chapter to specification (6). The resulting indifference curves are very similar in the two approaches.

11. Results from this equation are available on request.

12. In Fleurbaey, Luchini et al. (2012), the semi-parametric method of Donald (1995) was used to take into account the heteroskedasticity that is suggested in Figs. 2 and 3. In this chapter we preferred not to follow that procedure, because it complicates considerably the estimation of the parameters while leading to very similar results.

13. We discuss the pros and cons in more detail in Fleurbaey, Luchini et al. (2012).

14. The technique is well known within health economics to evaluate marginal changes — see, among others, Ferrer-i-Carbonell and Van Praag (2002), Groot, Maassen van den Brink, and Plug (2004), and Groot and Maassen van den Brink (2006).

ACKNOWLEDGMENTS

The authors thank Owen O'Donnell for his very useful comments. This research was supported by the Health Chair, a joint initiative by PSL, Université Paris-Dauphine, ENSAE, and MGEN under the aegis of the Fondation du Risque (FDR).

REFERENCES

Bleichrodt, H., & van Doorslaer, E. (2006). A welfare economics foundation for health inequality measurement. *Journal of Health Economics, 25*, 945–957.

Brekke, K., & Kverndokk, S. (2012). Inadequate bivariate measures of health inequality: The impact of income distribution. *Scandinavian Journal of Economics, 114*, 323–333.

Donald, S. (1995). Two-step estimation of heteroskedastic sample selection models. *Journal of Econometrics, 65*, 347–380.

Donaldson, D. (1992). On the aggregation of money measures of well-being in applied welfare economics. *Journal of Agricultural and Resource Economics, 17*, 88–102.

Erreygers, G., & Van Ourti, T. (2011). Measuring socioeconomic inequality in health, health care and health financing by means of rank-dependent indices: A recipe for good practice. *Journal of Health Economics, 30*, 685–694.

Ferrer-i-Carbonell, A., & Van Praag, B. (2002). The subjective costs of health losses due to chronic diseases. An alternative model for monetary appraisal. *Health Economics, 11*, 709–722.

Fleurbaey, M. (2006). Health, equity and social welfare. *Annales d'Economie et Statistique, 83-84*, 21–60.

Fleurbaey, M., & Blanchet, D. (2013). *Beyond GDP. Measuring welfare and assessing sustainability*. Oxford: Oxford University Press.

Fleurbaey, M., Luchini, S., Muller, C., & Schokkaert, E. (2013). Equivalent income and the economic evaluation of health care. *Health Economics, 22*, 711–729.

Fleurbaey, M., Luchini, S., Schokkaert, E., & Van de Voorde, C. (2012). Evaluation des politiques de santé: pour une prise en compte équitable des intérets des populations. *Economie et Statistique, 455–456*, 11–36.

Fleurbaey, M., & Maniquet, F. (2011). *A theory of fairness and social welfare*. Cambridge: Cambridge University Press.

Fleurbaey, M., & Schokkaert, E. (2009). Unfair inequalities in health and health care. *Journal of Health Economics, 28*, 73–90.

Fleurbaey, M., & Schokkaert, E. (2012). Inequity in health and health care. In P. Barros, T. McGuire & M. Pauly (Eds.), *Handbook of health economics* (Vol. 2, pp. 1003–92). New York, NY: Elsevier.

Fleurbaey, M., Schokkaert, E., & Decancq, K. (2012). *Happiness and respect for individual preferences*. Mimeo.

Groot, W., & Maassen van den Brink, H. (2006). The compensating income variation of cardiovascular disease. *Health Economics, 15*, 1143–1148.

Groot, W., Maassen van den Brink, H., & Plug, E. (2004). Money for health: The equivalent variation of cardiovascular disease. *Health Economics, 13*, 859–872.

Hausman, D. (2007). What's wrong with health inequalities? *Journal of Political Philosophy, 15*, 46–66.

Koolman, X., & van Doorslaer, E. (2004). On the interpretation of a concentration index of inequality. *Health Economics, 13*, 649–656.

Layard, R. (2005). *Happiness: Lessons from a new science*. London: Allan Lane.

O'Donnell, O., van Doorslaer, E., Wagstaff, A., & Lindelow, M. (2008). *Analyzing health equity using household survey data*. Washington, DC: World Bank.

Samuelson, P. (1974). Complementarity: An essay on the 40th anniversary of the Hicks–Allen revolution in demand theory. *Journal of Economic Literature, 12*, 1255–1289.

Samuelson, P., & Swamy, S. (1974). Invariant economic index numbers and canonical duality: Survey and synthesis. *American Economic Review, 64*, 566–593.

Sen, A. (1985). *Commodities and capabilities.* Amsterdam: North-Holland.

van Doorslaer, E., & Van Ourti, T. (2011). Measuring inequality and inequity in health and health care. In S. Glied & P. Smith (Eds.), *Oxford handbook on health economics* (pp. 837–869). Oxford: Oxford University Press.

REFERENCE VALUE SENSITIVITY OF MEASURES OF UNFAIR HEALTH INEQUALITY

Pilar García-Gómez, Erik Schokkaert and Tom Van Ourti

ABSTRACT

Most politicians and ethical observers are not interested in pure health inequalities, as they want to distinguish between different causes of health differences. Measures of "unfair" inequality — direct unfairness and the fairness gap, but also the popular standardized concentration index (CI) — therefore neutralize the effects of what are considered to be "legitimate" causes of inequality. This neutralization is performed by putting a subset of the explanatory variables at reference values, for example, their means. We analyze how the inequality ranking of different policies depends on the specific choice of reference values. We show with mortality data from the Netherlands that the problem is empirically relevant and we suggest a statistical method for fixing the reference values.

Keywords: Health inequality; inequality of opportunity; concentration index; reference value

JEL classifications: D63; I12; I14

INTRODUCTION

Most politicians and ethical observers are not interested in so-called pure health inequalities. They focus on some specific causes of health inequalities that are considered as especially troublesome from an ethical point of view. The most popular approach within health economics, which is based on the concentration index, is ultimately concerned about the correlation between socioeconomic status and health (see, e.g., O'Donnell, van Doorslaer, Wagstaff, & Lindelow, 2008; van Doorslaer & Van Ourti, 2011). The more recent approaches of the theory of fair allocation or of inequality of opportunity make an explicit distinction between two sets of variables: on the one hand the so-called "circumstance (or compensation) variables" for which individuals cannot be held responsible and that therefore lead to ethically illegitimate differences, and on the other hand variables for which individuals are held responsible and that therefore generate inequalities which are no cause for ethical concern (Fleurbaey & Schokkaert, 2009, 2012). Focusing on specific causes of inequalities implies, however, that one has to neutralize in one way or another the effects of the other variables underlying health differences. In the case of the concentration index it has become common practice to standardize the health data to control for the effects of demographic variables such as age and gender. In the theory of fair allocation the main purpose is to neutralize the effects of the responsibility variables, so that measured inequality only captures the effects of the circumstance variables. Conditional-egalitarian approaches and egalitarian-equivalent approaches (leading respectively to the notions of direct unfairness and of the fairness gap in Fleurbaey & Schokkaert, 2009) introduce reference values for the responsibility and the circumstance variables respectively. All this raises an obvious question: does the choice of reference values matter for the calculation of unfair inequality?

There is surprisingly little literature on this issue. In the case of the concentration index, it is common practice to fix the reference values in the standardization exercise at their sample means (Gravelle, 2003). This may seem a natural choice, but it remains one specific option for which there is in fact no strong theoretical support. In the same vein, the literature on fair allocation often remains silent about possible justifications for choosing specific reference values. For the fairness gap, Fleurbaey and Schokkaert (2012) suggest to pick as reference for the circumstance variables the values that lead to the best health outcomes, exploiting the intuitive idea that a fair situation corresponds to a state where everyone enjoys the best health prospect. For direct unfairness, no such proposal has been made. Luttens and Van de gaer (2007) have analyzed the issue in the context of optimal income taxation, but their results cannot be directly transferred to the health setting.

From this, one gets the impression that there is some general feeling in the literature that the choice of reference values is rather innocuous, in that it does not influence the ranking of the degree of inequality in different situations. In this chapter we analyze whether this optimistic feeling is justified, and we show that it is not. Of course, it is trivially true that different reference values will lead to different numerical outcomes for measured inequality. More interesting is the comparison of two different health distributions within the same society, that is, for two states of the world with the same underlying model of the relationship between health and other variables. Such a comparison is relevant, for example, when one wants to evaluate the equity effects of a specific policy. We analyze under which conditions the change in inequity in moving from one to the other distribution has the same sign irrespective of the chosen reference values. These conditions are intuitively easy to understand in the case of direct unfairness (or direct standardization for the concentration index). They are more complicated in the case of the fairness gap (or indirect standardization). We illustrate our results with an empirical analysis of mortality in the Netherlands. We analyze inequity in mortality with the variance and the absolute Gini of direct unfairness and the fairness gap for various ethical positions. We also show the results for the concentration index, with education as the measure of socioeconomic status. It turns out that in some cases the ranking of policies does depend on the chosen reference values.

Since the choice of reference values does matter, it is obvious that we are in need of a good theory for choosing these values, both in the case of the standardized concentration index and a fortiori in applications of the theory of fair allocation. The formulation of such a theory is beyond the objectives of this chapter, but we will introduce a statistical approach that provides a normative criterion for choosing reference values that is sufficiently simple for empirical work. The exploration of this research track is left for future work.

The structure of our chapter is as follows. The next section introduces the different inequity measures and shows where the reference values enter in the calculations. We then derive the general conditions for inequity comparisons to be independent of the chosen reference values. We illustrate our theoretical findings with an empirical analysis of inequity in mortality in the Netherlands. Finally we briefly present a possible way to move forward.

REFERENCE VALUES IN THE THEORY OF FAIR ALLOCATION AND IN THE STANDARDIZED CONCENTRATION INDEX

Let us start with some notation and definitions. We are interested in the distribution of health, denoted m_i.[1] Pure inequality in health as such is not a matter of ethical concern, however. The causes underlying these health differences do matter for the evaluation. In order to keep things simple, we assume that m_i is linearly linked to a set of $K+J$ characteristics of individual i, denoted by $x_i = x_{il}$, $l = 1, ..., K + J$

$$m_i = \alpha + \sum_{l=1}^{K+J} \alpha_l x_{il} + \varepsilon_i \tag{1}$$

where the unexplained part is picked up by an error term ε_i. To simplify matters, we assume that policy makers are not interested in inequality due to this unexplained part ε_i. This means that from now on, we only consider the deterministic part of Eq. (1), that is, $m_i^P = \alpha + \sum_l \alpha_l x_{il}$.[2] Our question is how to operationalize different ethical stances with respect to inequity in m_i taking into account that the drivers of health as presented in Eq. (1) are known.

Different ethical positions can be distinguished on the basis of their view on the ethical justifiability of the different drivers of health differences. They are therefore characterized by a specific subdivision of the vector of characteristics x_i into those elements reflecting individual responsibility $r_{ik}, k=1, ..., K$ — for which policy makers hold individuals responsible — and those for which individuals are not responsible and for which policy makers are willing to compensate, $c_{ij}, j=1,...,J$ (and which, if not compensated for, lead to health inequity, that is, to illegitimate health inequalities). We then write the deterministic part of Eq. (1) in terms of K responsibility and J circumstance variables

$$m_i^P = \alpha + \sum_{j=1}^{J} \beta_j c_{ij} + \sum_{k=1}^{K} \gamma_k r_{ik} + \sum_{j=1}^{J}\sum_{k=1}^{K} \delta_{jk} c_{ij} r_{ik} \tag{2}$$

where we stick to the linear specification, but allow for interactions between the circumstance and responsibility variables. Indeed, it will turn out that the choice of reference variables is important only when the function explaining m_i is not separable in the set of compensation and responsibility variables, that is, when at least one δ_{jk} differs from 0. The specification (2) is the simplest possible way to introduce nonseparability.[3] We will now first explain how reference values enter in the theory of fair allocation and then introduce the concentration index.

The Theory of Fair Allocation

When measuring the inequity of different health distributions, one wants to include the effects of differences in the circumstance variables, but at the same time neutralize the effects of the responsibility variables. The theory of fair allocation tries to combine this double concern. The first concern is captured by the *compensation principle*, stating that any health differences between individuals who are equally responsible are to be seen as unfair. The second concern is summarized in the *reward principle* which prescribes that health differences which are due to responsibility variables should not lead to an increase in measured unfairness.

Fleurbaey and Schokkaert (2009) explain that it is impossible to satisfy both principles together, unless Eq. (2) is additively separable in the circumstance and responsibility variables. It is instructive to illustrate this incompatibility for the functional form (2). Take first two individuals s and m with equal responsibility variables, that is, $r_{sk} = r_{mk} = r_k$, $k = 1, ..., K$. The health difference between these two individuals is given by

$$m_s^P - m_m^P = \sum_{j=1}^{J} \beta_j(c_{sj} - c_{mj}) + \sum_{j=1}^{J}\sum_{k=1}^{K} \delta_{jk}(c_{sj} - c_{mj})r_k \qquad (3)$$

which clearly depends on the values taken by r_k. Any measure that satisfies the compensation principle and that therefore takes up all effects of the differences between c-variables, will be unable to satisfy the reward principle because, due to the presence of the interaction terms, the effects of differences in the circumstance variables are "blown up" by the value of r_k. On the other hand, consider two individuals in equal circumstances, that is, $c_{pj} = c_{qj} = c_j$, $j = 1, ..., J$. The health difference between these two is

$$m_p^P - m_q^P = \sum_{k=1}^{K} \gamma_k(r_{pk} - r_{qk}) + \sum_{j=1}^{J}\sum_{k=1}^{K} \delta_{jk}c_j(r_{pk} - r_{qk}) \qquad (4)$$

which depends on the value taken by c_j. Any measure that satisfies the reward principle and therefore neglects the inequalities in Eq. (4) will at the same time miss the effects of differences in circumstance variables that work through the interaction effect. Note that the problem does not occur if Eq. (2) is additively separable in c_i and r_i, that is, if $\delta_{jk} = 0$, $\forall j, k$.

The theory then has proposed partial solutions, which satisfy only one of the two principles (see Fleurbaey & Schokkaert, 2009). These partial solutions define first an individual's *contribution* to overall inequality, and then calculate overall inequity as the inequality in these individual measures. The first (conditional-egalitarian) approach stresses *reward* by fixing the responsibility variables in Eq. (2) to a reference value ($\tilde{r}$). The resulting expression is called direct unfairness (du_i)

$$du_i(\tilde{r}_k) = \alpha + \sum_{k=1}^{K} \gamma_k \tilde{r}_k + \sum_{j=1}^{J} \left(\beta_j + \sum_{k=1}^{K} \delta_{jk} \tilde{r}_k \right) c_{ij} \qquad (5)$$

It is immediately clear that inequality in du_i will only reflect differences in the c-variables, since $\tilde{r}$ is fixed by construction. The multiplicative effects between actual c and r variables are not taken up in the measure of direct unfairness. The alternative approach stresses the *compensation* principle by comparing the actual health situation of each individual with the health he would obtain in a fair situation (i.e., where the influence of the circumstance variables would be ruled out). This leads to the fairness gap (fg_i) which is obtained by taking the difference between m_i^P and the hypothetical health level that would apply when circumstance is fixed at a fair reference value ($\tilde{c}$)

$$fg_i(\tilde{c}_j) = \sum_{j=1}^{J} \left(\beta_j + \sum_{k=1}^{K} \delta_{jk} r_{ik} \right) (c_{ij} - \tilde{c}_j) \qquad (6)$$

As Eq. (6) shows, the multiplicative effects now do enter the definition of the fairness gap. Both c_{ij} and r_{ik} appear in the fairness gap while only c_{ij} enters in direct unfairness. When Eq. (2) is additively separable, that is, $\delta_{jk} = 0, \forall j, k$, direct unfairness is equal to the fairness gap up to a constant, that is, $du_i(\tilde{r}_k) = fg_i(\tilde{c}_j) + \alpha + \sum_{k=1}^{K} \gamma_k \tilde{r}_k + \sum_{j=1}^{J} \beta_j \tilde{c}_j$. When additive separability does not hold, however, the reference values $\tilde{r}_k, \tilde{c}_j$ are going to matter.

Reference Value Sensitivity of Measures of Unfair Health Inequality 163

To measure overall inequity in the health distribution, one then calculates the inequality in the individual values of direct unfairness (5) or the fairness gaps (6). In line with the additive approach in Eqs. (2)–(6) and as we want direct unfairness and the fairness gap approach to give the same results when there are no interaction effects and both the reward and the compensation principles are satisfied, it is preferable to use an absolute inequality measure. In this chapter, we opt for two common measures of inequality. The first is the absolute Gini index (Yitzhaki, 1983), which can be written as

$$AG(y_i) = \frac{2}{n^2}\sum_{i=1}^{n} z_i^y y_i \qquad (7)$$

where $y_i = du_i(\tilde{r}_k)$ or $fg_i(\tilde{c}_j)$, and $z_i^y = (2i-(n+1))/2$ with the individuals $i=1,...,n$ being ranked from low to high y_i. The second is the variance which has been proposed for measuring absolute inequality of bounded variables (Lambert & Zheng, 2011), that is

$$VAR(y_i) = \frac{1}{n}\sum_{i=1}^{n}(y_i - \bar{y})^2 \qquad (8)$$

The Concentration Index

The concentration index (CI) approach takes a more restricted view on equity, in that it is only interested in the extent to which health inequalities are linked to an indicator of socioeconomic status. The absolute CI is very similar to the absolute Gini introduced in Eq. (7), except that individuals are ranked by their socioeconomic status (SES) (Wagstaff, van Doorslaer, & Paci, 1991)

$$AC(y_i, SES_i) = \frac{2}{n^2}\sum_{i=1}^{n} z_i^{SES} y_i \qquad (9)$$

In its simplest form, the CI approach is only interested in the extent of the association between SES and health inequalities — that is, $y_i = m_i$ — and is thus distinctly different from the approaches based on the fairness gap and direct unfairness. However, more subtle approaches, that standardize the health variables for differences in demographic variables have been developed in the CI approach (van Doorslaer et al., 1997; O'Donnell et al., 2008). This standardization implies that health differences due to age and gender are not considered as problematic. In a certain sense the concentration index approach then treats the standardizing variables in the same way as the responsibility/compensation variables are treated in the fair allocation approach.[4]

Direct standardization resembles direct unfairness as it puts the standardizing ("responsibility") variables to a reference (mostly mean) value. When the direct unfairness measure considers only SES as the circumstance variable ($J=1$) and when $\beta_1 + \sum_{k=1}^{K} \delta_{1k}\tilde{r}_k > 0$, Eq. (7) for direct unfairness will give the same results as Eq. (9), since $z_i^{du} = z_i^{SES}, \forall i$, that is, the rank of direct unfairness then equals the rank of the SES variable (see Eq. (5)). When $\beta_1 + \sum_{k=1}^{K} \delta_{1k}\tilde{r}_k < 0$, the ranking z_i^{du} is opposite to the ranking z_i^{SES}. The concentration index will then have the same magnitude, but with opposite sign.[5]

Indirect standardization resembles the fairness gap as it also compares actual m_i^P with a "standardized" fair situation. However, even if only SES is taken as circumstance variable, the absolute concentration index will in general deviate from the absolute Gini of the fairness gaps, since the ranking of the fairness gap does not in general coincide with the ranking of SES (see Eq. (6)).

REFERENCE-VALUE-CONSISTENT INEQUALITY COMPARISONS

The previous section has made clear that the values taken by the inequity measures will depend on the choice of the reference values. As such, this is of course a trivial result. In this section we will focus on a more interesting question. Compare two states of the world for which Eq. (2) holds, but with possibly different values for the regressors. Suppose we measure the inequity in both situations. Does the (in)equity ranking of the situations depend on the chosen reference values? A natural interpretation is the comparison of a baseline situation with the (simulated) state that would result as the consequence of a policy measure, such as increasing the education level of the population. This is the interpretation that we will favor in this section, but other applications are also possible, as long as Eq. (2) holds. While we assume that the actual and simulated states of the world refer to the same population, all our results also hold for comparisons between different populations. However, they cannot be used for evaluating a policy that changes the coefficients of Eq. (2) rather than the values of its regressors, or for comparisons between countries for which the coefficients in Eq. (2) differ. We first look at direct unfairness, then at the fairness gap and finally at the concentration index.

Direct Unfairness

We consider the comparison between two states of the world summarized by the vectors of the individual values of direct unfairness, that is, $du_i(\tilde{r}_k)$ and $du_i^S(\tilde{r}_k)$ where S refers to "simulated." The question at hand is whether the inequality ordering of the absolute Gini and the variance depend on the chosen reference values.

Absolute Gini
In case of the absolute Gini, we want to know whether the sign of $AG[du_i^S(\tilde{r}_k)] - AG[du_i(\tilde{r}_k)]$ depends on $\tilde{r}_k$. The expression one obtains is[6]

$$\begin{aligned}
&AG[du_i^S(\tilde{r}_k)] - AG[du_i(\tilde{r}_k)] \\
&= \frac{2}{n^2} \sum_{i=1}^{n} \left\{ z_i^{du^S(\tilde{r}_k)} \left[\alpha + \sum_{k=1}^{K} \gamma_k \tilde{r}_k + \sum_{j=1}^{J} \left(\beta_j + \sum_{k=1}^{K} \delta_{jk} \tilde{r}_k \right) c_{ij}^S \right] \right. \\
&\quad \left. - z_i^{du(\tilde{r}_k)} \left[\alpha + \sum_{k=1}^{K} \gamma_k \tilde{r}_k + \sum_{j=1}^{J} \left(\beta_j + \sum_{k=1}^{K} \delta_{jk} \tilde{r}_k \right) c_{ij} \right] \right\} \\
&= \sum_{j=1}^{J} \left(\beta_j + \sum_{k=1}^{K} \delta_{jk} \tilde{r}_k \right) \left\{ AC[c_{ij}^S, du_i^S(\tilde{r}_k)] - AC[c_{ij}, du_i(\tilde{r}_k)] \right\}
\end{aligned} \quad (10)$$

The interpretation of Eq. (10) is relatively straightforward. It decomposes the difference between the two values of the absolute Gini as a sum of components related to the different circumstance variables. For each variable the first term $(\beta_j + \sum_{k=1}^{K} \delta_{jk} \tilde{r}_k)$ gives its overall effect on health (with the responsibility variables set at their reference values). Somewhat loosely formulated, one can interpret the second term $\{AC[c_{ij}^S, du_i^s(\tilde{r}_k)] - AC[c_{ij}, du_i(\tilde{r}_k)]\}$ as an indication of the correlation between the circumstance variable and the overall measure $du_i(\tilde{r}_k)$. If that correlation is larger in the simulated situation and the effect of the variable is positive, the absolute Gini of direct unfairness increases.

Specific conclusions can be drawn for the easy but relevant case where there is only one circumstance variable, that is, $J = 1$. In this case, Eq. (10) simplifies to

$$\left(\beta_1 + \sum_{k=1}^{K} \delta_{1k}\tilde{r}_k\right)\{AC[c_{i1}^S, du_i^s(\tilde{r}_k)] - AC[c_{i1}, du_i(\tilde{r}_k)]\} \tag{11}$$

This expression will be positive (negative) when $\beta_1 + \sum_{k=1}^{K} \delta_{1k}\tilde{r}_k$ and $AC[c_{i1}^S, du_i^s(\tilde{r}_k)] - AC[c_{i1}, du_i(\tilde{r}_k)]$ have the same (opposite) sign. Since there is only one circumstance variable, the ranking of du_i and c_{i1} will be the same when $\beta_1 + \sum_{k=1}^{K} \delta_{1k}\tilde{r}_k > 0$, allowing us to rewrite the second term as $AG(c_{i1}^S) - AG(c_{i1})$, that is, the difference in absolute inequality in the circumstance variable in both states of the world. When $\beta_1 + \sum_{k=1}^{K} \delta_{1k}\tilde{r}_k < 0$, the ranking of du_i and c_{i1} will reverse and turn "upside down," and this will also change the sign, but not the magnitude of the second term. This all means that the *sign* of Eq. (11) is independent of the value of $\tilde{r}_k$, but interestingly also from the values of β_1 and δ_{1k}, and ultimately only depends on the absolute inequality in the circumstance variable.

When there is more than one circumstance variable, that is, $J \geq 2$, we cannot make any predictions in general since the effect of one circumstance variable may be outweighed by that of another. We cannot even derive general conclusions about the signs of the separate terms for each circumstance variable, since the ranking of direct unfairness depends on all the circumstance variables at the same time. The dependency of the difference in the absolute Gini indices on the chosen reference values then becomes an empirical problem, and there might be more than one unique set of reference values for which Eq. (10) turns 0, that is, the difference between absolute Gini indices need not be a monotonous function of the set of reference values.

Variance

We can develop a similar reasoning for the variance. The difference between the variance of direct unfairness under the simulated and the actual situation will not depend on the reference value when the sign of

$$VAR[du_i^S(\tilde{r}_k)] - VAR[du_i(\tilde{r}_k)]$$

$$= \frac{1}{n}\sum_{i=1}^{n}\left\{\left[\sum_{j=1}^{J}\left(\beta_j + \sum_{k=1}^{K}\delta_{jk}\tilde{r}_k\right)(c_{ij}^S - \overline{c_j^S})\right]^2 - \left[\sum_{j=1}^{J}\left(\beta_j + \sum_{k=1}^{K}\delta_{jk}\tilde{r}_k\right)(c_{ij} - \overline{c_j})\right]^2\right\}$$

$$= \sum_{j=1}^{J}\left\{\left(\beta_j + \sum_{k=1}^{K}\delta_{jk}\tilde{r}_k\right)^2 \left[VAR(c_{ij}^S) - VAR(c_{ij})\right]\right. \quad (12)$$

$$\left. + 2\sum_{l>j}^{J}\left(\beta_j + \sum_{k=1}^{K}\delta_{jk}\tilde{r}_k\right)\left(\beta_l + \sum_{k=1}^{K}\delta_{lk}\tilde{r}_k\right)\left[COV\left(c_{ij}^S, c_{il}^S\right) - COV(c_{ij}, c_{il})\right]\right\}$$

is fixed. The expression in Eq. (12) has a similar structure as the equivalent expression for the absolute Gini in Eq. (10). It again decomposes the change in the variance as the sum of J components, each related to one circumstance variable. The first term shows that the variance of direct unfairness will increase if the variance of the c variable increases. In addition, the change in the association between the circumstance variables also matters (through the covariance terms). Intuitively, this association captures whether high/low values of circumstance variables are more likely to be clustered among the same individuals. It is weighted by $(\beta_j + \sum_{k=1}^{K}\delta_{jk}\tilde{r}_k)(\beta_l + \sum_{k=1}^{K}\delta_{lk}\tilde{r}_k)$, that is, the product of the overall health effects of the variables j and l (with the responsibility variables put at their reference values). If these effects have the same sign for two circumstance variables, an increase in their covariance increases the variance of direct unfairness. If these effects have opposite signs, an increase in the covariance decreases the variance of direct unfairness. Again, all this is intuitively understandable and to some extent plays the same role in Eq. (12) as was played by the absolute concentration indices in Eq. (10) for the absolute Gini.

If there is more than one circumstance variable, it is difficult to derive from Eq. (12) general conclusions about the influence of the chosen reference values on the variance of direct unfairness, and there need not be a unique set of reference values for which Eq. (12) equals 0. However, when there is only one circumstance variable, the second term consisting of the sum of pairwise covariances drops out. The sign of the difference between the variance of direct unfairness under the simulated and actual direct unfairness is in this case only determined by the difference in the variances of the circumstance variables. This is completely analogous to the result for the absolute Gini. Here also, the choice of the reference values (and the value of the coefficients in Eq. (2)) do not influence the ranking of the values for the variance if there is only one circumstance variable.

The Fairness Gap

In this section, we repeat the analysis of the previous subsection for the fairness gap. In general, the expressions are more complicated functions of the reference values of the circumstance variables $\tilde{c}_j$. This is explained by the fact that both c_{ij} and r_{ik} appear in the expression for the fairness gap (see Eq. (6)).

Absolute Gini
The difference between the absolute Gini's of the simulated and actual fairness gaps equals

$$\begin{aligned}
&AG\left[fg_i^S(\tilde{c}_j)\right] - AG\left[fg_i(\tilde{c}_j)\right]\\
&= \frac{2}{n^2}\sum_{i=1}^{n}\left\{z_i^{fg^S(\tilde{c}_j)}\left[\sum_{j=1}^{J}\left(\beta_j + \sum_{k=1}^{K}\delta_{jk}r_{ik}^S\right)\left(c_{ij}^S - \tilde{c}_j\right)\right]\right.\\
&\qquad\left. - z_i^{fg(\tilde{c}_j)}\left[\sum_{j=1}^{J}\left(\beta_j + \sum_{k=1}^{K}\delta_{jk}r_{ik}\right)(c_{ij} - \tilde{c}_j)\right]\right\}\\
&= \sum_{j=1}^{J}\left\{\beta_j\left\{AC\left[c_{ij}^S, fg^S(\tilde{c}_j)\right] - AC[c_{ij}, fg(\tilde{c}_j)]\right\}\right.\\
&\qquad\left. + \sum_{k=1}^{K}\delta_{jk}\left\{AC\left[r_{ik}^S\left(c_{ij}^S - \tilde{c}_j\right), fg_i^S(\tilde{c}_j)\right] - AC[r_{ik}(c_{ij} - \tilde{c}_j), fg_i(\tilde{c}_j)]\right\}\right\}
\end{aligned} \tag{13}$$

Eq. (13) is a sum of J components, one for each circumstance variable. The first term in each of these components is very similar to the corresponding expression for direct unfairness, as it is the change in the concentration index of the circumstance variable (now ranked by the fairness gap) weighted by the health impact β_j. The second term is new and captures the effect of the interaction terms in Eq. (2). Remember that the fairness gap, contrary to direct unfairness, includes these interactions in the illegitimate part of inequality. For all interaction terms with $\delta_{jk} > 0$ the absolute Gini of the fairness gap increases with the absolute concentration index (with the fairness gap as the ranking variable) of the responsibility variables weighted by the deviation between the circumstance variable and its reference value.

Contrary to the case of direct unfairness, the sign of Eq. (13) is not independent of the reference value $\tilde{c}_j$ when there is only one circumstance variable. Indeed, as Eq. (13) shows, the change in ranking depends even in this simple case on the value of the responsibility variables r_{ik}. Even the sign of the first term cannot be predicted a priori. While in the case of direct unfairness the ranking of direct unfairness and the ranking of the circumstance variable coincide or are "upside down" after changing the reference value, this is not true for the fairness gap, which also depends on the responsibility variables (see Eq. (6)).

Variance
For the variance, we obtain

$$\begin{aligned}\text{VAR}\left[fg_i^S(\tilde{c}_j)\right] - \text{VAR}\left[fg_i(\tilde{c}_j)\right] = \frac{1}{n}\sum_{i=1}^{n}\Bigg\{&\left[\sum_{j=1}^{J}\left[\beta_j\left(c_{ij}^S-\overline{c_j^S}\right)\right.\right.\\&\left.+\sum_{k=1}^{K}\delta_{jk}\left(r_{ik}^S c_{ij}^S - \left(\frac{1}{n}\sum_{i=1}^{n}r_{ik}^S c_{ij}^S\right)\right) - \tilde{c}_j\sum_{k=1}^{K}\delta_{jk}\left(r_{ik}^S - \overline{r_k^S}\right)\right]\Bigg]^2 \\-&\left[\sum_{j=1}^{J}\left[\beta_j(c_{ij}-\overline{c_j})+\sum_{k=1}^{K}\delta_{jk}\left(r_{ik}c_{ij}-\left(\frac{1}{n}\sum_{i=1}^{n}r_{ik}c_{ij}\right)\right) - \tilde{c}_j\sum_{k=1}^{K}\delta_{jk}(r_{ik}-\overline{r_k})\right]\right]^2\Bigg\}\end{aligned} \quad (14)$$

Again this formula is different, but has a similar structure as the formula for the variance of direct unfairness. When there are no interactions between the circumstance and responsibility variables, both expressions are similar. In general, the change in the variance as the result of a policy change depends in a complicated way on the interplay between the different variables, including those that are fixed at reference values.

The Standardized Concentration Index

We finally derive similar expressions for the standardized concentration index, that is, the traditional approach in health economics. The concentration index (see Eq. (9)) focuses on socioeconomic health inequality, that is, on the relationship between health and socioeconomic status. It is natural to interpret this in our more general setting, but with SES_i as the ranking variable, which might (or not) be one of the elements in the vector c_{ij}. In the simplest approach, where $y_i = m_i$, there is no need to choose any reference values. However, as soon as one standardizes the health variable, reference values enter the picture again. It is common practice in the literature to fix the reference value to its mean value, but we provide here a more general treatment that allows to fix the reference value at any value. We denote the standardizing variables by r_{ik}, since they play the same role as the responsibility variables in the fair allocation approach.

Directly standardized health variables are then given by Eq. (5), that is, they correspond to the concept of direct unfairness. A change in policy leads to the following change in the concentration index

$$AC\left[du_i^S(\tilde{r}_k), \text{SES}_i^S\right] - AC[du_i(\tilde{r}_k), \text{SES}_i)]$$

$$= \frac{2}{n^2} \sum_{i=1}^{n} \left\{ z_i^{\text{SES}^s} \left[\alpha + \sum_{k=1}^{K} \gamma_k \tilde{r}_k + \sum_{j=1}^{J} \left(\beta_j + \sum_{k=1}^{K} \delta_{jk} \tilde{r}_k \right) c_{ij}^S \right] \right.$$

$$\left. - z_i^{\text{SES}} \left[\alpha + \sum_{k=1}^{K} \gamma_k \tilde{r}_k + \sum_{j=1}^{J} \left(\beta_j + \sum_{k=1}^{K} \delta_{jk} \tilde{r}_k \right) c_{ij} \right] \right\} \quad (15)$$

$$= \sum_{j=1}^{J} \left(\beta_j + \sum_{k=1}^{K} \delta_{jk} \tilde{r}_k \right) [AC(c_{ij}^S, \text{SES}_i^s) - AC(c_{ij}, \text{SES}_i)]$$

It is useful to compare this expression with the analogous expression Eq. (11) for the absolute Gini of direct unfairness. These expressions are similar except for the ranking variables in the absolute concentration indices. Hence, when SES_i is the sole circumstance variable, that is, $J = 1$ and $c_{i1} = SES_i$ both approaches are identical when $\beta_1 + \sum_{k=1}^{K} \delta_{1k} \tilde{r}_k > 0$.[7] Yet, contrary to the case of direct unfairness, the sign of Eq. (15) does change with $\beta_1 + \sum_{k=1}^{K} \delta_{1k} \tilde{r}_k$, and therefore may depend on the choice of the reference value $\tilde{r}_k$. Picking the mean value, even in the case where SES_i is the sole circumstance variable, is therefore not innocuous. Yet, it is important to remember that the sign of $\beta_1 + \sum_{k=1}^{K} \delta_{1k} \tilde{r}_k$ determines whether the concentration index is positive or negative. An increase in the absolute Gini of socioeconomic status will therefore always increase the *absolute* value of the concentration index, that is, the degree of inequity. When $J \geq 2$, we cannot make any predictions in general.

Indirect standardization leads to an expression that is similar to the absolute Gini of the fairness gap (see Eq. (13))

$$AC[fg_i^S(\tilde{c}), \text{SES}_i^S] - AC[fg_i(\tilde{c}), \text{SES}_i]$$
$$= \frac{2}{n^2}\sum_{i=1}^{n}\left\{z_i^{\text{SES}^s}\left[\sum_{j=1}^{J}\left(\beta_j + \sum_{k=1}^{K}\delta_{jk}r_{ik}^S\right)(c_{ij}^S - \tilde{c}_j)\right]\right.$$
$$\left. - z_i^{\text{SES}}\left[\sum_{j=1}^{J}\left(\beta_j + \sum_{k=1}^{K}\delta_{jk}r_{ik}\right)(c_{ij} - \tilde{c}_j)\right]\right\}$$
$$= \sum_{j=1}^{J}\beta_j\left\{AC\left[c_{ij}^S, \text{SES}_i^S\right] - AC[c_{ij}, \text{SES}_i]\right\}$$
$$+ \sum_{j=1}^{J}\sum_{k=1}^{K}\delta_{jk}\left\{AC\left[r_{ik}^S\left(c_{ij}^S - \tilde{c}_j\right), \text{SES}_i^S\right] - AC[r_{ik}(c_{ij} - \tilde{c}_j), \text{SES}_i]\right\}$$
(16)

For the same reasons as before, that is, the fact that indirect standardization takes into account the interaction effects between socioeconomic status and the standardizing variables, it is not straightforward to derive general conclusions from Eq. (16). The dependency of the equity evaluation of different policies on the choice of reference values is contingent on the actual structure of the data and can only be determined through empirical analysis.

Summary

The goal of this section was to understand whether inequality comparisons of direct unfairness and the fairness gap — based on the absolute Gini and the variance — are independent of the choice of the reference value. We also compared these results with the more traditional concentration index approach which uses indirect and direct standardization. Our most important findings are:

1. It is easier to find attractive interpretations for measures of direct unfairness than for measures with the fairness gap. This is the obvious consequence of the fact that direct unfairness is only a function of c_{ij}, while the fairness gap depends on both c_{ij} and r_{ik}.
2. The absolute Gini for direct unfairness summarizes the difference between two distributions as a weighted sum of the differences between the concentration indices for the individual circumstance variables (ranked by direct unfairness), where the weights refer to their effect on health at the reference values for the responsibility variables. The

variance applied to direct unfairness results in an expression containing the variances of and the covariances between the circumstance variables.
3. When there is only one circumstance variable, we get a strong result for the case of direct unfairness. The rankings of the absolute Gini and the variance for different policies are independent of the chosen reference values, and, maybe more surprising, are even independent of the coefficient estimates in Eq. (2).
4. No general results can be derived for direct unfairness if there is more than one circumstance variable or for the fairness gap, whatever the number of circumstance variables. When Eq. (2) and the distributions of all responsibility and circumstance variables are known, the results in this section illustrate the different forces at work, but the overall conclusions will be data-dependent. When the inequality comparison is found to depend on the reference values, one cannot guarantee a unique set of reference values for which inequality in the "simulated" and baseline case is identical.
5. The approach based on the concentration index with direct standardization is to some extent analogous to direct unfairness when SES is the only circumstance variable, while indirect standardization leads to expressions which bear some resemblance to those for the fairness gap. The common assumption of picking the average value for the reference value in the CI approach is not innocuous, as the choice of reference value may influence the results, even in the case of direct standardization.

EMPIRICAL ILLUSTRATION

We illustrate the results of the previous section with data on mortality in the Netherlands. Each individual is followed over a period of 10 years and we observe some of their initial characteristics x_{il} (age, gender, lifestyles, and education), and whether they have died by the end of the 10 year follow-up period. In the remainder of this section, we discuss the data, our empirical model for mortality, the resulting health inequality estimates, and the role of the reference values when comparing inequality between a baseline and two "simulated" situations.

Data

We use data from the Dutch cross-sectional survey on living conditions in 1998, 1999, and 2000. These surveys have been linked to the Dutch cause-of-death registry, and we use this linkage to reconstruct 10-year survival for all individuals, that is, for each individual observed in period $t = 1998$, 1999, 2000, we check whether this individual is deceased 10 years later ($t + 10$). We dropped individuals younger than 40 at the time of survey as they represent only about 3 percent of those who died by 2010, and since their causes of death are generally unrelated to the lifestyles we consider.

We link survival during the 10 year follow-up period to demographics, education, and unhealthy lifestyles in the baseline cross-sections 1998, 1999, and 2000. We consider four indicators of unhealthy lifestyles, whether individual: (i) is a smoker, (ii) does not exercise (or exercises less than 1 hour per week), (iii) is underweight (i.e., if $BMI < 18.5$), and (iv) is obese (i.e., if $BMI > 30$). Education is summarized with a binary variable measuring whether individuals had at most primary education, and we define demographics as the set of interactions between gender and the age categories 40−59, 60−74, and 75+ (females between 40 and 59 are the reference category). We present descriptive statistics in Table 1.

Mortality Model

Our goal is to estimate Eq. (2) with the simplest model available that still allows illustration of the results derived in the last section. For a more sophisticated mortality model with the same data, we refer to our earlier work (García-Gómez, Schokkaert, Van Ourti, & Bago d'Uva, 2012). Some

Table 1. Variable Description.

	Description	Mean
dead	1: when the individual died between $t+1$ and $t+10$, 0 otherwise	0.162
dM4059	1: when male and age between 40 and 59; 0 otherwise	0.297
dF4059	1: when female and age between 40 and 59; 0 otherwise*	0.320
dM6074	1: when male and age between 60 and 74; 0 otherwise	0.135
dF6074	1: when female and age between 60 and 74; 0 otherwise	0.139
dM75m	1: when male and age above 74; 0 otherwise	0.046
dF75m	1: when female and age above 74; 0 otherwise	0.063
lowedu	1: when at most primary education; 0 otherwise	0.256
smoke	1: when a current smoker; 0 otherwise	0.295
underweight	1: when $BMI < 18.5$; 0 otherwise	0.012
obese	1: when $BMI > 30$; 0 otherwise	0.123
nosport	1: exercising less than 1 hour per week; 0 otherwise	0.544

Note: *: reference category in the mortality model.

coefficient estimates are most likely driven by reverse causality, but we do not require causal estimates to illustrate our methods. We return to this point later.

We use a linear probability model with dummy explanatory variables, and initially allowed for all two-way interactions between education, demographics and unhealthy lifestyles. In our final model we have removed the interaction between the four lifestyles and low education as these are jointly insignificant. We also find that a majority of the individual estimates turn out insignificant even though all sets of included interactions are jointly significant.

Our estimation results are presented in Table 2. We find that 10-year mortality increases dramatically with age, and is higher for males (except in the 40–59 age group). Among the reference group of women 40–59 years, those with lower education have a slightly larger (and borderline significant) probability to die within 10 years, and those with unhealthy lifestyles experience a higher risk of mortality (although obesity and underweight are not individually statistically significant). In terms of the interaction effects, we find that the age gradient in mortality is stronger for (a) the lower educated, (b) those not exercising, (c) those smoking,[8] (d) those with underweight and the obese (although the effect is not very strong for the obese). Remember that these interaction effects are essential for our purpose: without interaction effects between circumstance and responsibility variables, direct unfairness and the fairness gap are identical and the choice of the reference values becomes irrelevant.

In the following sections, we use the estimates in Table 2 to calculate health inequality indices. We assume that policy makers are interested in ex-ante mortality differences, implying that we can neglect the inequality due to the unexplained part ε_i. This means that we work with the deterministic part of Eq. (1), that is, $m_i^P = \alpha + \sum_l \alpha_l x_{il}$, and the variable of interest is no longer binary but belongs to the unit interval.[9]

Health Inequity for Different Ethical Stances

As was mentioned before, different health inequity measures ultimately reflect different ethical positions. These positions can be differentiated along three dimensions. First, if one opts for the concentration index one is only interested in the relationship between health and socioeconomic status. Approaches in the theory of fair allocation take a broader perspective on inequality. Second, in the latter approaches one cannot satisfy compensation and reward at the same time. Direct unfairness measures satisfy the

Table 2. Estimates of 10-Year Mortality Follow up in the Netherlands, 1998−2010 (n = 12,527).

	OLS Coefficient	p-Value
dM4059	0.0002	0.979
dM6074	0.1487	0.000
dF6074	0.0471	0.000
dM75m	0.6155	0.000
dF75m	0.4625	0.000
lowedu	0.0141	0.110
smoke	0.0285	0.000
underweight	0.0520	0.131
obese	0.0104	0.308
nosport	0.0155	0.015
constant	0.0166	0.000
dM4059 * lowedu	0.0249	0.120
dM6074 * lowedu	0.0731	0.006
dF6074 * lowedu	0.0733	0.000
dM75m * lowedu	0.0616	0.103
dF75m * lowedu	0.0290	0.418
dM4059 * nosport	0.0188	0.057
dM6074 * nosport	0.0866	0.000
dF6074 * nosport	0.0393	0.030
dM75m * nosport	0.0522	0.257
dF75m * nosport	0.1451	0.001
dM4059 * smoke	0.0124	0.276
dM6074 * smoke	0.0750	0.004
dF6074 * smoke	0.0711	0.015
dM75m * smoke	−0.0020	0.965
dF75m * smoke	−0.0845	0.226
dM4059 * underweight	−0.0388	0.647
dM6074 * underweight	0.1536	0.283
dF6074 * underweight	0.1736	0.067
dM75m * underweight	0.2098	0.000
dF75m * underweight	0.1048	0.260
dM4059 * obese	−0.0009	0.956
dM6074 * obese	0.0304	0.470
dF6074 * obese	0.0369	0.179
dM75m * obese	0.0711	0.270
dF75m * obese	−0.0206	0.648

reward principle, but they do not satisfy compensation. Measures based on the fairness gap satisfy compensation at the cost of including some effects of responsibility differences in the measure of inequity. Third, one has to take a decision on which variables should be seen as part of circumstances and which should be seen as related to responsibility. In this respect, we will consider in this section four different possibilities as summarized in Table 3.[10] In the first option one considers all variables in Eq. (2) as leading to illegitimate health inequalities (row "all illegitimate"): inequity then coincides with "pure" health inequalities. The second option is most in the spirit of the theories of fair allocation or, for that matter, equality of opportunity (row "control/preference"): only differences that follow from the own choices of the respondents are legitimate, all other variables (including age and gender) belong to circumstances. A third option starts from the popular argument that only health inequalities that can be influenced by policy should be a cause of ethical concern and that health differences according to age and gender are largely unavoidable (row "standardization"). Illegitimate inequalities then follow from all the other variables. A last option includes lifestyles among the legitimate sources of inequalities (row "SES inequality"). Only education then remains as an "illegitimate" source of health inequalities.

The results for the various approaches in the (observed) baseline situation are shown in Table 4. In each case, we calculated the absolute Gini and the variance for three possible sets of reference values. The "best" values are those that give the best health results (the lowest mortality risks): these are the youngest females without lowest education and with healthy lifestyles (normal weight, nonsmoking, and exercising). The "worst" health results are achieved by the smoking oldest underweighted males with the lowest level of education and without exercise. We also calculate all measures with the "mean" values for the neutralized variables as the reference as this is the most common approach in health economics (Gravelle, 2003).

Finally, we calculate the concentration index with education as the ranking variable. In the "standardization" case, the concentration index is standardized for age and gender. This is the standard approach in health economics. In the "SES inequality" case, we also standardize for lifestyle differences. As described before, in the context of the concentration index,

Table 3. Ethical Stances.

	Responsibility	Circumstance
All illegitimate		Age-gender, education, lifestyles
Control/Preference	Lifestyles	Age-gender, education
Standardization	Age-gender	Lifestyles, education
SES inequality	Age-gender, lifestyles	Education

Table 4. Measures of Inequity in Mortality with Different Ethical Stances and Reference Values.

	Reference values	All Illegitimate DU	All Illegitimate FG	Control/ Preference DU	Control/ Preference FG	Standardization DU	Standardization FG	SES inequality DU	SES inequality FG
Variance	Best	0.0413	0.0413	0.0300	0.0404	0.0004	0.0048	0.0000	0.0008
	Worst	0.0413	0.0413	0.0757	0.0386	0.0048	0.0199	0.0011	0.0010
	Mean	0.0413	0.0413	0.0358	0.0392	0.0021	0.0033	0.0004	0.0007
Absolute Gini	Best	0.0956	0.0956	0.0746	0.0923	0.0106	0.0357	0.0027	0.0113
	Worst	0.0956	0.0956	0.1384	0.0941	0.0374	0.0739	0.0144	0.0167
	Mean	0.0956	0.0956	0.0875	0.0923	0.0250	0.0304	0.0088	0.0127
CI	Best					−0.0037	−0.0159	−0.0027	−0.0103
	Worst					−0.0190	−0.0018	−0.0144	−0.0083
	Mean					−0.0116	−0.0132	−0.0088	−0.0098

Note: DU = direct unfairness, FG = fairness gap. In the case of the concentration index (CI) the columns "DU" and "FG" correspond to direct and indirect standardization respectively.

"direct unfairness" and "fairness gap" correspond to direct and indirect standardization respectively.

The first columns in Table 4 show the results for "pure" inequality in mortality. In that case the choice of reference values is inconsequential. In all other cases, different reference values lead to different results for the measures of inequity. This is of course trivial, yet it is still worth pointing out that this general finding also holds for the concentration index. As was shown before, the concentration index is equal to the absolute Gini for direct unfairness if we take education as the only circumstance variable. The sign is different, however (compare in the column "SES inequality" the rows referring to the absolute Gini with those referring to the CI). The concentration index makes a distinction between health concentrated among individuals of low or high socioeconomic status. In our case the negative sign reflects the fact that there is concentration of mortality among the lower educated. In the fair allocation approach, the inequality measures can only take positive values.

Although it is not the main point of this chapter to compare the results for the different ethical stances, it is interesting to note the importance of age and gender. While this is not at all surprising in the light of the estimation results in Table 2, the implications for the inequity measures are still striking. Including age and gender among the "legitimate" sources of health inequalities (as in the standardization and SES approaches) leads to a sharp decrease in the measured inequity.

Fleurbaey and Schokkaert (2012) have argued that in the setting of the fairness gap, it might be most plausible to pick the set of reference values that leads to the lowest mortality risk, the intuition being that when comparing actual mortality with mortality in a fair situation, one should consider the fair situation as the situation where mortality risk due to the circumstance variables is lowest. This choice of reference values, as compared to the "worst" and "mean" case, has a limited impact on the inequity estimates for the fairness gap within the control/preference approach, but a larger impact in the other approaches.

It is tempting to take "pure health inequalities" as a kind of benchmark and then interpret all the other results in comparison to that benchmark. It is also tempting to think that the approach of the fairness gap which satisfies compensation should lead to a larger inequity than the direct unfairness approach since the fairness gap also includes some parts of the responsibility differences in the illegitimate part of inequality. However, the dependency of the results on the choice of reference values may go against these intuitions. Consider the results for direct unfairness in the preference/control approach. In the case of the "worst" reference values direct unfairness gives a higher value than the fairness gap (both for the absolute Gini and for the variance). Of course, the variables that are put at their "worst" value are different in the two cases: for direct unfairness the lifestyles are neutralized, for the fairness gap reference values are picked for the circumstances (age-gender and education). More strikingly, for these worst reference values the inequity as measured by the direct unfairness approach is larger than the pure health inequality. While this may seem surprising at first sight, it is easily understood. The direct unfairness approach with "worst" reference values measures inequality in the hypothetical situation where all individuals are underweight, are smoking and do not exercise. The interaction effects between these variables and the age-gender dummies are significant and show a clear pattern, in general becoming larger for the older respondents.

This result suggests that it is misleading to compare the numerical values in Table 4 as such if they refer to different ethical concepts or different reference values. That is why we have focused in the previous section on comparisons between different states of the world for a given ethical concept and for a fixed choice of reference values. We now turn to this issue with our empirical data.

Reference Value-Consistent Inequality Comparisons

In order to illustrate how reference values might affect inequality comparisons for a given ethical stance and a given inequity measure, we compare the degree of health equity in different counterfactual situations. In addition to the baseline, we consider an "education" scenario, in which everyone obtains at least a lower vocational or a lower secondary education degree, and an "exercise" scenario in which all individuals exercise more than 1 hour per week. Both scenarios are simulated by calculating the predicted probability to die from our estimated mortality model with the regressors lowedu and nosport put to 0 for all.[11] Our aim is to illustrate that the choice of the reference value may have important implications when measuring inequity in (opportunity of) health.

Table 5 reveals how reference values might impact on inequality comparisons. For each of the three scenarios (baseline, education, exercise) we calculate for the different ethical stances the health inequality according to the different measures that have been introduced before. We do this for all possible reference values. When there is only one reference variable (e.g., in the SES ethical stance with the fairness gap), this is relatively straightforward, but when there is more than one variable to be fixed at its reference value, this becomes more complicated. However, since we have only dummy variables in our mortality model, the number of potential 0/1 combinations of reference values is finite, and we can easily calculate the inequality for all potential combinations. We then calculate for each of these sets of reference values the differences in the resulting inequality values for two scenarios. Table 5 shows the largest and the smallest of these differences. If the inequality differences between two scenarios are always positive (e.g., in the "All illegitimate" ethical stance), then the second policy scenario would be preferred as its inequality is lower. For example, we find that a policy that achieves that all individuals exercise more than 1 hour per week attains always the lower inequality in the "All illegitimate" ethical stance. When these inequality differencse change sign, the inequality ranking of these two scenarios is not robust to the choice of reference value. We have reported these cases in bold. For example, notice that in the "standardization" ethical stance for all inequality measures inequality in mortality is lower for the "Education" policy reform compared to the "Exercise" policy reform for some reference values (the minimum value of the inequality difference between the Education and Exercise policy scenario is negative), while the opposite is true for another set of reference values (the maximum

Table 5. Difference in Inequity Between Pairwise Scenario Comparisons Calculated at Different Reference Values.

	Variance						Absolute Gini						Concentration Index			
	Direct unfairness		Fairness gap				Direct unfairness		Fairness gap				Direct standardization		Indirect standardization	
Comparison	Min	Max	Min	Max			Min	Max	Min	Max			Min	Max	Min	Max
All illegitimate																
Baseline-Education	0.0039	0.0039	0.0039	0.0039			0.0071	0.0071	0.0071	0.0071						
Baseline-Exercise	0.0104	0.0104	0.0104	0.0104			0.0152	0.0152	0.0152	0.0152						
Education-Exercise	0.0065	0.0065	0.0065	0.0065			0.0081	0.0081	0.0081	0.0081						
Preference/Control																
Baseline-Education	0.0029	0.0062	0.0031	0.0038			0.0068	0.0077	0.0050	0.0073						
Baseline-Exercise	0.0000	0.0000	0.0063	0.0096			0.0000	0.0101	0.0124	0.0142						
Education-Exercise	−0.0062	−0.0029	0.0032	0.0058			−0.0077	−0.0068	0.0056	0.0092						
Standardization																
Baseline-Education	0.0001	0.0024	**−0.0022**	**0.0017**			0.0012	0.0092	**−0.0039**	**0.0074**			−0.0167	−0.0027	−0.1025	−0.1025
Baseline-Exercise	0.0001	0.0065	**−0.0039**	**0.0031**			0.0021	0.0316	**−0.0074**	**0.0137**			−0.0067	−0.0007	−0.0044	−0.0044
Education-Exercise	**−0.0006**	**0.0056**	**−0.0021**	**0.0021**			**−0.0015**	**0.0277**	**−0.0054**	**0.0064**			0.0015	0.0144	0.0059	0.0059
SES																
Baseline-Education	0.0000	0.0015	0.0001	0.0008			0.0027	0.0167	0.0009	0.0113			−0.0167	−0.0027	−0.0103	−0.0103
Baseline-Exercise	0.0000	0.0000	0.0000	0.0000			0.0000	0.0000	0.0000	0.0000			0.0000	0.0000	0.0000	0.0000
Education-Exercise	−0.0015	−0.0000	−0.0008	−0.000			−0.0167	−0.0027	−0.0113	−0.0009			0.0027	0.0167	0.0103	0.0103

Note: For all ethical stances, the differences in the inequity measures between the two counterfactual situations (in the first column) were calculated for all possible sets of reference values. The table gives the minima and maxima for these differences. If maximum and minimum values of the difference have different sign, this points to a reversal in the inequity ranking of the counterfactual situations induced by the choice of reference values. These cases of rank reversal are indicated in bold.

value of the inequality difference between the Education and Exercise policy scenario is positive).

As predicted by the analysis in the previous section, we find that the reference values do not matter for the case of pure health inequalities. This happens since under "all illegitimate," there are no interactions between the compensation and responsibility variables. We also confirm that the reference value does not matter for the robustness of the inequality comparison when there is only one circumstance variable in the case of direct unfairness (see variance and absolute Gini for the SES scenario). Remember that in this case the change in the absolute Gini (the variance) of direct unfairness only depends on the change in the absolute Gini (the variance) of the single circumstance variable (here education). Therefore the scenario "exercise" has the same inequality as the baseline, as it does not change the distribution of education.[12] It might seem more striking that the "exercise" scenario does not differ from the baseline in the case of the fairness gap, but it is not. Eqs. (13) and (14) show that the "exercise" scenario would only be different for the fairness gap if there were an interaction between education and exercise in our mortality model (see Table 2). We also find — like in Table 4 — that the results for the concentration index with direct standardization are equal in absolute value to those for the absolute Gini under direct unfairness.

When there is more than one compensation variable, also direct unfairness may depend on the reference value and this happens in our case for the ethical stance "standardization" when comparing the education with the public health scenario. More generally, most sign reversals of the inequality comparisons are found for this "standardization" stance, in particular when we use the fairness gap.

In order to further improve the understanding of the results from the previous section, we provide some additional illustrations. Panel A of Table 6 illustrates the variance of direct unfairness in case of the ethical stance "standardization" for the comparison of the educational and the public health scenarios. Panel B provides an example for the absolute Gini of direct unfairness in case of the control approach. Similar examples can be provided for the fairness gap, but are left out for reasons of space and since these expressions are more complicated to interpret.

Let us start with the variance of direct unfairness under the ethical stance "standardization" (panel A in Table 6). The first term of Eq. (12) (see row "sum term 1") consists of a weighted sum of differences of variances, and only the weights depend on the reference value, that is, via $\sum_{k=1}^{K} \delta_{jk} \tilde{r}_k$. The variances of the lifestyles "smoke," "underweight," and

Table 6. Detailed Illustration of the Impact of Different Reference Values on Pairwise Inequity Comparisons: Two Examples.

Panel A: Eq. (12); variance; DU; standardization; education versus exercise

				$\tilde{r}_k = \mathbf{dF75m}$			$\tilde{r}_k = \mathbf{dF6074}$	
Circumstance	β_j	$VAR(c_{ij}^{educ})$	$VAR(c_{ij}^{exer})$	$\sum_{k=1}^{K}\delta_{jk}\tilde{r}_k$	term 1[a]	$\sum_{k=1}^{K}\delta_{jk}\tilde{r}_k$	term 1[a]
lowedu	0.0141	0.0000	0.1904	0.0290	−0.0004	0.0733	−0.0015
smoke	0.0285	0.2079	0.2079	−0.0845	0	0.0711	0
underweight	0.0520	0.0120	0.0120	0.1048	0	0.1736	0
obese	0.0104	0.1082	0.1082	−0.0206	0	0.0369	0
nosport	0.0155	0.2481	0.0000	0.1451	0.0064	0.0393	0.0007
sum term 1					0.0060		−0.0007
Sum term 2[£]					−0.0004		0.0001
diff. VAR*					0.0056		−0.0006

Panel B: Eq. (10); absolute Gini; DU; control; education versus exercise

		$\tilde{r}_k = \text{smoke, underweight, nosport}$				$\tilde{r}_k = \text{nosmoke, normal, sport}$		
circumstance	β_j	$\sum_{k=1}^{K}\delta_{jk}\tilde{r}_k$	AC^{educ}	AC^{exer}	eq. (10)	$\sum_{k=1}^{K}\delta_{jk}\tilde{r}_k$	AC^{educ}	AC^{exer}	eq. (10)
dM4059	0.0002	−0.0076	−0.2088	−0.1811	0.0002	0	−0.0186	−0.0510	0.0000
dM6074	0.1487	0.3152	0.0875	0.0875	0.0000	0	0.0875	0.0875	0.0000
dF6074	0.0471	0.2839	0.0520	0.0520	0.0000	0	0.0520	0.0520	0.0000
dM75m	0.6155	0.2600	0.0436	0.0436	0.0000	0	0.0436	0.0436	0.0000
dF75m	0.4625	0.1654	0.0531	0.0531	0.0000	0	0.0531	0.0531	0.0000
lowedu	0.0141			0.1157	−0.0016			0.1157	−0.0016
dM4059 * lowedu	0.0249			0.0083	−0.0002			0.0083	−0.0002
dM6074 * lowedu	0.0731			0.0255	−0.0019			0.0255	−0.0019
dF6074 * lowedu	0.0733	0		0.0275	−0.0020	0		0.0275	−0.0020

dM75* lowmedu	0.0616		0.0171	−0.0011	0.0171	−0.0011
dF75* lowedu	0.0290		0.0319	−0.0009	0.0319	−0.0009
sum Eq. (10)				−0.0075		−0.0077

Note: $^\mu$: term 1 = $(\beta_j + \sum_{k=1}^{K} \delta_{jk}\tilde{r}_k)^2 [VAR(c_{ij}^{educ}) - VAR(c_{ij}^{exer})]$.

$^\varepsilon$: sum term 2 = $\sum_{j=1}^{J} \{2\sum_{l>j}^{J}(\beta_j + \sum_{k=1}^{K} \delta_{jk}\tilde{r}_k)(\beta_l + \sum_{k=1}^{K} \delta_{lk}\tilde{r}_k) [COV(c_{ij}^{educ}, c_{il}^{educ}) - COV(c_{ij}^{exer}, c_{il}^{exer})]\}$.

*: diff. $VAR = VAR(du_i^{educ}) - VAR(du_i^{exer})$.

$AC^x = AC(c_{ij}^x; du_i^x(\tilde{r}_k))$.

"obese" are identical in the exercise and education scenarios. The variances of education and exercise become 0 in the "education" and "exercise" scenarios respectively. They therefore have an opposite effect on the difference between the inequality in the two scenarios, that is, the difference between the variances of education is −0.1904 and that of nosport is slightly larger in absolute terms (0.2481). The reference value will matter when it changes the relative weight of these two variances, and that is what happens in panel A. When we take women of 75 and older as the reference category, the full health impact of "nosport" (0.0155 + 0.1451) dominates that of "lowedu" (0.0141 + 0.02090) and thus we observe that inequality is larger under the education scenario. When we take women between 60 and 74 as the reference category, we come to the opposite conclusion. These findings are also intuitively plausible (see Table 2): the mortality reduction of doing sports is much larger for women aged 75+ compared to those between 60 and 75, and thus at the older age range, the inequality in exercise dominates. Eq. (12) also contains a second term, which is determined by the change in the clustering of the circumstance variables within individuals (weighted by their total health impact). We find that this second term is much smaller compared to the first one under both reference categories. This is plausible as our education and exercise scenarios are not targeted to reduce the within-individual clustering of the circumstance variables.[13]

In panel B of Table 6, we consider the absolute Gini applied to direct unfairness in the control approach. In this case there is no sign reversal in Table 5. We present the results for two sets of reference values: one where lifestyles are fixed at unhealthy levels ("smoke," "underweight," "nosport"), and another where these are fixed at healthy levels ("nosmoke," "normal," "sport"). In both cases, the absolute concentration indices for education and its interactions with the demographic variables equal 0 under the education scenario since everyone has now the same education level (i.e., "loweduc"=0).[14] Also in both cases, we find that the contributions of the demographic variables are 0 (rows dM6074-dM75m, column Eq. (10)) because their absolute concentration indices are identical in the exercise and education scenario, except for the youngest males.[15] The only sizeable contribution to the difference in the absolute Gini of direct unfairness therefore is due to the absolute concentration indices of education (and its interactions with the demographic variables) in the exercise scenario (see rows "lowedu" − "dF75*lowedu"). The upshot of all this is that the change in absolute Gini indices is driven by what happens to education, while the exercise scenario plays no role as exercise is a variable for which individuals are held responsible in the control approach. It is thus no surprise that the education scenario has a lower inequality with direct unfairness under this ethical stance, independent of the chosen reference values.

CHOOSING THE REFERENCE VALUE WHEN IT INFLUENCES INEQUALITY COMPARISONS

In the previous sections, we have analyzed how inequality comparisons based on the absolute Gini and the variance (and the concentration index) depend on the reference values. One could draw from this the pessimistic conclusion that in these cases it is in principle impossible to rank states of the world unambiguously. However, a more constructive approach can start from the idea that the choice of reference values is not arbitrary, that is, that not all reference values are equally good. Ideally, this would call for the construction of a *theory* on how to choose the "best" reference values. In this section we offer a cursory sketch of one possible direction to think about this issue. In the case of direct unfairness, reward is satisfied, and we will propose a value for the reference variable that minimizes the violation of compensation. In the case of the fairness gap, we minimize the violation of the reward principle. For this purpose, we introduce a statistical approach that is sufficiently simple for empirical work, but we leave the empirical exploration for future work.

Direct Unfairness: Minimizing the Violation of Compensation

We know that direct unfairness satisfies the reward principle, that is, that the resulting measures of inequality do not depend on the value of the responsibility variables. However, it violates the compensation condition that when two individuals share their responsibility variables, the measure of inequality should be equal to the mortality difference between them. We propose to choose the reference values in such a way that the deviation from this ideal situation is as small as possible.

To be more concrete, assume that there are M (mutually exclusive) subgroups $m = 1, 2, ..., M$ of individuals that share the same value for the responsibility variables, that is, for all i within each subgroup m, $r_{ik} = r_k^m$, $\forall k = 1, ..., K$. Let us first consider one such group m. We then should ideally have that $\forall i, l$ in group m, that is, with $r_{ik} = r_{lk} = r_k^m$, $\forall k = 1, 2, ..., K \Rightarrow du_i(\tilde{r}) - du_l(\tilde{r}) = m_i^P - m_l^P$. This implies that we should minimize

$$\sum_{j=1}^{J}\left(\beta_j + \sum_{k=1}^{K}\delta_{jk}\tilde{r}_k\right) c_{ij} - \sum_{j=1}^{J}\left(\beta_j + \sum_{k=1}^{K}\delta_{jk}\tilde{r}_k\right) c_{lj}$$
$$-\sum_{j=1}^{J}\left(\beta_j + \sum_{k=1}^{K}\delta_{jk}r_{ik}\right) c_{ij} + \sum_{j=1}^{J}\left(\beta_j + \sum_{k=1}^{K}\delta_{jk}r_{lk}\right) c_{lj} \quad (17)$$
$$= \sum_{j=1}^{J}\sum_{k=1}^{K}\delta_{jk}c_{ij}(\tilde{r}_k - r_k^m) - \sum_{j=1}^{J}\sum_{k=1}^{K}\delta_{jk}c_{lj}(\tilde{r}_k - r_k^m)$$

Eq. (17) is key to understanding our minimization approach. It shows that we must choose each $\tilde{r}_k$ such that the deviation with the actual value of the responsibility variable is minimized when the difference in the circumstance variables (weighted with the interaction coefficient) is large. When the difference between the latter is small, the value of the reference variables is not that important.

When we focus on one group only (e.g., because we care for normative reasons only about this group), Eq. (17) shows that we can always satisfy compensation for this group by choosing $\tilde{r}_k = r_k^m$, $\forall k = 1, ..., K$. When $J = K = 1$, this is the only solution, but when $K \geq 2$, there might be more than one set of values $\tilde{r}_1, \tilde{r}_2, ..., \tilde{r}_K$ for which Eq. (17) is satisfied. However, our proposal of picking $\tilde{r}_k = r_k^m, \forall k = 1, ..., K$ is the only solution that will always work independently of all possible values of the circumstance variables and the coefficients δ_{jk}.

When we want to take into account more than one group of individuals sharing the same values for the responsibility variables, we propose a separate solution for the variance and the absolute Gini. In the case of the variance, it is natural to use the (weighted) within-group variance of the left hand side of Eq. (18) as our objective function. In other words, one should minimize

$$\sum_{m=1}^{M}\frac{n_m}{n}\left\{\frac{1}{n_m}\sum_{i \in m}\left[\left(\sum_{j=1}^{J}\sum_{k=1}^{K}\delta_{jk}c_{ij}(\tilde{r}_k - r_{ik})\right) - \left(\frac{1}{n_m}\sum_{i \in m}\sum_{j=1}^{J}\sum_{k=1}^{K}\delta_{jk}c_{ij}(\tilde{r}_k - r_{ik})\right)\right]^2\right\}$$
$$= \sum_{m=1}^{M}\frac{n_m}{n}\left\{\frac{1}{n_m}\sum_{i \in m}\left[\sum_{k=1}^{K}(\tilde{r}_k - r_{ik})\sum_{j=1}^{J}\delta_{jk}(c_{ij} - \overline{c_{mj}})\right]^2\right\} \quad (18)$$

with respect to $\tilde{r}_k$, $k = 1, ..., K$, where n_m and $\overline{c_{mj}}$ correspond to respectively the population size and the average of c_{ij} of subgroup m.[16] Eq. (18) corresponds to a least squares framework, and can thus be related to the sum of squared residuals in a linear OLS regression.[17] Note that Eq. (18) assumes that we weigh each subgroup m with its population share while minimizing the within-variance. This might be found restrictive from a normative perspective and can be generalized to a weighted least squares procedure by replacing the population shares by any weighting scheme that sums to 1. Focusing on one group about which one is most concerned from an ethical point of view, is then just a special case of this more general approach.

A similar argument can be developed for the absolute Gini index (and the concentration index). Two complications arise though. First, the absolute Gini is not subgroup decomposable. This means that one has to choose between two suboptimal options: either one considers only the within absolute Gini, or one considers the sum of the within absolute Gini and the reranking term. Second, although it is possible to minimize by applying a minimization algorithm, there is in the Gini case no easy correspondence to a regression framework.

The Fairness Gap: Minimizing the Violation of Reward

The fairness gap satisfies the *compensation principle*, which prescribes that any difference in the probability of death is measured as unfair for individuals that are equally responsible. However, the fairness gap does not satisfy the reward principle which prescribes that a measure of inequality should not depend on the value of the responsibility variables (see Eq. (6)). To minimize the deviations from this reward principle, we suggest an approach which is conceptually similar to the approach in the previous subsection.

We now consider different subgroups $g = 1, ..., G$, consisting of individuals with the same values for the compensation variables. Reward will hold when the fairness gaps for two individuals $i \neq l$ within one such group are equal. In other words, $\forall i \neq l$ in group g with $c_{ij} = c_{lj} = c_j^g$, ideally $f_{gi}(\tilde{c}) = f_{gl}(\tilde{c})$. Minimizing the deviations from this ideal implies choosing $\tilde{c}$ in such a way that $\sum_{j=1}^{J}[\beta_j c_{ij} + \sum_{k=1}^{K} \delta_{jk} r_{ik} (c_{ij} - \tilde{c}_j)] - \sum_{j=1}^{J}[\beta_j c_{lj} + \sum_{k=1}^{K} \delta_{jk} r_{lk} (c_{lj} - \tilde{c}_j)]$ is minimized. The logic resembles the discussion of direct unfairness – the value of the reference variables will matter mostly when the responsibility variables differ – but there is also an overall scale effect due to the sum of the responsibility variables $\beta_j c_{ij}$.

Similar to the previous section, we propose for the variance a solution based on the within-variance so that one obtains a minimization problem that resembles a least squares framework.[18] The approach can be also generalized by allowing for "importance" weights for each group g. One can ascertain a unique solution when one gives priority to one single group (i.e., the weights of all other groups are 0) and when $J = K = 1$ (although also here picking the reference values equal to the actual values of the circumstance variables seems most sensible in case of giving priority to only one group when $J \geq 2$ and/or $K \geq 2$).

In case of the absolute Gini index (and the concentration index), the same complications arise as in case of direct unfairness, but in principle it is possible to obtain an objective function and derive the reference values.

CONCLUSION

The choice of reference values does matter when one wants to evaluate the (in)equity in different situations. This conclusion holds definitely when one applies the measures of direct unfairness and the fairness gap that have recently been proposed in the theory of fair allocation. While the concentration index as such does not require the choice of reference values, the standard approach in economics in which one first standardizes the health variable does. Indeed, its results may depend on the choice of the reference values in the standardization exercise. It is therefore surprising that this issue is largely neglected in the empirical literature and that there is little theoretical work on the topic.

Our approach has obvious limitations. We worked with a simple linear specification, where the essential nonlinearities were modeled as simple interaction terms between responsibility and circumstance variables. Moreover, we focused on the comparison of two situations for which it can be assumed that the underlying explanatory model of health remains the same. To extend the applicability of our results, one should go beyond these assumptions. This would require decomposing the differences in the inequality measures using methods that are extensions of the Oaxaca approach (see, e.g., Fortin, Lemieux, & Firpo, 2011).

Our results strongly suggest that we need a theory on how to choose the reference values. A general theory would probably imply the introduction of additional ethical considerations. One might try to elaborate the simple suggestion put forward by Fleurbaey and Schokkaert (2012), that from an ethical point of view it is natural to take as reference the best values of the circumstance variables.[19] In this chapter, we did not at all have the ambition to construct such a general theory. However, we suggested a statistical approach that could be used in the future to pick the reference values for direct unfairness and the fairness gap. While simple, our proposal has the obvious disadvantage that it makes the choice of reference values depend on the specific empirical features of the issue to be analyzed.

NOTES

1. We use this notation because our empirical work will refer to inequality in mortality. However, our theoretical analysis is general in that m_i can stand for all variables that are considered to be relevant for equity purposes, and need not even be a health variable.
2. We work with the population version of m_i^P in this section. Issues related to estimation (error) are discussed in the empirical part of the chapter.
3. In the context of standardization of the concentration index, Gravelle (2003) uses the term "essential nonlinearities" to capture the same idea.
4. In the context of equity in health care use, Van de Poel, van Doorslaer, and O'Donnell (2012) estimate different health care equations for different groups in the population. This can be written as in Eq. (2) if one introduces dummy variables that take the value 1 if the individual belongs to a specific group. They then introduce in the standardization procedure a notion of vertical equity based on the assumption that the "adequate" level of health care is that given to the richest urban groups in the population.
5. This is because the absolute concentration index belongs to the class of symmetric indices defined by Erreygers, Clarke, and Van Ourti (2012). The "symmetry" property implies that turning the world upside down (i.e., the poorest becomes the richest, the second poorest the second richest, and so on) leaves the magnitude of inequality unchanged, but reverses its sign.
6. In deriving Eq. (10), we have used that the absolute concentration index of a constant is 0, that is $AC[\alpha, du_i(\tilde{r}_k)] = AC[\alpha, du_i^S(\tilde{r}_k)] = AC[\gamma_k \tilde{r}_k, du_i(\tilde{r}_k)] = AC[\gamma_k \tilde{r}_k, du_i^S(\tilde{r}_k)] = 0$.
7. When SES_i is the only circumstance variable $AC(c_{i1}^S, SES_i^s) - AC(c_{i1}, SES_i) = AG(SES_i^s) - AG(SES_i)$.
8. The oldest age group is an exception. This is probably due to selection effects such as the healthy survivor effect.
9. The potential concern about predicted mortality being outside the unit interval is not very important for our analysis since we will consider absolute inequality. Nevertheless and reassuringly, no individual has a predicted mortality below 0, and only 2 individuals (out of 12,527) have a predicted mortality higher than 1.
10. See García-Gómez et al. (2012) for a more detailed discussion of these different positions. The philosophical literature on responsibility-sensitive egalitarianism makes a distinction between approaches in which people are held responsible for their

"preferences" (even if these are not chosen by them) and approaches in which they are held responsible for variables which are under their "control." In the simple model we use in this paper it is not really possible to distinguish these two approaches.

11. It is dangerous to interpret these counterfactual situations as resulting from simulated "policy changes," since our mortality model most likely suffers from reverse causality and other endogeneity issues. In this respect, our approach is perfectly comparable to the practice in most papers on inequity measurement in health, including the literature that intends to decompose inequalities in health into its contributing factors (see, e.g., Wagstaff, van Doorslaer, & Watanabe, 2003). In the huge literature on health inequity measurement, there are — as far as we know — only a few counterexamples that more carefully look at underlying endogeneity issues (such as Jones, Rice, & Rosa Dias 2012).

12. A similar argument explains why the variance and absolute Gini for direct unfairness under "control" are similar for the exercise and baseline scenarios.

13. This second term consists of a weighted sum of covariance differences (see Eq. (12)). Only the weights depend on the reference category. All the covariances with "lowedu" in the education scenario, and all the covariances with "nosport" in the exercise scenario drop out since these variables are 0 under the respective scenarios. The weighted sums of the remaining nonzero covariances, that is, those between "lowedu" and "under," "obese" and "smoke" in the exercise scenario, and those between "nosport" and "under," "obese" and "smoke" in the education scenario are small since the covariances and their weights are small, and since the weights are not strongly influenced by the reference categories.

14. Interactions among circumstance variables are treated in our linear probability model as just another circumstance variable.

15. The contribution of "dM4059" is nonzero (albeit small) since the absolute concentration indices are not identical under both scenarios. Since "dM4059" is identical in the education and exercise scenario, this derives from a difference in the ranking variable between both scenarios, that is, direct unfairness is different. This is the case since the coefficient of "dM4059" (see column β_j) is much smaller compared to the coefficient of "lowedu," and hence the ranking in terms of direct unfairness of the youngest males differs in both scenarios. This does not happen for the other demographic variables since their coefficients (and the differences between each of these coefficients) are much larger than that of "lowedu," and thus completely dominate direct unfairness. In other words, the ranking in terms of direct unfairness for the other demographic groups is similar under both scenarios.

16. Note that the variance is subgroup decomposable into between- and within-group variance. Here we only consider the within-group variance of the M mutually exclusive subgroups, since the between-group variance is irrelevant from the perspective of the compensation axiom.

17. One can obtain the reference values that minimize the violation of compensation by regressing $-\sum_{j=1}^{J} \sum_{k=1}^{K} \delta_{jk} (c_{ij} - \overline{c_{mj}}) r_{mk}$ on $\sum_{j=1}^{J} \delta_{j1}(c_{ij} - \overline{c_{mj}})$, $\sum_{j=1}^{J} \delta_{j2} (c_{ij} - \overline{c_{mj}})$, ..., $\sum_{j=1}^{J} \delta_{jK}(c_{ij} - \overline{c_{mj}})$ with an OLS regression *without* constant. The coefficients obtained from this regression should be used as reference values.

Note that this only holds when the responsibility variables are continuous and have cardinal measurement properties. In case one uses dummy variables (or categorical values), one should do a constrained OLS regression imposing that (sets) of coefficients should equal 0 or 1.

18. One should run an OLS model without constant of $\sum_{j=1}^{J} \left\{ \beta_j (c_{ij} - \overline{c_{gj}}) + \sum_{k=1}^{K} \delta_{jk} \left[r_{ik} c_{ij} - (\frac{1}{n_g} \sum_{i \in g} r_{ik} c_{ij}) \right] \right\}$ upon $\sum_{k=1}^{K} \delta_{1k} (r_{ik} - \overline{r_{gk}})$, $\sum_{k=1}^{K} \delta_{2k} (r_{ik} - \overline{r_{gk}})$, ..., $\sum_{k=1}^{K} \delta_{Jk} (r_{ik} - \overline{r_{gk}})$. The J coefficients provide the reference values. Constrained regression is required for dummy and categorical variables.

19. The choice of reference values is somewhat easier when analyzing equity in health care than when analyzing equity in health. In the former case the notion of vertical equity refers to some "ideal" way of adapting treatment to differences in needs. A nice example for the concentration index (in a somewhat different setting) is Van de Poel et al. (2012).

ACKNOWLEDGMENT

Pilar García-Gómez is a Postdoctoral Fellows of the Netherlands Organization for Scientific Research —Innovational Research Incentives Scheme —Veni. Tom Van Ourti acknowledges support from the National Institute on Ageing, under grant R01AG037398. We thank the Netherlands Central Bureau of Statistics for access to the linked data sets used for this research (POLS Gezondheid 1998–2000, DO 1999–2010). We have benefited from the comments and suggestions of Owen O'Donnell. We also thank Teresa Bago d'Uva who co-authored our earlier paper that developed a more sophisticated mortality model with the same data (García-Gómez et al., 2012). The usual caveats apply and all remaining errors are our responsibility.

REFERENCES

Erreygers, G., Clarke, P., & Van Ourti, T. (2012). Mirror, mirror, on the wall, who in this land is fairest of all? Distributional sensitivity in the measurement of socioeconomic inequality of health. *Journal of Health Economics, 31*, 257–270.

Fleurbaey, M., & Schokkaert, E. (2009). Unfair inequalities in health and health care. *Journal of Health Economics, 28*, 73–90.

Fleurbaey, M., & Schokkaert, E. (2012). Inequity in health and health care. In P. Barros, T. McGuire & M. Pauly (Eds.), *Handbook of Health Economics* (Vol. 2, pp. 1003–1092). New York, NY: Elsevier.

Fortin, N., Lemieux, T., & Firpo, S. (2011). Decomposition methods in economics. In O. Ashenfelter & D. Card (Eds.), *Handbook of Labor Economics* (Vol. 4a, pp. 1–102). New York, NY: Elsevier.

García-Gómez, P., Schokkaert, E., Van Ourti, T., & Bago d'Uva, T. (2012). *Inequity in the face of death*. CORE Discussion Paper 2012–2024. CORE, Université Catholique de Louvain.

Gravelle, H. (2003). Measuring income related inequality in health: standardization and the partial concentration index. *Health Economics, 12*, 803–819.

Jones, A., Rice, N., & Rosa Dias, P. (2012). Quality of schooling and inequality of opportunity in health. *Empirical Economics, 42*, 369–394.

Lambert, P., & Zheng, B. (2011). On the consistent measurement of achievement and shortfall inequality. *Journal of Health Economics, 30*, 214–219.

Luttens, R. & Van de gaer, D. (2007). Lorenz dominance and non-welfaristic redistribution. *Social Choice and Welfare, 28*, 281–302.

O'Donnell, O., van Doorslaer, E., Wagstaff, A., & Lindelow, M. (2008). *Analyzing health equity using household survey data*. Washington, DC: World Bank.

Van de Poel, E., van Doorslaer, E. & O'Donnell, O. (2012). Measurement of inequity in health care with heterogeneous response of use to need. *Journal of Health Economics, 31*, 676–689.

van Doorslaer, E. & Van Ourti, T. (2011). Measuring inequality and inequity in health and health care. In S. Glied & P. Smith (Eds.), *Oxford Handbook on Health Economics* (pp. 837–869). Oxford: Oxford University Press.

van Doorslaer, E., Wagstaff, A., Bleichrodt, H., Calonge, S., Gerdtham, U.-G., Gerfin, M., ... Winkelhake, O. (1997). Income-related inequalities in health: some international comparisons. *Journal of Health Economics, 16*, 93–112.

Wagstaff, A., van Doorslaer, E., & Paci, P. (1991). On the measurement of horizontal inequity in the delivery of health care. *Journal of Health Economics, 10*, 169–205.

Wagstaff, A., van Doorslaer, E., & Watanabe, N. (2003). On decomposing the causes of health sector inequalities with an application to malnutrition inequalities in Vietnam. *Journal of Econometrics, 112*, 207–223.

Yitzhaki, S. (1983). On an extension of the Gini inequality index. *International Economic Review, 24*, 617–628.

ACCOUNTING FOR POPULATION CHANGE IN THE LONGITUDINAL ANALYSIS OF INCOME-RELATED HEALTH INEQUALITIES

Paul Allanson and Dennis Petrie

ABSTRACT

Longitudinal data are required to characterise and measure the dynamics of income-related health inequalities (IRHI). This chapter develops a framework to evaluate the impact of population changes on the level of cross-sectional IRHI over time and thereby provides further insight into how health inequalities develop or perpetuate themselves in a society. The approach is illustrated by an empirical analysis of the increase in IRHI in Great Britain between 1999 and 2004 using the British Household Panel Survey. The results imply that levels of IRHI would have been even higher in 2004 but for the entry of youths into the adult population and deaths, with these natural processes of population turnover serving to partially mask the increase in IRHI among the resident adult population over the five-year period. We conclude that a failure to take demographic changes into account may lead to erroneous conclusions on the effectiveness of policies designed to tackle health inequalities.

Keywords: Income-related health inequality; population change; longitudinal data; Great Britain

JEL classifications: D63; I14

INTRODUCTION

The majority of work on income-related health inequality (IRHI) and its determinants has been conducted in static terms by providing (repeated) cross-sectional analyses based on 'snapshots' of the joint distribution of health and income at one or more points in time (see O'Donnell, Wagstaff, Van Doorslaer, & Lindelow, 2008). However this static approach by its very nature does not fully reveal the dynamic processes underlying the co-evolution of health and incomes over time, which may also be of interest from a welfare or policy perspective. For example, if half the population of a country is always poor and sick while half is rich and healthy then it will not be possible to determine whether it is always the same individuals in each category and hence whether IRHI arises from chronic or persistent social disadvantage as opposed to transitory episodes of both poverty and sickness, where the former state might be deemed less socially acceptable than the latter. Moreover, longitudinal or follow-up methods are required to determine the incidence and effectiveness of interventions designed to tackle such health inequalities in the population, where chronic inequalities might call for policies to tackle the structural problems that trap some individuals in deprivation and ill-health while transitory episodes might demand measures such as improvements in acute health services or temporary welfare assistance.

The inherent limitations of a static approach have led to the emergence of a small but growing literature that employs longitudinal data to characterise and measure the dynamics of income-related health inequalities. In particular, the pioneering paper by Jones and López Nicolás (2004) proposes an index of 'health-related income mobility', modelled on Shorrocks' (1978) income mobility index, that measures the extent to which IRHI is greater or smaller in the short run than in the long run. The ensuing empirical literature has revealed that IRHI, unlike income inequality (see Wodon & Yitzhaki, 2003), is typically greater the longer the time span over which the measurements are taken, with Allanson, Gerdtham, and Petrie (2010) demonstrating that this is likely to be explained by the stronger positive association between permanent disparities in income and health across individuals than between short-run changes in the income and health of individuals.

A second main use of longitudinal data has been to explore the evolution of health inequalities over time, where an understanding of the sources of changes in IRHI is critical for policy design and evaluation purposes. For example, Boyle, Norman, and Popham (2009) employ transition matrices to examine the impact of mobility on health inequalities and show that inequalities may widen even if the health of those who change (deprivation) class lies between that of the class they left and the class they joined. A starting point for understanding such findings is provided by the observation in Allanson et al. (2010) that any change in IRHI in a fixed population must arise from some combination of changes in health outcomes (i.e. 'health mobility') and changes in individuals' positions in the income distribution (i.e. 'income (rank) mobility'). Accordingly, they provide a decomposition of the change in the health concentration index (CI) between two periods into indices of income-related health mobility (IRHM) and health-related income mobility (HRIM). The IRHM index reflects the extent to which health changes are biased in favour of those with initially high or low incomes (progressivity), with its size also depending on the scale of health changes. The HRIM index captures the effect of the reshuffling of individuals within the income distribution, which may be expected to exacerbate IRHI since those who move up the income ranking tend to be healthier in the final period than those who move down.

Allanson and Petrie (2012) subsequently establish the normative implications of this type of decomposition by embedding the change in IRHI within a broader analysis of the change in the health of the population. In particular, they note that evaluating IRHM on the basis of the social weights associated with individuals' initial income ranks gives greater weight to the health prospects of those that start with lower income, where this asymmetric treatment of individuals may be justified on the grounds that the initially poor are disadvantaged to the extent that they face a worse lottery of future health possibilities than those who are better off. They further note that the same decomposition procedure may also be used to analyse the change in other rank-dependent IRHI indices, and with IRHI measured with respect to health shortfalls rather than attainments. The choice of health inequality measure is shown to imply a particular vertical equity judgement, which may be expressed in terms of a health inequality equivalence criterion that specifies how a given change in population health should be distributed so as to leave health inequality unchanged from its initial value (see Allanson & Petrie, 2013a, for further discussion).

Petrie, Allanson, and Gerdtham (2011) extend the original decomposition to take account of deaths, arguing that it is important to take mortality into account for the evaluation of policies that tackle health inequalities since a failure to do so would ignore perhaps the most important of all health outcomes. For example, a constant or even increasing cross-sectional population CI may not be a bad outcome if it is a result of efforts to keep the poor and sick alive for longer than previously may have been the case. Moreover, simply reweighting the sample to account for mortality-related attrition does not solve the problem as those who die between the two periods experience the most extreme health change possible and are thus significantly different from those with similar initial characteristics but who stay alive.

More generally, policy makers may wish to know how all sources of population change, including not only deaths but also births (or reaching some specified minimum age), immigration and emigration,[1] contribute to observed changes in the level of health inequalities within the population. In the next section, we develop a generalised framework for the analysis of changes in cross-sectional IRHI that allows for multiple sources of population entry and exit. This methodology is used in the third section to explore the contribution of population change to changes in cross-sectional health inequality using data from the British Household Panel Survey (BHPS). The final section concludes with a discussion of how the framework might be used to provide the basis for an extended analysis of the socio-economic determinants of IRHI change.

METHODS TO ACCOUNT FOR CHANGES IN IRHI USING LONGITUDINAL DATA

Let Ω_s^o and Ω_f^o be the overall populations of interest in some initial period s and final period f, where we are concerned about accounting for the difference in IRHI between these two populations (see Fig. 1). Ω_s^o is composed of $K(s)$ groups, where the non-mover population group Ω_s^1 consists of both the continuing population sub-group Ω_s^a who are still part of the population in the final period and the non-survivor population sub-group Ω_s^d who

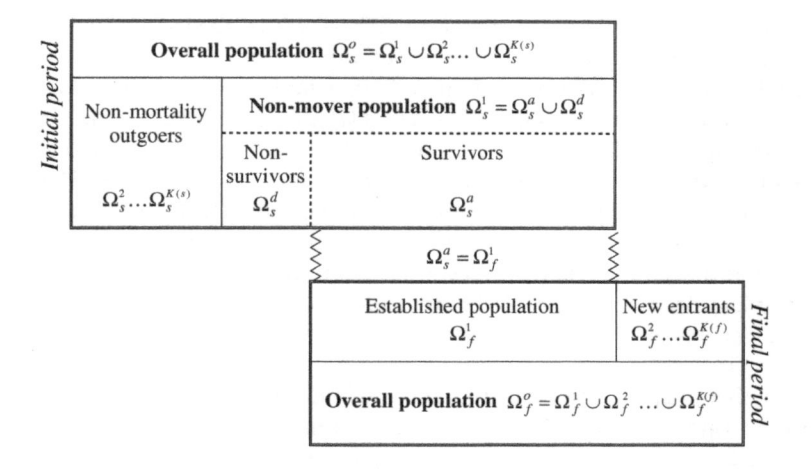

Accounting for the Impact of Population Change on IRHI 197

```
┌─────────────┬──────────────────────────────────────────────────────────┐
│             │ Overall population  $\Omega_s^o = \Omega_s^1 \cup \Omega_s^2 \cup \ldots \cup \Omega_s^{K(s)}$ │
│Initial period├──────────────┬───────────────────────────────────────────┤
│             │ Non-mortality│ Non-mover population $\Omega_s^1 = \Omega_s^a \cup \Omega_s^d$ │
│             │ outgoers     ├──────────────┬────────────────────────────┤
│             │              │ Non-         │ Survivors                  │
│             │              │ survivors    │                            │
│             │ $\Omega_s^2 \ldots \Omega_s^{K(s)}$ │ $\Omega_s^d$ │ $\Omega_s^a$ │
└─────────────┴──────────────┴──────────────┴────────────────────────────┘
                             $\Omega_s^a = \Omega_f^1$
              ┌──────────────────────────────┬──────────────────┐
              │ Established population       │ New entrants     │
              │ $\Omega_f^1$                 │ $\Omega_f^2 \ldots \Omega_f^{K(f)}$ │ Final period
              ├──────────────────────────────┴──────────────────┤
              │ Overall population $\Omega_f^o = \Omega_f^1 \cup \Omega_f^2 \cup \ldots \cup \Omega_f^{K(f)}$ │
              └─────────────────────────────────────────────────┘
```

{IRHI in final period within the overall population Ω_f^o} *less*

{IRHI in initial period within the overall population Ω_s^o}

=

{IRHI in final period within the overall population Ω_f^o} *less*

{IRHI in final period within the established population Ω_f^1}

+

{IRHI in final period within the established population Ω_f^1} *less*

{IRHI in initial period within the non-mover population Ω_s^1}

+

{IRHI in initial period within the non-mover population Ω_s^1} *less*

{IRHI in initial period within the overall population Ω_s^o}

Fig. 1. Decomposition of Difference in Cross-Sectional IRHI by Population Group.

die between the two periods; while the remaining groups $\Omega_s^2 \ldots \Omega_s^{K(s)}$ in Ω_s^o exit the population through other ways before the final period. Similarly, Ω_f^o is composed of $K(f)$ groups, where Ω_f^1 is the established population consisting of all those who were also part of the population in the initial period – and is therefore equal to Ω_s^a – while the remaining groups $\Omega_f^2 \ldots \Omega_f^{K(f)}$ are new entrants to the population.

In this context, Allanson et al. (2010) simply consider the change in IRHI in the continuing population $\Omega_s^a \equiv \Omega_f^1$ due to morbidity and income rank changes, while Petrie et al. (2011) also take deaths into account by providing an analysis of the difference between final period IRHI within the established population Ω_f^1 and initial period IRHI within the non-mover population Ω_s^1. In this section we further develop the methodology to take into account other sources of population change in order to provide a complete decomposition of the difference between IRHI in the final and initial periods within the overall populations Ω_f^o and Ω_s^o (see the bottom of Fig. 1).

For this purpose, we identify the contribution of entry as the difference between final period IRHI within the overall and established population groups, Ω_f^o and Ω_f^1 respectively. Similarly we identify the contribution of non-mortality exit as the difference between initial period IRHI within the non-mover and overall population groups, Ω_s^1 and Ω_s^o respectively. By definition, the resultant measures are static in nature since they do not allow for the possible effects of entry/exit on the health and income positions of individuals within the established/non-mover population. For example, the level of IRHI observed within the established population group in the final period will not in general be the same as that which would have existed in the absence of entry, although it may provide a reasonable first approximation to this unobserved counter-factual. In principle it may be possible to model and thereby allow for the induced effects of entry and non-mortality exit but this lies beyond the scope of the current chapter.

Accounting for Population Entry and Attrition

Our approach to analysing the contribution of population change to differences in IRHI is based on the Yitzhaki (1994) decomposition of the Gini coefficient by population sub-group. Let h_{it} and y_{it} represent the health and income respectively of individual i in period t ($t = s, f$). The mean health of the overall population in period t will be denoted by $\bar{h}_t^o$ and that of population group k ($k = 1, \ldots K(t)$) by $\bar{h}_t^k$. Thus if $p_t^k = n_t^k/n_t^o$ is the proportion of the overall population in the kth group then their share of total health will be $q_t^k = p_t^k \bar{h}_t^k / \bar{h}_t^o$. $F_k(y_t)$ will denote the cumulative distribution of income within population group k, with $F_o(y_t)$ being the overall cumulative income distribution. The mean fractional rank of group k within $F_k(y_t)$ is equal to

$\overline{F}_k^k(y_t) = 0.5$ by definition, while within the overall income distribution $F_o(y_t)$ it is equal to $\overline{F}_o^k(y_t)$.

Following Yitzhaki (1994), the overall CI in period t may be decomposed into[2]

$$CI(\Omega_t^o, h_t, F_o(y_t)) = CI(\Omega_t^o, \overline{h}_t^k, \overline{F}_o^k(y_t)) + \sum_{k=1}^{K(t)} q_t^k CI(\Omega_t^k, h_t, F_o(y_t)) \tag{1}$$

where $CI(\Omega_t^o, h_t, F_o(y_t)) = 2\text{cov}(\Omega_t^o, h_t, F_o(y_t))/\overline{h}_t^o$ is defined over the overall population Ω_t^o as twice the covariance between health and income rank normalised by average health; while $CI(\Omega_t^o, \overline{h}_t^k, \overline{F}_o^k(y_t))$ and $CI(\Omega_t^k, h_t, F_o(y_t))$ provide measures of between-group and within-group inequality respectively to be defined further below. Note that Eq. (1) exactly decomposes overall IRHI into a between-group component and a weighted sum of within-group components with weights equal to group shares in total health.

We first consider the contribution of entrants to IRHI in the final period, which we define as the difference in IRHI between the overall and established populations, Ω_f^o and Ω_f^1 respectively. Let $CI(\Omega_f^k, h_f, F_k(y_f)) = 2\text{cov}(\Omega_f^k, h_f, F_k(y_f))/\overline{h}_f^k$ be the intra-group CI of group k ($k = 1, \ldots K(f)$), which is defined over the kth population group Ω_f^k and is based on the fractional ranks of group k individuals in the group k income distribution $F_k(y_f)$. Thus $CI(\Omega_f^1, h_f, F_1(y_f))$ is the intra-group CI of the established population Ω_f^1 and the contribution of new entrants to IRHI in the final period can be written using Eq. (1) as

$$\begin{aligned} D^E &= CI(\Omega_f^o, h_f, F_o(y_f)) - CI(\Omega_f^1, h_f, F_1(y_f)) \\ &= CI\left(\Omega_f^o, \overline{h}_f^k, \overline{F}_o^k(y_f)\right) + \left\{\sum_{k=2}^{K(f)} q_f^k (CI(\Omega_f^k, h_f, F_o(y_f)) - CI(\Omega_f^1, h_f, F_o(y_f)))\right\} \\ &\quad + \left\{CI(\Omega_f^1, h_f, F_o(y_f)) - CI(\Omega_f^1, h_f, F_1(y_f))\right\} \\ &= D_B^E + D_W^E + D_R^E \end{aligned} \tag{2}$$

where the total difference in IRHI due to entry, D^E, is given as the sum of three factors, D_B^E, D_W^E and D_R^E, to be discussed in turn below.

First, IRHI will differ due to between-group IRHI

$$D_B^E = CI(\Omega_f^o, \overline{h}_f^k, \overline{F}_o^k(y_f)) = \frac{2\text{cov}(\Omega_f^o, \overline{h}_f^k, \overline{F}_o^k(y_f))}{\overline{h}_f^o} = 2\sum_{k=1}^{K(f)} p_f^k \frac{(\overline{h}_f^k - \overline{h}_f^o)(\overline{F}_o^k(y_f) - \overline{F}_o^o(y_f))}{\overline{h}_f^o} \tag{3}$$

That is, D_B^E is defined as twice the covariance between the mean health of each group and their mean fractional rank in the income distribution of the overall population, standardised by mean overall health.[3] D_B^E will equal zero if all groups have either the same level of mean health or the same average rank in the overall income distribution. D_B^E may be either positive or negative depending on the definition of the groups, even if there is a positive relationship between income and health within each population group. In particular, if considering IRHI in an adult population where entry consists largely of young healthy adults who are either in low-paid unskilled/junior jobs or unemployed then it may be that the mean health of new entrants will be above that of the established adult population whereas their mean income rank will be below average. In these circumstances, entry will result in a negative value of D_B^E due to the differences between group means, implying lower levels of IRHI than otherwise would have been the case holding all other factors constant.

Second, IRHI will differ due to differences between the level of IRHI within each entrant group and that within the established population

$$D_W^E = \sum_{k=2}^{K(f)} q_f^k (CI(\Omega_f^k, h_f, F_o(y_f)) - CI(\Omega_f^1, h_f, F_o(y_f)))$$

$$= \sum_{k=2}^{K(f)} q_f^k \left(2 \sum_{i \in \Omega_f^k} \frac{(h_{if} - \overline{h}_f^k)(F_o(y_{if}) - \overline{F}_o^k(y_f))}{n_f^k \overline{h}_f^k} - 2 \sum_{i \in \Omega_f^1} \frac{(h_{if} - \overline{h}_f^1)(F_o(y_{if}) - \overline{F}_o^1(y_f))}{n_f^1 \overline{h}_f^1} \right)$$

$$= \sum_{k=2}^{K(f)} q_f^k \left(\frac{2\text{cov}(\Omega_f^k, h_f, F_o(y_f))}{\overline{h}_f^k} - \frac{2\text{cov}(\Omega_f^1, h_f, F_o(y_f))}{\overline{h}_f^1} \right) = \sum_{k=2}^{K(f)} q_f^k P_f^k \quad (4)$$

where $CI(\Omega_f^k, h_f, F_o(y_f))$ is interpreted as the within-group CI for group k ($k = 1, \ldots K(f)$), which is defined over population group k (as for the intra-group CI) but is based on the fractional ranks of group k individuals in the income distribution of the overall population $F_o(y_f)$ not $F_k(y_f)$. Thus, holding between-group IRHI fixed, the contribution of each entrant group to IRHI is given as the product of: (1) a 'scale' effect q_f^k equal to the health share of the entrant group in the overall population; (2) a 'progressivity' index P_f^k equal to the difference between within-group IRHI in the entrant and established population groups. For example, entry of young healthy adults into low-paid jobs or unemployment might be expected to result in a negative value of D_W^E, implying lower levels of IRHI than otherwise would have been the case, due to the homogeneity of the entrant group relative to the established population, with the size of this equalising effect proportional to the entrants' share of overall population health.

The within-group difference index D_W^E can be further decomposed if we follow Yitzhaki (1994) in expressing each within-group CI as the product of a 'pure' intra-group CI and an overlapping index

$$D_W^E = \sum_{k=2}^{K(f)} q_f^k(O_f^k \ CI(\Omega_f^k, h_f, F_k(y_f)) - O_f^1 \ CI(\Omega_f^1, h_f, F_1(y_f))) \qquad (5)$$

where $CI(\Omega_f^k, h_f, F_k(y_f))$ is the intra-group measure of IRHI defined above, the overall overlapping index O_f^k is equal to

$$O_f^k = \sum_{j=1}^{K(f)} p_f^j \ O_f^{jk} = \sum_{j=1}^{K(f)} p_f^j \frac{CI(\Omega_f^k, h_f, F_j(y_f))}{CI(\Omega_f^k, h_f, F_k(y_f))}; \quad k=1,\ldots K(f) \qquad (6)$$

and the pairwise index O_f^{jk} may be interpreted as a measure of the degree to which incomes in group j are included in the income range of group k. In other words, each O_f^{jk} measures the degree of 'overlapping' of group j by group k, where overlapping should be thought of as the inverse of the sociological concept of stratification,[4] and the overall overlapping index for population group k, O_f^k, is given as the population-weighted average of these indices.

We note here that if expected health is a strictly increasing function of income within group k then O_f^{jk} will be non-negative, where this follows from the properties of the concentration curve as set out in Yitzhaki (2003, pp. 297–298).[5] Moreover, if this condition holds then the following four properties of O_f^{jk} can readily be inferred from the results presented in Yitzhaki (1994). First, O_f^{jk} is an increasing function of the fraction of group j that is located in the income range of group k. In particular, O_f^{jk} will take a value of zero when there is no overlap, which will be the case if there is perfect stratification in the sense of Lasswell (1965), since the ranks of members of the k'th group within the income distribution of group j will all be identical. Whereas O_f^{jk} will equal one if the income distributions of the two groups are identical, that is $F_j(y_f) = F_k(y_f)$ implying that $O_f^{kk} = 1$ by definition. Thus, $CI(\Omega_f^k, h_f, F_o(y_f)) = p_f^k CI(\Omega_f^k, h_f, F_k(y_f))$ if there is perfect stratification whereas $CI(\Omega_f^k, h_f, F_o(y_f)) = CI(\Omega_f^k, h_f, F_k(y_f))$ if the income distributions of the various groups are all identical, where the latter condition further implies that the within-group difference index D_W^E will differ from zero solely due to differences in the pure intra-group CIs. Second, holding the fraction of group j that is located in the income range of group k constant, O_f^{jk} will be larger the closer the incomes of group j lie to the level of income associated with mean health in group k, taking a maximum value when all the incomes in group j are concentrated at this point in the income distribution of group k. Third, this maximum value is unbounded from above if $CI(\Omega_f^k, h_f, F_k(y_f))$ is non-zero.[6] Fourth, higher values of O_f^{jk} will tend to be associated with lower values of O_f^{kj}, since the more group j is included in the income distribution of group k, the less of the income distribution of k is likely to lie in the range of j.[7] In short, if $O_f^{jk} > 1$ and $O_f^{kj} < 1$ then it may be said that the income distribution of group k encompasses that of group j, whereas if both values are less than one then this implies that the two income distributions form more or less separate strata.

Clearly, O_f^k and the intra-group IRHI index $CI(\Omega_f^k, h_f, F_k(y_f))$ are not independent terms. However the two indices do provide different insights. In particular, O_f^k is sensitive to the degree of inclusion of the income distribution of the overall population within that of population group k but is invariant to affine transformations of the health distribution of group k, whereas $CI(\Omega_f^k, h_f, F_k(y_f))$ is sensitive to the socio-economic gradient in health but is invariant to ordering-preserving transformations of the income distribution within the group. Thus there is value in reporting both O_f^k and $CI(\Omega_f^k, h_f, F_k(y_f))$, not just the measure of within-group IRHI $CI(\Omega_f^k, h_f, F_o(y_f))$. For example, the further decomposition may be used to explore in more detail the supposition made above that the entry of young adults will lead to lower levels of IRHI in the overall population because of lower levels of within-group IRHI. First, the assumption of a relatively shallow socio-economic gradient in the health of entrants implies that the intra-group CI of entrants $CI(\Omega_f^2, h_f, F_2(y_f))$ will be less than that of the established population $CI(\Omega_f^1, h_f, F_1(y_f))$, which will tend to lower IRHI all other things equal. Moreover, this equalising effect is likely to be reinforced to the extent that the incomes earned by entrants are concentrated in the lower half of the income distribution of the established population, since this will imply that the overall overlapping index of the established population O_f^1 will be greater than that of the entrant group O_f^2 and may even be greater than one if the income distribution of the established population is encompassing.[8]

Accounting for the Impact of Population Change on IRHI

Finally, D_R^E may be interpreted as a re-ranking index

$$D_R^E = CI(\Omega_f^1, h_f, F_o(y_f)) - CI(\Omega_f^1, h_f, F_1(y_f)) = (O_f^1 - 1) \, CI(\Omega_f^1, h_f, F_1(y_f)) \quad (7)$$

which will equal zero if the income ranks of individuals in the established population are the same in their own group as in the overall population, which will be the case if the income distribution of the new entrants is identical to that of the established population. In general, D_R^E may be either positive or negative with this depending on whether $O_f^1 < 1$ or $O_f^1 > 1$. For example, if entry consists largely of adults with either low-paid or no employment then O_f^1 may be either greater or less than one, as discussed above, and re-ranking may therefore be associated with either higher or lower levels of IRHI all other things equal.

Turning next to the impact of non-mortality exit on initial period IRHI then this may simply be thought of as the opposite of entry on final period IRHI. Hence, we obtain the following decomposition of the difference between initial period IRHI in the non-mover and overall populations, Ω_s^1 and Ω_s^O respectively

$$D^X = CI(\Omega_s^1, h_s, F_1(y_s)) - CI(\Omega_s^o, h_s, F_o(y_s))$$
$$= -CI(\Omega_s^o, \overline{h}_s^k, \overline{F}_o^k(y_s)) - \left\{ \sum_{k=2}^{K(s)} q_s^k (CI(\Omega_s^k, h_s, F_o(y_s)) - CI(\Omega_s^1, h_s, F_o(y_s))) \right\}$$
$$- (O_s^1 - 1) \, CI(\Omega_s^1, h_s, F_1(y_s))$$
$$= D_B^X + D_W^X + D_R^X \quad (8)$$

where D_B^X, D_W^X and D_R^X are defined conformably with D_B^E, D_W^E and D_R^E up to a change in sign. Thus, for example, emigration of retirees (from the United Kingdom) might be expected to exacerbate IRHI to the extent that these form a relatively prosperous group who are likely to be relatively healthy for their age but, nevertheless, with relatively low health on average compared to the initial population as a whole. Thus D_B^X would be positive, implying higher levels of IRHI as a result of their departure, as would be D_W^X due to the homogeneity of both health outcomes and income levels among emigrants relative to the non-mover population, while the re-ranking effect D_R^X may be either negative or positive depending on whether the income distribution of the non-mover population is encompassing or not.

Incorporation into a Complete Analysis of Changes in Cross-Sectional IRHI

Having established a methodology to identify the impact on IRHI of entry and non-mortality exit, we next incorporate our new measures into a full analysis of the sources of difference between the levels of IRHI in Ω_s^o and Ω_f^o. Our preferred approach makes use of the Petrie et al. (2011) decomposition, which treats death first and foremost as a form of health mobility rather than as just another source of population exit. Assigning the dead a health status of zero, the total difference in IRHI between the populations Ω_f^1 and Ω_s^1 may be decomposed as follows

$$\begin{aligned} M &= CI(\Omega_f^1, h_f, F_1(y_f)) - CI(\Omega_s^1, h_s, F_1(y_s)) \\ &= \left\{ CI(\Omega_f^1, h_f, F_1(y_f)) - CI(\Omega_s^1, h_f, F_1(y_s)) \right\} \\ &\quad + \left\{ CI(\Omega_s^1, h_f, F_1(y_s)) - CI(\Omega_s^1, h_s, F_1(y_s)) \right\} = M_R + M_H \end{aligned} \qquad (9)$$

where, following Petrie et al. (2011), M_H and M_R may be interpreted as IRHM and HRIM indices respectively, to be discussed further below. [9]

M_H captures the effect on IRHI of differences in relative health changes, due to both morbidity changes and mortality, between individuals with different levels of initial income. M_H will be positive if health changes are disequalising, which will be the case if the poor either enjoy a smaller share of net health gains or suffer a larger share of net heath losses compared to their initial share of health. M_H in turn depends on the progressivity and scale of health changes

$$M_H = \left\{ CI(\Omega_s^1, \Delta h_{f-s}, F_1(y_s)) - CI(\Omega_s^1, h_s, F_1(y_s)) \right\} \left\{ \frac{\sum_{i \in \Omega_s^1} \Delta h_{i,f-s}}{\sum_{i \in \Omega_s^1} h_{if}} \right\} = P_H q_H \qquad (10)$$

where $\Delta h_{f-s} = h_f - h_s$ is the change in health between the two periods; and $CI(\Omega_s^1, \Delta h_{f-s}, F_1(y_s))$ may be interpreted as the intra-group CI of health changes, which is defined over the non-mover population group Ω_s^1 and based on the fractional income ranks of non-movers within their own group in the initial period. To identify the separate effects of health changes due to morbidity changes (MB) and mortality (MT), M_H may be further broken down to yield

$$M_H = M_H^{MB} + M_H^{MT} = P_H^{MB} q_H^{MB} + P_H^{MT} q_H^{MT}$$

$$= \left\{ CI(\Omega_s^1, \Delta h_{f-s}^{MB}, F_1(y_s)) - CI(\Omega_s^1, h_s, F_1(y_s)) \right\} \left\{ \frac{\sum_{i \in \Omega_s^1} \Delta h_{i,f-s}^{MB}}{\sum_{i \in \Omega_s^1} h_{if}} \right\}$$

$$+ \left\{ CI(\Omega_s^1, \Delta h_{f-s}^{MT}, F_1(y_s)) - CI(\Omega_s^1, h_s, F_1(y_s)) \right\} \left\{ \frac{\sum_{i \in \Omega_s^1} \Delta h_{i,f-s}^{MT}}{\sum_{i \in \Omega_s^1} h_{if}} \right\} \quad (11)$$

where $\Delta h_{f-s} = \Delta h_{f-s}^{MB} + \Delta h_{f-s}^{MT}$, with Δh_{f-s}^{MB} set equal to the morbidity change for survivors and zero otherwise, and Δh_{f-s}^{MT} defined as the loss of health due to mortality for those who die and zero otherwise.

The HRIM index M_R may also be subject to further analysis to yield

$$\begin{aligned} M_R &= \left\{ CI(\Omega_f^1, h_f, F_1(y_f)) - CI(\Omega_s^1, h_f, F_1(y_s)) \right\} \\ &= \left\{ CI(\Omega_f^1, h_f, F_1(y_f)) - CI(\Omega_s^a, h_f, F_a(y_s)) \right\} \\ &\quad + \left\{ CI(\Omega_s^a, h_f, F_a(y_s)) - CI(\Omega_s^1, h_f, F_1(y_s)) \right\} \\ &= M_R^a + M_R^d \end{aligned} \quad (12)$$

which shows that it captures the effect on IRHI of income re-ranking not only due to the re-shuffling of survivors (NB : $\Omega_f^1 = \Omega_s^a$) within the income distribution, M_R^a, but also due to the loss of individuals from the population as a result of death, M_R^d. The former may be expected to exacerbate IRHI, as argued above, while the latter can be rewritten in the manner of Eq. (8) as

$$\begin{aligned} M_R^d &= - CI\left(\Omega_s^1, \overline{h}_f^v, \overline{F}_1^v(y_s)\right) - \left\{ CI(\Omega_s^a, h_f, F_1(y_s)) - CI(\Omega_s^a, h_f, F_a(y_s)) \right\} \\ &= -2(1-p_s^a)(\overline{F}_1^a(y_s) - \overline{F}_1^d(y_s)) - (O_f^a - 1) \, CI(\Omega_s^a, h_f, F_a(y_s)) \end{aligned} \quad (13)$$

where $\overline{h}_f^v$ is the mean health of population sub-group v ($v = a, d$) in the final period f, $\overline{F}_1^v(y_s)$ is the corresponding mean fractional rank in the income distribution of the non-mover population group Ω_s^1, there is no within-group term because non-survivors' share of health in the final period is zero by definition, and $O_f^a = CI(\Omega_s^a, h_f, F_1(y_s))/CI(\Omega_s^a, h_f, F_a(y_s))$ is to be interpreted as an overlapping term. Here the contribution of the between-group IRHI term will be negative if the average income rank of survivors in the initial period is higher than that of non-survivors, which is consistent with the observed socio-economic gradient in mortality rates. However this condition is not sufficient to ensure that M_R^d will be negative as the re-ranking term may be positive if the overlapping term O_f^a is less than one such that $(O_f^a - 1) < 0$. M_R^d will be zero if death is unrelated to initial income.

Summary

To summarise, our preferred decomposition of the change in cross-sectional IRHI between the two periods is given as

$$CI(\Omega_f^o, h_f, F_o(y_f)) - CI(\Omega_s^0, h_s, F_o(y_s)) = D^E + M + D^X \\ = \{D_B^E + D_W^E + D_R^E\} + \{M_R + M_H\} + \{D_B^X + D_W^X + D_R^X\} \quad (14)$$

It should be noted that this decomposition is path dependent in the sense that it is determined by the order in which the various factors are taken into account in the analysis. It follows that the particular decomposition pathway represented by Eq. (15) is not unique: for example, mortality could be treated as just another form of population exit in the decomposition of M with the fixed-population decomposition of Allanson et al. (2010) used to analyse the residual change in IRHI between the two periods. One might in principle seek to overcome this indeterminacy through the use of a 'Shapley value' average of all possible decomposition pathways (see Shorrocks, 2013), but in practice many of these pathways will prove impossible to evaluate due to data limitations.[10] Our preference for Eq. (14) is further based on the intelligibility of many of the components identified in the decomposition equation, particularly in relation to the treatment of the impact of morbidity changes and mortality on a common basis.

EMPIRICAL ANALYSIS

We use our methodology to explore the contribution of population change to changes in cross-sectional IRHI using data from the BHPS (University of Essex, Institute for Social and Economic Research, 2010). Established in 1991, the BHPS 'is primarily designed to be representative of all persons who are resident in Britain at multiple time points corresponding to the waves of data collection' (Lynn et al., 2006) and provides information on household organisation, employment, accommodation, tenancy, income and wealth, housing, health, socio-economic values, residential mobility, marital and relationship history, social support, and individual and household demographics. It thereby constitutes one of the main tools for understanding social and economic change at the individual and household level in Britain, with data from the survey integrated into both the European Community Household Panel and the Cross National Equivalent File (CNEF) for the purpose of international comparisons.

Sample Definition

The original sample was intended to be representative of all persons resident in private households in Great Britain (England, Scotland (south of the Caledonian Canal) and Wales) in 1991, with 13,840 persons of all ages identified in wave 1 as original sample members (OSMs) at 8,167 selected addresses (Lynn et al., 2006). In each subsequent wave, the potentially eligible sample includes three categories of members: (i) OSMs consisting of members of the wave 1 households and their natural children born after the start of the study; (ii) temporary sample members (TSMs) who are persons currently resident with an OSM, having formed a household with them after the start of the study; (iii) permanent sample members (PSMs) who have had a child with an OSM since the start of the study, whether or not they continue to live with either the OSM or child. However it should be noted that potential sample members who are resident outside of Great Britain at a given wave are deemed to be out of scope and therefore ineligible for interview unless and until they return. Moreover, potential sample members will also be ineligible for interview if they are resident in institutions where they cannot be interviewed; and are otherwise deemed inaccessible if they have adamantly refused to (continue to) take part in the panel at an earlier wave, or cannot be traced, or are too ill or elderly to be interviewed with no proxy possible. By construction, the BHPS is not designed to provide representative coverage of new immigrants since samples after wave 1 exclude, inter alia, persons in households where all the household members were resident outside of Britain at the time of wave 1.

Our analysis is restricted to waves 9 and 14 of the BHPS, 1999 and 2004, by the availability of data to construct our preferred measure of health, which is defined in terms of Quality Adjusted Life Years (QALYs) and derived from the responses to the SF-36 questionnaire using the SF-6D preference-based algorithm (Brazier, Roberts, & Deverill, 2002). The BHPS was boosted in wave 9 by the recruitment of new extension samples in Scotland and Wales, but these are not incorporated into the study given concerns about whether these independent samples can necessarily be assumed to represent the same population universe as the original sample. In particular, there may be reasons to doubt the comparability of the 1999 health and income data from these samples given that this was the initial wave of both these extension panels (see Frick, Goebel, Schechtman, Wagner, & Yitzhaki, 2006 for discussion). Moreover, attrition rates over the first few waves of these new panels may be expected to be higher than in the established original wave 1 panel over the same period. Thus the analysis is restricted to the original wave 1 sample to avoid any potential artefacts that might otherwise arise.

The BHPS provides cross-sectional respondent weights for the original wave 1 sample at each subsequent wave. These weights cover all individuals giving a full interview in a particular wave and allow use of the data in cross-sectional analyses by adjusting for attrition up to the latest wave, including new entrants and adjusting for within household non-response (see Taylor, Brice, Buck, & Prentice-Lane, 2010). However the use of these cross-sectional weights in the study leads to a further complication in that individuals who were present in both waves of the panel are assigned a different weight in each wave thereby giving rise to another potential source of difference between the cross-sectional estimates of IRHI in these two periods. To ensure that the decomposition is exact we include a further term in the empirical decomposition procedure that is equal to the difference between estimates of the intra-group CI of the established population in the final period using final and initial period weights. This reweighting correction specifically allows for changes in the relative weights of individuals within the group of survivors due to the reweighting procedure, but the reweighting will also have an effect through the estimated population share of the established population group in the final period.

The measure of individual income used in the study is equivalised household income, which takes into account the number of adults and children in the household using the McClements equivalence scale (Taylor et al., 2010). To prevent outlier income values exerting undue influence, we follow common practice when using the BHPS (see, e.g. Jenkins & van Kerm, 2011; Jones & López Nicolás, 2004) by excluding individuals from a particular wave if their equivalised household income fell in the top 1% or bottom 1% of the distribution in that wave. Sample weights were used throughout the analysis with these being given by adjusted BHPS cross-sectional respondent weights for each wave, where the adjustments were made using inverse probability weights (see Wooldridge, 2002) to allow for missing health data (see Petrie et al. (2011) for further discussion). Standard errors for all inequality and mobility measures were generated using a bootstrap procedure in which re-sampling was carried out by cluster (Primary Sampling Unit), rather than at the individual level, within each stratification class, reflecting the sample design. In particular, bootstrap standard errors for the mobility measures will reflect the correlation of both health and income between panel interviews for those individuals observed in both waves.[11]

Basic Descriptive Statistics

The trimmed samples comprise observations on 8,503 individuals in 1999 and 7,717 in 2004, of whom 6,188 were present in both waves. Of the 8,503 individuals in 1999, 1,939 failed to provide a full interview in 2004, despite there being no record of their death, among which we further identify two categories of exit: (1) 507 individuals who were known to have left the population of interest and were therefore ineligible for interview because they were either resident abroad or institutionalised or, in the case of TSMs, no longer resident with an eligible OSM (genuine outgoers); (2) 1,432 individuals who were either unable or unwilling to give a full interview or who were unable to be contacted for whatever reason (panel attrition group). Of the weighted sample in 1999, 21.3% were subject to some form of non-mortality related exit, with the population shares of the two exit groups equal to 4.3% and 17.0% respectively. Of the remainder of the sample in 1999, 376 are known to have died by 2004, implying a death rate of 7.1% over the five-year time span in the non-mover population, with the surviving 6,188 going on to represent the established population in 2004. With regard to entry in 2004, we distinguish three categories: (1) 600 individuals who received a full interview in 2004 who were ineligible for full interview in 1999 because they were younger than 16 at the time (youth entrants); (2) 555 individuals who received a full interview in 2004 having otherwise been ineligible for full interview in 1999 or any preceding wave (adult entrants); (3) 374 individuals who received a full interview in 2004 but not in 1999 despite having either provided a full interview in an earlier wave or been eligible to do so as an adult OSM (intermittent respondents). Of the weighted sample in 2004, 82.7% had provided a full interview in 1999 with the population shares of the three entry groups equal to 7.9%, 4.7% and 4.8% respectively.

Table 1 provides basic descriptive statistics on the health and income variables used in the analysis. The health variable is bounded in the unit interval with full health corresponding to a value of one, the lowest possible health utility of anyone alive being equal to 0.301, and with death assigned a score of zero. The average cross-sectional QALY score was 0.800 in 1999 and only marginally lower in 2004. Incomes are reported in nominal terms because the analysis only involves relative income ranks at each point in time. The incomes of genuine outgoers in 1999 were both higher on average and more variable than those of either the non-mover population or the panel attrition group. Youth entrants had both lower and less variable incomes than other population groups in 2004 while the opposite was broadly true of adult entrants. However, the group with the highest income variability was intermittent respondents, with the interquartile range indicating the presence of significant numbers of such individuals with both very low and very high incomes.

Change in IRHI Analysis

Table 2 shows that cross-sectional IRHI was 0.02066 in 1999 and 0.02358 in 2004.[12] The remainder of the table provides the decomposition of the increase in cross-sectional IRHI of 0.00292 between the two years, where this difference is significantly different from zero at the 5% level. The table shows that the dominant factor accounting for this increase in IRHI was the disequalising effect of 0.00338 due to health and income mobility in the non-mover population. However, the contributions of entry and non-mortality exit were also large and significantly different from zero, being equal to −0.00218 and 0.00161 respectively, even though the net effect of these changes in panel membership was relatively small as the equalising contribution of the former was almost entirely offset by the disequalising impact of the latter. Finally, the reweighting correction of 0.00011 made a negligible difference, being both small and insignificant.

Taken at face value these results point to the importance of taking all sources of population change into account in the analysis of differences in cross-sectional IRHI between years given that such differences cannot simply be ascribed to the changing circumstances of the non-mover population. However these raw findings should be interpreted with some care due to the existence and treatment of panel attrition and intermittent respondents in the BHPS. We consider this issue below when looking in more detail at the various components of the decomposition.

Table 1. Basic Summary Statistics.

A. Health (QALY)	Sample Size	Popⁿ Share (%)	Mean	Standard Deviation	Lower Quartile	Median	Upper Quartile	Mean Rank
1999								
Overall population	8,503	100.0	0.80021	0.130	0.731	0.845	0.887	—
Non-mover population	6,564	78.7	0.79723	0.130	0.728	0.845	0.887	—
Genuine outgoers	1,432	4.3	0.82052	0.116	0.763	0.845	0.887	—
Panel attrition group	507	17.0	0.80884	0.134	0.738	0.852	0.894	—
2004								
Overall population	7,717	100.0	0.79774	0.129	0.727	0.845	0.887	—
Established population	6,188	82.7	0.79267	0.131	0.717	0.845	0.887	—
Youth entrants	600	7.9	0.84480	0.097	0.793	0.887	0.894	—
Adult entrants	555	4.7	0.81513	0.117	0.747	0.845	0.887	—
Intermittent respondents	374	4.8	0.79081	0.139	0.706	0.845	0.887	—
B. Income (£'000)								
1999								
Overall population	8,503	100.0	21.825	13.493	12.004	18.435	27.705	0.50000
Non-mover population	6,564	78.7	21.642	13.232	12.034	18.334	27.281	0.49770
Genuine outgoers	1,432	4.3	25.103	15.945	13.142	22.264	32.823	0.55851
Panel attrition group	507	17.0	21.846	13.915	11.625	18.109	28.162	0.49591
2004								
Overall population	7,717	100.0	24.361	13.879	14.120	21.341	30.939	0.50000
Established population	6,188	82.7	24.355	13.805	14.223	21.331	30.709	0.50033
Youth entrants	600	7.9	20.931	11.021	12.420	19.070	27.662	0.43545
Adult entrants	555	4.7	28.598	15.339	17.597	26.022	37.814	0.58846
Intermittent respondents	374	4.8	25.943	16.295	12.919	21.395	34.646	0.51359

Table 2. Overall Decomposition of Difference in Cross-Sectional IRHI.

			Share
Concentration index in 2004 within the overall population		0.02358***	
		0.00113	
Concentration index in 2004 within established population		0.02576***	
(*using 2004 cross-sectional weights*)		*0.00121*	
Concentration index in 2004 within established population		0.02565***	
(*using 1999 cross-sectional weights*)		*0.00117*	
Concentration index in 1999 within non-mover population		0.02227***	
		0.00119	
Concentration index in 1999 within the overall population		0.02066***	
		0.00109	
Overall difference in IRHI		0.00292**	100%
Of which due to:		*0.00123*	
New entrants in final period	D^E	−0.00218***	−74.6%
Of which due to:		*0.00043*	
Between-group IRHI	D^E_B	−0.00043***	−14.8%
		0.00013	
Differences in within-group IRHI	D^E_W	−0.00154***	−52.7%
		0.00040	
Re-ranking in established population	D^E_R	−0.00021***	−7.1%
		0.00007	
Re-weighting correction		0.00011	3.9%
		0.00042	
Health and income mobility in non-mover population	M	0.00338***	115.6%
Of which due to:		*0.00123*	
Income-related health mobility	M^H	0.03146***	1075.9%
		0.00218	
Health-related income mobility	M^R	−0.02808***	−960.3%
		0.00236	
Non-mortality-related exit from initial population	D^X	0.00161***	55.0%
Of which due to:		*0.00045*	
Between-group IRHI	D^X_B	−0.00013*	−4.3%
		0.00007	
Differences in within-group IRHI	D^X_W	0.00150***	51.2%
		0.00044	
Re-ranking in non-mover population	D^X_R	0.00024***	8.1%
		0.00007	

Source: Authors' calculations based on Eq. (14). Bootstrapped standard errors in italics based on 2,000 replications. Statistical significance of difference from zero at 1%, 5% and 10% levels are denoted by ***, ** and * respectively.

The Impact of Entry on IRHI in 2004

Table 2 also presents the further decomposition of the difference in IRHI due to entry, $D^E = -0.00218$, which shows that between-group IRHI, within-group differences and re-ranking were all estimated to have made an equalising contribution to the level of IRHI within the overall population in the final period, with significant contributions of −14.8%, −52.7% and −7.1% respectively to the overall difference in IRHI. Tables 3 and 4 provide the basis for a more thorough understanding of the factors underlying these components.

Table 3 provides a further decomposition of the between-group IRHI term D_B^E, which shows that the major contribution to the overall negative effect of −0.00043 was due to youth entrants. Youth entrants were significantly healthier on average than the overall population in the final period but had a lower income rank than average, such that their entry into the population led to an estimated reduction in the level of IRHI observed in 2004 of −0.00060 all other things equal. However this was partly offset by effect of the entry of adult entrants who made a significantly disequalising contribution of 0.00018 to D_B^E due to a combination of above-average

Table 3. Analysis of the Between-Group IRHI Term D_B^E.

			Population Share	Difference between Group and Overall Population Means	
				Health	Income rank
Between-group IRHI	D_B^E	−0.00043***			
Of which due to:		0.00013			
Established population		0.00000	0.82687***	−0.00506***	0.00033
		0.00002	*0.00422*	*0.00057*	*0.00150*
Youth entrants		−0.00060***	0.07861***	0.04706***	−0.06455***
		0.00010	*0.00293*	*0.00348*	*0.00972*
Adult entrants		0.00018***	0.04696***	0.01739***	0.08846***
		0.00006	*0.00178*	*0.00465*	*0.01081*
Intermittent respondents		−0.00001	0.04756***	−0.00692	0.01359
		0.00002	*0.00279*	*0.00697*	*0.01559*

Source: Authors' calculations based on Eq. (3). Bootstrapped standard errors in italics based on 2,000 replications. Statistical significance of difference from zero at 1%, 5% and 10% levels are denoted by ***, ** and * respectively.

health and income ranks. Lastly, the contribution of intermittent respondents was negligible, being both small and insignificant.

Table 4 similarly provides additional analysis of D_W^E, where Panel A shows that the overall negative effect of −0.00154 due to within-group IRHI differences arose from the equalising contributions of both youth and adult entrants, which were only partially offset by the positive, disequalising contribution of intermittent respondents. These contributions are calculated as the product of the corresponding scale factor and progressivity index, where the former is the health share of the entrant group and the latter is equal to the difference between the within-group CIs of the entrant group and the established population. The negative progressivity indices for youth and adult entrants of −0.02019 and −0.01008 thus indicate that levels of IRHI in these groups within the overall population in 2004 were significantly lower than in the established population, whereas the positive value of 0.01325 for the intermittent respondent group implies the opposite.

Panel B further shows that the differences in within-group IRHIs largely arose because of corresponding differences in intra-group IRHIs rather than due to the overlapping terms. In particular, the health gradient among youth entrants was much shallower than in the established population, as reflected by the intra-group CIs of 0.00546 and 0.02576 respectively, such that their entry into the population contributed to lower levels of IRHI in 2004 all other things equal. Similarly, the lower level of intra-group IRHI among adult entrants compared to the established population underlies the equalising contribution due to the entry of this group, while the opposite effect may be observed in relation to intermittent respondents. To consider the role of the overlapping terms in mediating the impact of these differences in intra-group IRHIs, note first that the pairwise indices O_f^{jk} imply that the income distributions of the various population groups fit one within another like Russian dolls; from the completely encompassed youth entrant group through to the all-encompassing intermittent respondent group, consistent with the increasing levels of intra-group dispersion reported in Table 1 (see also Fig. 2). Thus the overall overlapping index of 1.1231 for the intermittent respondent group is significantly greater than one, while that of 0.99191 for the established population is significantly less than one, exacerbating the difference between the corresponding within-group CIs compared to the intra-group CIs and thereby reinforcing the disequalising impact resulting from the inclusion of intermittent respondents in the 2004 cross-sectional population. Similarly, the overall overlapping index of 1.05839 for the adult entrant group, which is not significantly

Table 4. Analysis of the Differences in Within-Group Term D_W^E.

Panel A

Differences in within-group IRHI	D_W^E	Scale Factor q_f^k	Progressivity Index p_f^k
	−0.00154***	—	—
	0.00040		
Of which due to:			
Youth entrants	−0.00168***	0.08325***	−0.02019***
	0.00020	0.00310	0.00225
Adult entrants	−0.00048***	0.04798***	−0.01008***
	0.00017	0.00187	0.00345
Intermittent respondents	0.00062**	0.04714***	0.01325**
	0.00029	0.00279	0.00616

Panel B

Group k	Within group CI	Intra-group CI	Overlapping Index O_f^k	Pairwise overlapping indices O_f^{jk}			
				Group j			
				1	2	3	4
1: Established population	0.02555***	0.02576***	0.99191###	1	1.00578	0.93052###	0.88894###
	0.00120	0.00121	0.00265		0.01921	0.02532	0.02758
2: Youth entrants	0.00536**	0.00546**	0.98244	0.98920	1	0.90995	0.90750
	0.00217	0.00229	0.27028	0.25886	—	0.68992	0.61112
3: Adult entrants	0.01547***	0.01462***	1.05839	1.06612	1.08156	1	0.94334
	0.00336	0.00313	0.04236	0.04450	0.05630	—	0.04324
4: Intermittent respondents	0.03880***	0.03488***	1.11231###	1.12089###	1.11211###	1.07530	1
	0.00613	0.00543	0.03358	0.03608	0.04038	0.04579	—

Source: Authors' calculations based on Eqs. (5) and (6). Bootstrapped standard errors in italics based on 2,000 replications. Statistically different from zero at 1%, 5% and 10% levels are denoted by ***, ** and * respectively. Statistically different from one at 1%, 5% and 10% levels are denoted by ###, ## and # respectively.

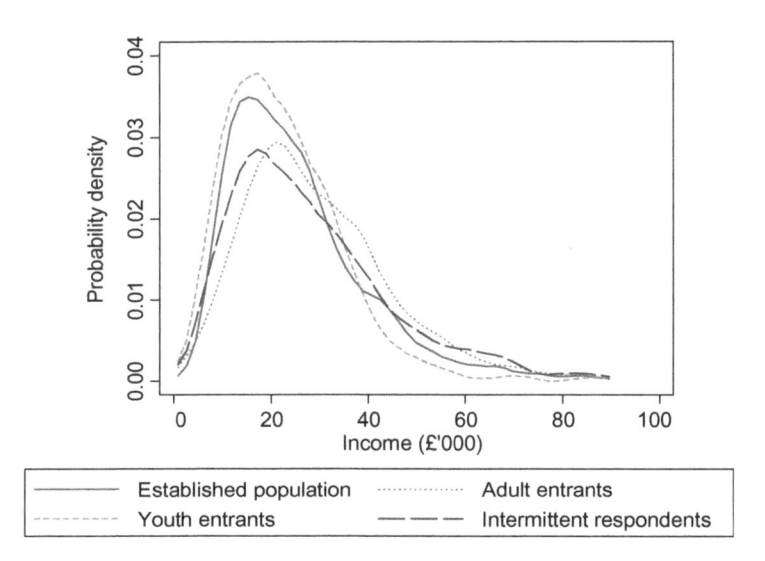

Fig. 2. Income Distributions by Population Group 2004.

different from one, gives rise to a higher estimate of within-group CI than intra-group CI thereby tending to reduce the equalising impact of the entry of this group into the population all other things equal. Finally, the overall overlapping index for the youth entrant group is marginally less than that of the established population though the resultant effect on IRHI is negligible, being both small in size and insignificant.

Lastly, the negative value of -0.00021 for the re-ranking term D_R^E in Table 2 results from the within-group CI for the established population being less than the corresponding intra-group CI in Table 4. As discussed above, this in turn is due to the overall overlapping index for the established population being significantly less than one as a result of the encompassing income distributions of both the adult entrant and intermittent respondent groups.

Overall, the results from the additional analysis of D^E support the conclusion that the bulk of the equalising effect due to entry arises from actual population changes rather than as an artefact of the intermittent response pattern of some individuals within the panel. More specifically, it is youth entrants that have the largest equalising effect both because they are healthier but poorer than the rest of the population on average and because they constitute a relatively homogenous group with comparatively low levels of both income inequality and IRHI.

Health and Income Mobility Analysis in the Non-Mover Population

The changing circumstances of the non-mover population were identified as the main factor accounting for the higher level of cross-sectional IRHI in 2004 than 1999. Table 5 provides a decomposition of the mobility index M in the manner of Petrie et al. (2011) in order to identify the relative contribution of income-related health and health-related income changes to this result.

Table 5. Decomposition of the Mobility Index M.

Health and Income Mobility in Non-Mover Population		
	M	0.00338***
		0.00123
Of which due to:		
Income-related health mobility	M_H	0.03146***
		0.00218
Due to: morbidity changes	M_H^{MB}	0.00445***
		0.00092
mortality	M_H^{MT}	0.02702***
		0.00200
Progressivity Index	P_H	−0.38966***
		0.02299
of: morbidity changes	P_H^{MB}	−0.28758***
		0.06271
mortality	P_H^{MT}	−0.41384***
		0.02293
Scale Index	q_H	−0.08075***
		0.00388
of: morbidity changes	q_H^{MB}	−0.01547***
		0.00170
mortality	q_H^{MT}	−0.06528***
		0.00341
Health-related income mobility	M_R	−0.02808***
		0.00236
Re-ranking among survivors	M_R^a	0.00782***
		0.00112
Exclusion of dead	M_R^d	−0.03590***
		0.00242

Source: Authors' calculations based on Eqs. (9)–(13). Bootstrapped standard errors in italics based on 2,000 replications. Statistical significance of difference from zero at 1%, 5% and 10% levels are denoted by ***, ** and * respectively.

IRHI, as measured by the mobility index M, rose by 0.00338 with the decomposition of this increase revealing three main points of interest. First, the positive value of 0.03146 for the income-related health mobility M_H indicates that health depreciation of 0.05975 in the non-mover population (cf. Table 1) had a disequalising effect, with the progressivity index P value of -0.38966 implying that relative health losses were concentrated among the worse-off. Second, 86.4% of the income-related health mobility was due to the effect of selective mortality, while 13.6% was due to selective health changes among the survivors. Mortality accounted for 80.8% of the net loss in health over the period with these losses more concentrated among the poor than net morbidity losses. Third, the negative value of -0.02808 for the health-related income mobility M^R indicates that the level of IRHI among the non-mover population still alive in 2004 was reduced as a result, with the disequalising impact of 0.00782 due to income re-ranking among the survivors outweighed by the -0.03590 effect of the dead dropping out of the population and therefore being excluded when calculating the level of IRHI in 2004 (see Petrie et al., 2011 for further discussion).

The Impact of Non-Mortality Related Exit on IRHI in 1999

Table 2 also presents the further decomposition of the difference in IRHI due to non-sample exit $D^X = 0.00161$, which shows that between-group IRHI had an insignificant effect on the level of IRHI within the overall population in the initial period, while within-group differences and re-ranking were both estimated to have made a disequalising contribution. Overall these three factors contributed -4.3%, 51.2% and 8.1% respectively to the overall difference in IRHI between 1999 and 2004. Tables 6 and 7 provide the basis for a more thorough understanding of the factors underlying these components.

Table 6 provides a further decomposition of the between-group IRHI term D_B^X, which is only marginally significant at conventional levels. Indeed the only significant contribution to the total derives from the combination of the above-average health and income rank of genuine outgoers, such that their exit from the population led to an estimated reduction in the level of IRHI observed in 1999 of -0.00013 all other things equal. In comparison, the contributions of both the non-mover population and the panel attrition group were negligible, being both small and insignificant.

Accounting for the Impact of Population Change on IRHI 219

Table 6. Analysis of the Between-Group IRHI Term D_B^X.

			Population Share	Difference between Group and Overall Population Means	
				Health	Income rank
Between-group IRHI	D_B^X	−0.00013*			
Of which due to:		*0.00007*			
Non-mover population		−0.00001	0.78713***	−0.00297***	−0.00230
		0.00001	*0.00530*	*0.00070*	*0.00171*
Genuine outgoers		−0.00013**	0.04283***	0.00864***	0.05851***
		0.00005	*0.00234*	*0.00301*	*0.01615*
Panel attrition		0.00002	0.17003***	0.02032***	−0.00409
		0.00003	*0.00502*	*0.00582*	*0.00689*

Source: Authors' calculations based on Eq. (8). Bootstrapped standard errors in italics based on 2,000 replications. Statistical significance of difference from zero at 1%, 5% and 10% levels are denoted by ***, ** and * respectively.

Table 7 similarly provides additional analysis of D_W^X, where Panel A shows that the overall positive effect of 0.00150 due to within-group IRHI differences arose from the disequalising contributions of both the genuine outgoer and panel attrition groups, with the positive values of the corresponding progressivity indices implying that levels of within-group IRHI in both groups were higher than in the non-mover population. Panel B further shows that these differences in within-group IRHIs largely arose because of corresponding differences in intra-group IRHIs. In particular, the health gradient among genuine outgoers was much shallower than in the non-mover population, as reflected by the intra-group CIs of 0.00360 and 0.02227 respectively, such that their exit may be expected to have had a disequalising effect all other things held constant. In comparison, the overlapping terms have a very limited mediating effect as the overall indices for all three population groups are very close to one in absolute terms.[13]

Lastly, the positive value of 0.00024 for the re-ranking term D_R^X in Table 2 is a consequence of the overall overlapping index of the non-mover population being significantly less than one, resulting in the within-group CI for the established population being less than the corresponding intra-group CI in Table 7.

Overall, these results imply that roughly half of the D^X value of 0.00161 might have been due to genuine outgoers, with the departure of individuals from the population of interest thus having the opposite effect of genuine

Table 7. Analysis of the Differences in Within-Group Term D_W^E.

Panel A

	D_W^X	Scale Factor q_f^k	Progressivity Index P_f^k
Differences in within-group IRHI	0.00150***	—	—
	0.00044		
Of which due to:			
Genuine outgoers	0.00081***	0.04392***	0.01847***
	0.00018	0.00246	0.00379
Panel attrition	0.00069*	0.17187***	0.00400*
	0.00038	0.00514	0.00221

Panel B

Group k	Within group CI	Intra-group CI	Overlapping Index O_f^k	Group j	Pairwise overlapping indices O_f^{jk}		
					1	2	3
1: Non-mover population	0.02203***	0.02227***	0.98936###			0.88236###	0.96707#
	0.00118	0.00121	0.00323			0.02692	0.01721
2: Genuine outgoers	0.00356	0.00360	0.98855		0.99721	1	0.94558
	0.00368	0.00337	8.04275		8.36989		8.56126
3: Panel attrition	0.01803***	0.01764***	1.02237		1.03422##	0.89336###	1
	0.00210	0.00208	0.01572		0.01913	0.03485	—

Source: Authors' calculations based on Eq. (8). Bootstrapped standard errors in italics based on 2,000 replications. Statistically different from zero at 1%, 5% and 10% levels are denoted by ***, ** and * respectively. Statistically different from one at 1%, 5% and 10% levels are denoted by ###, ## and # respectively.

population entry in that it contributed to higher levels of IRHI in 2004 than would have otherwise been the case. The other half was attributable to attrition from the panel, but this effect is in principle offset elsewhere in the overall decomposition of the difference in cross-sectional IRHI between the two years given that the cross-sectional weights for 2004 are meant to adjust for net attrition in order to correct for any selection bias due to non-random non-response (see Taylor et al., 2010).[14] In principle, if reweighting appropriately adjusts for intermittent respondents and panel attrition, only the impact of genuine population change needs to be taken into account in the analysis of trends in cross-sectional measures of population health performance, such as IRHI,[15] derived from panel surveys.

CONCLUSION

Cross-sectional IRHI can change over time for a number of reasons with very different implications for policy development. This chapter has examined the importance of population change as a source of differences in cross-sectional IRHI over time. The findings of the study reinforce the conclusion of Petrie et al. (2011) that taking death into account is important by further showing that the entry of youths into the adult population also served to reduce the level of cross-sectional IRHI in 2004 compared to what it would have otherwise been, with these natural processes of population turnover serving to partially mask an increase in IRHI among the adult population resident over the five-year period. Accordingly, it will prove necessary to either take into account the confounding effects of population change when seeking to monitor and evaluate policies to tackle health inequalities or identify and track a target population in order to avoid the need to do so. Failure to do so may lead to erroneous conclusions on the effectiveness of policies if these are either masked or exacerbated by broader demographic changes.

The results also imply the need to take population change into account when seeking to model the social determinants of IRHI change as this will allow policy makers to better understand how health inequalities develop in terms of the underlying social determinants or to identify population groups that may be of particular concern. For example, in the current analysis we identify youth entrants into the adult population as a group with significantly lower levels of IRHI than the established population. More generally there is a need to monitor the relative position and performance of both immigrant and emigrant populations though these are often under-represented groups in longitudinal household surveys such as the BHPS. This is likely to be particularly important in the analysis of IRHI in smaller regions where there are likely to be larger migrant groups in terms of the total population.

Allanson and Petrie (2013b) stress that longitudinal data is necessary to understand the evolution of IRHI and offer a methodology that allows for the identification of the determinants of health changes related to income status. Their methodology is based on a Two-Part Model consisting of a probit model of survival and a dynamic model of morbidity changes. However further work is required to extend this framework both to model the causes of all possible forms of population change and to allow for a genuine multi-period analysis of health changes related to income. There is also a wider need to understand how health inequalities develop and perpetuate themselves in society by further exploring the extent of intergenerational health and income mobility.

NOTES

1. Both immigration and emigration may be related to health status and income. Page, Begg, Taylor, and Lopez (2007) find that immigration significantly increases estimates of population life expectancy for Australia.

2. It should in principle be a straightforward exercise to extend the analytical procedures developed in this chapter to other rank-dependent IRHI indices.

3. Note that this definition differs from that which would be obtained by adapting the conventional approach to the group-wise decomposition of the Gini coefficient (see, e.g. Pyatt, 1976), which would yield a between-group CI based on the rank of mean income not the mean rank of income.

4. Yitzhaki and Lerman (1991, p. 314) quote the following explanation of the concept from Lasswell (1965, p. 10): 'In its general meaning, a stratum is a horizontal layer, usually thought of as between, above or below other such layers or strata. Stratification is the process of forming observable layers, or the state of being comprised of layers. Social stratification suggests a model in which the mass of society is constructed of layer upon layer of congealed population qualities.'

5. If $E(h_f|y_f)$ is an increasing function of y then: (i) the concentration curve of h ordered according to their respective values of y will be convex as $\partial E(h_f|y_f)/\partial y_f > 0$ by assumption; and (ii) the concentration curve will lie everywhere below the Line of Equality since $E(h_f|y_f) > 0$ implies that the covariance between health and income will also be positive. Condition (ii) guarantees non-negativity.

6. O_f^{jk} is not bounded from above, unlike the overlapping measure considered in Yitzhaki (1994), because the denominators in Eq. (6) are health concentration indices not health Gini coefficients.

7. Using Eqs. (1), (5) and (6) it is easy to prove this inverse relationship when the overall, between-group and intra-group IRHI measures are all held constant.

8. This follows since most entrants will fall within the income range of the established population whereas few members of the established population will have incomes within the range of entrants.

9. M_H is defined here as the negative of the IRHM index proposed in Petrie et al. (2011) so that positive values of M_H imply higher levels of IRHI in the final period, as is the case for all the other indices considered in the chapter. The change of sign is absorbed in the definition of the progressivity indices P_H, P_H^{MB} and P_H^{MT}.

10. In particular, it will typically only be possible to consider the impact of entry on final period IRHI since the health of entrants in the initial period will likely be unknown or otherwise of little concern. Similarly, the impact of non-mortality exit is evaluated in terms the impact this has on initial period IRHI since the health of individuals in the final period will not usually be known if they are no longer part of the relevant population.

11. However, the bootstrapping procedure did not include re-estimation of the individual weights that were constructed from the original sample. See Biewen (2002) on the use of bootstrap inference for inequality and mobility measurement.

12. The concentration indices in the current chapter are similar in magnitude to those found in other studies (see, e.g. van Doorslaer & Koolman, 2004). If there was a linear relationship between health and income rank then these levels of IRHI would imply that the difference in health utility between the poorest and richest individuals in the population was 0.099 in 1999 and of 0.113 in 2004, or just less than one standard deviation in health in both years. This follows since the Slope Inequality Index is equal to approximately six times the product of the health concentration index and mean health (see, e.g. Allanson & Petrie, 2012a).

13. The large standard errors associated with the estimates of the overlapping terms for the genuine outgoers group are a consequence of the small and insignificant value of the corresponding intra-group CI.

14. Note that the reweighting correction of 0.00011 reported in Table 2 only captures the impact of adjustments to the 2004 cross-sectional weights for net attrition on the level of final period IRHI within the established rather than the overall population.

15. The CI may be interpreted as the inequality component of the health achievement index of Wagstaff (2002).

ACKNOWLEDGEMENT

The authors bear sole responsibility for the further analysis and interpretation of the British Household Panel Survey data employed in this study.

REFERENCES

Allanson, P., Gerdtham, U.-G., & Petrie, D. (2010). Longitudinal analysis of income-related health inequality. *Journal of Health Economics*, 29, 78–86.

Allanson, P., & Petrie, D. (2012). On the choice of health inequality measure for the longitudinal analysis of income-related health inequalities. *Health Economics, 22*, 353–365.

Allanson, P. & Petrie, D. (2013a, forthcoming). Understanding the vertical equity judgements underpinning health inequality measures. *Health Economics.* doi:10.1002/hec.2984

Allanson, P. & Petrie, D. (2013b). Longitudinal methods to investigate the role of health determinants in the dynamics of income-related health inequality. *Journal of Health Economics, 32*, 922–937.

Biewen, M. (2002). Bootstrap inference for inequality, mobility and poverty measurement. *Journal of Econometrics, 108*, 317–342.

Boyle, P. J., Norman, P., & Popham, F. (2009). Social mobility: Evidence that it can widen health inequalities. *Social Science & Medicine, 68*, 1835–1842.

Brazier, J., Roberts, J., & Deverill, M. (2002). The estimation of a preference-based measure of health from the SF-36. *Journal of Health Economics, 21*, 271–292.

Frick, J. R., Goebel, J., Schechtman, E., Wagner, G. G., & Yitzhaki, S. (2006). Using analysis of Gini (ANOGI) for detecting whether two subsamples represent the same universe. *Sociological Methods & Research, 34*, 427–468.

Jenkins, S. P. & Van Kerm, P. (2011). *Trends in individual income growth: Measurement methods and British evidence.* ISER Working Paper Series 2011-06, Institute for Social and Economic Research, University of Essex.

Jones, A. M., & López Nicolás, A. (2004). Measurement and explanation of socioeconomic inequality in health with longitudinal data. *Health Economics, 13*, 1015–1030.

Lasswell, T. E. (1965). *Class and stratum.* Boston, MA: Houghton Mifflin.

Lynn, P. (Ed.), Buck, N., Burton, J., Laurie, H., & Noah Uhrig, S. C. (2006). *Quality profile: British Household Panel Survey*, Version 2.0: Waves 1 to 13: 1991–2003. Institute for Social and Economic Research, University of Essex.

O'Donnell, O., Wagstaff, A., Van Doorslaer, E., & Lindelow, M. (2008). *Analyzing health equity using household survey data: A guide to techniques and their implementation.* Washington, DC: The World Bank.

Page, A., Begg, S., Taylor, R., & Lopez, A. (2007). Global comparative assessments of life expectancy: The impact of migration with reference to Australia. *Bulletin of the World Health Organisation, 85*(6), 474–81.

Petrie, D., Allanson, P., & Gerdtham, U.-G. (2011). Accounting for the dead in the longitudinal analysis of income-related health inequalities. *Journal of Health Economics, 30*, 1113–1123.

Pyatt, G. (1976). On the interpretation and disaggregation of Gini coefficients. *The Economic Journal, 86*, 243–254.

Shorrocks, A. (1978). Income inequality and income mobility. *Journal of Economic Theory, 19*, 376–393.

Shorrocks, A. (2013). Decomposition procedures for distributional analysis: A unified framework based on the Shapley value. *Journal of Economic Inequality, 11*, 99–126.

Taylor, M. F. (Ed.), Brice, J. Buck, N., & Prentice-Lane, E. (2010). *British Household Panel Survey User Manual*, Volume A: Introduction. Technical Report and Appendices, University of Essex, Colchester.

University of Essex, Institute for Social and Economic Research. (2010, June). British Household Panel Survey: Waves 1–18, 1991–2009 [computer file] (7th ed.). Colchester, Essex: UK Data Archive [distributor]. SN: 5151.

van Doorslaer, E., & Koolman, X. (2004). Explaining the differences in income-related health inequalities across European countries. *Health Economics, 13*, 609–628.

Wagstaff, A. (2002). Inequality aversion, health inequalities, and health achievement. *Journal of Health Economics, 21*(4), 627–641.

Wodon, Q., & Yitzhaki, S. (2003). Inequality and the accounting period. *Economics Bulletin, 4*(36), 1–8.

Wooldridge, J. M. (2002). *Econometric analysis of cross-section and panel data.* Cambridge, MA: MIT Press.

Yitzhaki, S. (1994). Economic distance and overlapping of distributions. *Journal of Econometrics, 61*, 147–159.

Yitzhaki, S. (2003). Gini's mean difference: A superior measure of variability for non-normal distributions. *METRON – International Journal of Statistics, 51*, 285–316.

Yitzhaki, S., & Lerman, R. (1991). Income stratification and income inequality. *Review of Income and Wealth, 37*, 313–329.

REGRESSION-BASED DECOMPOSITIONS OF RANK-DEPENDENT INDICATORS OF SOCIOECONOMIC INEQUALITY OF HEALTH

Guido Erreygers and Roselinde Kessels

ABSTRACT

In this chapter we explore different ways to obtain decompositions of rank-dependent indices of socioeconomic inequality of health, such as the Concentration Index. Our focus is on the regression-based type of decomposition. Depending on whether the regression explains the health variable, or the socioeconomic variable, or both, a different decomposition formula is generated. We illustrate the differences using data from the Ethiopia 2011 Demographic and Health Survey (DHS).

Keywords: Inequality measurement; Concentration Index; decomposition methods

JEL classifications: D63; I00

INTRODUCTION

Inequality decomposition techniques have been developed and used extensively over the last four to five decades. In the income inequality literature various methods have been proposed to decompose inequality by subgroups as well as by income sources (see, e.g., Rao, 1969; Bourguignon, 1979 for early contributions). Typical for subgroup decompositions is that they involve partitions of the population into distinct subsets, such as urban and rural, or male and female. In the literature on subgroup decomposability the focus has been on additively decomposable indicators, i.e. inequality measures which can be written as a weighted sum of within-group inequality levels and a between-group term (see, e.g., Shorrocks, 1980), but some attention has also been paid to inequality measures satisfying more general decomposability criteria (see, e.g., Shorrocks, 1984). Income source decompositions refer to divisions of income into different components, such as wage and non-wage income. For these decompositions, the main issue has been whether it is possible to identify the proportional contribution of each income component to the measured level of inequality (see, e.g., Shorrocks, 1982).

Both decompositions are based on pre-determined identities which split either the population or individual incomes into distinct categories. By contrast, in regression-based decompositions the identities are replaced by regressions in which the independent variables are the determinants of income, such as education, sex, and age. Because of the presence of an error term in the regression equation, these decompositions typically end up with a residual component. The origins of this approach can be traced back to the influential work of Oaxaca (1973), but especially Morduch and Sicular (2002) and Fields (2003) have developed the technique further by building on insights from the literature on income source decompositions. Cowell and Fiorio (2011) provide a good overview of recent contributions in this field.

Some income inequality decomposition methods have been applied to measures of socioeconomic inequality of health. Simple decomposition formulas by both subgroups and health components were suggested by Clarke, Gerdtham, and Connelly (2003). Regression-based decomposition methods were introduced by Gravelle (2003) and Wagstaff, Van Doorslaer and Watanabe (2003). Using results on the decomposition of the Gini coefficient obtained by Podder (1993), Wagstaff, Van Doorslaer, and Watanabe (2003) not only proposed a procedure to decompose the Concentration Index into contributing factors, but also indicated how the decomposition could serve as a framework to analyse changes in socioeconomic inequality over time. Their results have been used and extended in many ways (see, e.g., Jones & López Nicolás, 2004; O'Donnell, Van Doorslaer, & Wagstaff, 2006; O'Donnell, Van Doorslaer, Wagstaff, & Lindelow, 2008, chapter 13; Van Ourti, Van Doorslaer, & Koolman, 2009) and led to numerous empirical applications (see, e.g., Hosseinpoor et al., 2006; Van de Poel, Hosseinpoor, Jehu-Appiah, Vega, & Speybroeck, 2007). Some of this work is covered in a recent survey by Van Doorslaer and Van Ourti (2011).

In this chapter we focus on regression-based decompositions of rank-dependent indicators of socioeconomic inequality of health, of which the Concentration Index is the best known example. Our starting point is that inequality of income is of a different nature than socioeconomic inequality of health: while the former is univariate, the latter is bivariate. In other words, whereas income inequality indicators measure the degree of inequality of incomes as such, socioeconomic inequality indicators measure the degree of *correlation* between socioeconomic status and health. This difference in character is visible in the range of values of the indicators: univariate indicators are always nonnegative (e.g., limited to the interval [0,1], with 0 indicating minimum inequality and 1 maximum inequality), but bivariate indicators can be both negative and positive (e.g., limited to the interval [−1, +1], with −1 indicating an extreme pro-poor distribution of health and +1 an extreme pro-rich distribution of health). This difference is not always properly acknowledged, although there are exceptions (see, e.g., Abul Naga & Geoffard, 2006). The challenge, therefore, is to find decompositions which explain the degree of correlation between two variables rather than the degree of inequality in one variable.

After a preliminary section, we first deal with one-dimensional decompositions, including the Wagstaff–Van Doorslaer–Watanabe decomposition. Then, we explore various two-dimensional decompositions, and make a comparison between one- and two-dimensional decompositions. By means of an empirical analysis of child malnutrition in Ethiopia, we illustrate the differences between the main decompositions. We discuss the results and draw a number of conclusions.

PRELIMINARIES

Consider a population consisting of n individuals. The health level of individual i is represented by the real number h_i. The health variable is assumed to be either a ratio-scale variable which takes nonnegative values, only or a cardinal variable with a finite lower bound. The average health level in the population is equal to $\mu_h = \frac{1}{n}\sum_{i=1}^{n} h_i$.

As argued by Erreygers and Van Ourti (2011), the use of the health Concentration Index can be defended when we are dealing with a ratio-scale health variable which is unbounded, i.e. which does not have a finite upper bound. However, when we are dealing with a variable which has a finite upper bound, a modified version is called for. For this situation, Wagstaff (2005) and Erreygers (2009) each proposed a variant of the Generalized Concentration Index.

All of these indices are rank-dependent indices in the sense that they are in essence weighted sums of health levels with the weights determined by socioeconomic ranks. The socioeconomic rank of individual i is determined by his/her position according to the variable which is supposed to measure socioeconomic well-being, e.g. income. Let the value of this variable for individual i be y_i. Then the natural number $r_i(y)$ measures the position of individual i in the rank-order according to variable y, with the rank $r_i(y) = 1$ assigned to the person who is least well-off, and the rank $r_i(y) = n$ assigned to the person who is most well-off. (In what follows we will simplify $r_i(y)$ to r_i if it is obvious that y is the variable used for ranking.) In the case of ties, we assign to every individual of the tied group the average rank of the group. Over the population as a whole the average rank is $\mu_r = \frac{n+1}{2}$. The fractional rank f_i is defined as $f_i \equiv \frac{1}{n}(r_i - \frac{1}{2})$, and varies between $\frac{1}{2n}$ and $1 - \frac{1}{2n}$. The average fractional rank is $\mu_f = \frac{1}{2}$. Finally, the deviation of the fractional rank of individual i from the average fractional rank, denoted as $d_i \equiv f_i - \mu_f$, has an average of $\mu_d = 0$.

The Generalized health Concentration Index $GC(h;y)$, or more simply GC whenever it is clear that the health variable is h and the socioeconomic variable y, is defined as:

$$GC = \frac{2}{n}\sum_{i=1}^{n} h_i d_i \qquad (1)$$

The standard health Concentration Index, $C(h;y) = C$, as well as the indices introduced by Wagstaff (2005), $W(h;y) = W$, and by Erreygers (2009), $E(h;y) = E$, can be expressed as simple functions of GC:

$$C = \frac{1}{\mu_h} GC \qquad (2)$$

$$W = \frac{b_h - a_h}{(b_h - \mu_h)(\mu_h - a_h)} GC \qquad (3)$$

$$E = \frac{4}{b_h - a_h} GC \qquad (4)$$

where a_h and b_h stand for the lower and upper bounds of the health variable. In the remainder of the chapter we will concentrate on the decomposition of the Generalized Concentration Index; formulas (2), (3) and (4) can be used to convert the outcome into corresponding decompositions of the other rank-dependent indices.

To end this preliminary section, it may be useful to point out a well-known connection between the rank-dependent indices and the covariance concept. Since $Cov(h, d) = \frac{1}{n}\sum_{i=1}^{n} h_i d_i - \mu_h \mu_d$ and $\mu_d = 0$, it follows that we have:

$$GC = 2Cov(h, d) \qquad (5)$$

Both Eqs. (1) and (5) can be used to generate decompositions of the Generalized Concentration Index. Although one expects to obtain the same decompositions irrespective of which of the two formulas is used, we will show below that this need not be the case.

ONE-DIMENSIONAL DECOMPOSITIONS

We begin our analysis with the case in which only one of the two variables is subject to a regression. This has been the dominant approach in the literature on regression-based decompositions of the Concentration Index. Following Wagstaff et al. (2003) health has been unanimously preferred as the relevant variable for regression. We therefore first recapitulate the results of this health-oriented decomposition and then introduce rank-oriented decompositions.

The Health-Oriented Decomposition

Wagstaff et al. (2003), who have pioneered this type of decomposition analysis, start from the assumption that the health variable h is determined by a number of explanatory variables $x_1, x_2, ..., x_k$. Suppose that we have the following linear regression equation:

$$h_i = \beta_0 + \beta_1 x_{1,i} + \beta_2 x_{2,i} + ... + \beta_k x_{k,i} + \varepsilon_i \tag{6}$$

where ε_i is an error term. Substituting the right-hand side of Eq. (6) for h_i in Eq. (1) we obtain:

$$GC = \frac{2}{n}\sum_{i=1}^{n}[\beta_0 + \beta_1 x_{1,i} + \beta_2 x_{2,i} + ... + \beta_k x_{k,i} + \varepsilon_i]d_i \tag{7}$$

$$= \beta_0 \frac{2}{n}\sum_{i=1}^{n} d_i + \sum_{j=1}^{k} \beta_j \left(\frac{2}{n}\sum_{i=1}^{n} x_{j,i} d_i\right) + \frac{2}{n}\sum_{i=1}^{n} \varepsilon_i d_i \tag{8}$$

Since $\sum_{i=1}^{n} d_i = 0$, the first term vanishes. Given that $\frac{1}{n}\sum_{i=1}^{n} x_{j,i} d_i = Cov(x_j, d)$ and $\frac{1}{n}\sum_{i=1}^{n} \varepsilon_i d_i = Cov(\varepsilon, d)$, this leads to the following decomposition:

$$GC = 2\sum_{j=1}^{k} \beta_j Cov(x_j, d) + 2Cov(\varepsilon, d) \tag{9}$$

This decomposition splits the Generalized Concentration Index into two components: a deterministic and a residual component. The first consists of a sum of k contributions, one for each explanatory variable. If the x_j variables are ratio-scale or cardinal variables, we can apply definition (1) to each of the k individual terms. In fact, in that case the contribution of the explanatory variable x_j to socioeconomic inequality, $2\beta_j Cov(x_j, d)$, can also be expressed as a Generalized Concentration Index, since it is equal to $\beta_j GC(x_j; y)$. If the error term of Eq. (6) were uncorrelated with the socioeconomic rank, one would expect the residual component $Cov(\varepsilon, d)$ to be close to zero.

It has been customary to interpret the deterministic component as the 'explained' part and the residual component as the 'unexplained' part of the decomposition. However, the validity of that interpretation may be questioned. In fact, the residual component $Cov(\varepsilon, d)$ can always be reduced to zero by including the fractional rank deviation variable d as a regressor. In a well-behaved regression model all covariances between the explanatory variables and the error term are zero; this is needed in order for the coefficients to be BLUE (Best Linear Unbiased Estimators). A clear example is the simple case where the variable d is taken to be the *only* explanatory variable of h, i.e. $x_1 = d$. Since the OLS estimator of β_1 is then equal to $Cov(h,d)/Var(d)$, it follows that the deterministic component of the decomposition is identical to GC and therefore the residual component is equal to zero. But it is difficult to maintain that in this case we have explained anything at all. If instead of the fractional rank deviation variable d a strongly correlated proxy variable is used, e.g. income or socioeconomic status, the residual component will be very small, i.e. close to, but not equal to zero. Again, that should not be taken as a sign that the decomposition provides a good explanation of socioeconomic inequality.

This issue is relevant in view of the fact that it has become standard practice in empirical work (see, e.g., Hosseinpoor et al., 2006; Van de Poel et al., 2007) to include socioeconomic status in the set of explanatory variables of the regression of health. Moreover, in many of these studies the socioeconomic status variable typically contributes more to the explanation of socioeconomic inequality than any other variable included in the model. Although we agree there is a strong case for the inclusion of socioeconomic status as an explanatory variable of *health* per se, we think it is unjustified to include it among the factors which explain *socioeconomic inequality of health*. Therefore, in our decomposition analysis we choose not to include socioeconomic status or income as an explanatory variable in the regression of health.

Rank-Oriented Decompositions

Instead of starting from an equation which predicts health levels, we could also start from an equation which predicts the socioeconomic ranks. Two methods suggest themselves. The first consists of predicting the levels of the variable which defines the socioeconomic ranks. Assuming that y is determined by the variables $z_1, z_2, ..., z_q$, the first step would be to estimate the linear equation:

$$y_i = \gamma_0 + \gamma_1 z_{1,i} + \gamma_2 z_{2,i} + ... + \gamma_q z_{q,i} + \eta_i \tag{10}$$

where η_i is an error term. The predicted value of y_i, i.e. $\hat{y}_i = \hat{\gamma}_0 + \hat{\gamma}_1 z_{1,i} + \hat{\gamma}_2 z_{2,i} + ... + \hat{\gamma}_q z_{q,i}$, could then be used to generate the predicted rank of person i, $\hat{r}_i = r_i(\hat{y})$. Let us call the difference between the actual and the predicted ranks the unexplained rank deviation, and let us denote it as ρ_i. Given that $r_i = \hat{r}_i + \rho_i$, we also have, using an obvious notation, $f_i = \hat{f}_i + \omega_i$ and $d_i = \hat{d}_i + \omega_i$, where $\omega_i = \rho_i/n$. Substituting this into Eq. (1) we obtain:

$$GC = \frac{2}{n}\sum_{i=1}^{n} h_i(\hat{d}_i + \omega_i) \qquad (11)$$

and so the Generalized Concentration Index can be decomposed into a deterministic and a residual component:

$$GC = 2Cov(h, \hat{d}) + 2Cov(h, \omega) \qquad (12)$$

The drawback of this first method, which determines the socioeconomic ranks indirectly, is that it allows only a very rough decomposition of the index. As an alternative, we could try to determine the socioeconomic ranks directly. Hence, assuming that the variables $z_1, z_2, ..., z_q$ are the relevant variables, instead of estimating Eq. (10) we could start from an equation which estimates the fractional rank deviations:

$$d_i = \alpha_0 + \alpha_1 z_{1,i} + \alpha_2 z_{2,i} + ... + \alpha_q z_{q,i} + \xi_i \qquad (13)$$

where ξ_i is an error term. Substituting this into Eq. (1) we now obtain the following result:

$$GC = 2\alpha_0 \mu_h + 2\sum_{g=1}^{q} \alpha_g \left(\frac{1}{n}\sum_{i=1}^{n} h_i z_{g,i}\right) + \frac{2}{n}\sum_{i=1}^{n} h_i \xi_i \qquad (14)$$

This equation suggests a three-component decomposition:

$$GC = 2\alpha_0 \mu_h + 2\sum_{g=1}^{q} \alpha_g [Cov(h, z_g) + \mu_h \mu_{z_g}] + 2Cov(h, \xi) \qquad (15)$$

We now have (i) a constant term, $2\alpha_0 \mu_h$; (ii) a sum of contributions of the q explanatory variables, with the contribution of variable g equal to $2\alpha_g [Cov(h, z_g) + \mu_h \mu_{z_g}]$; and (iii) a residual component, $2Cov(h, \xi)$.

One may feel uncomfortable with this decomposition because of the presence of a constant term, which has no obvious interpretation. Following Eq. (5) rather than Eq. (1) suggests a way out. Since $Cov(h,d) = Cov(h, \alpha_0 u + \alpha_1 z_1 + \alpha_2 z_2 + ... + \alpha_q z_q + \xi)$, where u is a vector of ones, it follows that $Cov(h,d) = \alpha_0 Cov(h,u) + \alpha_1 Cov(h,z_1) + \alpha_2 Cov(h,z_2) + ... + \alpha_q Cov(h,z_q) + Cov(h,\xi)$. Knowing that $Cov(h,u) = 0$, we arrive at the following decomposition:

$$GC = 2\sum_{g=1}^{q} \alpha_g Cov(h,z_g) + 2Cov(h,\xi) \qquad (16)$$

The modified decomposition is written as a sum of two components, of which one might be interpreted as the 'explained' part and the other as the 'unexplained' part. The contribution of variable z_g to the explained component is now equal to $2\alpha_g Cov(h,z_g)$. Actually, we could have derived Eq. (16) from Eq. (15); we have in fact $\alpha_0 + \sum_{g=1}^{q} \alpha_g \mu_{z_g} = 0$, which follows from Eq. (13) if one takes into account that $\mu_d = 0$ and $\mu_\xi = 0$. Comparing Eq. (16) to Eq. (15), it is as if the value of the constant term is distributed over the contributions of the explanatory variables, with $-2\alpha_g \mu_h \mu_{z_g}$ being added to the contribution of variable z_g. Note that in the special case where all the independent variables $z_1, z_2, ..., z_q$ are themselves rank variables, or more specifically fractional rank deviation variables, all dependent and independent variables of Eq. (13) have zero means, so that $\alpha_0 = -\mu_\xi = 0$ and the two decompositions (15) and (16) coincide.

Decomposition (16) has a similar structure as the Wagstaff–Van Doorslaer–Watanabe decomposition (9). In each case we arrive at an expression which decomposes the Generalized Concentration Index into a sum of q explained contributions, with each of these equal to a covariance weighted by a regression coefficient, and a residual or unexplained component, which is also a covariance. Although decomposition (15) is slightly different, it has a similar residual term. If the error term ξ were uncorrelated with the health variable h, the covariance $Cov(h,\xi)$ would be close to zero and the residual term very small. Finally, note that, in line with our recommendation to exclude socioeconomic status as an explanatory variable in the health-oriented decomposition, we also advise against the inclusion of the health variable h in Eq. (13) because it would artificially result in a zero residual covariance in the decompositions (15) and (16).

FROM ONE-DIMENSIONAL TO TWO-DIMENSIONAL DECOMPOSITIONS

So far we have limited ourselves to one-dimensional decompositions. These are based on regressions of only one of the two variables under consideration. It should be remembered, however, that we are interested in the *correlation* between the two variables. It may be doubted whether focusing on one dimension only is enough to fully understand how the two dimensions are related. Therefore, it seems appropriate to extend the analysis and to adopt a framework which allows one to look at both variables simultaneously.

Three approaches suggest themselves, and we will explore each one of them briefly. The first approach consists of making a super-decomposition based on two separate regressions, one for each variable. In the second approach the two regressions are made simultaneously, using a common set of independent variables. The final approach looks for a direct way to explain the correlation between the two variables.

A Combined Super-Decomposition

Let us assume that each of the two variables of interest can be explained by a separate regression equation. More specifically, let health levels be predicted by Eq. (6) and socioeconomic ranks by Eq. (13). A combination of these two equations results in what we will call a combined super-decomposition.

Once again, two paths can be followed to obtain a decomposition formula. If we start from Eq. (1) the Generalized health Concentration Index will be expressed as:

$$GC = \frac{2}{n} \sum_{i=1}^{n} \left[\beta_0 + \sum_{j=1}^{k} \beta_j x_{j,i} + \varepsilon_i \right] \left[\alpha_0 + \sum_{g=1}^{q} \alpha_g z_{g,i} + \xi_i \right] \qquad (17)$$

Working out the terms and assuming that $\mu_\varepsilon = \mu_\xi = 0$, we can expand this to:

$$GC = 2\beta_0 \alpha_0 + 2\alpha_0 \sum_{j=1}^{k} \beta_j \mu_{x_j} + 2\beta_0 \sum_{g=1}^{q} \alpha_g \mu_{z_g} + 2 \sum_{j=1}^{k} \sum_{g=1}^{q} \beta_j \alpha_g Cov(x_j, z_g)$$

$$+ 2 \left[\sum_{j=1}^{k} \beta_j Cov(x_j, \xi) + \sum_{g=1}^{q} \alpha_g Cov(\varepsilon, z_g) + Cov(\varepsilon, \xi) \right] \qquad (18)$$

In comparison to what we obtained before, this result looks awfully complicated. Adopting a two-dimensional approach leads to a dramatic increase in the number of terms. We can simplify the decomposition a bit by making the plausible assumption that the $k + q$ covariance terms $Cov(x_j, \xi)$ and $Cov(\varepsilon, z_g)$ are all equal to zero. This gives:

$$GC = 2\beta_0\alpha_0 + 2\alpha_0\sum_{j=1}^{k}\beta_j\mu_{x_j} + 2\beta_0\sum_{g=1}^{q}\alpha_g\mu_{z_g} + 2\sum_{j=1}^{k}\sum_{g=1}^{q}\beta_j\alpha_g Cov(x_j, z_g) + 2Cov(\varepsilon, \xi) \quad (19)$$

which is only marginally less complicated.

As before, starting from Eq. (5) generates a more simple decomposition. Since $Cov(h, d) = Cov(\beta_0 u + \beta_1 x_1 + \beta_2 x_2 + ... + \beta_k x_k + \varepsilon, \alpha_0 u + \alpha_1 z_1 + \alpha_2 z_2 + ... + \alpha_q z_q + \xi)$, we obtain:

$$GC = 2\sum_{j=1}^{k}\sum_{g=1}^{q}\beta_j\alpha_g Cov(x_j, z_g) + 2Cov(\varepsilon, \xi) \quad (20)$$

Instead of just k or q explained contributions, we now have kq terms which may be said to capture the explained component of the Generalized Concentration Index. It is, however, much harder than before to give a clear interpretation to the many terms involved in the decomposition. For instance, saying that the total explained effect of variable x_j equal to $2\beta_j\sum_{g=1}^{q}\alpha_g Cov(x_j, z_g)$ and that of variable z_g equal to $2\alpha_g\sum_{j=1}^{k}\beta_j Cov(x_j, z_g)$ would lead to double counting.

A Simultaneous Super-Decomposition

A special case would occur if the set of variables which determine the health levels, the x_j's, coincided with the set of variables which determine the socioeconomic positions, the z_g's. Suppose we have a common set of p variables $s_1, s_2, ..., s_p$ which determine both the health levels h and the fractional rank deviations d. Then we could run a bivariate multiple regression of the following form:

$$h_i = \lambda_0 + \lambda_1 s_{1,i} + \lambda_2 s_{2,i} + ... + \lambda_p s_{p,i} + \psi_i \quad (21)$$

$$d_i = \pi_0 + \pi_1 s_{1,i} + \pi_2 s_{2,i} + ... + \pi_p s_{p,i} + \chi_i \quad (22)$$

where ψ_i and χ_i are error terms. We take it for granted that $\mu_\psi = \mu_\chi = 0$, and moreover that the $2p$ covariances $Cov(s_j, \chi)$ and $Cov(\psi, s_j)$ are zero.

We can again start from either Eq. (1) or Eq. (5). In the first case, the application of formula (19) gives the following expression:

$$GC = 2\lambda_0\pi_0 + 2\sum_{j=1}^{p}(\lambda_0\pi_j + \lambda_j\pi_0)\mu_{s_j} + 2\sum_{j=1}^{p}\sum_{g=1}^{p}\lambda_j\pi_g[Cov(s_j, s_g) + \mu_{s_j}\mu_{s_g}] + 2Cov(\psi, \chi)$$

(23)

Although this might already be considered as a decomposition formula, we propose to group the terms slightly differently. The second component of the right-hand side of Eq. (23) consists of a sum of p terms, one for each independent variable s_j, where $j = 1, \ldots, p$. The third component, by contrast, has p^2 terms, one for each pair of independent variables (s_j, s_g), where $j, g = 1, \ldots, p$. Of these p^2 terms, exactly p refers to only one variable. Let us add these terms to each of the corresponding terms of the second component. Given that $Cov(s_j, s_j) = Var(s_j)$ and $Cov(s_j, s_g) = Cov(s_g, s_j)$, this gives the following:

$$GC = 2\lambda_0\pi_0 + 2\sum_{j=1}^{p}\{(\lambda_0\pi_j + \lambda_j\pi_0)\mu_{s_j} + \lambda_j\pi_j[Var(s_j) + (\mu_{s_j})^2]\}$$

$$+ 2\sum_{j=1}^{p}\sum_{g=j+1}^{p}\{(\lambda_j\pi_g + \lambda_g\pi_j)[Cov(s_j, s_g) + \mu_{s_j}\mu_{s_g}]\} + 2Cov(\psi, \chi) \quad (24)$$

In other words, we now have: (i) a constant term, $2\lambda_0\pi_0$; (ii) p single-variable terms $2(\lambda_0\pi_j + \lambda_j\pi_0)\mu_{s_j} + \lambda_j\pi_j[Var(s_j) + (\mu_{s_j})^2]$ which might be said to capture the direct effect of the p independent variables; (iii) $\frac{p(p-1)}{2}$ two-variable terms $2(\lambda_j\pi_g + \lambda_g\pi_j)[Cov(s_j, s_g) + \mu_{s_j}\mu_{s_g}]$ which capture the correlation structure between the independent variables; and (iv) a residual component which is equal to the covariance between the two error terms. For a well-specified model with negligible multicollinearity between the independent variables, one expects the correlation effects to be small relative to the direct effects.

If we start from Eq. (5) rather than Eq. (1), we have to apply formula (20). Isolating the terms of the first component which involve only one of the independent variables, and keeping in mind that all $Cov(s_j, \chi)$

Regression-Based Decompositions of Socioeconomic Inequality of Health

and $Cov(\psi, s_j)$ are by assumption equal to zero, we arrive at the following decomposition:

$$GC = 2\sum_{j=1}^{p} \lambda_j \pi_j Var(s_j) + 2\sum_{j=1}^{p}\sum_{g=j+1}^{p} (\lambda_j \pi_g + \lambda_g \pi_j) Cov(s_j, s_g) + 2Cov(\psi, \chi) \quad (25)$$

In comparison to decomposition (24) it is as if the value of the constant term has been distributed over both the direct and combined or correlated contributions.

A Direct Explanation of the Correlation Between Health and Socioeconomic Status

The two super-decompositions outlined above are based on two regressions, one for each of the two dimensions involved. Each regression equation explains the variability in one dimension only. The product of the two regression equations is then supposed to provide an explanation of the correlation between the two dimensions. But does this indirect procedure really work? Should we not aim for a direct explanation of the observed correlation between the two dimensions?

The question is whether it is possible to do some kind of regression where the dependent variable measures the variability of the *correlation* between the two variables, rather than the variability in one of them only. There is no natural unit to measure correlation at the individual level. But knowing that $GC = \frac{2}{n}\sum_{i=1}^{n} h_i d_i$, a proxy variable suggests itself. Let us define the composite variable $v_i \equiv h_i d_i$ and treat it as a measure of correlation between h_i and d_i. Assuming that the independent variables $s_1, s_2, ..., s_p$ are the determining factors of the degree of correlation, we can perform the following linear regression to explain this new composite variable:

$$v_i = \phi_0 + \phi_1 s_{1,i} + \phi_2 s_{2,i} + ... + \phi_p s_{p,i} + \zeta_i \quad (26)$$

where ζ_i is an error term. Given that $GC = \frac{2}{n}\sum_{i=1}^{n} v_i$ and assuming that $\mu_\zeta = 0$, it follows that we have:

$$GC = 2\phi_0 + 2\phi_1 \mu_{s_1} + 2\phi_2 \mu_{s_2} + ... + 2\phi_p \mu_{s_p} \quad (27)$$

We therefore arrive at a decomposition consisting of a constant term $2\phi_0$, which again is difficult to interpret, and p terms $2\phi_j\mu_{s_j}$, of which the jth term may be interpreted as the contribution of factor s_j to GC. In contrast to the previous decompositions, there is no residual component.

A COMPARISON

Now that we have identified several decomposition possibilities, let us take a step back and see how they compare to one another. We no longer take into consideration the very rough decomposition (12) based on the indirectly estimated ranks derived from the regression of the underlying socioeconomic variable. As a matter of fact, in order to make the comparison meaningful, we limit ourselves to decompositions based on regressions with a common set of independent variables $s_1, s_2, ..., s_p$. We therefore assume that $\{x_1, x_2, ..., x_k\} = \{z_1, z_2, ..., z_q\} = \{s_1, s_2, ..., s_p\}$. It follows that the coefficients and the error terms of the original health regression (6) and of the original fractional rank deviation regression (13) coincide with those of the bivariate multiple regression (21)–(22), i.e. $\beta = \lambda$, $\alpha = \pi$, $\varepsilon = \psi$ and $\xi = \chi$.

There are six remaining decompositions to be compared. Three of these are one-dimensional:

(I) the health-oriented decomposition based on regression (6) and represented by Eq. (9);

(IIa) the rank-oriented decomposition based on regression (13) and represented by Eq. (15), which has a constant term;

(IIb) the rank-oriented decomposition based on regression (13) and represented by Eq. (16), without a constant term.

The other three are two-dimensional:

(IIIa) the super-decomposition based on the bivariate multiple regression model (21)–(22) and represented by Eq. (24), which has a constant term;

(IIIb) the super-decomposition based on the bivariate multiple regression model (21)–(22) and represented by Eq. (25), without a constant term;

(IV) the decomposition based on the regression of the health-fractional rank deviation product (26) and represented by Eq. (27).

Table 1 summarizes the components of each decomposition.

Some observations are in order with regard to these decompositions. First, it can be shown (see the appendix) that the residual terms of decompositions (I), (IIa), (IIb), (IIIa) and (IIIb) are all the same. This remarkable

Table 1. Components of the Six Decompositions for Comparison.

Decomposition	Constant	Contribution of s_j	Correlation between s_j and s_g	Residual
I	—	$2\lambda_j Cov(s_j, d)$	—	$2Cov(\psi, d)$
IIa	$2\pi_0 \mu_h$	$2\pi_j[Cov(h, s_j) + \mu_h \mu_{s_j}]$	—	$2Cov(h, \chi)$
IIb	—	$2\pi_j Cov(h, s_j)$	—	$2Cov(h, \chi)$
IIIa	$2\lambda_0 \pi_0$	$2(\lambda_0 \pi_j + \lambda_j \pi_0)\mu_{s_j}$ $+ 2\lambda_j \pi_j [Var(s_j) + (\mu_{s_j})^2]$	$2(\lambda_j \pi_g + \lambda_g \pi_j)$ $\times [Cov(s_j, s_g) + \mu_{s_j}\mu_{s_g}]$	$2Cov(\psi, \chi)$
IIIb	—	$2\lambda_j \pi_j Var(s_j)$	$2(\lambda_j \pi_g + \lambda_g \pi_j)Cov(s_j, s_g)$	$2Cov(\psi, \chi)$
IV	$2\phi_0$	$2\phi_j \mu_{s_j}$	—	—

result comes from the fact that the two regressions on which they are based have exactly the same set of independent variables. Second, the p individual contributions of decompositions (I) and (IIb) can be related to the direct and combined contributions of decomposition (IIIb). In fact, our assumption that the $2p$ covariance terms $Cov(s_j, \chi)$ and $Cov(\psi, s_j)$ are zero implies:

$$2\lambda_j Cov(s_j, d) = 2\lambda_j \sum_{g=1}^{p} \pi_g Cov(s_j, s_g) \quad (28)$$

$$= 2\lambda_j \pi_j Var(s_j) + 2 \sum_{g=1, g\neq j}^{p} \lambda_j \pi_g Cov(s_j, s_g) \quad (29)$$

$$2\pi_j Cov(h, s_j) = 2\pi_j \sum_{g=1}^{p} \lambda_g Cov(s_g, s_j) \quad (30)$$

$$= 2\lambda_j \pi_j Var(s_j) + 2 \sum_{g=1, g\neq j}^{p} \lambda_g \pi_j Cov(s_j, s_g) \quad (31)$$

A slightly more complex relationship holds between the terms of decompositions (I), (IIa) and (IIIa).

AN EMPIRICAL ILLUSTRATION

Data Description

The data come from the 2011 Demographic and Health Survey (DHS) of Ethiopia and are confined to children under the age of five.

First, we constructed the response variables, the health variable h, the fractional rank deviation d and the composite variable v, for use in the six decompositions. The health variable h we have chosen is actually an ill-health variable: the degree of stunting or malnutrition. It is defined on the unit interval, i.e. $a_h = 0$ and $b_h = 1$, and provides information on the depth of malnutrition with children. We obtained this measure from the child's height-for-age standard deviation or z-score which is the difference between the height of a child and the median height of a child of the same age and sex in a well-nourished reference population divided by the standard deviation in the reference population. We used the new WHO child growth population as reference population. We measured the degree of stunting relative to the threshold of minus two standard deviations of the median of the reference population. Children with a z-score greater than this threshold are not stunted and are assigned a zero degree value. The other children are stunted and are assigned a value in the unit interval that is proportional to the magnitude of their z-score with a z-score of minus six standard deviations corresponding to the maximum value of one. In total, taking into account the sample weights provided by DHS, we found that 44% of the children in our dataset (see below for further description) are stunted. To obtain the fractional rank deviation d, we ranked the children's households according to their wealth status. We used the wealth indices constructed by DHS from a principal component analysis on all household living conditions and assets. We computed the fractional rank deviation taking into account the sample weights so that, in effect, the variable d stands for the weighted fractional rank deviation. To create the composite variable v, we multiplied the variables h and d for all children in our dataset.

Second, we selected a set of nine explanatory variables for use in the decompositions. Based on previous stunting regressions performed by Wagstaff et al. (2003) and Van de Poel et al. (2007), we included a number of child-level characteristics such as age and sex of the child, maternal characteristics such as education of the mother and her partner or husband and household-level characteristics such as urban or rural residence, time to a water source, access to safe drinking water and satisfactory sanitation. In addition to that, we specified the child's age nonlinearly in the regression models using a squared term. Because Wagstaff et al. (2003) found a significant inverted u-shaped relationship for child's age in their stunting regressions for Vietnam, we expected to obtain a similar result. We mean-centred the squared term, however, to remove multicollinearity with the linear term. Furthermore, we defined the safe drinking water and satisfactory sanitation variables along the lines proposed by the WHO and UNICEF. We identified the following sources of water supply as safe drinking water: piped water (piped into dwelling, piped into yard or plot, or public tap), water from a protected well, tube well or borehole, water from a protected spring and rainwater. We identified the following sanitation infrastructure as satisfactory sanitation: a flush toilet (flush to piped sewer system, septic tank or pit latrine), a pit latrine with slab, a Ventilated Improved Pit (VIP) latrine and a composting toilet. Note that, as opposed to the regressions made by Wagstaff et al. (2003) and Van de Poel et al. (2007), we did not include a wealth-related variable in our set of explanatory variables. The reason is that we used the wealth indices for the construction of one of our response variables, the weighted fractional rank deviation d.

Table 2 shows a summary of all variables with their descriptive statistics taking into account the sample weights. We encountered missing values in 20.5% of a total of 11,654 registered children under the age of five. The final sample thus contains information on 9,262 children. We observed most of the missing data, involving 17.5% of the children, for the height-for-age z-score. The remaining missing data resulted from education of the mother's partner, time to a water source, safe drinking water and satisfactory sanitation. We performed all data manipulations and subsequent analyses (see sections Regression Results and Decomposition Results) using the statistical software package SAS, version 9.3 (SAS Institute, Cary, NC, USA).

Regression Results

The six decompositions for comparison are based on the four regressions (6), (13), (21)–(22) and (26) that relate the degree of stunting h, the weighted fractional rank deviation d, both univariate as well as bivariate, and the composite variable v, to the set of nine explanatory variables. In each of the regressions, we used the sample weights to weigh the observations by household cluster. The estimated coefficients of the bivariate regression model (21)–(22) coincide with those from fitting the two univariate models (6) and (13) using the same set of explanatory variables. In other words, the regression coefficients for h and d from a univariate or bivariate estimation procedure are the same using the same set of explanatory variables. Table 3 shows the regression coefficients for h, d and v. It also contains the t- and F-statistics and significances, for the univariate

Table 2. Mean, Standard Deviation and Description of All Variables.

Variable	Mean	Standard Deviation	Description
Degree of stunting	0.1252	0.2073	Height-for-age z-score (WHO) scaled to the interval [0,1]
Weighted fractional rank deviation	0	0.2952	Degree of stunting > 0 if height-for-age z-score < −2 SD
Composite variable	−0.0068	0.0674	Based on the wealth indices provided by DHS
Age of child	29.8571	17.8084	Degree of stunting × Weighted fractional rank deviation
Squared age of child	303.3724	270.6317	In months
Sex of child	0.5140	0.5110	Term is mean-centred: (age of child − 29.8571)^2
Residence type	0.1237	0.3366	Male (1), female (0)
Education of mother	1.3446	2.8587	Urban (1), rural (0)
Education of partner/husband	2.7439	3.8141	In years
Time to water source	0.8653	1.1756	In years
Safe drinking water	0.4614	0.5097	In hours
Satisfactory sanitation	0.1234	0.3362	Available (1), not available (0)

Table 3. Univariate Regressions for the Degree of Stunting h, the Weighted Fractional Rank Deviation d and the Composite Variable $v \equiv hd$.

	h		d		v	
	Coefficient	t-Stat	Coefficient	t-Stat	Coefficient	t-Stat
Constant	0.1307	22.37***	−0.1683	−25.07***	−0.0227	−11.88***
Age of child	0.0016	13.82***	0.0003	2.57*	−0.0001	−1.32
Squared age of child	−0.0001	−18.72***	0.0000	0.00	0.0000	2.09*
Sex of child	0.0135	3.34***	0.0067	1.43	−0.0003	−0.24
Residence type	−0.0257	−3.48***	0.2441	28.72***	0.0236	9.77***
Education of mother	−0.0036	−3.89***	0.0106	9.93***	−0.0004	−1.27
Education of partner/husband	−0.0030	−4.37***	0.0147	18.60***	0.0014	6.33***
Time to water source	−0.0003	−0.17	−0.0042	−2.06*	0.0005	0.79
Safe drinking water	0.0034	0.78	0.1298	25.91***	0.0175	12.30***
Satisfactory sanitation	−0.0171	−2.60**	0.1114	14.73***	0.0096	4.46***
F		85.82**		681.26***		72.47***
R^2		0.0770		0.3986		0.0659

*$p < 0.05$, **$p < 0.01$, ***$p < 0.001$, else $p > 0.1$.

regressions. On the other hand, the bivariate regression provides bivariate test statistics and significances, which appear in Table 4.

The F-tests for the univariate regressions in Table 3 reveal that each of the univariate models is highly significant. The R^2 values of the models show that much of the variation in h, d and v remains unexplained. That should not come as a surprise; for instance, Wagstaff et al. (2003) also observed R^2 values of low explicative power for their stunting regressions (equal to 0.188 and 0.247) despite the fact that household consumption as a wealth-related variable was included in the models. Furthermore, the t-tests for the individual explanatory variables in the univariate regressions indicate that all variables are significant in at least one model.

Regarding the significant variables of the univariate regression models, we wish to highlight the following results. Apart from the absence of a wealth-related variable, our stunting model h resembles the stunting models presented by Wagstaff et al. (2003) and Van de Poel et al. (2007). Similar to Wagstaff et al. (2003), the t-statistics indicate that child's age is the most important determinant of malnutrition with coefficients for the linear and squared term describing an inverted u-shaped relationship. Other determinants of malnutrition are, in order of importance, the education of the mother and her partner, the residence type, the sex of the child and satisfactory sanitation. Furthermore, in line with our expectations, the most

Table 4. Bivariate Analysis of Variance of the Degree of Stunting h and the Weighted Fractional Rank Deviation d.

	Wilks' Lambda	Bivariate F
Constant	0.8969	531.59***
Age of child	0.9785	101.43***
Squared age of child	0.9634	175.91***
Sex of child	0.9985	6.92***
Residence type	0.9179	413.94***
Education of mother	0.9883	54.65***
Education of partner/husband	0.9629	178.20***
Time to water source	0.9995	2.16
Safe drinking water	0.9318	338.38***
Satisfactory sanitation	0.9768	109.88***
Overall model	0.5605	345.05***
At least one distinct response	0.5605	345.05***
Two distinct responses	0.9346	80.90***

***$p < 0.001$, else $p > 0.1$.

important effects on the fractional rank deviation d result from the residence type and safe drinking water, followed by the education of the mother's partner, satisfactory sanitation and the education of the mother. Except for the education of the mother, these variables are also important to explain v. In addition to that, v depends nonlinearly on child's age which is demonstrated by a normal u-shaped relationship.

Using the models h and d in a bivariate estimation procedure, we obtain bivariate test statistics that are more powerful than the univariate t- or F-tests at detecting significant relationships when the responses are correlated. Moreover, the bivariate tests provide a way to understand the structure of relationships across the two responses. In particular, they point at the number of relevant response dimensions and at a significant set of explanatory variables to describe them. The bivariate significances in Table 4 are based on Wilks' lambda or the likelihood ratio test that performs the same role as the univariate t- or F-test. Using Wilks' lambda, an approximation to F has been derived that closely fits its value (see, e. g., Tabachnick & Fidell, 2012). The F-test for the overall bivariate regression model for h and d shows that the model is highly significant. The F-tests for the bivariate response character confirm that the two response dimensions are appropriate and the F-tests for the individual explanatory variables show that all variables have a significant effect on the bivariate response except for time to a water source. Regarding these significant variables, the F-statistics indicate that the residence type and safe drinking water affect the two responses h and d most. They are followed by the education of the mother's partner and the linear and squared term of child's age.

Decomposition Results

Using either the 'product definition' in Eq. (1) or the 'covariance definition' in Eq. (5) of the Generalized Concentration Index, we obtained a value for the GC of -0.0136. Its negative sign reveals higher rates of child malnutrition among the poor or a socioeconomic inequality of malnutrition to the disadvantage of the poor. We present the six decompositions in percentages, setting the value of the GC to 100%.

Table 5 shows the percentage contributions of decompositions (I), (IIa), (IIb) and (IV) represented by Eqs. (9), (15), (16) and (27). They are based on the univariate regressions for h, d and v. As opposed to decomposition (IV), decompositions (I), (IIa) and (IIb) are characterized by a residual

Table 5. Percentage Contributions from Decompositions (I), (IIa), (IIb) and (IV).

	I	IIa	IIb	IV
Constant	–	309.98	–	333.72
Age of child	−1.04	−21.69	−2.77	22.10
Squared age of child	0.20	−0.01	0.01	−23.38
Sex of child	−0.27	−6.62	−0.32	2.41
Residence type	18.41	−33.65	21.92	−42.94
Education of mother	17.66	−16.21	10.02	7.65
Education of partner/husband	20.58	−55.19	18.92	−57.29
Time to water source	−0.12	7.00	0.24	−5.90
Safe drinking water	−2.86	−105.38	4.94	−118.97
Satisfactory sanitation	7.66	−18.03	7.26	−17.41
Residual	39.79	39.79	39.79	–
Total	100.00	100.00	100.00	100.00

term. These residuals are the same as a result from using the same set of nine explanatory variables in the regression models for h and d. Their contribution equals 39.79%, which is substantial. Another result from comparing the four decompositions is the contrast between decompositions (I) and (IIb) without a constant term and decompositions (IIa) and (IV) with a constant term that exceeds more than three times the value of the GC in both decompositions. In addition to that, the rank-oriented decompositions (IIa) and (IIb) with and without a constant term, which are supposed to give similar results, are completely different. There is more similarity in decompositions (I) and (IIb) without a constant term and in decompositions (IIa) and (IV) with a constant term than in decompositions (IIa) and (IIb) that are based on the same regression model. The presence or absence of the constant term clearly dominates the decompositions. In decompositions (I) and (IIb), the residence type and the education of the mother and her partner are the most important contributors to socioeconomic inequality. Their contributions have the same sign as the GC, which means that they can be seen as factors which are responsible for the pro-poor character of socioeconomic inequality of malnutrition. In other words, living in towns and having parents with more years of education tend to be associated with less malnutrition. In decompositions (IIa) and (IV), on the other hand, the most important contributors are safe drinking water, followed by the education of the mother's partner and the residence type. However, the sign of their contributions is opposite to the sign of the GC, which means that they have a pro-rich effect on socioeconomic inequality of malnutrition. From a formal point of view, one might say that in these two cases the very large positive percentage for the constant term forces negative percentages on most of the other terms.

Next, Tables 6 and 7 contain the individual percentage contributions of decompositions (IIIa) and (IIIb) represented by Eqs. (24) and (25) where decomposition (IIIa) includes a constant term. They are based on the bivariate regression for h and d. Both decompositions examine the relationship between h and d, but also relate to the one-dimensional decompositions for h and d. In particular, the column and row totals of the contributions of decomposition (IIIa) in Table 6 relate to decompositions (I) and (IIa) and the column and row totals of the contributions of decomposition (IIIb) in Table 7 relate to decompositions (I) and (IIb). As a result, the contribution of the residual term in decompositions (IIIa) and (IIIb) is the same as in decompositions (I), (IIa) and (IIb), amounting to 39.79%.

Tables 8 and 9 contain summary presentations of decompositions (IIIa) and (IIIb) showing the direct and combined or correlated percentage contributions of the decompositions. Similar to decompositions (IIa) and (IV), the constant term in decomposition (IIIa) exceeds more than three times the value of the GC. It is offset by the direct contributions of the decomposition which sum to a large negative percentage. In contrast, the correlated contributions of the decomposition sum to a positive percentage that is about half the value of the GC. For decomposition (IIIb) without a constant term, the percentage totals from the direct and correlated contributions are all positive and therefore smaller in magnitude. In addition, the total of the correlated contributions is about twice as large as the total of the direct contributions.

The most important direct contributions to inequality in decomposition (IIIa) come from the same variables that determine inequality in decompositions (IIa) and (IV). Noting that in decomposition (IIIa) the large direct contributions of the linear and squared term of child's age balance each other out, these determinants are safe drinking water, followed by the education of the mother's partner and the residence type. Similarly, the direct contributions to inequality in decomposition (IIIb) correspond to those in decompositions (I) and (IIb) and come from the residence type and the education of the mother and her partner. As an overview, Figs. 1 and 2 show the direct percentage contributions of decompositions (I), (IIb) and (IIIb) without a constant term and decompositions (IIa), (IIIa) and (IV) with a constant term.

Table 6. Percentage Contributions from Decomposition (IIIa) in Relationship with Decompositions (I) and (IIa).

	Constant	Age of Child	Squared Age of Child	Sex of Child	Residence Type	Education of Mother	Education of Partner	Time to Water	Safe Water	Satisfactory Sanitation	χ	Total (I)
Constant	323.63	−19.74	−0.02	−6.57	−58.02	−27.38	−77.37	7.06	−115.17	−26.41	—	—
Age of Child	119.23	−9.75	−0.01	−2.44	−21.22	−9.50	−27.54	2.60	−42.89	−9.52	—	−1.04
Squared Age of Child	−107.85	6.39	0.01	2.22	19.64	9.32	26.53	−2.32	37.50	8.77	—	0.20
Sex of Child	17.22	−1.06	0.00	−0.68	−3.06	−1.44	−4.12	0.38	−6.09	−1.43	—	−0.27
Residence Type	−7.88	0.48	0.00	0.16	11.42	2.19	4.55	−0.07	5.50	2.07	—	18.41
Education of Mother	−12.03	0.69	0.00	0.24	7.09	5.42	7.64	−0.22	6.46	2.37	—	17.66
Education of Partner	−20.36	1.20	0.00	0.41	8.81	4.57	13.87	−0.41	9.39	3.10	—	20.58
Time to Water	−0.64	0.04	0.00	0.01	0.05	0.05	0.14	−0.04	0.24	0.04	—	−0.12
Safe Water	3.88	−0.24	0.00	−0.08	−1.36	−0.50	−1.20	0.09	−3.00	−0.46	—	−2.86
Satisfactory Sanitation	−5.21	0.31	0.00	0.11	3.01	1.06	2.33	−0.08	2.69	3.45	—	7.66
ψ	—	—	—	—	—	—	—	—	—	—	39.79	39.79
Total (IIa)	309.98	−21.69	−0.01	−6.62	−33.65	−16.21	−55.19	7.00	−105.38	−18.03	39.79	100.00

Table 7. Percentage Contributions from Decomposition (IIIb) in Relationship with Decompositions (I) and (IIb).

	Age of Child	Squared Age of Child	Sex of Child	Residence Type	Education of Mother	Education of Partner	Time to Water	Safe Water	Satisfactory Sanitation	χ	Total (I)
Age of Child	−2.48	0.00	−0.02	0.16	0.58	0.96	−0.01	−0.46	0.21	−	−1.04
Squared Age of Child	−0.19	0.00	0.03	0.30	0.19	0.75	0.04	−0.88	−0.03	−	0.20
Sex of Child	−0.01	0.00	−0.33	0.03	0.02	0.00	0.01	0.04	−0.03	−	−0.27
Residence Type	0.00	0.00	0.00	10.01	1.52	2.66	0.10	2.69	1.43	−	18.41
Education of Mother	−0.04	0.00	0.00	4.93	4.40	4.76	0.04	2.18	1.38	−	17.66
Education of Partner	−0.04	0.00	0.00	5.16	2.85	9.00	0.04	2.14	1.44	−	20.58
Time to Water	0.00	0.00	0.00	−0.07	−0.01	−0.01	−0.02	0.01	−0.01	−	−0.12
Safe Water	0.00	0.00	0.00	−0.67	−0.17	−0.27	0.00	−1.61	−0.14	−	−2.86
Satisfactory Sanitation	−0.01	0.00	0.00	2.07	0.62	1.08	0.03	0.84	3.02	−	7.66
ψ	−	−	−	−	−	−	−	−	−	39.79	39.79
Total (IIb)	−2.77	0.01	−0.32	21.92	10.02	18.92	0.24	4.94	7.26	39.79	100.00

Table 8. Percentage Direct and Combined Contributions from Decomposition (IIIa).

| | Direct Effect | Combined Effect ||||||||
		Age of child	Squared age of child	Sex of child	Residence type	Education of mother	Education of partner	Time to water	Safe water
Age of child	89.73								
Squared age of child	−107.86	6.38							
Sex of child	9.97	−3.49	2.22						
Residence type	−54.48	−20.74	19.64	−2.90					
Education of mother	−33.99	−8.81	9.32	−1.20	9.28				
Education of partner	−83.87	−26.34	26.53	−3.71	13.35	12.21			
Time to water	6.38	2.64	−2.32	0.40	−0.02	−0.17	−0.27		
Safe water	−114.28	−43.13	37.50	−6.17	4.13	5.97	8.18	0.33	
Satisfactory sanitation	−28.17	−9.21	8.77	−1.33	5.08	3.43	5.43	−0.05	2.23
Component total	−316.56								53.15
Constant	323.63								
Residual	39.79								
Total									100.00

Table 9. Percentage Direct and Combined Contributions from Decomposition (IIIb).

| | Direct Effect | Combined Effect |||||||
		Age of child	Squared age of child	Sex of child	Residence type	Education of mother	Education of partner	Time to water	Safe water
Age of child	−2.48								
Squared age of child	0.00	−0.19							
Sex of child	−0.33	−0.02	0.03						
Residence type	10.01	0.15	0.30	0.03					
Education of mother	4.40	0.54	0.19	0.01	6.45				
Education of partner	9.00	0.92	0.75	0.00	7.82	7.61			
Time to water	−0.02	−0.01	0.04	0.01	0.03	0.04	0.02		
Safe water	−1.61	−0.46	−0.88	0.04	2.02	2.01	1.87	0.01	
Satisfactory sanitation	3.02	0.20	−0.03	−0.03	3.50	2.01	2.52	0.02	0.70
Component total	21.99					38.22			
Residual	39.79								
Total					100.00				

254 GUIDO ERREYGERS AND ROSELINDE KESSELS

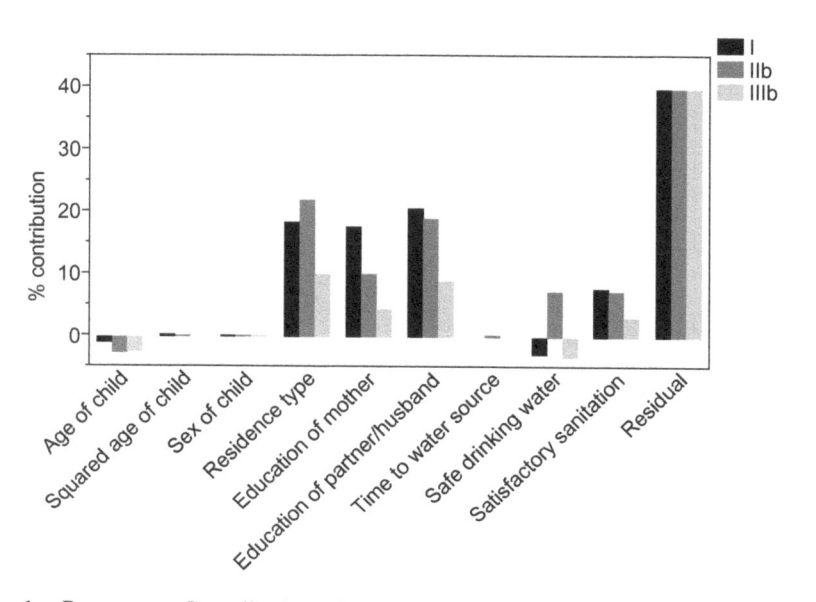

Fig. 1. Percentage Contributions from Direct Effects Related to Decompositions (I), (IIb) and (IIIb).

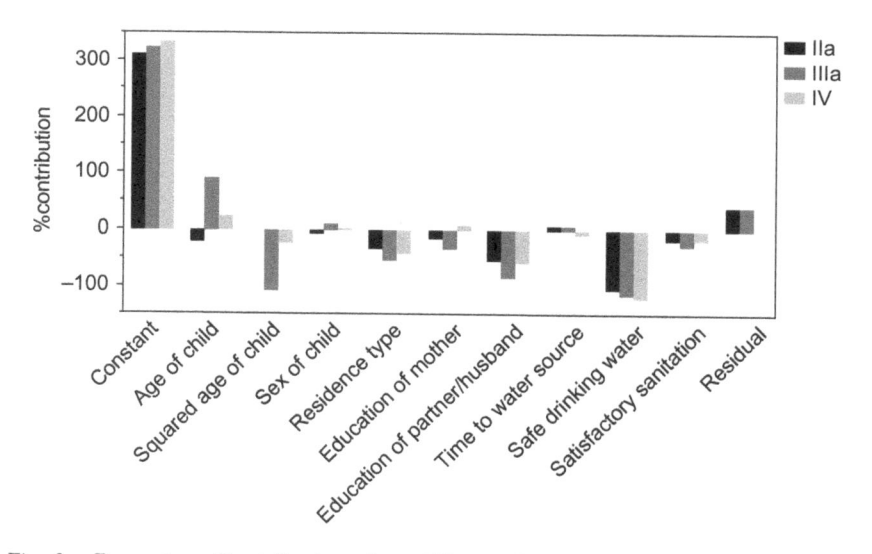

Fig. 2. Percentage Contributions from Direct Effects Related to Decompositions (IIa), (IIIa) and (IV).

DISCUSSION

Both the theoretical framework and the empirical illustration reveal that there are many ways to generate regression-based decompositions of socio-economic inequality of health, and that the results may be very different. We do not always find that the estimated individual contributions of the explanatory variables have the same sign, let alone the same magnitude. Three of the six decompositions have very large constant terms (by 'very large' we mean that these terms exceed by far the magnitude of the index itself), which seem difficult to interpret. The two super-decompositions involve a lot of correlation terms which on the whole may be more important than the direct contributions of the explanatory variables. Except for the decomposition based on the regression of the health-fractional rank deviation product, all decompositions have a residual term which may be very substantial in magnitude.

Both the one-dimensional rank-oriented approach and the two-dimensional simultaneous approach lead to two distinct decomposition formulas, one with and one without constant term. A comparison of the two sets of results shows huge differences. It is hard to understand why two equivalent starting points – the 'product definition' and the 'covariance definition' of the Generalized Concentration Index – produce so widely divergent outcomes. One might be tempted to conclude that any decomposition formula has a large amount of arbitrariness in it.

As far as the empirical aspects are concerned, perhaps we should have tried to increase the explanatory power of our regression equations by including more variables. Although this might improve the reliability of the empirical estimates, we doubt whether it would change much to the essence of our results. It seems highly unlikely that the constant term will fade away, that the correlation effects will become negligible or that the residual term will disappear. Anyhow, additional empirical work (more years, more countries, more health variables, etc.) might be useful to try and discern a pattern in the various decompositions.

Finally, we repeat our recommendation not to include socioeconomic status as an explanatory variable in the regression of health, or likewise, health as an explanatory variable in the regression of socioeconomic status. Our motivation is that including either of these variables distorts the explanation of the correlation between health and socioeconomic status. By doing so, it is almost as if we are treating the variable in question both as a dependent and as an independent variable. It seems to us that the typically high contributions of socioeconomic status in many decomposition analyses — e.g., more than one third in the study on child mortality in Iran by Hosseinpoor et al. (2006) and about 30% in the study on malnutrition in Ghana by Van de Poel et al. (2007) — are largely artificial results. These are mainly due to the high degree of correlation between the socioeconomic variable which is chosen as explanatory variable and the fractional rank deviation variable which is used for the calculation of the inequality index. In effect, much of what otherwise would end up in the residual term appears as a contribution of the socioeconomic variable. In our view, this calls for restraint when interpreting the results of decompositions of socioeconomic inequality of health.

CONCLUSION

In the past, research on the measurement of socioeconomic inequality of health has often been a copy of research on the measurement of income inequality. To a great extent, this has also been the case with regard to decomposition analysis. We believe that more caution should be exerted when adopting methods and results from one field to the other. The main reason is that bivariate inequality is of a different nature than univariate inequality. Secondary, the health variable taken into consideration is almost always not an unbounded variable such as income. What we have tried to show in this chapter is that there are many ways of obtaining decomposition results for rank-dependent indicators of socioeconomic inequality of health, and that therefore decomposition results should not be taken for granted. In our opinion, one way to proceed from here is to use an axiomatic approach. This may be helpful first to identify which properties a good decomposition should have, and then to derive which decompositions possess the desired properties.

ACKNOWLEDGEMENTS

The research described in this chapter was carried out while Roselinde Kessels was a postdoctoral fellow of the Research Foundation — Flanders (FWO). We thank Tom Van Ourti and Philip Clarke for discussions related to decomposition analysis, Ellen Van de Poel for assistance with regard to the Ethiopian data, and Owen O'Donnell for his detailed and constructive comments which have led to significant additions and improvements to the chapter. We are also grateful to seminar participants at the Centre of Health Economics Research (COHERE) of the University of Southern Denmark, and the Department of Economics of the University of Antwerp.

REFERENCES

Abul Naga, R. H., & Geoffard, P.-Y. (2006). Decomposition of bivariate inequality indices by attributes. *Economics Letters*, *90*(3), 362–367.

Bourguignon, F. (1979). Decomposable income inequality measures. *Econometrica*, *47*(4), 901–920.

Clarke, P. M., Gerdtham, U.-G., & Connelly, L. B. (2003). A note on the decomposition of the health concentration index. *Health Economics*, *12*(6), 511–516.

Cowell, F. A., & Fiorio, C. V. (2011). Inequality decompositions – a reconciliation. *Journal of Economic Inequality*, *9*(4), 509–528.

Erreygers, G. (2009). Correcting the concentration index. *Journal of Health Economics*, *28*(2), 504–515.

Erreygers, G., & Van Ourti, T. (2011). Measuring socioeconomic inequality in health, health care and health financing by means of rank-dependent indices: A recipe for good practice. *Journal of Health Economics*, *30*(4), 685–694.

Fields, G. S. (2003). Accounting for income inequality and its change: A new method, with application to the distribution of earnings in the United States. In S. W. Polachek (Ed.), *Worker well-being and public policy* (Vol. 22, pp. 1–38). Research in Labor Economics. Bingley, UK: Emerald.

Gravelle, H. (2003). Measuring income related inequality in health: Standardisation and the partial concentration index. *Health Economics*, *12*(10), 803–819.

Hosseinpoor, A. R., Van Doorslaer, E., Speybroeck, N., Naghavi, M., Mohammad, K., Majdzadeh, R., Delavar, B., Jamshidi, H., Vega, J. (2006). Decomposing socioeconomic inequality in infant mortality in Iran. *International Journal of Epidemiology*, *35*(5), 1211–1219.

Jones, A. M., & López Nicolás, A. (2004). Measurement and explanation of socioeconomic inequality in health with longitudinal data. *Health Economics*, *13*(10), 1015–1030.

Morduch, J., & Sicular, T. (2002). Rethinking inequality decomposition, with evidence from rural China. *Economic Journal*, *112*(476), 93–106.

Oaxaca, R. (1973). Male-female wage differentials in urban labor markets. *International Economic Review*, *14*(3), 693–709.

O'Donnell, O., Van Doorslaer, E., & Wagstaff, A. (2006). Decomposition of inequalities in health and health care. In A. M. Jones (Ed.), *The Elgar companion to health economics* (pp. 179–192). Cheltenham, UK: Edward Elgar.

O'Donnell, O., Van Doorslaer, E., Wagstaff, A., & Lindelow, M. (2008). *Analyzing health equity using household survey data. A guide to techniques and their implementation*. Washington, DC: World Bank.

Podder, N. (1993). The disaggregation of the Gini coefficient by factor components and its applications to Australia. *Review of Income and Wealth*, *39*(1), 51–61.

Rao, V. M. (1969). Two decompositions of concentration ratio. *Journal of the Royal Statistical Society, Series A (General)*, *132*(3), 418–425.

Shorrocks, A. F. (1980). The class of additively decomposable inequality measures. *Econometrica*, *48*(3), 613–625.

Shorrocks, A. F. (1982). Inequality decomposition by factor components. *Econometrica*, *50*(1), 193–211.

Shorrocks, A. F. (1984). Inequality decomposition by population subgroups. *Econometrica*, *52*(6), 1369–1385.

Tabachnick, B. G., & Fidell, L. S. (2012). *Using multivariate statistics* (6th ed.), Boston, MA: Pearson Education.

Van de Poel, E., Hosseinpoor, A. R., Jehu-Appiah, C., Vega, J., & Speybroeck, N. (2007). Malnutrition and the disproportional burden on the poor: The case of Ghana. *International Journal for Equity in Health*, *6*(21). doi:10.1186/1475-9276-6-21

Van Doorslaer, E., & Van Ourti, T. (2011). Inequality and inequity in health and health care. In S. Glied & P. C. Smith (Eds.), *The Oxford handbook of health economics* (pp. 837–869). Oxford: Oxford University Press.

Van Ourti, T., Van Doorslaer, E., & Koolman, X. (2009). The effect of income growth and inequality on health inequality: Theory and empirical evidence from the European Panel. *Journal of Health Economics*, *28*(3), 525–539.

Wagstaff, A. (2005). The bounds of the concentration index when the variable of interest is binary, with an application to immunization inequality. *Health Economics*, *14*(4), 429–432.

Wagstaff, A., Van Doorslaer, E., & Watanabe, N. (2003). On decomposing the causes of health sector inequalities with an application to malnutrition inequalities in Vietnam. *Journal of Econometrics*, *112*(1), 207–223.

APPENDIX

In conventional matrix notation, the two regressions (21) and (22) can be written as $h = S\lambda + \psi$ and $d = S\pi + \chi$, where $S = [u, s_1, s_2, ..., s_p]$ and u is a vector of ones. The OLS estimators of λ and π are equal to $\hat{\lambda} = (S'S)^{-1} S'h$ and $\hat{\pi} = (S'S)^{-1} S'd$. This implies that the estimated errors are $\hat{\psi} = h - S\hat{\lambda} = Mh$ and $\hat{\chi} = d - S\hat{\pi} = Md$, where $M = I - S(S'S)S'$. Matrix M is both symmetric and idempotent.

From $\hat{\psi} = Mh$ it follows that $d'\hat{\psi} = d'Mh$, and from $\hat{\chi} = Md$ that $h'\hat{\chi} = h'Md$. Since M is symmetric, we have $h'Md = h'M'd$ and of course $h'M'd = d'Mh$. Hence we have $d'\hat{\psi} = h'\hat{\chi}$. Given that $Cov(d, \hat{\psi}) = \frac{1}{n} d'\hat{\psi}$ and $Cov(h, \hat{\chi}) = \frac{1}{n} h'\hat{\chi}$, it follows that $Cov(d, \hat{\psi}) = Cov(h, \hat{\chi})$. Moreover, we also have $\hat{\psi}'\hat{\chi} = (Mh)'(Md) = h'M'Md$. Since M is symmetric and idempotent, we know that $M'M = MM = M$, and so we find that $\hat{\psi}'\hat{\chi} = h'Md$. This means that $Cov(d, \hat{\psi}) = Cov(h, \hat{\chi}) = Cov(\hat{\psi}, \hat{\chi})$.

PART II
DETERMINANTS OF HEALTH INEQUALITY

HEALTH INEQUALITIES THROUGH THE LENS OF HEALTH-CAPITAL THEORY: ISSUES, SOLUTIONS, AND FUTURE DIRECTIONS

Titus J. Galama and Hans van Kippersluis

ABSTRACT

We explore what health-capital theory has to offer in terms of informing and directing research into health inequality. We argue that economic theory can help in identifying mechanisms through which specific socioeconomic indicators and health interact. Our reading of the literature, and our own work, leads us to conclude that non-degenerate versions of the Grossman (1972a, 1972b) model and its extensions can explain many salient stylized facts on health inequalities. Yet, further development is required in at least two directions. First, a childhood phase needs to be incorporated, in recognition of the importance of childhood endowments and investments in the determination of later-life socioeconomic and health outcomes. Second, a unified theory of joint investment in skill (or human) capital and in health capital could provide a basis for a theory of the relationship between education and health.

Keywords: Health; inequality; socioeconomic status; human capital theory

JEL classifications: D91; I12; I14

INTRODUCTION

Health is a basic necessity of life. Inequalities in health constitute inequalities in people's capability to function. The right to the highest attainable level of health is enshrined in the charter of the World Health Organization (WHO) and in many international treaties (e.g. article 25 of the Universal Declaration of Human Rights). Yet, the majority of people in the world do not enjoy the health that is biologically possible (WHO, 2008); the socially and economically disadvantaged generally experience worse health outcomes (e.g. Mackenbach, Kunst, Cavelaars, Groenhof, & Geurts, 1997).

Health inequality is not only an infringement of equity: the avoidable mortality and morbidity of lower socioeconomic groups also impedes productivity and threatens to undermine economic growth and prosperity (WHO, 2001). It is no surprise then that a primary goal of many governments' health policies is the reduction of health inequities (e.g. US Healthy People 2020 Initiative, 2010).

A significant body of research across multiple disciplines has been devoted to documenting and explaining the substantial disparities in health between socioeconomic groups. The recent literature has concentrated on estimating causal effects. It has been established that causality runs in both directions: evidence is strong that health affects socioeconomic characteristics such as employment and income (e.g. Garcia-Gomez, van Kippersluis, O'Donnell, & Van Doorslaer, forthcoming; Smith, 1999), and the evidence base is growing that socioeconomic characteristics, in particular education, affect health (e.g. Conti, Heckman, & Urzua, 2010; Lleras-Muney, 2005; Van Kippersluis, O'Donnell, & Van Doorslaer, 2011).[1]

A major limitation of the existing literature is the failure to uncover the mechanisms underlying the causal relationships: for example, it is not known how the educated achieve their health advantage (Cutler & Lleras-Muney, 2010). Case and Deaton (2005) note that 'it is extremely difficult to untangle the links between work, earnings, health, and education, without some sort of guiding framework.' In this chapter we explore what economic theory, and in particular health-capital theory developed in the seminal work of Michael Grossman (1972a, 1972b), can offer in terms of improving understanding of the causes of health inequalities.

We will argue that economic theory can help in identifying mechanisms through which specific socioeconomic indicators, such as education, income and wealth, and health interact. Identifying the mechanisms is vital to evaluation of the normative case for reducing health inequalities and the design of policies that are effective in doing so (Deaton, 2002).

Based on our reading of the literature, and our own work, we conclude that the Grossman (1972a, 1972b) model provides a solid foundation for the study of health inequalities across socioeconomic groups. With the extensions proposed by Ehrlich and Chuma (1990), Case and Deaton (2005), and Galama and Van Kippersluis (2010), health-capital theory can explain important stylized facts on health inequalities. Yet, further development is required in at least two directions. First, theories of health inequalities need to include a childhood phase, recognizing the importance of childhood endowments and investments in the determination of later-life socioeconomic and health outcomes (e.g. Cunha & Heckman, 2007; Heckman, 2006). Second, the human- and health-capital literatures have developed separately and currently no unifying theory exists. As a result, both theories fall short of explaining the strong association between education and health. We outline our initial thoughts on both of these areas for future research. We believe advancements in these directions are feasible and anticipate them to occur in the next few years.

This chapter is organized as follows. In the next section we discuss some salient empirical stylized facts on health inequality that economic theory should be able to capture. The third section focuses on health-capital theory: it starts from the conventional Grossman model, presents issues with the model, proposes solutions and discusses possible future directions of theory development. Finally, we summarize our findings and conclude.

STYLIZED FACTS ON HEALTH INEQUALITY

In this section we discuss six of the most important stylized facts that emerge from the rich empirical literature on socioeconomic inequalities in health. This list is not meant to be exhaustive, or even comprehensive. It reflects our personal view of stylized facts that ought to be captured by an economic theory aiming to provide insight into health inequalities. Further, we stress that the focus is on socioeconomic inequalities only, and we do not discuss racial or gender disparities in health (see, e.g., Annandale & Hunt, 2000; Arber & Cooper, 1999; Levine et al., 2001; Williams & Jackson, 2005 for discussions of those). Also, we restrict attention to the developed world (see Cutler & Lleras-Muney, 2012 for a review including developing countries).

Our six stylized facts on health inequality are as follows:

1. Health is strongly associated with socioeconomic status, irrespective of the measures used, and irrespective of the institutional setting.

Disparities in health across socioeconomic status (SES) groups are substantial. For example, Case and Deaton (2005) show how in the United States, a 20-year-old low-income (bottom quartile of family income) male, on average, reports to be in similar health as a 60-year-old high-income (top quartile) male. Inequalities in health exist across all measures of SES, such as education, income and wealth, and across all indicators of health, including subjective measures of health, and more objective measures such as the onset of chronic diseases, disability and mortality (e.g. Adler et al., 1994; Marmot, 1999; Smith, 1999). Disparities are found in countries with relatively low levels of protection from loss of work and health risks, such as the United States, and those with stronger welfare systems, such as the Netherlands (Case & Deaton, 2005; House et al., 1994; Smith, 1999, 2007; van Kippersluis, O'Donnell, Van Doorslaer, & Van Ourti, 2010).

2. Health inequalities between low- and high-SES groups increase over the life cycle until age 60, after which they narrow.

In cross-sectional data, health differences across low- and high-SES groups exist already by age 20, and increase gradually until around age 60, after which the health differences appear to narrow. Fig. 1 illustrates how these relations are remarkably similar between countries (the United States and the Netherlands shown).

Interpretations of the observed widening and subsequent narrowing of the SES-health gradient with age differ in the extent to which the observed pattern is presumed to reflect substantive changes in the relationship between SES and health over the life course, as opposed to simply being the product of methodological limitations. According to the *cumulative-advantage hypothesis*, the SES-health gradient increases over the life course due to gestation of the effects. For example, the health effects of socioeconomic differences in smoking become apparent only in middle

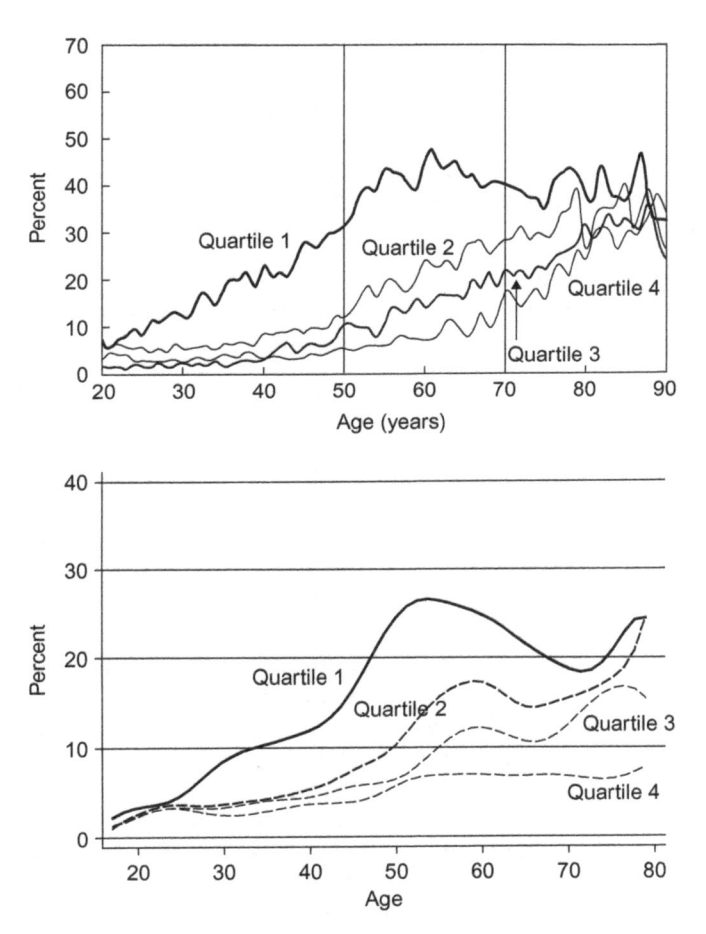

Fig. 1. Percentage Reporting Fair or Poor Health (bottom two categories of Self-Reported Health) by Age-Specific Household Income Quartiles. Top: US National Health Interview Surveys, 1991–1996, taken from Smith (2004) and reproduced with permission of John Wiley & Sons, Inc. Bottom: Dutch CBS Health Interview Surveys, 1983–2000, own calculations.

age (Lynch, 2003; Ross & Wu, 1996). Selective mortality and cohort effects obscure this process, as lower SES people are more likely to die, resulting in an apparently healthier surviving disadvantaged population, and explaining the narrowing of disparities in old age. The competing view, the *age-as-leveller hypothesis*, proposes that biological determinants increase in importance relative to socioeconomic determinants at older ages (Herd, 2006), leading to smaller socioeconomic inequalities at later ages. Generally, the evidence is consistent with a cumulative-advantage process operating until middle age, with age indeed acting as a leveller in old age (Beckett, 2000; Case & Deaton, 2005; Deaton & Paxson, 1998; House et al., 1994; Smith, 2007).

3. Health insurance and access to health care only explain a small fraction of health inequalities − occupation, health behaviours and the ability to process information seem more important.

It has been argued that utilization of medical services and access to care explain only part of the observed inequalities in health by SES (Adler, Boyce, Chesney, Folkman, & Syme, 1993). Physical and psychosocial hazards at work seem to play a larger role: low-SES individuals more often perform physically demanding manual labour or are employed in jobs associated with greater psychosocial stressors than high-SES individuals, and their health deteriorates faster as a consequence (Borg & Kristensen, 2000; Case & Deaton, 2005; Marmot, Ryff, Bumpass, Shipley, & Marks, 1997; see also Ravesteijn, Van Kippersluis, & Van Doorslaer, this volume).

Additionally, inequalities arise due to differences in health behaviours: higher SES people are less likely to smoke, drink heavily, or be obese (Cutler, Lleras-Muney, & Vogl, 2011). Fuchs (1986) even argues that in developed countries, it is personal lifestyles that cause the greatest variation in health. How SES affects health behaviours is largely unclear, yet the ability to process new information and to take advantage of new medical technologies seems important (Goldman & Smith, 2002; Glied & Lleras-Muney, 2008; Lleras-Muney & Lichtenberg, 2005). This suggests that access to health care and technology does have an indirect role in generating health inequalities.

4. There exists an important 'reverse causality' effect of ill-health on labour force participation, income and wealth.

One of the dominant pathways responsible for the association between health and economic circumstances is the strong effect health has on labour force participation, earnings and wealth, especially in middle age. Unhealthy individuals drop out of the labour force sooner, and lose income as a result. This explanation was proposed by Smith (1999, 2007) and Case and Deaton (2005), and has been corroborated by quasi-experimental evidence of the effect of sudden health shocks on earnings and income

(Garcia-Gomez et al., forthcoming; Halla & Zweimuller, forthcoming; Møller Dano, 2005).

5. Among dimensions of socioeconomic status, education seems to be the most important determinant of health.

Cutler et al. (2011) argue that the evidence points to no or only very limited impact of income or wealth on health (see also Adams, Hurd, McFadden, Merrill, & Ribeiro 2003; Michaud & Van Soest, 2008; Smith, 1999). Yet, this view is not unequivocally accepted. For example, Lynch, Kaplan, and Shema (1997) suggest that accumulated exposure to economic hardship causes bad health.

Far less controversy exists on education being a powerful determinant of health. There is accumulating evidence that education has a causal effect on health (e.g. Conti et al., 2010; Lleras-Muney, 2005; Oreopoulos, 2006; Van Kippersluis et al., 2011), although not all studies find this (Albouy & Lequien, 2008; Clark & Royer, forthcoming).

6. A large part of the health gradient may be due to early childhood endowments and investments.

In a series of papers, David Barker and co-authors demonstrated the importance of foetal growth on later-life health outcomes (e.g. Barker, 1995; see also Almond & Currie, 2011). More recently, James Heckman and colleagues have emphasized the role of childhood cognitive and non-cognitive abilities in determining both education and health outcomes in later life (e.g. Conti et al., 2010; Cunha & Heckman, 2007; see also Currie & Almond, 2011).

This evidence, combined with strong evidence that parental, especially maternal, SES influences the evolution of child health (Case et al., 2002; Currie, 2009; Currie & Stabile, 2003), suggests that a large part of the SES-health gradient may be determined very early in life. As Cutler et al. (2011, p. 154) note, this suggests also an intergenerational aspect of inequalities: 'poor childhood health begets limited means in adulthood, which in turn begets poor childhood health for the next generation.'

HEALTH-CAPITAL THEORY

A natural framework of analysis is provided by human-capital theory, the foundations of which have been laid by the seminal works of Schultz

(1961), Becker (1964), Ben-Porath (1967), and Mincer (1974). While this theory has proven very effective in contributing to the understanding of decisions with respect to education and (on-the-job) training, it falls short in this regard with respect to health. For example, Becker (1964) observes that investments in human capital should fall with age as the period over which returns can be accrued decreases. Yet, investments in health clearly increase with age, even after retirement when health has lost its importance in generating earnings. This, and other distinctions identified by, e.g., Mushkin (1962) between health and other types of human capital led to the development of the so-called health-capital model by Grossman (1972a, 1972b, 2000). The health-capital model has served as the workhorse model in health economics, and has greatly contributed to the understanding of a wide range of phenomena in health and health care.

Model Formulation

In the health-capital model, health is treated as a stock that provides direct utility:

$$\int_0^T U[C(t), H(t)] e^{-\beta t} dt \tag{1}$$

where utility $U[\cdot]$ is provided by consumption $C(t)$ and health $H(t)$ and β is the rate at which individuals discount future utility. Health depreciates with age at the biological ageing rate $d(t)$:

$$\frac{\partial H(t)}{\partial t} = f[I(t)] - d(t)H(t) \tag{2}$$

The ageing process $d(t)$ can be countered through health investments $I(t)$, which improve health through the production process $f[I(t)]$ and consists of direct outlays $m(t)$ (e.g. medical expenses) and own time inputs $\tau_I(t)$ (e.g. exercise). Assets $A(t)$ increase with the rate of return to capital r,

$$\frac{\partial A(t)}{\partial t} = rA(t) + Y[H(t)] - p_C(t)X_C(t) - p_m(t)m(t) \tag{3}$$

with earnings from labour $Y[H(t)]$ (a function of health), and decrease with expenditures on consumption goods and services $X_C(t)$ and expenditures on health investment goods and services $m(t)$ at prices $p_C(t)$ and $p_m(t)$ respectively. Earnings consist of the time spent working in a period $\tau_w(t)$ multiplied by the wage rate $w(t)$: $Y[H(t)] = w(t)\tau_w(t)$. The total time available in a period Ω is the sum of all its possible uses:

$$\Omega = \tau_w(t) + \tau_I(t) + \tau_C(t) + s[H(t)] \tag{4}$$

where $\tau_w(t)$ is time devoted to work, $\tau_I(t)$ is time devoted to health investment, $\tau_C(t)$ is time devoted to consumption and $s[H(t)]$ is sick time. Last, we have initial and end conditions: $A(0), A(T), H(0), H(T)$, and individuals die when health reaches a minimum level $H(T) = H_{\min}$.

A few key concepts of the model are as follows:

1. Individuals demand good health (i) for its production benefit: health increases earnings (reduced sick time, enhanced productivity[2]), and (ii) for its consumption benefit: health provides utility. This is in contrast to other components of human capital, which are generally not modelled as providing a consumption (utility) benefit.
2. The demand for health investment is a derived demand: individuals invest in health due to the underlying demand for good health, e.g., not because they enjoy consuming care.
3. The efficiency of the health investment process $I(t) = I[m(t), \tau_I(t); E]$ increases with knowledge E as the more educated are assumed to be more efficient consumers and producers of health care.

Issues

Is the Grossman model and its extensions able to explain our six stylized facts on health differences across SES groups? It does an adequate job in capturing stylized fact 1. The model predicts a positive association between health and socioeconomic indicators such as education and wealth. However, Case and Deaton (2005) have argued that health-capital models are unable to explain differences in the rate of health decline (not just the level) between SES groups, i.e. it fails to describe stylized fact 2. They note: 'If the rate of biological deterioration is constant, which is perhaps implausible but hardly impossible, ... people will "choose" an infinite life ...'. Hence, a feature of the model is that complete health repair is possible if the rate of biological ageing $d(t)$ is constant. Declines in health status are driven not by the rate of biological ageing $d(t)$, but by its rate of increase

$\partial d(t)/\partial t$. Only if SES differences exist in this rate of increase can the widening of the gradient until old age be explained.

An important stylized fact of the demand for medical care is that it is the unhealthy, not the healthy, that uses medical services most intensively, and this is true regardless of whether bad health was the result of a sudden health shock or the result of more gradual health deterioration. However, as Wagstaff (1986) and Zweifel and Breyer (1997) have pointed out, health-capital models are unable to predict this observed negative relation between health and the demand for medical care. Introspection and casual observation further suggest that healthy individuals are those who began life healthy and that have invested in health over the life course. Yet, Usher (1976) has pointed to the lack of 'memory' in the model. The solution for health does not depend on its initial value or the histories of health investment and biological ageing (see, e.g., Eqs. (42), (45) and (47) in Grossman, 2000). Thus the model would, for example, not be able to reproduce the observation that health and investments in early childhood have sustained effects on adult outcomes (Currie & Almond, 2011). The static nature of the derived solution for health is also incompatible with the inherently dynamic nature of the model formulation (see Eq. (2) above).

In our own work (Galama, 2011; Galama & Van Kippersluis, 2010) we have come to the conclusion that there is a fairly simple, but so far largely misunderstood, solution to these limitations of the Grossman model as follows. The health-capital literature makes two important assumptions, for mathematical convenience, which lead to a *degeneracy* of the solution to the optimization problem. To recall the definition, in mathematics, a degenerate case is a limiting case in which a class of solutions changes its nature so as to belong to another, usually simpler, class. A degenerate case thus has special features, which depart from the properties that are generic in the wider class, and the nature of the degenerate solution is generally lost under a small perturbation of the degenerate system. This is exactly the case with the Grossman model under the commonly used assumptions of (i) a health production function in the dynamic (transition) equation for health (see Eq. (2)) that is linear in health investment, i.e., $f[I(t)] = I(t)$ and (ii) a Cobb–Douglas constant returns to scale (CRTS) relation between investment in health $I(t)$ and its inputs of own time $\tau_I(t)$ and health investment goods/services purchased in the market $m(t)$, i.e. $I(t) = \mu(t)m(t)^k \tau_I(t)^{1-k}$.

Under these two assumptions the Hamiltonian of the constrained optimization problem is linear in $I(t)$, $\tau_I(t)$ and $m(t)$. Since the optimality condition for these three (related) controls are derived by taking the derivative of the Hamiltonian with respect to the controls, the controls themselves are no longer part of the optimality condition (they drop out because of the imposed linearity) and their value cannot be determined (see Galama, 2011, for more detail).[3] Ehrlich and Chuma (1990) were the first to note this indeterminacy ('bang-bang') problem. Still, the importance of this observation appears to have gone largely unnoticed: contributions to the literature that followed the publication of Ehrlich and Chuma's work in 1990 have continued to make the two standard assumptions[4] and the issue is not touched upon in a very recent debate on the model (Kaestner, forthcoming; Zweifel, 2012).

In Galama (2011) we develop the Grossman model with a health-production process with decreasing returns to scale (DRTS) in health investment (addressing the degeneracy, as in Ehrlich & Chuma, 1990) and show that it addresses major criticisms levelled at the model.[5] Under plausible assumptions, the theory now shows that the health of wealthy and educated individuals declines more slowly, initially widening the gradient, and that the gradient subsequently narrows as a result of mortality selection and increased health investment by lower SES individuals due to rapidly declining health. In short, with these changes the health-capital model can account for stylized fact 2. Further, current health status is found to be a function of the initial level of health and the histories of prior health investments (addressing concerns raised by Usher, 1976); health investment rapidly increases near the end of life; and length of life is finite as a result of limited life-time resources (addressing concerns raised by Case & Deaton, 2005).

Thus, the Grossman model, in our opinion, provides a solid foundation for a theory of health inequalities. The criticisms of the model have largely overlooked the fact that the literature has focussed on a highly unusual degenerate case and that reformulations of the theory can address its major limitations.[6]

Towards a Theory of Health Inequality

In Galama and Van Kippersluis (2010) we developed a theory of disparities in health between SES groups, based on the Grossman model with six additional features in order to capture the stylized facts described above.

First, we assume DRTS in health investment of the health production function, which addresses the degeneracy of linear investment models (Ehrlich & Chuma, 1990; Galama, 2011) and, in addition to predicting the observed association between measures of health and SES (stylized fact 1), captures the widening and subsequent narrowing of health inequalities with age (stylized fact 2).

Second, following Case and Deaton (2005) individuals choose among jobs with characteristics $z(t)$ which potentially have health consequences. This might be referred to as 'job-related health stress' and can be interpreted broadly, ranging from physical working conditions (e.g. hard or risky labour) to psychosocial aspects of work (e.g. low social status, lack of control and repetitive work). The decision to engage in unhealthy labour is governed by the relative benefit of a possible wage premium $\partial Y(t)/\partial z(t) > 0$ versus the cost in terms of a higher health deterioration rate $\partial d(t)/\partial z(t) > 0$ (stylized fact 3).

Third, lifestyles and consumption patterns may affect the biological ageing rate (Case & Deaton, 2005; see also Forster, 2001). We distinguish healthy consumption $C_h(t)$ (such as the consumption of healthy foods, sports and exercise) from unhealthy consumption $C_u(t)$ (such as smoking and excessive alcohol consumption). Healthy consumption provides utility $\partial U(t)/\partial C_h(t) > 0$, and is associated with health benefits in that it lowers the biological ageing rate $\partial d(t)/\partial C_h(t) < 0$. Unhealthy consumption provides consumption benefits $\partial U(t)/\partial C_u(t) > 0$ but increases the biological rate of ageing $\partial d(t)/\partial C_u(t) > 0$ (stylized fact 3).

Fourth, we include an endogenous retirement decision that captures possible reverse causality from health to SES (stylized fact 4). Earlier attempts at including a retirement decision in the Grossman model (Galama, Kapteyn, Fonseca, & Michaud, forthcoming) have had to rely on numerical analyses. But a transversality condition for the optimal retirement age can be obtained from the dynamic envelope theorem (e.g. Caputo, 2005, p. 293).

Fifth, individuals endogenously optimize length of life as in Ehrlich and Chuma (1990). Last, the causal effect of education on income is included in a straightforward manner by assuming a Mincer-type wage relation in which earnings are increasing in the level of education and the level of experience of workers (e.g. Mincer, 1974).

We perform detailed comparative dynamic analyses to assess the characteristics of the model and generate empirically testable predictions. We find that greater initial wealth, permanently higher earnings (over the life cycle) and a higher level of education induce individuals to invest more in health, shift consumption towards healthy consumption, and enable individuals to afford healthier working environments (associated with lower levels of physical and psychosocial health stresses) and living environments. As a result, they live longer.

The mechanism through which initial wealth, permanent income and education (our measures of SES) operates is by increasing the relative marginal value of health (the ratio of the marginal value of health to the marginal value of wealth), thereby increasing the demand for health investment, increasing the health benefit of (and hence demand for) healthy consumption and increasing the health cost of (and hence reduced demand for) unhealthy working and living environments, and of unhealthy consumption. The more rapidly worsening health of low-SES individuals leads to early withdrawal from the labour force, widening the gradient in early- and mid-age, and to shorter lives. Jointly these behavioural choices gradually lead to growing health advantage for higher SES groups with age.

Interestingly, the model predicts a subsequent narrowing of the SES-health gradient, due to mortality selection and because low-SES individuals increase their health investment and improve their health-related behaviour faster as a result of their more rapidly worsening health. Thus, consistent with empirical data, the model (in contrast to those extant in the literature) successfully predicts a widening and a subsequent narrowing with age of the gradient in health by SES, and that high-SES individuals have greater longevity and years of good health.

The theory further suggests that unhealthy consumption is not only a function of the direct monetary cost (e.g. the price of a pack of cigarettes) but also of an indirect health cost (value of health lost), which increases with wealth and with the degree of unhealthiness of the good. As a result, the effect of wealth on unhealthy consumption consists of the usual positive *direct* effect and an offsetting *indirect* effect. This leads to the prediction that an unexpected wealth shock increases demand for healthy and moderately unhealthy consumption goods, but decreases demand for severely unhealthy goods. Our theory may thus provide an economic rationale for the observation that wealthy individuals are more likely to drink moderately, but less likely to drink heavily and smoke (Cutler & Lleras-Muney, 2010). In an empirical test exploiting both lottery winnings and inheritances as plausibly exogenous variation in wealth, we present evidence that differences in health costs may indeed provide an explanation for behavioural differences, and ultimately health outcomes, between wealth groups (Van Kippersluis & Galama, 2013).

On-going and Future Directions

Our theory of health disparities includes lifestyle, health behaviour, job environment, retirement and longevity (in addition to health investment), and is capable of replicating a large number of the stylized facts concerning health inequalities. Two important stylized facts (5 and 6), however, are not yet accommodated.

Regarding stylized fact 6, an important extension of the theory would be the inclusion of a distinct childhood phase of life. Important socioeconomic differences exist in the evolution of child health (Currie, 2009), and the impact of foetal and early-childhood conditions on health in adulthood are substantial (e.g. Barker, 1995; Almond & Currie, 2011; Currie & Almond, 2011). James Heckman and co-authors discuss the complexity of early childhood skill formation, pointing out that abilities matter, that abilities are multiple in nature, that socio-emotional or non-cognitive skills foster the development of cognitive skills, that there are sensitive and critical periods in the development of child abilities, that ability gaps form at early ages and are difficult to remediate at late but not early ages (or stated in a different way – that the rate of return to investments in disadvantaged children is high compared to interventions targeted to disadvantaged adolescents) and that early investments in children need to be followed up with later investments (e.g. Conti et al., 2010; Cunha & Heckman, 2007). They offer a model of childhood skill formation that exhibits *self-productivity*, where higher stocks of skills in one period create higher stocks of skills in the next period, and *dynamic complementarity*, where stocks of skills in one period make investments in the next period more productive (see also Currie & Almond, 2011).

Extending the theory in this direction would entail adding a distinct childhood period. One might treat the child as passive, in the sense that parents make decisions regarding time investment and financial investment in their children, but the children themselves do not. Parents are motivated by altruism or by an implicit contract with their children to devote time to care for them or support them financially in old age (see, e.g., Ehrlich & Lui, 1991). This would most likely take the form of an overlapping generations model. Each distinct period of life (e.g. childhood, working life and retirement) however can be modelled as consisting of an infinite number of periods (i.e. using continuous time) rather than the commonly employed two or three discrete period models, so that the theory can describe rich life cycle behaviour and inter-temporal trade-offs between and within generations. Such a childhood phase could be added as an extension to the Grossman-type models discussed in this chapter.

An interesting series of papers by Jacobson (2000) and Bolin et al. (2001, 2002) have modelled the production of health by the family (including the health of the child) using the Grossman framework and modelling spouses with common preferences, as Nash-bargainers and as strategic actors. Their models build on the degenerate linear investment case, however, and it would be of interest to develop them for the general, non-degenerate case.

Regarding stylized fact 5, as Michael Grossman himself observed, '... we still lack comprehensive theoretical models in which the stocks of health and knowledge are determined simultaneously. ... The rich empirical literature treating interactions between schooling and health underscores the potential payoffs to this undertaking ...' (Grossman, 2000). Indeed, the human- and health-capital literatures have developed relatively separately, with the human-capital literature either modelling health as a form of human capital that is not very distinct from other forms or it has treated health as exogenously given. Similarly, health-capital theory has taken knowledge or skill as exogenously given. As a result, both theories fall short of explaining the strong association between education and health.

An important next step in a theory of health inequalities would be the merging of what we term skill- (or human) capital theory with health-capital theory. A basic formulation of a unifying theory would consist of a dynamic model in which skill capital primarily determines the wage rate, while health capital primarily determines the period over which returns accrue (determining the amount of time spent working in a day, retirement and longevity). Investment in skill capital raises the return to investment in health capital, and vice versa, as lifetime earnings are strongly multiplicative in skill and health. Allowing the efficiencies of the skill- and health-capital production processes to be functions of skill capital and health capital may provide several additional reinforcing mechanisms, such as self-productivity and dynamic complementarity (as in Cunha & Heckman, 2007).

DISCUSSION

Health inequalities across socioeconomic groups raise both ethical and economic concerns, and their reduction is a key priority on the health policy agenda of many nations and regions. Yet, despite numerous policy efforts aimed at reducing disparities over the past decades, if anything, health inequalities seem to have widened rather than narrowed (Meara, Richards, & Cutler, 2008).

While the scientific evidence on this topic has rapidly expanded, the mechanisms through which health differences across socioeconomic groups emerge and persist are still relatively poorly understood. Economic theory can help guide empirical studies in identifying mechanisms through which specific socioeconomic indicators and health interact.

We identified six stylized facts about health inequalities that we argue a theoretical framework should aim to reproduce. These are as follows: (i) health differences exist across all socioeconomic indicators, irrespective of the institutional setting, (ii) socioeconomic health inequality widens until around age 60, after which it narrows, (iii) occupation, health behaviours and the ability to process information are important mechanisms, (iv) there exists an important 'reverse causality' effect of ill-health on labour force participation, income and wealth, (v) education seems very important in determining health and (vi) a large part of the health gradient may be due to early childhood endowments and investments.

While the literature has identified several shortcomings of the traditional health-capital model due to Grossman (1972a, 1972b), our claim is that most major limitations can be attributed to the use of a health production process that is linear in health investment. In our work we have found that this widely used but highly unusual degenerate case bears little resemblance to the more general non-degenerate case.

Introducing a health investment process subject to diminishing returns (which removes the degeneracy), the Grossman model can account for the widening and narrowing of health differences across socioeconomic groups over the life cycle, for the empirically observed negative association between health and medical care, and addresses several other major issues identified in the literature (Galama, 2011). Thus, we strongly believe that non-degenerate versions of the Grossman model provide a suitable foundation for a theory of health inequalities.

Yet, additional extensions of the traditional Grossman model are required in order to account for stylized facts 3 and 4. In recent work, we made a first attempt towards this aim (Galama & Van Kippersluis, 2010). In that paper, we incorporate six additional features, among which the introduction of DRTS in health investment, the introduction of retirement as an endogenous choice, the trade-off between health-detrimental working conditions and a wage premium, and the distinction between healthy and unhealthy consumption goods are the most important. With these additions, the model can account for stylized facts 1–4.

The remaining challenges are to reproduce stylized facts 5 and 6. Achieving the first requires further extension to incorporate a childhood phase in which parents invest in the cognitive skills, non-cognitive skills and health of children. Meeting the second challenge will require a theoretical model that explicitly distinguishes between health and other forms of human capital in order to improve understanding of the role of education in health inequalities.

NOTES

1. Yet, see Albouy and Lequien (2008) and Clark and Royer (2013) for studies that failed to identify an effect of education on mortality.
2. In case the wage rate is also a function of health.
3. A small perturbation from linearity in health investment results in drastically different model solutions. Even if we were to believe that the health production process was linear (and few, we believe, will make this argument) it surely won't be so with very exact precision.
4. E.g., Bolin et al. (2001, 2002), Case and Deaton (2005), Erbsland, Ried, and Ulrich (1995), Jacobson (2000) and Ried (1998).
5. We further argue for a different interpretation of the health stock equilibrium condition, one of the most central relations in the health capital literature. It is not the relation that determines the equilibrium level of health as it is commonly interpreted (as, e.g., in Ehrlich & Chuma, 1990; Grossman 1972a, 1972b) but rather the optimality (first-order) condition for the level of health investment.
6. An interesting consequence of the literature's focus on the degenerate case is that empirical tests of the Grossman model are still in their infancy. Thus far tests of the Grossman model have almost exclusively relied on the degenerate model (e.g. Erbsland et al., 1995; Gerdtham & Johannesson, 1999; Gerdtham, Johannesson, Lundberg, & Isacson 1999; Grossman, 1972a; Leu & Doppmann, 1986; Leu & Gerfin, 1992; Nocera & Zweifel, 1998; Van de Ven & Van der Gaag, 1982; Wagstaff, 1986, 1993; Van Doorslaer, 1987). See Galama, Hullegie, Meijer and Outcault (2012) for a first attempt at estimating a linearized equation derived from the more general (non-degenerate) version of the Grossman model. A more recent literature has solved and estimated dynamic formulations (sometimes loosely) based on health-capital theory using dynamic programming techniques, and taking into account a health investment process that is subject to decreasing returns to scale (e.g. Ehrlich & Yin, 2005; Fonseca, Michaud, Kapteyn & Galama 2013; Gilleskie, 1998, 2010; Hugonnier, Pelgrin & St-Amour 2013; Khwaja, 2010; Scholz and Seshadri, 2012; Yogo, 2009).

ACKNOWLEDGEMENTS

Research reported in this publication was supported by the National Institute on Aging of the National Institutes of Health under Award Numbers K02AG042452 and R01AG037398. The content is solely the responsibility of the authors and does not necessarily represent the official views of the National Institutes of Health. Titus Galama is grateful to the

Erasmus School of Economics of Erasmus University Rotterdam for a Visiting Professorship in the Economics of Human Capital. We thank the editors for helpful comments and suggestions.

REFERENCES

Adams, P., Hurd, M. D., McFadden, D., Merrill, A., & Ribeiro, T. (2003). Healthy, wealthy and wise? Tests for direct causal paths between health and socioeconomic status. *Journal of Econometrics, 112*, 3–56.

Adler, N. E., Boyce, T., Chesney, M. A., Cohen, S., Folkman, S., Kahn, R. L., & Syme, S. L. (1994). Socioeconomic status and health: The challenge of the gradient. *American Psychologist, 49*(1), 15–24.

Adler, N. E., Boyce, W. T., Chesney, M. A., Folkman, S., & Syme, L. S. (1993). Socioeconomic inequalities in health: No easy solution. *JAMA, 269*, 3140–3145.

Albouy, V., & Lequien, L. (2008). Does compulsory education lower mortality. *Journal of Health Economics, 28*(1), 155–168.

Almond, D., & Currie, J. (2011). Killing me softly: The fetal origins hypothesis. *The Journal of Economic Perspectives, 25*(3), 153–172.

Annandale, E., & Hunt, K. (Eds.). (2000). *Gender inequalities in health*. Buckingham: Open University Press.

Arber, S., & Cooper, H. (1999). Gender differences in health in later life: The new paradox? *Social Science & Medicine, 48*(1), 61–76.

Barker, D. J. (1995). Fetal origins of coronary heart disease. *BMJ: British Medical Journal, 311*(6998), 171.

Becker, G. (1964). *Human capital*. New York, NY: National Bureau of Economic Research.

Beckett, M. (2000). Converging health inequalities in later life: An artifact of mortality selection? *Journal of Health and Social Behavior, 41*, 106–119.

Ben-Porath, Y. (1967). The production of human capital and the life cycle of earnings. *The Journal of Political Economy, 75*(4), 352–365.

Bolin, K., Jacobson, L., & Lindgren, B. (2001). The family as the producer of health. When spouses are Nash bargainers. *Journal of Health Economics, 20*, 349–362.

Bolin, K., Jacobson, L., & Lindgren, B. (2002). The family as the health producer – When spouses act strategically. *Journal of Health Economics, 21*, 475–495.

Borg, V., & Kristensen, T. S. (2000). Social class and self-rated health: Can the gradient be explained by differences in life style or work environment? *Social Science & Medicine, 51*(7), 1019–1030.

Caputo, M. R. (2005). *Foundations of dynamic economic analysis*. Cambridge: Cambridge University Press.

Case, A., & Deaton, A. (2005). Broken down by work and sex: How our health declines. In D. A. Wise (Ed.), *Analyses in the economics of aging* (pp. 185–212). Chicago, IL: The University of Chicago Press.

Clark, D., & Royer, H. (forthcoming). The effect of education on adult mortality and health: Evidence from Britain. *American Economic Review*.

Conti, G., Heckman, J. J., & Urzua, S. (2010). The education-health gradient. *American Economic Review Papers and Proceedings, 100*, 234–238.

Cunha, F., & Heckman, J. J. (2007). The technology of skill formation. *American Economic Review, 97*(2), 31–47.

Currie, J. (2009). Healthy, wealthy, and wise: Socioeconomic status, poor health in childhood, and human capital development. *Journal of Economic Literature, 47*(1), 87–122.

Currie, J., & Almond, D. (2011). Human capital development before age five. *Handbook of labor economics* (Vol. 4, pp. 1315–1486).

Currie, J., & Stabile, M. (2003). Socioeconomic status and child health: Why is the relationship stronger for older children? *American Economic Review, 93*, 1813–1823.

Cutler, D. M., & Lleras-Muney, A. (2010). Understanding differences in health behaviors by education. *Journal of Health Economics, 29*(1), 1–28.

Cutler, D. M., & Lleras-Muney, A. (2012). *Education and health: Insights from international comparisons*. NBER Working Paper 17738.

Cutler, D. M., Lleras-Muney, A., & Vogl, T. (2011). Socioeconomic status and health: Dimensions and mechanisms. In. S. Glied & P. C. Smith (Eds.), *Oxford handbook of health economics*. Oxford, UK: Oxford University Press.

Deaton, A. (2002). Policy implications of the gradient of health and wealth. *Health Affairs, 21*(2), 13–30.

Deaton, A. S., & Paxson, C. H. (1998). Aging and inequality in income and health. *American Economic Review, 88*, 248–253.

Ehrlich, I., & Chuma, H. (1990). A model of the demand for longevity and the value of life extension. *Journal of Political Economy, 98*(4), 761–782.

Ehrlich, I., & Lui, F. T. (1991). Intergenerational trade, longevity, and economic growth. *Journal of Political Economy, 99*(5), 1029–1059.

Ehrlich, I., & Yin, Y. (2005). Explaining diversities in age-specific life expectancies and values of life saving: A numerical analysis. *Journal of Risk and Uncertainty, 31*(2), 129–162.

Erbsland, M., Ried, W., & Ulrich, V. (1995). Health, health care, and the environment. Econometric evidence from German micro data. *Health Economics, 4*, 169–182. (Reprinted in A. M. Jones & O. O'Donnell (2002). *Econometric analysis of health data* (pp. 25–36). New York, NY: Wiley.)

Fonseca, R., Michaud, P.-C, Kapteyn, A., & Galama, T. J. (2013). *Accounting for rise of health spending and longevity*. IZA Discussion Paper, 7522.

Forster, M. (2001). The meaning of death: Some simulations of a model of healthy and unhealthy consumption. *Journal of Health Economics, 20*(4), 613–638.

Fuchs, V. R. (1986). *The health economy* (1st ed.). Cambridge, MA: Harvard University Press.

Galama, T. J. (2011). *A contribution to health capital theory*. RAND Working Paper No. WR-831.

Galama, T. J., Hullegie, P., Meijer, E., & Outcault, S. (2012). Is there empirical evidence for decreasing returns to scale in a health capital model? *Health Economics, 21*(9), 1080–1100. DOI: 10.1002/hec.2843

Galama, T. J., Kapteyn, A., Fonseca, R., & Michaud, P. C. (forthcoming). A health production model with endogenous retirement. *Health Economics*. doi:10.1002/hec.2865

Galama, T. J., & van Kippersluis, H. (2010). *A theory of socioeconomic disparities in health*. RAND Working Paper No. WR-773.

Garcia-Gomez, P., van Kippersluis, H., O'Donnell, O., & van Doorslaer, E. (forthcoming). Long term and spillover effects of health shocks on employment and income. *Journal of Human Resources*.

Gerdtham, U. G., & Johannesson, M. (1999). New estimates of the demand for health: Results based on a categorical health measure and Swedish micro data. *Social Science & Medicine, 49*, 1325–1332.

Gerdtham, U. G., Johannesson, M., Lundberg, L., & Isacson, D. (1999). The demand for health: Results from new measures of health capital. *European Journal of Political Economy*, 15, 501–521.

Gilleskie, D. (1998). A dynamic stochastic model of medical care use and work absence. *Econometrica*, 66(1), 1–45.

Gilleskie, D. (2010). Work absences and doctor visits during an illness episode: The differential role of preferences, production, and policies among men and women. *Journal of Econometrics*, 156(1), 148–163.

Glied, S., & Lleras-Muney, A. (2008). Technological innovation and inequality in health. *Demography*, 45(3), 741–761.

Goldman, D. P., & Smith, J. P. (2002). Can patient self-management help explain the SES health gradient? *Proceedings of the National Academy of Science*, 99, 10929–10934.

Grossman, M. (1972a). *The demand for health: A theoretical and empirical investigation*. New York, NY: National Bureau of Economic Research.

Grossman, M. (1972b). On the concept of health capital and the demand for health. *Journal of Political Economy*, 80(2), 223–255.

Grossman, M. (2000). The human capital model. In Culyer & J. P. Newhouse (Eds.), *Handbook of health economics* (Vol. 1, pp. 347–408). Amsterdam, The Netherlands: Elsevier Science.

Halla, M., & Zweimuller, M. (2013). The effect of health on income: Quasi-experimental evidence from commuting accidents. *Labour Economics*, 24, 23–38.

Heckman, J. J. (2006). Skill formation and the economics of investing in disadvantaged children. *Science*, 312(5782), 1900–1902.

Herd, P. (2006). Do functional health inequalities decrease in old age? *Research on Aging*, 28(3), 375–392.

House, J. S., Lepkowski, J. M., Kinney, A. M., Mero, R. P., Kessler, R. C., & Herzog, A. R. (1994). The social stratification of aging and health. *Journal of Health and Social Behavior*, 35, 213–234.

Hugonnier, J., Pelgrin, F., & St-Amour, P. (2013). Health and (other) asset holdings. *Review of Economic Studies*, 80(2), 663–710.

Jacobson, L. (2000). The family as producer of health — an extension of the Grossman model. *Journal of Health Economics*, 19, 611–637.

Kaestner, R. (forthcoming). The Grossman model after 40 years: A reply to Peter Zweifel. *European Journal of Health Economics*.

Khwaja, A. (2010). Estimating willingness to pay for Medicare using a dynamic life-cycle model of demand for health insurance. *Journal of Econometrics*, 156(1), 130–147.

Leu, R. E., & Doppmann, R. J. (1986). Gesundheitszustandsmessung und Nachfrage nach Gesundheitsleistungen. In E. Wille (Ed.), *Informations- und Planungsprobleme in öffentlichen Aufgabenbereichen* (pp. 1–90). Frankfurt am Main, Germany: Lang.

Leu, R. E., & Gerfin, M. (1992). Die nachfrage nach gesundheit: ein empirischer test des grossman-modells, In. P. Oberender (Ed.), *Steuerungsprobleme im gesundheitswesen* (pp. 61–78). Baden-Baden, Germany: Nomos.

Levine, R. S., Foster, J. E., Fullilove, R. E., Briggs, N. C., Hull, P. C., Husaini, B. A., & Hennekens, C. H. (2001). Black-white inequalities in mortality and life expectancy, 1933–1999: Implications for healthy people 2010. *Public Health Reports*, 116, 474–483.

Lleras-Muney, A. (2005). The relationship between education and adult mortality in the United States. *Review of Economic Studies*, 72, 189–221.

Lleras-Muney, A., & Lichtenberg, F. (2005). The Effect of Education on Medical Technology Adoption: Are the More Educated More Likely to Use New Drugs. *Annalesd'Economie et Statistique* (pp. 671–696), special issue in memory of Zvi Griliches, No 79/80.

Lynch, J. W., Kaplan, G. A., & Shema, S. J. (1997). Cumulative impact of sustained economic hardship on physical, cognitive, psychological, and social functioning. *New England Journal of Medicine, 337*(26), 1889–1895.

Lynch, S. M. (2003). Cohort and life-course patterns in the relationship between education and health: A hierarchical approach. *Demography, 40*, 309–331.

Mackenbach, J. P., Kunst, A. E., Cavelaars, A. E. J. M., Groenhof, F., Geurts, J. J. M., and the EU Working Group on Socioeconomic Inequalities in Health. (1997). Socioeconomic inequalities in morbidity and mortality in western Europe. *Lancet, 349*, 1655–1659.

Marmot, M. (1999). Multi-level approaches to understanding social determinants. In L. Berkman & I. Icawachi (Eds.), *Social epidemiology*. Oxford: Oxford University Press.

Marmot, M., Ryff, C. D., Bumpass, L. L., Shipley, M., & Marks, N. F. (1997). Social inequalities in health: Next questions and converging evidence. *Social Science and Medicine, 44*(6), 901–910.

Meara, E. R., Richards, S., & Cutler, D. (2008). The gap gets bigger: Changes in mortality and life expectancy, by education, 1981–2000. *Health Affairs, 27*(2), 350–360.

Michaud, P.-C., & van Soest, A. (2008). Health and wealth of elderly couples: Causality tests using dynamic panel data models. *Journal of Health Economics, 27*(5), 1312–1325.

Mincer, J. A. (1974). *Schooling, experience, and earnings*. New York, USA: Columbia University Press.

Møller Dano, A. (2005). Road injuries and long-run effects on income and employment. *Health Economics, 14*(9), 955–970.

Mushkin, S. (1962). Health as an investment. *Journal of Political Economy, 70*(5), 129–157.

Nocera, S., & Zweifel, P. (1998). The demand for health: An empirical test of the Grossman model using panel data. In P. Zweifel (Ed.), *Health, the medical profession, and regulation* (pp. 35–49). Boston, MA: Kluwer.

Oreopoulos, P. (2006). Estimating average and local average treatment effects of education when compulsory schooling laws really matter. *American Economic Review, 96*(1), 152–175.

Ravesteijn, B., van Kippersluis, H., & van Doorslaer, E. (2013). The contribution of occupation to health inequality. In P. R. Dias & O. O'Donnell (Eds.), *Health and inequality* (Vol. 21). Research on Economic Inequality. Bingly, UK: Emerald Group Publishing Limited.

Ried, W. (1998). Comparative dynamic analysis of the full Grossman model. *Journal of Health Economics, 17*(4), 383–425.

Ross, C. E., & Wu, C. L. (1996). Education, age, and the cumulative advantage in health. *Journal of Health and Social Behavior, 37*, 104–120.

Scholz, J. K., & Seshadri, A. (2012). *The interplay of wealth, retirement decisions. Policy and economic shocks*. Michigan Retirement Research Center Research Paper No. WP, 2012–271.

Schultz, T. (1961). Investment in human capital. *American Economic Review, 51*, 1–17.

Smith, J. P. (1999). Healthy bodies and thick wallets. *Journal of Economic Perspectives, 13*(2), 145–166.

Smith, J. P. (2004). Unraveling the SES: Health connection. *Population and Development Review, Supplement: Aging, Health, and Public Policy, 30*, 108–132.

Smith, J. P. (2007). The impact of socioeconomic status on health over the life-course. *Journal of Human Resources, 42*(4), 739–764.

US Healthy People 2020 Initiative. (2010, July 26). *Healthy People 2020: An opportunity to address the societal determinants of health in the United States.* Secretary's Advisory Committee on Health Promotion and Disease Prevention Objectives for 2020.

Usher, D. (1976). Comments on the correlation between health and schooling. In N. E. Terleckyj (Ed.), *Household production and consumption* (pp. 212–220). New York, NY: National Bureau of Economic Research. Retrieved from http://www.nber.org/chapters/c3962.pdf

Van de Ven, W. P. M. M., & Van der Gaag, J. (1982). Health as an unobservable: A MIMIC-model of demand for health care. *Journal of Health Economics, 1,* 157–183.

Van Doorslaer, E. K. A. (1987). *Health, knowledge and the demand for medical care: An econometric analysis.* Assen, the Netherlands: Van Gorcum.

Van Kippersluis, H., & Galama, T. J. (2013). *Why the rich drink more but smoke less: The impact of wealth on health behaviors.* RAND Working Paper, WR-988.

Van Kippersluis, H., O'Donnell, O., & van Doorslaer, E. (2011). Long run returns to education: Does schooling lead to an extended old age? *Journal of Human Resources, 46*(4), 695–721.

Van Kippersluis, H., O'Donnell, O., van Doorslaer, E., & Van Ourti, T. (2010). Socioeconomic differences in health over the life cycle in an Egalitarian country. *Social Science and Medicine, 70*(3), 428–438.

Wagstaff, A. (1986). The demand for health: Some new empirical evidence. *Journal of Health Economics, 5,* 195–233.

Wagstaff, A. (1993). The demand for health: An empirical reformulation of the Grossman model. *Health Economics, 2,* 189–198.

Williams, D. R., & Jackson, P. B. (2005). Social sources of racial disparities in health. *Health Affairs, 24*(2), 325–334.

World Health Organization. (2001). *Macroeconomics and health: Investing in health for economic development.* Report of the Commission on Macroeconomics and Health, Geneva.

World Health Organization. (2008). *Closing the gap in a generation: Health equity through action on the social determinants of health.* Final Report of the Commission on Social Determinants of Health, World Health Organization, Geneva.

Yogo, M. (2009). *Portfolio choice in retirement: Health risk and the demand for annuities, housing, and risky assets.* PARC Working Papers, Population Aging Research Center.

Zweifel, P. (2012). The Grossman model after 40 years. *European Journal of Health Economics, 13*(6), 677–682.

Zweifel, P., & Breyer, F. (1997). *Health economics.* New York, NY: Oxford University Press.

THE DEVELOPMENTAL ORIGINS OF HEALTH INEQUALITY

Gabriella Conti

ABSTRACT

In this chapter, I review recent evidence on the developmental origins of health inequality. I discuss the origins of the education-health gradient, the long-term costs caused by early life adversity, and how early life experiences affect the biology of the body. Additionally, I provide complementary evidence on enrichment interventions which can at least partially compensate for these gaps. I highlight emerging lines of scientific inquiry which are likely to have a significant impact on the field. I argue that, while the evidence that early life conditions have long-term effects is now uncontroversial, the literature needs to be expanded both in a theoretical and empirical direction. On the one hand, a model linking early life origins to ageing needs to be developed; on the other hand, a better understanding of the mechanisms — both biological and socioeconomic — is required, in order to design more effective interventions.

Keywords: developmental origins; health inequality; deprivation; enrichment; early childhood interventions

JEL classifications: I12; I21; J24; C31; C93

INTRODUCTION

Noncommunicable diseases (NCDs) are responsible for about two-thirds of worldwide deaths. The WHO has set the goal of a 25% reduction in preventable NCD mortality by 2025 (UN, 2011). Most policies that combat disease currently focus on treatment after disease occurs and on reducing risk factors in adult life. Recent discussions of effective ways to control the soaring costs of the US health care system emphasize tertiary prevention, that is, reducing the worsening of conditions of those already ill (see, e.g., Emanuel, 2012). Indeed, most of the cost of medical care in the United States arises from a minority of individuals with multiple chronic conditions, such as cardiovascular and metabolic diseases and cancer (Cohen & Yu, 2012).

A complementary approach is to prevent disease entirely, or at least to substantially delay its onset. A consolidated body of evidence shows that adult illnesses are more prevalent and problematic among individuals who have experienced adverse early life conditions (Galobardes, Lynch, & Davey-Smith, 2008). The exact mechanisms through which early life experiences translate into later life health are actively being investigated, although there is increasing evidence which points to an important role played by biological − in addition to socioeconomic − mechanisms (Hertzman & Boyce, 2010). The importance of the social determinants of health (Marmot & Wilkinson, 2006) emphasizes the need to adopt a different approach to tackle health disparities, which recognizes the importance of prevention and the dynamic nature of the process of human capital formation, which starts in the womb, and consequently the role of economic and social policy as health policy.

Since the seminal work of Wilhelm Roux (1888) on the "developmental mechanics," to the more recent literature on "predictive adaptive response" (Gluckman et al., 2008), understanding the role of nature and nurture in evolution and the relevance of "functional adaptation" since the early stages of development, has become a central feature of the biological sciences. The concept of developmental health has been influential in life-course epidemiology (Davey Smith, 2003; Kuh & Ben-Shlomo, 2004; Power, Kuh, & Morton, 2013); however, it has been only recently introduced in the economic literature. A developmental approach to health inequality is both promising and challenging. This chapter reviews recent evidence on it and sets out a few directions for future research. It is structured in the following way. The second section reviews some basic facts on the developmental origins of health inequality. The third section focuses on the early origins of the education-health gradient. The fourth section presents evidence on some biological mechanisms underlying the long-term effects of early life adversity. The fifth section presents some evidence of remediation by environmental enrichment. The sixth section concludes and discusses some avenues for future research.

SOME STYLIZED FACTS ON THE DEVELOPMENTAL ORIGINS OF HEALTH INEQUALITY

I start by presenting some stylized facts on the early emergence and transmission of health inequalities.

(1) Health inequalities by family environments are already present at birth (Currie, 2011). Fig. 1 shows the proportion of children born with low

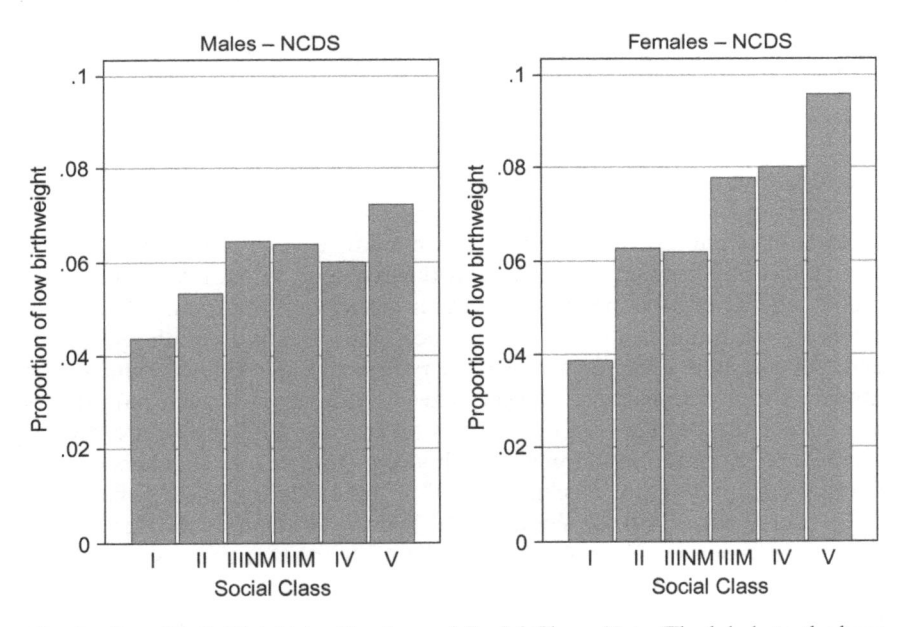

Fig. 1. Low Birth Weight by Gender and Social Class. *Note:* The labels to the bars refer to the social class at birth of the mother's husband. The NCDS (National Child Development Study) uses the Registrar General's classification of Social Class (SC): Social Class I (I) includes professional occupations; Social Class II (II) includes managerial and technical occupations; Social Class IIIN (IIIN) includes skilled nonmanual occupations; Social Class IIIM (IIIM) includes skilled manual occupations; Social Class IV (IV) includes partly-skilled occupations; Social Class V (V) includes unskilled occupations. Source: Conti and Heckman (2013).

birth weight (weight at birth less than 2,500 grams) in the 1958 British cohort (National Child Development Study, NCDS). For both genders, we observe a clear SES-health gradient: children born in more disadvantaged households have almost twice the chance of being born with a low birth weight as compared to those born in more affluent families.

(2) Health inequalities get amplified during childhood (Case, Lubotsky, & Paxson, 2002). Poor children both are hit by a greater number of shocks (Currie & Stabile, 2003), and are less able to respond to them (Condliffe & Link, 2008). Additionally, differences in parental health behaviors by socioeconomic status affect child health beyond health insurance (Case & Paxson, 2002).

(3) Given these mechanisms, in the absence of interventions, inequalities present at birth can get under the skin and affect the biology of the body, propagate throughout childhood, and persist into adulthood (Hertzman, 1999). In Fig. 2, we see evidence of a gradient in C-Reactive Protein (an inflammatory marker associated with a variety of cardiovascular risk factors) at age 44 by social class at birth which mimics the gradient in low birth weight seen in Fig. 1.

This emerging complex evidence needs to be conceptualized and interpreted within a lifecycle framework linking early-life conditions to late-life outcomes by accounting for intervening mechanisms and a variety of exposures at different levels. While there is abundance of empirical studies,[1] the theory has not kept up the pace with the evidence. As noted in Heckman (2007), the workhorse health production model by Grossman (1972) only refers to the adult health investment decisions, treating childhood health endowments and adult preferences as parameters determined outside the model. The accumulated evidence, instead, suggests that such parameters are in fact the output of a developmental model. While there are several models of parental investment in children (Caucutt & Lochner, 2012; Cunha, 2013; Cunha & Heckman, 2007; Cunha, Heckman, & Schennach, 2010; Del Boca, Flinn, & Wiswall, 2012; Gayle, Golan, & Soytas, 2013), they all in general refer to the human capital formation process (under the form of a single "skill," with the exception of Cunha et al., 2010), and none of them explicitly incorporates the specific features of a health capital model. Additionally, they focus on how preferences and endowments are determined by parental investments in their children, but do not model late-life outcomes (with the exception of Gayle et al., 2013). Galama and van Kippersluis (2010) and Galama (2011) have extended the Grossman framework, but on the other hand they do not model how preferences or childhood endowments are determined. There is the need to incorporate a

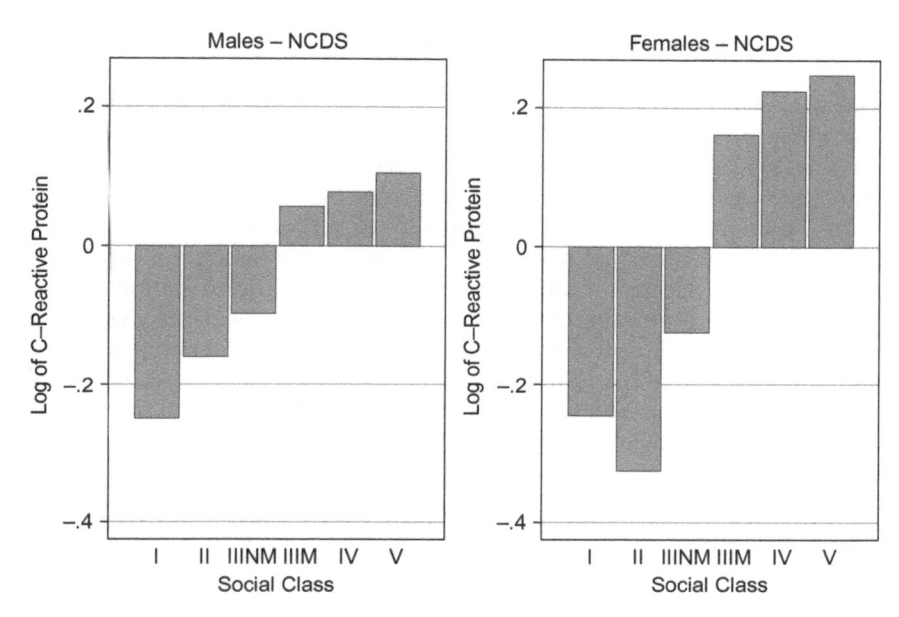

Fig. 2. Log of C-Reactive Protein by Gender and Social Class at Birth. *Note*: The labels to the bars refer to the social class at birth. The NCDS uses the Registrar General's classification of Social Class (SC): Social Class I (I) includes professional occupations; Social Class II (II) includes managerial and technical occupations; Social Class IIIN (IIIN) includes skilled nonmanual occupations; Social Class IIIM (IIIM) includes skilled manual occupations; Social Class IV (IV) includes partly-skilled occupations; Social Class V (V) includes unskilled occupations. Source: Conti and Heckman (2013).

childhood phase in the Grossman model, so that the effects of early life experiences can be modeled to affect later life outcomes through multiple pathways, and both genetic inheritance and epigenetic mechanisms can be allowed to affect the human capital formation process, in a life-cycle theory of parent and own investment in health.[2]

THE EARLY ORIGINS OF THE EDUCATION-HEALTH GRADIENT

Disparities in health across socioeconomic status (SES) groups, often termed the "health gradient," are substantial. Inequalities in health exist across all measures of SES, such as education, income and wealth, and across all indicators of health, including both subjective and objective measures (Marmot, 1999; Smith, 1999). While understanding the sources of disparities in health has been for a long time a topic of active interdisciplinary research, only recently the attention has been steered toward the early years, (see e.g. Case et al. (2002) on the income-health gradient).

In Conti and Heckman (2010) and in Conti, Heckman and Urzua (2010), I have contributed to this line of research by taking a novel developmental approach to the study of health disparities by education. I have estimated a developmental model of how early life endowments give rise to labor market and health disparities by education, which complement the traditional studies which have relied on quasi-experimental evaluations (see Lochner, 2011, for a recent review). I have developed a general latent variable model that explicitly accounts for how early cognitive, socio-emotional and health endowments affect the selection process into post-compulsory education, and how these early life endowments and education in turn affect later outcomes. The model allows to separately identifying selection effects from causal effects, and provides guidance on the impacts of educational interventions. I have analyzed data from the British Cohort Study — a survey of all babies born after the 24th week of gestation from Sunday, April 5, to Saturday, April 11, 1970, in the United Kingdom. There have been seven follow-ups to track all members of this birth cohort: 1975, 1980, 1986, 1996, 2000, 2004, and 2008. Very rich information has been collected from several sources (parents, teachers, and doctors during a medical visit). I have analyzed family background characteristics taken from the birth sweep (1970), cognitive, personality and anthropometric measurements from the second sweep (1980), and education, labor market and health outcomes from the fifth follow-up sweep (2000). Here I review the results on the effects of the early life endowments on smoking and obesity. Fig. 3 plots the average probability of being a daily smoker (left panel) or of being obese (right panel) along the distribution of each of the three endowments, while fixing the other two at their mean values.[3] The figure is constructed so that such probabilities are normalized to zero for an individual at the bottom of each dimension of the endowment distribution at age 10, to set the scale and ease comparisons of the magnitude of the effects both across the different endowments, and across genders. The first striking result is that, while child cognition displays an important role in determining educational choices and labor market outcomes, it plays very little role in determining health and risky behaviors, especially for males, in contrast to what argued by much of the cognitive epidemiology literature (Deary,

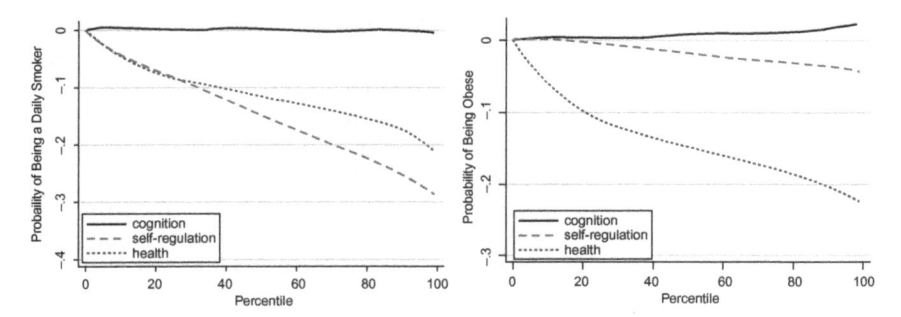

Fig. 3. Effect of Age 10 Endowments on Smoking (Left Panel) and Obesity (Right Panel), Males. Source: Conti and Heckman (2010).

Weiss, & Batty, 2010). In Conti and Heckman (2010), I show that, when human capital is modeled to be uni-dimensional, cognition shows significant effects on all the adult outcomes considered. Its role, instead, greatly diminishes and it is driven to insignificance once a three-endowment model is estimated. The second result is that both noncognitive dimensions (self-regulation and early physical health) are important determinants of adult outcomes, of equal strength for the non-labor market outcomes. The left panel of Fig. 3 shows that an early intervention which improves the capacity of the child to self-regulate (holding his cognitive ability and health endowment constant at their mean levels) by moving him up from the 20th to the 80th percentile of the distribution, would reduce the probability of being a daily smoker at age 30 by more than 10 percentage points. An effect of comparable magnitude is obtained for the physical health of the child. The only exception to this pattern is found for obesity, for which the early health dimension is the single most important determinant. As shown in the right panel of Fig. 3, an early intervention that would improve the physical health of the child (by moving her from the bottom to the top percentile of the distribution) would bring about a reduction in the probability of being obese at age 30 by approximately 20 percentage points. While this evidence comes from observational data, in the fifth section I present complementary evidence from two early childhood interventions — the Perry and the Abecedarian program — which led to a reduction in externalizing behavior and obesity in childhood, and smoking prevalence and cardiovascular risk factors in adulthood, respectively.

While evidence on the importance of early life endowments for late life outcomes has been studied in more than one paper, previous work

(Carneiro, Crawford, & Goodman, 2007; Heckman, Stixrud, & Urzua, 2006),[4] had not quantified their importance in explaining health disparities. A notable exception is Cutler and Lleras-Muney (2010), who examine different explanations for the relationship between education and health behaviors. They find that income, health insurance, and family background can account for about 30% of the gradient, and that knowledge and measures of cognitive ability explain an additional 30%. Surprisingly, they find no role for time and risk preferences, or for personality. In Conti and Hansman (2013) I revisit their findings on the NCDS data, and using early measures of personality (rather than adult measures), I show that childhood behavioral traits contribute to the education-health gradient to an extent nearly as large as that of cognition.[5]

In addition to analyze their effects on labor market and health outcomes, in Conti and Heckman (2010) and Conti, Heckman, and Urzua (2010), I also quantify the importance of early life endowments in accounting for disparities in adulthood. The main results are displayed in Fig. 4, where the length of each bar shows the mean differences at age 30 in a number of outcomes between individuals who have dropped out at the minimum compulsory school leaving age (16 years in Britain at the time considered), and

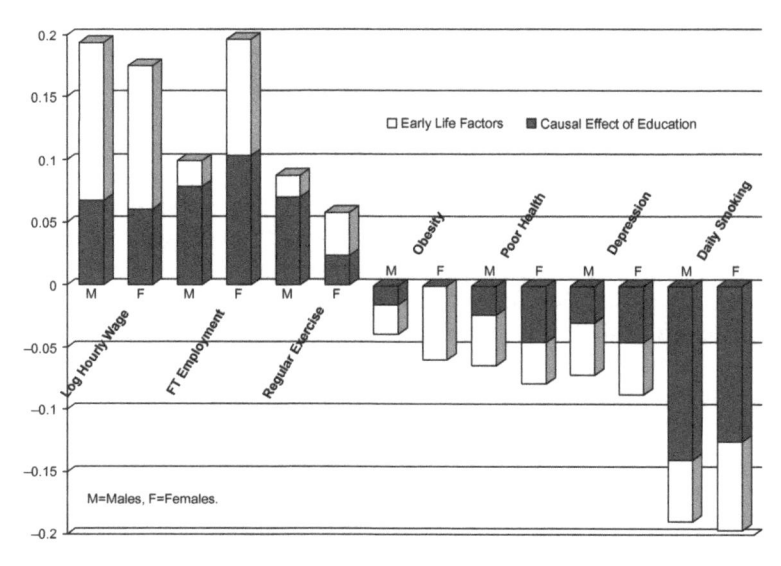

Fig. 4. Early Origins of the Education-Health Gradient. Source: Conti and Heckman (2010).

those who have stayed on beyond 16 to achieve a post-compulsory educational qualification. These raw differentials are then decomposed into a selection component attributable to early life factors (the white portion of the bar), and into a causal component which is the treatment effect of education (the dark portion of the bar). This decomposition exercise shows that education has a stronger effect on health behaviors than on health. It also shows that early life factors (endowments and family environments) account for at least half of the adult disparities in poor health, depression, and obesity. Finally, I go beyond the mean effects traditionally considered in the literature, to analyze distributions of treatment effects (the proportion of individuals who benefit and are harmed by the treatment) and treatment effect heterogeneity − to assess whether the success of later interventions depends on the quality of earlier ones. I show that indeed the effect of education on health varies as function of these early life endowments: for example, the effect of education on smoking is stronger for males with higher cognition and lower self-regulation. Recognizing this heterogeneity − and the fact that individuals can select into certain the treatment on the basis of their idiosyncratic gains − has been proved crucial to reconcile the disparate findings in the literature on the effect of education on health.

Future research in this area should focus on understanding which endowments at which ages matter for particular health outcomes, at which point in the lifecycle they are more malleable, and which are the cost-effective interventions to promote them.[6] Additionally, an understanding of the formation of the education gradient in health will be improved by comparing the results from different methodologies, such as selection models with a factor structure (of different degrees of complexity) guided by economic theory, and conventional propensity score matching and instrumental variable analyses − so to understand the different margins of choice at which effects are identified, and attempt to reconcile the discordant findings present in the literature. Finally, a deeper exploration of the various mechanisms and pathways through which education affects health (ranging from the provision of information to the availability of resources) is warranted, in order to gain a more thorough understanding of the nature of the gradient.

THE LONG-RUN COSTS OF EARLY LIFE ADVERSITY

A long line of research from several disciplines has documented the importance of early life conditions, starting in the prenatal period, for health and well-being throughout the lifecourse (Barker, 1997; Fogel, 2004; Gluckman & Hanson, 2004). Developmental plasticity implies that social environments and experiences during sensitive periods can profoundly influence human health (Hochberg et al., 2011). While there is now a consolidated body of evidence that early conditions matter for health, knowledge on the mechanisms is still relatively scarce. In recent years, we have begun to gain a more sophisticated understanding of how the circumstances in which the children are born and raised "get under the skin" and affect the biological development of the brain and of the rest of the body. Studies of stress response pathways (McEwen and Stellar, 1993), allostatic load (Geronimus, Hicken, Keene, & Bound, 2006), neuronal development, and epigenetic mechanisms (Waterland & Michels, 2007), have shown that the environment can become biologically embedded in the body. Identifying the mechanisms is vital to design policies that are effective at reducing health inequalities. However, one major obstacle when undertaking this endeavor is that in humans it is not easy to separate out biological effects from behavioral responses that might alleviate or exacerbate the effects of early conditions. The use of animal models might provide a useful complement to the human evidence, since external manipulation of the environment and controlled experimental conditions allow analyzing the long-term health effects of early circumstances which occur because of biological embedding. Along these lines, the seminal work by Meaney and Szyf (Weaver et al., 2004) has already shown the importance of maternal care in the development of stress response in rats, and the role played by epigenetic changes.

In Cole et al. (2012) and Conti et al. (2012), I show that adverse early life conditions (non-maternal rearing) in rhesus monkeys have long-term negative effects on both physical and mental health; that they are not ameliorated by a normal social environment later in life; and that they operate at least in part through stress-response pathways and changes in the expression of leukocyte genes related to immune function. These findings provide robust evidence that the environment can causally affect the biology of the body — and that at the same time intervention is possible at a biological level before disease becomes manifest. This project uses data from an experiment on rhesus monkeys raised in the Laboratory of Comparative Ethology in Poolesville (MD). I now briefly describe the experimental protocol. At birth, monkeys are randomized into one of three rearing conditions: mother reared (MR), peer reared (PR), and surrogate peer reared (SPR). MR monkeys remain with their biological mothers from birth and are raised in large cages with other monkeys (other females with their kids, and two males), whereas both PR and SPR are taken from their mothers and individually raised by humans in a nursery until the 37th day of life. On the 37th day, PR monkeys are placed in groups of four with the three monkeys closest in age, and they spend 24 hours together in a cage. SPR monkeys spend 22 h/d alone in a cage with a surrogate mother (a hot water bottle wrapped with soft and cuddling terrycloth, hanging from the cage ceiling) and are placed with a peer group of three other SPR monkeys in a play cage for 2 hours each day. At the end of the experimental period, that is, between 6 months[7] and 1 year, all monkeys born in the same year are put together in a single mixed social group (the size of the group is bigger than 20, in some cases it reaches 30). Thus, we can distinguish two phases: an experimental phase, since birth until 6 months/1 year of age and a post-experimental phase. The basic idea underlying the experimental design is for the PR condition to give the effect of maternal deprivation, while for the SPR condition to give the effect of both maternal and social deprivation.[8]

In Cole et al. (2012) I analyze RNA extracted from blood samples of 4-month-old rhesus monkeys to examine changes in basal leukocyte gene expression profiles as function of rearing conditions. I couple microarray-based assessment of the entire macaque transcriptome with recent advances in computational bioinformatics and econometrics to map large sets of differentially expressed genes into a small number of higher-order biological themes regarding their functional consequences (using Gene Ontology functional annotations), and to test whether the monkeys not reared by their mothers had at least a twofold or greater difference in average expression values as compared to the control group of monkeys reared by their mothers. I find that the monkeys not raised by their mothers have enhanced expression of genes involved in inflammation, cytokine signaling and T-lymphocyte activation, and suppression of genes involved in several innate antimicrobial defenses, including type I Interferon (IFN) antiviral response. This particular biological configuration reflects a state of "general alert" of the body, and an increased susceptibility to disease. Fig. 5 gives a heat plot representation of gene expression values for transcripts showing a twofold or greater difference in average expression between peripheral blood mononuclear cells (PBMCs) from surrogate-peer reared (SPR) rhesus macaques and those from maternally reared macaques (MR). I then used promoter-based bioinformatics analyses to understand how the information from the social environment gets transmitted under the skin. I find an increased activity of transcription factors linked to stress-responsive "social signal transduction" pathways such as the sympathetic nervous system (SNS) and a decreased activity of IFN response factors implicated in

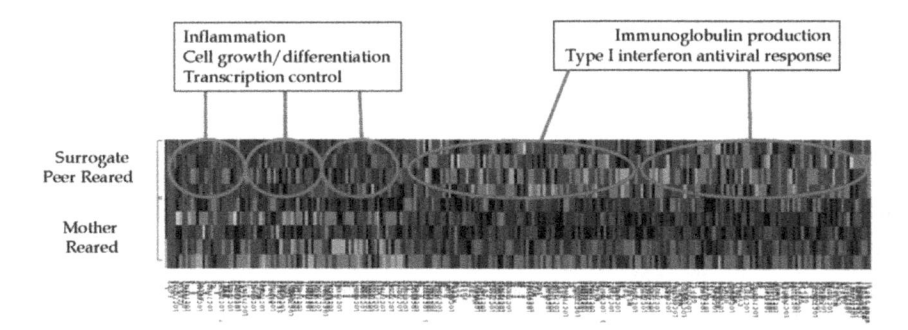

Fig. 5. Differential Gene Expression in Leukocytes from Mother-Reared vs. Surrogate-Peer-Reared Monkeys. *Note*: Each row displays values for an animal; each column displays values for a gene transcript. In dark grayscale (top left and bottom right), up-regulated gene expression; in light grayscale (top right and bottom left), down-regulated gene expression. Source: Cole et al. (2012).

the observed differences in gene expression. This work shows that adverse social conditions in early life can become embedded within the basal transcriptome of primate immune cells within the first 4 months of life, and implicate transcription control pathways as candidate mediators of these effects and potential targets for health interventions.[9]

While in Cole et al. (2012) I have shown that being raised in adverse conditions leads to biological changes, an important question is whether the consequences of early life adversity can be reversed if children are moved to more "normal" environments. To answer this question, in Conti et al. (2012) I have analyzed data from medical records based on quarterly veterinarian visits for a population of 231 rhesus macaques born between 2002 and 2007 (122 MR, 57 PR and 52 SPR). I compared average health outcomes across the two treated groups (PR and SPR) and the control group (MR) pairwise after the first year of life, once the monkeys have all been put together in a single mixed social group, to examine whether early life adversity carries out late health effects. The main finding of this study is that the health effects of adverse early conditions last even after the end of the experimental period. The most striking effects are found for male monkeys raised with a surrogate mother: they show higher probability and frequency of developing an illness (Fig. 6) than those raised by the mother (nearly every SPR male monkey had an illness at some point during the experimental period). In particular, they were sick of stress-related diseases, like diarrhea. Complementary analysis of the blood test results for a

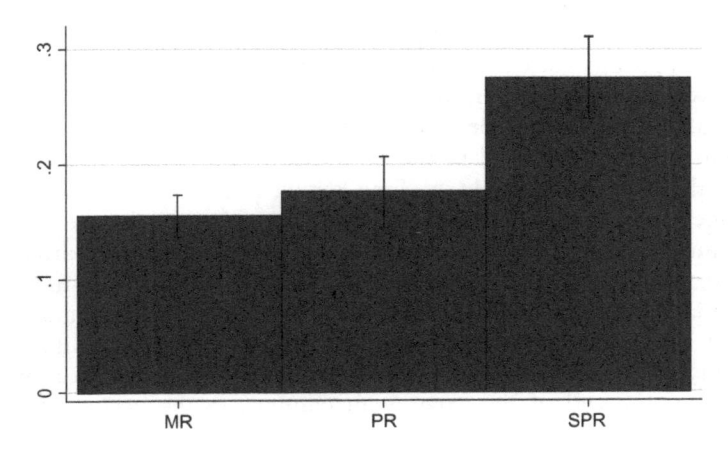

Fig. 6. Frequency of Illness in Mother-Reared (MR) vs. Peer-Reared (PR) vs. Surrogate-Peer-Reared (SPR) Monkeys. Source: Conti et al. (2012).

subsample of monkeys affected by these conditions showed that they presented alterations in the blood very similar to those found in humans. I then looked for precursors of these late diseases in the experimental phase, and I found that SPR monkeys had higher levels of the stress hormone cortisol following a stress challenge, and also lower levels of 5-HIAA, which is the main metabolite of the mood-related neurotransmitter serotonine. Similar stress-related responses have been found, for example, in children adopted after being raised in orphanages (Gunnar, Fisher, & TEESPN, 2006). Additionally, both male and female monkeys not raised by their mothers showed higher probability of developing mental health problems; in particular, the males SPR were more than five times as likely to show stereotyped behavior, while the males PR were about three times more likely, as compared to those raised by their mothers.[10] These effects are consistent with the attachment theory elaborated by Bowlby (1951), according to which the lack of a warm and continuous relationship with a caregiver might have irreversible mental health consequences. Additionally, I find that PR female monkeys are more likely to suffer from wounds and alopecia, and to have a higher weight than MR ones: actually, they weigh just as much as their male counterparts. By again searching for possible mechanisms in the experimental phase, I find that they display more aggressive behavior (and no self-grooming) in the first 30 weeks of life as compared to those reared by their mothers. I interpret this as evidence of the influence of the early social environment on the emergence of behavioral differences, since the peer groups are of mixed gender, and for males, both groups not reared by their mothers show more aggressive behavior. Given the early behavioral changes observed in this group, I conjectured that wounds and alopecia might be due to fighting and hair pulling, and that the traits acquired in the early years as an adaptive response to the social environment might be long-lasting and not reversible. Finally, the gender differences I find are consistent with existing evidence that, both in the animal and in the human kingdom, males are more affected by adversity, while females are more resilient (Rutter, 1981). This study shows that the lack of a secure attachment relationship in the early years has detrimental consequences for both physical and mental health later in life, with long-lasting effects that vary by gender. The persistence of these effects after the end of the experiment emphasizes the need to intervene early in life to prevent long-term damage. It also provides strong biological foundations to all the body of observational evidence which has shown long-term health consequences in children being maltreated or neglected (Danese, Pariante, Caspi, Taylor, & Poulton, 2007; Felitti et al., 1998), in which causality might be difficult to establish (Rutter, 2012). It complements the compelling human evidence on the consequences of maternal deprivation which comes from children raised in the adverse settings of the Romanian orphanages of the 1980s and 1990s. The most recent evidence shows, like for the nonhuman primates, a high degree of persistence (until 15 years of age) of cognitive impairment, suboptimal physical development, and behavioral problems (Rutter, 2010).

Future research in this area should focus on disentangling biological versus behavioral mechanisms, in particular understanding how parental investments respond to child endowments. The evidence to date suggests that parents exacerbate initial endowment differences by engaging in reinforcing investments (Almond & Mazumder, 2013). In such case, at least part of the observed late-life differences might not be solely due to purely biological mechanisms. An important aspect of this endeavor is to uncover which measures of maternal, newborn and infant health best capture the effects of the fetal environment. Most of the studies in the literature have used birth weight. However, birth weight is an imperfect proxy of newborn health (Almond & Currie, 2011). Along these lines, using unique data on fetal development from ultrasound scans, in Conti et al. (2013) I show that the use of an imperfect measure like birth weight might indeed underestimate the importance of the prenatal period. Future work should investigate which are the best markers of early environments (and predictors of later disease), assessed both prospectively and retrospectively.

Another fruitful line of research in this area would be to investigate the role of epigenetic changes: what is their quantitative importance, and whether they are on a causal pathway between early life conditions and late life disease. Identifying the epigenetic consequences of early life environments could have important applications, in terms of developing both epigenetic biomarkers for early diagnosis of disease, and epigenetic drugs to prevent or cure them. Finally, research to date has mostly focused on the negative consequences of being hit by a shock early in life. However, many children who have experienced adverse conditions ultimately manage to overcome them — and even to thrive. Understanding what are the factors promoting resilience (Feder, Nestler, & Charney, 2009) could provide important insights into how to help children overcome troubled early environments.

THE LONG-RUN BENEFITS OF ENVIRONMENTAL ENRICHMENT

Policies to promote health in adulthood have traditionally focused on reducing the prevalence of unhealthy habits (Ezzati & Riboli, 2012). Even when the importance of taking a lifecourse perspective has been recognized, policies to promote health in childhood have traditionally focused on improving physical health, by promoting the use of health inputs such as prenatal care, immunizations and good nutritional intake, and by raising rates of health insurance coverage. However, for the first time, mental health problems have displaced physical conditions as leading causes of disabilities in US children (Slomski, 2012). Additionally, the evidence reviewed in the previous sections suggests that interventions outside traditional health policy might be effective at improving child — and adult — health. Strategies aimed at supporting the family, beyond merely providing financial support, for example by raising parents' knowledge about practices to promote healthy child development, and by nurturing strong attachment relationships, have been proved effective at improving child well-being. In this regard, the most reliable evidence on the effectiveness of early interventions comes from experiments that substantially enriched the early environments of children born in disadvantaged families. Here I briefly review recent evidence from two iconic interventions, the Perry Preschool Project and the Abecedarian Project, since they have been evaluated by the method of random assignment, they have long-term follow-ups, and their health effects have recently been investigated.

The High/Scope Perry Preschool Project (PPP) is a social experiment designed to evaluate the impact of the novel Perry curriculum on highly disadvantaged[11] African-American children of 3–5 years of age. It was administered to five cohorts of children during the early- to mid-1960s in the district of the Perry Elementary School in Ypsilanti, Michigan. The intervention consisted of 2.5 hours classes for 5 days per week during the regular school year (30 weeks), and included weekly home visits lasting 1/1.5 hours. The curriculum was based on the concept of *active learning*, which is centered around play, based on problem-solving, and placed within a structured daily routine.[12] The final sample consisted of 123 children over five entry cohorts.

The Carolina Abecedarian Project (ABC) is a social experiment designed to test if an intellectually stimulating environment could prevent the development of mild mental retardation for disadvantaged children. The intervention was much more intensive than the Perry. It was year-round and full-day. It consisted of a two-stage treatment: a preschool treatment targeting early childhood education (from 0.4 months until 5 years), and a subsequent school-age treatment targeting initial schooling (from 5 to 8 years). It used a systematic curriculum specially developed by Sparling and Lewis (1979, 1984) that consisted of a series of "learning games," but also included a nutritional and health care component. It was administered to four cohorts of children born between 1972 and 1977 and living in or near Chapel Hill, North Carolina (NC). Eligibility was based on a High-Risk Index computed from 13 socioeconomic factors capturing disadvantage. The final sample consisted of 111 children recruited over a 5-year period, resulting in four cohorts. Unlike PPP, ABC provided access to basic pediatric health care to participants as well as adequate nutrition (breakfast, lunch, and an afternoon snack).

Both the Perry and the Abecedarian interventions have shown consistent patterns of successful outcomes for treatment group members as compared to control group members for both boys and girls (Campbell et al., 2008; Heckman et al., 2010). While among Perry participants, an initial increase in IQ gradually faded out in the 4 years following the intervention, still at the oldest age studied (age 40), treated individuals had attained higher levels of education, earned higher wages, and were less likely to be on welfare and to commit crime than the controls.

Heckman, Pinto, and Savelyev (2013) show that the effects of the Perry intervention on life outcomes operate primarily through the program's reduction in child's externalizing behavior. Much less is known about the health effects of these interventions, and previous attempts at analyzing the effects of these programs on health and risk behaviors (Muennig,

Schweinhart, Montie, & Neidell, 2009; Muennig et al., 2011) have not accounted for the variety of statistical challenges that these small sample Randomized Controlled Trials (RCTs) pose, have not investigated gender differences in the treatment effects, and have not considered health effects across the whole lifecourse of the subjects. In Conti et al. (2013) I have overcome all these limitations and carried out an extensive analysis by taking advantage of all the health information available in the Abecedarian and Perry samples, since early childhood, and including newly collected unique biomedical data. I find statistically significant and economically important treatment effects for both males and females which were not uncovered in the pooled gender analysis, and which survive when simultaneously tackling all the statistical challenges. The Perry participants show a significant reduction in unhealthy behaviors, in particular smoking and adherence to safe traffic practices. For example, among males in the control group the prevalence of non-smokers was 46% at age 27, and 47% at age 40, while that in the treatment group was 58% and 63%, respectively. The Abecedarian participants had a leaner physical constitution in childhood[13]; additionally, the analysis of the biomarkers recently collected for this sample reveals that they were in better physical health also by the time they reached their mid-30s. For example, treated males were less likely to have hypertension, dyslipidemia, and to be affected by the metabolic syndrome, as compared to males in the control group.

Other studies – such as the Nurse-Family Partnership (Kitzman et al., 1997), in which nurses visit pregnant girls and teach them prenatal health practices and parenting – also provide evidence of a variety of positive health effects to both the child and the mother (Olds, 2002).[14] Prenatal home visiting programs such as the NFP are also particularly appealing, both because they reach at-risk families as early as possible, and because they intervene at the same time on children and adolescent mothers, by affecting those traits still amenable to change during adolescence (Brown & Hurlock, 1977).[15]

There are several fruitful avenues for future research which can be pursued in this area. The first one involves understanding the *mechanisms* through which these programs achieved their observed effects. This is of primary importance since as of today we do not know yet whether, for example, enrichment interventions work in humans by restoring the same pathways which have been damaged by early life adversity, or by developing alternative ones. Some interventions might work by changing directly the traits which were targeted by the curriculum (such as, for example, cognition in the Abecedarian), while others were achieved by changing certain behavioral habits which led to a change in those traits (for example, eating habits which led to a reduction in obesity in the Abecedarian). A proper understanding of the mechanisms through which these programs achieved their effects cannot be undertaken without a thorough analysis of the various curricula. And our ability to understand the mechanisms will also improve as the collection of biomarkers is routinely integrated in the evaluations of interventions. In addition, the way the parents respond to interventions, that is, if they crowd out, or act as a supplement to, private resources, has to be thoroughly investigated. So far the evidence is that the interventions supplement and complement the investments made by the parents in the children (Bradley, Casey, & Caldwell, 1997; Gelber & Isen, 2011). Finally, important practical issues are related to the design and the actual implementation of these programs, and involve their timing, mode of delivery, and scalability. With regard to the first aspect, a question for future research involves the effectiveness of prenatal versus postnatal interventions, that is, the extent to which programs targeted to pregnant women (or to adolescent girls in fertile age) have higher returns than programs targeted to the early years. This is closely linked to the second aspect, that is, mode of delivery: prenatal interventions are usually delivered in the home by means of nurse or paraprofessional visiting, while postnatal programs are mostly center based, and might involve or not a home visiting component (e.g., the Perry Preschool program involved 1.5 hours per week of home visits, while the Abecedarian program included home visits only in the school-age treatment). Finally, while there is evidence that carefully designed, high-quality early childhood interventions produce long-term benefits, an important issue is to produce successful results by going up to scale. In order to achieve this, a first step is the need to assess different interventions on a comparable metric, in terms of rate of return, and to carry out rigorous cost-effectiveness analyses.

Lastly, recent discoveries in biology and neuroscience have shown the possibility to re-open windows of plasticity later in life (Bardin, 2012). It has already been shown in animals that environmental enrichment (Francis et al., 2002), methyl supplementation (Weaver et al., 2005) and histone deacetylase inhibitor (Weaver et al., 2004) reverse the effects of low maternal care on stress reactivity in adult rats. While the reversibility of structural and functional changes in the brain following alterations of the social environment has not been systematically investigated, recent research in humans is beginning to document the effects of specific interventions to reduce stress and promote well-being on brain structure and function (see Davidson & McEwen, 2012, for a recent review), and restoration in telomere function by diet, exercise and stress reduction (Puterman & Epel, 2012). The optimal timing and duration of such interventions might be, however, quite specific, and depend upon the nature of the early life adversity. This is an exciting line of future research which is just at the beginning.

CONCLUSIONS AND FUTURE DIRECTIONS

The field of the effects of early life conditions on health inequality has been a very fertile area of research in the recent years. The evidence that something happened very early in life might have long-term consequences seems now irrefutable. At the same time, though, such evidence is sparse. Not the same long-term outcomes are affected by different forms of early life adversity. Comparability across studies is also made more complicated by the fact that different early life insults act through different biological mechanisms, and might elicit different behavioral responses.

In this chapter, I have reviewed recent evidence which shows that a substantial portion of late-life disparities have origins early in life; that experiences occurring during critical periods of development can have long-term effects; and that, while children can be permanently damaged, the damage can often be remediated. However, the literature will benefit from a greater degree of specificity, both in the definition of exposures and outcomes of interest, and in a more in depth study of the mechanisms. One particularly interesting challenge, which is receiving a lot of attention recently, is the need to disentangle biological pathways versus behavioral responses. Recent advances in biology and the use of animal models will allow us to develop a better understanding of how much of the observed late life disparities is due to the biological embedding of early life experiences, and how much is due to behavioral processes, which might reduce or magnify the effects of early conditions.

Particularly important from a policy perspective is to understand whether trajectories from early life exposures to unfavorable outcomes can be altered, and at which times it is most effective to intervene. Undoubtedly, our ability to design effective policies will increase as evidence from the biological sciences on windows of plasticity for specific dimensions will sharpen. The key message which emerges from this chapter is the need to nurture human development at a time when biology is most amenable to change. Designing and implementing biologically − based interventions is the key to prevent the emergence and widening of health disparities in the future generation, while not abandoning the current one.

NOTES

1. See Almond and Currie (2010) for a recent review.
2. See also Strauss and Thomas (2008) for a review of theoretical and empirical evidence on health across the lifecourse, with a focus on developing countries.
3. The adult outcomes and the child capabilities are simulated from the estimates of our model and from the data.
4. See also Goodman, Joyce, and Smith (2011) and Kaestner and Callison (2011) for more recent evidence.
5. A limitation common to all this work is the assumption of a fixed structure for the early life endowments, and for the mapping of the endowments to the measurements. Conti, Heckman, Fruhwirth-Schnatter, and Piatek (2013) overcome this limitation and propose a novel Bayesian exploratory factor-analytic procedure which attempts to uncover the structure of early life traits without any a priori information.
6. A related issue is the harmonization of constructs across studies, since the use of different measurements has often hindered comparability.
7. Weaning is usually completed at 6–7 months.
8. The SPR condition is similar to that used in the "cloth mother" primate experiments by Harry Harlow (1958), who had previously shown that proper development of infants requires nurturing from an attentive caregiver, not just the provision of food and water. In that research, socially isolated baby monkeys that were removed from their mothers were found to prefer clinging to a cloth-covered surrogate, rather than to a harsh wire sculpture, even when only the latter provided milk. This research has been critical in helping change policies in human orphanages that had treated infants inhumanely.
9. See Tung et al. (2012) for complementary evidence on the effects of social status (dominance rank) on gene expression, and Tung and Gilad (2013) for a review of the evidence on the effects of social environmental conditions on gene regulation.
10. Stereotypies displayed by the monkeys were digit sucking (the most frequent), pacing, head tossing, self-grasping, saluting, spinning, rocking, circling, and swinging.
11. The initial IQ was below 85.
12. The teacher encouraged the children to engage in play activities that involved "plan, do and review" tasks each day.
13. Childhood health measures are not available for the Perry sample.
14. The NFP targets pregnant adolescent girls, with no previous live births, low income, and unmarried. The program has been implemented in a series of randomized trials conducted in Elmira (New York, $n=400$), Denver (Colorado, $n=735$) and Memphis (Tennessee, $n=1,135$). In each of these three sites, women were randomized to receive either home visitation services during the pregnancy and the first 2 years of life, or to receive comparison services.
15. Another emerging area of research is related to the cost-effectiveness of adolescent interventions. We have already noticed that education seems to be effective at changing behaviors, while early life endowments have both a direct effect on health, and an indirect effect mediated by education. Recent evidence on adolescent interventions in humans (Chapter 10 in Heckman, Humphries, & Kautz, 2013) shows that for later remediation to be effective, it should focus on noncognitive

traits. Indeed, environmental enrichment in puberty has shown positive effects in animals (Burdge et al., 2009; Imemaka et al., 2008).

ACKNOWLEDGMENTS

This chapter draws in part on my work with James Heckman, to whom I am very grateful for many stimulating discussions on the developmental origins of health and for continuous support and encouragement. The research was supported in part by NICHD 1R01HD54702, and a European Research Council grant hosted by University College Dublin, DEVHEALTH 269874.

REFERENCES

Almond, D., & Currie, J. (2010). Human capital development before age five. *Handbook of labor economics* (Vol. 4b), Elsevier, Amsterdam.
Almond, D., & Currie, J. (2011). Killing me softly: The fetal origins hypothesis. *Journal of Economic Perspectives*, 25(3), 153–172.
Almond, D., & Mazumder, B. (2013). Fetal origins and parental responses. *Annual Review of Economics*, 5(3), 1–3, 20.
Assembly, U. G. (2011). Political declaration of the high-level meeting of the General Assembly on the prevention and control of non-communicable diseases. *United Nations*.
Barker, D. J. P. (1997). Fetal nutrition and cardiovascular disease in later life. *British Medical Bulletin*, 53(1), 96–108.
Bowlby, J. (1951). *Maternal care and mental health*. World Health Organization Monograph.
Bradley, R. H., Casey, P. H., & Caldwell, B. M. (1997). Quality of the home environment. In R. T. Gross, D. Spiker, & C. W. Haynes (Eds.), In *Helping low birth weight, premature babies: The infant health and development program*. Stanford University Press, Stanford.
Brown, M., & Hurlock, J. (1977). Mothering the mother. *The American Journal of Nursing*, 77(3), 439–441.
Burdge, G. C., Lillycrop, K. A., Phillips, E. S., Slater-Jefferies, J. L., Jackson, A. A., & Hanson, M. A. (2009). Folic acid supplementation during the juvenile-pubertal period in rats modified the phenotype and epigenotype induced by prenatal nutrition. *The Journal of Nutrition*, 139(6), 1054–1060.
Campbell, F. A., Wasik, B. H., Pungello, E., Burchinal, M., Barbarin, O., Kainz, K., ... Ramey, C. T. (2008). Young adult outcomes of the Abecedarian and CARE early childhood educational interventions. *Early Childhood Research Quarterly*, 23(4), 452–466.
Carneiro, P., Crawford, C., & Goodman, A. (2007). The impact of early cognitive and non-cognitive skills on later outcomes. *CEE dp 92*.
Case, A., Lubotsky, D., & Paxson, C. (2002). Economic status and health in childhood: The origins of the gradient. *American Economic Review*, 92(5), 1308–1334.

Case, A., & Paxson, C. (2002). Parental behavior and child health. *Health Affairs, 21*(2), 164–178.

Caucutt, E. M., & Lochner, L. (2012). *Early and late human capital investments, borrowing constraints, and the family.* NBER Working Paper 18493.

Cohen, S. B., & Yu, W. (2012). The Concentration and persistence in the level of health expenditures over time: Estimates for the U.S. Population, 2008–2009. *Statistical Brief 354*, Agency for Healthcare Research and Quality.

Cole, S. W., Conti, G., Arevalo, J. M., Ruggiero, A. M., Heckman, J. J., & Suomi, S. J. (2012). Transcriptional modulation of the developing immune system by early life social adversity. *PNAS, 109*(50), 20578–20583.

Condliffe, S., & Link, C. R. (2008). The relationship between economic status and child health: Evidence from the United States. *American Economic Review, 98*(4), 1605–1618.

Conti, G., Godfrey, K., Hanson, M., Inskip, H., Cooper, C., & the SWS Study Group. (2013). *Beyond birthweight: The origins of health capital.* Mimeo.

Conti, G., & Hansman, C. (2013). Personality and the education-health gradient. *Journal of Health Economics, 32*(2), 480–485.

Conti, G., Hansman, C., Heckman, J. J., Novak, M., Ruggiero, A. M., & Suomi, S. J. (2012). Primate evidence on the late health effects of early life adversity. *PNAS, 109*(23), 8866–8871.

Conti, G., & Heckman, J. J. (2010). Understanding the early origins of the education-health gradient: A framework that can also be applied to analyze gene-environment interactions. *Perspectives on Psychological Science, 5*(5), 585–605.

Conti, G., & Heckman, J. J. (2013). The economics of child well-being. In A. Ben-Arieh, I. Frones, F. Casas, & J. E. Korbin (Eds.), *The handbook of child well-being*. Springer, New York.

Conti, G., Heckman, J. J. Fruhwirth-Schnatter, S., & Piatek, R. (2013). *Bayesian exploratory factor analysis.* Mimeo.

Conti, G., Heckman, J. J., Moon, S., & Pinto, R. (2013). *The long-term health effects of early childhood interventions.* Mimeo.

Conti, G., Heckman, J. J., & Urzua, S. (2010). The education-health gradient. *American Economic Review Papers & Proceedings, 100*, 234–238.

Cunha, F. (2013). *Preferences, beliefs, and investments in the human capital of young children.* University of Pennsylvania, unpublished manuscript.

Cunha, F., & Heckman, J. J. (2007). The technology of skill formation. *American Economic Review, 97*(2), 31–47.

Cunha, F., Heckman, J. J., & Schennach, S. (2010). Estimating the technology of cognitive and noncognitive skill formation. *Econometrica, 78*(3), 883–931.

Currie, J. (2011). Inequality at birth: Some causes and consequences. *American Economic Review Papers & Proceedings, 101*(3), 1–22.

Currie, J., & Stabile, M. (2003). Socioeconomic status and child health: Why is the relationship stronger for older children? *American Economic Review, 93*(5), 1813–1823.

Cutler, D., & Lleras-Muney, A. (2010). Understanding differences in health behavior by education. *Journal of Health Economics, 29*, 1–28.

Danese, A., Pariante, C. M., Caspi, A., Taylor, A., & Poulton, R. (2007). Childhood maltreatment predicts adult inflammation in a life-course study. *PNAS, 104*(4), 1319–1324.

Davey Smith, G. (Ed.). (2003). *Health inequalities: Lifecourse approaches.* Bristol: The Policy Press.

Deary, I. J., Weiss, A., & Batty, G. D. (2010). Intelligence and personality as predictors of illness and death: How researchers in differential psychology and chronic disease epidemiology are collaborating to understand and address health inequalities. *Psychological Science in the Public Interest, 11*(2), 53–79.

Emanuel, E. (2012). Prevention and cost control. *Science, 337*, 1433–1433.

Ezzati, M., & Riboli, E. (2012). Can noncommunicable diseases be prevented? Lessons from studies of populations and individuals. *Science, 337*(6101), 1482–1487.

Feder, A., Nestler, E. J., & Charney, D. S. (2009). Psychobiology and molecular genetics of resilience. *Nature Reviews Neuroscience, 10*, 446–457.

Felitti, V. J., Anda, R. F., Nordenberg, D., Williamson, D. F., Spitz, A. M., Edwards, V., ... Marks, J. S. (1998). Relationship of childhood abuse and household dysfunction to many of the leading causes of death in adults. The Adverse Childhood Experiences (ACE) study. *American Journal of Preventive Medicine, 14*(4), 245–258.

Fogel, R. W. (2004). Health, nutrition, and economic growth. *Economic Development and Cultural Change, 52*(3), 643–658.

Galama, T. (2011). *A contribution to health capital theory.* RAND Working Paper, WR-831.

Galama, T., & van Kippersluis, H. (2010). *A theory of socioeconomic disparities in health.* RAND Working Paper, WR-773.

Galobardes, B., Lynch, J. W., & Davey-Smith, G. (2008). Is the association between childhood socioeconomic circumstances and cause-specific mortality established? Update of a systematic review. *Journal of Epidemiology and Community Health, 62*, 387–390.

Gayle, G.-L., Golan, L., & Soytas, M. A. (2013). *What accounts for the racial gap in time allocation and intergenerational transmission of human capital?* Washington University working paper.

Gelber, A. M., & Isen, A. (2011). *Children's schooling and parents' investment in children: Evidence from the head start impact study.* NBER Working Paper 17704.

Gluckman, P. D., & Hanson, M. A. (2004). Living with the past: Evolution, development, and patterns of disease. *Science, 305*, 1733–1736.

Gluckman, P. D., Hanson, M. A., Cyrus, C., & Thornburg, K. L. (2008). Effect of in utero and early-life conditions on adult health and disease. *New England Journal of Medicine, 359*(1), 61–73.

Goodman, A., Joyce, R., & Smith, J. P. (2011). The long shadow cast by childhood physical and mental problems on adult life. *PNAS, 108*(15), 6032–6037.

Grossman, M. (1972). On the concept of health capital and the demand for health. *Journal of Political Economy, 80*(2), 223–255.

Gunnar, M. R., Fischer, P. A., & The Early Experience, Stress, and Prevention Network. (2006). Bringing basic research on early experience and stress neurobiology to bear on preventive interventions for neglected and maltreated children. *Development and Psychopathology, 18*, 651–677.

Harlow, H. F. (1958). The nature of love. *American Psychologist, 13*, 673–685.

Heckman, J. J. (2007). The economics, technology, and neuroscience of human capability formation. *PNAS, 104*(33), 13250–13255.

Heckman, J. J., Humphries, J. E., & Kautz, T. (2013). *The GED and the Role of Character in American Life.* Forthcoming, University of Chicago Press.

Heckman, J., Pinto, R., & Savelyev, P. (2013). Understanding the mechanisms through which an influential early childhood program boosted adult outcomes. *American Economic Review, 103*(6), 2052–2086.

Heckman, J. J., Stixrud, J., & Urzua, S. (2006). The effects of cognitive and noncognitive abilities on labor market outcomes and social behavior. *Journal of Labor Economics, 24*(3), 411–482.

Hertzman, C. (1999). The biological embedding of early experience and its effects on health in adulthood. *Annals New York Academy of Sciences*, 85–95.

Hertzman, C., & Boyce, T. (2010). How experience gets under the skin to create gradients in developmental health. *Annual Review of Public Health, 31*, 329–347.

Kaestner, R., & Callison, K. (2011). Adolescent cognitive and noncognitive correlates of adult health. *Journal of Human Capital, 5*(1), 29–69.

Kitzman, H., Olds, D. L., Henderson, C. R., Hanks, C., Cole, R., Tatelbaum, R., ... Barnard, K. (1997). Effect of prenatal and infancy home visitation by nurses on pregnancy outcomes, childhood injuries, and repeated childbearing: A randomized controlled trial. *Journal of the American Medical Association, 278*(8), 644–652.

Kuh, D., & Ben-Shlomo, Y. (Eds.). (2004). *A life course approach to chronic disease epidemiology*. Oxford University Press, Oxford.

Lochner, L. (2011). Non-production benefits of education: Crime, health, and good citizenship. In E. Hanushek, S. Machin, & L. Woessmann (Eds.), *Handbook of the economics of education* (Vol. 4, Ch. 2), Amsterdam: Elsevier Science.

Marmot, M. (1999). Epidemiology of socioeconomic status and health: Are determinants within countries the same as between countries? *Annals New York Academy of Science, 896*, 16–29.

Marmot, M. G., & Wilkinson, R. G. (2006). *Social determinants of health*. Oxford University Press, Oxford.

Muennig, P., Robertson, D., Johnson, G., Campbell, F., Pungello, E., & Neidell, M. (2011). The effect of an early education program on adult health: The carolina abecedarian project randomized controlled trial. *American Journal of Public Health, 101*(3), 512–516.

Muennig, P., Schweinhart, L., Montie, J., & Neidell, M. (2009). Effects of a prekindergarten educational intervention on adult health: 37-year follow-up results of a randomized controlled trial. *American Journal of Public Health, 99*(8), 1431–1437.

Olds, D. (2002). Prenatal and infancy home visiting by nurses: From randomized trials to community replication. *Prevention Science, 3*(3), 153–172.

Power, C., Kuh, D., & Morton, S. (2013). From developmental origins of adult disease to life course research on adult disease and aging: Insights from birth cohort studies. *Annual Review of Public Health, 34*, 7–28.

Puterman, E., & Epel, E. (2012). An intricate dance: Life experience, multisystem resiliency, and rate of telomere decline throughout the lifespan. *Social and Personality Psychology Compass, 6*(11), 807–825.

Roux, W. (1888). Contributions to the developmental mechanics of the embryo. Translated from the German in 1974. In B. H. Willer & J. M. Oppenheimer (Eds.), *Foundations of experimental embriology* (pp. 2–37). New York, NY: Hafner.

Rutter, M. (1981). *Maternal deprivation reassessed* (2nd ed.). Harmondsworth: Penguin.

Rutter, M. (2010). *Deprivation-specific psychological patterns: Effects of institutional deprivation*. Boston, MA: Wiley-Blackwell.

Rutter, M. (2012). Achievements and challenges in the biology of environmental effects. *PNAS, 109*(2), 17149–17153.

Slomski, A. (2012). Chronic mental health issues in children now loom larger than physical problems. *JAMA, 308*(3), 223–225.

Smith, J. P. (1999). Healthy bodies and thick wallets: The dual relation between health and economic status. *Journal of Economic Perspectives*, *13*(2), 145–166.

Strauss, J., & Thomas, D. (2008). Health over the life course. *Handbook of Development Economics*, *4*.

Tung, J., Barreiro, L. B., Johnson, Z. P., Hansen, K. D., Michopoulos, V., Toufexis, D., ... Gilad, Y. (2012). Social environment is associated with gene regulatory variation in the rhesus macaque immune system. *PNAS*, *109*(17), 6490–6495.

Tung, J., & Gilad, Y. (2013). Social environmental effects on gene regulation. *Cellular and Molecular Life Sciences*, *70*(22), 4323–4339

Weaver, I. C. G., Cervoni, N., Champagne, F. A., D'Alessio, A. C., Sharma, S., Seckl, J. R., ... Meaney, M. J. (2004). Epigenetic programming by maternal behavior. *Nature Neuroscience*, *7*(8), 847–854.

THE CONTRIBUTION OF OCCUPATION TO HEALTH INEQUALITY

Bastian Ravesteijn, Hans van Kippersluis and Eddy van Doorslaer

ABSTRACT

Health is distributed unequally by occupation. Workers on a lower rung of the occupational ladder report worse health, have a higher probability of disability and die earlier than workers higher up the occupational hierarchy. Using a theoretical framework that unveils some of the potential mechanisms underlying these disparities, three core insights emerge: (i) there is selection into occupation on the basis of initial wealth, education and health, (ii) there will be behavioural responses to adverse working conditions, which can have compensating or reinforcing effects on health and (iii) workplace conditions increase health inequalities if workers with initially low socio-economic status choose harmful occupations and don't offset detrimental health effects. We provide empirical illustrations of these insights using data for the Netherlands and assess the evidence available in the economics literature.

Keywords: Health; labour; occupation; lifecycle; the Netherlands

JEL classifications: I14 and J24

INTRODUCTION

Health and mortality are distributed unequally by occupation (Mackenbach et al., 2008; Marmot et al., 1991). For example, Davey-Smith et al. (1998) show that in the United Kingdom, those in the highest occupational classes had a 70% lower mortality rate over a 21-year period than those in the bottom occupational class. Not only mortality rates differ: Case and Deaton (2005) find that in the United States those employed in manual occupations self-report lower health than those who work in professional occupations, and that their health declines more rapidly with age. Van Kippersluis et al. (2010) similarly find that among working Dutch males, health differences across manual and non-manual workers widen until around early retirement age and decline thereafter. Does this evidence mean that lower skilled occupations exert a higher health toll and thereby contribute to observed health disparities by socio-economic status (SES)?

In this chapter we review the literature on whether occupation affects health and, if so, to what extent this contributes to socio-economic inequalities in health. The discussion is illustrated with descriptive evidence from the Netherlands, which provides an interesting context in which there is a heated ongoing debate on whether certain 'hard' occupations should be exempted from a proposed rise in the statutory retirement age, and where it only recently became possible to link occupational information to administrative registers containing mortality and disability figures. Our assessment of the literature is guided by a theoretical framework, which indicates that it is vital to understand the association between occupation and health along three dimensions.

First, it is unclear whether the strong and persistent association between occupation and health derives from a direct, causal effect of occupation on health. Alternatively, the association between occupation and health could stem from health enabling and/or limiting factors that induce individuals to self-select into certain types of occupation. A third possibility is that predetermined characteristics such as education or initial endowments affect both occupation and health, implying that health inequalities by occupation are simply a reflection of 'deeper' societal inequalities across socio-economic groups. Even if a causal effect of occupation on health is established, it is essential to understand which occupational characteristics are most important in producing these health differentials. Is it simply the manual aspect of the job in terms of hard physical labour, or are health differences mostly caused by the psychosocial stressors, such as low job control and high work load? The answers to these questions have implications for policies that aim to prolong working lives and provide foundations for possible differentiation of the statutory retirement age on the basis of individual occupational histories.

Second, individual choices are not made in isolation. Decisions regarding occupational choice are made simultaneously with decisions regarding health investment and consumption. Hence, workers may (partially) offset the occupation-related damage to their health by investing in health, or may add to this health risk by engaging in unhealthy types of consumption.

Third, given a heavily constrained occupational choice set, workers with worse endowments may choose to 'sell' part of their health by engaging in harmful occupations, in return for higher earnings. If this health risk is not fully compensated, it implies that occupation could exacerbate socio-economic inequalities in health. If workers with poor endowments are more likely to choose such harmful occupations and are not fully compensated financially, there is scope for compensating labour market policies to offset health inequalities resulting from 'hard' occupations.

Our review suggests that the evidence on the causal impact of occupation on health − in contrast to evidence on the association − is fairly thin. Identification of causal effects is particularly hampered by the sheer difficulty of finding suitable sources of exogenous variation in occupational and working conditions. Recent contributions do suggest that, while health differences across occupations largely reflect health-based selection, at least some part of the effect runs through physical working conditions affecting health outcomes, thereby exacerbating socio-economic inequalities in health.

The chapter is organized as follows. In the next section we document patterns of occupation, health and longevity in the Netherlands. In the third section we describe the basics of an economic model of health behaviour across the lifecycle which can help us understand occupational differences in health. In the penultimate section we review the scientific evidence guided by the core insights derived from the theory. The final section concludes.

PATTERNS OF OCCUPATION AND HEALTH IN THE NETHERLANDS

The association between occupation and self-reported health, as well as other measures of morbidity, has been widely documented, both internationally and for the Netherlands (Cavelaars et al., 1998; Kunst, Looman, & Mackenbach, 1990; Mackenbach et al., 2008). There is some evidence of an association between occupation and mortality (Kunst et al., 1990), but less on the association between occupation and the onset of disability (e.g. Currie & Madrian, 1999). We add to this with evidence from the Netherlands, made possible through the recent linking of surveys and administrative registers by Statistics Netherlands.

We use the Dutch *Permanent Survey of Living Conditions* (Dutch acronym POLS) which has been linked to the registers since 1997. POLS is a repeated cross section survey which includes questions on measures of self-assessed health (SAH) and a measure of type of occupation based on the Dutch Standard Classification of Occupations (Dutch acronym SBC, see CBS, 2012). We use observations of individuals in the years 1997 through 2006, 115,888 of whom report an occupational title. The earliest cross-sections are much larger, with the first four years accounting for 70% of observations.

We distinguish between five major occupational groups: elementary, low-level, mid-level, high-level and university-level occupations (CBS, 2012). The 1992 SBC occupational classification is based on the skill level that is required for each occupation.[1] Examples of elementary occupations include conveyer belt workers or cleaners; low-level occupations include lumberjacks, miners and construction workers; mid-level occupations include foremen, building contractors or mechanics; high-level occupations include primary school teachers, mid-level managers, and head nurses; university-level occupations include medical doctors, accountants and architects.[2] We investigate the association between occupational type and three measures of health. We find that workers in a 'higher' type of occupation on average report better health, are less likely to become disabled and live longer than workers in lower ranked occupations.

Occupation and Self-Assessed Health

In the survey years 1997–2001, respondents were asked to assess their health on a five-point scale from poor to very good. We restrict the sample to working-age individuals between 20 and 65 years old, which is the current legal retirement age. Fig. 1 shows the health self-reports, uncontrolled for age and gender, for workers in five occupational groups, for those on disability benefits and for those not working. Only a very small proportion of people on disability benefits reports good health. People on disability benefits report worse health than others who are not in paid employment. The figure shows that health status monotonically improves with higher levels of occupation: 81% of elementary workers report good or very good health as opposed to 90% of those in high-level and university-level occupations.

Fig. 2 shows the proportion in good or very good health of individuals in the five occupational groups at different ages. It is striking that already at age 25 marked differences in health are observed across occupational groups. Since occupation is unlikely to have had much of an effect on health already at that age, this strongly suggests that there is health-related selection into occupations. The health disparities between occupational groups increase with age, suggesting rapid health deterioration among workers in the lower occupational groups, yet it should be kept in mind that these are not lifecycle profiles and hence could reflect cohort effects,

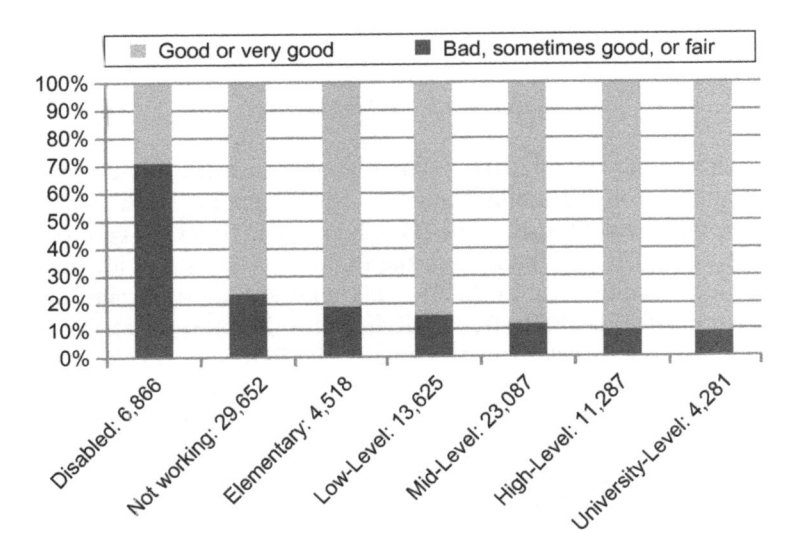

Fig. 1. Self-Assessed Health by Disability, Employment and Occupation (Netherlands POLS Surveys 1997–2006).

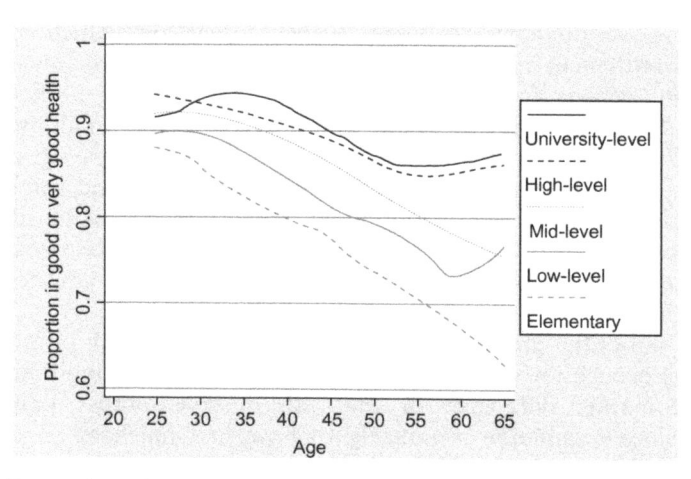

Fig. 2. Proportion of Workers in Good or Very Good Health by Occupation and Age (Netherlands POLS Surveys 1997–2006).

selective promotion between occupational groups, selective mortality and other sources of confounding. The occupational health gradient by age is somewhat steeper for men than for women (not shown).

Occupation and Disability

In the Netherlands, people who become unable to work because of health reasons qualify for a disability benefit. Using a linkage with longitudinal data from the Social Statistics File (Dutch acronym SSB), we can follow up all workers aged 20–65 observed in the POLS survey data to identify those moving into disability (until 2006). This allows analysis of the duration until exit out of a disability-free spell and into disability of all individuals who reported to be working at the time of the POLS survey. We take into account the left-truncation resulting from the fact that we start to observe individuals at different ages and we take into account right-censoring because of death, reaching the retirement age of 65 or the fact that we observe disability only until 2006. We estimate a Cox proportional hazard model of the duration until exit to disability. The base category is elementary work and the likelihood of exiting into disability monotonically decreases with level of occupation. Taking into account the 95% confidence intervals, individuals in low-level occupations are between 17% and

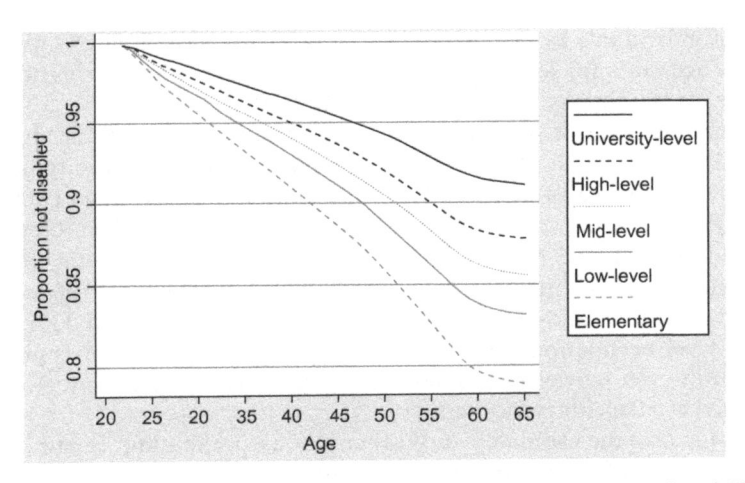

Fig. 3. Survival until Exit to Disability by Occupation. Cox Proportional Hazard Model (Netherlands, POLS Surveys and SSB Follow-Up until 2006).

33% less likely to exit into disability than elementary workers at any age. Individuals in mid-level occupations are between 38% and 51% less likely to exit to disability. For individuals in high-level occupations this is between 45% and 57% and for university-level occupations this is between 56% and 70%.

Fig. 3 shows the proportion of the working population that survives disability-free until the age of 65. At the age of 55, already 18% of elementary workers have exited to disability while only 7% of university-level workers are receiving disability benefits. Also very striking is the monotonicity of the gradient: with every step down the occupational ladder, the risk of disability increases significantly. The survivor function flattens after the age of 60, most likely reflecting the increased likelihood of exiting the labour force into early retirement instead of disability.

Occupation and Mortality

Occupational disparities in health are also reflected by differential survival. While these have been documented for many countries, hitherto they could not be examined for the general Dutch population because of absence of mortality data by occupation. Linkage of the POLS survey to the Cause of Death registry (Dutch acronym DO) enables analysis of the duration until death of individuals by occupational status. As for disability, our duration analysis accounts for left-truncation and we also account for right censoring because we observe mortality only until 2010.

Again, we estimate a Cox proportional hazard model of the duration until exit due to death. At any age, individuals receiving disability benefits are more than twice as likely to die in the period of observation compared to individuals who were in an elementary occupation when they were observed in the POLS survey. In our sample, taking into account the 95% confidence intervals, individuals in low-level occupations are between 7% and 23%, those in mid-level occupations are between 20% and 32%, those in high-level occupations are between 32% and 44%, and university-level occupation even between 45% and 57% less likely to die at any given age compared to elementary workers.

Fig. 4 shows the estimated survival curves by occupation. It can be seen that, at the age of 65, more than 20% of individuals who were on disability benefits have passed away — around 13% of elementary workers and around 7% of university-level workers. In the coming years, the legal retirement age in the Netherlands will be increased to 67. At that age, and not taking into account any increase in life expectancy, 16% of elementary workers will have passed away, as opposed to 8% of individuals in

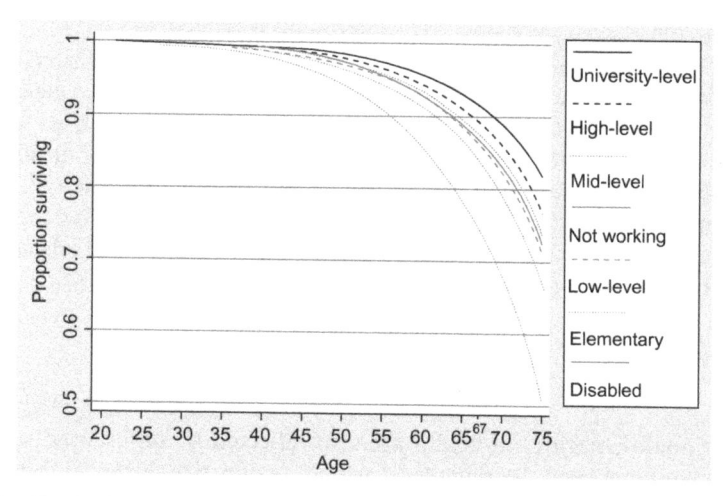

Fig. 4. Survival until Exit to Death by Employment and Occupation, Cox Proportional Hazard Model (Netherlands POLS Surveys 1997–2006 and Cause-of-Death Follow-Up until 2010).

university-level occupations. It is clear that both the probability of reaching retirement age and the survival chances beyond that age decrease monotonically with lower occupations.

All in all, the analysis confirms that in the Netherlands — as in many other industrialized countries — patterns of morbidity, disability and mortality differ by occupation. Health and survival prospects generally improve monotonically when moving up the occupational ladder. This raises the question of the extent to which these disparities reflect selection of healthier individuals into higher occupations, as opposed to these occupations offering a health advantage. In the case that the differences do reflect a causal effect of occupation on health, it is still of crucial importance to know to what extent this derives directly from the physical or psychosocial working conditions or rather follows from different life styles caused by occupation (e.g. through peer effects).

THEORETICAL FRAMEWORK

In this section, we present a theoretical framework based upon Grossman (1972), Case and Deaton (2005) and Galama and Van Kippersluis (2010) (see also Galama & Van Kippersluis, 2013), which represents choices of occupation, health investment, and consumption levels. It should help us to better understand (a) the empirical patterns observed in the previous section and (b) the evidence obtained so far in the wider literature.

Model Formulation

The individual maximizes discounted lifetime utility, which depends on consumption c and health h in each period, by choosing a level of consumption, of health investment m, and of physical and psychosocial occupational attributes in vector o, given his information set I_t which includes all state variables at time t.

$$\max_{\{c_{t+j}, m_{t+j}, o_{t+j}\}_{j=0}^{T-t}} E\left[\sum_{j=0}^{T-t} \beta^j u(c_{t+j}, h_{t+j}) | I_t\right] \quad (1)$$

The individual faces a health and a budget constraint. In each period, health is determined by permanent health p, the biological aging rate a, the history of idiosyncratic health shocks η, and the history of health investments and occupational choices.

$$h_{t+j} = f(p, a_1, ..., a_{t+j}, \eta_1, ..., \eta_{t+j}, m_1, ..., m_{t+j-1}, \mathbf{o}_1, ..., \mathbf{o_{t+j-1}}) \qquad (2)$$

Permanent, time-invariant health is a function of endowments $p = g(e)$ and reflects characteristics and circumstances that are stable over time, such as genetic predisposition for certain illnesses. Health deteriorates with age and with exposure to harmful occupational characteristics, but can be improved by health investments. Initial health is viewed as the health level at the beginning of the working career, and it is determined by permanent health, health depreciation due to age, and the effects of all past health shocks on current health. The effect of the history of health shocks is typically smaller than the sum of these health shocks.

Expenditures on consumption and health investment (at prices p_c and p_m) may not exceed total earnings. Wages w depend on endowments, current health, and on the current level of harmful workplace conditions, which can be chosen in each period. Current health and endowments determine the maximum wage (the 'wage frontier') the individual can attain. The wage can be increased by undertaking jobs with harmful workplace conditions that have a deleterious impact on health, leading to health compensating wage differentials. There is no initial wealth in this simple model, endowments take the form of human capital.

$$\sum_{k=1}^{T}(p_c c_k + p_m m_k) \leq \sum_{k=1}^{T} w(\mathbf{o_k}; h_k, e) \qquad (3)$$

The model emphasizes that the realization of lifetime utility depends on endowments, effort and institutions. Endowments are characteristics of the individual that are not chosen by the individual, like gender, race or genetic predisposition for learning, athletic ability or disease. But individuals are also endowed with their family background. For example, later-life outcomes may be determined by the level of education and income of the parents or by their ability to raise children. Second, lifetime utility is determined by individual effort, for example investment in health is costly but this type of effort is rewarded in terms of earnings potential and future health. Similarly, working may be harmful to health, but work is rewarded with earnings. Third, institutions determine how initial endowments and effort are rewarded in terms of utility and they determine the parameters of the constraints. For example, remedial teaching programs may reduce the importance of endowments while payroll taxes reduce the rewards of endowments and effort in terms of earnings.

Equilibrium Conditions

If we make the simplifying assumption that the time preference rate is equal to the interest rate, then, in each period, consumption and health investment are each chosen to equate the respective marginal benefit and marginal cost represented by the conditions

$$\frac{\partial u}{\partial c_t} = \lambda p_c \qquad (4)$$

$$\sum_{j=1}^{T-t-1} \frac{\partial h_{t+j}}{\partial m_t} \left[\frac{\partial u_{t+j}}{\partial h_{t+j}} \beta^j + \lambda \frac{\partial w_{t+j}}{\partial h_{t+j}} \right] = \lambda p_m \qquad (5)$$

where λ is the 'value' (or shadow price) of lifetime wealth and the LHS of Eq. (5) distinguishes the direct utility and indirect production benefits of health investment. These benefits include the future returns to current health investment through earnings and the discounted marginal utility of health in future periods.

The optimal level of harmful occupational characteristics is determined by

$$\lambda \frac{\partial w_t}{\partial o_{l,t}} = - \sum_{j=1}^{T-t-1} \frac{\partial h_{t+j}}{\partial o_{l,t}} \left[\frac{\partial u_{t+j}}{\partial h_{t+j}} \beta^j + \lambda \frac{\partial w_{t+j}}{\partial h_{t+j}} \right] \qquad (6)$$

for all l.

where the LHS represents the marginal return to entering an occupation that pays a wage premium in compensation for health hazards imposed and the RHS is the marginal health cost weighted by its direct and indirect consequences. The marginal costs include the effect of current occupational damage on future health and consequently on future earnings. Hence, there is an instantaneous wage benefit of harmful occupational attributes, yet future wages and future utility will be lower due to lower future health.

CORE INSIGHTS AND EMPIRICAL EVIDENCE

The economic framework yields several insights that are relevant for the interpretation of empirical evidence on occupation and health. In this section we discuss three core insights and the extent to which the empirical evidence in the economics literature is in line with them.

Selection and the Estimation of Causal Effects

Individuals select into types of occupation on the basis of endowments, education and health. Initial endowments influence one's health, but also one's wage prospects, since the marginal benefits of harmful occupational characteristics depend on endowments. Ravesteijn, Van Kippersluis, and Van Doorslaer (2013a) describe that in the Netherlands, those in 'higher ranked' occupations are generally better educated. It is therefore important to account for all factors that simultaneously influence both occupational choice and health outcomes if we want to obtain estimates of the causal effects of occupation on health. Moreover, not only do occupational characteristics affect health, but health may influence occupational choices. Health, which is subject to shocks, co-determines the wage rate, and the marginal benefits of engaging in harmful occupations. In simple terms, health determines the type of occupation one is able and willing to perform. Both unobserved heterogeneity and reverse causality prevent us from making statements about a causal effect of occupation on health on the basis of simple associations, such as those identified in US data by Case and Deaton (2005), Cutler, Lleras-Muney, and Vogl (2011) and Morefield, Ribar, and Ruhm (2011).

Several recent papers have made an attempt to go beyond the description of the occupation-health association and to estimate the health *effects* of occupation. Using an estimator that partially allows for correlation of regressors with time invariant unobservables, Datta-Gupta and Kristensen (2008) find that working in a satisfactory job environment improves self-reported health and reduces limitations in activities of daily living (ADL) in Denmark, France and Spain. Using data from 15 European countries, Cottini and Lucifora (2010) find that adverse working conditions negatively affect mental health, with the largest effect due to working at very high speed and tight deadlines, low job autonomy and being involved in complex tasks. They seek to address the potential problem of endogeneity of job conditions by instrumenting working conditions with (i) occupational health

Occupation and Health Inequality

and safety regulation by country and (ii) job control defined by industry and occupation. Both instruments are based upon the idea that institutions or competition at an aggregate level are plausibly exogenous to the working conditions in a particular firm. Estimates exploiting these instruments show even larger effects of working conditions on mental health. Using Danish panel data with detailed information on physical and psychosocial workplace conditions, as well as physical and mental health, and allowing for correlated unobservable determinants of health, lifestyles and work conditions, Cottini and Ghinetti (2012) find that bad working conditions reduce especially mental health.[3]

Using US data and controlling for initial and lagged health using a random effects specification to allow for time-invariant and time-varying factors that may affect both health and occupation, Fletcher, Sindelar, and Yamaguchi (2011) find that physically demanding work has a strong negative effect on self-rated health for white women but not for men and nonwhite women, and that harsh environmental working conditions have a strong negative effect for young men but not for young women.

On the basis of analysis of German panel data, and exploring several empirical panel data approaches, Ravesteijn, Van Kippersluis, and Van Doorslaer (2013b) claim that 50% of the association between workplace conditions and self-rated health is due to the causal effect on health, while the remaining 50% reflects selection effects.

Compensating Behaviours and Clustering of Occupational Attributes

A second core insight from the theory is that choices are not made in isolation. An individual simultaneously selects his occupation and investment in health. Health behaviour may be adjusted in response to occupational choice, since the marginal benefits of health investment depend on occupation, through the terms $\partial h_{t+j}/\partial m_t$ and $\partial w_{t+j}/\partial h_{t+j}$ from Eq. (5). Note that the behavioural adjustment is different from the selection issue in terms of timing. Ravesteijn et al. (2013a) describe that workers in lower occupations are more likely to smoke and less likely to engage in physical exercise. If these smoking differences in adolescence reflect different preferences across individuals which then lead to different occupational choices, this is considered selection. In contrast, if workers in certain occupations initiate smoking to cope with stress on the job or due to peer effects among colleagues, then these are considered behavioural adjustments. Therefore, the total health effect of a change in occupation is the sum of the direct effect of the occupational characteristics on health, and the indirect effect on health behaviour. In the absence of estimates of a full-fledged structural model — which inevitably requires strong functional form assumptions and very detailed data — or an experimental setting, it is extremely difficult to obtain an unbiased estimate of the direct effect since we only observe the total effect after the behavioural response.

Choo and Denny (2006) claim on the basis of Canadian data that even though the health effect of manual work is reduced by around 10% after controlling for health behaviours, there seems to be a direct effect of occupation on health. Cutler et al. (2011) similarly observe from US data that controlling for health behaviours reduces, but does not eliminate, occupational differences in health. Kelly, Dave, Sindelar, and Gallo (forthcoming) claim to be the first to estimate the causal impact of initial occupation on health behaviours. They find that entering the labour market as a blue collar worker raises the probability of obesity by 4% and of smoking by 3%. At least part of the observed health differences across occupational groups would appear to arise from differences in health behaviour differences.

Each occupation is characterized by psychosocial and physical workplace conditions. It is important to distinguish between the contributions of each of these attributes to health outcomes. Occupations with heavy manual work duties may simultaneously be characterized by low job control. Researchers should be careful in attributing certain health effects of an occupation to a specific attribute if this characteristic is simultaneously associated with other characteristics within occupational types.

In the Dutch POLS survey, individuals are asked to describe the characteristics of their jobs, including physical exertion, inconvenient work postures, repetitive work movements and psychosocial aspects, such as time pressure and control over daily work activities. Table 1 shows clear gradients in both physical and psychosocial job characteristics favouring the higher occupations. The only exception is working under time pressure, which is reported more often among the higher-ranked occupations. There appears to be clustering of different job characteristics that are potentially damaging to health in certain occupations.

Karasek (1979) defines job strain as the interaction effect between decision latitude and job demands. Decision latitude refers to the degree to which a worker can influence his workplace situation (job control). Job demands are simply stressors on the job. Karasek argues that the combination of low decision latitude and high job demands is particularly bad for health.

Table 1. Occupational Class and Attributes. Percentage of Respondents Sometimes or Regularly Exposed to Respective Job Attribute versus No Exposure.

Occupation Level	Physically Demanding (%)	Inconvenient Work Postures (%)	Repetitive Work Movements (%)	Job Control (%)	Under Time Pressure
Elementary	58	39	70	63	49
Low	51	40	63	68	54
Mid	39	39	57	81	70
High	16	19	39	81	72
University	9	18	41	94	86

According to the effort-reward imbalance model (Siegrist, 1996),[4] it is imbalance between job demands in terms of physical and psychosocial effort, on the one hand, and recognition/reward in terms of wages, esteem, job stability and career opportunities, on the other, that leads to a negative impact on health. Bosma, Pieter, Siegrist, and Marmot (1998) compare the job demand-control model of Karasek with the effort-reward imbalance model of Siegrist using data from the Whitehall II study. They confirm that the imbalance between personal efforts and rewards predicts higher risk of coronary heart disease. They also find that low job control in itself is strongly related to heart disease, while job strain or more generally high job demands are not.

The *Whitehall I and II studies* by Marmot, Shipley, and Rose (1984, 1991), Marmot, Bosma, Hemingway, Brunner, and Stansfeld (1997a) and Marmot, Ryff, Bumpass, Shipley, and Marks (1997b) brought the concepts of 'rank' and 'social status' into the theory on psychosocial job demands. These studies showed that male British civil servants in low employment grades suffered from higher mortality and morbidity rates than their colleagues in high employment grades, despite a great deal of homogeneity across the six employment grades. After 10 years, mortality for the highest employment grade was about one third of the mortality rate of the lowest for a wide range of causes of death. Marmot and colleagues argue that differences in health outcomes between civil servants of higher and lower rank are due primarily to seniority in the employment hierarchy — rank. They show that low job control seems important, yet they reject the Karasek hypothesis that high demand at work plays an important role.

Case and Paxson (2011) confirm that entry grade and current occupational grade in Whitehall are significantly related to SAH, yet they show that the associations are eliminated after controlling for *future* occupational grades. This suggests that occupational grade may be more of a marker than a cause of poor health. Using first-difference models, they find *no* association between current civil service grade and future SAH. In contrast, they *do* find a significant association between current SAH and future civil service grade. These findings support the health selection hypothesis, rather than the hypothesis that social position in adulthood influences changes in health status.[5]

Fletcher et al. (2011) combine information on physical requirements of work and environmental work conditions identified in the in the *Dictionary of Occupational Titles* (DOT) with US panel data and find that both physical demands and harsh environmental conditions harm self-reported health. Fletcher (2012) uses the DOT to construct a 'bad job' factor including ten adverse job conditions, including mostly physical job hazards and perceived reward. While he finds that starting a career in a 'bad job' is detrimental for later life self-reported health, he is unable to disentangle the individual contributions of the 10 job conditions. Ravesteijn et al. (2013b) find that the annual effect of a one standard deviation increase of physical occupational demands is equal to the health deterioration experienced in six months of aging for German workers. The effect of psychosocial workplace conditions is only apparent at higher ages.

In sum, there is little doubt that physical demands of a job matter for health. There is more controversy surrounding the question whether and how psychosocial aspects of the job matter for health.

Occupational Characteristics and Socio-Economic Inequalities in Health

The third insight from the theoretical model is that occupational choices may contribute to socio-economic inequalities in health. Agents with low endowments, for example in terms of parental background and intelligence, have lower permanent health and lower earnings for each choice of occupation. They may choose to 'sell' part of their health capital — by choosing harmful occupational attributes — to obtain an earnings bonus (Smith, 1776; see also Viscusi, 1978, 1979). Hence, the choice for a compensating wage differential may be induced partly by initial endowments, and therefore represents a heavily constrained choice.

This phenomenon could occur through multiple channels. First, since the marginal utility of consumption is higher for low levels of consumption, marginal increases in consumption are more attractive for agents with low endowments. Second, the marginal benefit of engaging in harmful occupational characteristics increases in the value of lifetime wealth, λ, as can be seen in Eq. (6). The value of lifetime wealth is generally assumed to decrease with more wealth (e.g. Galama & van Kippersluis, 2010), such that those with low endowments will have a higher value of lifetime wealth and hence higher marginal benefits for harmful workplace conditions. Finally, Case and Deaton (2005) argue that the marginal benefit of harmful job characteristics decrease with endowments and education, that is $\partial^2 w/\partial o \partial e < 0$, since *'professors, unlike construction workers, (...), get no increase in earnings by wearing out their bodies more rapidly'*. This would imply an additional reason for those with fewer endowments to accept an unhealthy job.

The compensating wage premium historically was associated with a potentially dangerous occupation requiring hard physical labour, for example mining, yet a modern-era variant is perhaps an investment banker who depletes his health capital through high levels of job stress and long working hours in exchange for a relatively high wage. Hence, the sign of $\partial^2 w/\partial o \partial e$ may depend on the actual type of workplace condition, for example plausibly negative for physical demands, yet potentially positive for psychosocial stressors on the job.

The gradient between SES and health becomes steeper if workers with a lower SES in terms of education, parental background and financial wealth are more likely to choose occupations with harmful workplace conditions, and if they don't fully offset these negative effects on health by making health investments. This implies that workplace conditions could directly contribute to health inequalities.

In the epidemiological literature there have been numerous attempts to assess the contribution of occupation to health inequalities by SES. Typically, the bivariate association between health and one particular socio-economic indicator is estimated, after which occupation or occupational characteristics are added to the regression to assess how the association changes (e.g. Borg & Kristensen, 2000; Marmot et al., 1997a). These studies suggest a large role for occupation, for example Borg and Kristensen estimate that as much as 59% of socio-economic disparities can be attributed to occupation and the work environment. Yet, simply adding occupation to a regression of health outcomes on other socio-economic indicators does not provide a reliable estimate of the contribution of occupation to socio-economic inequalities in health. Since occupation is 'intervening' in the relationship between some other socio-economic indicators and health, and occupation is clearly endogenous, this provides a particular form of the 'bad controls' problem (Angrist & Pischke, 2009), that is elaborated upon in this context by Ravesteijn (2013). One requires sources of exogenous variation in *both* the socio-economic indicator (the regressor of interest) *and* in occupation (the intervening control variable) in order to identify the contribution of the latter to socio-economic-related health inequality, which is obviously a tall order.

CONCLUSION

There is a strong and persistent association between occupation and health. We have verified that occupation is correlated with SAH, risk of disability and longevity in the Netherlands. For example, those in professional occupations are on average 63% less likely to enter into disability, and 51% less likely to die at any given point in time, when compared to those in elementary occupations.

While this evidence is often interpreted as indicating unfair health inequalities, a fully informed normative policy response requires knowledge of why health is related to occupation. We have sketched a theoretical model of choices with respect to occupation and health. Three core insights emerge: (i) there is selection into occupation on basis of initial endowments and health, (ii) there will be behavioural responses to adverse working conditions, which can be compensating in the form of health investment, or worsening in terms of unhealthy behaviours and (iii) workplace conditions increase health inequalities if workers with initially low SES choose harmful occupations and do not offset detrimental health effects.

Guided by these insights, four main conclusions emerge from our review of the evidence. First, while health inequalities across occupational largely reflect health-related selection into occupations, recent evidence suggests that there also exists a causal effect of occupation on health, that mainly derives from physical work conditions. We believe future research should go beyond the unravelling of (partial) associations to unveil the underlying *causal* health effects of job conditions. While the panel-data approaches are promising, an alternative would be to look for exogenous variation in occupational characteristics that might be obtained from changes in regulation, unanticipated firm downsizing or plant closures.

Second, observed health outcomes across occupational groups may be the result from a behavioural response to changing job conditions rather than the direct effects of occupational characteristics. It is known that health behaviours differ across occupational groups – in the Netherlands close to 50% of workers in elementary occupations smoke versus just over 20% in university-level occupations. There is some evidence that at least part of these differences in health behaviours is caused by (first) occupation (Kelly et al., forthcoming). Future research should focus on disentangling the direct effects of occupation and the indirect effects resulting from behavioural response, which is crucial for policy purposes.

Third, research should attempt to separate the contributions of the various physical and psychosocial aspects of work places. While there is convincing evidence both from the epidemiological literature (e.g. Bernard, 1997) and the economic literature (Fletcher et al., 2011; Ravesteijn et al., 2013b) that physical characteristics of occupations impact on health, there is more controversy on the impact of psychosocial aspects. Since adverse physical and psychosocial job conditions tend to be clustered, much remains to be learned on their relative contributions.

Finally, more effort should be devoted to establishing the cumulative effects of occupation on health, and the extent to which occupation contributes to the association between (childhood) SES and health. This is the most challenging, but potentially also the most rewarding item on the research agenda. Improved understanding of the interrelation between (childhood) SES, occupation and health is not only helpful for addressing SES-health inequalities, but is equally important in guiding policy choices regarding the regulation of occupational safety and regarding premature labour market exits for health reasons.

NOTES

1. The idea here is to present associations of an occupational measure and health outcomes. While we acknowledge that this classification is likely to pick up not just the effects of occupation, but additionally the effects of education and other individual characteristics, similar issues would plague other classifications of occupation into, for example, blue and white-collar jobs.
2. Due to changes in the coding procedure, 17,897 observations of occupational titles had to be excluded from the analyses.
3. Limitations of the study are that it uses only two waves of the panel, fixed effects are not taken into account and there are no exclusion restrictions, with non-linearity relied on for identification.
4. We refer to Bakker and Demerouti (2007) for a complete overview and review of the two models and proposed alternatives.
5. A recent study by Anderson and Marmot (2012) does find evidence that promotion on the job reduces the risk of heart disease.

ACKNOWLEDGEMENT

This chapter was prepared with funding from Netspar to the Theme 'Income, health, work and care across the life cycle II' and a panel paper grant. The authors further acknowledge funding from the National Institute on Aging of the National Institutes of Health under Award Number R01AG037398. We are grateful to Statistics Netherlands for (remote) access to the linked datasets used in this research, and to the editors for helpful comments and suggestions.

REFERENCES

Anderson, M., & Marmot, M. (2012). The effects of promotions on heart disease: Evidence from whitehall. *The Economic Journal*, *122*(561), 555–589.

Angrist, J. D., & Pischke, J.-S. (2009). *Mostly harmless econometrics: An empiricist's companion*. Princeton, NJ: Princeton University Press.

Bakker, A. B., & Demerouti, E. (2007). The job demands-resources model: State of the art. *Journal of Managerial Psychology*, *22*(3), 309–328.

Bernard, B. P. (Ed.) (1997). Musculoskeletal disorders and workplace factors: A critical review of epidemiologic evidence for work-related musculoskeletal disorders of the neck, upper extremity, and low back). Cincinnati, OH: Department of Health and Human Services, National Institute for Occupational Safety and Health.

Borg, V., & Kristensen, T. S. (2000). Social class and self-rated health: Can the gradient be explained by differences in life style or work environment? *Social Science & Medicine*, *51*, 1019–1030.

Bosma, H., Pieter, R., Siegrist, J., & Marmot, M. (1998). Two alternative job stress models and the risk of coronary heart disease. *American Journal of Public Health*, *88*(1), 68–74.

Case, A., & Deaton, A. S. (2005). Broken down by work and sex: How our health declines. In *Analyses in the economics of aging*. NBER Chapters:185–212. National Bureau of Economic Research, Inc.

Case, A., & Paxson, C. (2011). The long reach of childhood health and circumstance: Evidence from the Whitehall II study. *The Economic Journal*, *121*(554), F183–F204.

Cavelaars, A. E. J. M., Kunst, A. E., Geurts, J. J. M., Helmert, U., Lundberg, O., Mielck, A., ... Mackenbach, J. P. (1998). Morbidity differences by occupational class among men in seven European countries: An application of the Erikson–Goldthorpe social class scheme. *International Journal of Epidemiology*, *27*(2), 222–230.

CBS. (2012). Retrieved from http://www.cbs.nl/nl-NL/menu/methoden/classificaties/overzicht/sbc/1992/default.htm. Accessed on October 31, 2012.

Choo, E., & Denny, M. (2006). *Wearing out – The decline in health*. Working Papers tecipa-258. Department of Economics, University of Toronto, Toronto.

Cottini, E., & Ghinetti, P. (2012). *Working conditions, lifestyles and health*. Economics Working Papers 2012-28. Aarhus University.

Cottini, E., & Lucifora, C. (2010). *Mental health and working conditions in European countries*. IZA Discussion Paper No. 4717. Bonn, Germany.

Currie, J., & Madrian, B. C. (1999). Health, health insurance and the labor market. *Handbook of labor economics, 3*, 3309–3416.

Cutler, D., Lleras-Muney, A., & Vogl, T. (2011). Socioeconomic status and health: Dimensions and mechanisms. In S. Glied & P. C. Smith (Eds.), *Oxford handbook of health economics* (pp. 124–163). Oxford University Press, New York, USA.

Datta Gupta, N., & Kristensen, N. (2008) Work environment satisfaction and employee health: Panel evidence from Denmark, France and Spain, 1994–2001. *European Journal of Health Economics, 9*(1), 51–61.

Davey Smith, G., Hart, C., Hole, D., MacKinnon, P., Watt, G., Blane, D., & Hawthorne, V. (1998). Education and occupational social class: Which is the more important indicator of mortality risk? *Journal of Epidemiology & Community Health, 52*(3), 153–160.

Fletcher, J. M. (2012). The effects of first occupation on long term health status: Evidence from the Wisconsin Longitudinal Study. *Journal of Labor Research, 33*(1), 49–75.

Fletcher, J. M., Sindelar, J. L., & Yamaguchi, S. (2011). Cumulative effects of job characteristics on health. *Health Economics, 20*(5), 553–570.

Galama, T. J., & van Kippersluis, H. (2010). *A theory of socioeconomic disparities in health over the life cycle*. Tinbergen Institute Discussion Papers. Tinbergen Institute, Tinbergen.

Galama, T. J., & van Kippersluis, H. (2013). Health inequalities through the lens of health capital Theory: Issues, solutions, and future directions. In P. Dia & O. O'Donnell (Eds.), *Health and inequality*. Bingley, UK: Emerald.

Grossman, M. (1972). On the concept of health capital and the demand for health. *Journal of Political Economy, 80*(2), 223–255.

Karasek, R. A. J. (1979). Job demands, job decision latitude, and mental strain: Implications for job redesign. *Administrative Science Quarterly, 24*(2), 285–308.

Kelly, I. R., Dave, D. M., Sindelar, J. L., & Gallo, W. T. (forthcoming). *The impact of early occupational choice on health behaviors*. Review of Economics of the Household.

Kunst, A. E., Looman, C. W. N., & Mackenbach, J. P. (1990). Socio-economic mortality differences in the Netherlands in 1950–1984: A regional study of cause-specific mortality. *Social Science & Medicine, 31*(2), 141–152.

Mackenbach, J. P., Stirbu, I., Roskom, A. R., Schaap, M. M., Menvielle, G., Leinsalu, M., & Kunst, A. E. (2008). Socioeconomic inequalities in health in 22 European countries. *New England Journal of Medicine, 358*, 2468–2481.

Marmot, M., Bosma, H., Hemingway, H., Brunner, E., & Stansfeld, S. (1997a). Contribution of job control and other risk factors to social variations in coronary heart disease incidence. *The Lancet, 350*(9073), 235–239.

Marmot, M., Ryff, C. D., Bumpass, L. L., Shipley, M., & Marks, N. F. (1997b). Social inequalities in health: Next questions and converging evidence. *Social Science and Medicine, 44*(6), 901–910.

Marmot, M. G., Shipley, M. J., & Rose, G. (1984). Inequalities in death-specific explanations of a general pattern?. *The Lancet, 1*(8364), 1003–1006.

Marmot, M. G., Stansfeld, S., Patel, C., North, F., Head, J., White, I., Brunner, E., Feeney, A., & Smith, G. D. (1991). Health inequalities among British civil servants: The Whitehall II study. *The Lancet, 337*(8754), 1387–1393.

Morefield, B., Ribar, D. C., & Ruhm, C. J. (2011). Occupational status and health transitions. *BE Journal of Economic Analysis & Policy, 11*(3), 1–27.

Ravesteijn, B. (2013). *Good, bad, and ugly controls. On intervening control variables*. Mimeo, Erasmus University Rotterdam.

Ravesteijn, B., van Kippersluis, H., & van Doorslaer, E. (2013a). *Long and healthy careers? The relationship between occupation and health and its implications for the statutory retirement age*. Netspar Panel Paper, Tilburg.

Ravesteijn, B., van Kippersluis, H., & van Doorslaer, E. (2013b). *The wear and tear on health: what is the role of occupation?* Mimeo, Erasmus University Rotterdam.

Siegrist, J. (1996). Adverse health effects of high-effort/low-reward conditions. *Journal of Occupational Health Psychology*, 1(1), 27–41.

Smith, A. (1776). *An inquiry into the nature and causes of the wealth of nations*. London, UK: Methuen & Co.

Van Kippersluis, H., O'Donnell, O., Van Doorslaer, E., & Van Ourti, T. (2010). Socioeconomic differences in health over the life cycle in an egalitarian country. *Social Science and Medicine*, 70(3), 428–438.

Viscusi, W. K. (1978). Wealth effects and earnings premiums for job hazards. *The Review of Economics and Statistics*, 60(3), 408–416.

Viscusi, W. K. (1979). *Employment hazards: An investigation of market performance*. Boston, USA: Harvard Economic Studies.

PART III
INEQUALITY OF OPPORTUNITY IN HEALTH

INEQUALITY OF OPPORTUNITIES IN HEALTH AND THE PRINCIPLE OF NATURAL REWARD: EVIDENCE FROM EUROPEAN COUNTRIES

Damien Bricard, Florence Jusot, Alain Trannoy and Sandy Tubeuf

ABSTRACT

This chapter aims to quantify and compare inequalities of opportunity in health across European countries considering two alternative normative ways of treating the correlation between effort, as measured by lifestyles, and circumstances, as measured by parental and childhood characteristics, championed by Brian Barry and John Roemer. This study relies on regression analysis and proposes several measures of inequality of opportunity. Data from the Retrospective Survey of SHARELIFE, which focuses on life histories of European people aged 50 and over, are used.

In Europe at the whole, inequalities of opportunity stand for almost 50% of the health inequality due to circumstances and efforts in Barry

scenario and 57.5% in Roemer scenario. The comparison of the magnitude of inequalities of opportunity in health across European countries shows considerable inequalities in Austria, France, Spain and Germany, whereas Sweden, Poland, Belgium, the Netherlands and Switzerland present the lowest inequalities of opportunity. The normative principle on the way to treat the correlation between circumstances and efforts makes little difference in Spain, Austria, Greece, France, Czech Republic, Sweden and Switzerland, whereas it would matter the most in Belgium, the Netherlands, Italy, Germany, Poland and Denmark.

In most countries, inequalities of opportunity in health are mainly driven by social background affecting adult health directly, and so would require policies compensating for poorer initial conditions. On the other hand, our results suggest a strong social and family determinism of lifestyles in Belgium, the Netherlands, Italy, Germany, Poland and Denmark, which emphasises the importance of inequalities of opportunity in health within those countries and calls for targeted prevention policies.

Keywords: Equality of opportunity; principle of natural reward; Europe; inequality decomposition; efforts; circumstances

JEL classifications: D63; I14; N30

INTRODUCTION

Inspired by the philosophical concept of equality of opportunity developed by Dworkin (1981), Arneson (1989), Cohen (1989), Roemer (1998) and Fleurbaey (2008), a number of recent publications in health economics have focused on drawing the line between legitimate and illegitimate causes of health inequalities (Fleurbaey, 2006; Fleurbaey & Schokkaert, 2009, 2012; Garcia Gomez, Schokkaert, Van Ourti, & Bago d'Uva, 2012; Jusot, Tubeuf, & Trannoy, 2013; Rosa-Dias, 2009, 2010; Rosa-Dias & Jones, 2007; Sen, 2002; Tubeuf, Jusot, & Bricard, 2012; Trannoy, Tubeuf, Jusot, & Devaux, 2010). The main argument is that differences in observed health outcomes are explained by factors for which the individual can be held responsible, called effort, such as healthy lifestyles, and by factors for which the individual should not be held responsible, called circumstances, such as social and family background. The distinction between efforts and circumstances is at the core of the implementation of equality of opportunity policies and is based on the concept of individual responsibility. Equality of opportunity principles recommend first to respect the impact of individual responsibility, namely effort, on the outcome; this is the principle of natural reward, and second to compensate the impact of characteristics independent of individual responsibility, namely circumstances; this is the principle of compensation (Fleurbaey, 1995). One requires therefore distinguishing the respective contributions of efforts and circumstances to overall health inequalities, so that policy-makers are able to identify the effort which should be rewarded and the circumstances that should be compensated. The challenge when doing so is that the two components cannot be assumed to be independent and one needs to decide how the correlation between efforts and circumstances should be treated. Two main alternative views have been debated in the literature within this context (for a more extensive presentation of debates on the distinction between legitimate and illegitimate inequalities in health, see Fleurbaey & Schokkaert, 2012). According to Roemer (1998) effort should be respected inasmuch as effort is disembodied from the impact of circumstances; in other words the correlation between efforts and circumstances is considered as circumstances and is independent from individual responsibility. On the other hand, according to Barry (transcription of Barry position according to Roemer, 1998, p. 21; Barry, 2005) effort should be entirely rewarded and the correlation of effort and circumstances does not require to be acknowledged. To illustrate the debate, let us consider the case of smokers; would we hold sons of smokers less responsible to smoke than sons of non-smokers? From Roemer viewpoint, sons of smokers are less responsible than sons of non-smokers; from Barry viewpoint, parental circumstances are not relevant and sons of smokers are as responsible as sons of non-smokers for smoking. According to the viewpoint adopted, the magnitude of inequalities of opportunity in smoking will differ and this will have important implications on the implementation of the principle of natural reward and the principle of compensation. Empirical applications of this debate remain scarce (Jusot et al., 2013) and this issue has never been considered at the European level. In the case of France, Jusot et al. (2013) have shown that inequalities of opportunity represent about 46% of observed health inequalities regardless of the normative viewpoint adopted. They concluded that the philosophical view on the correlation between efforts and circumstances does not matter empirically and the share of inequality related to circumstances is very large in comparison with the share of inequalities related to efforts in France.

This chapter quantifies and compares inequality of opportunity in health in different European countries and assess whether it empirically matters to adopt Barry or Roemer view on the magnitude of inequalities of opportunity in each of these countries. In particular, the chapter investigates whether the correlation between effort and circumstances differ from one country to another. We use data from the Retrospective Survey of SHARELIFE, which focuses on life histories of European people aged 50 and over in 2008/2009.

A large strand of recent European studies have shown persistent socioeconomic health inequalities on general population data (Hernandez-Quevedo, Jones, Lopez, & Rice, 2007; Mackenbach, Stirbu, & Roskam, 2008; van Doorslaer & Koolman, 2004), as well as on sample of older adults (Crimmins & Cambois, 2003; Masseria, Mossalios, & Allin, 2006). Most of them have highlighted the importance of social aspects in the explanation of systematic differences in health status using various contemporary socioeconomic indicators, such as education, income, occupation, wealth, etc. and only one study has investigated the contribution of family and social background to socioeconomic inequalities in health in Europe (Tubeuf & Jusot, 2011). Based on the first wave of the Survey of Health Ageing and Retirement Survey, Jusot, Tubeuf, and Trannoy (2009, 2010) have compared inequalities of opportunity in health due to a small set of circumstances across European countries. As effort variables were not considered, this study only provided a partial picture of inequalities of opportunity in health and did not allow disentangling illegitimate and legitimate sources of inequalities.

Our results show differences in inequalities of opportunity across European countries with larger inequalities in Austria, France, Spain and Germany, and lower inequalities in Sweden, Poland, Belgium, the Netherlands and Switzerland. The share of inequalities of opportunity in health inequalities due to circumstances and efforts varies from 30% in the less unequal countries to 80% in the most unequal countries, whereas it represents 50% at the aggregate level. The way the correlation between efforts and circumstances is changing the measure of inequalities of opportunity also varies between countries where the difference between the alternative scenarios is not significant such as Switzerland and Sweden and countries where adopting a Roemerian approach matters more and induces a maximum of about 20% increase of the measurement of inequalities of opportunity. At the aggregate level, the difference between the alternative scenarios represents an increase of 16.8% in the Roemer measure of inequalities of opportunity comparing to the Barry measure.

The remainder of the chapter is as follows. The second section presents the methods and in particular the econometric model, the third section describes the data, the fourth section presents results on the explanatory factors of overall health inequalities in Europe and focuses on the findings on inequalities of opportunity in health between European countries. A discussion and concluding remarks form the final section.

METHODS

We empirically assess how Roemer and Barry respective viewpoints matter for the measurement of inequalities of opportunity in health in Europe using a regression-based methodology as suggested in Jusot et al. (2013). In the first step, reduced-form models are estimated in each country to measure the association between health status and respectively circumstances and efforts.[1] In the second step, predicted variables are used to measure the magnitude of health inequalities and to compare inequality of opportunity in health between European countries.

Estimation Strategy

Let us assume that individual health status H is a function of circumstances C, efforts E, demographic variables D and an error term u

$$H = f(C, E, D, u) \tag{1}$$

The vector of circumstances C consists of a set of variables beyond individual control related to health status in adulthood such as childhood conditions and family background. The vector of efforts E captures individual responsibility for health, such as lifestyles. Circumstances are considered as a source of illegitimate inequalities and efforts are considered as a source of legitimate inequalities.

The vector of demographic variables D captures biological determinants such as age and sex. Controlling for demographics is essential for international comparisons in order to control for differences in population composition. These biological determinants are circumstances in the very sense of the word. It could also be argued that health differences by age classes reflect the human destiny and everyone will experiment them soon or later over the life cycle. The error term u represents unobserved variables such as unobserved efforts or circumstances as well as luck. If we assume that we have a complete description of all factors, the residual term appeals to pure luck and others random factors (accident for example) which cannot be captured by the other determinants. In a regression, the residual term will be uncorrelated to other factors and its distribution will be even-handed with respect to circumstances as required for equality of opportunity (see Lefranc, Pistolesi, & Trannoy, 2009).[2] Whether this makes health differences due to biological factors as well as any unobserved variables a legitimate source of health inequality is not straightforward, and we therefore consider that demographics and the error term are two other sources of health inequality.

According to Barry, individual effort has to be fully respected whatever the influence of past circumstances on effort decisions. This position allows directly regressing circumstances and effort variables on health status to measure the correlation between health status and individual effort in health capital investment on the one hand, and the correlation between health status and circumstances on the other. The health status H_{ij} of individual i in country j within Barry context can then be written as follows

$$H_{ij} = \lambda_j^B + \alpha_j^B C_{ij} + \beta_j^B E_{ij} + \gamma_j^B D_{ij} + u_{ij} \tag{2}$$

Eq. (2) allows us to test the condition of equality of opportunity in Barry view by testing the equality of $\hat{\alpha}_j^B$ to zero. Independence between C_{ij} and E_{ij} is not required.

According to Roemer (1998), equality of opportunity requires that effort is purged from any contamination coming from circumstances so that it represents pure individual effort. This concept leads us to estimate an auxiliary equation regressing the effort E_{ij} of individual i in country j against their circumstances C_{ij}. It allows isolating a residual term e_{ij}, the relative efforts, which represent individual efforts purged from any circumstances

$$E_{ij} = \lambda_j + \delta_j \cdot C_{ij} + e_{ij} \tag{3}$$

We then substitute the vector of actual efforts E_{ij} for the estimated relative efforts $\hat{e}_{ij}$ in the equation of health status (Eq. (2)) and the health status H_{ij}^R of individual i in country j within Roemer context can be written in as follows

$$H_{ij} = \lambda_j^R + \alpha_j^R C_{ij} + \beta_j^R \hat{e}_{ij} + \gamma_j^R D_{ij} + u_{ij} \tag{4}$$

Eq. (4) allows us to test the condition of equality of opportunity in Roemer view by testing the equality of $\hat{\alpha}_j^R$ to zero since C_{ij} and e_{ij} are independent.

We estimate both health equations (Eqs. (2) and (4)) and the auxiliary equation (Eq. (3)) using linear probability models. These models allow us to have a perfect orthogonalisation of the auxiliary equations and to obtain comparable models in Eqs. (2) and (4) according to the Frisch–Waugh–Lowell theorem. It provides us with $\hat{\beta}_j^B$ in the first health equation (Eq. (2)) being the same as $\hat{\beta}_j^R$ in the second health equation (Eq. (4)). However $\hat{\beta}_j^R$ and $\hat{\alpha}_j^B$ remain different because in Roemer approach the coefficient of circumstances additionally incorporates the indirect effect of circumstances on efforts, which corresponds to the product of the coefficient of efforts in Barry approach and the coefficient of circumstances in the auxiliary equation ($\alpha_j^R = \alpha_j^B + \beta_j^B \delta_j$). We can note that predicted health is the same in the alternative specifications according to Barry or to Roemer as the set of regressors of both models contains the same information.

Inequality Measurement

We are interested in quantifying and decomposing the magnitude of health inequality into its components and for this purpose we use the variance. The variance presents a natural decomposition and has properties of consistency, symmetry and independence of the level of disaggregation (Shorrocks, 1982).

Using the previous estimation strategy, we can isolate the four main components of health namely circumstances $\hat{H}_C^k$, efforts $\hat{H}_E^k$, demographics $\hat{H}_D^k$, and residual $\hat{H}_{res}^k$ in each context $k = \{$B (Barry); R (Roemer)$\}$.

The decomposition of the variance of health status $\sigma^2(H)$ is therefore given by

$$\sigma^2(H) = \text{cov}(\hat{H}_C^k, H) + \text{cov}(\hat{H}_E^k, H) + \text{cov}(\hat{H}_D^k, H) + \text{cov}(\hat{H}_{res}^k, H) \qquad (5)$$

We use this decomposition to measure inequalities of opportunities IOP^k and inequalities related to efforts IEF^k. We also propose another measure of inequalities of opportunities as a share of inequalities related to circumstances and efforts SOP^k.

The measure of inequality of opportunities in health IOP^k is simply equal to the component of health inequality related to illegitimate factors, namely circumstances and is written as follows

$$IOP_k = \text{cov}(\hat{H}_C^k, H) \text{ with } k = B, R \qquad (6)$$

Similarly, the measure of health inequality related to efforts IEF^k is equal to the component of health inequality related to legitimate factors, namely efforts and is written as follows

$$\text{IEF}_k = \text{cov}(\hat{H}_E^k, H) \text{ with } k = B, R \tag{7}$$

The second measure of inequality of opportunities in health SOP^k assesses the magnitude of inequalities of opportunity in health as a share of health inequality explained by the two main sources of interest from a normative point of view, namely efforts and circumstances.

$$\text{SOP}_k = \frac{\text{IOP}_k}{\text{IOP}^k + \text{IEF}^k} = \frac{\text{cov}(\hat{H}_C^k, H)}{\text{cov}(\hat{H}_C^k, H) + \text{cov}(\hat{H}_E^k, H)} \text{ with } k = B, R \tag{8}$$

In order to compare the extent to which the inequality of opportunity in health varies between Barry and Roemer approaches, we rely on a measure of the difference between the alternative scenarios as follows

$$\text{Diff}^{R-B} = \frac{\text{IOP}^R - \text{IOP}^B}{\text{IOP}^B} \tag{9}$$

We note that Diff^{R-B} will be the same regardless of the measure of inequality of opportunities (IOP$_k$ or SOP$_k$) being considered.

Statistical Inference and Empirical Strategy for the International Comparison

A bootstrap procedure is implemented to calculate standard errors for the estimated coefficients within the two health equation of each scenario and standard errors for the various inequality measures taking into account the whole process of estimation using 1,000 replications. This is particularly relevant for the two-step estimation needed for the Roemer scenario as estimated residuals from the auxiliary equations introduced in the main health equation are likely to introduce uncertainty.

Before we undertake the health regression models for each country and each viewpoint, we carry out a pooled health regression at the European level including country dummies. Comparisons of inequality of opportunity in health across countries are made using IOP^k, IEF^k and SOP$_k$ as computed separately in each country. The calculation of standard errors allows us to test all inequality measures within each country being equal to zero and to make pairwise comparisons across countries. In particular, unilateral t-tests are undertaken to test the ranking across countries and allow distinguishing three groups of countries: countries having high inequality measure which are never dominated by another country; countries with low inequality measure which never dominate another country; and countries with an intermediate level of inequality measure.

DATA

For the purpose of this study, we mainly use the third wave of the Survey of Health, Ageing and Retirement in Europe (SHARE) which was collected in 2008/2009. This wave is called SHARELIFE — the Retrospective Survey — as it focuses on people's life histories and thus provides a unique set of information on circumstances and health status for several European countries. We also use additional information on lifestyles and circumstances collected at wave 1 in 2004 and wave 2 in 2006/2007. SHARE is a multidisciplinary database representative of the European population aged 50 and over in Scandinavia (Denmark and Sweden), Western Europe (Austria, France, Germany, Switzerland, Belgium and the Netherlands) and the Mediterranean countries (Spain, Italy and Greece), as well as two transition countries (the Czech Republic and Poland). Additional information about the dataset is available in Börsch-Supan et al. (2005).

We consider a sample of 20,946 individuals (9,447 men and 11,499 women) aged between 50 and 80 years. The variable of interest is health in adulthood as measured by self-assessed health (SAH) in wave 3. Respondents were asked to rate their own health on a five-point categorical scale ranging from poor to excellent health status. We used SAH as a binary variable taking the value one if the individuals rate their health as 'good' or better, and zero if they rate their health less than 'good'. On the one hand, self-assessed health has been shown to be a good predictor of mortality, morbidity, and subsequent use of health care (Idler & Benyamini, 1997) and has largely been used in cross-country comparisons (Jusot et al., 2009, 2010; Mackenbach et al., 2008; Masseria et al., 2006; Tubeuf & Jusot, 2011; van Doorslaer & Koolman, 2004). On the other hand, Jürges (2007) found large cross-country variation in SAH using the 2004 wave of SHARE, with the healthiest respondents living in the Scandinavian countries and the least healthy in Southern Europe. He concluded that differences are partly explained by differences in health status and the remaining part come from reporting styles. Danish and Swedish respondents are found to overrate their health whereas Germans are found to underrate. These results suggest a bias on comparing average health across countries. If we assume that this bias on national average health is not linked to circumstances and efforts, then we can assume that there is no bias on the estimation of the covariances between health and circumstances and efforts, respectively.

Table 1 provides the distribution of the sample according to self-assessed health. 62.5% of the European sample reports a good, very good or excellent self-assessed health status. The proportion of individuals reporting a good health status varies from 34% in Poland to 79.7% in Switzerland. Health status also varies within countries; the variance of self-assessed health is significantly different from zero in each country and ranges from 0.162 in Switzerland to 0.249 in Spain (first row in Table 4).[3]

Three sets of variables are considered in the study: circumstances, efforts and demographics. The set of circumstances includes variables related to parents' characteristics that have been shown to matter for health (Jusot et al., 2013; Rosa-Dias, 2009, 2010; Trannoy et al., 2010; Tubeuf et al., 2012). Effort is proxied by health-related behaviours that are available at wave 1 and wave 2 in SHARE. Table 2 presents the descriptive statistics of the sample at European level.

Table 1. Distribution of 'Good' Health Status Across European Countries (20,946 Observations).

	Percentage
Europe	62.5
Austria (AT)	58.0
Germany (DE)	56.7
Sweden (SW)	70.2
Netherlands (NL)	68.9
Spain (SP)	46.7
Italy (IT)	56.1
France (FR)	62.1
Denmark (DK)	72.3
Greece (GR)	73.3
Switzerland (CH)	79.7
Belgium (BE)	69.4
Czech Republic (CZ)	56.4
Poland (PL)	34.0

Table 2. Descriptive Statistics at European Level (20,946 Observations).

	Percentage
Sex	
Men	45.1
Women	54.9
Age	
50–54	11.5
55–59	21.1
60–64	21.0
65–69	17.9
70–74	15.0
75–80	13.5
Main breadwinner occupation	
Senior managers and professionals	8.1
Technicians, associate professionals and armed forces	6.1
Office clerks, service workers and sales workers	13.5
Skilled agricultural and fishery workers	26.8
Craftsmen and skilled workers	26.2
Elementary occupations and unskilled workers	17.7
No main breadwinner	1.6
Number of books at home	
None or very few (0–10 books)	43.2
Enough to fill one shelf (11–25 books)	22.6
Enough to fill one bookcase (26–100 books)	21.5
Enough to fill two or more bookcases (more than 100 books)	12.7
Number of rooms per household member (mean)	0.7
Number of facilities at home	
None	26.7
One	19.7
Two or three	29.0
Four or five	24.6
Period of difficulties during childhood	
Economic hardships	2.3
Hunger	5.9
Parent's longevity	
Mother prematurely deceased	38.6
Mother deceased in later ages	35.2
Mother alive	26.3
Father prematurely deceased	47.6
Father deceased in later ages	42.0
Father alive	10.4
Parent's health-related behaviours	
No regular dentist visits for their children	47.9

Table 2. (*Continued*)

	Percentage
Parents' smoking	63.6
Parents' alcohol consumption	8.4
Lifestyle/Effort variables	
Reported smoking status at least once in the past waves	21.3
Obesity at least once in the past waves	18.9
Reported sedentary lifestyles at least once in the past waves	8.7

The vector of circumstances includes a number of social conditions in childhood, parents' longevity and parents' health-related behaviours. Social conditions include the occupation of the main breadwinner during childhood, which is described with the ISCO classification (International Standard Classification of Occupations) into six groups (i) 'senior managers and professionals', (ii) 'technicians and associate professionals and armed forces', (iii) 'office clerks, service and sales workers', (iv) 'skilled agricultural and fishery workers', (v) 'craftsmen and skilled workers', (vi) 'elementary occupations and unskilled workers' and an additional category is added if individuals reported no breadwinner at home during their childhood. Most of the respondents in Europe have a parent who was a skilled agricultural or fishery worker (26.8%) or craftsman or skilled worker (26.2%) whereas only 8.1% of the sample is born from a father who was manager or professional. Social conditions also include the number of books at home when the respondent was a child; this could be used as a proxy of parents' educational level. The number of books at home is a four categories variable starting from a first category with individuals declaring to have none or very few books (0–10 books) to a last category with individuals describing to have enough to fill two or more bookcases (more than 100 books). We also use information on living conditions at home; this included the number of rooms per household member at home when the respondent was 10, the number of facilities available in the accommodation when the respondent was 10 such as having cold running water supply or central heating for example. Finally, social conditions include two indicators of financial difficulties during childhood: individual report of economic hardships and report of hunger episodes before the respondent was aged 16. Parental health is also considered and a variable of the longevity of each parent is created using their vital status at the time of the survey in 2008/2009 or their age at death when applicable. For deceased parents, we use the national median age at death on the basis of SHARELIFE data and the age at death to divide those parents into two groups: those who died earlier and those who died at the median age or later. As expected on a cohort of respondents aged 50 and over, only 10.4% of the fathers and 26.3% of the mothers are still alive. In addition, we used three parental health-related lifestyles when the respondent was 10: smoking, alcohol problem and particular aspects of health care use. The smoking indicator takes the value one if at least one of the two parents was reported to be a smoker; the alcohol variable takes the value one if at least one of the two parents was reported to have a problem with alcohol; the health care behaviour variable indicates the lack of regular visits to the dentist for their children.

The vector of efforts includes three past lifestyles variables reported in waves 1 or 2: smoking status, obesity status[4] and sedentary lifestyles (defined as binary variables). Smoking status variable takes the value one if the respondent reported to be a current smoker in at least one of the past waves and zero otherwise. Obesity status is constructed using reported height and weight and calculating the body mass index (BMI); it takes the value one if the respondent is obese (BMI higher than 30) in at least one of the past waves and zero otherwise. Sedentary lifestyles are measured using respondent's reported involvement in activities requiring a moderate level of physical energy; it equals one if the respondent reports engaging hardly ever or not at all in activities in one of the past waves and zero otherwise.

RESULTS

The main results of interest of the chapter are the cross-country comparisons of the magnitude of inequality of opportunity and of the differences observed by alternative normative viewpoints. We primarily give an overview of the determinants of health inequalities in Europe and in each country commenting the regression analysis results for the health equations in the two alternative viewpoints. We then focus on the results of cross-country differences in inequality of opportunity in health.

Regression Analysis

The results of both linear probability models are presented in Table 3 and are provided as coefficients[5] associated to circumstances and efforts on the probability of reporting excellent, very good or good health at the European level within each scenario (columns 2 and 3). Results of auxiliary equations at the European level are available in Table A1. Findings of

Table 3. Regressions Coefficients of the Probability of Reporting Good Health Status from Barry and Roemer Specifications at the European Level (with Bootstrapped Standard Errors).

	Barry Specification		Roemer Specification	
Sex (ref: Female)				
Male	0.042***	(0.006)	0.042***	(0.006)
Age (ref: 50−54)				
55−59	−0.025**	(0.011)	−0.025**	(0.010)
60−64	−0.061***	(0.012)	−0.061***	(0.011)
65−69	−0.094***	(0.013)	−0.094***	(0.012)
70−74	−0.140***	(0.014)	−0.140***	(0.013)
75−80	−0.215***	(0.015)	−0.215***	(0.014)
Main breadwinner (ref: Elementary occupations and unskilled workers)				
Senior managers and professionals	0.054***	(0.014)	0.061***	(0.014)
Technicians, associate professionals and armed forces	0.019	(0.015)	0.025	(0.016)
Office clerks, service workers and sales workers	0.029**	(0.012)	0.033***	(0.012)
Skilled agricultural and fishery workers	0.006	(0.010)	0.013	(0.010)
Craftsmen and skilled workers	0.010	(0.010)	0.012	(0.010)
No main breadwinner	0.028	(0.026)	0.027	(0.027)
Number of books at home (ref: None or very few (0−10 books))				
Enough to fill one shelf (11−25 books)	0.049***	(0.009)	0.056***	(0.009)
Enough to fill one bookcase (26−100 books)	0.060***	(0.010)	0.071***	(0.010)
Enough to fill two or more bookcases (more than 100 books)	0.050***	(0.013)	0.058***	(0.013)
Number of room/household member	0.026***	(0.009)	0.037***	(0.009)
Number of facilities (ref: None)				
One	0.005	(0.010)	0.015	(0.010)
Two or three	0.025**	(0.010)	0.032***	(0.010)
Four or five	0.037***	(0.012)	0.046***	(0.012)
Period of difficulties during childhood				
Economic hardships	−0.117***	(0.022)	−0.119***	(0.022)
Hunger	−0.056***	(0.015)	−0.057***	(0.015)
Mother's longevity (ref: mother prematurely deceased)				
Mother deceased in later ages	0.018**	(0.007)	0.024***	(0.008)
Mother alive	0.029***	(0.008)	0.036***	(0.008)
Father's longevity (ref: father prematurely deceased)				
Father deceased in later ages	0.035***	(0.007)	0.041***	(0.007)
Father alive	0.038***	(0.012)	0.047***	(0.011)
Parents' health-related behaviours				
No regular dentist visits for their children	−0.029***	(0.008)	−0.035***	(0.008)
Parents' smoking	−0.017***	(0.007)	−0.019***	(0.007)
Parents' alcohol consumption	−0.066***	(0.012)	−0.072***	(0.012)

Table 3. (*Continued*)

	Barry Specification		Roemer Specification	
Lifestyle variables/Residuals				
Smoking	−0.056***	(0.008)	−0.056***	(0.008)
Obesity	−0.130***	(0.008)	−0.130***	(0.008)
Sedentarity	−0.206***	(0.012)	−0.206***	(0.011)
Country (ref: Austria (AT))				
Germany (DE)	−0.064***	(0.022)	−0.064***	(0.022)
Sweden (SW)	0.025	(0.023)	0.025	(0.022)
Netherlands (NL)	0.038*	(0.022)	0.038*	(0.021)
Spain (SP)	−0.076***	(0.023)	−0.076***	(0.022)
Italy (IT)	0.013	(0.022)	0.013	(0.021)
France (FR)	−0.002	(0.022)	−0.002	(0.020)
Denmark (DK)	0.054**	(0.022)	0.054**	(0.021)
Greece (GR)	0.154***	(0.021)	0.154***	(0.020)
Switzerland (CH)	0.129***	(0.023)	0.129***	(0.022)
Belgium (BE)	0.076***	(0.021)	0.076***	(0.020)
Czech Republic (CZ)	−0.069***	(0.022)	−0.069***	(0.023)
Poland (PL)	−0.202***	(0.023)	−0.202***	(0.022)
Constant	0.655***	(0.025)	0.576***	(0.025)
Obs	20946		20946	
R^2	0.143		0.143	

Standard errors in parenthesis and significance levels of test of rejecting the hypothesis of the nullity of the coefficient from 1,000 bootstrapped replications: ***1%, **5%, *10%.

health equations separately carried out for each country are presented in Table A2 and auxiliary equations for each country are available in Bricard, Jusot, Trannoy, and Tubeuf (forthcoming).

There are clear differences in the magnitude of the coefficients of circumstance variables in both scenarios in Europe; the coefficients of circumstances being in average 31% larger in Roemer scenario than in Barry scenario (Table 3). However results remain similar in terms of signs and relatively close in terms of significance levels in both specifications. It appears that any circumstances included in the model are significantly associated with the probability of reporting good health in Europe.

Higher social background is strongly and significantly associated with the probability of reporting a good health status. Individuals born in a family where the main breadwinner was a senior manager or professional worker have a probability 5.4 percentage points higher to report a better health status than individuals born of an elementary occupation or an unskilled worker in Barry model. The coefficient reaches 6.1 percentage points in Roemer scenario because of the strong correlation between self-assessed health and obesity indicated in the related auxiliary equation (Table A1). The number of books at home during childhood is also found to be strongly related to a better health status in adulthood as individuals reporting to have had enough books to fill at least one shelf significantly reported a better health status than those reporting none or very few books at home. Moreover, we note a significant and positive effect of housing characteristics during childhood; the probability of reporting a good health status is increasingly associated with the number of rooms per household members and the number of facilities at home. The coefficients associated with parental education proxy and housing conditions are noticeably higher in Roemer context than in Barry context, which suggest their strong correlation with lifestyles in auxiliary equations (Table A1). Periods of difficulties during childhood also significantly contribute to the probability of reporting a good health status with an 11.7 percentage points decrease in the case of economic hardships and a 5.6 percentage points decrease in the case of hunger episodes. However, despite their strong association with health status, we note a weaker difference in the magnitude of the coefficient across scenarios, due to contradictory correlations with the various lifestyles. Parents' health also drives health disparities: having a father or a mother who died in older ages or who is still alive at the time of the survey is associated with a higher probability of good health status in adulthood. Those associations are particularly large in Roemer scenario due to their strong negative correlation with all lifestyles. For instance, the coefficient associated to having a father died in older age increases from 3.5 percentage points in Barry scenario to 4.1 percentage points in Roemer scenario. Finally, we find a negative and significant effect of parents' poor health-related behaviours such as the lack of regular visits to the dentist for their children, parents' smoking and parents' alcoholic consumption during childhood. As expected, we note an increase in their coefficients in Roemer scenario, parents' poor health-related behaviours being positively correlated to individual poor health-related behaviours.

If we now turn our attention to the coefficients of the three past efforts variables, smoking, being obese and lack of activity are found significantly and negatively associated with good health. The coefficient of sedentary lifestyles is particularly striking as compared to other effort variables. Individuals with weak involvement in physically demanding activities are 20.6 percentage points less likely to report good health. Similarly, obesity is significantly associated with a decrease of 13 percentage points in the probability of being in good health. Finally, smoking is an important determinant of health but the marginal effect is considerably smaller than the previous ones, with a magnitude of 5.6 percentage points.

Table A2 shows the findings of health equations separately conducted in each country in both contexts. Lifestyles are significantly associated with health in most countries. Obesity is significant in all countries except Denmark; adopting sedentary behaviour is significantly associated with poorer health in all countries except Austria and smoking is significant for health in most of the European countries. Conversely, significant circumstances differ from one country to the other and there are also countries where circumstances are not significantly related to health. It is particularly noticeable in Poland and in Switzerland where most of the coefficients of the circumstances are not significantly different from zero. In Barry context, social background matters in most of the countries except in Poland and Switzerland. The association between SAH and parental longevity is found weaker than the association between SAH and social background in most of the countries except in the Netherlands, Denmark and France where parental longevity is strongly related to SAH. We found a weak association between SAH and parental behaviours, excepted in Belgium, Denmark, Greece, Spain and Poland. It is important to be cautious with those results as the lack of significance in the regression models might also come from a limited statistical power. Consistently with the results found at the European level, coefficients associated with circumstances are higher in Roemer model than in Barry model and this coefficients' increase varies across countries. The increase is particularly large in Germany where the coefficient associated with parental longevity is not significant in Barry context but reaches 5% level significance in Roemer context. We also find a large increase in Belgium and the Netherlands where coefficients associated with the number of books at home are particularly higher in Roemer context than in Barry context.

Inequalities Measurement

Using the estimated coefficients of the health equations, we can assess how the magnitude of legitimate health inequalities and illegitimate health inequalities, namely inequalities of opportunity in health, differs between the alternative views. Roemer's view is expected to amplify the magnitude of inequalities of opportunities in health if circumstances associated with poor health status are also associated to unhealthy lifestyles.

Table 4 gives the magnitude of health inequalities using the variance of health status and provides then various insights on the differences in

Table 4. Inequalities of Opportunity in Health and Inequalities Related to Efforts According to Barry and Roemer Scenario Across European Countries.

	Europe	AT	DE	SW	NL	ES	IT	FR	DK	GR	CH	BE	CZ	PL
Variance	0.234*** (0.001)	0.244*** (0.003)	0.246*** (0.002)	0.209*** (0.005)	0.214*** (0.004)	0.249*** (0.001)	0.246*** (0.001)	0.236*** (0.003)	0.200*** (0.005)	0.196*** (0.004)	0.162*** (0.007)	0.212*** (0.004)	0.246*** (0.002)	0.225*** (0.004)
Barry scenario														
IOP^B	0.009*** (0.001)	0.023*** (0.006)	0.013*** (0.003)	0.009*** (0.003)	0.006*** (0.002)	0.014*** (0.003)	0.009*** (0.002)	0.014*** (0.003)	0.011*** (0.003)	0.010*** (0.002)	0.004** (0.002)	0.007*** (0.002)	0.013*** (0.003)	0.007*** (0.003)
IEF^B	0.009*** (0.001)	0.013*** (0.004)	0.016*** (0.003)	0.007*** (0.002)	0.011*** (0.002)	0.006*** (0.002)	0.013*** (0.002)	0.008*** (0.002)	0.011*** (0.002)	0.004*** (0.001)	0.006*** (0.002)	0.015*** (0.002)	0.004** (0.002)	0.006*** (0.002)
SOP^B	49.172*** (2.730)	63.733*** (8.461)	44.395*** (6.598)	54.944*** (9.147)	33.902*** (7.166)	70.044*** (7.349)	42.219*** (6.543)	65.597*** (6.735)	50.727*** (7.134)	71.542*** (6.669)	40.908*** (11.829)	31.111*** (6.192)	78.252*** (7.104)	56.579*** (9.246)
Roemer scenario														
IOP^R	0.010*** (0.001)	0.025*** (0.006)	0.015*** (0.003)	0.009*** (0.003)	0.007*** (0.002)	0.015*** (0.003)	0.011*** (0.002)	0.015*** (0.003)	0.013*** (0.003)	0.011*** (0.002)	0.004*** (0.002)	0.008*** (0.002)	0.013*** (0.003)	0.008*** (0.003)
IEF^R	0.007*** (0.001)	0.011*** (0.004)	0.014*** (0.003)	0.007*** (0.002)	0.010*** (0.002)	0.005*** (0.002)	0.011*** (0.002)	0.007*** (0.002)	0.010*** (0.002)	0.003*** (0.001)	0.006*** (0.002)	0.014*** (0.002)	0.003** (0.001)	0.005*** (0.002)
SOP^R	57.424*** (2.579)	69.804*** (7.785)	50.691*** (6.535)	57.029*** (8.645)	40.093*** (7.212)	76.824*** (6.456)	48.650*** (6.446)	69.584*** (6.278)	57.192*** (6.976)	77.849*** (5.725)	42.480*** (11.592)	37.179*** (6.423)	82.921*** (6.219)	64.520*** (8.456)
Difference between Roemer and Barry														
$Diff^{R-B}$	16.782*** (1.570)	9.526** (4.314)	14.181*** (4.118)	3.796 (4.167)	18.261*** (4.828)	9.680*** (2.926)	15.233*** (4.127)	6.078** (2.405)	12.744*** (3.532)	8.816*** (2.617)	3.843 (5.407)	19.505*** (4.617)	5.967*** (2.172)	14.035*** (4.610)
N	20946	648	1550	1193	1794	1439	2094	1800	1746	2466	1032	2250	1514	1420

Standard errors in parenthesis and significance levels of test of rejecting the hypothesis of the nullity of the coefficient from 1,000 bootstrapped replications: ***1%, **5%, *10%.

magnitude of inequalities of opportunities in health and inequalities related to lifestyles within each scenario for all countries separately as well as for Europe as a whole. We find inequalities of opportunity in health in all countries. When we consider IOP_k regardless of the scenario, inequalities of opportunity are significantly different from zero in all countries. Moreover, the inequality of opportunity in inequalities due to circumstances and efforts (SOP_k) is significantly different from zero in all countries in both scenarios as are the inequalities related to efforts (IEF_k). However there are some differences between countries in the magnitude of these inequalities according to the scenario and the measure being used.

Figs. 1 and 2 respectively show the magnitude of the inequalities of opportunity IOP_k and of the inequalities related to efforts IEF_k according to Barry and Roemer scenarios in the European countries with confidence intervals obtained from bootstrapped standard errors; the countries are ranked from the most to the least unequal. Fig. 3 shows the ranking of countries according to the magnitude of the inequalities of opportunity in health inequalities due to circumstances and efforts SOP_k in both scenarios. Differences between countries are calculated using unilateral t-tests (tables of results are available in Bricard et al., forthcoming). For each inequality measure, t-tests allow distinguishing three groups of countries separated by the dashed lines in the figures: countries with a high inequality measure which are never dominated by another country; countries with a low inequality measure which never dominate another country; and countries with an intermediate inequality measure.

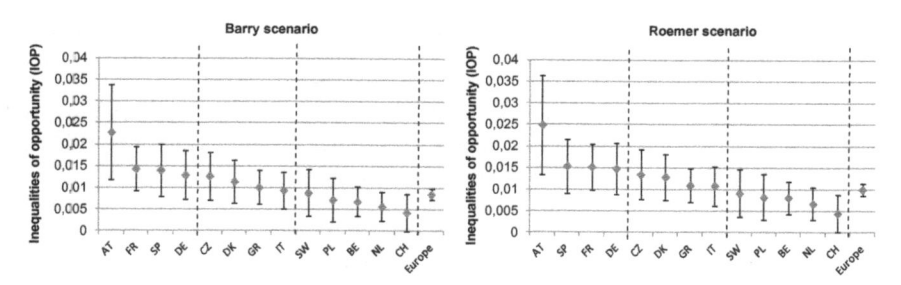

Fig. 1. Inequalities of Opportunity According to Barry and Roemer Scenario Across European Countries (IOP), with 95% Confidence Intervals. *Note*: The dashed lines are based on the *t*-tests values; they divide countries into countries with a high inequality measure which are never dominated by another country, countries with a low inequality measure which never dominate another country, countries with an intermediate inequality measure and finally inequality at European level.

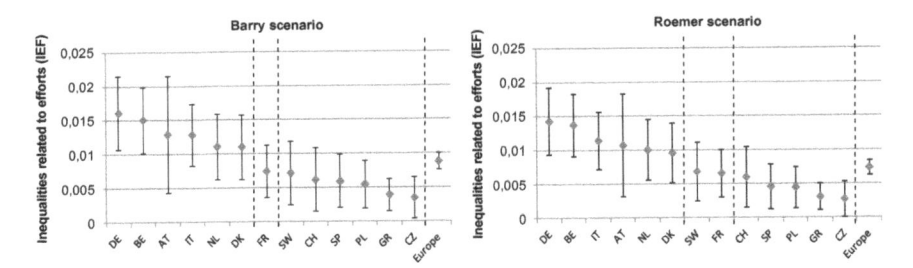

Fig. 2. Inequalities Related to Efforts According to Barry and Roemer Scenario Across European Countries (IEF), with 95% Confidence Intervals. *Note*: The dashed lines are based on the *t*-tests values; they divide countries into countries with a high inequality measure which are never dominated by another country, countries with a low inequality measure which never dominate another country, countries with an intermediate inequality measure and finally inequality at European level.

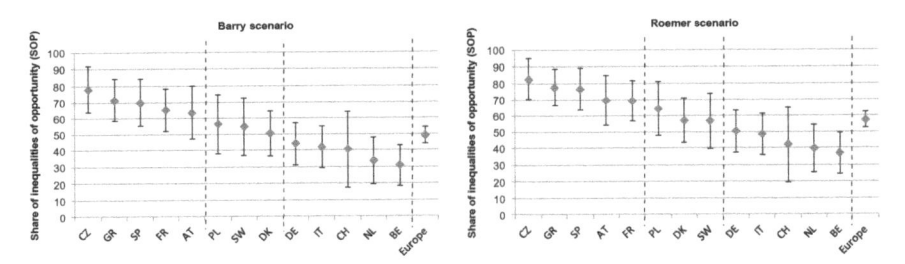

Fig. 3. Share of Inequalities of Opportunity in Health Inequalities Due to Circumstances and Efforts Across European Countries According to Barry and Roemer Scenario (SOP), with 95% Confidence Intervals. *Note*: The dashed lines are based on the *t*-tests values; they divide countries into countries with a high inequality measure which are never dominated by another country, countries with a low inequality measure which never dominate another country, countries with an intermediate inequality measure and finally inequality at European level.

According to the Barry scenario, we find that inequalities of opportunity in health when measured with IOP^B are significantly the largest in Austria, France, Spain and Germany whereas they are the lowest in Sweden, Poland, Belgium, the Netherlands and Switzerland. Czech Republic, Denmark, Greece and Italy show an intermediate position. Inequalities of opportunity represent a quite small proportion of the total health inequality; IOP_B as a share of total variance varying from 2.7% in Switzerland and the Netherlands to 9.3% in Austria. Considering inequalities related to efforts (IEF$_B$), they also vary across countries and are the highest in Germany, Belgium, Austria, Italy, the Netherlands and Denmark whereas they are the lowest in Sweden, Switzerland, Spain, Poland, Greece and Czech Republic. France has an intermediate position in this ranking.

If we now turn our attention to the magnitude of inequalities of opportunity in health relative to the sole inequalities which can be classified from a normative point of view, namely circumstances and effort, as measured by SOP$_B$, the ranking of countries is considerably changing. Inequalities of opportunity in health measured as SOP$_B$ are now significantly larger in Czech Republic, Greece, Spain, France and Austria; intermediate in Poland, Sweden and Denmark; and lower in Germany, Italy, Switzerland, the Netherlands and Belgium. SOP$_B$ equals 30% in Belgium and the Netherlands whereas it equals more than 70% in Spain, Greece and Czech Republic. We can remark that there are two potential explanations for the high level of SOP$_B$: either having a high value for IOP$_B$ such as in Austria and in France and Spain, or having a small share of inequalities related to efforts IEF$_B$ as observed in Czech Republic and Greece. On the contrary, SOP^B is particularly low in Switzerland, Belgium, the Netherlands because of the small value of IOP$_B$, and also in Germany because of a large share of inequalities related to efforts (IEF$_B$).

If we turn to the Roemer scenario, results are very similar in terms of the ranking of countries for the two measures of inequalities of opportunity and for the measure of inequalities related to efforts. The magnitude of inequalities of opportunity is higher in Roemer scenario in most countries, which can be illustrated when computing the difference between the measures between Roemer and Barry scenarios (Diff^{R-B}). Fig. 4 shows the ranking of the countries according to Diff^{R-B} providing confidence intervals constructed using bootstrapped standard errors. The difference between the Roemer and Barry scenarios is found significant within most countries, except in Sweden and in Switzerland where the difference is not significantly different from zero and in France and Austria, the difference is only significant at the 10% level. Using unilateral t-tests of the magnitude of the differences, we can distinguish two groups of countries: countries which are never dominated by another country and countries which never dominate another country. The first group is composed of countries where the difference between normative scenarios is particularly important, for example Belgium, the Netherlands, Italy, Germany, Poland and Denmark; in those countries, adopting the Roemer viewpoint leads to an increase of the extent of inequalities of opportunity of more than 10% with comparison to the

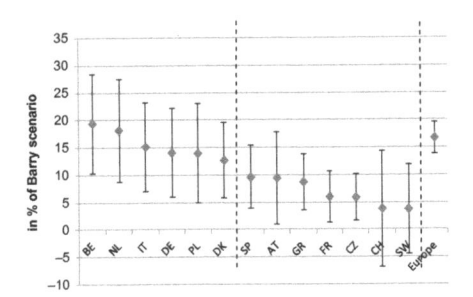

Fig. 4. Relative Difference between Barry and Roemer Measure of Inequalities of Opportunity in Health Across European Countries (Diff^{R-B}), with 95% Confidence Intervals. *Note*: The dashed lines are based on the *t*-tests values; they divide countries into countries with a high inequality measure which are never dominated by another country, countries with a low inequality measure which never dominate another country and finally inequality at European level.

Barry approach. On the other hand, the second group gathers countries where the difference between scenarios is small or non-significant as it is the case in Spain, Austria, Greece, France, Czech Republic, Switzerland and Sweden.

Those findings illustrate the strong link between efforts and circumstances within the countries where the difference across scenarios is large, that is individuals' efforts (lifestyles) are likely to be strongly determined by circumstances (family and social background). Conversely, the small difference within other countries is either due to a weak correlation between efforts and circumstances or a weak influence of efforts on health status.

If we now turn to the results in Europe as a whole, we find significant inequalities of opportunity in both Barry and Roemer scenarios and for both IOP_k and SOP_k inequality of opportunities indicators. Concerning their magnitude, inequalities of opportunity represent a small proportion of total health inequality; $IOP_B = 3.7\%$ of the total variance in Barry and $IOP_R = 4.3\%$ in Roemer scenario. However, when we compare illegitimate inequalities to the sole inequalities which can be classified from a normative point of view as measured by SOP_k, inequalities in opportunity stand for almost 50% of the health inequality due to circumstances and efforts in the Barry scenario and 57.5% in the Roemer scenario. The difference between Roemer and Barry Diff^{R-B} is significant and represents 16.8% of the health inequality measured in Barry scenario.

DISCUSSION

The aim of this chapter is to quantify and compare inequalities of opportunity in health in Europe and to assess whether it matters empirically to adopt Barry or Roemer viewpoint on the treatment of the correlation between efforts and circumstances. Our results firstly attest the existence of inequalities of opportunity in health in Europe. Moreover, the comparison of the magnitude of inequalities of opportunity in health across European countries and across scenarios provides interesting results. Inequalities of opportunities are the largest in Austria, France, Spain and Germany and the lowest in Sweden, Poland, Belgium, the Netherlands and Switzerland. The share of inequalities of opportunity in health inequalities due to circumstances and efforts varies from 30% in the less unequal countries to 70% in the most unequal countries, whereas it represents 50% at the aggregate level. The way the correlation between efforts and circumstances matters for the assessment of inequalities of opportunity also varies across countries. The difference between scenarios is negligible in Switzerland and Sweden but is particularly important in Belgium and the Netherlands where taking into account the indirect effect of circumstances through lifestyles induces a 20% increase in inequalities of opportunity.

We have to bear in mind that our study is based on a subjective indicator of health status. As mentioned before, reporting styles will not be problematic for the assessment and the comparison of inequalities of opportunity across countries if reporting biases are orthogonal to circumstances and to efforts. However, we cannot exclude the existence of such reporting bias. Moreover, our empirical model specification suffers from potential unobserved circumstances and effort variables. It is therefore important to underline that our study is likely to assess only the lower bound of inequality of opportunity in health.

Inequalities of opportunity in Europe represent on average half of the health inequalities due to circumstances and efforts and there are large variations across countries. Moreover, inequalities of opportunity are found to be more correlated to the magnitude of health inequalities than legitimate inequalities. Fig. 5 explores the relationship between overall health inequality and respectively inequalities of opportunity in health and inequalities related to efforts. It shows a positive correlation between inequalities of opportunity in health and health inequality with a coefficient of correlation of about 0.39. The correlation between inequalities related to efforts and health inequalities is relatively small and is about 0.06. This result is in line

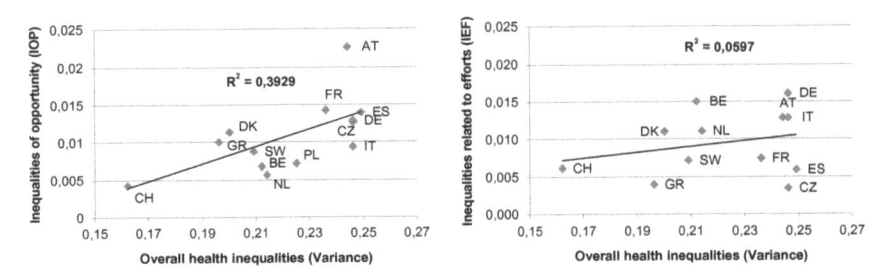

Fig. 5. Relationship between Inequalities of Opportunity (IOP) and Inequalities Related to Efforts (IEF) with Overall Health Inequalities (Variance).

with a recent paper that has provided evidence of a positive link between inequalities of opportunity and inequalities of outcomes in the case of income inequalities (Lefranc, Pistolesi, & Trannoy, 2008).

The difference induced by the adopted normative viewpoint is more important in countries with high inequalities due to efforts. Conversely, we do not find a general pattern on the relationship between the extent of inequalities of opportunities and the way the correlation between efforts and circumstances matters for the assessment of inequalities of opportunity. Sweden and Switzerland combine low inequalities of opportunities in health and weak differences between Roemer and Barry's viewpoints whereas Germany, Italy, Spain and Denmark combine high inequalities of opportunity in health and strong differences between Roemer and Barry's viewpoints. However, some countries do not fit with these patterns; Austria, France and Czech Republic show high inequalities of opportunity in health but the two alternative normative viewpoints do not appear to matter much. Finally, Belgium, the Netherlands and Poland do not show very important inequalities of opportunity in health but differences between the two scenarios are considerable.

These results contribute to the debate on whether it is individual health-related behaviours (efforts) or poor past conditions (circumstances) that should be tackled to reduce effectively inequalities of opportunity in health and health inequalities in general. Social background, parents' health and parents' health-related behaviours represent factors beyond the realm of individual responsibility (Fleurbaey, 2008; Fleurbaey & Schokkaert, 2009; Roemer, 1998; Trannoy et al., 2010), they are socially or morally unacceptable sources of inequality and they legitimate public interventions. The recent report of the World Health Organization's Commission on the Social Determinants of Health (Marmot et al., 2008) highlights the role of childhood conditions as primary sources of unfair inequality in health. Causal estimates of the effect of circumstances and efforts on health are required to define precisely the policy interventions that matter to tackle inequality of opportunity and our chapter does not explore causality inference. However, given the magnitude of the inequalities of opportunity in health and the strong correlation between social background and health that are observed in each country, our research work recommends improving childhood conditions and equality of opportunity in education and in income acquisition to reduce inequality of opportunity in health.

According to Roemer's viewpoint, targeting determinants of health-related behaviours which are beyond individual responsibility would be also normatively justified. Empirically, the choice between the alternative normative viewpoints about the legitimacy of the correlation between efforts and circumstances seems to matter more in some European countries than in others. This suggests differences in the underlying public health policies that could be put in place to fight against inequalities of opportunity in health. Even if this analysis does not provide causal findings, it suggests a strong social and family determinism of lifestyles in Belgium, the Netherlands, Italy, Germany, Poland and Denmark which emphasised the importance of inequalities of opportunity in health within those countries according to the Roemerian approach. In terms of public health and social policies, reducing social reproduction and the intergenerational transmission of unhealthy lifestyles would be appropriate in those countries if they endorse the Roemerian ethical viewpoint on equality of opportunity. On the other hand, Austria, France, Spain and Czech Republic show high inequalities of opportunities in health mainly driven by social and family background affecting adult health directly, and so those countries would require policies compensating for poorer initial conditions mainly, regardless of the normative point of view adopted.

NOTES

1. We rely on a reduced form model because we are primarily interested in capturing correlations between health and effort, health and circumstances and finally effort and circumstances. In particular, we do not include contemporary socioeconomic characteristics among the regressors because they are endogenous and may be correlated with past health, parental characteristics as well as individual effort (see Jusot et al., 2013 for more details).

2. See Fleurbaey and Schokkaert (2012) for a more consideration on the role of luck.

3. In the case of a binary indicator, the variance is directly derived from the proportion of individuals who report good health status and is bounded from 0 to 0.25.

4. There might be a debate on whether obesity can be considered as an individual effort or as an outcome because of its link with nature and nurture. We consider that obesity status captures aggregated effects of lifestyles in our context. This view is supported by public health decision makers such as the NICE. In the NICE guideline (2006) with respect regard to the treatment of obesity, it is stated that '*People choose whether or not to change their lifestyle or agree to treatment. Assessing their readiness to make changes affects decisions on when or how to offer any intervention*' (p. 6).

5. It is important to remind that effort variables are different from a mathematical point of view in each scenario. Actual efforts are measured as dummy variables in Barry model whereas relative efforts are measured as continuous variables in Roemer model. However, according to Frisch–Waugh–Lowell theorem and because we use linear probability models in the auxiliary equation, the coefficients of effort variables are identical in both scenarios. Conversely, circumstances variables are introduced in the same mathematical form in both models but their coefficients differ in Roemer scenario according to the extent to which circumstances are correlated to efforts.

ACKNOWLEDGEMENTS

We gratefully acknowledge the financial support of the Health Chair, a joint initiative by PSL, Université Paris-Dauphine, ENSAE and MGEN under the aegis of the Fondation du Risque (FDR). Damien Bricard also benefited from a PhD studentship from the *Régime Social des Indépendants* (RSI).

We thank Bénédicte Apouey, Andrew Clark, Martin Karlsson, Erik Schokkaert and the participants to the 2013 PhD Seminar on Health Economics and Policy (Grindelwald, Switzerland) and to the 12th Journées Louis-André Gérard-Varet Conference in Public Economics for their helpful comments. We would like to thank the editors of this special issue for valuable remarks.

This chapter uses data from wave 1 and 2 release 2.5.0, as of 24 May 2011 and SHARELIFE release 1, as of 24 November 2010. The SHARE data collection has been primarily funded by the European Commission through the 5th Framework Programme (project QLK6-CT-2001-00360 in the thematic programme Quality of Life), through the 6th Framework Programme (projects SHARE-I3, RII-CT-2006-062193, COMPARE, CIT5-CT-2005-028857 and SHARELIFE, CIT4-CT-2006-028812) and through the 7th Framework Programme (SHARE-PREP, No. 211909, SHARE-LEAP, No. 227822 and SHARE M4, No. 261982). Additional funding from the U.S. National Institute on Aging (U01 AG09740-13S2, P01 AG005842, P01 AG08291, P30 AG12815, R21 AG025169, Y1-AG-4553-01, IAG BSR06-11 and OGHA 04-064) and the German Ministry of Education and Research as well as from various national sources is gratefully acknowledged (see www.share-project.org for a full list of funding institutions).

REFERENCES

Arneson, R. J. (1989). Equality and equal opportunity of welfare. *Philosophical Studies, 56*, 77–93.

Barry, B. (2005). *Why social justice matters*. Cambridge: Polity Press.

Börsch-Supan, A., Brugiavini, A., Jürges, H., Mackenbach, J. P., Siegrist, J., & Weber, G. (2005). *Health, ageing and retirement in Europe — First results from the Survey of Health, Ageing and Retirement in Europe*. Mannheim: Mannheim Research Institute for the Economics of Aging (MEA).

Bricard, D., Jusot, F., Trannoy, A., & Tubeuf, S. (forthcoming). Inequality of opportunity in health and the principle of natural reward: Evidence from European countries. *Cahiers de la chaire santé*.

Cohen, G. A. (1989). On the currency of egalitarian justice. *Ethics, 99*, 906–944.

Crimmins, E., & Cambois, E. (2003). Social inequalities in health expectancy. In J.-M. Robine, C. Jagger, C. Mathers, E. Crimmins, & R. Suzman (Eds.), *Determining health expectancies* (pp. 111–126). Chichester: John Willey & Sons.

Dworkin, R. (1981). What is equality? Part I: Equality of welfare. *Philosophy and Public Affairs* 10, 185–246.

Fleurbaey, M. (1995). Equality and responsibility. *European Economic Review, 39*, 683–689.

Fleurbaey, M. (2006). Health, equity, and social welfare. *Annales d'Économie et de Statistique, 83/84*, 21–59.

Fleurbaey, M. (2008). *Fairness, responsibility, and welfare*. Oxford: Oxford University Press.

Fleurbaey, M., & Schokkaert, E. (2009). Unfair inequalities in health and health care. *Journal of Health Economics, 28*(1), 73–90.

Fleurbaey, M., & Schokkaert, E. (2012). Equity in health and health care. *Handbook of Health Economics, 2*, 1003–1092.

Garcia Gomez, P., Schokkaert, E., Van Ourti, T., & Bago d'Uva, T. (2012). *Inequity in the face of death*. CORE Discussion Paper No. 2012/24. Louvain-la-Neuve, Université Catholique de Louvain.

Hernandez-Quevedo, C., Jones, A., Lopez, A. N., & Rice, N. (2007). Socio-economic inequalities in health: A comparative longitudinal analysis using the European Community Household Panel. *Social Science and Medicine, 63*, 1246–1262.

Idler, E. L., & Benyamini, Y. (1997). Self-rated health and mortality: A review of twenty-seven community studies. *Journal of Health and Social Behaviour, 38*, 21–37.

Jürges, H. (2007). True health vs response styles: Exploring cross-country differences in self-reported health. *Health Economics, 16*(2), 163–178.

Jusot, F., Tubeuf, S., & Trannoy, A. (2009). Tel père, tel fils: l'influence de l'origine sociale et familiale sur la santé des descendants en Europe. *Retraite et Société*, *58*(2), 63–85.

Jusot, F., Tubeuf, S., & Trannoy, A. (2010). *Inequality of opportunities in health in Europe: Why so much difference across countries?* HEDG Working Paper No. 10/26. University of York.

Jusot, F., Tubeuf, S., & Trannoy, A. (2013). Circumstances and efforts: How important is their correlation for the measurement of inequality of opportunity in health? *Health Economics*. doi:10.1002/hec.2896

Lefranc, A., Pistolesi, N., & Trannoy, A. (2008). Inequality of opportunities vs inequality of outcomes: Are Western societies all alike? *Review of Income and Wealth*, *54*(4), 513–546.

Lefranc, A., Pistolesi, N., & Trannoy, A. (2009). Equality of opportunity and luck: Definitions and testable conditions, with an application to income in France. *Journal of Public Economics*, *93*(11–12), 1189–1208.

Mackenbach, J. P., Stirbu, I., Roskam, A.-J., & et al. (2008). Socioeconomic inequalities in health in 22 European countries. *The New England Journal of Medicine*, *358*(23), 2468–2481.

Marmot, M., Friel, S., Bell, R., Houweling, T., Taylor, S., & the Commission on Social Determinants of Health (2008). Closing the gap in a generation: Health equity through action on the social determinants of health. *The Lancet*, *372*, 1661–1669.

Masseria, C., Mossalios, E., & Allin, S. (2006). *Measurement of socioeconomic inequality of health in 10 European countries: An exploratory analysis of SHARE using three approaches.* European Commission – Research Note, LSE.

NICE. (2006). *Obesity guidance on the prevention, identification, assessment and management of overweight and obesity in adults and children.* NICE clinical guideline 43. Retrieved from http://www.nice.org.uk/CG043

Roemer, J. (1998). *Equality of opportunity*. Cambridge: Harvard University Press.

Rosa-Dias, P. (2009). Inequality of opportunity in health: Evidence from the UK cohort study. *Health Economics*, *18*(9), 1057–1074.

Rosa-Dias, P. (2010). Modelling opportunity in health under partial observability of circumstances. *Health Economics*, *19*(3), 252–264.

Rosa-Dias, P., & Jones, A. (2007). Giving equality of opportunity a fair innings. *Health Economics*, *16*, 109–112.

Sen, A. K. (2002). Why health equity? *Health Economics*, *11*, 659–666.

Shorrocks, A. F. (1982). Inequality decomposition by factor components. *Econometrica*, *50*(1), 193–211.

Trannoy, A., Tubeuf, S., Jusot, F., & Devaux, M. (2010). Inequality of opportunities in health in France: A first pass. *Health Economics*, *19*(8), 921–938.

Tubeuf, S., & Jusot, F. (2011). Social health inequalities among older Europeans: The contribution of social and family background. *European Journal of Health Economics*, *12*(1), 61–77.

Tubeuf, S., Jusot, F., & Bricard, D. (2012). Mediating role of education and lifestyles in the relationship between early-life conditions and health: Evidence from the 1958 British cohort. *Health Economics*, *21*(Suppl. S1), 129–150.

van Doorslaer, E., & Koolman, X. (2004). Explaining the differences in income-related health inequalities across European countries. *Health Economics*, *13*(7), 609–628.

APPENDIX

Table A1. Regressions Coefficients of Auxiliary Equations at the European Level (with Bootstrapped Standard Errors).

	Smoking		Obesity		Sedentarity	
Main breadwinner (ref: Elementary occupations and unskilled workers)						
Senior managers and professionals	0.008	(0.013)	−0.055***	(0.013)	−0.001	(0.009)
Technicians, associate professionals and armed forces	−0.002	(0.014)	−0.034**	(0.013)	−0.007	(0.009)
Office clerks, service workers and sales workers	0.015	(0.011)	−0.027***	(0.010)	−0.003	(0.007)
Skilled agricultural and fishery workers	−0.019**	(0.009)	−0.029***	(0.008)	−0.009	(0.006)
Craftsmen and skilled workers	0.009	(0.009)	−0.020**	(0.009)	0.001	(0.006)
No main breadwinner	−0.009	(0.023)	0.003	(0.022)	0.005	(0.016)
Number of books at home (ref: None or very few (0–10 books))						
Enough to fill one shelf (11–25 books)	−0.012	(0.008)	−0.013*	(0.007)	−0.023***	(0.005)
Enough to fill one bookcase (26–100 books)	−0.015*	(0.009)	−0.020**	(0.008)	−0.037***	(0.006)
Enough to fill two or more bookcases (more than 100 books)	0.005	(0.011)	−0.018*	(0.011)	−0.030***	(0.008)
Number of room/household member	−0.020***	(0.007)	−0.035***	(0.007)	−0.027***	(0.005)
Number of facilities (ref: None)						
One	0.002	(0.009)	−0.018**	(0.008)	−0.040***	(0.006)
Two or three	0.036***	(0.008)	−0.034***	(0.008)	−0.022***	(0.006)
Four or five	0.056***	(0.010)	−0.052***	(0.010)	−0.026***	(0.007)
Period of difficulties during childhood						
Economic hardships	−0.025	(0.019)	−0.020	(0.018)	0.029**	(0.013)
Hunger	−0.071***	(0.012)	−0.003	(0.012)	0.024***	(0.008)
Mother's longevity (ref: mother prematurely deceased)						
Mother deceased in later ages	−0.028***	(0.007)	−0.018***	(0.006)	−0.007	(0.005)
Mother alive	0.040***	(0.007)	−0.031***	(0.007)	−0.021***	(0.005)
Father's longevity (ref: father prematurely deceased)						
Father deceased in later ages	−0.036***	(0.006)	−0.016***	(0.006)	−0.011**	(0.004)
Father alive	−0.013	(0.010)	−0.021**	(0.010)	−0.023***	(0.007)
Parents' health-related behaviours						
No regular dentist visits for their children	0.027***	(0.006)	0.006	(0.006)	0.019***	(0.004)

Table A1. (*Continued*)

	Smoking		Obesity		Sedentarity	
Parents' smoking	0.075***	(0.006)	−0.006	(0.006)	−0.007*	(0.004)
Parents' alcohol consumption	0.043***	(0.010)	0.029***	(0.010)	0.000	(0.007)
Constant	0.164***	(0.012)	0.296***	(0.012)	0.154***	(0.008)
Obs	20946		20946		20946	
R^2	0.024		0.015		0.019	

Standard errors in parenthesis and significance levels of test of rejecting the hypothesis of the nullity of the coefficient from 1,000 bootstrapped replications: ***1%, **5%, *10%.

Table A2. Regressions Coefficients of the Probability of Reporting Good Health Status from Barry and Roemer Scenario Across European Countries (with Bootstrapped Standard Errors).

	Austria (AT) Barry specification		Austria (AT) Roemer specification		Germany (DE) Barry specification		Germany (DE) Roemer specification		Sweden (SW) Barry specification		Sweden (SW) Roemer specification		Netherlands (NL) Barry specification		Netherlands (NL) Roemer specification	
Sex (ref : Female)																
Male	−0.014	(0.038)	−0.014	(0.039)	0.001	(0.024)	0.001	(0.025)	0.060**	(0.027)	0.060**	(0.025)	−0.018	(0.022)	−0.018	(0.021)
Age (ref : 50−54)																
55−59	−0.049	(0.089)	−0.049	(0.090)	0.050	(0.047)	0.050	(0.047)	−0.127**	(0.057)	−0.127**	(0.059)	0.105**	(0.041)	0.105**	(0.042)
60−64	−0.131	(0.088)	−0.131	(0.089)	−0.002	(0.051)	−0.002	(0.053)	−0.145**	(0.058)	−0.145**	(0.058)	0.094**	(0.042)	0.094**	(0.043)
65−69	−0.112	(0.089)	−0.112	(0.093)	−0.008	(0.053)	−0.008	(0.056)	−0.109*	(0.061)	−0.109*	(0.062)	0.016	(0.048)	0.016	(0.048)
70−74	−0.145	(0.092)	−0.145	(0.097)	−0.028	(0.057)	−0.028	(0.060)	−0.151**	(0.066)	−0.151**	(0.068)	0.052	(0.053)	0.052	(0.055)
75−80	−0.266***	(0.098)	−0.266***	(0.097)	−0.110*	(0.060)	−0.110*	(0.062)	−0.215***	(0.070)	−0.215***	(0.073)	0.025	(0.055)	0.025	(0.055)
Main breadwinner (ref : Elementary occupations and unskilled workers)																
Senior managers and professionals	0.200**	(0.085)	0.218**	(0.090)	0.081	(0.064)	0.123**	(0.063)	−0.018	(0.060)	0.004	(0.062)	0.064	(0.046)	0.077	(0.048)
Technicians, associate professionals and armed forces	0.178*	(0.097)	0.198**	(0.098)	−0.040	(0.062)	−0.015	(0.063)	0.037	(0.065)	0.067	(0.064)	0.045	(0.049)	0.049	(0.053)
Office clerks, service workers and sales workers	0.139*	(0.073)	0.139*	(0.071)	0.095*	(0.052)	0.125**	(0.054)	−0.073	(0.057)	−0.045	(0.058)	0.021	(0.047)	0.035	(0.047)
Skilled agricultural and fishery workers	0.013	(0.065)	0.011	(0.070)	−0.004	(0.052)	0.017	(0.054)	−0.025	(0.052)	0.003	(0.053)	0.082*	(0.044)	0.101**	(0.044)
Craftsmen and skilled workers	0.030	(0.062)	0.046	(0.063)	0.015	(0.047)	0.037	(0.048)	0.020	(0.049)	0.037	(0.051)	0.020	(0.039)	0.023	(0.040)
No main breadwinner	0.034	(0.103)	0.044	(0.103)	0.127	(0.078)	0.138*	(0.080)	0.076	(0.120)	0.081	(0.139)	−0.038	(0.087)	−0.027	(0.092)
Number of books at home (ref: None or very few (0−10 books))																
Enough to fill one shelf (11−25 books)	0.135***	(0.048)	0.126***	(0.047)	−0.037	(0.034)	−0.027	(0.035)	0.084*	(0.046)	0.083*	(0.045)	0.067**	(0.029)	0.082***	(0.029)
Enough to fill one bookcase (26−100 books)	0.157***	(0.054)	0.142**	(0.059)	−0.017	(0.036)	−0.000	(0.037)	0.106**	(0.045)	0.123***	(0.045)	0.061**	(0.030)	0.083***	(0.032)
Enough to fill two or more bookcases (more than 100 books)	0.052	(0.087)	0.039	(0.090)	0.037	(0.044)	0.046	(0.045)	0.102**	(0.050)	0.110**	(0.051)	−0.039	(0.038)	−0.026	(0.041)
Number of room/household member	−0.016	(0.044)	−0.022	(0.045)	0.020	(0.035)	0.024	(0.035)	0.029	(0.030)	0.028	(0.032)	0.030	(0.033)	0.027	(0.033)
Number of facilities (ref: None)																
One	−0.002	(0.055)	0.029	(0.054)	0.110***	(0.041)	0.111***	(0.041)	0.109**	(0.056)	0.095*	(0.055)	0.023	(0.056)	0.030	(0.065)
Two or three	0.060	(0.055)	0.095*	(0.055)	0.116***	(0.041)	0.126***	(0.041)	0.127**	(0.060)	0.130**	(0.062)	0.041	(0.055)	0.048	(0.062)
Four or five	0.024	(0.063)	0.036	(0.065)	0.182***	(0.046)	0.185***	(0.048)	0.122**	(0.053)	0.119***	(0.054)	0.048	(0.065)	0.061	(0.070)
Period of difficulties during childhood																
Economic hardships	0.118	(0.090)	0.111	(0.088)	−0.132*	(0.077)	−0.134*	(0.079)	0.044	(0.140)	0.023	(0.150)	0.007	(0.133)	−0.029	(0.172)
Hunger	0.077	(0.079)	0.072	(0.078)	−0.073*	(0.038)	−0.067*	(0.039)	−0.017	(0.133)	0.033	(0.135)	−0.049	(0.051)	−0.030	(0.051)

Table A2. *(Continued)*

	Austria (AT)				Germany (DE)				Sweden (SW)				Netherlands (NL)			
	Barry specification		Roemer specification		Barry specification		Roemer specification		Barry specification		Roemer specification		Barry specification		Roemer specification	
Sex (ref : Female)																
Mother's longevity (ref: mother prematurely deceased)																
Mother deceased in later ages	0.047	(0.043)	0.043	(0.044)	0.044	(0.028)	0.059**	(0.029)	0.032	(0.033)	0.043	(0.032)	0.050*	(0.026)	0.064**	(0.025)
Mother alive	0.048	(0.058)	0.059	(0.061)	0.028	(0.034)	0.043	(0.035)	0.015	(0.035)	0.009	(0.035)	0.055*	(0.029)	0.064**	(0.029)
Father's longevity (ref: father prematurely deceased)																
Father deceased in later ages	0.054	(0.042)	0.062	(0.041)	0.035	(0.026)	0.057**	(0.028)	0.033	(0.028)	0.036	(0.028)	0.044*	(0.024)	0.051**	(0.024)
Father alive	0.134*	(0.074)	0.128	(0.080)	0.066	(0.045)	0.088*	(0.047)	0.059	(0.045)	0.050	(0.045)	0.084***	(0.038)	0.098***	(0.037)
Parents' health-related behaviours																
No regular dentist visits for their children	-0.019	(0.041)	-0.016	(0.042)	-0.002	(0.026)	0.003	(0.027)	-0.048	(0.046)	-0.058	(0.048)	0.022	(0.027)	0.016	(0.027)
Parents' smoking	-0.008	(0.039)	-0.028	(0.037)	0.020	(0.025)	0.019	(0.026)	0.011	(0.027)	0.012	(0.027)	-0.032	(0.030)	-0.044	(0.031)
Parents' alcohol consumption	-0.117*	(0.067)	-0.162**	(0.067)	-0.029	(0.046)	-0.072	(0.045)	-0.054	(0.048)	-0.054	(0.050)	0.046	(0.050)	0.020	(0.053)
Lifestyles variables/residuals																
Smoking	0.010	(0.049)	0.010	(0.051)	-0.137***	(0.033)	-0.137***	(0.033)	-0.127***	(0.039)	-0.127***	(0.036)	-0.101***	(0.028)	-0.101***	(0.027)
Obesity	-0.242***	(0.045)	-0.242***	(0.046)	-0.256***	(0.031)	-0.256***	(0.031)	-0.182***	(0.041)	-0.182***	(0.041)	-0.207***	(0.033)	-0.207***	(0.035)
Sedentarity	-0.097	(0.059)	-0.097	(0.061)	-0.234***	(0.051)	-0.234***	(0.051)	-0.206**	(0.086)	-0.206**	(0.091)	-0.211***	(0.046)	-0.211***	(0.049)
R^2	0.169		0.169		0.130		0.130		0.096		0.096		0.087		0.087	

	Spain (SP)				Italy (IT)				France (FR)			
	Barry specification		Roemer specification		Barry specification		Roemer specification		Barry specification		Roemer specification	
Sex (ref : Female)												
Male	0.103***	(0.027)	0.103***	(0.026)	0.100***	(0.021)	0.100***	(0.021)	0.034	(0.022)	0.034	(0.021)
Age (ref : 50–54)												
55–59	-0.019	(0.049)	-0.019	(0.047)	-0.026	(0.041)	-0.026	(0.043)	-0.041	(0.039)	-0.041	(0.039)
60–64	-0.125**	(0.051)	-0.125**	(0.050)	-0.103**	(0.043)	-0.103**	(0.043)	0.002	(0.041)	0.002	(0.041)
65–69	-0.056	(0.055)	-0.056	(0.052)	-0.154***	(0.046)	-0.154***	(0.044)	-0.115**	(0.046)	-0.115**	(0.046)
70–74	-0.103*	(0.055)	-0.103*	(0.055)	-0.230***	(0.049)	-0.230***	(0.048)	-0.173***	(0.047)	-0.173***	(0.050)
75–80	-0.197***	(0.058)	-0.197***	(0.055)	-0.305***	(0.051)	-0.305***	(0.051)	-0.253***	(0.048)	-0.253***	(0.049)
Main breadwinner (ref : Elementary occupations and unskilled workers)												
Senior managers and professionals	-0.006	(0.084)	-0.001	(0.084)	0.082	(0.058)	0.093	(0.061)	0.031	(0.045)	0.036	(0.047)
Technicians, associate professionals and armed forces	-0.012	(0.069)	0.003	(0.067)	-0.001	(0.056)	-0.001	(0.056)	-0.015	(0.048)	-0.005	(0.048)

Office clerks, service workers and sales workers	−0.033	(0.046)	−0.031	(0.047)	0.048	(0.036)	0.025	(0.038)	−0.050	(0.042)	−0.053	(0.042)
Skilled agricultural and fishery workers	0.006	(0.033)	0.012	(0.032)	0.015	(0.026)	0.016	(0.026)	−0.011	(0.034)	0.004	(0.035)
Craftsmen and skilled workers	−0.010	(0.038)	−0.008	(0.037)	0.063**	(0.032)	0.061*	(0.033)	−0.062*	(0.034)	−0.060*	(0.035)
No main breadwinner	0.001	(0.134)	0.011	(0.137)	0.053	(0.112)	0.051	(0.107)	0.011	(0.130)	−0.018	(0.139)
Number of books at home (ref: None or very few (0–10 books))											
Enough to fill one shelf (11–25 books)	0.087**	(0.035)	0.085**	(0.035)	0.082**	(0.033)	0.103***	(0.033)	0.045	(0.030)	0.054*	(0.031)
Enough to fill one bookcase (26–100 books)	0.079	(0.049)	0.087*	(0.048)	0.027	(0.043)	0.048	(0.042)	0.093***	(0.032)	0.108***	(0.035)
Enough to fill two or more bookcases (more than 100 books)	0.143**	(0.061)	0.151***	(0.061)	0.106*	(0.056)	0.131**	(0.057)	0.094**	(0.041)	0.102**	(0.041)
Number of room/household member	0.047	(0.030)	0.057*	(0.031)	0.051	(0.040)	0.070	(0.043)	0.036	(0.030)	0.039	(0.031)
Number of facilities (ref: None)											
One	0.016	(0.035)	0.024	(0.036)	−0.001	(0.031)	0.004	(0.031)	0.026	(0.036)	0.022	(0.036)
Two or three	0.065*	(0.035)	0.073**	(0.036)	0.013	(0.028)	0.005	(0.029)	0.077**	(0.037)	0.076**	(0.038)
Four or five	0.083	(0.054)	0.089*	(0.054)	0.043	(0.040)	0.038	(0.039)	0.065	(0.041)	0.059	(0.042)
Period of difficulties during childhood											
Economic hardships	−0.014	(0.061)	−0.019	(0.061)	−0.127***	(0.049)	−0.146***	(0.052)	−0.194**	(0.084)	−0.175**	(0.077)
Hunger	0.002	(0.042)	−0.001	(0.042)	−0.076*	(0.042)	−0.072*	(0.040)	−0.020	(0.048)	−0.028	(0.048)
Mother's longevity (ref: mother prematurely deceased)											
Mother deceased in later ages	0.008	(0.029)	0.014	(0.029)	0.027	(0.024)	0.034	(0.024)	0.056**	(0.028)	0.062**	(0.028)
Mother alive	0.083**	(0.039)	0.091**	(0.037)	0.005	(0.030)	0.021	(0.029)	0.052*	(0.029)	0.052*	(0.029)
Father's longevity (ref: father prematurely deceased)											
Father deceased in later ages	0.035	(0.027)	0.035	(0.026)	0.030	(0.021)	0.038*	(0.021)	0.049*	(0.026)	0.059**	(0.026)
Father alive	−0.011	(0.052)	−0.006	(0.050)	0.002	(0.040)	0.011	(0.041)	0.058**	(0.034)	0.071**	(0.035)
Parents' health-related behaviours											
No regular dentist visits for their children	−0.021	(0.043)	−0.034	(0.040)	−0.037	(0.029)	−0.049*	(0.028)	−0.042*	(0.024)	−0.047*	(0.025)
Parents' smoking	−0.039	(0.027)	−0.040	(0.027)	−0.027	(0.021)	−0.029	(0.022)	−0.007	(0.023)	−0.001	(0.022)
Parents' alcohol consumption	−0.148***	(0.044)	−0.151***	(0.046)	0.011	(0.033)	0.013	(0.035)	−0.065*	(0.038)	−0.063*	(0.036)
Lifestyles variables/residuals											
Smoking	0.009	(0.036)	0.009	(0.038)	−0.025	(0.026)	−0.025	(0.028)	−0.091***	(0.031)	−0.091***	(0.031)
Obesity	−0.114***	(0.028)	−0.114***	(0.029)	−0.090***	(0.027)	−0.090***	(0.027)	−0.124***	(0.031)	−0.124***	(0.032)
Sedentarity	−0.116***	(0.039)	−0.116***	(0.038)	−0.256***	(0.027)	−0.256***	(0.027)	−0.184***	(0.038)	−0.184***	(0.040)
R^2	0.116		0.116		0.147		0.147		0.139		0.139	

Table A2. (*Continued*)

Sex (ref.: Female)	Danemark (DK) Barry specification		Danemark (DK) Roemer specification		Greece (GR) Barry specification		Greece (GR) Roemer specification		Switzerland (CH) Barry specification		Switzerland (CH) Roemer specification	
Male	0.039*	(0.020)	0.039*	(0.021)	0.074***	(0.017)	0.074***	(0.018)	0.031	(0.025)	0.031	(0.025)
Age (ref.: 50–54)												
55–59	−0.022	(0.031)	−0.022	(0.032)	−0.053**	(0.024)	−0.053**	(0.024)	−0.033	(0.038)	−0.033	(0.038)
60–64	0.010	(0.035)	0.010	(0.035)	−0.121***	(0.029)	−0.121***	(0.029)	−0.045	(0.042)	−0.045	(0.043)
65–69	−0.031	(0.039)	−0.031	(0.042)	−0.174***	(0.032)	−0.174***	(0.032)	−0.026	(0.045)	−0.026	(0.046)
70–74	−0.046	(0.047)	−0.046	(0.047)	−0.293***	(0.035)	−0.293***	(0.035)	−0.086*	(0.050)	−0.086*	(0.050)
75–80	−0.137***	(0.049)	−0.137***	(0.050)	−0.409***	(0.036)	−0.409***	(0.037)	−0.212***	(0.054)	−0.212***	(0.053)
Main breadwinner (ref.: Elementary occupations and unskilled workers)												
Senior managers and professionals	0.054	(0.040)	0.059	(0.043)	−0.017	(0.041)	−0.015	(0.043)	0.022	(0.060)	0.027	(0.063)
Technicians, associate professionals and armed forces	0.057	(0.054)	0.058	(0.054)	−0.057	(0.051)	−0.048	(0.053)	−0.067	(0.069)	−0.057	(0.068)
Office clerks, service workers and sales workers	0.008	(0.038)	0.018	(0.039)	−0.050*	(0.029)	−0.043	(0.029)	0.022	(0.052)	0.022	(0.052)
Skilled agricultural and fishery workers	0.047	(0.032)	0.077**	(0.034)	−0.117***	(0.026)	−0.121***	(0.025)	0.013	(0.054)	0.011	(0.054)
Craftsmen and skilled workers	0.002	(0.034)	0.014	(0.036)	−0.054*	(0.030)	−0.048	(0.030)	−0.023	(0.049)	−0.022	(0.051)
No main breadwinner	0.016	(0.190)	0.003	(0.199)	−0.051	(0.070)	−0.058	(0.074)	0.151	(0.113)	0.128	(0.110)
Number of books at home (ref.: None or very few (0–10 books))												
Enough to fill one shelf (11–25 books)	0.107***	(0.036)	0.111***	(0.035)	0.001	(0.022)	0.002	(0.021)	−0.003	(0.037)	−0.002	(0.037)
Enough to fill one bookcase (26–100 books)	0.112***	(0.034)	0.115***	(0.034)	0.001	(0.030)	0.002	(0.030)	0.012	(0.035)	0.014	(0.035)
Enough to fill two or more bookcases (more than 100 books)	0.069*	(0.037)	0.072*	(0.037)	−0.015	(0.055)	−0.019	(0.056)	−0.010	(0.041)	0.002	(0.041)
Number of room/household member	0.040	(0.026)	0.048*	(0.026)	0.094***	(0.036)	0.099***	(0.038)	−0.016	(0.037)	−0.034	(0.038)
Number of facilities (ref.: None)												
One	0.003	(0.045)	0.021	(0.045)	−0.014	(0.021)	−0.015	(0.020)	0.042	(0.075)	0.050	(0.077)
Two or three	−0.014	(0.045)	0.003	(0.047)	−0.040*	(0.024)	−0.040*	(0.023)	0.099	(0.073)	0.115	(0.074)
Four or five	0.029	(0.045)	0.044	(0.048)	−0.045	(0.034)	−0.048	(0.034)	0.150**	(0.074)	0.159**	(0.074)
Period of difficulties during childhood												
Economic hardships	−0.274**	(0.133)	−0.267**	(0.131)	−0.101**	(0.045)	−0.105**	(0.046)	0.081	(0.092)	0.100	(0.099)
Hunger	−0.129	(0.173)	−0.190	(0.161)	−0.123***	(0.044)	−0.129***	(0.043)	−0.089	(0.086)	−0.118	(0.096)
Mother's longevity (ref.: mother prematurely deceased)												
Mother deceased in later ages	0.028	(0.025)	0.030	(0.026)	−0.002	(0.022)	−0.007	(0.021)	−0.023	(0.030)	−0.024	(0.031)
Mother alive	0.032	(0.027)	0.041	(0.028)	0.012	(0.021)	0.016	(0.022)	−0.050	(0.031)	−0.045	(0.033)
Father's longevity (ref.: father prematurely deceased)												
Father deceased in later ages	0.055***	(0.023)	0.063***	(0.024)	0.031*	(0.018)	0.032*	(0.019)	0.012	(0.028)	0.018	(0.029)
Father alive	0.093***	(0.032)	0.089***	(0.032)	0.051**	(0.024)	0.056**	(0.023)	0.005	(0.040)	0.013	(0.039)

	Belgium (BE)				Czech Republic (CZ)				Poland (PL)			
	Barry specification		Roemer specification		Barry specification		Roemer specification		Barry specification		Roemer specification	
Sex (ref : Female)												
Male	0.055***	(0.019)	0.055***	(0.019)	0.007	(0.026)	0.007	(0.024)	0.004	(0.025)	0.004	(0.025)
Age (ref : 50–54)												
55–59	−0.043	(0.032)	−0.043	(0.033)	−0.086**	(0.041)	−0.086**	(0.041)	−0.066	(0.044)	−0.066	(0.043)
60–64	−0.079**	(0.033)	−0.079**	(0.036)	−0.086*	(0.044)	−0.086**	(0.043)	−0.167***	(0.047)	−0.167***	(0.046)
65–69	−0.138***	(0.038)	−0.138***	(0.041)	−0.106**	(0.048)	−0.106***	(0.048)	−0.213***	(0.052)	−0.213***	(0.052)
70–74	−0.134***	(0.039)	−0.134***	(0.040)	−0.158***	(0.054)	−0.158***	(0.053)	−0.259***	(0.055)	−0.259***	(0.053)
75–80	−0.170***	(0.042)	−0.170***	(0.043)	−0.276***	(0.057)	−0.276***	(0.055)	−0.254***	(0.058)	−0.254***	(0.056)
Main breadwinner (ref : Elementary occupations and unskilled workers)												
Senior managers and professionals	0.007	(0.038)	0.024	(0.042)	0.257***	(0.072)	0.269***	(0.073)	0.155*	(0.081)	0.165**	(0.083)
Technicians, associate professionals and armed forces	0.012	(0.038)	0.014	(0.042)	0.147**	(0.063)	0.154**	(0.064)	0.049	(0.083)	0.069	(0.079)
Office clerks, service workers and sales workers	−0.012	(0.033)	−0.014	(0.035)	0.183***	(0.059)	0.186***	(0.058)	0.078	(0.072)	0.100	(0.069)
Skilled agricultural and fishery workers	0.059**	(0.029)	0.071**	(0.030)	0.055	(0.053)	0.058	(0.057)	0.049	(0.043)	0.053	(0.044)
Craftsmen and skilled workers	0.036	(0.026)	0.029	(0.027)	0.076	(0.048)	0.077	(0.051)	0.075	(0.047)	0.083*	(0.046)
No main breadwinner	−0.072	(0.071)	−0.075	(0.073)	0.157	(0.103)	0.159	(0.106)	0.011	(0.205)	0.069	(0.208)
Number of books at home (ref: None or very few (0–10 books))												
Enough to fill one shelf (11–25 books)	0.044*	(0.026)	0.059**	(0.026)	0.029	(0.042)	0.034	(0.042)	0.037	(0.034)	0.042	(0.033)
Enough to fill one bookcase (26–100 books)	0.067***	(0.026)	0.090***	(0.027)	0.083*	(0.042)	0.085*	(0.044)	−0.043	(0.042)	−0.039	(0.042)
Enough to fill two or more bookcases (more than 100 books)	0.095***	(0.034)	0.109***	(0.035)	0.021	(0.053)	0.024	(0.052)	0.031	(0.063)	0.036	(0.062)
Number of room/household member	−0.009	(0.020)	−0.006	(0.021)	0.070	(0.049)	0.080	(0.050)	−0.028	(0.054)	−0.025	(0.055)
Parents' health-related behaviours												
No regular dentist visits for their children	−0.081***	(0.028)	−0.094***	(0.029)	−0.040**	(0.026)	−0.041**	(0.020)	−0.038	(0.031)	−0.027	(0.032)
Parents' smoking	−0.011	(0.028)	−0.023	(0.029)	−0.037**	(0.016)	−0.036**	(0.016)	0.010	(0.027)	0.005	(0.026)
Parents' alcohol consumption	−0.028	(0.038)	−0.041	(0.039)	−0.090**	(0.037)	−0.093**	(0.037)	−0.009	(0.043)	−0.021	(0.046)
Lifestyles variables/residuals												
Smoking	−0.122***	(0.025)	−0.122***	(0.025)	0.042**	(0.017)	0.042**	(0.018)	−0.109***	(0.035)	−0.109***	(0.034)
Obesity	−0.036	(0.033)	−0.036	(0.032)	−0.085***	(0.022)	−0.085***	(0.022)	−0.120***	(0.043)	−0.120***	(0.043)
Sedentarity	−0.380***	(0.056)	−0.380***	(0.056)	−0.115***	(0.039)	−0.115***	(0.039)	−0.278***	(0.082)	−0.278***	(0.083)
R^2	0.129		0.129		0.186		0.186		0.095		0.095	

Table A2. (Continued)

	Belgium (BE) Barry specification		Belgium (BE) Roemer specification		Czech Republic (CZ) Barry specification		Czech Republic (CZ) Roemer specification		Poland (PL) Barry specification		Poland (PL) Roemer specification	
Sex (ref : Female)	-0.063**	(0.027)	-0.069**	(0.028)	-0.058	(0.045)	-0.063	(0.046)	0.005	(0.051)	0.017	(0.051)
Number of facilities (ref: None)												
One	-0.010	(0.029)	-0.017	(0.029)	-0.043	(0.039)	-0.054	(0.039)	0.008	(0.046)	0.016	(0.047)
Two or three	-0.044	(0.034)	-0.056*	(0.035)	-0.035	(0.043)	-0.041	(0.046)	0.088	(0.062)	0.085	(0.060)
Four or five												
Period of difficulties during childhood												
Economic hardships	-0.298***	(0.110)	-0.358***	(0.105)	0.162	(0.156)	0.177	(0.151)	-0.063	(0.082)	-0.077	(0.083)
Hunger	-0.088	(0.055)	-0.088	(0.054)	-0.172	(0.128)	-0.148	(0.126)	-0.040	(0.047)	-0.043	(0.048)
Mother's longevity (ref: mother prematurely deceased)												
Mother deceased in later ages	-0.001	(0.022)	0.003	(0.023)	0.012	(0.030)	0.015	(0.029)	-0.026	(0.027)	-0.022	(0.027)
Mother alive	-0.007	(0.025)	-0.003	(0.027)	0.044	(0.035)	0.056	(0.034)	0.010	(0.037)	0.019	(0.038)
Father's longevity (ref: father prematurely deceased)												
Father deceased in later ages	0.038**	(0.019)	0.050**	(0.020)	0.023	(0.027)	0.027	(0.027)	-0.024	(0.025)	-0.023	(0.025)
Father alive	-0.025	(0.034)	-0.015	(0.036)	0.031	(0.048)	0.039	(0.049)	0.041	(0.059)	0.061	(0.058)
Parents' health-related behaviours												
No regular dentist visits for their children	-0.024	(0.020)	-0.033	(0.021)	-0.062	(0.043)	-0.070*	(0.039)	-0.041	(0.028)	-0.048*	(0.029)
Parents' smoking	-0.002	(0.021)	-0.005	(0.021)	-0.060**	(0.026)	-0.063**	(0.025)	-0.052**	(0.026)	-0.045*	(0.026)
Parents' alcohol consumption	-0.111***	(0.034)	-0.123***	(0.035)	-0.047	(0.057)	-0.042	(0.056)	-0.086**	(0.041)	-0.081*	(0.045)
Lifestyles variables/residuals												
Smoking	-0.135***	(0.027)	-0.135***	(0.027)	-0.016	(0.032)	-0.016	(0.031)	-0.027	(0.030)	-0.027	(0.030)
Obesity	-0.151***	(0.026)	-0.151***	(0.026)	-0.066**	(0.029)	-0.066**	(0.029)	-0.073***	(0.027)	-0.073***	(0.026)
Sedentary	-0.334***	(0.040)	-0.334***	(0.039)	-0.131***	(0.040)	-0.131***	(0.043)	-0.140***	(0.030)	-0.140***	(0.031)
R^2	0.120		0.120		0.096		0.096		0.108		0.108	

EX-ANTE AND *EX-POST* MEASUREMENT OF INEQUALITY OF OPPORTUNITY IN HEALTH: EVIDENCE FROM ISRAEL

Adi Lazar

ABSTRACT

The chapter suggests two methodologies to measure inequality of opportunity in health in Israel, an ex-ante and an ex-post approach. In both cases, following the strategy recently suggested by Trannoy, Tubeuf, Jusot, and Devaux (2010), the chapter starts by introducing the production function of health, taking into account circumstances (the father's years of education, his country of birth, the religion of the individual, his or her country of birth, age and gender) as well as effort variables (the level of education of the individual, his or her occupation and a variable describing his or her smoking habits).

The chapter also suggests then a decomposition of the overall health inequality into a legitimate and an illegitimate component, using the mean logarithmic deviation as inequality index, such a breakdown being applied to both the ex-ante and the ex-post approaches to equality of opportunity.

Keywords: Health inequality; inequality of opportunity; Israel

JEL classification: I14

INTRODUCTION

The reduction of health inequalities is a priority for many policymakers and international organizations. Nonetheless, in general, policymakers do not aim at eliminating all differences in health status in society. While health inequality arising from differences in choices and in effort exerted is often tolerated, inequalities arising from differences in circumstances, for which individuals are not responsible, are usually viewed as fundamentally unfair. Reducing the degree of inequality in opportunities for good health is supposed to 'level the playing field' so that circumstances such as skin colour, gender, birthplace, or family background, which are beyond the control of an individual, do not influence a person's health status.

Measuring health inequality is different from measuring inequality in health opportunity. Measuring health inequality means measuring unequal health outcomes such as the inequality in some health status variable or in infant mortality rates. These unequal outcomes may show inequalities that stem at least partially from circumstances that lie beyond an individual's control. This share of the unequal outcome that can be attributed to circumstance reflects inequality of opportunity. As a result, one way to measure inequality in health opportunity is to decompose unequal health outcomes into a share resulting from circumstances (which the individual cannot be held accountable for, because he or she is not responsible for them), and a residual component that is, for example, the consequence of his choice of lifestyle. The component resulting from circumstances that lie beyond the individual's control reflects, as was mentioned previously, inequality in health opportunity (see Paes de Barros, Ferreira, Vega, & Chanduvi, 2008a).

The analysis of inequality in health opportunity belongs actually to the broader topic of inequality of opportunity. The concept of equality of opportunity requires that unchosen inequalities should be eliminated but that inequalities that are the consequence of individual choices, assuming equal initial conditions, should not be eliminated (see Kranich, 1996; Ooghe,

Schokkaert, & Van de gaer, 2007; Roemer, 1998; Van de gaer, 1993). In other words, differences related to factors beyond individual control which are defined as circumstances or types should be compensated by society and this is called the *Principle of Compensation* (see Checchi & Peragine, 2010). There are however differences in achievements for which the individual is responsible (this refers to what is generally called effort, as was previously mentioned). Such differences should not be compensated and this is what is called the *Principle of Natural Reward* (see Fleurbaey, 2011).

Economists have taken an ordinal as well as a cardinal approach when trying to implement the concept of equality of opportunity (for the ordinal point of view, see Lefranc, Pistolesi, & Trannoy, 2009 and Zheng, 2011; for the cardinal approach, see Bourguignon, Ferreira, & Menendez, 2007; Ferreira & Gignoux, 2011 and Paes de Barros et al., 2008a). In a recent work, using a cardinal approach, Checchi and Peragine (2010) proposed to build a matrix where the rows refer to the *types* and the columns to what Peragine (2004a, 2004b) has called *tranche*s. They make then a distinction between an ex-ante types approach and an *ex-post* tranches approach. The latter approach is an illustration of the principle of compensation because it stresses inequality within effort groups. The former approach looks at the ex-ante prospects of individual with identical circumstances, hence its focus on inequality between types.

The purpose of this chapter is to measure inequality in health opportunities in Israel on the basis of both the ex-ante and ex-post approaches proposed by Checchi and Peragine (2010).[1] This chapter innovates by being the first inequality opportunity analysis using Israeli data.

The chapter is organized as follows. The second section introduces the production function of health, taking into account circumstances as well as effort variables. The third section suggests a decomposition of the overall health inequality into a legitimate and an illegitimate component, using the mean logarithmic deviation as inequality index. Such a breakdown is being applied to both the ex-ante and the ex-post approaches to equality of opportunity. Finally, the fourth section gives an empirical illustration using data from the 2003 Israeli Social Survey.

THE HEALTH PRODUCTION FUNCTION

Health is essentially a multi-dimensional phenomenon and as a consequence it is difficult to represent it using only one indicator. Given the difficulties one faces in measuring health, the latter is often apprehended via what is called self-assessed health (SAH) (see Li Donni et al., 2013; Malmusi, Borrell, & Benach, 2010; Trannoy et al., 2010; Tubeuf & Jusot, 2011). This measure of health is derived on the basis of the respondent's subjective assessment of his or her health status. It is presented as a categorical variable, measured on a four-point scale ranging from *not good at all* to *very good*. In the Israeli Social Survey for 2003 the SAH variable is based on the question:' How is your health, overall' and the answer is framed in the following four categories: not good at all, not so good, good and very good. Despite its subjectivity, this measure has been found to contribute more to supplementary health information than other health indicators.

Let us consider a society in which the health status of each individual is determined on one hand by circumstances beyond his or her responsibility and on the other hand by responsibility characteristics (or efforts). The first step of our analysis will be to estimate a health production function, assuming that the determinants of health are the individual circumstances and efforts. It is however likely that individual efforts are not orthogonal to circumstances and this implies that at least some of them are correlated with his or her circumstances. Accordingly, we can say that the link between circumstances and the individual health status takes two forms: a direct association, which reflects the way various circumstances affect individual health, and an indirect association going through the influence of circumstances on the efforts of the individual. Since Roemer (1998) assumed that effort was orthogonal to circumstances, we will assume that the components of effort which are correlated with his or her circumstances are circumstances as well.

In order to estimate the direct as well as indirect association of circumstances with individual health, we adopt the strategy presented recently by Trannoy et al. (2010) and which is based on a two-step procedure: First, we regress each effort variable in a separate equation against the vector of circumstances, the number of equations being identical to the number of effort variables. For each of these regressions we compute the estimated residuals, which are then introduced in the subsequent equations describing individual effort. More precisely, after regressing the first effort variable we compute its estimated residual and introduce it into the second equation of the next effort measure. Then we compute the estimated residual of the second equation and introduce the *two* residuals (from the first and the second regressions) into the third equation of the individual effort (in which we regress the third effort variable), and so on. In the second stage of the analysis we regress the individual health status against the vector of circumstances along with the estimated residuals of the effort equations described previously.

Given the data available in the 2003 Israeli Social Survey we have included the following variables as circumstances: the father's years of education,[2] his country of birth (which is represented by two dummy variables — one equal to 1 when the father was born in Israel and another equal to 1 when the father was born in Europe or America[3]), an indicator for the religion (equal to 1 if the individual is Jewish[4]), the product of the country of birth indicator by the individual religion (represented by two dummy variables — one equal to 1 if the individual is Jewish and was born in Israel and another equal to 1 if he or she is Jewish and was born in Europe or America[5]) and also two demographic factors — age[6] and gender (which takes the value of 1 if the individual reports being a male). To describe the effort we included three binary variables: the level of education of the individual (equal to 1 if individual obtained at least an academic degree), his or her occupation (equal to 1 if he or she reported having a professional or managerial occupation) and a variable describing his or her smoking habits (equal to 1 if individual is not currently a smoker).

Let us label $Education_i$, $Occupation_i$ and $NoSmoking_i$, these three effort variables, for individual i, and $Health_i$ his or her health status, the latter variable being assumed to be a continuous latent variable derived from the answers of the individual to the questions on his or her health status. Let us also call $FatherYearsEduc_i$, $FatherIsrael_i$, $FatherEuropeAmerica_i$, $Jewish_i$, $JewishIsrael_i$ and $JewishEuropeAmerica_i$ the individual circumstances described previously. The model we estimate consists then of four equations:

$$Education_i = \alpha_0 + \alpha_1 Gender_i + \alpha_2 Age_i + \alpha_3 Age_i^2 + \alpha_4 Father\ Years\ Educ_i \\ + \alpha_5 FatherIsrael_i + \alpha_6 FatherEuropeAmerica_i + \alpha_7 Jewish_i \\ + \alpha_8 JewishIsrael_i + \alpha_9 JewishEuropeAmerica_i + u_{1i} \quad (1)$$

$$Occupation_i = \beta_0 + \beta_1 Gender_i + \beta_2 Age_i + \beta_3 Age_i^2 + \beta_4 FatherYearsEduc_i \\ + \beta_5 FatherIsrael_i + \beta_6 FatherEuropeAmerica_i + \beta_7 Jewish_i \\ + \beta_8 JewishIsrael_i + \beta_9 JewishEuropeAmerica_i + \beta_{10} \hat{u}_{1i} + u_{2i} \\ \quad (2)$$

$$NoSmoking_i = \gamma_0 + \gamma_1 Gender_i + \gamma_2 Age_i + \gamma_3 Age_i^2 + \gamma_4 FatherYearsEduc_i \\ + \gamma_5 FatherIsrael_i + \gamma_6 FatherEuropeAmerica_i + \gamma_7 Jewish_i \\ + \gamma_8 JewishIsrael_i + \gamma_9 JewishEuropeAmerica_i + \gamma_{10} \hat{u}_{1i} \\ + \gamma_{11} \hat{u}_{2i} + u_{3i} \quad (3)$$

$$\begin{aligned} Health_i = {} & \delta_1 Gender_i + \delta_2 Age_i + \delta_3 Age_i^2 + \delta_4 FatherYearsEduc_i \\ & + \delta_5 FatherIsrael_i + \delta_6 FatherEuropeAmerica_i + \delta_7 Jewish_i \\ & + \delta_8 JewishIsrael_i + \delta_9 JewishEuropeAmerica_i + \delta_{10}\hat{u}_{1i} + \delta_{11}\hat{u}_{2i} \\ & + \delta_{12}\hat{u}_{3i} + u_{4i} \end{aligned} \quad (4)$$

In this model the first three equations (Eqs. (1)–(3)) are estimated via a binary logit model, while Eq. (4) is estimated via an ordered logit regression. Since our model is not linear the residuals $\hat{u}_{1i}$, $\hat{u}_{2i}$ and $\hat{u}_{3i}$ are computed as generalized residuals corresponding to the conditional expected value of the residuals given the outcomes $E(u_{1i}/Education_i^{High})$, $E(u_{2i}/Occupation_i^{High})$ and $E(u_{3i}/NoSmoking_i)$ (Gourieroux, Monfort, Renault, & Trognon, 1987).[7]

It should be stressed that, as a consequence of the estimation procedure, the coefficients associated to circumstance variables in Eq. (4) represent the sum of the direct as well as indirect associations of circumstances with individual health status. On the other hand, the estimated residuals in that equation, written as $\hat{u}_{1i}$, $\hat{u}_{2i}$ and $\hat{u}_{3i}$, represent only the individual effort,[8] since in Eq. (4) they are orthogonal to the circumstances.

To obtain a measure of individual health status we first predict health levels, based on the estimates from the health equation, including the predicted residuals of the education, occupation and 'non-smoker' equations. At the next stage, since our methodology cannot be applied when there are negative values, we standardize the predicted health variable described above by transforming it so that its value varies between 0 and 1. More precisely, the standardized predicted health status is computed as being equal to $(He\hat{a}lth_i - \min(He\hat{a}lth)) / (\max(He\hat{a}lth) - \min(He\hat{a}lth))$, where $He\hat{a}lth_i$ is the predicted health level of the individual, $\min(He\hat{a}lth)$ is the minimum value of the predicted health variable and $\max(He\hat{a}lth)$ is its maximum value.

MEASURING INEQUALITY IN HEALTH OPPORTUNITY

Let us recall our assumption that the health status of each individual in our society is completely described by two sets of traits: circumstances which are beyond an individual's responsibility, and responsibility characteristics (or effort). The first set, represented by an individual's set of circumstances **c**, belongs to a finite set $\Omega = \{\mathbf{c}_1, ..., \mathbf{c}_k\}$, which includes gender, religion, country of birth and family background. The second set, represented by all the other background traits of the individual that might affect his or her success, but that are excluded from the list of circumstances (this second set refers to what is called effort), is a scalar belonging to the set $\Theta = \{e_1, ..., e_m\}$. In our study effort will refer to the individual's education, his or her occupation and his or her smoking behaviour.

Let us now consider a data matrix H whose rows i correspond to the individual circumstances and whose columns j correspond to his or her responsibility characteristics (or effort). According to the previous definitions of circumstances and effort that matrix has k rows, corresponding to the set of k circumstances and m columns, corresponding to the set of m effort characteristics. In the simple case, suppose that individual health status, written here as h, is generated by a function $g : \Omega \times \Theta \rightarrow R_+$, which links an individual's SAH to his or her combinations of effort and circumstances, that is:

$$h_{i,j} = g(c_i, e_j) \tag{5}$$

where $h_{i,j}$ denotes the health status of an individual with circumstances c_i and effort e_j. It should be noted that the overall health distribution of population size n is actually a vector $\mathbf{H} = \{h_1, h_2, ..., h_n\}$, which was described previously in the form of a matrix H.

Now let us assume that each element of this matrix, denoted by $H_{i,j}$, gives the *average* levels of health of individuals with circumstances c_i and chosen effort e_j. Recall that the predicted health level of each individual is represented by the standardized value of his or her predicted health status, where the latter is assumed to be equal to the sum of the multiplications of the explanatory variables by their coefficients in the health regression, including the predicted residuals of the education, occupation and' no-smoker' equations. The average health level in each cell in the matrix is then simply the arithmetic mean of the standardized predicted health levels of the individuals whose circumstances and effort correspond to the specific row and column of the cell.

Applying a suitable inequality measure to this matrix H, which represents the distribution of the health levels of the total population, would capture the *overall* health inequality in our society. However, in order to determine the share of the overall health inequality that can be attributed to unequal health opportunity, the remaining part of the inequality being due to individual responsibility, we can implement either an 'ex-ante' or an 'expost' methodology (see Checchi & Peragine, 2010, as well as Fleurbaey & Schokkaert, 2009).

The Tranches (Ex-Post) Approach

Implementation Procedure
Given a distribution of individual health levels, represented by a vector $\mathbf{H} = \{h_1, h_2, ..., h_n\}$, let us classify the total population by levels of the effort variable, so that each group in this partition, called a 'tranche', includes the set of individuals assumed to have applied the same level of effort. Calling $\mathbf{h}_j$ the health distribution for tranche $j, j = 1, ..., m$, where tranche j includes all the individuals with identical effort e_j, the overall health distribution for the entire population may also be written as $\mathbf{H} = (\mathbf{h}_1, \mathbf{h}_2, ..., \mathbf{h}_m)$. This approach focuses on ex-post inequalities within effort groups, inequalities that are attributed to the different circumstances, and consequently should be compensated for. It is commonly accepted that this tranches (ex-post) approach is in some sense an expression of the principle of compensation. On the other hand, differences between the tranches are interpreted as equitable and should not be compensated for since they are due to autonomous choices made by the individuals.

To decompose the overall health inequality into an ethically acceptable component (which is due to individual effort) and an ethically unacceptable component (which is due to initial circumstances and consequently represents inequality in health opportunity), let us take the following steps.

Step 1: Transform the overall health distribution $\mathbf{H} = (\mathbf{h}_1, \mathbf{h}_2, ..., \mathbf{h}_m)$ into a hypothetical distribution, in which each individual's health level is replaced with the average health status of the tranche to which he or she belongs. Let us call $\mu_{\mathbf{h}_j}$ the average health status of tranche j and $1_{(n/m)}$ the unit vector of length (n/m), where n refers to the population size and m to the number of effort groups.[9] We can then construct a hypothetical distribution, represented by a vector $\mathbf{H}_B$, written as

$$\mathbf{H}_B = \left(\mu_{\mathbf{h}_1} 1_{n/m}, ..., \mu_{\mathbf{h}_j} 1_{n/m}, ..., \mu_{\mathbf{h}_m} 1_{n/m}\right) \tag{6}$$

In fact such a distribution $\mathbf{H}_B$ can also be represented by a matrix with m columns and k rows, where each column consists of k identical elements, each equal to the average health status of the column. Such a technique removes hence any within-tranches inequality, that is it eliminates the inequality in health opportunity and leaves unchanged the health inequality *between* tranches. Therefore, any inequality index applied to such a distribution represents only inequality due to individual responsibility (his or her effort).

Step 2: Transform the overall health distribution $\mathbf{H} = (\mathbf{h}_1, \mathbf{h}_2, ..., \mathbf{h}_m)$ into a standardized distribution, in which each individual's health level is multiplied by the average health status of the overall distribution and divided by the average health status of its tranche. More precisely, for all $j = 1, ..., m$ and $i = 1, ..., k$ the health status of each individual, written as h_{ij}, is replaced with $h_{i,j} * \mu_\mathbf{H} / \mu_{\mathbf{h}_j}$, where $\mu_\mathbf{H}$ is the average health status of the overall distribution while $\mu_{\mathbf{h}_j}$ is the average health status of tranche j. Such a standardized distribution, represented by $\mathbf{H}_W$, can be expressed as

$$\mathbf{H}_W = \left(\mathbf{h}_1 \frac{\mu_\mathbf{H}}{\mu_{\mathbf{h}_1}}, ..., \mathbf{h}_j \frac{\mu_\mathbf{H}}{\mu_{\mathbf{h}_j}}, ..., \mathbf{h}_m \frac{\mu_\mathbf{H}}{\mu_{\mathbf{h}_m}} \right) \tag{7}$$

This procedure guarantees that all tranches will have the same average health status as the overall distribution and therefore removes any inequality between tranches but leaves unchanged health inequality *within* tranches. Hence, any inequality index applied to this distribution measures only the inequality due to circumstances, that is, inequality in health opportunity.

In a matrix format, that distribution is actually a transformation of the original matrix $\mathbf{H}$, represented with m columns and k rows. Each element denoted by $h_{i,j}$ in the original matrix $\mathbf{H}$, representing the average standardized predicted health levels of all individuals belonging to tranche j and type (circumstances) i, is now replaced by $h_{i,j} * \mu_\mathbf{H} / \mu_{\mathbf{h}_j}$, where $\mu_\mathbf{H}$ is the average health status of the overall distribution and $\mu_{\mathbf{h}_j}$ is the average health status of tranche j, as mentioned previously.

Step 3: Let us apply as a measure of inequality the *mean logarithmic deviation* (*MLD*), which is a *path independent* decomposable index, which guarantees that overall inequality will be equal to the sum of the within- and between-groups inequalities (see Foster & Shneyerov, 2000, as well as Ferreira & Gignoux, 2011). In our case, path independence requires that the sum of the inequality in health opportunity (which, in the tranches approach, is represented by the within-groups inequality) and that in effort (which, in the tranches approach, is represented by the between-groups inequality) is equal to the overall health inequality. For the overall health distribution $\mathbf{H} = \{h_1, h_2, ..., h_n\}$ with its average $\mu_\mathbf{H}$, the *MLD* is then defined as

$$MLD(\mathbf{H}) = \frac{1}{n} \sum_{i=1}^{n} \ln \frac{\mu_\mathbf{H}}{h_i} \tag{8}$$

where n is the population size and h_i is the health status of individual i. Eq. (8) represents the overall health inequality of the total population.

A Measure of Inequality in Health Opportunity

In order to quantify the part of the health inequality due to initial circumstances, the *MLD* measure has to be applied to the distribution that removes all inequalities between tranches and leaves unchanged the health inequality *within* tranches. Such a distribution was defined previously as $\mathbf{H}_W = (h_1 \mu_\mathbf{H}/\mu_{\mathbf{h}_1}, ..., h_j\mu_\mathbf{H}/\mu_{\mathbf{h}_j}, ..., h_m\mu_\mathbf{H}/\mu_{\mathbf{h}_m})$. Therefore, in the tranche approach, inequality in health opportunity is expressed as $MLD(\mathbf{H}_W)$ or, in relative terms, as

$$OI_W = \frac{MLD(\mathbf{H}_W)}{MLD(\mathbf{H})} \qquad (9)$$

where OI_W, the abbreviation of 'opportunity inequality', is the share of overall health inequality that attributed to inequality in health opportunity. Since the *MLD* measure has a path-independent decomposition, the share of the unequal health opportunity presented in Eq. (9) can alternatively be expressed using the distribution $\mathbf{H}_B = (\mu_{\mathbf{h}_1} 1_{n/m}, ..., \mu_{\mathbf{h}_j} 1_{n/m}, ..., \mu_{\mathbf{h}_m} 1_{n/m})$ as

$$OI_B = 1 - \frac{MLD(\mathbf{H}_B)}{MLD(\mathbf{H})} \qquad (10)$$

where $MLD(\mathbf{H}_B)$ is health inequality due to effort and $MLD(\mathbf{H}_B)/MLD(\mathbf{H})$ represents the share of overall health inequality that is attributed to individual effort. The interpretation of these measures is as follows. In order to quantify the part of the health inequality due to individual responsibility, the *MLD* measure has to be applied to the distribution that removes all inequalities within tranches and leaves unchanged the health inequality *between* tranches. This measure was defined previously as $\mathbf{H}_B = (\mu_{\mathbf{h}_1} 1_{n/m}, ..., \mu_{\mathbf{h}_j} 1_{n/m}, ..., \mu_{\mathbf{h}_m} 1_{n/m})$. Therefore, in the tranches approach, the health inequality due to individual effort is expressed as $MLD(\mathbf{H}_B)$ or, in relative terms, as

$$EI = \frac{MLD(\mathbf{H}_B)}{MLD(\mathbf{H})} \qquad (11)$$

where *EI*, the abbreviation of 'effort inequality', is the share of overall health inequality that is attributed to individual responsibility.[10] Since the measure of inequality in health opportunity can be written as OI_W or OI_B the decomposition of the overall health inequality can be presented, in relative terms, as

$$1 = EI + OI \qquad (12)$$

where *EI* is the share of overall health inequality attributed to effort inequality and $OI = OI_W = OI_B$ is the share of overall health inequality attributed to inequality in health opportunity. In absolute terms, the overall health inequality is decomposed as the sum of inequality in effort and in opportunities, that is, as

$$MLD(\mathbf{H}) = MLD(\mathbf{H}_B) + MLD(\mathbf{H}_W) \qquad (13)$$

where $MLD(\mathbf{H})$ is the overall health inequality, $MLD(\mathbf{H}_B)$ the effort health inequality and $MLD(\mathbf{H}_W)$ the inequality in health opportunity, as defined above.

The Types (Ex-Ante) Approach

Implementation Procedure
Instead of classifying the total population by levels of effort, let us introduce another partition based on the set of circumstances $\Omega = \{\mathbf{c}_1, ..., \mathbf{c}_k\}$. In such a partition each group is called a 'type' and includes all individuals sharing the same circumstances. Calling $\mathbf{g}_i$ the health distribution for type i, $i = 1, ..., k$, where type i is the set of individuals with set of circumstances $\mathbf{c}_i$, the overall health distribution for the entire population can also be written as $\mathbf{H} = (\mathbf{g}_1, \mathbf{g}_2, ..., \mathbf{g}_k)$. The focus of this approach is hence on inequalities between types. It assumes that differences in the ex-ante prospects of individuals with identical circumstances are fair and should not be compensated for. In other words, differences in individual achievements that are attributed to effort (and result in within-types inequality) are interpreted as equitable. This is why this types (ex-ante) approach can be considered as an expression of the principle of reward. On the other hand, differences in individual achievements which are due to circumstances and

represented by the inequality between types are assumed to be illegitimate and should be compensated for.

As for the analysis presented for the tranches (ex-post) approach, let us now decompose the overall health inequality into legitimate and illegitimate components (which refer to effort and opportunity inequalities respectively).

Step 1: Transform the overall health distribution $\mathbf{H} = (\mathbf{g}_1, \mathbf{g}_2, ..., \mathbf{g}_k)$ into a hypothetical distribution, in which each individual's health level is replaced with the average health status of the type to which he or she belongs. Let us call $\mu_{\mathbf{g}_i}$ the average health status of type i and $1_{n/k}$ the unit vector of length n/k, where n refers to the population size and k to the number of circumstance groups.[11] Then the hypothetical distribution, represented by a vector $\mathbf{H}_B^{Ante}$, can be written as

$$\mathbf{H}_B^{Ante} = \left(\mu_{\mathbf{g}_1} 1_{n/k}, ..., \mu_{\mathbf{g}_i} 1_{n/k}, ..., \mu_{\mathbf{g}_k} 1_{n/k}\right) \quad (14)$$

That distribution can also be represented by a matrix with m columns and k rows, where each row consists of m identical elements, each equals to the average health status of the row. Such a technique removes any within-types inequality, eliminates the inequality due to individual responsibility, and leaves unchanged the *between*-types health inequality. Hence, any inequality index applied to this distribution reflects only the inequality due to circumstances, that is inequality in health opportunity.

Step 2: Transform the overall health distribution $\mathbf{H} = (\mathbf{g}_1, \mathbf{g}_2, ..., \mathbf{g}_k)$ into a standardized distribution, in which each individual's health level is multiplied by the average health status of the overall distribution and divided by the average health status of its type. More precisely, for all $j = 1, ..., m$ and $i = 1, ..., k$ the health status of each individual, denoted by $h_{i,j}$, is replaced with $h_{i,j} * \mu_\mathbf{H}/\mu_{\mathbf{g}_i}$, where $\mu_\mathbf{H}$ is the average health status of the overall distribution and $\mu_{\mathbf{g}_i}$ is the average health status of type i. Such standardized distribution, represented by $\mathbf{H}_W^{Ante}$, can be expressed as

$$\mathbf{H}_W^{Ante} = \left(\mathbf{g}_1 \frac{\mu_\mathbf{H}}{\mu_{\mathbf{g}_1}}, ..., \mathbf{g}_i \frac{\mu_\mathbf{H}}{\mu_{\mathbf{g}_i}}, ..., \mathbf{g}_k \frac{\mu_\mathbf{H}}{\mu_{\mathbf{g}_k}}\right) \quad (15)$$

Such a procedure guarantees for all types the same average health status as the overall distribution. It therefore removes any *between-types* inequality and leaves unchanged the health inequality *within types*. Hence, any suitable inequality index applied to this distribution represents only the inequality due to individual responsibility (his or her effort).

In a matrix format, this distribution is actually a transformation of the original matrix **H**, represented with m columns and k rows. Each element denoted by $h_{i,j}$ in the original matrix **H**, representing the average standardized predicted health levels of all individuals belonging to tranche j and type (circumstances) i, is now replaced by $h_{i,j}{}^*\mu_\mathbf{H}/\mu_{\mathbf{g}_i}$, where $\mu_\mathbf{H}$ is the average health status of the overall distribution and $\mu_{\mathbf{g}_i}$ is the average health status of type i, as noted previously.

Step 3: Let us use as a measure of inequality the *MLD*, which guarantees that the overall health inequality will be equal to the sum of the inequality in health opportunity (which, in the types approach, is represented by the between-groups inequality) and in effort (which, in the types approach, is represented by the within-groups inequality).

A Measure of Inequality in Health Opportunity
In order to quantify the part of health inequality due to initial circumstances, the *MLD* measure has to be applied to the distribution that removes any within-types inequality and leaves unchanged the health inequality *between* types, defined previously as $\mathbf{H}_B^{Ante} = (\mu_{\mathbf{g}_1} 1_{n/k}, \ldots, \mu_{\mathbf{g}_i} 1_{n/k}, \ldots, \mu_{\mathbf{g}_k} 1_{n/k})$. Therefore, in the types approach, the inequality in health opportunity is expressed as $MLD(\mathbf{H}_B^{Ante})$ or, in relative terms, by

$$OI_B^{Ante} = \frac{MLD(\mathbf{H}_B^{Ante})}{MLD(\mathbf{H})} \qquad (16)$$

where OI_B^{Ante}, an abbreviation for 'opportunity inequality' according to the ex-ante approach, is the share of overall health inequality that is attributed to inequality in health opportunity. Since the decomposition of the *MLD* measure is path-independent, the share of the unequal health opportunity presented in Eq. (16) can alternatively be expressed, using the distribution $\mathbf{H}_W^{Ante} = (\mathbf{g}_1 \mu_\mathbf{H}/\mu_{\mathbf{g}_1}, \ldots, \mathbf{g}_i \mu_\mathbf{H}/\mu_{\mathbf{g}_i}, \ldots, \mathbf{g}_k \mu_\mathbf{H}/\mu_{\mathbf{g}_k})$, as

$$OI_W^{Ante} = 1 - \frac{MLD(\mathbf{H}_W^{Ante})}{MLD(\mathbf{H})} \qquad (17)$$

where $MLD(\mathbf{H}_W^{Ante})$ measures health inequality due to effort and $MLD(\mathbf{H}_W^{Ante})/MLD(\mathbf{H})$ is a relative term, expressing the share of overall health inequality attributed to individual effort.

The interpretation of these measures is as follows. In order to quantify the part of health inequality due to individual responsibility, the *MLD* measure has to be applied to the distribution that removes any between-types inequality and leaves unchanged the *within*-types inequality. The latter was defined previously as $\mathbf{H}_W^{Ante} = (\mathbf{g}_1 \mu_\mathbf{H}/\mu_{\mathbf{g}_1}, ..., \mathbf{g}_i \mu_\mathbf{H}/\mu_{\mathbf{g}_i}, ..., \mathbf{g}_k \mu_\mathbf{H}/\mu_{\mathbf{g}_k})$. Therefore, in the types approach, the health inequality due to individual effort is expressed as $MLD(\mathbf{H}_W^{Ante})$ or, in relative terms, as

$$EI^{Ante} = \frac{MLD(\mathbf{H}_W^{Ante})}{MLD(\mathbf{H})} \qquad (18)$$

where EI^{Ante}, an abbreviation of 'effort inequality' according to the ex-ante approach, is the share of overall health inequality that is attributed to health inequality due to individual responsibility.[12] Since the measure of inequality in health opportunity can be written as OI_W^{Ante} or OI_B^{Ante}, the decomposition of the overall health inequality is expressed, in relative terms, as

$$1 = EI^{Ante} + OI^{Ante} \qquad (19)$$

where EI^{Ante} is the share of overall health inequality that is attributed to effort inequality and $OI^{Ante} = OI_W^{Ante} = OI_B^{Ante}$ is the share of the overall health inequality that is attributed to inequality in health opportunity. In absolute terms, the overall health inequality is decomposed as the sum of effort and opportunity inequality, that is, as

$$MLD(\mathbf{H}) = MLD(\mathbf{H}_B^{Ante}) + MLD(\mathbf{H}_W^{Ante}) \qquad (20)$$

where $MLD(\mathbf{H})$ is the overall health inequality, $MLD(\mathbf{H}_W^{Ante})$ the inequality in health opportunity and $MLD(\mathbf{H}_W^{Ante})$ the inequality in health due to effort.

EMPIRICAL APPLICATION

In this section we illustrate both the ex-post and the ex-ante approaches to the measurement of inequality in health opportunity, using the Israeli Social Survey for 2003. That survey, based on around 3,000 individuals, contains information on the self-assessed health status of the respondents, their socioeconomic background (circumstances) and effort. In order to apply the ex-post and the ex-ante approaches to the SAH measure, we have first considered the correlation of the individual effort with his or her circumstances by regressing the effort measures within three separate equations against the vector of circumstances. For the SAH regression we have also included, in addition to the circumstances, the residuals we had computed for each of the effort equations.

Results of the Regressions for the Individual's Characteristics

The results show that the probability of individuals reporting better health decreases with age, with an increasing marginal association; the probability of reaching an advanced educational level increases and then decreases with age, while the probability of being a non-smoker decreases and then increases with the age of the individual. The estimated turning points[13] are 52.8 years for the individual's education and 32.3 years for his or her smoking behaviour.

The results also reveal that compared to women the probability to have a better SAH is higher but that of being a non-smoker is smaller among males. In the other two equations (individual education and occupation) there are no significant gender differences.

Other things constant we also observe that the education of the father has a positive association with individual health and the probability of reaching an advanced education and a high professional status. The association of the father's years of schooling is the same for the individual's occupation and health and higher for his or her education.

The SAH is highest among Jews who were born in Israel and lowest among non-Jews. Jews have also a higher probability of having a high professional status and of being a non-smoker.

Our results reveal also that when the father was born in Israel, Europe or America, the health status of the individual and the probability of reaching an advanced education, having a high professional status and being a non-smoker are all higher. A positive association with the individual's characteristics appears also for the individual's country of birth (assuming he or she is a Jewish). Moreover, the value of the coefficients of Jews born in Israel is greater than that of Jews born in Europe or America.

As far as the coefficients of the generalized residuals in the three effort equations (referring to individual education, occupation and smoking behaviour respectively) are concerned, the results show that only the coefficient of the generalized residual referring to education is significant and it appears then that education has a positive association with the probabilities of having a higher health status, and a high professional status and with that of being a non-smoker. It is important to stress that the correct interpretation of this result is that education has a positive association with individual health, the occupational status and the smoking behaviour of an individual, independently from his or her social background (circumstances). In contrast the coefficients of the generalized residuals of the occupation and of the smoking behaviour variables indicate that occupation and the smoking behaviour have no significant association with an individual's health. In addition it appears also that occupation has no significant association with the probability for an individual to be a non-smoker. These findings mean that *efforts and luck* in social status (represented by the individual's occupation) do not affect an individual's health and smoking behaviour. What may be more surprising is that the effort and luck of an individual, as far as his or her smoking behaviour is concerned, have no association with his or her health status. There is however an indirect association of an individual's smoking behaviour (and occupation), one that works via his or her circumstances. In other words the social background of an individual (his or her circumstances) has an association with his or her occupation and smoking behaviour and this in turn influences his or her health status.

Results of the Ex-Ante and Ex-Post Approaches

In the second stage of the empirical analysis we have built the health matrix **H**, representing the actual overall health distribution of the 3,011 individuals in our survey. For that purpose, we have first computed for each individual i the predicted value of his or her circumstances, using the results of the health regression, presented in Appendix D. We therefore wrote that

$$Circum_i = 0.351^*Gender_i + 0.023^*FatherYearsEduc_i + 0.611^*FatherIsrael_i$$
$$+ 0.129^*FatherEuropeAmerica_i + 1.080^*Jewish_i$$
$$+ 0.440^*JewishIsrael_i - 0.692^*JewishEuropeAmerica_i \quad (21)$$

where $Circum_i$, the predicted value of the circumstances of individual i, is actually the sum of the cross-products of his or her circumstances, excluding the age[14] by the corresponding coefficients in the health regression.

From this computation we derived a distribution of the individual circumstances in the whole population in the survey. We then divided this distribution of the individual circumstances in quintiles, each of them representing 20% of the individuals.

Using the same health regression, we also computed for each individual i the predicted value of his or her effort, that is, we wrote that

$$\hat{Effort}_i = 0.558^*\hat{u}_{1i} + 0.057^*\hat{u}_{2i} + 0.109^*\hat{u}_{3i} \quad (22)$$

where $\hat{Effort}_i$, the predicted value of the effort of individual i, is actually the sum of the multiplications of his or her efforts by the corresponding coefficients in the health regression. These efforts, as was mentioned previously, are represented by $\hat{u}_{1i}$, $\hat{u}_{2i}$ and $\hat{u}_{3i}$, which refer respectively to the education, occupation and smoking behaviour of individual i. From this computation we derived the distribution of the predicted individual efforts for the whole population in the survey. As for the individual circumstances, we then divided this distribution of individual efforts in quintiles, representing each 20% of the individuals in the population surveyed.

Then we built a five-by-five matrix **H**, the five rows corresponding to the five groups of the distribution of individual circumstances and the five columns to the five groups of the distribution of individual efforts.

In the next stage of the analysis we identified the individuals who were in each cell. For example, in the upper left cell, we obviously found all the individuals who belong to the lowest quintile of the distribution of circumstances as well as to the lowest quintile of the distribution of efforts. Then, we attributed to each individual his or her standardized predicted health level on the basis of the distribution of the latent variable derived from the ordered logit regression. Then we computed in each cell the average value of the standardized predicted values of this latent variable among the individuals located in the cell.

By transforming the health matrix **H** into two different matrices, depending on the approach selected, and using the mean logarithmic deviation (*MLD*), we could implement the ex-post and ex-ante approaches to the measurement of inequality in health opportunity. For each component of the health inequality we also give confidence intervals based on the Jackknife approach.[15]

The results of this procedure, which are summarized in Appendix F, show that the two components of the health inequality, the between- as well as the within-groups (tranches or types) inequalities, in both the ex-post and the ex-ante approaches, are always different one from the other and also significantly different from zero (they are all statistically significant at 5% level). Moreover the mean logarithmic deviation $MLD(\mathbf{H})$ measuring the overall health inequality is equal to 0.0455, for both the ex-post and ex-ante approaches (see the third and ninth rows of Appendix F). Since the mean logarithmic deviation is equal to the difference in logarithmic terms between the arithmetic and geometric means, we can say that there is approximately a 4.5% difference between these two means of the latent variable measuring the health status of individuals.

As far as the decomposition of the overall health inequality is concerned, we observe that, in both the ex-post and ex-ante approaches, this inequality is mainly due to unequal circumstances. In the ex-post procedure, inequality in health opportunity (i.e. the inequality within tranches, defined above as $OI_W = MLD(\mathbf{H}_W)/MLD(\mathbf{H})$) represents 92% of the overall health inequality (see the sixth line of Appendix F). In the ex-ante approach, inequality in health opportunity (i.e. the inequality between types, defined above as $OI_B^{Ante} = MLD(\mathbf{H}_B^{Ante})/MLD(\mathbf{H})$), is slightly lower and equal to 89% of the overall health inequality (see the last line of Appendix F). These findings clearly show that individual circumstances have a great association with the inequality in individual health status and tend to justify any public policy aiming at reducing that part of health inequality which is the consequence of differences in individual circumstances.

CONCLUSIONS

This chapter proposes two methodologies for the measurement of inequality of opportunity in health, known as the ex-ante and the ex-post approaches, and illustrates them using data from Israel. In both approaches, assuming that the SAH is determined by circumstances as well as effort variables, the overall health inequality is decomposed into a legitimate and an illegitimate component, using the mean logarithmic deviation as a measure of inequality. Using the 2003 Israeli Social Survey, it first examines the correlation between the individual effort and his or her circumstances by regressing the effort measures against the vector of circumstances and, subsequently, estimating the individual health status equation. The results show that the SAH is highest among Jews who were born in Israel and lowest among non-Jews. Jews have also a higher probability of having a high professional status and of being a non-smoker. Furthermore, education has a positive association with individual health, and the probability of individuals having a professional or managerial job and being non-smokers, independently from his or her social background (circumstances).

The results also show that the proposed decomposition analysis can be, in practice, a very useful tool for understanding the determinants of health inequality. In the case of Israel, in both the ex-post and ex-ante approaches, most of the inequality in health opportunity is due to unequal circumstances, which account for approximately 90% of the overall inequality. This provides researchers and policymakers with key information on the main sources of health inequality, thereby facilitating the design of policies aimed at tackling them.

NOTES

1. For another analysis contrasting the ex-ante and ex-post approaches in the case of health, see Li Donni, Peragine, and Pignataro (2013).
2. Father's years of education is a quantitative variable equal to 8 for elementary school, 12 for secondary school (whether he/she received a matriculation certificate or not), 14 for post secondary education without an academic certificate, 15 for a BA (academic certificate or similar certificate), 17 for an MA, MD or similar certificate and 21 for a PhD or similar certificate.
3. The excluded categories refer to cases for which the father was born in Asia or Africa.
4. The excluded categories refer to individuals who are Muslim, Christian, Druze or atheist.
5. The excluded categories refer to Jews who were born in Asia or Africa and non-Jews.
6. The age of the individual is actually the average age in each range of ages.
7. It should be noted that in this model each equation is estimated separately. Following the strategy recently suggested by Trannoy et al. (2010), since our model is not linear, we regress each effort variable in a separate equation against the vector of circumstances and then introduce the estimated residuals of these three equations into the fourth equation explaining the individual health status. This technique is designed to avoid estimating the four equations as a system. For estimation as a system with fully correlated error terms, see Rosa Dias (2009, 2010).
8. To be more accurate, these estimated residuals actually represent also individual luck and unobserved circumstances permitting the individual to reach a high educational level or/and a high occupational level as well as to avoid smoking.
9. By dividing n by m we assume that the number of individuals in each column is the same and is equal to n/m.
10. Similar to the opportunity index, the effort inequality can also be expressed, using the distribution $\mathbf{H}_W$, as $EI_W = 1 - MLD(\mathbf{H}_W)/MLD(\mathbf{H})$, where EI defined in Eq. (11) and EI_W are equal.

11. By dividing n by k we assume that the number of individuals in each row is the same and equal to n/k.

12. Note that the effort inequality may be also expressed, using the distribution $\mathbf{H}_B^{Ante}$, as $EI_B^{Ante} = 1 - MLD(\mathbf{H}_B^{Ante})/MLD(\mathbf{H})$, where EI^{Ante} given in Eq. (18) and EI_B^{Ante} are equal.

13. A turning point, in this context, refers to the age at which the derivative of the probability distribution changes sign. In our case, the turning points refer to the ages at the maximum and minimum points of the individual's education and his or her smoking behaviour's distributions respectively.

14. The coefficients of the circumstances are obtained from the health regression taking into account also the age variable as one of the explanatory variables. However, for the health matrix, we have excluded the age from the distribution of the individual circumstances, since otherwise the results of the inequality decomposition lose value due to the great influence of the age variable on the health inequality. In that way, age is taken into account indirectly, ensuring that the associations of the individual circumstances are calculated given his or her age.

15. Jackknife is similar to bootstrapping and used in statistical inference to estimate the standard error of a statistic, when a random sample of observations is used to calculate it. The basic idea behind the Jackknife approach lies in systematically recomputing the statistic estimate when one leaves out one observation at a time from the sample of observations.

ACKNOWLEDGEMENT

I gratefully thank Jacques Silber for his very useful suggestions.

REFERENCES

Bourguignon, F., Ferreira, F. H. G., & Menendez, M. (2007). Inequality of opportunity in Brazil. *Review of Income and Wealth, 53*(4), 585–618.

Checchi, D., & Peragine, V. (2010). Inequality of opportunity in Italy. *Journal of Economic Inequality, 8*(4), 429–450.

Ferreira, F. H. G., & Gignoux, J. (2011). The measurement of inequality of opportunity: Theory and an application to Latin America. *Review of Income and Wealth, 57*(4), 622–657.

Fleurbaey, M. (2011). Four approaches to equal opportunity. In C. Knight & Z. Stemplowska (Eds.), *Responsibility and distributive justice*. USA: Oxford University Press. Chapter 3.

Fleurbaey, M., & Schokkaert, E. (2009). Unfair inequalities in health and health care. *Journal of Health Economics, 28*, 73–90.

Foster, J. E., & Shneyerov, A. A. (2000). Path independent inequality measures. *Journal of Economic Theory, 91*, 199–222.

Gourieroux, C., Monfort, A., Renault, E., & Trognon, A. (1987). Generalised residuals. *Journal of Econometrics, 34*(1–2), 5–32.

Kranich, L. (1996). Equitable opportunities: An axiomatic approach. *Journal of Economic Theory*, *71*, 132–147.

Lefranc, A., Pistolesi, N., & Trannoy, A. (2009). Equality of opportunity: Definitions and testable conditions, with an application to income in France. *Journal of Public Economics*, *93*, 1189–1207.

Li Donni, P., Peragine, V., & Pignataro, G. (2013). Ex-ante and ex-post measurement of equality of opportunity in health: A normative decomposition. *Health Economics*. doi: 10.1002/hec.2908

Malmusi, D., Borrell, C., & Benach, J. (2010). Migration-related health inequalities: Showing the complex interactions between gender, social class and place of origin. *Social Science & Medicine*, *71*(9), 1610–1619.

Ooghe, E., Schokkaert, E., & Van de gaer, D. (2007). Equality of opportunity versus equality of opportunity sets. *Social Choice and Welfare*, *28*, 209–230.

Paes de Barros, R., Ferreira, F. H. G., Vega, J. R. M., & Chanduvi, J. S. (2008a). *Measuring inequality of opportunities in Latin America and the Caribbean*. Washington, DC: The World Bank.

Peragine, V. (2004a). Measuring and implementing equality of opportunity for income. *Social Choice and Welfare*, *22*, 1–24.

Peragine, V. (2004b). Ranking income distributions according to equality of opportunity. *Journal of Economic Inequality*, *2*(1), 11–30.

Roemer, J. E. (1998). *Equality of opportunity*. Cambridge: Harvard University Press.

Rosa Dias, P. (2009). Inequality of opportunity in health: Evidence from a UK cohort study. *Health Economics*, *18*, 1057–1074.

Rosa Dias, P. (2010). Modelling opportunity in health under partial observability of circumstances. *Health Economics*, *19*, 252–264.

Trannoy, A., Tubeuf, S., Jusot, F., & Devaux, M. (2010). Inequality of opportunities in health in France: A first pass. *Health Economics*, *19*(8), 921–938.

Tubeuf, S., & Jusot, F. (2011). Social health inequalities among older Europeans: The contribution of social and family background. *The European Journal of Health Economics: HEPAC*, *12*(1), 61–77.

Van de gaer, D. (1993). *Equality of opportunity and investment in human capital*. Ph.D. dissertation, Katholieke Universiteit Leuven.

Zheng, B. (2011). A new approach to measure socioeconomic inequality in health. *Journal of Economic Inequality*, *9*(4), 555–577.

APPENDIX A: LOGIT REGRESSION – DEPENDENT VARIABLE: ATTAINMENT OF, AT LEAST, ONE ACADEMIC QUALIFICATION

Explanatory Variable	Coefficient	Std. Error	Wald[a]	Sig.
Gender[b]	−0.044	0.075	0.335	0.563
Age	0.191	0.017	124.120	0.000
Square of age	−0.002	0.000	107.184	0.000
Father's years of education[c]	0.175	0.012	202.499	0.000
Father's country of birth: Israel[d]	0.546	0.136	16.162	0.000
Father's country of birth: Europe or America	0.568	0.129	19.365	0.000
Jewish[e]	−0.225	0.237	0.898	0.343
Jewish Israel[f]	0.451	0.196	5.277	0.022
Jewish Europe or America	0.444	0.219	4.100	0.043
Constant	−7.784	0.464	281.029	0.000

Note: Number of observations: 3,553; pseudo R-square: 0.174; log-likelihood: −2,080.893 (The log likelihood reflects how likely it is (the odds) that the observed values of the dependent variable may be predicted from the observed values of the independent variables.)

[a]This is the Wald chi-square test that tests the null hypothesis that the coefficient (parameter) equals 0. This hypothesis is rejected when the *p*-value (listed in the column called 'Sig.') is smaller than the critical *p*-value of 0.05 (or 0.01).

[b]The gender variable is equal to 1 if the individual reports being a male.

[c]Father's years of education is a variable which is equal to 8 for elementary school, 12 for secondary school (whether he received a matriculation certificate or not), 14 for post-secondary education but non-academic certificate, 15 for BA (academic certificate or similar certificate), 17 for MA, MD or similar certificate and the highest value of 21 for PhD or similar certificate.

[d]For the father's country of birth there are two dummy variables – one which is equal to 1 when the father was born in Israel and another which is equal to 1 when the father was born in Europe or America. The excluded categories refer to cases where the father was born in Asia or Africa.

[e]The religion variable is equal to 1 if the individual is Jewish. The excluded categories refer to individuals who are Muslim, Christian, Druze or atheist.

[f]For the product of an individual's country of birth by his or her religion there are two dummy variables – one which is equal to 1 if the individual is Jewish and was born in Israel and another which is equal to 1 if he or she is a Jewish and was born in Europe or America. The excluded categories refer to Jews who were born in Asia or Africa and non-Jews.

APPENDIX B: LOGIT REGRESSION – DEPENDENT VARIABLE: PROFESSIONAL OR MANAGERIAL JOB

Explanatory Variable	Coefficient	Std. Error	Wald	Sig.
Gender	−0.122	0.079	2.381	0.123
Age	0.021	0.017	1.537	0.215
Square of age	0.000	0.000	1.247	0.264
Father's years of education	0.023	0.012	3.452	0.063
Father's country of birth: Israel	0.393	0.136	8.410	0.004
Father's country of birth: Europe or America	0.277	0.131	4.473	0.034
Jewish	0.680	0.234	8.410	0.004
Jewish Israel	−0.096	0.183	0.274	0.601
Jewish Europe or America	−0.348	0.210	2.760	0.097
Residuals: Education equation[a]	0.151	0.086	3.053	0.081
Constant	−2.149	0.449	22.925	0.000

Note: Number of observations: 3,015; pseudo R-square: 0.015; log-likelihood: −1,882.59.

[a]The estimated residual of the education equation is computed using the following formula: $Education_i - (1/(1 + e^{-\hat{Education}_i}))$ where $Education_i$, the individual education level, is a binary variable equal to 1 when the individual has an academic education (BA, MA or PhD) and to 0 otherwise; $\hat{Education}_i$ is the estimated education level of the individual, and is equal to the sum of the multiplications of the explanatory variables by their coefficients in the education regression.

APPENDIX C: LOGIT REGRESSION – DEPENDENT VARIABLE: NON-SMOKER STATUS

Explanatory Variable	Coefficient	Std. Error	Wald	Sig.
Gender	−0.633	0.088	51.166	0.000
Age	−0.058	0.020	8.079	0.004
Square of age	0.001	0.000	16.550	0.000
Father's years of education	0.003	0.014	0.054	0.815
Father's country of birth: Israel	0.575	0.146	15.445	0.000
Father's country of birth: Europe or America	0.520	0.143	13.165	0.000
Jewish	1.045	0.253	17.079	0.000
Jewish Israel	−0.281	0.207	1.845	0.174
Jewish Europe or America	−0.585	0.241	5.888	0.015
Residuals: Education equation	0.753	0.104	52.888	0.000
Residuals: Occupation equation[a]	0.045	0.095	0.226	0.635
Constant	1.091	0.508	4.622	0.032

Note: Number of observations: 3,015; pseudo R-square: 0.106; log-likelihood: −1,568.147.

[a]The estimated residual of the occupation equation is computed on the basis of the following formula: $Occupation_i - (1/(1 + e^{-\hat{Occupation}_i}))$, where $Occupation_i$, the individual occupation, is a binary variable which is equal to 1 if an individual reports having a professional or managerial occupation and to 0 otherwise; $\hat{Occupation}_i$ is the estimated occupation of the individual, and is equal to the sum of the multiplications of the explanatory variables by their coefficients in the occupation regression, including also the estimated residual from the education equation.

APPENDIX D: ORDERED LOGIT REGRESSION – DEPENDENT VARIABLE: GOOD OR VERY GOOD SELF-ASSESSED HEALTH

Explanatory Variable	Coefficient	Std. Error	Wald	Sig.
Gender	0.351	0.074	22.460	0.000
Age	−0.024	0.016	2.233	0.135
Square of age	0.000	0.000	4.319	0.038
Father's years of education	0.023	0.012	3.685	0.055
Father's country of birth: Israel	0.611	0.139	19.449	0.000
Father's country of birth: Europe or America	0.129	0.125	1.076	0.300
Jewish	1.080	0.211	26.228	0.000
Jewish Israel	0.440	0.166	7.074	0.008
Jewish Europe or America	−0.692	0.193	12.900	0.000
Residuals: Education equation	0.558	0.082	45.913	0.000
Residuals: Occupation equation	0.057	0.079	0.524	0.469
Residuals: No-Smoker equation[a]	0.109	0.088	1.535	0.215

Note: Number of observations: 3,011; pseudo R-square: 0.333; log-likelihood: −2,114.81.

[a] The estimated residual of the no-smoker equation is computed on the basis of the following formula: $NoSmoking_i - (1/(1 + e^{-No\hat{S}moking_i}))$, where $NoSmoking_i$ is a binary variable which is equal to 1 if an individual is not currently a smoker and to 0 otherwise; $No\hat{S}moking_i$ is a variable equal to the sum of the multiplications of the explanatory variables by their coefficients in the no-smoking regression, including also the estimated residuals from the education and occupation equations.

APPENDIX E: BOUNDS OF THE ORDERED CATEGORIES IN THE HEALTH EQUATION

Level of Health	Corresponding Health Status	Coefficient From	Coefficient To	Std. Error	Marginal Percentage[a]
1	Not good at all		−4.417	0.428	3.2%
2	Not so good	−4.417	−2.248	0.423	14.2%
3	Good	−2.248	0.122	0.421	37.9%
4	Very good	0.122		0.000	44.7%

[a] This column shows the proportion of individuals at each level of health.

APPENDIX F: MEAN LOGARITHMIC DEVIATION DECOMPOSITION

Components of the Inequality	Value of the *MLD* index	Conf. Int. Lower Bound (95%)	Conf. Int. Upper Bound (95%)
		Jackknife	
Ex-post approach			
Overall health inequality	0.0455	0.045476	0.045606
Inequality of opportunity	0.0418	0.041753	0.041873
Inequality of responsibility	0.0037	0.0037183	0.003743
Incidence of inequality in health opportunity	0.9181	0.91777	0.91837
Ex-ante approach			
Overall health inequality	0.0455	0.045476	0.045606
Inequality of opportunity	0.04075	0.04072	0.040837
Inequality of responsibility	0.00475	0.0047454	0.0047828
Incidence of inequality in health opportunity	0.8954	0.89499	0.8958

PART IV
EMPIRICAL STUDIES OF HEALTH INEQUALITY

EARLY LIFE CONDITIONS AND LATER LIFE INEQUALITY IN HEALTH

Maarten Lindeboom and Reyn van Ewijk

ABSTRACT

Prenatal exposure to adverse conditions is known to affect health throughout the life span. It has also been shown that health is unevenly distributed at advanced ages. This chapter investigates whether health inequalities at old age may be partially caused by prenatal circumstances. We use a sample of people aged 71−91 from eight European countries and assess how shocks in GDP that occurred while the respondents were still in utero affect four important dimensions of later-life health: cognition, depression, functional limitations, and grip strength. We find that early-life macro-economic circumstances do not affect health at advanced ages, nor do they affect inequalities in health. In additional analyses, we show that the least healthy people may not enter our sample as the probability of dying before reaching age 71 is high, and mortality rates among those who were prenatally exposed to adverse GDP shocks are higher. We conclude that selective mortality may mask effects of early-life circumstances on health and health inequality at old age.

Keywords: Health and inequality; health production; economics of the elderly

JEL classifications: I14; I12; J14

INTRODUCTION

There is a recent and growing literature that links conditions early in life to later-life socio-economic position, health and mortality. It is postulated that exposure to adverse nutritional conditions during pregnancy results in alterations in the development of vital organs and these alterations may be detrimental in the long term as they may increase the risk of chronic diseases (notably cardiovascular diseases, diabetes, and hypertension) later in life. This mainly biological mechanism is also known as the "Fetal Origins Hypothesis" (Godfrey & Barker, 2001). Alternatively, indirect mechanism may be at work. For instance, those exposed to adverse conditions early in life may have worse child health, which may lead to worse educational outcomes and worse health outcomes at adolescent ages when people enter the labor market. This in turn may influence socio-economic position, health, and mortality later in life. See also Kuh and Ben-Shlomo (2004) for more on direct and indirect mechanisms linking early-life conditions and later-life health and socio-economic position. Most findings of the literature point at long-run effects (see for instance the review paper by Almond & Currie, 2011). It is also known that health is unevenly distributed at advanced ages (Manton & Stallard, 1991, Portrait, Lindeboom, & Deeg, 2001) and the above suggests that part of this inequality in health may originate early in life. It is this chapter's aim to further explore this issue.

We examine for a set of eight European countries whether early-life conditions contribute to later-life inequality in health. We proceed in three stages. First, as our sample consists of people age 71 and older, we assess whether mortality before reaching age 71 is affected by early life conditions. If this is the case, this might lead to a bias toward the zero in the subsequent stage of the analyses. Second, we investigate whether in utero conditions causally affect old age measures of mental and physical health. Third, we calculate concentration indices (Kakwani, Wagstaff, & Van Doorslaer, 1997) and look whether these indices are related to early-life conditions. The explicit link between the literature on long-run effects and the literature on health inequalities distinguishes our chapter from previous contributions in the respective fields.

It is difficult to assess causal effects with observational data, mainly because observed associations between indicators of conditions early in life and later-life health (inequality) generally cannot be interpreted as causal. For instance, some studies on long-run effects use birth weight (see Davey Smith, 2005 for an overview) to proxy the intrauterine environment, but there may exist unobserved (biological) factors that both relate birth weight and later-life health and this may confound the results. To be able to detect causal effects one needs independent variation in early life conditions. The approach taken in the more recent literature is to rely on exogenous variation implied by aggregated events that affect the individual environment but that do not directly affect later-life health, other than via the conditions in early childhood. Examples of such approaches are studies that use epidemics (Almond, 2006), month of birth (Doblhammer, 2004), famines (Roseboom et al., 2000), and business cycles (Van den Berg, Lindeboom, & Portrait, 2006). In this chapter we follow the latter approach.

We use individual data from eight countries from the Study of Health, Ageing and Retirement in Europe (SHARE) and link these to macro GDP data at the year of birth of the included cohorts. The cohorts considered in this chapter are all born between 1920 and 1939, a period where social insurance systems were less developed than nowadays and therefore recessions could have a dramatic effect on the individual socio-economic position. Most countries in our sample experienced a boom during this period that ended with a deep recession: the great depression. We consider two mental health and two physical health measures that each measure important dimensions of old age health: cognition, depression, functional limitations, and grip strength. Furthermore, we note that in general, analyses on effects of early-life events on health at advanced ages might be biased by mortality. If early-life events increase mortality rates, then samples of elderly will consist of the relatively healthy survivors, which might mask effects of such events. An additional contribution of this chapter is that we investigate how prenatally experienced GDP shocks affect mortality rates, which gives us a sense of the selectivity of samples of elderly.

This chapter proceeds as follows: the second section describes the data we use in our main analyses. The third section analyzes how mortality rates are affected by prenatal GDP shocks. The fourth section presents the empirical implementation and results of our main analyses on how health and inequality in health at advanced ages are affected by prenatal GDP shocks. The fifth section concludes.

DATA

We link GDP shocks that occurred during the period that people were in utero to their health outcomes at old age. The health outcomes come from the fourth wave of the SHARE. SHARE is a survey that collects detailed information on health and socio-economic variables among a large random sample of people aged 50 or over residing in various European countries (Malter & Börsch-Supan, 2013). We focus on individuals born between 1920 and 1939, who were between 71 and 91 years old at the time of the survey. This period coincides with the inter-bellum, which has the great advantage that no respondents were born or conceived during the world wars, which might have autonomous effects on later-life health that could easily be confounded with effects of GDP shocks. For this reason, we also excluded persons born in 1919, as many of them were conceived during World War I. We identify the country where respondents were born and include only those countries participating in SHARE that had more or less unchanged borders since the time the respondents were born.[1] Our sample includes respondents from Scandinavia (Sweden), Northern Europe (Austria, Belgium, France, the Netherlands, Switzerland) and Southern Europe (Italy and Spain). For these countries we include the primary respondents as well as their partners who were born in the 1920–1939 time period, leading to a total sample size of 9,177.

Our analyses focus on whether poor economic circumstances during the period in utero lead to inequalities in health at old age. We take four health variables that each measure important dimensions of health at old age. First, respondents read a list of 10 words by the interviewer. Immediately after hearing the words, they had to repeat as many of the words as they were able to remember. A few minutes later, and after completing a few other cognitive performance tasks, the respondents had to repeat as many words as possible from the same list again. Our cognitive performance variable is defined as the sum of both tests: learning and delayed recall. It has a minimum value of 0 and a maximum value of 20. Second, depressive symptoms were measured using the EURO-D depression scale (Prince et al., 1999). Respondents reported which of 12 symptoms had been present recently: depression, pessimism, suicidal feelings, feelings of guilt, trouble sleeping, lack of interests, irritability, lack of appetite, fatigue, difficulties concentrating, lack of enjoyment, and tearfulness. After summing up these item scores, the depression scale has a minimum score of 0 and a maximum of 12. Third, respondents reported whether they had limitations with six activities of daily living (dressing, including putting on shoes and socks; walking across a room; bathing or showering; eating, such as cutting up your food; getting in and out of bed; using the toilet, including getting up or down) and they also reported whether they had limitations with seven instrumental activities of daily living (using a map to figure out how to get around in a strange place; preparing a hot meal; shopping for groceries; making telephone calls; taking medications; doing work around the house or garden; managing money, such as paying bills and keeping track of expenses). Our limitations variable is the total number of limitations of either type that respondents reported. Our fourth health variable is grip strength, which is measured by letting respondents squeeze a handle as hard as they can.

For some analyses, we use binary indicators for scoring poorly on the health variables. We define poor scores as having a depression score of 3 or higher, having at least one limitation, and being in the lowest quartile in one's country/sex group for cognitive performance and grip strength. Tables 1 and 2 give means, the ratio of the top and bottom quartile, and the share with a poor score for the eight different countries. The table indicates that there are quite a few differences between the countries. Switzerland and Austria have the highest cognitive scores (8.01 and 7.74 for males, respectively) and Spain the lowest (5.35). France, Italy, and Spain have high depression scores, whereas the Netherlands and Switzerland have low ones. With respect to the physical health measures, the Netherlands, Sweden, and Switzerland do relatively well.

The individual data of the cohorts in our sample are linked to historical GDP data (Bolt & Van Zanden, 2013).[2] To avoid measuring spurious correlations between GDP around birth and later-life health we detrend the series using a Hodrick−Prescott filter with smoothing parameter 500. The resulting deviations from trends in GDP serve as input for our analyses. Fig. 1 presents the GDP data along with the trend for the eight countries in our sample. The figure shows that most countries experience a light upward trend during the period considered. The deviation between the trend and the series shows that most countries experience a boom and a recession. For instance, Austria had a boom for the period 1923−1932 and a subsequent recession from 1932 to 1937. In Belgium similar periods of booms and recession can be identified, but the fluctuations in GDP are clearly less

Table 1. Descriptives of Main Outcome Variables – Females.

		Cognitive Performance	Depressive Symptoms	Limitations	Grip Strength
Austria	Mean (SD)	7.95 (3.68)	2.73 (2.26)	1.24 (2.26)	23.07 (6.74)
	Ratio 75th/25th percentile	2.0	4.0	(*)	1.4
	Share with poor score	26%	31%	42%	26%
Belgium	Mean (SD)	7.1 (3.6)	3.11 (2.26)	1.82 (2.96)	22.13 (5.69)
	Ratio 75th/25th percentile	2.5	5.0	(*)	1.4
	Share with poor score	25%	39%	48%	25%
France	Mean (SD)	6.85 (3.6)	3.49 (2.45)	1.28 (2.45)	21 (6.07)
	Ratio 75th/25th percentile	2.3	2.5	(*)	1.5
	Share with poor score	29%	44%	40%	26%
Italy	Mean (SD)	5.95 (3.59)	3.87 (2.65)	1.60 (2.78)	21.23 (6.14)
	Ratio 75th/25th percentile	2.7	3.0	(*)	1.5
	Share with poor score	28%	51%	44%	26%
Netherlands	Mean (SD)	8.31 (3.57)	2.39 (2.09)	0.88 (1.88)	23.36 (5.25)
	Ratio 75th/25th percentile	1.8	4.0	(*)	1.4
	Share with poor score	29%	26%	34%	31%
Spain	Mean (SD)	4.76 (2.97)	4.42 (2.85)	2.28 (3.59)	18.81 (7)
	Ratio 75th/25th percentile	2.3	3.5	(*)	1.5
	Share with poor score	39%	57%	50%	34%
Sweden	Mean (SD)	8.35 (3.66)	2.57 (2.07)	0.95 (2.28)	23.65 (6.1)
	Ratio 75th/25th percentile	1.8	4.0	(*)	1.4
	Share with poor score	30%	29%	30%	30%
Switzerland	Mean (SD)	8.63 (3.39)	2.40 (1.98)	0.67 (1.88)	22.37 (5.93)
	Ratio 75th/25th percentile	1.8	4.0	(*)	1.4
	Share with poor score	25%	27%	24%	31%
Total	Mean (SD)	7.08 (3.71)	3.22 (2.47)	1.42 (2.68)	21.77 (6.33)
	Ratio 75th/25th percentile	2.21	3.68	(*)	1.44
	Share with poor score	29%	40%	41%	28%

(*), the ratio cannot be calculated since 25th percentile score equals 0.
Poor score: lowest quartile of cognitive performance/grip; strength: 3 or higher on EURO-D depression scale; at least one limitation.

marked as in Austria. The figures show that for most countries the great depression arrived at the start of the 1930s. Exceptions are Italy, where the depression was less pronounced, and Spain, where the start of a recession in 1936 corresponds to the onset of the Spanish civil war. In our analyses we will relate the cyclical values of the GDP that occurred while people were in utero to our four later-life health measures. More specifically, we

Table 2. Descriptives of Main Outcome Variables – Males.

		Cognitive Performance	Depressive Symptoms	Limitations	Grip Strength
Austria	Mean (SD)	7.74 (3.76)	1.98 (2.11)	1.01 (2.36)	36.96 (9.72)
	Ratio 75th/25th percentile	2.0	(*)	(*)	1.4
	Share with poor score	26%	19%	31%	27%
Belgium	Mean (SD)	7.03 (3.45)	2.35 (2.1)	1.18 (2.42)	36.66 (8.11)
	Ratio 75th/25th percentile	1.8	3.0	(*)	1.4
	Share with poor score	34%	23%	36%	26%
France	Mean (SD)	6.49 (3.38)	2.73 (2.18)	0.94 (2.17)	34.79 (8.63)
	Ratio 75th/25th percentile	2.3	4.0	(*)	1.4
	Share with poor score	29%	31%	31%	25%
Italy	Mean (SD)	6.35 (3.59)	2.55 (2.29)	1.07 (2.62)	34.05 (8.94)
	Ratio 75th/25th percentile	2.3	4.0	(*)	1.4
	Share with poor score	33%	28%	26%	27%
Netherlands	Mean (SD)	7.82 (3.31)	1.57 (1.61)	0.53 (1.53)	38.32 (8.04)
	Ratio 75th/25th percentile	1.7	(*)	(*)	1.3
	Share with poor score	35%	14%	20%	27%
Spain	Mean (SD)	5.35 (3.16)	2.54 (2.4)	1.39 (3.16)	31.09 (8.11)
	Ratio 75th/25th percentile	2.7	4.0	(*)	1.5
	Share with poor score	32%	29%	29%	26%
Sweden	Mean (SD)	7.67 (3.28)	1.93 (1.86)	0.86 (2.29)	39.36 (8.6)
	Ratio 75th/25th percentile	1.7	3.0	(*)	1.3
	Share with poor score	34%	19%	26%	27%
Switzerland	Mean (SD)	8.01 (3.24)	1.80 (1.91)	0.43 (1.29)	36.25 (7.55)
	Ratio 75th/25th percentile	1.7	(*)	(*)	1.3
	Share with poor score	31%	16%	20%	25%
Total	Mean (SD)	6.94 (3.52)	2.26 (2.14)	0.97 (2.37)	35.67 (8.81)
	Ratio 75th/25th percentile	2.05	3.65	(*)	1.39
	Share with poor score	32%	23%	28%	26%

(*), the ratio cannot be calculated since 25th percentile score equals 0.
Poor score: lowest quartile of cognitive performance/grip; strength: 3 or higher on EURO-D depression scale; at least one limitation.

define GDP shocks during the period in utero as a weighted mean of the deviation from GDP trend in the year of birth and the deviation in the preceding year to the extent that gestation started in the pre-birth year. We assume a 9 month gestation period for each respondent. Since we know only month of birth, and not day of birth, we assign each respondent a

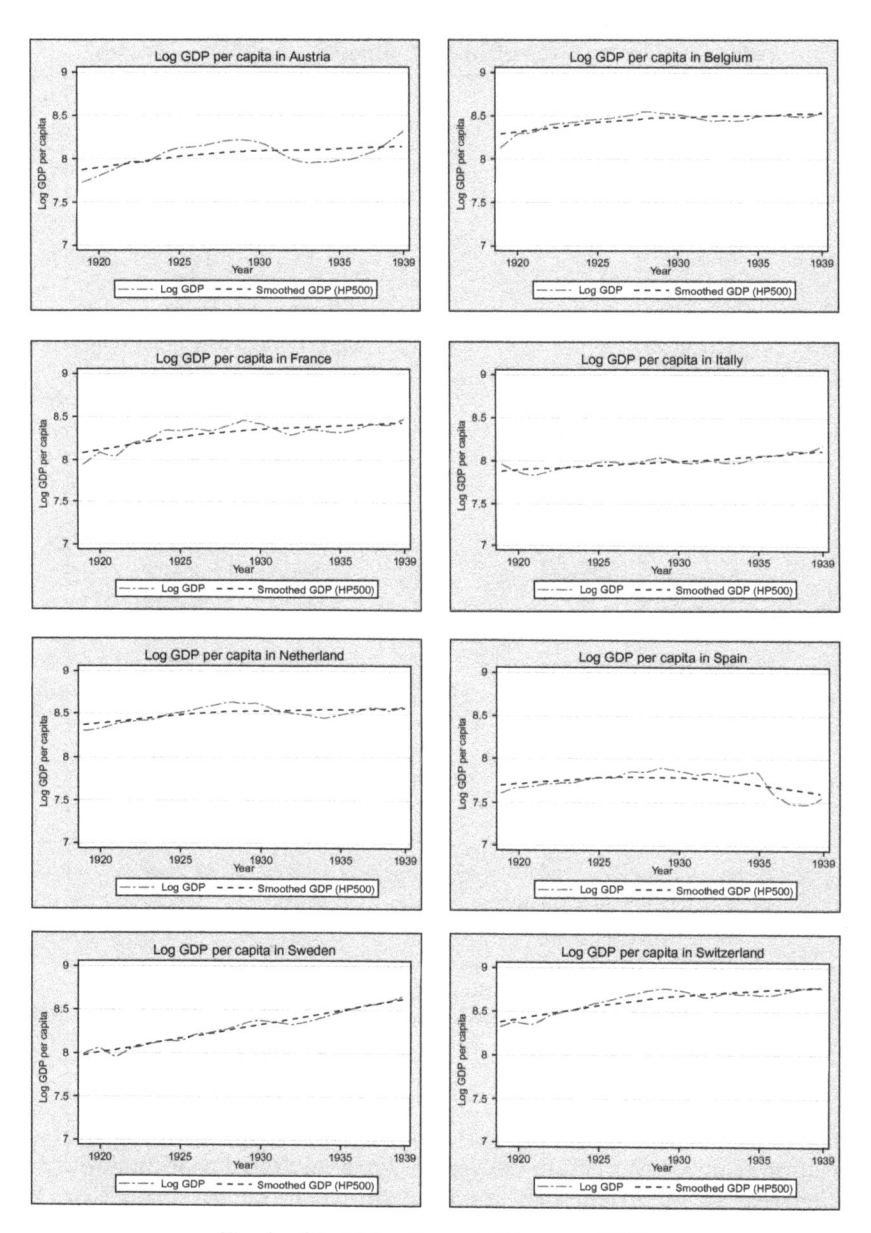

Fig. 1. Hodrick–Prescott filters on GDP.

birth date exactly in the middle of his/her birth month. For instance, for someone born in January, the in utero GDP shock is 8.5, nine times the shock in the pre-birth year, and 0.5, nine times the GDP shock in the year of birth, and analogously for all other birth months. It is important to note that the prenatal shock as defined by our GDP data cannot be strictly interpreted as the effect of economic conditions. This is perhaps best illustrated with the case of Spain, where during the civil war period GDP was substantially lower. As predicted by the "fetal origins hypothesis," stress and instability resulting from both reduced income and war may have impacts on fetal development. The result for Spain is hence relevant in its own right, but as the interpretation of the results for Spain may be somewhat different than for other countries, for all our analyses, we also conduct a version where Spain is excluded.

It should be noted that our sample consists of respondents aged 71–91, so that even if it would be the case that mortality rates before reaching age 71 are unaffected, selective mortality might still lead us to underestimate effects of prenatal circumstances on later-life health if people who are exposed to adverse prenatal conditions are more likely to die between age 71 and 91. For the sample without Spain, we ran additional regressions of the probability of dying between age 71 and 81 on in utero GDP shocks and indeed found suggestive evidence that mortality rates were higher among those who experienced poorer prenatal circumstances.[3]

PRENATAL EVENTS AND MORTALITY

It is important to note that our analyses relate individuals who are currently alive to the conditions they have faced early in life. The same holds for most other papers in this area. For instance, Almond (2006) examines the socio-economic position of older individuals whose mothers have been exposed to the 1918 famine. A similar setup is used by the papers on the Chinese famine (see, e.g., Meng & Qian, 2009) or the famine caused by the Leningrad siege (Stanner et al., 1997). We include cohorts born from 1920 to 1939 and at the time of the survey our respondents were between 71 and 91 years old. In this sample the frail individuals may have died prior to reaching age 71 and as a consequence the resulting sample will consist of the relatively healthy survivors. This selection effect will lead to an underestimation of the long-run effect of in utero exposure to economic shocks on later-life health and health inequality. The selection will also lead to less

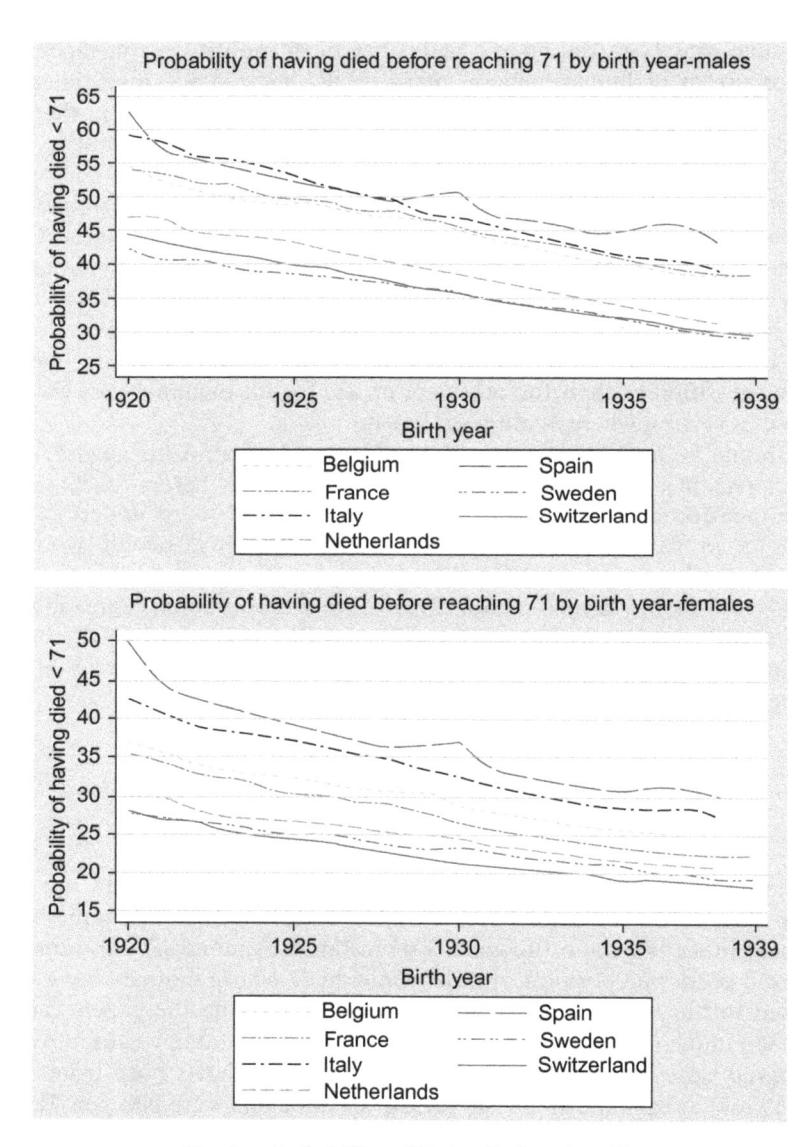

Fig. 2. Probability of Dying Before Age 71.

dispersion in health at advanced ages (i.e., lower values of inequality measures such as the concentration index that we will employ in the third section). To have an idea of the magnitude of these selection effects and whether these effects differ per country, we use the Human Mortality Database (2013) to construct survival probabilities (up to age 71) per country for different birth years. Fig. 2 reports these for men and women.

The most important thing to note from these figures is that mortality rates are substantial and that these can vary considerably across countries and age cohorts. Spain, Belgium, France, and Italy are countries with high mortality rates; Sweden, Switzerland, and the Netherlands have lower mortality rates. The mortality rates imply that for some cohorts more than 50% of the individuals has died before age 71. Note also that there is a clear downward trend in mortality for all countries. This reflects the steady increase in life expectancy in the past decades. For Spain one can see a clear jump in the mortality rates around birth year 1930 and the years of the civil war. The main question here is whether the survival rates vary with the business cycle at birth. A pooled regression of the probability of dying prior to age 71 on the cyclical value of GDP and country-fixed effects indeed indicates that higher cyclical values (booms) are associated with lower probabilities of dying before age 71 (−3.9 percentage points (SE 1.8) for males and −4.4 percentage points (SE 1.7) for females). In additional analyses, where we interacted the cyclical GDP value with country dummies, it is found that the business cycle effect on mortality rates is primarily driven by Spain. Indeed, leaving out Spain from the analyses leads to insignificant effects of the business cycle on death before age 71 (−0.3 percentage points (SE 1.9) for males and −0.5 percentage points (SE 1.7) for females). If Spain's effect is not driven by GDP shocks but by effects of war that are of a different nature, then no effect of GDP in utero on the probability of dying prior to age 71 remains.

EMPIRICAL ANALYSES ON HEALTH AND INEQUALITY IN HEALTH

Empirical Specification

The epidemiological and economic literature on the long-run effects of adverse conditions has revealed effects on socio-economic outcomes (see, e.g., Almond, 2006; Chen & Zhou, 2007), mortality (see, e.g., Doblhammer & Vaupel, 2001, Van den Berg et al., 2006) and health (see for instance the large number of studies about the Dutch Hunger Winter cited in Lumey, Stein, & Susser, 2011). We start our analysis with simple models for the effect of economic conditions on the four health outcomes: low cognition scores, high depressions scores, at least one limitation, and low grip strength. We define GDP shocks during the period in utero as a weighted mean of the deviation from GDP-trend in the year of birth and the deviation in the preceding year, assuming a 9 month gestation period. As we take the binary versions of our health variables, these are linear probability models of the form:

$$y_{ij} = \alpha_j + \beta age_{ij} + \theta GDPut_{ij} + \varepsilon_{ij} \qquad (1)$$

and

$$y_{ij} = \alpha_j + \beta age_{ij} + \sum_j \theta_j GDPut_{ij} + \varepsilon_{ij} \qquad (2)$$

In the second set of regressions, we allow the effect of GDP in utero to differ between countries. We perform Wald tests to test for the equality of these effects between countries. In both specifications, we assume the effect of age on the health outcomes, y, to be the same for each country, j. Note that Fig. 2 seems to indicate that this may indeed be a valid assumption, but as a robustness check, we also estimate models where the age effect is allowed to differ between countries. This does not substantially change the results. We run all regressions separately for males and for females. Note that these regressions are not of prime importance for our main research question, the importance in utero conditions on later life inequality in health. We extend on this below.

The literature on income-related inequity in health care utilization uses extensively the concentration index (Kakwani et al., 1997; Wagstaff, Van Doorslaer, & Watanabe, 2003). By analogy we calculate concentration indices to define inequalities in later-life health that are associated with GDP shocks experienced while being in utero. In our context the concentration curve relates the cumulative proportion of health (vertical axis) to the cumulative proportion of the sample, ranked by the intensity of the GDP shocks experienced in utero (horizontal axis). In Fig. 3 we plot a hypothetical example. The concentration curve (solid line) coincides with the diagonal (dotted line) when there are no health inequalities between

Early Life Conditions and Later Life Inequality in Health 411

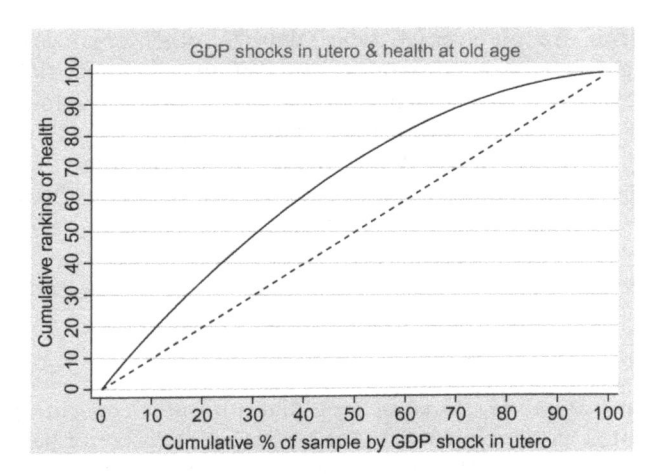

Fig. 3. Hypothetical Example of a Concentration Curve. *Note*: Figure shows the concentration curve (solid line) for a hypothetical country where health is concentrated among people with negative GDP shocks, as can be seen from the fact that the solid line lies above the diagonal (dotted line).

people with different GDP shocks. The farther both lines are away from each other, the greater the inequality related to in utero conditions. If the concentration curve lies above the diagonal, health is concentrated among people with negative GDP shocks; if it is below the diagonal it is concentrated among those with high shocks. The concentration index, C, is defined as twice the area between the curve and the diagonal and has a minimum value of -1 and a maximum value of $+1$ and can be estimated using the convenient regression:

$$2\sigma_{rank}^2 \left(\frac{health_{ij}}{\sum_{i=1}^{N} health_{ij}/N} \right) = \gamma + \delta rank_{ij} + v_{ij} \qquad (3)$$

where $rank_{ij}$ is the fractional rank number for individual i in country j in the distribution of the GDP shocks. δ gives the concentration index; v is an error term. We calculate robust standard errors (O'Donnell, Van Doorslaer, Wagstaff, & Lindelow, 2008). Health is strongly dependent on age in our sample of elderly persons and moreover there may be systematic differences in health outcomes between countries. For instance, grip strength may be higher for Sweden and the Netherlands (Table 2) because individuals in these countries are on average taller than in other countries and grip strength might be correlated with height.[4] We therefore adjust the regressions (3) to specify γ as a function of age and country dummies: $\gamma = \gamma_j + \varphi age_{ij}$. This is effectively indirect standardization of Eq. (3) (O'Donnell et al., 2008). We also estimated versions of our model where we allow the concentration index to differ between countries, so that we estimate:

$$2\sigma^2_{rank}\left(\frac{health_{ij}}{\sum_{i=1}^{N} health_{ij}/N}\right) = \gamma_j + \varphi age_{ij} + \sum_j \delta_j rank_{ij} + v_{ij} \quad (4)$$

From Eqs. (3) and (4) it can be seen that a positive concentration index (δ) is associated with a higher share of health, i.e., that better health is concentrated among those who have experienced, on average, positive GDP shocks in utero. This holds for health scores where higher scores imply a better health (e.g., cognition and grip strength); the reverse holds for health scores where higher scores imply worse health (e.g., depressive symptoms and limitations).

RESULTS

The results of the simple models for the effect of economic conditions on our four health outcomes are reported in Table 3. All outcome variables are binary and for all outcomes a positive coefficient implies a higher probability of observing the outcome for individuals with high GDP shocks and a negative coefficient the opposite. The first row of Table 3 presents the coefficients of a pooled regression, where the effect of the GDP cycle is assumed to be constant (Eq. (1)). None of the coefficients is statistically significant at the standard levels, indicating that being exposed in utero to economic upturns or downturns does not affect any of our four health outcomes. This contrasts with the findings of the previous epidemiological literature where long-run effects of in utero exposure to adverse conditions were found to impact the prevalence of chronic conditions. What distinguishes our study from the previous ones is that our sample is relatively old. A substantial share of the findings in the literature come from the studies on the Dutch Hunger Winter (see Lumey et al., 2011), where prevalence of certain conditions is only established for individuals younger than 60. Our sample consists of individuals aged between 71 and 91 and as we have seen in Fig. 2, of these cohorts up to 60% has already died. This leads to an overrepresentation of the relatively healthy individuals in our sample and thus to an underestimate of the true effect of in utero exposure to economic shocks on later-life health. Table 3 also contains country-specific results (estimates of Eq. (2)). These regressions corroborate the previous results. Some of these coefficients are larger than others and in some occasions even significant. It has to be noted, however, that such cases are rare and that with 68 coefficients, at a 5% significant level, these could equally well be a result of chance.

Table 4 reports estimates of the coefficient δ of Eqs. (3) and (4): the concentration indices for the (in)equality in later-life health associated with GDP shocks in utero. As in Table 3, the first row presents the results from a pooled regression, where δ is assumed to be constant across all countries (Eq. (3)). The lower panel presents the country-specific indices (Eq. (4)). All health variables represent scores. For cognitive performance and grip strength, higher values of the score are associated with better health and a *positive* coefficient means that good health is concentrated among those born in good economic times. For depressive symptoms and limitations, higher scores are associated with worse health outcomes, and consequently a *negative* coefficient δ means that good health is concentrated among those born in good economic times.

A first glance at the table indicates that in general the value of the concentration indices is rather small. This is not uncommon in such studies. For instance, Van Doorslaer, Koolman, and Puffer (2002) find similar sized concentration indices (with respect to income-related inequality, need, and equity) (see, e.g., Van Doorslaer et al., 2002, Table 10, p. 235). It is interesting to note that in the first row, for women, the standard errors are generally smaller, implying larger t-statistics. This results in a significant positive concentration index for cognitive performance and a non-negligible negative effect of limitations (t-stat is 1.6) for women. Note that female selection effects are also smaller than for males (see Fig. 2). Both estimates imply that better health outcomes are concentrated among those who have been exposed to favorable conditions in utero.

The country-specific concentration indices give a more varied picture, but only a few of the coefficients are significantly different from zero. Some significant coefficients are in the expected direction. For instance, Austrian females have a positive concentration index for cognitive performance, Swiss males and Spanish women a negative concentration index for limitations and Dutch women a positive concentration index for grip strength.

Table 3. The Effect of GDP Cycle on Various Health Measures: Results from Linear Probability Models

	Low Cognition		High Depression Score		At Least One Limitation		Low Grip Strength	
	Males	Females	Males	Females	Males	Females	Males	Females
All countries	0.070 (0.114)	−0.099 (0.097)	0.044 (0.107)	0.045 (0.106)	0.066 (0.109)	−0.099 (0.102)	0.009 (0.111)	−0.108 (0.103)
All countries without Spain	0.110 (0.132)	−0.069 (0.109)	0.054 (0.122)	0.164 (0.121)	0.127 (0.126)	−0.005 (0.116)	0.089 (0.129)	−0.058 (0.118)
Austria	−0.001 (0.183)	−0.113 (0.149)	0.169 (0.171)	0.028 (0.163)	0.136 (0.175)	−0.089 (0.158)	0.284 (0.181)	0.016 (0.161)
Belgium	−0.317 (0.478)	−0.251 (0.391)	−0.635 (0.443)	0.382 (0.426)	−0.165 (0.454)	0.504 (0.411)	0.078 (0.448)	0.047 (0.404)
France	0.683* (0.303)	0.066 (0.238)	0.140 (0.286)	0.299 (0.262)	0.298 (0.288)	0.079 (0.251)	−0.584* (0.295)	0.103 (0.258)
Italy	0.801 (0.563)	0.071 (0.577)	1.133* (0.524)	−0.152 (0.633)	0.633 (0.540)	−0.160 (0.609)	0.383 (0.551)	−0.289 (0.636)
Netherlands	−0.332 (0.453)	−0.222 (0.407)	−0.493 (0.424)	0.334 (0.449)	−0.326 (0.439)	0.043 (0.433)	0.677 (0.431)	−0.831+ (0.426)
Spain	−0.036 (0.220)	−0.159 (0.195)	0.029 (0.207)	−0.240 (0.212)	−0.112 (0.210)	−0.416* (0.204)	−0.219 (0.209)	−0.241 (0.203)
Sweden	1.201 (0.761)	0.124 (0.770)	−0.581 (0.701)	0.002 (0.844)	1.452* (0.719)	−0.227 (0.816)	−0.877 (0.706)	−0.253 (0.798)
Switzerland	−0.838+ (0.485)	−0.093 (0.422)	−0.495 (0.449)	0.275 (0.460)	−0.707 (0.465)	0.111 (0.447)	0.014 (0.452)	−0.314 (0.423)
p Equal coefficient	0.063+	0.995	0.145	0.764	0.187	0.605	0.097+	0.642
Sample size	3950	4879	3924	4866	4082	5031	3681	4296

+ $p < 0.10$; * $p < 0.05$; ** $p < 0.01$.
Table shows regression coefficients, and standard errors (in parentheses) of OLS regressions of the outcome variable on age, country-fixed effects, and GDP shock in utero.

Low cognition: being in the lowest quartile within country * sex combination.
High depression score: scoring 3 or higher on the EURO-D depression scale.
Having at least one limitation with activities of daily living or with instrumental activities of daily living.
Low grip strength: being in the lowest quartile within country * sex combination.

Table 4. Concentration Indices for the (In)equality in Later Life Health due to GDP Shocks In Utero.

	Cognitive Performance		Depressive Symptoms		Limitations		Grip Strength	
	Male	Female	Male	Female	Male	Female	Male	Female
All countries	−0.004	0.008*	0.003	0.009	−0.012	−0.024	−0.002	0.003
	(0.005)	(0.004)	(0.009)	(0.006)	(0.023)	(0.015)	(0.002)	(0.003)
All countries without Spain	−0.004	0.007+	0.001	0.013+	0.013	0.003	−0.002	0.001
	(0.005)	(0.004)	(0.010)	(0.007)	(0.025)	(0.017)	(0.002)	(0.003)
Austria	0.000	0.013+	0.009	0.003	−0.032	−0.017	−0.005	0.001
	(0.010)	(0.007)	(0.017)	(0.011)	(0.044)	(0.023)	(0.005)	(0.005)
Belgium	0.002	0.001	−0.043	0.039*	−0.036	0.101+	0.003	−0.008
	(0.015)	(0.014)	(0.028)	(0.019)	(0.078)	(0.058)	(0.007)	(0.007)
France	−0.015	−0.002	0.013	0.017	0.095+	−0.022	0.006	−0.003
	(0.010)	(0.009)	(0.023)	(0.015)	(0.055)	(0.031)	(0.005)	(0.006)
Italy	−0.021	0.026	0.064+	−0.006	0.111	−0.010	−0.010	0.004
	(0.018)	(0.019)	(0.035)	(0.031)	(0.082)	(0.067)	(0.009)	(0.012)
Netherlands	0.006	0.023	−0.034	0.011	−0.065	−0.040	−0.013*	0.016*
	(0.015)	(0.016)	(0.025)	(0.021)	(0.045)	(0.040)	(0.006)	(0.008)
Spain	−0.004	0.011	0.017	−0.001	−0.079	−0.098*	−0.001	0.009
	(0.009)	(0.008)	(0.022)	(0.017)	(0.056)	(0.040)	(0.004)	(0.006)
Sweden	−0.016	−0.004	−0.043	0.018	0.260*	0.102	−0.011	0.008
	(0.018)	(0.024)	(0.042)	(0.031)	(0.110)	(0.066)	(0.011)	(0.013)
Switzerland	0.012	−0.003	−0.031	0.015	−0.212**	−0.042	0.002	0.007
	(0.016)	(0.015)	(0.027)	(0.020)	(0.046)	(0.046)	(0.007)	(0.008)
p Equal coefficient	0.738	0.676	0.143	0.805	<0.001**	0.085+	0.299	0.329
Sample size	3950	4879	3924	4866	4082	5031	3681	4296

+p <0.10; *p < 0.05; **p < 0.01.
Table shows concentration indices, and standard errors in parentheses. Concentration index regressions control for age. For cognitive performance and grip strength, higher scores indicate better health and a positive concentration index score means that good health is concentrated among people with positive average GDP shocks in utero. For depressive symptoms and limitations, higher scores indicate worse health and a negative concentration index means that bad health is concentrated among people with positive average GDP shocks in utero.

Others have unexpected signs, such as the negative coefficient for males for grip strength of Dutch males. This implies that worse (better) grip strength is concentrated among those who have been exposed to good (bad) in utero conditions. Given the number of coefficients that we estimate, this result might be due to chance. For Swedish males we find a similar effect for limitations, but this effect is much larger than the other coefficients in the table. Sweden has in general little variation in the health outcomes (see, e.g., the 75th/25th percentile ratios in Table 2) and relatively small fluctuations in GDP (see Fig. 1), and it may be that it is difficult to separate age effects from the rank effect in such regressions.

We estimated similar regressions in which we allowed the effect of age to differ between countries. This may not aid in the separation of the age effect from the GDP effect, but it at least allows for differential age effects across countries. These regression results also confirm our findings. It could be that mean scores are not picking up relevant differences between individuals. We therefore also repeated the analyses in which we use the binary versions of the health variables instead of the continuous scores. This also did not change our main findings. As indicated earlier, our findings may be affected by the age of the cohorts that we consider. The cohorts are aged between 71 and 91 and a substantial part of the cohorts have already died (cf. Fig. 2). This selective mortality will reduce the inequality in the distribution of health at advanced ages and therefore also the role of any factor that may influence later-life inequality in health. Alternatively, it may be that our measure of exposure (the business cycle) does not have sufficient 'bite' to influence later-life health outcomes. Indeed, epidemiological and economic studies have found some effects of famines on later-life morbidity, mortality, and socio-economic status (e.g., Chen & Zhou, 2007; Meng & Qian, 2009; Lindeboom, Portrait, & Van den Berg et al., 2010), but these conditions are generally worse than deviations from the trend in GDP. However, the time period includes the great depression, a period with massive unemployment and poverty. Indeed, Van den Berg, Portrait, Lindeboom, and Deeg (2010) also exploit business cycles in the 1920s and 1930s to look at the effect of life events on later-life cognition and find effects. It has to be noted that in their study the individuals are generally slightly younger, but this also indicates that variation in the business cycle can have an effect on later life health of the survivors in the cohorts. Finally, fertility patterns may also change over the business cycle (see, for instance, Deheija & Lleras-Muney, 2004). In our case it may explain the absence of finding strong effects if those born in recessions are generally from families with a higher socio-economic background. Indeed, Deheija and Lleras-Muney find that infant mortality decreases during recessions and that this may be due to the fact that parents of higher socio-economic status get more children than those of lower socio-economic status. In our application this may give a further downward bias to our results over and above the effect of selective mortality. Unfortunately we cannot check this with our data as this requires individual data about the socio-economic status of the parents of the respondents in our sample.

CONCLUSIONS

We examine for a set of eight European countries whether early-life conditions contribute to later-life inequality in health. We proceed in three stages. First, we analyze whether early-life conditions affect mortality rates, which might lead to a bias toward the zero in the second and third stage of the analyses. In the second stage, we assess whether early childhood conditions causally affect old age measures of mental and physical health. Finally, in our main analysis we calculate concentration indices (Kakwani et al., 1997) and examine whether these indices are related to early-life conditions. We follow the literature on the long-run effects of childhood conditions and instrument these conditions with more aggregate events. Using a more aggregate measure that cannot be influenced by individual decisions facilitates the assessment of causal effects on later-life outcomes. Here we use the state of the business cycle as measured by the cyclical deviation from the trend of GDP. We use the fourth wave of the SHARE data of eight European countries and select respondents who have been born in the inter-bellum, i.e., the years 1920–1939, that includes the great depression. We link these data to yearly GDP data and estimate models that relate the cognition, depression, functional limitations, and grip strength to macroeconomic conditions at the time that the individual was in utero. We use the method suggested by Kakwani et al. (1997) to derive concentration indices for the (in)equality in later-life health due to GDP shocks in utero. We find in general small or no significant effects of GDP shocks in utero on later-life inequality in health. We conclude that selective mortality that is particularly important for our cohorts of individuals born between 1920 and 1939 (and who are at the time of the interview between the ages of 71 and 91) may mask long-run effects on later-life inequality.

NOTES

1. Poland, Slovenia, Estonia, the Czech Republic, and Germany were excluded for this reason.
2. See http://www.ggdc.net/MADDISON/Historical_Statistics/vertical-file_02-2010.xls
3. Note that our data do not allow us to estimate similar regressions on the probability of dying between age 71 and 91, as we have too few cohorts in our data that have already reached age 91.
4. Alternatively, it could be the case that these countries have experienced less fluctuations in GDP and that therefore average grip strength is higher in these countries. This could imply that part of the GDP cycle effect may be picked up by country effects when these are included in the regressions.

ACKNOWLEDGMENTS

This chapter uses data from SHARE wave 4 release 1, as of November 30, 2012. The SHARE data collection has been primarily funded by the European Commission through the 5th Framework Programme (project QLK6-CT-2001-00360 in the thematic programme Quality of Life) through the 6th Framework Programme (projects SHARE-I3, RII-CT-2006-062193, COMPARE, CIT5-CT-2005-028857, and SHARELIFE, CIT4-CT-2006-028812) and through the 7th Framework Programme (SHARE-PREP, N° 211909, SHARE-LEAP, N° 227822 and SHARE M4, N° 261982). Additional funding from the U.S. National Institute on Aging (U01 AG09740-13S2, P01 AG005842, P01 AG08291, P30 AG12815, R21 AG025169, Y1-AG-4553-01, IAG BSR06-11 and OGHA 04-064) and the German Ministry of Education and Research as well as from various national sources is gratefully acknowledged (see www.share-project.org for a full list of funding institutions).

REFERENCES

Almond, D. (2006). Is the 1918 influenza pandemic over? Long-term effects of in-utero influenza exposure in the post-1940 US population. *Journal of Political Economy, 114*, 672–712.

Almond, D., & Currie, J. (2011). Killing me softly: The fetal origins hypothesis. *The Journal of Economic Perspectives, 25*(3), 153–172.

Bolt, J., & Van Zanden, J. L. (2013). *The first update of the Maddison Project: Re-estimating growth before 1820*. Maddison Project Working Paper 4. University of Groningen, The Netherlands.

Chen, Y., & Zhou, L. (2007). The long-term health and economic consequences of the 1959–1961 famine in China. *Journal of Health Economics, 26*, 659–681.

Davey Smith, G. (2005). Epidemiological Freudianism. *International Journal of Epidemiology, 34*, 1–2.

Deheija, R., & Lleras-Muney, A. (2004). Booms, busts and babies health. *Quarterly Journal of Economics, 119*, 1091–1130.

Doblhammer, G. (2004). *The late life legacy of very early life. Demographic research monographs*. Rostock: Max Planck Institute for Demographic Research, ISSN: 1613-5220.

Doblhammer, G., & Vaupel, J. W. (2001). Lifespan depends on month of birth. *Proceedings of the National Academy of Sciences, 98*(5), 2934–2939.

Godfrey, K. M., & Barker, D. J. P. (2001). Fetal programming and adult health. *Public Health Nutrition, 4*, 611–624.

Human Mortality Database. (2013). University of California, Berkeley (USA), and Max Planck Institute for Demographic Research (Germany). Retrieved from www.mortality.org or www.humanmortality.de. Data downloaded on March 4, 2013.

Kakwani, N., Wagstaff, A., & Van Doorslaer, E. (1997). Socioeconomic inequalities in health: Measurement, computation, and statistical inference. *Journal of Econometrics, 77*(1), 87–103.

Kuh, D., & Ben-Shlomo (Eds.). (2004). *A life course approach to chronic disease epidemiology.* New York: Oxford University Press; 1997.

Lindeboom, M., Portrait, F., & Van den Berg, G. J. (2010). Long-run effects on longevity of a nutritional shock early in life: The Dutch potato famine of 1846–1847. *Journal of Health Economics, 29*(5), 617–629. Elsevier.

Lumey, L. H., Stein, A. D., & Susser, E. (2011). Prenatal famine and adult health. *Annual Review of Public Health, 32*, 24.1–24.26.

Malter, F., & Börsch-Supan, A. (Eds.), (2013). SHARE Wave 4: Innovations & methodology. MEA, Max Planck Institute for Social Law and Social Policy, Munich.

Manton, K. G., & Stallard, E. (1991). Cross-sectional estimates of active life expectancy for the US elderly and oldest-old populations. *Journal of Gerontology, 46*(3), S170–S182.

Meng, X., & Qian N., (2009). *The long term consequences of famine on survivors: Evidence from a unique natural experiment using China's Great Famine.* NBER Working Paper No. 14917. National Bureau of Economic Research, Cambridge, MA.

O'Donnell, O., Van Doorslaer, E., Wagstaff, A., & Lindelow, M. (2008). *Analyzing health equity using household survey data.* Washington, DC: The World Bank.

Portrait, F., Lindeboom, M., & Deeg, D. (2001). Life expectancies in specific health states – results from a joint model of health status and mortality of older persons. *Demography, 38*, 525–538.

Prince, M. J., Reischies, F., Beekman, A. T., Fuhrer, R., Jonker, C., Kivela, S. L., & Copeland, J. R. (1999). Development of the EURO-D scale – a European Union initiative to compare symptoms of depression in 14 European centres. *The British Journal of Psychiatry, 174*(4), 330–338.

Roseboom, T. J., van der Meulen, J. H., Osmond, C., Barker, D. J., Ravelli, A. C., Schroeder-Tanka, J. M., & Bleker, O. P. (2000). Coronary heart disease after prenatal exposure to the Dutch famine, 1944–45. *Heart, 84*(6), 595–598.

Stanner, S. A., Bulmer, K., Andres, C., Lantseva, O. E., Borodina, V., Poteen, V. V., & Yudkin, J. S. (1997). Does malnutrition in utero determine diabetes and coronary heart disease in adulthood? Results from the Leningrad Siege study, a cross sectional study. *British Medical Journal, 315*(7119), 1342.

Van den Berg, G. J., Lindeboom, M., & Portrait, F. (2006). Economic conditions early in life and individual mortality. *American Economic Review, 96*(1), 290–302.

Van den Berg, G. J., Portrait, F., Lindeboom, M., & Deeg, D. (2010). The role of early life conditions in the cognitive decline due to adverse events. *Economic Journal, 120*, F411–F428.

Van Doorslaer, E., Koolman, X., & Puffer, F. (2002). Equity in the use of physician visits in OECD countries: Has equal treatment for equal need been achieved?. In OECD (Ed.), *Measuring up: Improving health systems performance in OECD countries* (pp. 225–248). Paris: OECD.

Wagstaff, A., Van Doorslaer, E., & Watanabe, N. (2003). On decomposing the causes of health sector inequalities with an application to malnutrition inequalities in Vietnam. *Journal of Econometrics, 112*(1), 207–223.

WEALTH, HEALTH, AND THE MEASUREMENT OF MULTIDIMENSIONAL INEQUALITY: EVIDENCE FROM THE MIDDLE EAST AND NORTH AFRICA

Mohammad Abu-Zaineh and Ramses H. Abul Naga

ABSTRACT

Recent decades have witnessed a rising interest in the measurement of inequality from a multidimensional perspective. This literature has however remained largely theoretical. This chapter presents an empirical application of a recent methodology and in doing so offers practical insights on how multidimensional inequality can be measured over two attributes (wealth and health) in the developing country context. Following Abul Naga and Geoffard (2006), a methodological framework allowing the decomposition of multidimensional inequality into two univariate Atkinson–Kolm–Sen equality indices and a third term measuring the association between the attributes is implemented. The methodology is then illustrated using data from the World Health Surveys 2002−2003. Specifically, this study presents the first comparative analysis on multidimensional inequality for a set of Middle East and North African (MENA) countries. Results reveal that the multidimensional (in-)equality indices tend to mimic the (in-)equality ordering of the wealth distributions as the latter are always less equally distributed than health. An empirical conclusion that emerges is that reducing the correlation between the attributes may help to reduce overall welfare inequality, specifically when socioeconomic inequality in health is pro-poor. The finding that the correlation between attributes has a significant contribution in the quantification of inequality has important policy implications since it reveals that it is not only wealth and health inequalities *per se that matter in the measurement of welfare inequality but also the associations between them.*

Keywords: Health; wealth; welfare; multidimensional inequalities; aversion to correlation increasing transformations; developing countries

JEL classifications: D31; D63; D71; D78; I31

INTRODUCTION

Perhaps the most commonly cited development indicator to date is GDP per capita. Yet this measure of average income neglects distributional aspects. Since, it is unlikely that two distributions exhibiting an identical average income will also be identically distributed, one cannot convert average income to aggregate social welfare via a functional relation; specifically, the distribution with the greater level of equality will entail a higher level of welfare. The 1970s and 1980s have thus witnessed a great interest in the measurement of income inequality and social welfare (Atkinson, 1970; Atkinson & Bourguignon, 1982; Sen, 2000).

More recently, however, there has been a rising interest in the measurement and explanation of socioeconomic inequality and social welfare from a multidimensional perspective (Bleichrodt & van Doorslaer, 2006). Following the pioneering contributions of Sen (1973), Kolm (1977), Atkinson and Bourguignon (1982), Massoumi (1986), Tsui (1995, 1999), Duclos, Sahn, and Younger (2011), the underlying theoretical foundation of multivariate inequality analysis are now well-established (Bourguignon, 1999). Yet, as far as empirical analysis is concerned, several interesting practical questions arise. These are related to the applicability of the proposed multidimensional inequality indices, particularly, in the case where one of the attributes in question may pertain to health — a concept the accumulation of which is mainly governed by biological laws in addition to a variety of lifestyle variables as well as access to health care — while the other relates to wealth — a concept the accumulation of which is largely governed by institutional laws.[1] These questions might take on a particular significance when the subject of empirical investigations is a group of lower-middle income countries.

An attempt to explore the role of health in the context of the multidimensional analysis of the distribution of welfare was undertaken in the Chinese context (Zhong, 2009). However, to our knowledge, there has been hitherto no attempt to explore the applicability of the aforementioned theoretical foundations of multidimensional inequality analysis in the context of cross-country comparative analyses. This study attempts, therefore, to fill this gap with the aim of illustrating how multidimensional inequality relates to wealth inequality in practice. The study presents the first comparative analysis on the assessment of multidimensional inequality for a set of countries belonging to the Middle East and North Africa region (hereinafter MENA region). These countries vary in terms of their income levels — ranging from low-income countries such as Comoros and Mauritania, to lower-middle-income economies such as Morocco, upper-middle-income countries such as Tunisia, and finally, high-income countries such as the United Arab Emirates. These countries also vary in terms of their demographic structures as well as the health status of their populations and the nature of their health care systems (Bibi & Nabili, 2010).

Of course, contrasted evolutions between these countries can be related to the significant differences in their epidemiological situations: while infectious diseases remain the main public health problem in low-income countries, with AIDS, tuberculosis, and malaria epidemics leading to a decrease in global life expectancy, in most middle-income countries, the epidemiologic transition versus noncommunicable chronic diseases is already on going, sometimes with a polarization of the epidemiological profiles of the main death causes between the poorest sectors and the rest of the population (Coutts et al., 2013). However, such variations in the socioeconomic, demographic, and morbidity characteristics of the targeted countries, would allow for further methodological improvements that can enrich our empirical analysis of multidimensional inequality in the context of developing countries. Beside the important usefulness that results of the present chapter are expected to have from a policy perspective, the results can also be useful for extracting conclusions with wider international connotations.

Following this line of thought, the present chapter seeks to address the following specific practical questions:

1. When measuring welfare inequality, does the definition of welfare indicators (e.g., wealth versus health) matter?
2. Is the country with less wealth (or income) inequality the one with less health inequality?
3. If not, how do we choose to measure inequality over two attributes? More specifically, should a multidimensional inequality index be sensitive, other things equal, to the correlation between attributes?
4. If the two dimensions of well-being are wealth and health, to which of these two dimensions would a bivariate inequality index be most sensitive?

The method of empirical analysis we adopt follows the framework proposed by Abul Naga and Geoffard (2006). This allows the researcher to decompose a multidimensional inequality index into a function of unidimensional inequality indices as well as a measure of association between the various attributes. The empirical analysis is based on data taken from the World Health Surveys (WHS), collected by the World Health Organization (WHO) during the years 2002 and 2003. The remit of the chapter is organized as follows. The second section defines our basic notation and concepts. The third section presents the family of inequality indices and the decomposition framework of multidimensional inequality which form the theoretical basis of our empirical analysis. The dataset and variable definitions used in the analysis are summarized in the fourth section. Our main empirical findings are presented in the fifth section while the sixth section discusses the results and concludes the chapter with some policy recommendations and directions for further research.

METHOD

For the purpose of our empirical study, we shall consider a population consisting of n individuals. Individual i has resources $x_i = [x_{i1}, x_{i2}]$, where $x_i \in R^2_{++}$. The joint distribution is a matrix $X = \begin{pmatrix} x_1 \\ \vdots \\ x_n \end{pmatrix} \in M^n$, the set of all

$n \times 2$ matrices with strictly positive elements. Accordingly, the jth column of X, X_j, gives a distribution (an $n \times 1$ vector) for the jth attribute in the population, and we also write $X = [X_1 \; X_2]$. To clarify our notation, consider the following two matrices:

$$X = \begin{pmatrix} 2 & 1 \\ 1 & 2 \\ 4 & 5 \end{pmatrix}, \quad Y = \begin{pmatrix} 2 & 2 \\ 1 & 1 \\ 4 & 5 \end{pmatrix} \tag{1}$$

Both X and Y are elements of M^3, and the marginal distributions X_1 and Y_1 are equal, while X_2 and Y_2 are identical up to a single permutation of the elements.

A bidimensional inequality index is a real valued function $I(X)$: $M^n \to R_+$. Underlying I is a *social welfare function* $W(X)$: $M^n \to R_+$. We take $W(.)$ to be the average of individual welfare levels. We also assume that W is continuous, strictly increasing, strictly quasi-concave, and ratio-scale invariant. Following Abul Naga, and Geoffard (2006), we refer to the above five properties of W as *the basic axioms*. The increasing property entails that W satisfies the Pareto principle, while quasi-concavity entails that W satisfies a preference for equality.

Let $\mu \doteq (\mu_1, \mu_2)$ denote the vector of means of the welfare attributes and let $w^o = W(X)$ be the level of welfare attained by X. Then, if $W(.)$ satisfies the basic axioms, following Kolm (1977), we may define a scalar $\theta(X)$ in the unit interval, such that $u(\theta\mu) = (1/n) \sum_{i=1}^{n} u(x_i) = w^o$. Starting from a distribution X, a fraction θ of the sum-total of each attribute would lead to the same level of welfare as X, provided each attribute were equally distributed in the population. Therefore, θ is a measure of equality in X, and

$$I(X) = 1 - \theta(X) \tag{2}$$

is the corresponding welfare inequality index.

We shall consider two generic forms for the underlying utility function pertaining to $W(.)$, namely:

$$u(x_{i1}, x_{i2}) = x_{i1}^{\alpha} x_{i2}^{\beta} \quad \alpha, \beta > 0, \quad \alpha + \beta \leq 1 \tag{3}$$

$$u(x_{i1}, x_{i2}) = x_{i1}^{\alpha} x_{i2}^{\beta} \quad \alpha, \beta < 0 \tag{4}$$

The first of the above utility functions has $u_{12}>0$, while for the second, $u_{12}<0$. To provide some intuition for our empirical results to follow, suppose x_1 is wealth and x_2 is health. Then, with $u_{12}<0$, the marginal utility of wealth is higher for the unhealthy, while for $u_{12}>0$ better health increases the marginal utility of wealth. Returning to the joint distributions X and Y of Eq. (1), we would thus expect $W(X)>W(Y)$ when the underlying utility function is Eq. (4) with a negative cross-derivative, whereas $W(Y)>W(X)$ when social welfare is measured in relation to the utility function (3) where the cross-derivative is positive. For instance, when $\alpha=\beta=0.5$ in Eq. (3), $W(X)=2.43 < W(Y)=2.49$. On the other hand, when $\alpha=\beta=-0.5$ in Eq. (4), $W(X)=-0.55 > W(Y)=-0.57$.

Clearly, if we were to compute separate inequality indices on the marginal distributions we would arrive at the conclusion that X_1 and Y_1 exhibit the same level of inequality, and likewise, X_2 and Y_2 have identical levels of dispersion. The two distributions X and Y however differ in one important respect: Y has been obtained from X via a (single) *correlation increasing transformation* (CIT). Specifically: we have: $y_{11} = \max\{x_{11}, x_{21}\} = 2$, $y_{12} = \max\{x_{12}, x_{22}\} = 2$. Likewise, $y_{21} = \min\{x_{11}, x_{21}\} = 1$, and $y_{22} = \min\{x_{12}, x_{22}\} = 1$. Thus the rank-correlation between the two attributes of well-being was increased in moving from X to Y, though the marginal distributions have remained unchanged.

Assume $W(.)$ satisfies the basic axioms. Atkinson and Bourguignon (1982) show that if in addition W has an aversion for correlation increasing transformations of the data (i.e., *CITs* reduce social welfare) then $u_{12}\leqslant 0$. Thus, for the utility function (4) where $u_{12}\leqslant 0$ the social welfare function is said to satisfy an aversion to correlation increasing transformations.

DECOMPOSITION OF INEQUALITY

In what follows, we shall apply a decomposition of multidimensional inequality introduced by Abul Naga, and Geoffard (2006), that emphasizes the role of the *rank-correlation* between attributes in shaping social value judgments on the underlying level of inequality. Note that other decompositions of multidimensional inequality for cardinal variables such as income and anthropometric measures have been proposed in the literature; for instance Kobus (2012) introduces a strong decomposability property, and characterizes the relevant class of strongly attribute decomposable inequality indices.

Let $\omega = \alpha/(\alpha+\beta)$. The logarithm of the *equality* index $\theta(X)$ underlying Eqs. (3)–(4) was shown by Abul Naga, and Geoffard (2006) to be decomposable in the form

$$\ln \theta(X) = \omega \ln \gamma_1(X_1) + (1-\omega)\ln \gamma_2(X_2) + \frac{1}{\alpha+\beta} \ln \kappa(X) \quad (5)$$

where $\gamma_i(X_i)$ is the Atkinson–Kolm–Sen equality index for attribute i and the function

$$\kappa(X) = \frac{n \sum_{i=1}^{n} x_{i1}^{\alpha} x_{i2}^{\beta}}{\sum_{i=1}^{n} x_{i1}^{\alpha} \sum_{i=1}^{n} x_{i2}^{\beta}} \quad (6)$$

is a measure of association that has the property of being increasing in the *rank-correlation* between the two attributes. For instance, when $\alpha = \beta = -0.5$, we have for the matrices of Eq. (1), $\kappa(X) = 1.0334$, and $\kappa(Y) = 1.0875$. Interestingly, however, in the decomposition (5), $\theta(\cdot)$ is increasing in $\kappa(\cdot)$ when $\alpha, \beta > 0$, but decreasing in κ when α, β are both negative. The parameter ω also finds an intuitive interpretation in the decomposition (5): ω is the elasticity of the equality index in the first attribute with respect to θ. Thus, a 1% increase in equality of the first attribute would result in a ω% increase in the overall multidimensional equality index θ.

Following Zhong (2009), we also note that the index κ can be interpreted as a measure of socioeconomic inequality in health, where a value of 1 captures a situation where each attribute is equally distributed. A value greater than (*less*) 1 of the index κ indicates pro-rich (*pro-poor*) socioeconomic inequality in health. Accordingly, the index κ could be used as an alternative to the Concentration Index in the measurement of socioeconomic related inequality health. Again a simple example can illustrate. Consider the following two distributions:

$$A = \begin{pmatrix} 3 & 1 \\ 1 & 3 \end{pmatrix} \quad B = \begin{pmatrix} 3 & 3 \\ 1 & 1 \end{pmatrix}$$

Clearly, here B is obtained via a correlation increasing transformation of A. Letting α and β both be equal to -1, we have $\kappa(A) = 0.75 < 1 < 1.25 = \kappa(B)$. Also note that resources are equally distributed for $E = \begin{pmatrix} 2 & 2 \\ 2 & 2 \end{pmatrix}$, and there obtains $\kappa(E) = 1$.

Note finally, that the decomposition (5) is easily extended to the context of $p > 2$ attributes. The utility function that generalizes Eq. (4) is of the form $u(x_1,\ldots,x_p) = -x_1^{\alpha_1}\ldots x_p^{\alpha_p}$, where each α_j is strictly smaller than zero. The decomposition now takes the form (see in particular Brambilla & Peluso, 2010)

$$\sum_j \alpha_j \ln \theta = \sum_j \alpha_j \ln \gamma_j + \ln \kappa \qquad (7)$$

$$\kappa(X) = \frac{n^{p-1} \sum_{i=1}^{n} x_{i_1}^{\alpha_1}\ldots x_{i_p}^{\alpha_p}}{\sum_{i=1}^{n} x_{i_1}^{\alpha_1} \ldots \sum_{i=1}^{n} x_{i_p}^{\alpha_p}} \qquad (8)$$

We now turn to our empirical application, where we focus on the case of two specific attributes of well-being, namely wealth and health.

DATA SET AND VARIABLE DEFINITIONS

Our empirical analysis is based on a multi-country dataset drawn from the World Health Survey (WHS). The WHS was undertaken by the World Health Organization (WHO) during the years 2002 and 2003. The WHS is a representative, multiple-topic survey collecting information from the population using a two-stage stratified selection process. Beside the household's socio-demographic and socioeconomic characteristics, the WHS survey provides detailed and comparable data on various health outcomes (e.g., health expenditure, illnesses, coverage, risk factors, etc.) of household adult members (aged 18 years and older) in about 70 countries spreading over all the regions of the world (Üstün et al., 2003). For the purpose of this chapter, an analysis is performed on a sample of five countries belonging to the aforementioned MENA region countries: Morocco ($n = 611$), Tunisia ($n = 1,547$), Mauritania ($n = 1,372$), Comoros ($n = 618$), and United Arab Emirates ($n = 362$). For all countries, the data has been obtained by means of a survey questionnaire with samples being probabilistically selected so that every individual is assigned a known nonzero probability of being selected. The WHS samples are nationally representative and post-stratification corrections are made to sampling weights in order to adjust for the population distribution as per the UN Statistical Division (http://unstats.un.org/unsd/default) and to compensate for nonresponse cases (Moussavi et al., 2007).

This study uses individual-level data. Its target population comprises *adult women of reproductive age* (18–49). It is clear that the relation between height and age differs across sex and meaningful results cannot be obtained by analyzing anthropometric data pertaining to men and women together in one sample. For this reason, the anthropometric data in most developing country surveys are only collected for women in reproductive age, as is the case in the context of our data. As mentioned above, the approach undertaken in this study assumes that individuals' utility (or welfare) is derived from two attributes, namely wealth and health. The WHS offers alternative sources on data upon which a measure of wealth can be constructed; these include the direct measures of living standards: household gross income and gross consumption expenditures. In addition, data on household assets and other characteristics, which can be used to construct alternative (indirect) measures of welfare are also made available. Among these three sources of data, household gross expenditures are generally preferred, relative to data on income and assets as a more reliable measure of the households' living standards, particularly in the context of developing countries (Deaton & Grosh, 2000; McKenzie, 2005). This is also in line with various economic theories of consumption, such as Freidman's (1957) permanent-income hypothesis, suggesting that consumption is a better indicator of household welfare when compared with transitory or short-run income (Browning & Crossley, 2001; Deaton, 1997). Thus, the wealth concept adopted here is gross consumption expenditure per equivalent adult. Household expenditure has thus been equivalized using the same *equivalence scale* in each country, namely that proposed by Aronson et al. (1994) (Aronson & Lambert, 1994).

The WHS also provides a wide range of indicators on individual health. Yet, our approach requires that the health variable be measured in a continuous fashion. Although, several methods to cardinalize an ordinal health variable such as *self-assessed health* (SAH) have been proposed in the literature; for example, dichotomization, ordered probit, and interval regressions (cf., e.g., Van Doorslaer & Jones, 2003), we have alternatively opted to make use of the available cardinal measures of health. Our choice is mainly motivated by the fact that health inequality measures have been argued to be sensitive to the different cardinal-transformation methods of categorical variables (Allison & Foster, 2004). Our health variable is, thus, captured using anthropometric measures in the adult women population.

Alternative anthropometric measures for adult household members can be constructed based on the WHS data, namely, Length/Height-For-Age (LFA), Weight/Mass-For-Age (WFA), and the Body Mass Index (BMI). Separate analyses were conducted over each of these anthropometric measures to explore the sensitivity of our results to the chosen measure of health. However, given that our results were qualitatively broadly similar, we have opted to present in this chapter results related to the first of these measures, the LFA. Results pertaining to the other anthropometric measures are available from the authors.

EMPIRICAL FINDINGS

Table 1 reports basic summary statistics (including the *mean, standard deviation, coefficient of variation*, and the *Kendall rank-correlation coefficient* — referred to as *Kendall's tau* (τ) — for the variables included in the

Table 1. Summary Statistics.

	Mean	Standard Deviation	Coefficient of Variation	Kendall's Tau Coefficient (τ)
	Morocco ($n=611$)			
Wealth	963.1673	6418.352	6.6638	0.0374
Health	0.05481	0.01631	0.2974	
	Tunisia ($n=1,547$)			
Wealth	1523.642	22883.08	15.0187	−0.0433
Health	0.05373	0.0157614	0.2934	
	Mauritania ($n=1,372$)			
Wealth	466.1304	985.3966	2.1140	0.0187
Health	0.05573	0.017048	0.3059	
	Comoros ($n=618$)			
Wealth	594.0779	1391.162	2.3417	*−0.0156*
Health	0.0548895	0.0164885	0.3004	
	UAE ($n=362$)			
Wealth	3208.689	4139.5	1.2901	*−0.0443*
Health	0.0527722	0.0149378	0.2831	

study. The mean per capita expenditure (measured in international dollars adjusted for purchasing power parity (PPP)) ranges from 466.13 and 594.1 in Mauritania and Comoros, respectively, to 3208.7 and 1523.6 in UAE and Tunisia, respectively. The wealth *coefficient* of variation appears to be highest in Tunisia (a value of 15.0) and lowest in UAE. By contrast, mean health shows slightly less variations across the countries (ranging from 0.053 in UAE to 0.056 in Mauritania). This is also reflected in the respective health coefficients of variation which range from 0.28 in UAE to 0.31 in Mauritania. Finally, the *Kendall's tau* (τ) coefficient (presented in the last column of Table 1) provides a measure of rank-correlation between the two attributes in question. Accordingly, the coefficient τ has a negative value when there is disagreement between the two rankings as is the case in Tunisia, Comoros, and UAE, and vice versa, it has a positive value when there is agreement between the two rankings as is the case in Morocco and Mauritania.

Results on the bidimensional welfare equality indices, θ, are presented in Table 2 as per different values of the *inequality aversion parameters*, α, β, ranging from -0.25 to -4. These values are set assuming that for a given *wealth-health ratio*: (i) the inequality aversion parameters for the wealth and health are the same ($\alpha = \beta$); (ii) the social planner is "more averse" to inequality in wealth than in health, that is, $\alpha < \beta$ (*NB: the absolute value of α is greater than β*), and (iii) $\alpha > \beta$ (*the absolute value of β is greater than α*). Furthermore, in order to reflect the likely aversion to income-related health inequality in the population, both parameters are set to be negative (α, $\beta < 0$). This corresponds to Eq. (4) where the utility function leads to an in-*equality index* satisfying the *property of* aversion to *correlation increasing transformations*. Thus, as the rank-correlation between health and wealth increases, the value the bidimensional equality index θ takes is expected to decrease.

As can be seen from the first row of Table 2, the multidimensional equality index θ appears to be sensitive to the way we model attitudes vis-à-vis inequality: the values of the index θ ranging from a smaller value of 0.0181 for the case $\alpha < \beta$: (α, β)=(-1.5, -1) to a larger value of 0.7252 for the case $\alpha > \beta$: (α, β)=(-1, -4). Thus, the overall ranking of countries in terms of multidimensional (in-)equality vary across the three cases we study. For instance, by considering the case of equal coefficients of aversion to inequalities in both wealth and health (case 1: $\alpha = \beta$), important variations in the level of overall welfare (in-)equality across countries emerge: for the case $\alpha = \beta = -0.5$, *equality* in welfare appears to be the least in Tunisia, with the equality index θ taking a value of 0.3051. This is

Table 2. Inequality in Welfare, Wealth, and Health (*Univariate and Multidimensional Inequality Indices*)[a,b].

CIT Aversion ($\alpha, \beta < 0$)		$\alpha = \beta$		$\alpha > \beta$ (In Absolute Value)		$\alpha < \beta$ (In Absolute Value)	
Inequality aversion parameters		$\alpha = -0.5$, $\beta = -0.5$	$\alpha = -1$, $\beta = -1$	$\alpha = -1.25$, $\beta = -1$	$\alpha = -1.5$, $\beta = -1$	$\alpha = -1$, $\beta = -2$	$\alpha = -1$, $\beta = -4$
Morocco	Welfare (θ)	0.6530	0.5409	0.4976	0.4049	0.6648	0.7252
	Wealth (γ_1)	0.4477	0.2991	0.2899	0.2252	0.2991	0.2991
	Health (γ_2)	0.9382	0.9193	0.9193	0.9193	0.8847	0.8288
	κ	0.9925	0.9402	0.9402	0.9380	0.7967	0.7035
Tunisia	Welfare (θ)	0.3051	0.2756	0.2263	0.1860	0.4017	0.5126
	Wealth (γ_1)	0.0997	0.0833	0.0724	0.0641	0.0833	0.0833
	Health (γ_2)	0.9419	0.9244	0.9244	0.9244	0.8926	0.8399
	κ	1.0045	1.0139	1.0124	1.0044	1.0233	1.0337
Mauritania	Welfare (θ)	0.4578	0.0856	0.0352	0.0181	0.1928	0.3562
	Wealth (γ_1)	0.2174	0.0074	0.0024	0.0013	0.0074	0.0074
	Health (γ_2)	0.9294	0.9051	0.9051	0.9051	0.8529	0.7253
	κ	0.9818	0.8944	0.9013	0.9482	0.7519	0.3570
Comoros	Welfare (θ)	0.5914	0.1106	0.0446	0.0215	0.2055	0.3357
	Wealth (γ_1)	0.3949	0.0172	0.0049	0.0021	0.0172	0.0172
	Health (γ_2)	0.9328	0.9074	0.9074	0.9074	0.8576	0.7007
	κ	1.0263	1.2774	1.2884	1.2901	1.4565	0.9733
UAE	Welfare (θ)	0.6233	0.2873	0.1613	0.0972	0.4169	0.5502
	Wealth (γ_1)	0.4142	0.0916	0.0408	0.0224	0.0916	0.0916
	Health (γ_2)	0.9439	0.9262	0.9262	0.8993	0.8917	0.8212
	κ	1.0032	1.0285	1.0308	1.0288	1.0058	0.8262

[a] Note that α is the inequality aversion parameter for wealth and β is the inequality aversion parameter for health.
[b] κ is the measure of association between attributes.

followed by Mauritania ($\theta = 0.4578$), Comoros ($\theta = 0.5914$), UAE (0.6233), with the highest observed value of the index θ being observed for Morocco ($\theta = 0.6530$).

Assigning greater aversion to inequality in wealth (case 2: $\alpha < \beta$) results in smaller values of the multidimensional equality index θ for all the countries, that is, a higher level of welfare inequality. Although Morocco preserves its rank as the country with the lowest inequality, some changes in the ranking order can be observed: equality in welfare appears now to be the lowest in Mauritania (0.0352 and 0.0181 for the two cases $\alpha = -1.25$

and $\alpha = -1.5$, β held fixed at -1, respectively), followed by Comoros (0.0446 and 0.0215), UAE (0.1613 and 0.0972), and Tunisia (0.2263 and 0.1860). By contrast, the levels of multidimensional inequality fall as more weight is assigned to the health dimension (case 3: $\alpha > \beta$; α held fixed at -1 and β assigned values -2 and -4, respectively). However, the overall ranking of countries is only slightly different in comparison with case 2. For instance, while Morocco and Mauritania remain the countries with the highest and lowest levels of welfare equality, respectively, welfare inequality levels in UAE and Tunisia appear now to be much less worse than in the case where a larger value is assigned to the wealth inequality aversion parameter (case 2: $\alpha < \beta$).

Given these trends, the more interesting question from the perspective of our empirical analysis is, thus, holding other things equal, *what are the dimensions of well-being that are more likely to reflect such variations in overall multidimensional inequalities across countries* and *what is the contribution of the correlation between both dimensions of well-being, that is, the contribution of "the socioeconomic inequalities in health" to the overall welfare inequality?* However, before having a closer look at the decomposition results of the equality index θ it is of interest to examine, first, the ranking of the countries in terms of both dimensions of well-being: wealth and health inequalities. Table 2 presents results on the two univariate Atkinson–Kolm–Sen equality measures γ_1, γ_2 measuring, respectively, the inequalities in wealth and health, and a third term, κ, capturing the association between two attributes.

Among the countries we study, Mauritania appears to have the lowest level of equality in wealth (e.g., $\gamma_1 = 0.0074$ when $\alpha = \beta = -1$) versus Morocco which has the highest level of equality in wealth (e.g., $\gamma_1 = 0.2991$). Assigning more weight to the aversion parameter of wealth does not change the picture: Mauritania remains the country with the lowest equality in wealth ($\gamma_1 = 0.0024$ and 0.0013 when $\alpha = -1.25$ and -1.5 respectively with β fixed at -1) while Morocco preserve its rank as the one with the highest level of equality in wealth ($\gamma_1 = 0.2899$ and 0.2252).

Interestingly, however, countries exhibiting more wealth inequality do not necessarily exhibit more health inequality. For instance, for almost all the cases reported in this study, health inequality appears to be lower in the UAE and Tunisia compared with Morocco which has the lowest level of wealth inequality. Also of note, compared to wealth equality indices, the health equality indices appear to be fairly less sensitive to the changes in the inequality aversion parameters. Nonetheless, in almost all countries the health equality index takes on values approximately three times larger than that of the wealth equality index, and even more so when $\alpha<\beta$. This is unsurprising given the fact that the distribution of wealth tends to exhibit far more extreme values than the distribution of health, hence, a larger range for γ_1. Indeed, while our measure of wealth can grow indefinitely, the range of values the anthropometric measure of health takes is bounded by biological laws. Therefore, some caution should be exercised as regards to the comparison of the magnitudes of inequalities in health and wealth. Note also that though this need not be a general rule; it emerges in our data that the level of multidimensional equality increases as more weight is assigned to the health dimension. For instance, in Morocco, the value taken by the equality index stands at 0.6530 when $\alpha=\beta=-0.5$; at 0.6648 when $(\alpha, \beta)=(-1, -2)$, but falls significantly to 0.4976 and 0.4049 when $(\alpha, \beta)=(-1.25, -1)$ and $(-1.5, -1)$, respectively. Such trends are broadly similar across all other countries.

The above decomposition results reveal that the multidimensional (in-)equality indices tend to mimic the (in-)equality ordering of the wealth distributions, as the latter remain substantially less equally distributed than health. Recall that these equality indices are computed with the aversion parameters α and β being negative. Under such circumstances, an increase in the *rank-correlation* between the attributes results in an increase in inequality. In other words, the index θ embodies an aversion to correlation increasing transformations between the attributes. A closer look at Table 2 reveals that although the values κ takes is sensitive to the choice of inequality aversion parameters, the ranking of countries in terms of this measure is somewhat consistent for all the choices on the values of α and β. For instance, the values of κ are always less than 1 in the case of Morocco and Mauritania ($\kappa=0.9402$ and 0.8944 for $\alpha=\beta=-1$ and $\kappa=0.9380$ and 0.9482 when $\alpha=-1.5$ and $\beta=-1$, respectively), while they are always greater than 1 in all other countries, indicating a *pro-rich* socioeconomic related inequality in health. These trends are preserved across all the values of α and β reported here.

Lastly, to give sense on the relative contributions of each of the two univariate inequality indices as well as the association measure κ to the overall level of welfare inequality, the multidimensional welfare index $\theta(X)$ is decomposed as per Eq. (5). The contributions of the three terms on the right-hand side of Eq. (5) are, then, expressed in a percentage terms of value of $\ln\theta(X)$. To clarify how the contributions are calculated, take for instance the calculations pertaining to $(\alpha, \beta)=(-0.5, -0.5)$. Eq. (5) then takes the form $\ln \theta(X) = 0.5 \ln \gamma_1(X_1) + 0.5 \ln \gamma_2(X_2) - \ln \kappa(X)$. It is to be noted that each of $\ln\theta$, $\ln\gamma_1$, and $\ln\gamma_2$ is a negative number. Hence, the weights $\varphi_1 = \omega \ln \gamma_1(X_1)/\ln \theta(X)$ and $\varphi_2 = (1-\omega)\ln \gamma_2(X_2)/\ln \theta(X)$ are such that $0 \leq \varphi_1, \varphi_2$. Given these definitions, there are several limitations in the use of these weights that we must draw to the reader's attention. First, it is important to bear in mind that it is possible that a given weight exceeds the value 1. Second, note that when examining inequality over wealth and health, in most practical cases φ_1 will be decreasing in γ_1, and hence φ_1 will increase with the level of inequality in X_1. But cases may also occur where φ_1 increases as γ_1 rises.[2] Finally, upon defining $\varphi_\kappa = \frac{1}{\alpha+\beta} \cdot \frac{\ln \kappa(X)}{\ln \theta(X)}$, φ_κ is positive when $\ln \kappa > 1$, that is when the socioeconomic inequality in health is pro-rich, and hence contributes to reducing overall equality. Conversely, $\varphi_\kappa < 0$ when $\kappa < 1$ and socioeconomic inequality in health is pro-poor and contributes to reducing inequality. Returning to parameterization $(\alpha, \beta) = (-0.5, -0.5)$, in the Moroccan context, $\ln \theta = -0.4262$ and $\ln \kappa = -0.0075$. Thus, the weight φ_κ takes the value of -0.0177 as health inequality is pro-poor.

Table 3 reports the weights φ_1, φ_2, and φ_κ for the various values of inequality aversion parameters (α, β) considered above. For all cases, the

Table 3. Percentage Contribution of Wealth, Health and Association Measure to the Total Inequality in Welfare[a].

CIT Aversion ($\alpha, \beta < 0$)		$\alpha = \beta$		$\alpha > \beta$ (In Absolute Value)		$\alpha < \beta$ (In Absolute Value)	
Inequality aversion parameters		$\alpha=-0.5$, $\beta=-0.5$	$\alpha=-1$, $\beta=-1$	$\alpha=-1.25$, $\beta=-1$	$\alpha=-1.5$, $\beta=-1$	$\alpha=-1$, $\beta=-2$	$\alpha=-1$, $\beta=-4$
Morocco	Wealth (φ_1)	94.29%	98.17%	98.56%	98.93%	98.54%	75.13%
	Health (φ_2)	7.48%	6.85%	5.37%	3.90%	20.02%	46.76%
	Association (φ_κ)	−1.77%	−5.02%	−3.93%	−2.83%	−18.56%	−21.89%
Tunisia	Wealth (φ_1)	97.10%	96.41%	97.25%	98.00%	90.83%	74.31%
	Health (φ_2)	2.52%	3.05%	2.38%	1.90%	8.33%	20.89%
	Association (φ_κ)	0.38%	0.54%	0.37%	0.10%	0.84%	4.80%
Mauritania	Wealth (φ_1)	97.66%	99.80%	99.93%	99.38%	99.35%	95.06%
	Health (φ_2)	4.69%	2.52%	1.45%	0.9942%	6.44%	24.90%
	Association (φ_κ)	−2.35%	−2.32%	−1.38%	−0,3742%	−5.79%	−19.96%
Comoros	Wealth (φ_1)	88.44%	92.23%	95.01%	96.35%	85.59%	74.43%
	Health (φ_2)	6.62%	2.21%	1.37%	1.00%	6.49%	26.07%
	Association (φ_κ)	4.94%	5.56%	3.62%	2.65%	7.92%	−0.50%
UAE	Wealth (φ_1)	93.21%	95.80%	97.39%	97.69%	91.05%	80.01%
	Health (φ_2)	6.11%	3.07%	1.87%	1.82%	8.73%	26.38%
	Association (φ_κ)	0.68%	1.13%	0.74%	0.49%	0.22%	−6.39%

[a]For definitions of weights φ_1, φ_2, and φ_κ see section "Data Set and Variable Definitions."

most important contributor to welfare inequality is wealth, with a contribution ranging from about 72% to 99% of the overall welfare equality. However, the magnitude of the contributions of wealth and health to welfare inequality varies across the three cases. For instance, the contribution of health becomes larger, as expected, when more weight $\beta/\alpha+\beta$ is attached to the aversion parameter of health and vice versa.

DISCUSSION AND CONCLUSION

This chapter applies recent methodological advances in the area of multidimensional inequality measurement in the context of developing countries. It implements empirically a method for the decomposition of multidimensional inequality introduced by Abul Naga, and Geoffard (2006), that emphasizes the role of the *rank-correlation* between attributes in shaping social value judgments on the underlying level of inequality. This methodology is applied to assess bivariate inequalities in a set of developing countries. Several interesting findings and key implications that emerge from our empirical analysis are worth making in light of the practical questions raised in the outset. First, the health attribute of well-being, as captured by the anthropometric measure, appears to be *circa* much more equally distributed in most of the countries under consideration than the distribution of wealth (as measured by *equivalent expenditure*). Thus, when comparing countries in terms of welfare inequality the choice of welfare attributes does matter to a large extent. Second, countries exhibiting more wealth inequality do not necessarily exhibit more health inequality. Also of note, compared to wealth inequality, the values taken by the health inequality index appear to be fairly less sensitive to the changes in the inequality aversion parameters. Indeed, unlike wealth which can grow indefinitely, our health attribute is captured using an anthropometric measure, which has its own "*biological*" bounds dictated by the process of accumulation of nutritional status (e.g., length-to-age and body mass). Therefore, caution should be exercised as regards to the comparison of the magnitudes of inequalities in health per se. Third, given that our results have systematically documented less inequalities in the health attribute, the decomposition results reveal that the multidimensional inequality indices tend to mimic the inequality ordering of the wealth distributions.

The finding that the *rank-correlation* between attributes — as measured by the association measure (κ) — has a significant contribution in the quantification of inequality has important policy implications since it reveals that it is not only wealth and health inequalities per se that matters in the measurement of welfare inequality but also the associations between them. Thus, reducing inequalities in welfare seems to be also a matter of reducing these associations through appropriate health-related policies than only direct measures of redistributing wealth. Typically, polices that subsidize the consumption of essential food elements for the poor improve the health outcomes of these groups. Such policies make the patterns of socioeconomic inequalities pro-poor and in doing so reduce the health gradient, hence, contribute to promote greater welfare equality.

This chapter has only considered two attributes of well-being. Analyzing inequality in welfare in this sort of way is promising, since it offers a distinctive angle and useful information on how to think about justice − at least in an economic sense. Yet, a broader way of looking at the matter might also be required. First, many variables used to measure health status are ordinal. For such variables the approach we have implemented is not directly applicable, as it relies on cardinal definitions of the variables. In this respect, recent methodological advances, of which we cite Kobus (2012), Apouey and Silber (2013), Zheng (2008, 2011), and Cowell and Flachaire (2012) are more appropriate. Second, the assessment of welfare inequality of the type undertaken in this study, as in the empirical literature to date, leaves behind a number of issues unsolved, or sidestepped, and thus, open for future work by scholars in related fields. A distinction is to be drawn between correlation preferring and correlation averse inequality indices. Inequality rankings reflect judgments about equity; this is more so when we consider multiple attributes of well-being. Indeed, the analysis of welfare inequality need not be confined to the narrow space of wealth. To borrow Sen's terminology: *"incomes and commodity holdings are only contingently important as instruments to ends and the freedom to achieve ends"* (Sen, 1993). Future research ought to address the multidimensionality character by including inequalities in other spheres of well-being than the direct measures of wealth and health.

NOTES

1. Wealth also depends on individual ability, quality of education, and career choices.
2. While a finite number of Pigou−Dalton transfers on X_1 will increase the resulting value of γ_1, the effect of such progressive transfers on $\kappa(X)$ are undetermined: $\kappa(\cdot)$ may increase, or decrease, as X_1 becomes more equally distributed.

ACKNOWLEDGMENTS

We would like to thank The *French National Research Agency* (ANR) for its financial support to the research project *INEGSANTE-Les Suds-Aujourd'hui II-2010-2013*. The views expressed in this chapter are those of the authors and do not necessarily represent the views or policies of the World Health Organization or the ANR. We are also grateful to the editors Pedro Rosa Dias and Owen O'Donnell for many helpful suggestions.

REFERENCES

Abul Naga, R., & Geoffard, P. (2006). Decomposition of bivariate inequality indices by attributes. *Economics Letters*, *90*, 362−367.

Allison, & Foster, J. (2004). Measuring health inequality using qualitative data. *Journal of Health Economics*, *23*(3), 505−524.

Apouey, B., & Silber, J. (2013). Inequality and bi-polarization in socioeconomic status and health: Ordinal approaches. In P. R. Dias & O. O'Donnell (Eds.), *Health and inequality* (Vol. 21). Research on Economic Ineuqality. Bingley, UK: Emerald Group Publishing Limited.

Aronson, J. R., & Lambert, P. J. (1994). Decomposing the Gini coefficient to reveal the vertical, horizontal, and reranking effects of income taxation. *National Tax Journal*, *47*(2), 273−294.

Atkinson, A. B. (1970). On the measurement of inequality. *Journal of Economic Theory*, (2), 244−263.

Atkinson, A. B., & Bourguignon, F. (1982). The comparison of multi-dimensioned distributions of economic status. *Review of Economic Studies*, *49*, 183−201.

Bibi, S., & Nabili, K. M. (2010). Equity and inequality in the Arab region. PRR No. 33, Economics Research Forum (ERF), Cairo.

Bleichrodt, H., & van Doorslaer, E. (2006). A welfare economics foundation for health inequality measurement. *Journal of Health Economics*, *25*, 945−957.

Bourguignon, F. (Ed.). (1999). Comment to 'Multidimensioned Approaches to Welfare Analysis' by Maasoumi, E. In *Handbook of income inequality measurement*. London: Kluwer Academic.

Brambilla, M., & Peluso, E. (2010). A remark on decomposition of bivariate inequality indices by attributes by Abul Naga and Geoffard. *Economics Letters*, *90*(2006), 362−367. Economics Letters, *108*, 100.

Browning, M., & Crossley, T. F. (2001). The life-cycle model of consumption and saving. *The Journal of Economic Perspectives*, *15*(3), 3−22.

Coutts, A., Stuckler, D., Batniji, R., Ismail, S., Maziak, W., & McKee, M. (2013). The Arab spring and health: Two years on. *International Journal of Health Services*, *43*(1), 49−60.

Cowell, F. A., & Flachaire, E. (2012). *Inequality with ordinal data*. Working Paper, London School of Economics and GREQAM, Aix-Marseille University.

Deaton, A. (1997). *The theory of household survey*. Baltimore, MD: The John Hopkins University Press.

Deaton, A., & Grosh, M. (Eds.). (2000). *Consumption in designing household survey questionnaires for developing countries: Lessons from 15 years of living standards measurement study.* Washington, DC: The World Bank.

Duclos, J.-Y., Sahn, D., & Younger, S. (2011). Partial multidimensional inequality orderings. *Journal of Public Economics, 95*(3–4), 225–238.

Friedman, M. (1957). *A theory of the consumption function.* Princeton, NJ: Princeton University Press.

Kobus, M. (2012). Attribute decomposition of multidimensional inequality indices. *Economics Letters, 117,* 189–191.

Kolm, S. (1977). Multidimensional equalitarianisms. *Quarterly Journal of Economics, 91,* 1–13.

Massoumi, E. (1986). The measurement and decomposition of multi-dimentional inequity. *Econometrica, 54,* 991–997.

McKenzie, D. J. (2005). Measuring inequality with asset indicators. *Journal of Population Economics, 18*(2), 229–260.

Moussavi, S., Chatterji, S., Verdes, E., Tandon, A., Patel, V., & Ustun, B. (2007). Depression, chronic diseases, and decrements in health: Results from the World Health Surveys. *Lancet, 370,* 851–858.

Sen, A. (2000). Social justice and the distribution of income. Chapter 1. In A. B. Atkinson & F. Bourguignon (Eds.), *Handbook of income distribution* (Vol. 1, pp. 59–85). Amsterdam: Elsevier.

Sen, A. K. (1973). *On economic inequality.* Oxford: Clarendon Press.

Sen, A. K. (1993). Capability and well-being. In M. Nussbaum & A. Sen (Eds.), *The quality of life* (pp. 30–53). New York, NY: Oxford Clarendon Press.

Tsui, K. Y. (1995). Multidimensional generalizations of the relative and absolute inequality indices: The Atkinson-Kolm-Sen approach. *Journal of Economic Theory, 67,* 251–265.

Tsui, K. Y. (1999). Multidimensional inequality and multidimensional entropy measures: An axiomatic derivation. *Social Choice and Welfare, 16,* 145–157.

Üstün, T., Chatterji, S., Villanueva, M., Celik, B. L. C., Sadana, R., Valentine, N., … Murray, C. J. L. (2003). WHO multi-country survey study on health and responsiveness 2000–2001. In Christopher J. L. Murray & D. B. Evans (Eds.), *Health systems performance assessment debates, methods and empiricism.* Geneva: World Health Organization.

Van Doorslaer, E., & Jones, A. (2003). Inequalities in self-reported health: Validation of a new approach to measurement. *Journal of Health Economics, 22*(1), 61–87.

Zheng, B. (2008). A note on measuring inequality with ordinal data. *Research on Economic Inequality, 16,* 177–188.

Zheng, B. (2011). A new approach to measure socioeconomic inequality in health. *The Journal of Economic Inequality, 9*(4), 555–577.

Zhong, H. (2009). A multivariate analysis of the distribution of individual's welfare in China: What is the role of health? *Journal of Health Economics, 28,* 1062–1070.

INCOME INEQUALITY, HEALTH AND DEVELOPMENT – IN SEARCH OF A PATTERN

Therese Nilsson and Andreas Bergh

ABSTRACT

There is an on-going debate as to whether health is negatively affected by economic inequality. Still, we have limited knowledge of the mechanisms relating inequality to individual health and very little evidence comes from less-developed economies. We use individual and multi-level data from Zambia on child nutritional health to test three hypotheses consistent with a negative correlation between income inequality and population health: the absolute income hypothesis (AIH), the relative income hypothesis (RIH) and the income inequality hypothesis (IIH). The results confirm that absolute income positively affects health. For the RIH we find sensitivity to the reference group used. Most interestingly, we find higher income inequality to robustly associate with better child health. The same pattern appears in a cross country regression. To explain the conflicting results in the literature we suggest examining potential mediators such as generosity, food sharing, trust and purchasing power.

Keywords: Inequality; health; development

JEL classifications: D31; I10; I12; O10

INTRODUCTION

In the early 1990s the income inequality hypothesis — that is the idea that income inequalities in society are detrimental for everyone's health — gained popularity among social scientists and public health scholars. Economic historian and epidemiologist Richard Wilkinson has received a lot of attention for popularizing the idea. In their book *The Spirit Level*, Wilkinson and Pickett (2009) cite an impressive number of studies to support their claims that the negative health effect is independent of whether you are at the top or at the bottom of the income distribution, and also that the income distribution in wealthy countries actually plays a larger role in the determination of health than the actual level of income. The mechanism emphasized by Wilkinson is that poorer individuals feel stress, shame, loss of respect and distrust when comparing themselves to their richer counterparts (Wilkinson, 1996). Other mechanisms mentioned in the literature include political processes or increased violence in unequal societies, in turn affecting health outcomes.

While Wilkinson holds that the negative health effects of inequality are much stronger in rich countries, Deaton (2003) notes that many of the arguments put forward by Wilkinson and others are plausible for poor, as well as rich, countries. Still almost no studies have examined the relationship between inequality and health in developing countries. To some extent, the reason is that data from developing countries are more scarce, especially regarding the often used subjective, self-assessed health measures.

For objective health measures, there are data available also from developing countries that can be used to examine if the relationship between health and inequality varies across levels of development. Fig. 1(a) shows the cross-country correlation between the Gini coefficient for disposable household income in 2000 and the prevalence of child stunting, which is caused by malnourishment.[1] This health measure is particularly interesting from a development perspective. Research increasingly emphasizes the important role of child health as a major factor influencing future economic outcomes (cf. Bengtsson & Lindström, 2000; Currie, 2009). Moreover, anthropometrical indicators are objective, relatively precise and consistent across subgroups (Heltberg, 2009).

Although there is a good deal of variation, Fig. 1(a) suggests that stunting is more prevalent in more unequal societies. But this relationship appears to reflect the association between inequality and average child health status in developed countries. While Fig. 1(b) reveals a positive

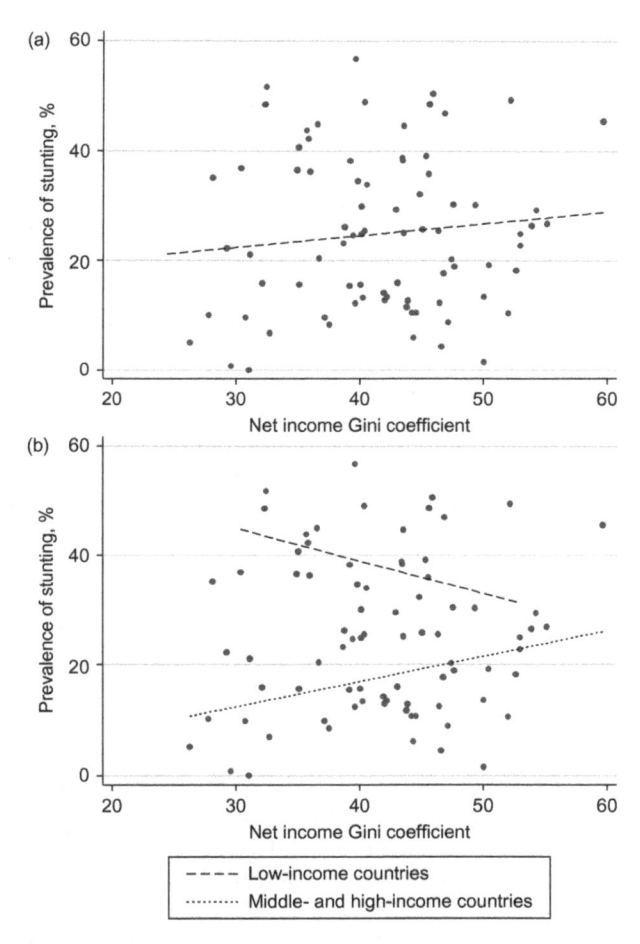

Fig. 1. The Cross-Country Correlation between Income Inequality and Prevalence of Stunting, 2000. *Source*: World Bank (2008) and Solt (2008).

correlation between income inequality and stunting among middle- and high-income countries, inequality actually correlates with better child health in low-income countries.[2]

While the correlations in Fig. 1(b) seem supportive of the idea that inequality associates with worse health in rich countries but not in poor, this conclusion would be premature. Even if more control variables are added in a multivariate analysis, a negative partial correlation between an income inequality measure and the average health status of a population does not necessarily indicate a negative relationship between inequality and health at the individual level or at the household level.[3] From Rodgers (1979) and Gravelle (1998) we know that such aggregate associations might stem from a concave relationship between income and individual health. In other words, older studies that typically use aggregate data may suffer from the ecological fallacy. Without controlling for individual income, a negative relationship between inequality and population health may be partially or fully explained by a non-linear relationship between individual income and individual health. The intuition is that in a more unequal society the health losses caused by individuals having low absolute incomes will be greater than the health gains to those having high absolute incomes, and therefore average health will be lower − even if there is no effect of inequality per se. By using individual level data and controlling for individual or household income, the problem can be avoided and different theoretical hypotheses, all consistent with a negative aggregate association between inequality and population health, can be examined (Wagstaff & van Doorslaer, 2000).

Recently, a number of high-quality studies using individual level data have been published. Interestingly, these tend to produce much more contradictory conclusions than older aggregate level studies. Some of the most consistent evidence of a negative association between income inequality and individual health is found in analyses of data from the United States using subjective (self-assessed) health measures (e.g. Kennedy, Kawachi, Glass, & Prothrow-Stist, 1998; Lopez, 2004; Submramanian, Kawachi, & Kennedy, 2001). In contrast, studies focusing on other developed countries, and using both subjective and objective health measures, often reject the hypothesis that income inequality has a detrimental effect on individual health (e.g. Shibya et al., 2002 on Japan; Gerdtham & Johannesson, 2004 on Sweden; Jones, Duncan, & Twigg, 2004 and Gravelle & Sutton, 2009 on the United Kingdom).[4]

In all, the evidence for a negative correlation between income inequality and average population health in rich countries weakens substantially when individual income is controlled for. But what about the surprising positive correlation between child health and inequality we see in Fig. 1(b)? Sadly, we possess very limited knowledge of the relationship between inequality and individual health in less-developed economies. For this reason, the next section probes deeper into the determinants of stunting in Zambia, classified as one of the poorest and most unequal countries in the world with poor key indicators on health (WHO, 2007). Using a detailed dataset, we test three hypotheses:

1. the *absolute income hypothesis* (AIH), stating that individual income has a positive but diminishing effect on individual health;
2. the *relative income hypothesis* (RIH), according to which health is influenced by the relation of individual income to the average income in a reference group;
3. the *income inequality hypothesis* (IIH), stating that individual health is negatively influenced by inequality in the distribution of income.

Our dependent variable is child nutritional status expressed by height-for-age z-scores. In relation to Figs. 1(a) and (b), a child is classified as stunted when its z-score is below -2, implying that the child's height in relation to her age is 2 standard deviations below the international referenced median of a well-nourished population of children.

Using average household expenditures and expenditure Gini coefficients calculated at three geographical levels (provincial, district and constituency), we confirm the absolute income hypotheses but find no consistent evidence supporting the relative income hypothesis. Most interestingly, we find a positive association between contextual inequality and child health, robust to measuring inequality at different geographical levels, to alternative inequality measures and to alternative specifications.

THEORY AND PREVIOUS EMPIRICAL FINDINGS[5]

The *absolute income hypothesis* (AIH) states that economic resources improve health with diminishing marginal impact. Higher income may improve health through ability to purchase medical care and other health-enhancing goods. Richer households may also be more efficient at producing child health if they possess better health-related information and provide healthier environments (Khanam, Nghiem, & Connelly, 2009).[6] If poor child health interferes with the mother or father's ability to earn income, then causality will be bidirectional (cf. Deaton, 2003; Smith, 1999).

The literature examining the health-inequality relationship using individual level data generally confirms the AIH (Karlsson, Nilsson, Lyttkens, & Leeson, 2010; Mellor & Milyo, 2002). A positive relationship between household income and child health is also well documented, particularly in poor countries where malnutrition is a phenomenon, although the precise mechanisms by which income transmits to better health remain unresolved (Khanam et al., 2009).

The *relative income hypothesis* (RIH) states that individual health is affected by the individual's economic situation relative to others in some reference group. Holding individual income constant, higher average income in the reference group will through *psychosocial* mechanisms translate to worse health.[7] Wilkinson (1996) emphasizes that health status is determined by perceptions of place in the social hierarchy. Poorer individuals feel stress, loss of respect, distrust and shame when comparing themselves to their richer counterparts. These perceptions could translate directly into physical afflictions through biochemical responses to stress and anxiety, increasing the probability of disease (Brunner & Marmot, 1999), or into unhealthy behaviour such as smoking (Lynch, Smith, Kaplan, & House, 2000). Psychosocial stress is typically assumed to directly impact health negatively, but it may also indirectly influence child health negatively through household income, or through lower levels of stimulation to the child and decreased capacity for supportive parenting (Olivius, Ostergren, Hanson, & Lyttkens, 2004). With stunting as outcome variable, the causal chain will include the transmission from parental factors to child health. If this link dampens the effect, results will be biased towards zero. However, it is well-known that family stress affects children's social and emotional well-being, and recent studies also document associations with objective health measures. Wyman et al. (2008) find family stress to associate with increased illnesses in children and conclude that impaired parental functioning may be a mechanism linking family stress with adverse effects on child health. Similarly, Caserta et al. (2008) find an association between family psychosocial stress and rates of illness and immune function in children. Parental stress and depression have also been linked to children's inflammatory profiles (Wolf, Miller, & Chen, 2008).

The RIH has mainly been tested by examining the individual health impact of average incomes in the geographical area where the individual resides, but many scholars note that the reference group to which the individual compares could differ (Deaton, 2003; Karlsson et al., 2010; Miller & Paxon, 2006). The empirical evidence for the RIH is relatively weak, with several studies finding virtually no such effects (Li & Zhu, 2006; Lorgelly & Lindley, 2008), with scattered evidence of both negative effects (Luttmer, 2005) and positive effects (Gerdtham & Johanesson, 2004; Miller & Paxson, 2006).

Finally, as discussed at the beginning of this chapter, the *income inequality hypothesis* (IIH) posits a direct negative effect on individual health from income inequality, independent of individual income. Several mechanisms may cause this effect. One relates to trust and *social capital*, as inequality may create distrust at the individual level, translating to antisocial behaviour and reduced civic participation at the societal level.[8] Low social capital or lack of social connectedness may in turn have health consequences (Durkheim, 1992 [1897]; Kawachi, Subramanian, & Kim, 2007; Putnam, 2000).[9] For example, socially integrated people have been shown to display greater immunological resistance to certain diseases while social isolation correlates with unhappiness (Argyle, 1999). Social capital may also promote child health (Berkman & Kawachi, 2000; Morrow, 2004). In particular, higher levels of maternal social capital may improve child nutritional status by permitting mothers greater access to more services and assets, improving maternal health and promoting health awareness (Baum, 1999; De Silva & Harpham, 2007) or by providing protection in times of crisis (Harpham, De Silva, & Tran, 2006).[10]

A second mechanism potentially underlying the IIH is *political*. Greater differences between rich and poor are assumed to coexist with less common resources (e.g. public health care) in turn affecting individual health (Kaplan, Pamuk, Lynch, Cohen, & Balfour, 1996; Lynch et al., 2000). Inequality may translate into less public spending as large income differences often reflect heterogeneity in interests between the rich and the poor (Alesina, Baqir, & Easterly, 1999; Krugman, 1996). In developing contexts, public hospitals and a public infrastructure are generally found to be important determinants of child health (cf. Rajkumar & Vinaya, 2008). Underinvestment in common resources, in particular, can affect child nutrition as it may affect maternity care, the number of child medical check-ups performed and immunization rates.[11] Importantly, the mechanism is not obvious from the perspective of a simple median voter model: Depending on how the income distribution changes, the median voter demand for health care could either decrease or increase.

As empirical evidence shows that income inequality and violence are positively correlated (Demombynes & Berk, 2005), *violent crime* is a third factor potentially mediating the relationship between income inequality and health status. Obviously, violence can directly affect health, and it could increase stress among those worrying about violence. For child health, violence is a likely mechanism if violence triggers higher parental stress.

As discussed by Karlsson et al. (2010) it could be that the IIH is only confirmed when inequality is measured at the same level as the one where mechanisms are at work. For example, finding evidence of an inequality effect may require measuring inequality as the same level as where, for example decisions are taken on public spending on health care. In Zambia the district is the geographical level closest to the jurisdiction at which public provision of health-enhancing services suggesting this is where we assume to find evidence of the IIH if the political mechanism is relevant. On the other hand, if social capital and general trust is the more important mediator the inequality effect on health should be stronger when income differences are measured close to the children's homes (in the Zambian case this would be the constituency level) rather than when the income differences reflect a large geographical area.[12]

Several articles review the existing literature in this research field (Deaton, 2003; Submaranian & Kawachi, 2004; Wilkinson & Picket, 2007; Wagstaff & van Doorslaer, 2000). Subramanian and Kwachi (2004) review the literature using individual level data and conclude that the results are mixed. As mentioned above, studies testing the IIH in the United States often find that income inequality correlates with adverse health impacts. For example, individuals living in states with higher income inequality are at increased risk of mortality, hypertension and having harmful levels of BMI (Diaz-Roux, Link, & Northridge, 2000; Lochner, Pamuk, & Makuc, 2001). On the other hand, Chang and Christakis (2005) find an inverse association between inequality and obesity, and controlling for state-specific effects Mellor and Milyo (2002) do not find a significant association between income inequality and self-assessed heath in the United States. Studies within other developed countries seem more prone to rejecting the IIH. For example, Shibuya, Hashimoto, and Yano (2002) conclude that income inequality does not have a detrimental effect on self-rated health in Japan. Blakely et al. (2006), Gerdtham and Johannesson (2004) and Jones et al. (2004) come to similar conclusions in studies of mortality within New Zealand, Sweden and the United Kingdom, respectively. Moreover, Lorgelly and Lindeley (2008) and Gravelle and Sutton (2009) reject the IIH using panel data on self-assessed health in Britain. Using a cross-national individual level panel, however, Hildebrand and van Kerm (2009) find consistent evidence of a negative effect from income inequality on self-assessed health in Europe. For self-assessed health, support for the IIH in richer countries is also found by Karlsson et al. (2010). In the studies mentioned above, health is typically measured at adult ages. However, Holstein et al. (2009) find support for the IIH among 11- to 15-year-olds using self-reported health complaints in 37 rich countries.

A couple of studies test the IIH using data from middle-income countries. In Chile, community inequality is found to increase the probability of reporting poor health (Subramanian, Delgado, Jadue, Vega, & Kawachi, 2003). Similar results are found among men in Russia (Carlson, 2005).

Studying child health in Ecuador, Larrea and Kawachi (2005) find support for IIH when income inequality is measured at the provincial level, but not for smaller geographical areas. For China, Li and Zhu (2006) find a negative effect in high inequality communities. However, neither Bobak, Pikhart, Rose, Hertzman, and Marmot (2000), nor Karlsson et al. (2010) find any negative health impact from inequality on individuals residing in middle-income countries. To our knowledge, the poorest country in which the IIH has been tested using individual level data is India. Using information on state level income inequality and the body mass index of ever married women, Subramanian, Kawachi, and Smit (2007) find that state level inequality relate to both under-nutrition as well as over-nutrition.

DATA AND EMPIRICAL MODEL

Country Background

Despite considerable efforts to improve the health situation over the past decade, key health indicators in Zambia are very poor. Life expectancy at birth decreased from 45.8 years in 1990 to 38.4 years in 2005 and the mortality rate of children under five increased from 180 to 182 (per 1,000 individuals) in the same time period (World Bank, 2008). As in many developing countries, household per capita expenditures are on average low and monetary poverty levels high. Sixty-eight per cent of the Zambian population has a consumption level below the national poverty line. Economic resources are also unequally distributed. With a national Gini coefficient of 0.54 Zambia is classified as one of the most unequal societies in the world.

Data and Variables

Data come from the 2004 Zambian Living Condition Monitoring Survey (LCMS IV), carried out from October 2004 to January 2005. The survey is nationally representative covering individuals in 19,340 households.[13]

Dependent Variable: Health Status
Using data on physical body measurement for all children aged 0–59 months in surveyed households, we derive the anthropometric measure *height-for-age*. Reflecting the accumulation of health and nutrition over a

child's entire lifetime, height-for-age is generally not affected by acute episodes of poor nutritional intake or sickness (Falkner & Tanner, 1986). The measure is acknowledged as a good, objective indicator of children's general health (Mosley & Chen, 1984; Thomas, Strauss, & Henriques, 1991; Zere & McIntyre, 2003).[14]

More specifically, we use the height-for-age z-score (HAZ) defined as the difference between a child's height and that of the median height of children of the same age and gender in a well-nourished reference population divided by the standard deviation of height in that population (WHO, 1995).[15] Following WHO (1995) recommendations we exclude observations with a z-score lower than −6 or larger than +3. Children younger than three months are also excluded as their health status might be explained by the weight of the mother (Skoufias, 1998). Our final sample contains health status for 10,316 children.[16]

Fig. 2 illustrates a histogram of the HAZ distribution and the corresponding distribution for the healthy reference population. The average value is −1.79, significantly lower than the mean value of the healthy population which is 0 and close to the threshold of −2 at which a child is defined as stunted.

Income, Mean Income and Income Inequality
To test the AIH we include the log of *household monthly per capita expenditure* in our regressions. To test the RIH we include a log of *average*

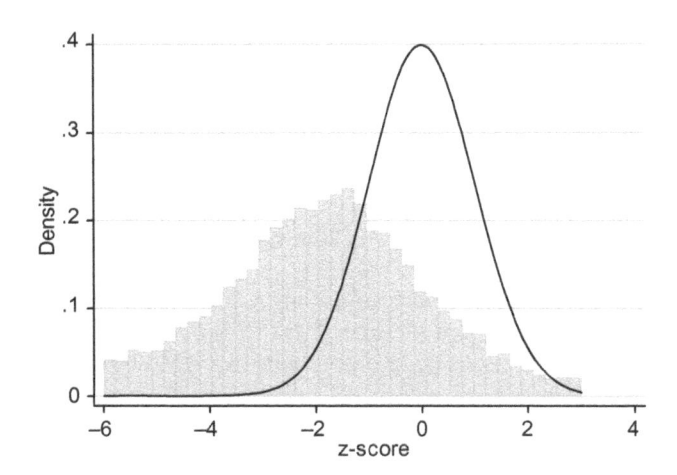

Fig. 2. Height-for-Age z-Score Distribution in Zambia (2004) and in Well-Nourished Population of Children Under 5 Years.

expenditures per capita in the geographical area where respondents reside. To test the IIH, our primary inequality measure is the *Gini* coefficient, increasing with higher inequality.

Zambia is demarcated into 9 provinces, which are further divided into 72 districts and 155 constituencies. We test the RIH and the IIH at three different aggregation levels — province, district and constituency. As changes in income distributions are unlikely to have an instantaneous health impact we examine the association between inequality and health under different lag lengths, using both current and past inequality levels (from the 1998 LCMS II survey). The variables *average per capita expenditures* and *Gini* are calculated from the full data set. To correct for differential representation, sample weights are applied in these calculations.

Additional Control Variables

All specifications control for *gender* (1 if female) and *age* (measured in months). As stunting may be more prevalent during the first two years of life, we also include *age square*. Because children with a higher birth order are generally at higher risk of being malnourished (Behrman, 1988), we include the *birth order* of the children in each household. We also include the maximum *level of education of any person in the household* older than 12, as education is related to family decision-making processes and child feeding practices. The variable is categorized into one of four levels corresponding to the Zambian education system: none (no years of schooling), primary (1–7 years of schooling), secondary (8–12 years of schooling) and higher education (>12 years of schooling).

In line with theories of household economics (Becker, 1965; Behrman, Pollak, & Taubman, 1986), variables for household composition and characteristics are included: *female household head* (1 for female-headed households), and *female household share*, measuring the percentage of female household members older than 12 years. We also include *household size*, and an indicator for households in *rural* areas.

As sanitary standards might affect nutritional status we include two dummy variables for access to *piped water* and *toilet facilities*. Furthermore, as malnutrition is commonly caused by insufficient energy and proteins, we include *meals* (1 if the household normally have more than two meals a day excluding snacks) and *animal products* (1 if the household eats fish, poultry or animal products more than once a week). Note that water supply, sanitation and food intake are possible mechanisms in the income–health relationship, and should thus not always be included in the regressions. Table 1 provides summary statistics for variables in our analysis.

Table 1. Summary Statistics.

Variable	Mean	SD	Min.	Max.	Obs.
Individual level					
HAZ	−1.79	1.82	−5.99	3	10,316
Gender	0.50	0.50	0	1	10,316
Age (months)	28.80	15.81	3	59	10,316
Age^2 (months)	1,079	963.62	9	3,600	10,316
Birth order	2.84	1.508	1	18	10,316
Household level					
HH expenditure per capita (in Zambian Kwacha)	94468.2	102994.6	285.7	1,967,600	10,316
Rural	0.60	0.49	0	1	10,316
HH head fern ale	0.15	0.35	0	1	10,316
HH gender share	0.54	0.18	0	1	10,316
HH size	6.81	3.12	2	33	10,316
HH edu 0	0.03	0.16	0	1	10,316
HH edu 1	0.36	0.48	0	1	10,316
HH edu 2	0.52	0.50	0	1	10,316
HH edu 3	0.10	0.29	0	1	10,316
Meals	0.47	0.50	0	1	10,316
Animal products	0.49	0.50	0	1	10,316
Water	0.38	0.49	0	1	10,316
Toilet facility	0.84	0.36	0	1	10,316
Contextual level					
Gini province	0.51	0.04	0.47	0.59	10,316
Gini district	0.51	0.05	0.43	0.68	10,316
Gini constituency	0.49	0.06	0.31	0.70	10,316
GE(0) province	0.51	0.08	0.40	0.63	10,316
GE(0) district	0.48	0.11	0.31	0.87	10,316
GE(0) constituency	0.46	0.13	0.17	1.02	10,316
GE(1) province	0.63	0.2	0.46	1.14	10,316
GE(1) district	0.57	0.22	0.34	1.3	10316
GE(1) constituency	0.54	0.28	0.17	2.55	10,316
Average expenditures province	121,708.4	35,708.8	78,300	204,000	10,316
Average expenditures district	117,805.6	41,118.2	51,700	227,000	10,316
Average expenditures constituency	118,818	52,422.7	37,700	439,000	10,316

HH edu corresponds to the highest educational level of a household member older than 12 years. Education is categorized into one of four levels of schooling corresponding to the educational system in Zambia: none (no years of schooling), primary (1−7 years of schooling), secondary (8−12 years of schooling), and higher education (more than 12 years of schooling). Meals is a dummy equalling 1 if the household normally has more than two meals a day. Animal products is a dummy equalling 1 if the household eats fish, poultry, or animal products more than once a week. Water refers to whether the household has a safe water source. Toilet facility refers to the sanitary standard of the household toilet facility. The exchange rate USD/ZMK in January 2004 was 4,789.

Empirical Model

The empirical model, where individuals are indexed by *i*, the households by *j* and geographical level by *g*, is formulated as

$$\text{HAZ}_{ijg} = \alpha + v'_i\beta_i + x'_j\beta_j + z'_g\beta_g + \varepsilon_{ijg}$$

The dependent variable is increasing with better child health. The vector v_i contains individual characteristics of children, the vector x_j features of households where children live and z_g contains contextual factors. The error term ε_{ijg} captures unobserved child, household and community characteristics. As stressed in the previous literature endogeneity problems are a major challenge for research on inequality and health (cf. Deaton, 2003; Subramanian & Kwachi, 2004). As unit fixed effects interfere with the possibility to test RIH and IIH, results should be interpreted with care as our aggregate measures may correlate with unobservable determinants of child health at the chosen geographical levels.

EMPIRICAL RESULTS

Baseline Results

We first examine the relationships using *Ordinary Least Squares* (OLS). Importantly, the hypotheses AIH, RIH and IIH are not mutually exclusive, and can all be tested in the same specification. Each one could be a partial explanation of the aggregate relationship between inequality and population health. As clustering and stratification may skew standard errors, these survey design features are accounted for.[17] Table 2 present baseline results when inequality and average expenditures are aggregated at the provincial, the district and the constituency level, respectively. Table A1 presents complete estimates and the effects of most individual and household level control variables are as expected.

Results confirm the AIH by showing that the log of household expenditure correlates with child health. Without controlling for other observable household characteristics, a one standard deviation increase in household per capita expenditures associates with an increase of the HAZ by roughly one standard deviation, a substantial improvement. Controlling for additional household variables somewhat decreases the magnitude of the

Table 2. OLS Estimates of Height-for-Age z-Score Function with Average Expenditure and Inequality Defined at Different Geographic Levels.

Province						
LogHH expenditures per capita	0.168*** [0.024]	0.124*** [0.025]	0.130*** [0.025]	0.071*** [0.025]	0.045* [0.026]	0.076*** [0.025]	0.051** [0.025]
Average province expenditures		0.650*** [0.094]	0.636*** [0.094]	0.485*** [0.098]	0.494*** [0.101]	0.588*** [0.099]	0.583*** [0.102]
Gini province			1.784** [0.744]	2.400*** [0.759]	1.947** [0.775]		
Gini province $t-1$						3.648*** [0.706]	3.263*** [0.708]
Observations	10,316	10,316	10,316	10,316	10,316	10,316	10,316
R^2	0.03	0.04	0.04	0.05	0.06	0.06	0.06
District						
LogHH expenditures per capita	0.168*** [0.024]	0.140*** [0.025]	0.136*** [0.025]	0.086*** [0.026]	0.059** [0.026]	0.092*** [0.025]	0.065** [0.026]
Average district expenditures		0.244*** [0.079]	0.254*** [0.079]	0.075 [0.084]	0.071 [0.085]	0.085 [0.085]	0.079 [0.087]
Gini district			−0.618 [0.520]	−0.404 [0.512]	−0.584 [0.507]		
Gini district $t-1$						0.771** [0.314]	0.680** [0.310]
Observations	10,316	10,316	10,316	10,316	10,316	10,316	10,316
R^2	0.03	0.03	0.03	0.05	0.05	0.05	0.05

Table 2. (Continued)

Constituency						
LogHH expenditures per capita	0.168*** [0.024]	0.140*** [0.026]	0.133*** [0.025]	0.089*** [0.026]	0.063** [0.026]	0.092*** [0.026]	0.067** [0.026]
Average constituency expenditures		0.185*** [0.069]	0194*** [0.070]	0.021 [0.073]	0.018 [0.073]	0.031 [0.073]	0.025 [0.073]
Gini constituency			−0.649 [0.435]	−0.280 [0.428]	−0.388 [0.426]		
Gini constituency $t-1$						0.673*** [0.245]	0.620** [0.243]
Observations	10,316	10,316	10,316	10,316	10,316	10,316	10,316
R^2	0.03	0.03	0.03	0.05	0.05	0.05	0.05

Complex survey design accounted for. Standard errors in brackets. *Significant at 10%; **significant at 5%; ***significant at 1%. All regressions include controls for gender, age, age square, birth order, female household head, female household share, household size, household location (urban/rural), household educational level, source of water, toilet facility, number of meals, and intake of animal products.

association, suggesting that the relationship between household expenditures and child health is partially mediated through, for example food consumption.

The baseline analysis provides no support for the RIH. In fact, holding household and individual characteristics constant, children in households residing in richer provinces are less malnourished. The positive relationship remains when evaluating expenditures at the district and constituency level, but these results are not robust to the inclusion of household characteristics. The protective health impact of living in a richer province suggests there might be spill-over effects on disadvantaged children from living among richer households, for example better environment and better provision of public goods in general.

For the IIH, we find that both present and lagged inequality in household expenditures at the provincial level associate with better, rather than worse, child health. At the district and constituency level, lagged inequality also correlates positively with child health, whereas present levels of inequality are negative but not statistically significant. It is noteworthy that the positive relationship seems to be stronger when using lagged inequality, and that inequality matters also at lower geographical levels.

Controlling for Endogeneity of Income

If households spend more money on health care, medicines or food consumption when children are ill, the effect of household expenditure on health will be biased downwards. The opposite bias occurs if bad child health causes low parental incomes (Attanasio, Gomez, Rojas, & Vera-Hernandez, 2004).[18] To avoid biased estimates, we follow Skoufias (1998) and Lawson (2004) in using the *value of electrical goods* (excluding radio and TV) and the type of energy used for *lighting* in the household as instruments for household expenditure.[19] The estimates in Table 3 show that the effect of household expenditures per capita remains significantly positive and similar across specifications. The IV-estimates are in general larger than OLS estimates suggesting that the latter are biased downward. The estimated effect of inequality is robust to this exercise.

Controlling for endogeneity produces marginally more support for the RIH with the constituency level as reference group, but the negative association is not robust to the inclusion of lagged inequality. The positive relationship between provincial level average expenditures and better health in baseline estimations remains robust (columns 1 and 2).

Table 3. 2SLS Estimates of Height-for-Age z-Score Function with Average Expenditure and Inequality Defined at Different Geographic Levels.

	(1)	(2)	(3)	(4)	(5)	(6)
Log HH expenditures per capita	0.317*	0.240*	0.403*	0.382*	0.513**	0.430**
	[0.181]	[0.127]	[0.207]	[0.203]	[0.200]	[0.215]
Average province expenditures	0.401***	0.509***				
	[0.129]	[0.127]				
Gini province	1.960**					
	[0.784]					
Gini province $t-1$		3.440***				
		[0.737]				
Average district expenditures			−0.136	−0.101		
			[0.149]	[0.142]		
Gini district			−0.189			
			[0.579]			
Gini district $t-1$				0.838**		
				[0.335]		
Average constituency expenditures					−0.247*	−0.196
					[0.148]	[0.146]
Gini constituency					0.245	
					[0.503]	
Gini constituency $t-1$						0.678***
						[0.249]
Constant	−8.484***	−10.318***	−1.639	−2.467**	−0.998	−1.496
	[1.276]	[1.305]	[1.107]	[1.133]	[1.003]	[1.037]
Observations	10,302	10,302	10,302	10,302	10,302	10,302

Complex survey design accounted for. Standard errors in brackets. *Significant at 10%; **significant at 5%; ***significant at 1%. All regressions include controls for gender, age, age square, birth order, female household head, female household share, household size, household location (urban/rural), household educational level, source of water, toilet facility, number of meals, and intake of animal products.

Sensitivity Analysis

We conduct an extensive series of sensitivity tests of our main results.[20] The main results — support for AIH, no or very weak support for RIH and a positive correlation between lagged inequality and child health, rejecting the IIH, are robust to the following changes:

Using alternative inequality indices: Using the generalized entropy measures GE(0) and GE(1) instead of the Gini coefficient. GE(0) gives more weight to distances between incomes in the lower tail, while GE(1) applies equal weights across the distribution (cf. Cowell, 1995).

Removing outliers: Re-estimating results excluding the lowest and then the highest deciles in the expenditure distribution, and also excluding constituencies with fewer than 50 and 100 observations.

Using alternative explanatory variables: Replacing *animal products* with a proxy for the *proportion of high protein foods in diet*. Replacing the indicator on the standard of a household's *toilet facility* with information on its method of *garbage disposal*.

Using alternative instruments: Replacing the set of instruments used in the two stage estimations with information on housing conditions (type of *floor* and *roof*) and type of *energy* used in cooking. Doing this, results with respect to the AIH, RIH and IIH are confirmed, but some covariates such as household education and the rural dummy become insignificant, suggesting a correlation with these alternative instruments.

Including weights in regressions: Following Deaton's (2000) and Korn and Graubard's (2003) recommendations on regression analysis of survey data, we initially do not apply weighting procedures in the econometric modelling. As a sensitivity test we take them into account, with no change in baseline results.

Alternative estimation techniques: Running a two-level (household and geographic unit) random intercept model including individual characteristics, household expenditures as well as the contextual variables.

DISCUSSION AND CONCLUDING REMARKS

When comparing recent studies to earlier research, it is clear that the evidence of a negative link between income inequality and population health in developed countries weakens when using micro data and controlling for individual income (cf. Deaton, 2003; Karlsson et al., 2010; Kawachi & Kennedy, 1997; Mellor & Milyo, 2001). On the other hand, we show that the positive correlation between inequality and average child health across less developed countries is also present using individual level data and within-country inequality variation at three different geographical levels in Zambia. Thus, while Wilkinson seems to be wrong about the robustness of the evidence for the income inequality hypothesis in rich countries, he seems to be right in claiming that rich and poor are different in how population health is related to inequality.

In our opinion, Deaton (2003) is also right in noting that the mechanisms pointed to as explanations of the income inequality hypothesis in rich countries are plausible also for poor ones, suggesting that these mechanisms do not help us understand the diverse pattern of results in the literature. Several theoretical pathways by which inequality may adversely impact on health outcomes have been proposed. But what could explain a positive association between inequality and health?

As argued by Goldthorp (2010), income inequality may well be associated with stressful social comparisons, but there is no obvious reason why these social comparisons lead to more stress when income differences are bigger. Having less than one's peer group may be just as stressful (or even more so) when one has slightly less compared to when the difference is big. If inequality negatively affects health via social stress, but the effect is independent of the Gini coefficients,[21] then other factors correlated with income inequality but not captured in previous studies could explain the diverse findings in the literature.

Consider for example the contrast between Zambia, with very low average income and extremely high inequality levels, and rich, egalitarian Norway. In Zambia, we find inequality to be linked to improved physiological health. In Norway, Dahl et al. (2006) find the opposite. This is the opposite of what one would expect based on the income inequality hypothesis where the size of inequality is what matters. Are there omitted factors such that in Norway, inequality correlates with behaviours that actually have adverse health effects — while in Zambia, some omitted factors that correlate with inequality are actually beneficial for health? We see a number of possible explanations.

A first possibility is the social sharing of food and other consumption (cf. Gurven, 2004; Kaplan & Hill, 1985). With social sharing of food, the distribution of actual consumption will be more equal than the measured distribution of expenditure. In contexts with high inequality it is possible that the rich are very generous towards the poor. If growth comes with higher inequality, and those who benefit from growth share with those who do not benefit, the marginal health gain in poor households is likely to exceed the health losses for those who share voluntarily. In this case the actual consumption by the poor will be higher than indicated by their income or their expenditure. Evidence in developing contexts indicate that consumption sharing among households is taking place (Udry, 1995), and according to Deininger, Jin, and Yu (2007) households have a better ability to insure caloric consumption than total consumption. In all, the hypothesis goes well with the evidence presented from Zambia.

A second possible explanation concerns the exact way in which inequality increases. Even in societies with high total inequality, within-group inequality may still be rather low. For example, the information in Table 1 on the alternative inequality measures GE(0) and GE(1) indicates that differences at the bottom of the expenditure distribution in Zambia are smaller than overall expenditure differences, when every observation in the distribution is given an equal weight.[22] It is not very far-fetched to hypothesize that inequality in a situation with a few very rich and a large number of poor has less negative health effects compared to a society drifting apart throughout the income distribution.

In the former case, trust among the relatively poor is likely to remain relatively high: the evidence suggests that income differences among people in the bottom half of the distribution are particularly strongly negatively associated with trust (Gustavsson & Jordahl, 2008). Moreover, when inequality is high because some are richer but a majority is poor, the median voter will be poor, and thus the political channels in the income inequality hypothesis are weaker.

Finally, a relatively large number of poor means a relatively bigger market for products aimed towards the poor, and thus such products become more profitable to produce. This mechanism is analysed by Bergh and Nilsson (2013), who show that there are circumstances where high inequality is associated with higher purchasing power of the poor. The purchasing power mechanism may have important implications for the well-being and health of the poor.

Altogether, our findings merit further research on the relationship between inequality and health in developing contexts. As indicated by the association between higher income inequality and lower prevalence of stunting at the population level across low-income countries in Fig. 1(b), the relationship between inequality and child health may not be atypical for Zambia. A possible direction for further studies is to include proxies for various mediators in order to determine through what linkages the positive income inequality−health relationship mediates. It is also desirable to move beyond the correlation strategy used in this analysis to enable an identification of causal effects. In addition, the theoretical aspects on the relationship between inequality and health need to be revisited, examining how the health effects of inequality depend on the shape of the income distribution.

NOTES

1. The prevalence of stunting refers to the share of children under 5 years of age with a height-for-age z-score lower than -2.
2. NB: Few OECD member countries (3 out of 30) report prevalence of stunting.
3. Though such a correlation among aggregate variables is precisely the type of evidence referred to in *The Spirit level*.
4. For an exception, see Dahl, Ivar Elstad, Hofoss, and Martin-Mollard (2006) on the effect of regional inequality on mortality in Norway.
5. There are hypotheses in addition to the three presented in this paper, for example the relative deprivation hypothesis and the relative position hypothesis, both relating to the relationship between relative income and individual health. As a result, the RIH has been defined differently in parts of the literature and is sometimes used as a heading for all hypotheses. We follow the definitions in Wagstaff and van Doorslaer (2000).
6. Moreover education may mediate the household income—child health relationship. Education might also be an unobserved factor that makes people both healthier and wealthier. If education and not income matters to health, correlation between income and health is induced by effects of education on income (Grossman, 1975, 2000).
7. According to the RIH an individual's health may worsen both if someone richer or poorer in her reference group see their income rise, that is health may be affected by upward and downward comparisons.
8. Several empirical studies find income inequality to display a strong, negative correlation with the extent to which people trust each other (see, e.g. Gustavsson & Jordahl, 2008; Knack & Keefer, 1997).
9. Social capital is defined differently in various paradigms. In general social capital can however be defined as the sum of trust and respect of individuals in a society and by the features of social organization that facilitate cooperation of mutual benefit (cf. Bourdieu, 2007; Putnam, 2000).
10. Crisis protection is likely of great importance to the physical condition of young children and infants who rely on household's strategies to ensure basic health needs.
11. The WHO (2007) states that poor feeding practices and infections often undermine child nutritional status. These outcomes likely correlate with the access to and quality of maternity care and to whether children are immunized.
12. Wilkinson and Pickett (2009), however, argue that the income inequality manifest in a smaller geographical area most likely does not properly reflect the level of inequality which exists in society as a whole and, therefore, that inequality at the smaller geographical level has a lower probability of correlating with health.

13. The survey was conducted by the Zambian Central Statistical Office (CSO) using a multiple stage sample selection survey design, where clusters and households within clusters are randomly selected, and a stratified survey sample.

14. As height, length and weight are measured by survey enumerators, anthropometric indices are not susceptible to self-reported bias. Errors in measurement, therefore, are unlikely to be correlated with socio-economic characteristics of the household where children reside.

15. The dependent variable was derived by using the anthropometric statistical software Epi-Info. We use the sex specific 2000 CDC normalized version of the NCHS reference.

16. In all, the original sample is reduced by 14.8 per cent due to exclusions or missing data.

17. The LCMS IV has eight strata and 1,048 PSUs.

18. A Durbin–Wu–Hausman test indicates that baseline results could be biased due to such endogeneity.

19. Standard testing raises no concern about the validity of the instruments: The Anderson canonical correlation LR test is rejected in all specifications. The instruments are uncorrelated with the error term and excluded instruments are correctly excluded as p-values of Sargan's test of overidentifying restrictions are large.

20. Detailed regression output is available from the authors.

21. While this might sound implausible, it follows for example if the procedure generating the distribution matters, as suggested by the literature on procedural justice and equality of opportunity (cf. Nozick, 1974; Roemer, 1998).

22. GE(0) corresponds to the mean-log deviation and is particularly sensitive to low values in the expenditure distribution, while GE(1) corresponds to Theil's inequality index which allots equal weight to all observations in the distribution.

ACKNOWLEDGEMENTS

The authors are thankful for comments and suggestions from Carl Hampus Lyttkens, Jesper Roine, Mireia Jofre-Bonet, Pernilla Johansson, Björn Ekman and seminar participants at Lund University for useful comments and suggestions. Financial support from SIDA/SAREC, and Jan Wallander and Tom Hedelius foundation is gratefully acknowledged.

REFERENCES

Alesina, A., Baqir, R., & Easterly, W. (1999). Public goods and ethnic divisions. *Quarterly Journal of Economics, 114*, 1243–1284.

Argyle, M. (1999). Causes and correlates of happiness: Well-being. In D. Kahneman, E. Diener & N. Schwarz (Eds.), *The foundations of hedonic psychology* (pp. 353–373). New York, NY: Russell Sage Foundation.

Arimond, M., & Ruel, M. T. (2004). Dietary diversity is associated with child nutritional status: Evidence from 11 demographic and health surveys. *Journal of Nutrition, 134*(10), 2579–2585.

Attanasio, O., Gomez, L. C., Rojas, A. G., & Vera-Hernandez, M. (2004). Child health in rural Colombia: Determinants and policy interventions. *Economics and Human Biology, 2*(3), 411–438.

Babones, S. J. (2008). Income inequality and population health: Correlation and causality. *Social Science & Medicine, 66*(7), 1614–1626.

Baum, F. (1999). Social capital: Is it good for your health? Issues for a public health agenda. *Journal of Epidemiology and Community Health, 53*, 195–196.

Becker, G. (1965). The theory of the allocation of time. *Economic Journal, 75*, 493–517.

Behrman, J. R. (1988). Nutrition, health, birth order and seasonality: Intra-household allocation among children in rural India. *Journal of Development Economics, 28*(1), 43–62.

Behrman, J. R., Pollak, R. A., & Taubman, P. (1986). Do parents favor boys? *International Economic Review, 17*(1), 33–54.

Bengtsson, T., & Lindström, M. (2000). Childhood misery and disease in later life: The effects on mortality in old age of hazard experienced in early life, southern Sweden, 1760–1894. *Population Studies, 54*, 263–277.

Bergh, A. (2008). A critical note on the theory of inequity aversion. *Journal of Socio-Economics, 37*(5), 1789–1796.

Bergh, A., & Nilsson, T. (2013). When more poor means less poverty: On income inequality and purchasing power. *Southern Economic Journal*.

Berkman, L. F., Kawachi, I. (Eds.). (2000). *Social epidemiology.* New York, NY: Oxford University Press.

Blakely, T., Atkinson, J., Ivory, V., Collings, S., Wilton, J., & Howden-Chapman, P. (2006). No association of neighbourhood volunteerism with mortality in New Zealand: A national multilevel cohort study. *International Journal of Epidemiology, 35*(4), 981–989.

Bobak, M., Pikhart, H., Rose, R., Hertzman, C., & Marmot, M. (2000). Socioeconomic factors, material inequalities, and perceived control in self-rated health: Cross-sectional data from seven post-communist countries. *Social Science and Medicine, 51*, 1343–1350.

Bourdieu, P. (2007). The forms of capital. In A. R. Sadovnik (Ed.), *Sociology of education*. New York, NY: Routledge.

Brunner, E., & Marmot, M. (1999). Social organization, stress and health. In M. Marmot & R. G. Wilkinson (Eds.), *Social determinants of health*. Oxford: Oxford University Press. Chap. 2

Carlson, P. (2005). Relatively poor, absolutely ill? A study of regional income inequality in Russia and its possible health consequences. *Journal of Epidemiology and Community Health, 59*(5), 389–394.

Caserta, M. T., O'Connor, T. G., Wyman, P. A., Wang, H., Moynihan, J., Cross, W., Tu, X., & Jin, X. (2008). The associations between psychosocial stress and the frequency of illness, and innate and adaptive immune function in children. *Brain, Behaviour and Immunity, 22*(6), 933–40.

Chang, V. W., & Christakis, N. A. (2005). Income inequality and weight status in US metropolitan areas. *Social Science & Medicine, 61*, 83–96.

Cowell, F. A. (1995). *Measuring inequality* (2nd ed.). Hemel Hempstead: Harvester Wheatsheaf.

Currie, J. (2009). Healthy, wealthy, and wise: Socioeconomic status, poor health in childhood, and human capital development. *Journal of Economic Literature, 47*, 87–122.

Dahl, E., Ivar Elstad, J., Hofoss, D., & Martin-Mollard, M. (2006). For whom is income inequality most harmful? A multi-level analysis of income inequality and mortality in Norway. *Social Science and Medicine, 63*(10), 2562−2574.

De Silva, M. J., & Harpham, S. R. (2007). Maternal social capital and child nutritional status in four developing countries. *Health and Place, 13*(2), 341−355.

Deaton, A. (2000). *The analysis of household surveys − A microeconomteric approach to development policy.* London: World Bank.

Deaton, A. (2003). Health, inequality and economic development. *Journal of Economic Literature, 41*, 113−158.

Deininger, K., Jin., S., & Yu, X. (2007). Risk coping and starvation in rural China. *Applied Economics, 39*(11), 1341−1352.

Demombynes, G., & Berk, O. (2005). Crime and local inequality in South Africa. *Journal of Development Economics, 76*(2), 265−292.

Diaz-Roux, A. V., Link, B. G., & Northridge, M. E. (2000). A multilevel analysis of income inequality and cardiovascular disease. *Social Science & Medicine, 50*, 673−687.

Durkheim, E. (1992 [1897]). *Suicide.* London: Routledge.

Ettner, S. L. (1996). New evidence on the relationship between income and health. *Journal of Health Economics, 15*(1), 67−86.

Falkner, F., & Tanner, J. M. (1986). *Human growth* (2nd ed.). New York, NY: Plenum Press.

Gerdtham, U., & Johannesson, M. (2004). Absolute income, relative income, income inequality, and mortality. *The Journal of Human Resources, 39*, 228−247.

Goldthorpe, J. H. (2010). Analysing social inequality: A critique of two recent contributions from economics and epidemiology. *European Sociological Review, 26*(6), 731−744.

Graitcer, P., & Gentry, E. (1981). Measuring children: One reference for all. *The Lancet, 318*(8241), 297−299.

Gravelle, H. (1998). How much of the relation between population mortality and unequal distribution of income is a statistical artefact? *British Medical Journal, 316*, 382−385.

Gravelle, H., & Sutton, M. (2009). Income, relative income, and self-reported health in Britain 1979−2000. *Health Economics, 18*(2), 125−145.

Grossman, M. (1975). The correlation between health and schooling. In N. Terleckyj (Ed.), *Household production and consumption* (pp. 147−211). New York, NY: Columbia University Press for NBER.

Grossman, M. (2000). The human capital model. In A. J. Culyer & J. P. Newhouse (Eds.), *Handbook of health economics* (Vol. 1A, pp. 347−408). Amsterdam: Elsevier.

Gurven, M. (2004). Reciprocal altruism and food sharing decisions among Hiwi and Ache hunter-gatherers. *Behavioral Ecology and Sociobiology, 56*, 366−380.

Gustavsson, M., & Jordahl, H. (2008). Inequality and trust in Sweden: Some inequalities are more harmful than others. *Journal of Public Economics, 92*(1−2), 348−365.

Habicht, J.-P., Yarbrough, C., Martorell, R., Malina, R., & Klein, R. (1974). Height and weight standards for preschool children − How relevant are ethnic differences in growth potential? *The Lancet, 303*(7858), 611−615.

Harpham, T., De Silva, M. J., & Tran, T. (2006). Maternal social capital and child health in Vietnam. *Journal of Epidemiology and Community Health, 60*(10), 865−871.

Heltberg, R. (2009). Malnutrition, poverty, and economic growth. *Health Economics, 18*, S77−S88.

Hildebrand, V., & Van Kerm, P. (2005). *Income inequality and self-rated health status: Evidence from the European community household panel.* Social and Economic Dimensions of an Aging Population Research Papers, McMaster University.

Hildebrand, V., & Van Kerm, P. (2009). Income inequality and self-rated health status: Evidence from the European community household panel. *Demography, 46*(4), 805–825.

Holstein, B. E., Currie, C., Boyce, W., Damsgaard, M. T., Gobina, I., Kökönyei, G., Hetland, J., de Looze, M., Richter, M., & Due, P. (2009). Socio-economic inequality in multiple health complaints among adolescents: International comparative study in 37 countries. *International Journal of Public Health, 54*(2), 260–270.

Hox, J. (2002). *Multilevel analysis: Techniques and applications.* London: Lawrence Erlbaum Ass. Publisher.

Jones, K., Duncan, C., & Twigg, L. (2004). Evaluating the absolute and relative income hypothesis in an exploratory analysis of deaths in the health and lifestyle survey. In P. Boyle, S. Curtis, & E. Graham (Eds.), *The geography of health inequalities in the developed world.* London: Ashgate Press.

Kahn, B., Zuckerman, H., Bauchner, C. J., Homer, & Wise, P. H. (2002). Women's health after pregnancy and child outcomes at age 3 years: A prospective cohort study. *American Journal of Public Health, 92*, 1312–1318.

Kaplan, H., & Hill, K. (1985). Food sharing among Ache foragers: Tests of explanatory hypotheses. *Current Anthropology, 26*, 223–245.

Kaplan, G. A., Pamuk, E. R., Lynch, J. W., Cohen, R. D., & Balfour, J. L. (1996). Inequality in income and mortality in the United States: Analysis of mortality and potential pathways. *British Medicine Journal, 312*, 999–1003.

Karlsson, M., Nilsson, T., Lyttkens, C. H., & Leeson, G. (2010). Income inequality and health: Importance of a cross-country perspective. *Social Science & Medicine, 70*, 875–885.

Kawachi, I., & Kennedy, B. P. (1997). The relationship of income inequality to mortality: Does the choice of indicator matter? *Social Science Medicine, 45*, 1121–1127.

Kawachi, I., & Kennedy, B. P. (1999). Income inequality and health: Pathways and mechanisms. *Health Services Research, 34*(1), 215–227.

Kawachi, I., Subramanian, S. V., & Kim, D. (2007). *Social capital and health.* New York, NY: Springer.

Kennedy, B. P., Kawachi, I., Glass, R., & Prothrow-Stist, D. (1998). Income distribution, socio-economic status, and self-related health in the US: Multilevel analysis. *British Medical Journal, 317*(7163), 917–921.

Khanam, R., Nghiem, H. S., & Connelly, L. B. (2009). Child health and the income gradient: Evidence from Australia. *Journal of Health Economics, 28*(4), 805–817.

Knack, S., & Keefer, P. (1997). Does social capital have an economic payoff? A cross-country investigation. *Quarterly Journal of Economics, 112*(4), 1252–1288.

Korn, E. L , & Graubard, B. I. (2003). Estimating variance components by using survey data. *Journal of the Royal Statistical Society, Series B (Methodological), 65*(1), 175–190.

Krugman, P. (1996). The spiral of inequality. *Mother Jones,* November/December, pp. 44–49.

Larrea, C., & Kawachi, I. (2005). Does economic inequality affect child malnutrition? The case of Ecuador. *Social Science and Medicine, 60*, 165–178.

Lawson, D. (2004). *Determinants of health seeking behaviour in Uganda – Is it just income and user fees that are important?* Working Paper, University of Manchester, Manchester, UK.

Leigh, A., & Jencks, C. (2007). Inequality and mortality: Long-run evidence from a panel of countries. *Journal of Health Economics, 26*(1), 1–24.

Li, H., & Zhu, Y. (2006). Income, income inequality and health – Evidence from China. *Journal of Comparative Economics, 34*, 668–693.

Lochner, K., Pamuk, E., & Makuc, D. (2001). State-level income inequality and individual mortality risk: A prospective, multilevel study. *American Journal of Public Health, 91*(3), 385–392.

Lopez, R. (2004). Income inequality and self-rated health in US metropolitan areas: A multilevel analysis. *Social Science & Medicine, 59*, 2409–2419.

Lorgelly, P. K., & Lindley, J. K. (2008). What is the relationship between income inequality and health? Evidence from the BHPS. *Health Economics, 17*(2), 249–265.

Luttmer, E. F. P. (2005). Neighbors as negatives: Relative earnings and well-being. *Quarterly Journal of Economics, 120*(3), 963–1002.

Lynch, J. W., Smith, G. D., Kaplan, G. A., & House, J. S. (2000). Income inequality and mortality: Importance to health of individual income, psychosocial environment, or material conditions. *British Medical Journal, 320*, 1200–1204.

Mellor, J. M., & Milyo, J. D. (2001). Income inequality and health. *Journal of Policy Analysis and Management, 20*(1), 151–55.

Mellor, J. M., & Milyo, J. D. (2002). Income inequality and individual health: Evidence from the current population survey. *Journal of Human Resources, 37*, 510–539.

Miller, D. L., & Paxson, C. (2006). Relative income, race, and mortality. *Journal of Health Economics, 25*(5), 979–1003.

Morrow, V. (2004). Children's "social capital": Implications for health and well-being. *Health Education, 104*(4), 211–225.

Mosley, W. H., & Chen, L. C. (1984). An analytical framework for the study of child survival in developing countries. *Population and Development Review, 10*, 25–45.

Nozick, R. (1974). *Anarchy, state and Utopia*. New York, NY: Basic Books.

Olivius, G., Ostergren, P. O., Hanson, B. S., & Lyttkens, C. H. (2004). Parental economic stress. *European Journal of Public Health, 14*(4), 354–360.

Osler, M., Christensen, U., Due, P., Lund, R., Andersen, I., Diderichsen, F., & Prescott, E. (2003). Income inequality and ischaemic heart disease in Danish men and women. *International Journal of Epidemiology, 32*, 375–380.

Preston, S. H. (1975). The changing relation between mortality and level of economic development. *Populations Studies, 29*, 231–248.

Putnam, R. D. (2000). *Bowling alone. The collapse and revival of American community*. New York, NY: Touchstone.

Rajkumar, A., & Vinaya, S. (2008). Public spending and outcomes: Does governance matter? *Journal of Development Economics, 86*(1), 96–111.

Ram, R. (2006). Further examination of the cross-country association between income inequality and population health. *Social Science and Medicine, 62*(3), 779–791.

Rodgers, G. B. (1979). Income and inequality as determinants of mortality: An international cross-section analysis. *Population Studies, 33*, 343–351.

Roemer, J. E. (1998). *Equality of opportunity*. Cambridge: Harvard University Press.

Senik, C. (2004). When information dominates comparison: Learning from Russian subjective panel data. *Journal of Public Economics, 88*, 2099–2123.

Shibuya, K., Hashimoto, H., & Yano, E. (2002). Individual income, income distribution, and self rated health in Japan: Cross sectional analysis of nationally representative sample. *British Medical Journal, 324*, 16.

Skoufias, E. (1998). Determinants of child health during the economic transition in Romania. *World Development, 26*(11), 2045–2056.

Smith, J. P. (1999). Healthy bodies and thick wallets: The dual relation between health and economic status. *Journal of Economic Perspectives, 13*, 145–166.

Solt, F. (2008). Standardizing the world income inequality database. *Social Science Quarterly, 90*(2), 231–242.

Subramanian, S. V., Delgado, I., Jadue, L., Vega, J., & Kawachi, I. (2003). Income inequality and health: Multilevel analysis of Chilean communities. *Journal of Epidemiology and Community Health, 57*, 844–848.

Subramanian, S. V., & Kwachi, I. (2004). Income inequality and health: What have we learned so far? *Epidemiologic Reviews, 26*, 78–91.

Submramanian, S. V., Kawachi, I., & Kennedy, B. P. (2001). Does the state you live in make a difference? Multilevel analysis of self related health in the US. *Social Science and Medicine, 53*(1), 9–19.

Subramanian, S. V., Kawachi, I., & Smit, G. D. (2007). Income inequality and the double burden of under- and overnutrition in India. *Journal of Epidemiology and Community Health, 61*, 802–809.

Thomas, D., Strauss, J., & Henriques, M.-H. (1991). How does mother's education affect child height? *Journal of Human Resources, 26*(2), 183–211.

Udry, C. (1995). Risk and saving in Northern Nigeria. *American Economic Review, 85*(5), 1287–1301.

Wagstaff, A., & van Doorslaer, E. (2000). Income inequality and health: What does the literature tell us? *Annual Review of Public Health, 21*, 543–567.

Waldman, R. (1992). Income distribution and infant mortality. In I. Kawachi, B. Kennedy, & R. G. Wilkinson (Eds.), *The society and population health reader* (pp. 14–27). New York, NY: New Press.

WHO. (1995). Physical status: The use and integration of anthropometry. Report of a WHO expert committee. World Health Organization Technical Report Series, *854*, 1–452.

WHO. (2007). Retrieved from http://www.who.int/nutgrowthdb/database/countries/zmb/en/

Wilkinson, R., & Pickett, K. (2006). Income inequality and population health: A review and explanation of the evidence. *Social Science & Medicine, 62*, 1768–1784.

Wilkinson, R. G. (1992). National mortality rates: The impact of inequality? *American Journal of Public Health, 82*(8), 1082–1084.

Wilkinson, R. G. (1996). *Unhealthy societies: The afflictions of inequality.* London: Routledge.

Wilkinson, R. G., & Pickett, K. (2009). *The spirit level: Why equality is better for everyone.* London: Allen Lane.

Wolf, J. M., Miller, G. E., & Chen, E. (2008). Parent psychological states predict changes in inflammatory markers in children with asthma and healthy children. *Brain Behaviour and Immunity, 22*(4), 433–441.

World Bank. (2008). *World development indicators 2008.* Development Data Group, World Bank, Washington DC.

Wyman, P. A., Moynihan, J., Eberly, S., Cox, C., Cross, W., Jin, X., & Caserta, M. T. (2008). Association of family stress with natural killer cell activity and the frequency of illnesses in children. *Brain, Behaviour and Immunity, 22*(6), 933–940.

Zere, E., & McIntyre, D. (2003). Inequities in under-five child malnutrition in South Africa. *International Journal for Equity in Health, 2*(1), 7–10.

APPENDIX

Table A1. Complete OLS Estimates of Height-for-Age z-Score Function with all Included Controls.

	Province	District	Constituency
Gender	0.200***	0.205***	0.205***
	[0.034]	[0.035]	[0.035]
Age	−0.053***	−0.052***	−0.052***
	[0.005]	[0.005]	[0.005]
Age^2	0.001***	0.001***	0.001***
	[0.000]	[0.000]	[0.000]
Birth order	−0.069***	−0.071***	−0.071***
	[0.018]	[0.018]	[0.018]
Female household head	0.010	0.010	0.008
	[0.065]	[0.065]	[0.065]
Female HH share (adult)	0.227*	0.215*	0.217*
	[0.120]	[0.120]	[0.121]
HH size	0.044***	0.046***	0.047***
	[0.009]	[0.009]	[0.009]
Rural	−0.197***	−0.222***	−0.228***
	[0.059]	[0.063]	[0.062]
HH edu1	0.269**	0.297**	0.302**
	[0.123]	[0.124]	[0.124]
HH edu2	0.340***	0.363***	0.368***
	[0.127]	[0.129]	[0.128]
HH edu3	0.516***	0.540***	0.541***
	[0.145]	[0.147]	[0.147]
Water	−0.012	0.003	0.009
	[0.046]	[0.046]	[0.046]
Toilet facility	−0.004	−0.075	−0.071
	[0.065]	[0.063]	[0.063]
Meals	0.182***	0.248***	0.248***
	[0.044]	[0.043]	[0.043]
Animal products	0.118***	0.064	0.060
	[0.045]	[0.045]	[0.045]
Log HH expenditures per capita	0.045*	0.059**	0.063**
	[0.026]	[0.026]	[0.026]
Average expenditures	0.494***	0.071	0.018
	[0.101]	[0.085]	[0.073]
Gini	1.947**	−0.584	−0.388
	[0.775]	[0.507]	[0.426]
Constant	−8.592***	−2.369**	−1.881**
	[1.256]	[1.007]	[0.845]
Observations	10,316	10,316	10,316
R-squared	0.06	0.05	0.05

Complex survey design accounted for standard errors in brackets.
*significant at 10%; **significant at 5%; ***significant at 1%

PART V
EQUITY IN HEALTH CARE

EQUITY IN HEALTH CARE DELIVERY: SOME THOUGHTS AND AN EXAMPLE

John E. Roemer

ABSTRACT

Equality of opportunity (EOp) for health is defined and advocated as the right conceptualization of equity in the allocation of health care resources. EOp is contrasted with the traditional view that equity consists in "horizontal equity," a state in which all persons in a society with similar health needs receive similar amounts of medical resources. We argue the horizontal equity is neither sufficient nor necessary for distributive justice in this domain. The EOp view holds individuals partially responsible for the quality of lifestyle that they live, in so far as it affects their health, but compensates individuals for the effect on health of circumstances beyond their control, including the effect of circumstances on their lifestyle. EOp generally recommends a distribution of medical resources that is more egalitarian than the utilitarianism recommends, but less egalitarian than the (Rawlsian) maximin view recommends.

An example is computed to illustrate the difference between opportunity equalizing and utilitarian health delivery policies.

Keywords: Equal opportunity; circumstances; effort; horizontal equity; utilitarianism

JEL classifications: I14; D63

INTRODUCTION

In what does equity in health care delivery consist? Perhaps the most accepted view is that that delivery be horizontally equitable, which is to say, that two individuals who suffer from the same disease should receive the same treatment. (For example, this definition of equity is offered in van Doorslaer et al. (2000) and O'Donnell, van Doorslaer, Wagstaff, and Lindelow (2008).) Surely, the most unjust aspects of health care delivery, either within or across nations, can be captured with this notion, because the greatest injustice consists in the difference in expenditure in treating the rich and the poor. I shall argue, however, that horizontal equity is *insufficient* as a characterization of what constitutes a just distribution of resources in the health sector. I shall even claim, but more contestably, that horizontal equity is not *necessary* for such justice. That second claim, however, is not the focus of my argument.

We can easily see that horizontal equity is insufficient to characterize justice in the distribution of health resources with the following example. Suppose there is a society consisting of rich and poor people. The rich are either healthy or suffer from gout, and the poor are either healthy or suffer from tuberculosis (TB). Society spends $1,000 on each case of gout, and $5 on each case of TB. This distribution is horizontally equitable: any citizen, regardless of his social position, receives the same health resources if he suffers from gout, and the same is true for any citizen who suffers from TB. In this society, that is to say, the health resources an ill person receives are a function *only* of the disease she manifests, not of her social class or income. Yet we would probably say that the distribution of health resources is massively unjust in this society, because of the correlation between diseases and income.

One might think that the example is artificial, but I believe it is not, for one of the major aspects of health inequity in the world is that more is spent on *diseases* of the rich than on diseases of the poor. One might also think that one could preserve the horizontal-equity characterization of justice by changing the definition of horizontal equity – by referring to "equal health needs" in place of "equal disease characteristics." But I do not think that is easily accomplished. For it may well be begging the question of what constitutes justice to define horizontal equity in terms of "equal treatment for equal health needs," *unless* "equal health needs" is an objectively clear phrase, referring to equal disease characteristics.

In what follows, I shall propose that a distribution of health resources in a society is just if it *equalizes opportunities for health* in the population. I will be thinking of a society as that of a country, although one could, in principle, apply the view internationally. The word "opportunities" in the phrase suggests that the goal is not to equalize health outcomes, but rather, *chances* for acquiring good health. How we parse out what equality of chances means will determine, of course, how egalitarian the view is.

I will apply the theory of equal opportunity that I have expounded elsewhere (Roemer, 1993, 1998, 2001, 2012). In that theory, the language consists in five critical words. The *objective* is that condition of people for which we wish to equalize opportunities – in the present case, some measure of health (QALYs or life expectancy, for example). *Circumstances* are aspects of a person's environment – physical, social, or biological – that influence her health status and over which she has no control. In the case of health, these would typically constitute some set of social and biological characteristics. A *type* is the set of people in the society who share the same circumstances. *Effort* is the constellation of those behaviors of a person that influence her health and over which she has at least some control. Finally, the *instrument* is the tool by which opportunities are to be equalized: in the present case, a distribution of health resources.

The goal of an equal opportunity policy is to make it the case that the degree to which a person achieves the objective is independent of his circumstances, and is a function only of his effort. Thus, a person is effectively held responsible only for the consequences of his effort, and is insured against bad outcomes due to his having disadvantaged circumstances. Given a finite amount of resource to devote to the problem, it will usually be impossible to realize this goal, and so we will settle for a compromise, as follows. We wish to make it the case that, at every "degree of effort," the level of objective of the worst-off individuals is as high as possible, regardless of their type. (Thus we substitute "maximin" for "equalize.") But even this goal is unachievable, for we cannot maximize an infinite number of quantities (here, the level of the worst-off person *at every effort level*) at once. So a further compromise is in order, whose description will await the formal treatment below.

Other important examples of considerations of personal responsibility for equity in health care are developed in Fleurbaey and Schokkaert (2009, 2012). Both my approach and theirs derive from the rich philosophical debate which began with Rawls (1971) and reached its apex in the 1980s, following Ronald Dworkin's (1981) important contribution. A discussion of this chapter in contemporary political philosophy can be found in Roemer (2010).

In the case of health, I propose that the relevant effort is what is called lifestyle quality: whether or not the person smokes, how much she exercises, what her diet consists in, and so on. A person's life style is not entirely voluntary, but it is surely in part voluntary and, I will claim, it is not wrong to hold persons at least partially responsible for their lifestyle, in so far as it affects their health. Let me first explain what I mean by "in part."

Consider an example, in which society consists of several types of person, defined by their socio-economic status (SES). Although a person's SES may not be entirely beyond his control, the society in question may wish to treat it so for the purposes of health policy: that is, society may wish to indemnify citizens against the consequences of their SES for their health. To this end, it would be appropriate to take a person's circumstances to include his SES. Suppose, for simplicity, this is the only circumstance. At any distribution of the health resource among the population, there will ensue a *distribution of effort* in each type: that is, a distribution of lifestyle qualities within each social class.[1] Let us suppose that we can measure lifestyle quality with a single index, so we can speak of an individual's having a lifestyle quality of q. In general, we will observe different distributions of q in the different types (social classes). The *distribution* of lifestyle quality is a *characteristic of the type*: it reflects the social conditions of the type as a whole, not of any individual, and as a characteristic of type, it is rightly considered to be an aspect of circumstance. Thus, it would be incorrect to say that two individuals, of different SES, but who exhibit the same q, have expended "equal degrees of effort" as far as the theory of equal opportunity is concerned – because for one, q may be far above the average of his type, while for the other, it may be far below the average. In other words, the absolute measure of lifestyle quality, q, is polluted, with respect to its usability in the theory, by the fact that it confounds two elements: an element of volition by the individual, and the influence of circumstances (SES). Observed lifestyle quality is a reflection of *effort*, which we cannot observe directly. We wish to deduce the degree of effort from its reflection.

How can we sterilize the measure q of its circumstantial component, and replace it with a measure that more accurately captures the volitional element of choice, the thing for which we think the individual can be held responsible? One way is to measure an individual's effort not by the raw value of q, but by the *rank* of his lifestyle index in the distribution of lifestyle qualities of persons of his or her type. Thus, we measure how much effort an individual has made by comparing him or her only to others in the individual's type. The *rank* of a person's effort in the effort distribution of his/her type is taken to be the "sterilized" measure of effort.

We then state that two individuals in society have expended the same degree of effort if and only if they lie at the same rank of the lifestyle distributions of their respective types. The degree of effort, so defined, judges a person only against others of his type. The judgment so made is then said to be a relevant inter-type measure of effort.

The equal opportunity (EOp) policy is now defined to be that distribution of resources under which, for every number π between zero and one, the health outcome (e.g., life expectancy) for all those at the πth rank (or quantile) of their type lifestyle distributions are equal. In actual problems, this cannot achieved, so we will require a measure of closeness to the ideal of equality. (A precise mathematical statement will appear below.)

Consider this example. Suppose, for the sake of concreteness, that lifestyle quality consists in just one factor, how much an individual smokes. Suppose that smoking is correlated with SES, so that individuals of disadvantaged SES smoke more, on average. Perhaps the intensity of smoking varies between zero and 100 with a median of 70 in a low SES type, and it varies between 0 and 90 with a median of 20 in a high SES type. Then we would declare that a person in the disadvantaged type who smoked with intensity 70 and a person in the high type who smoked with intensity 20 had expended the same *degrees of effort*, because they each sit at the 0.5 rank (50th centile) of the effort distributions of their type. The EOp policy would attempt to equalize their health outcomes – say, life expectancies. Clearly, this would in general require spending more on the individual from the disadvantaged type. On the other hand, that policy would not attempt to equalize the life expectancies of these two individuals *and* the life expectancy of someone from the disadvantaged type who smoked with intensity 50: there would be no inequity if that person had a greater life expectancy.

Clearly, the claim of equity, here, depends on our having captured in circumstances all, or the main, effects on health which lie beyond the person's control. That is presumed in the example.

Some readers will doubtless say, at this point, that it is wrong to hold people responsible, even in part, for their health status. They may say, for example, that the EOp view contravenes horizontal equity, because it *requires* us to spend more on the person with disease X who had a high quality life style than on another person of disease X who had a low quality life style. That conclusion, however, is false: we can, in fact, construct EOp policies which *respect* horizontal equity, and I will do that below. Others may say that it is wrong, tout court, to hold people responsible for their health. Before responding that in section 4, it will be useful to formulate the EOp view of health in a more precise way.

A MORE PRECISE FORMULATION

We consider a population partitioned into J types, where we denote the generic type as j. There are I diseases which afflict members of this society, with the generic disease denoted i. There is available in the health sector an amount of resource (money) R per capita. We do not address how much of a society's product should be dedicated to health, but only how to spend the amount that has been so dedicated.

The set of possible resource allocations is defined to be a set of vectors $r = (R^1, R^2, ..., R^I)$, where R^i will be the amount spent on treating a case of disease i. We call r a *policy*. Thus, *by definition*, we restrict ourselves to policies that are horizontally equitable: any person suffering from disease i, regardless of her type and lifestyle quality, will receive the same treatment. There are, however, many different policies r that could be chosen.

For any given vector r there will ensue a distribution of lifestyle quality in each type j, and a consequent distribution of disease occurrences in each type. (As I wrote above, lifestyle quality may not be responsive to the policy, but we allow for the general case in which it is.) Let us denote the fraction of individuals in type j who contract disease i when the policy is r by $f^{ij}(r)$. Let p^j denote the fraction of the population of type j. Then the policy is *feasible* when:

$$\sum_{i,j} p^j f^{ij}(r) \le R$$

and it exhausts the budget precisely when:

$$\sum_{i,j} p^j f^{ij}(r) = R \tag{1}$$

We now define the set of *admissible policies* as all those for which (1) holds: call this set A. We must locate the equal-opportunity policy in A.

It bears repeating that *all policies in A are horizontally equitable:* thus horizontal equity is *insufficient* as a criterion of justice in health expenditures. For there will be an infinite number of policies in A, among which the horizontal equity criterion is indifferent.

We next suppose that we know the *health production functions* for each type; these are functions which give the probability that a person of type j will contract disease i if she lives a lifestyle of quality q. We denote these functions s^{ij}; thus $s^{ij}(q)$ is the probability that a j- type will contract disease i if she lives lifestyle quality q. We presume it is the case that $\{s^{ij}\}$ are monotone decreasing functions: that is, raising lifestyle quality reduces the probability of disease.

We also have as data of the problem the mapping from the policy space A to the space of cumulative distribution functions on the non-negative real numbers. Denote that class of distribution functions by Γ. The map:

$$F^j : A \to \Gamma$$

gives us the distribution of lifestyle qualities that will occur in type j, at any policy r in A. We write $F_r^j = F^j(r)$. Thus an individual with lifestyle quality q in type j lies at rank π of the effort distribution of her type, when the policy is r, if $F_r^j(q) = \pi$. We denote this value of q by $q_r^j(\pi)$.

Finally, we need to postulate the relationship between treatment of disease and health outcome. For the sake of concreteness, let us take the outcome to be life expectancy. We therefore suppose that we know the life expectancy for those in type j who have contracted disease i and who are treated with resource level x. Denote this life expectancy by $\lambda^{ij}(x)$. We could further complexify, here, by assuming that life expectancy is a function, in addition, of the life style quality of the individual, but I choose not to do so, to avoid further notational complexity.

Consider, now, a policy r, which induces a distribution of lifestyle quality in each type. Consider a type j and all those at rank π of j's lifestyle quality distribution. Assume there is a large number of people in each type, so that the fraction of people in a type who contract a disease is equal to the probability that people in that type will contract the disease. Then[2] the average life expectancy of all such people – the (j,π) cohort – will be

$$\frac{\sum_i s^{ij}(q_r^j(\pi))\lambda^{ij}(R^i)}{\sum_i s^{ij}(q_r^j(\pi))} \equiv L^j(\pi, r)$$

We are finally ready to define the EOp policy. Fix, for the moment, a particular value of π. We would like to find a policy that makes the numbers $\{L^j(\pi,r)\}$ equal, for all j: such a policy would make it the case that the life expectancy for a person of degree of lifestyle quality π who becomes ill is independent of his type. There may be no such policy; we therefore replace "equalize" with "maximin," and we define the desirable policy as:

$$r(\pi) = \arg\max_r \min_j L^j(\pi, r)$$

This is the policy that makes, for the "tranche" of people of lifestyle degree π, the life expectancy of the most disadvantaged type as large as possible.

Now unfortunately, there will be, in general, a different policy $r(\pi)$ for each $\pi \in [0, 1]$. Thus, some (further) compromise is required. The compromise that I prefer is to choose that policy that maximizes the average of the life expectancies of the worse off type, overall effort levels, that is:

$$r^{EOp} = \arg\max_r \int_0^1 \min_j L^j(\pi, r)\, d\pi \qquad (2)$$

In the averaging procedure (2), we show no favoritism for those according to their effort level.[3]

Although we need a lot of data to compute the EOp policy, it is only the Department of Health that must have these data: once the policy is computed, a hospital need only diagnose a patient to know what treatment is appropriate (i.e., how much resource to spend on the case). No patient need ever be asked her type or her lifestyle characteristics. There is, that is to say, no incursion of privacy necessitated by applying the policy – apart from the initial incursion in the research project that assembles the data set to compute the health production functions. And furthermore, as I have emphasized, the policy is horizontally equitable.

I can now explain why horizontal equity is not *necessary* for equality of opportunity. I began, in this section, with a restriction to horizontally equitable policies. But, more generally, we might define a policy as a *matrix* $\{r^{ij}\}$, where r^{ij} is the resource to be spent on a case of disease i in a person of type j. We could then repeat the above analysis, and compute the associated EOp policy. It would generally *not* be the case that *that* EOp policy would be horizontally equitable: it would likely spend different amounts on the occurrence of a given disease in different types. Indeed, the polices $\{r^{ij}\}$ are less restrictive than the policies $\{r^i\}$, and so we would with them achieve a higher value of the EOp program — that is, equality of opportunity is enhanced by *dropping* horizontal equity.

Nevertheless, there may be norms that recommend horizontal equity as well as equality of opportunity, which motivated my first specification of the problem. Dropping horizontal equity would require a hospital to do a (generalized) means test on a patient before treating him, which would be objectionable for other reasons. So I here assume that we compute the equal-opportunity policy (or the one that best approaches that ideal) among only those policies which are horizontally equitable.

AN EXAMPLE

In this section, I compute the EOp policy for a hypothetical example. I posit a society with two types, the rich and the poor. I suppose that a person is not to be held accountable for his socio-economic status, as far as his health is concerned. The poor have lifestyles whose qualities q are uniformly distributed on the interval $[0,1]$, while the rich have lifestyle qualities that are uniformly distributed on the interval $[0.5, 1.5]$. The probability of contracting cancer, as a function of lifestyle quality (q) is the same for both types, and given by:

$$s^{CP}(q) = s^{CR}(q) = 1 - \frac{2q}{3}$$

Only the poor are at a risk of TB; their probability of contracting TB is:

$$s^{TP}(q) = 1 - \frac{q}{3}$$

Suppose that life expectancy for a rich individual is given by 70, if cancer is not contracted, and $60 + 10(x_c - 1)/(x_c + 1)$, if cancer is contracted, and x_c is spent on its treatment.

Thus, if the disease is contracted, life expectancy will lie between 50 and 70, depending on how much is spent on treatment (from zero to an infinite amount). (This is a simple way of modeling the fact that nobody dies of cancer before age 50.)

Suppose that life expectancy for a poor individual is 70 if neither disease is contracted, $60 + 10(x_c - 1)/(x_c + 1)$ if cancer is contracted and x_c is spent on its treatment, and $50 + 20(.1x_t - 1)/(.1x_t + 1)$ if TB is contracted and x_t is spent on its treatment.

In addition, if both cancer and TB are contracted, life expectancy (for the poor person) will be the minimum of the two cancer and TB expectancies. Thus, the poor can die at age 30 if they contract TB and it is not treated. With large expenditures, a person who contracts TB can live to age 70. Furthermore, it is expensive to raise life expectancy above 30 if TB is contracted.

Finally, I assume that 25% of the population is poor and 75% is rich, and that the national health budget is $3,000 per capita.

With these data, one can compute that 33% of the rich will contract cancer, 9.3% of the poor will contract only cancer, 26% of the poor will contract only TB, and 57% of the poor will contract both TB and cancer. (Here, we do not exclude the possibility that a person could contract both diseases.)

Our instrument is (R^C, R^T), the schedule of how much will spent on treating an occurrence of each disease. The objective is to equalize opportunities, for the rich and the poor, for life expectancy.

The calculation of the optimal solution is presented in the appendix. The solution is $R^C = \$686$, $R^T = \$13,027$. In Fig. 1, I present the life expectancies of the rich and the poor, as a function of the rank at which they sit on the effort distribution of their type, at this solution.

The higher curve is that of the rich. We see that, at the EOp solution, the rich still have greater life expectancy than the poor – despite the large amounts being spent on treating TB. Moreover, life expectancy increases with lifestyle quality – this inequality of outcome is an aspect that EOp does *not* attempt to eliminate.

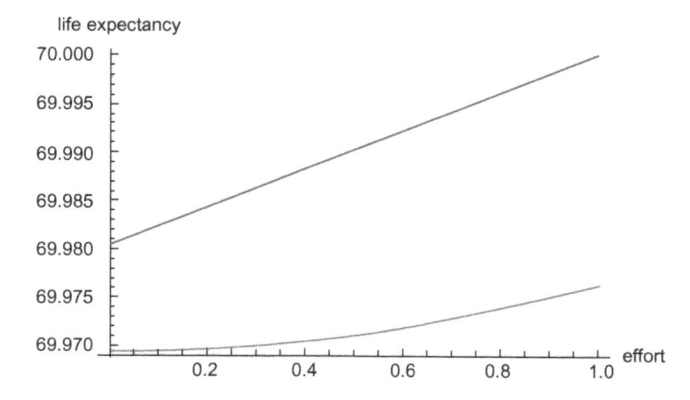

Fig. 1. Life Expectancies as a Function of Effort at the EOp Solution, Rich and Poor.

Let us compare this solution to the *utilitarian* solution, the expenditure schedule at which *life expectancy in the population as a whole* is maximized. The solution turns out to be $R^C = \$1,915$, $R^T = \$10,571$. Three times as much as spent on cancer as in the EOp solution! Fig. 2 graphs the life expectancy of the two types in the utilitarian solution (dashed lines) as well as the EOp solution (thick lines).

We see that the utilitarian solution narrows the life-expectancy differential between the types a good deal less than does the EOp solution. The difference between the life expectancies of the lowest effort people under the utilitarian policy is about three times what that difference is under the EOp policy. The EOp solution is more egalitarian, across the types, than the utilitarian solution — the utilitarian cares only about average life expectancy in aggregate, not on the distribution of life expectancy across types. The social life expectancy under the utilitarian policy is 69.9857 years and, under the EOp policy, 69.9717 years — not very different in this example.

It should be remarked that the distribution of life expectancies across types will be even more differentiated in a society with private financing of medical care than in the utilitarian solution. For our utilitarian solution is horizontally equitable — the same amount is expended on treating the occurrence of a disease in a person, regardless of his type. That is not the case in a private system, where more is spent on treatment of given diseases in rich people than in poor people. In the United States, the utilitarian solution would surely be more just than what we observe.

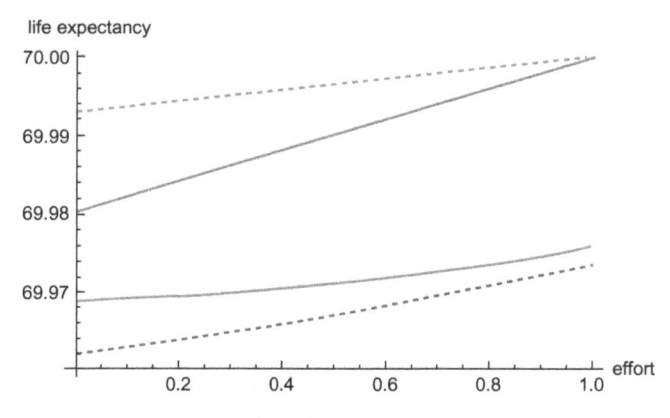

Fig. 2. Life Expectancies, Rich and Poor, EOp Policy (Thick Lines), Utilitarian Policy (Dashed Lines).

The reader may be surprised that the EOp solution does not narrow the type differential of life expectancies more than it does. This is because of our choice of instrument, and because of the limited amount of total resource. Note that an occurrence of a given disease in either type receives the same treatment. If we were willing to spend more on treating cancer in poor individuals than in rich individuals, then the life-expectancy differential between types could be narrowed much more. But this would violate horizontal equity. Thus, to repeat what I said earlier, horizontal equity and equality of opportunity are in conflict. Both are perhaps desirable, but for different reasons, and the compromise I have made in the above formulation is to find that policy that equalizes opportunities from among those that are horizontally equitable.

Before proceeding let us consider whether we want to include sex in the list of circumstances. In many parts of the world, this would be a good thing — it would serve to shift medical resources to women, who are receiving fewer of them than they should. It must be remarked, however, that in the advanced countries, this may not be the correct approach. In all advanced countries, life expectancy is greater for women than for men; if we included sex in the list of circumstances, the effect would be to shift medical resources from women to men, in an effort to equalize their life expectancies. This point has been discussed by Kekes (1997), in the context of a Rawlsian theory of health care. It is pertinent to note that WHO, in its definition of equity, specifically excepts differences in health status due to natural, biological variation, from the list of inequities in health. The issue of male–female life expectancy may well be a case in point. If having a shorter life is a biological attribute of maleness, normal and ubiquitous in the species, then trying to equalize life expectancies across the sexes is not necessary to equalize opportunities for health. On the other hand, if shorter male life spans are due to greater occupational stresses, and so on, then it would be appropriate to include sex as a component of circumstance.

THE BIGGER PICTURE

I have proposed a solution to what we could call the micro-allocation problem of health care resources. There are, however, at least three other problems that should be addressed in the larger picture:

(i) What fraction of GNP should be devoted to health care?

(ii) What preventive measures should be taken to *change* the distribution of lifestyle quality in the population?
(iii) What should be the incidence of costs of health care upon the population?

Note that, in the example above, the total amount of health resource was given (i), the distributions of lifestyle quality were taken as given (ii), and there was no discussion of how the health budget was financed (iii).

One could apply equal-opportunity principles to analyze the second question. Given the total budget for health, one could decide how to allocate it between prevention and treatment in order to equalize opportunities for life expectancy across types. In the example given in the last section, one would tend to spend more money on preventing TB than cancer, because TB was the greater risk for the worse-off (poor) type.

One could also apply principles of distributive justice to solve the third problem, but more decisions would be required. At one extreme, health care could be privately financed; at the other extreme, it could be state financed. In the latter case, one must decide what the tax incidence for the health care budget upon the population should be. To do so using principles of equal opportunity would require a decision of what condition among the population should be the predicate of the opportunity equalization – the equalisandum. In reality, countries rarely have the luxury of solving this problem from the normative viewpoint, as politics usually solves it. It is beyond the scope of this chapter to further pursue that question.

The first problem is also solved through political competition today.

CRITIQUE AND CONCLUSION

I have contrasted the equal-opportunity approach to equity in health care with the common view that horizontal equity is the necessary and sufficient condition for equity. I should mention that there is a series of welfarist views expounded in the literature, as well. A view of equity in health care is *welfarist* or *consequentialist* if it defines equity in terms of the maximization of some social welfare function, where the arguments of that function are the degrees of health of members of the population. Those degrees could be measured in QALYs or DALYs or life expectancies, for example. The key is that the justice of a situation is measured by knowing only the health statuses of members of the population. Authors who advocate theories of this kind include, from the recent literature, Bleichrodt (1997), Lindholm and Rosén (1998), and Sheldon and Smith (2000). Indeed the horizontal equity view, of van Doorslaer et al. (2000) is, as well, a consequentialist view, because "need" is a measure of health status. Under the EOp view, however, we cannot assess the equity of a situation without knowing, in addition to the health statuses of society's members, the *efforts* that they expended toward good health. Thus, the EOp view is non-welfarist and non-consequentialist.

A simple way of summarizing the contrast between a welfarist and non-welfarist theory is to consider the data that are needed to answer the question of how resources should be spent. A welfarist, in our case, need only know the distribution of illness in the population as a whole. The non-welfarist needs to know, in addition, the *circumstances* of individuals (in our examples, social class) and the distribution of lifestyle quality in each type.

Indeed, it is the non-consequentialist aspect of the EOp view that many will find objecitonable, for they will find the proposal to hold individuals responsible in part for their lifestyle qualities to be too libertarian. I think the objections are of three kinds:

(a) There is no such thing as autonomous volition; behaviors are all, in the end, induced by "circumstances" beyond a person's control;
(b) Lifestyle quality is not the person's responsibility because it, in particular, is induced by social influences;
(c) Health is too an important an input into well-being for which to hold individuals responsible. (Some say good health is a right.)

In responding to (a), one must distinguish between the *causal thesis*, on the one hand, which is the claim that all behaviors are, deep enough down, determined by chemical and neurological events that are beyond the control of the person, and, on the other hand, the view that persons can be held responsible for aspects of their behavior. Those who simultaneously hold both of these views are called, by philosophers, compatibilists. Perhaps most philosophers are compatibilists. Thomas Scanlon(1988), for example, subscribes to the causal thesis, but argues that is correct to hold a person responsible for an action if he undertook it after due deliberation. Clearly, every human society has embraced conceptions of responsibility. Thus, even if (a) is true, that is insufficient grounds (say the compatibilists) for denying that people should be held in some part responsible for their lifestyle quality.

Position (b) differs from (a) in admitting that volition can play a role in human action, but in denying that *in this particular case* it does. For instance, one can say that whether or not a person smokes is due to how vulnerable he is to pernicious advertising, or how insecure he felt as a teenager – both causes which may be properly considered "circumstances." The response to this position is that we attempt to capture the circumstances that make a person at risk of becoming a smoker in the definition of type. Of course, in any practical exercise, we cannot delineate all the circumstances, and hence some of the variation in smoking within a type – or the variation in other aspects of lifestyle quality – will be due to circumstances that we have ignored. But this objection then becomes a statistical one, not a principled one. For if the advocate of (b) does not endorse (a), then he must admit that some variation in lifestyle quality is due to volition.

Turning to (c), I do not see why health is in principle a more important an input into well-being than education or income. A person with a level of health *or* education *or* income below certain respective levels leads a miserable life. And a person who is partially healthy, or partially educated, or has an income somewhat above the subsistence level can lead a life that is better than miserable. This leads me to believe that there may be minimal levels of health *and* education *and* income that a society should guarantee to all its members, without consideration of questions of responsibility and volition. But once that level is achieved, *if* equality of opportunity is a legitimate idea in any sphere, then I do not see why it should apply less to health than to education or income.

If resources are not scarce, then there is no reason to decide how to allocate them among competing individuals according to an equal-opportunity ethic: we should simply give each person as much as he needs, independently of what the cause of that need is – whether it be low effort or disadvantaged circumstances. I endorse this view with respect to health, education, and income. But resources are scarce. If degree of responsibility can justify divergence from full equality in education or income, why not in health outcome? Health resources are scarce, I believe, in all countries today. Countries with public financing of health care face issues of how to ration it. What principles would those who hold view (b) advocate instead of EOp?

In defense of applying EOp to health care, let me quote from Margaret Whitehead (1992), who writes, in explaining the position of the WHO, that the results of "health-damaging behavior if freely chosen, such as participation in certain sports and pastimes," should not be considered to constitute an inequity. She further elaborates:

> Judgments on which situations are unfair will vary from place to place and from time to time, but one widely used criterion is the degree of *choice* involved. Where people have little or no choice of living and working conditions, the resulting health differences

are more likely to be considered unjust than those resulting from health risks that were chosen voluntarily. (Emphasis in original)

And, using our terminology, Whitehead states:

Equity is therefore concerned with creating equal *opportunities* for health, and with bringing health differentials down to the lowest possible level. (Emphasis in original)

Now Whitehead, and WHO, choose a relatively non-contentious example — namely, accidents incurred while playing dangerous sports — to illustrate the point about autonomous volition and responsibility. But exactly the same reasoning applies to harder examples, like smoking and lung cancer, to the extent that smoking is a choice.

(As I said earlier, some maintain that smoking is not a choice. But many of those who maintain that also advocate raising taxes on tobacco to reduce smoking. These two views are inconsistent. If raising taxes changes behavior, then is not smoking, at least to some extent, a choice? If one agrees that smoking has an aspect of choice, that does not imply that tobacco companies should not pay damages to sufferers from lung cancer, for they purposefully mislead consumers about the dangers of tobacco, and altered the nicotine content of cigarettes to make them more addictive. There is plenty of reason to hold tobacco companies responsible for damages even if smokers have some choice.)

Let me conclude by focusing upon the egalitarian facet of EOp, rather than on its inegalitarian one. As I showed in the third section, the equal-opportunity approach is *more egalitarian* across types (there, the rich and the poor) than the policy of *maximizing life expectancy in society as a whole*. To be precise, EOp is egalitarian in compensating individuals with disadvantageous circumstances for the low quality lifestyles that they have. It does this by treating the *distribution* of lifestyle quality within a type as an aspect of the type, and hence compensable at the bar of justice. Utilitarianism does not do this. Yet, EOp is less egalitarian than full maximin — what we might call the Rawlsian prescription — which would attempt to maximize the life expectancy of the worst-off individuals, regardless of lifestyle quality.

In countries with private systems of health care financing, a utilitarian policy would be a great improvement over the status quo. Life expectancy in the US population as a whole could be increased if resources were allocated in order to maximize (average) life expectancy across all citizens. Moreover, in the United States, the utilitarian policy would also probably be more *egalitarian* with respect to the life expectancies of the rich and the poor than present policy.[4] This, however, is not the most just policy in my view. I would sacrifice some amount of *average* life expectancy in a society in order to reduce further the *differences* in life expectancy between rich and poor, black and white, schooled and unschooled. The equal-opportunity view puts value on reducing *differences* in outcomes due to disadvantageous circumstances, such as being poor, black, or uneducated, while the utilitarian view does not; however, the EOp view holds that not all inequalities of outcome are inequitable, in contrast to the full maximin view.

Critics of the equal-opportunity approach, as I have formulated it, concentrate upon the fact that it takes effort into account, which they consider to be a quasi-libertarian move. What they overlook is that, perhaps, the *central* part of the EOp approach is that it attempts to equalize outcomes *across types,* and in that move, it is progressive in the normal sense of the word. In addition, as I have shown, and as is – I believe – generally the case (although my demonstration was limited here to an example), the EOp policy is considerably more egalitarian than the utilitarian policy, which dominates the field of health policy.

NOTES

1. Thus, I am assuming that the distribution of resources can affect the effort (lifestyle quality) that people expend. That effect could be very small or even nil. The case in which effort is adversely affected by the resource distribution is the problem of moral hazard.
2. In the formula that follows, I have assumed for the sake of simplicity that an individual contracts either no or one disease. Of course, the formula can be generalized to the case where we drop this assumption.
3. Other compromises than (2) are possible. For two others which I have occasionally used, see Roemer (2002).
4. This would be the case if switching some dollars from treatment of the rich to treatment of the poor would increase the total number of years of life in the population, which is arguably the case.

REFERENCES

Bleichrodt, H. (1997). Health utility indices and equity considerations. *Journal of Health Economics, 16,* 65–91.

Dworkin, R. (1981). What is equality? Part 2: Equality of resources. *Phil. & Public Affairs, 10,* 283–345.

Fleurbaey, M., & Schokkaert, E. (2009). Unfair inequalities in health and health care. *Journal of Health Economics, 28,* 73–90.

Fleurbaey, M., & Schokkaert, E. (2012). Equity in health and health care. In *Handbook of health economics* (Vol. 2, pp. 1004–1092). Amsterdam: North Holland.

Kekes, J. (1997). A question for egalitarians. *Ethics, 107*, 658–669.

Lindholm, L., & Rosén, M. (1998). On the meaurement of the nation's equity adjusted health. *Health Economics, 7*, 621–628.

O'Donnell, O., van Doorslaer, E., Wagstaff, A., & Lindelow, M. (2008). *Analyzing health equity using household survey data: A guide to techniques and their implementation.* Washington, DC: World Bank.

Rawls, J. (1971). *A theory of justice.* Cambridge MA: Harvard University Press.

Roemer, J. E. (1993). A pragmatic theory of responsibility for the egalitarian planner. *Philosophy and Public Affairs, 22*, 146–165.

Roemer, J. E. (1998). *Equality of opportunity.* Cambridge MA: Harvard University Press.

Roemer, J. E. (2002). Equality of opportunty: A progress report. *Social Choice and Welfare, 19*, 455–472.

Roemer, J. E. (2010). Equality: Its justification, nature, and domain. In W. Salverda, B. Nolan, & T. Smeeding (Eds.), *Oxford handbook on economic inequality.* Oxford University Press.

Roemer, J. E. (2012). On several approaches to equality of opportunity. *Economics & Philosophy, 28*, 165–200.

Scanlon, T. (1988). The significance of choice. In S. McMurrin (Ed.), *The tanner lectures on human values (Vol. 8)*, Salt Lake City, UT: University of Utah Press.

Sheldon, T., & Smith, P. C. (2000). Equity in the allocation of health care resources. *Health Economics, 9*, 571–574.

van Doorslaer, E., Wagstaff, A., van der Burg, H., Christiansen, T., De Graeve, D., Duchesne, I., ... Gross, L. (2000). Equity in the delivery of health care in Europe and the US. *Journal of Health Economics, 19*, 553–583.

Whitehead, M. (1992). The concepts and principles of equity and health. *International Journal of Health Services, 22*, 429–445.

APPENDIX

This appendix solves the EOp problem for the example of the third section. The notation below follows that or Roemer (1998).

We must first define the life-expectancy functions of the individuals in the two types. Converting from absolute efforts to centiles of effort, the probability that a rich person at centile π of his effort distribution contracts cancer is $1-2(\pi+.5)/3$; the probability that a poor person contracts cancer is $1-2\pi/3$; the probability that a poor person contracts TB is $1-\pi/3$; the probability that a poor person contracts both diseases is $(1-2\pi/3)(1-\pi/3)$. Thus, we can write the life expectancy of a rich person as:

$$L^R(\pi, x_c) = \frac{2}{3}(\pi+.5)70 + \left(1 - \frac{2}{3}(\pi+.5)\right)\left(60 + 10\frac{x_c - 1}{x_c + 1}\right)$$

The life expectancy of a poor person is:

$$L^P(\pi, x_c, x_t) = \frac{\pi}{3}\frac{2\pi}{3}70 + \frac{\pi}{3}\left(1 - \frac{2\pi}{3}\right)\left(60 + 10\frac{x_c - 1}{x_c + 1}\right)$$
$$+ \left(1 - \frac{\pi}{3}\right)\frac{2\pi}{3}\left(50 + 20\frac{.1x_t - 1}{.1x_t + 1}\right)$$
$$+ \left(1 - \frac{\pi}{3}\right)\left(1 - \frac{2\pi}{3}\right)\min\left[\left(50 + 20\frac{.1x_t - 1}{.1x_t + 1}\right), \left(60 + 10\frac{x_c - 1}{x_c + 1}\right)\right]$$

Letting f_c^R be the fraction of the Rich who contract cancer, p^R and p^P be the fraction of Rich and Poor in society, and R be the per capita health budget, the budget constraint is: $(p^R f_c^R + p^P f_c^P)x_c + p^P f_t^P x_t = R$.

We easily compute from the data the various fractions of types who contract diseases.

Our objective is to choose (x_c, x_t) to:

$$\text{Maximize} \int_0^1 \min[L^R(\pi, x_c), L^P(\pi, x_c, x_t)]d\pi$$

The utilitarian program is:

$$\text{Maximize} \int_0^1 (p^R L^R(\pi, x_c) + p^P L^P(\pi, x_c, x_t))d\pi$$

the solution is easily found by using *Mathematica*'s NMaximize program; the code can be supplied to readers upon request.

MEASURING HEALTH INEQUALITY IN THE CONTEXT OF COST-EFFECTIVENESS ANALYSIS

Miqdad Asaria, Susan Griffin and Richard Cookson

ABSTRACT

In this chapter we discuss the cost-effectiveness analysis (CEA) of public health interventions where there are combined, and potentially conflicting, objectives of increasing total population health and reducing unfair health inequalities in the population. Our focus is on identifying appropriate health inequality measures in this context to quantify the impacts of interventions on unfair health inequality and, where necessary, analyse equity-efficiency trade-offs between improving total population health and reducing unfair health inequality. We recognise that this requires a number of important social value judgements to be made, and so prefer measures that facilitate transparency about these social value judgements. We briefly summarise the literature on health inequality and health-related social welfare functions, and conclude that while valuable it is not entirely suitable for our purpose. We borrow instead from the wider literature on economic inequality, highlighting how this translates to a health setting, and identify appropriate measures for CEA. We conclude with a stylised example illustrating how we would apply a battery of dominance rules and social welfare indices to evaluate the health distributions associated with two hypothetical health interventions.

Keywords: Health inequalities; cost effectiveness; equity; public health; trade-off; social value judgements

JEL classification: I14

INTRODUCTION

Public health interventions often have dual objectives of improving population health and reducing unfair health inequalities. Cost-effectiveness analysis (CEA) is often used to evaluate such interventions, but typically only ranks interventions based on the first of these objectives. While quantitative analysis is occasionally conducted to explore the distribution of the reach or uptake of interventions, this is rarely worked through to understand the impact the interventions have on the final distribution of health.

We propose in this chapter that to evaluate interventions of this kind we must estimate and compare the expected population health distributions associated with the interventions considered. Social value judgements need to be made when comparing such distributions regarding the unfairness of health variation (as it is only unfair health variation that we aim to minimise) as well as the degree of aversion to inequality (to allow us to trade-off more overall health on average with more equal distributions of health). We draw on the general economic inequalities literature to identify methods that are meaningful in a health inequalities context and are transparent about the social value judgements that are imposed in evaluating distributions.

We have written the chapter with two audiences in mind: specialists in economic inequality who may not be familiar with methods of CEA, and specialists in CEA who may not be familiar with measures of economic inequality. We apologise to both audiences for reviewing material they are familiar with, but nevertheless hope that readers of both kinds will find something of interest in our attempt to combine ideas and methods from these two different literatures with a view to developing practical tools that can help inform important public policy decisions.

We start this chapter by briefly describing how CEA is used to evaluate health interventions and describe how this must be adapted to generate distributions of health outcomes and health opportunity costs. We review some principles underlying the quantification of economic inequality then briefly describe the methods from the health economics literature to evaluate distributions of health in terms of health inequality. We next describe the health economics literature on addressing inequality concerns in health distributions using health related social welfare functions (SWFs), before looking at the more general economic inequalities literature on SWFs. We conclude by presenting a stylised example to demonstrate how such methods could be used in the CEA of health interventions.

Using Cost-Effectiveness Analysis to Estimate Net Health Benefits

The role of CEA is to provide information to decision makers to help them identify which of a set of investment opportunities would provide the greatest payoff. We take as a starting point a societal decision making framework and describe a typical CEA conducted from a health sector perspective.[1] That is, we assume a fixed budget for the provision of health interventions, and that the interventions do not have important non-health benefits or impose costs outside the health sector. Health outcomes are quantified in terms of a single cardinal measure of health that reflects mortality and morbidity, for example a quality adjusted life year (QALY). This common measure of health can be applied to all evaluations, allowing comparisons to be made across a range of health conditions. The resources of interest, which determine the cost burden of the interventions, are simply those that fall on the budget constraint, that is resources within the health sector. A primary objective of the decision maker is assumed to be maximisation of expected population health gains, conventionally calculated as the sum total of expected individual discounted health gains, from available resources.

The health budget is assumed to be fully allocated, so introducing a new health intervention displaces some currently funded activity. Should one of the mutually exclusive options be found to offer an improvement in health but at a greater cost than the currently funded alternative, the potential improvement in health outcomes must be compared to the health lost as a result of discontinuing other currently funded activities by reallocating resources to fund the new intervention. The health gains forgone by displacing existing health interventions represent the opportunity cost of introducing the new intervention. If the health gains from the new intervention exceed this opportunity cost then it is regarded as cost-effective.

Identifying and evaluating displaced health service activity is not often undertaken. Instead an estimation of the shadow price of the budget constraint provides a threshold for assessing cost-effectiveness. This threshold represents an estimate of the impact of the displacement that would occur by diverting resources to the new intervention in terms of health forgone. When the amount of additional resources demanded by each intervention has only a marginal impact on existing services the cost-effectiveness threshold will not alter with each reallocation of resources, and a common estimate can be used within each budgetary period. This cost-effectiveness threshold can be used to describe the cost burden of interventions in terms of health, and these can be subtracted from the expected health gains attributed to an intervention in order to describe its net health benefit (Fig. 1).

With this approach cost-effectiveness analyses identify and characterise the eligible patient population for the intervention being evaluated, but the characteristics and health levels of non-recipients are left undetermined. Changes in health levels between the interventions being compared are typically calculated from the point at which the treatment decision is made, leaving health achieved up to that point unspecified. Furthermore, from the point of the treatment decision outcomes that do not differ according

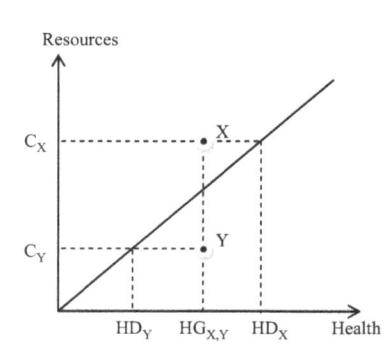

The slope of the diagonal line represents the amount of health that can be generated per unit of resources used to provide existing health interventions. Two new interventions (X and Y) are evaluated to determine whether they should be provided within the health sector.

Intervention X offers a health gain HG_X at a cost of C_X. Reducing provision of existing services to fund X would displace amount of health HD_X, resulting in a loss of health overall as $HG_X - HD_X < 0$

Intervention Y offers a health gain HG_Y at an additional cost of C_Y. Reducing provision of existing services to fund Y would displace amount of health HD_Y, resulting in a gain of health overall as $HG_Y - HD_Y > 0$

Fig. 1. Evaluating the Cost Effectiveness of New Health Interventions.

to the intervention received may also be left unspecified. So, interventions are evaluated by focusing on changes in health, without explicitly characterising the resulting levels of health.

EXTENDING COST-EFFECTIVENESS ANALYSIS TO ESTIMATE HEALTH DISTRIBUTIONS

In order to extend this analysis to allow us to evaluate health inequalities we first require information on the distribution of total health levels without the interventions. We augment this with estimates of the distributions of health changes to be produced by the interventions being compared to give the modelled health distributions resulting from the respective interventions. The distribution of changes in health attributed to an intervention is informed by the distribution of the health gains among recipients of the intervention, and the distribution of the opportunity costs among those who would have received the displaced activities. The key additional data requirements for this analysis are the distributions of:

1. total health levels without the intervention;
2. incidence or eligibility for the interventions being evaluated;
3. treatment effect in terms of health gains and resource use;
4. health opportunity cost;
5. equity relevant characteristics (e.g. income, ethnicity) to allow us to isolate unfair inequality.

It is important to note that because we are operating within the framework of CEA we assume that health is measured on a fixed cardinal scale such as quality adjusted life expectancy (QALE).

Evaluating Health Inequalities

The literature on measuring health inequality draws heavily from the literature on income inequalities. However, while there are many similarities between health and income there are also some important differences that should be considered, and the application and interpretation of income inequality measures to health inequality must be done in light of these differences between the two domains. Health and income both make vitally important contributions to individual wellbeing, and both are 'goods' in the sense that more is generally considered to be better. In addition, both can act as stores of future value ('capital') as well as current value ('consumption'). Income can be invested as well as spent on non-durable goods, and health is a form of human capital as well as a consumption good. Furthermore, both concepts can in principle be measured on fixed ratio scales that enable comparisons between all individuals. However, key differences include:

- Levels of income and wealth are defined as a current flow and a current stock respectively, whereas levels of health are often defined as a sum total of past, current and/or expected future flows (e.g. life expectancy)
- Income is unbounded while health has an upper bound
- Full equality of income between individuals is in principle achievable but some inequality in health between individuals is irremediable and incompensable
- Income has only instrumental value, whereas health has intrinsic value (e.g. the value of being alive, mentally alert, free of pain) as well as instrumental value (e.g. as a pre-requisite for undertaking household and employment tasks)
- Individual income is usually assumed to have diminishing marginal value, whereas any such assumption about individual health is controversial

With these differences in mind it is useful to examine some of the key properties of inequality measures as outlined below.

Weak principle of transfers/Pigou–Dalton transfer principle (Dalton, 1920)

In terms of income inequalities it is possible to remove income earned by one individual in the form of a tax and transfer it directly to another in the form of a benefit. In the context of health care it would not be possible to remove health gained by one individual and transfer it to another. Instead it is future expected health gains that can be transferred between individuals.

Scale independence versus translation independence

Scale independence focuses attention on concern for relative inequality between individuals, rather than the size or scale of absolute differences between individuals. While this is relatively uncontroversial when applied to changes in the scale used to measure health – analogous to nominal changes in income due to inflation – it is harder to justify when looking at real differences in health. For example, if everyone's life span doubles then a ten year absolute health gap will grow into a 20 year absolute health gap. It is not self-evident that any reasonable person must deem the new health distribution to be just as 'equal' or 'fair' as the old one.

Translation independence on the other hand focuses on concern for absolute inequality between individuals. This is perhaps a more attractive property in domains such as health where fixed upper bounds exist and ideas of diminishing marginal value do not necessarily hold.

A brief review of health inequality measures

The health inequalities literature can broadly be categorised into studies using univariate measures of health inequality, directly translated from the income inequalities domain, and studies using bivariate measures, measuring health inequality with respect to some socioeconomic variable.

The univariate literature makes use of tools such as the Lorenz curve and it associated Gini coefficient which characterises all variation in health (Le Grand, 1987). It has been argued that pure measures of health variation have limited ethical or policy interest: what generates public policy concern is systematic association between health and an equity relevant social variable such as income (Hausman, 2007).

This has led to the development of bivariate measures of socio-economic inequality in health such as the concentration curve and its associated concentration index — for more on these and other similar socio-economic inequality measures see Mackenbach and Kunst (1997) and Wagstaff, Paci, and van Doorslaer (1991). Concentration curves can be thought of as analogous to Lorenz curves with individuals ordered according to some other socio-economic variable apart from health, most commonly income. The concentration curve allows one to see how the distribution of health varies with a variable that is considered to be an unfair determinant of health. Where ranking by income and ranking by health coincide, the Lorenz curve and the concentration curve for a distribution will be identical. While these measures come closer to capturing what we are after — a characterisation of the unfair health inequalities in the health distribution — they only allow us to look at one unfair dimension at a time and typically limit us to looking at ordinal dimensions.

More sophisticated measures of health inequality have been proposed based on standardisation of health distributions, using regression techniques to directly or indirectly standardise health distributions for variation in health considered fair allowing only the unfair variation in health to be characterised (Fleurbaey & Schokkaert, 2009). The health distribution thus adjusted simultaneously captures unfair health inequality in all dimensions and can be evaluated using the standard univariate health inequality measures. This approach requires the decision maker to make explicit social value judgements about which dimensions of inequality are deemed fair and which unfair. The ability to simultaneously isolate and evaluate all dimensions of the unfair inequality and the explicitness of the social value judgements underpinning the adjustment process makes this approach most amenable to use in the CEA process.

Social Welfare Functions Combining Concern for Improving Health and Reducing Health Inequality

Once we have appropriately modelled our health distributions and measured the corresponding levels of total health and unfair health inequality, we need to combine these two objectives in order to rank the interventions. We can do this by means of SWFs. A health-related SWF can in principle be used to describe social welfare as a function of the health distribution, other things equal — that is setting aside non-health aspects of the social state. A health related SWF may yield either a partial or a complete ordering of health distributions, depending on the strength of the social value judgements it embodies.

Some key properties used when defining SWFs include that they can be individualistic, non-decreasing, symmetric, additive, concave, and have constant relative/absolute inequality aversion. For more details on these properties see Sen (1973) and Cowell (2011). We can use these properties to derive rules to help us determine which of two health distributions are socially preferable. The following rules are listed in order from least restrictive to most restrictive and allow us to determine a partial ordering of estimated health distributions A and B associated with two different health interventions that we are considering:

- *Rule 1 — Pareto dominance*: for any individualistic, increasing and additive SWF: distribution A is preferred to distribution B if every person in distribution A has more health than they do in distribution B.
- *Rule 2 — Re-ranked Pareto dominance*: for any individualistic, increasing, additive and *symmetric* SWF: distribution A is preferred to distribution B if every person in distribution A has more health than the equivalently ranked person in distribution B.

- *Rule 3a – Atkinson's theorem*: for any individualistic, increasing, additive, symmetric, and *strictly concave* SWF where the mean health in distributions A and B is the same: distribution A is preferred to distribution B if and only if the Lorenz curve for A lies wholly inside the Lorenz curve for B (Atkinson, 1970).
- *Rule 3b – Shorrocks' theorem*: for any individualistic, increasing, additive, symmetric, and strictly concave SWF and states A and B where the mean health in distributions A and B is not the same: distribution A is preferred to distribution B if the generalised Lorenz curve for A lies wholly inside the generalised Lorenz curve for B (Shorrocks, 1983).

By using these dominance rules we do not need to specify the exact nature of the SWF but can describe broad characteristics that encompass whole classes of SWFs, under any of which the welfare rankings of particular interventions would be the same. It is important to recognise that these rules cannot assess trade-offs between health inequality and total health: the rules would never rank a distribution with lower overall health higher than one with greater overall health. This does not mean that we always prefer the distribution with higher overall health, as there will be cases under Rule 3 where higher overall health combined with a higher level of inequality leaves us unable to rank distributions.

Social Welfare Indices

Where dominance rules do not apply, in order to obtain a complete ranking of health distributions we need more fully to describe the SWF. Adding a final assumption about the type and level of inequality aversion that our SWF entails, e.g. constant relative inequality aversion or constant absolute inequality aversion, allows us to construct a social welfare index (SWI). The key idea used in these SWF based indices is that if health is distributed unequally then, given that we have an aversion to inequality, more overall health would be required to produce the same social welfare than if health were distributed equally. Social welfare can be represented in these measures using a simple and convenient 'equally distributed equivalent' (EDE) health: the common level of health in a hypothetical equal distribution of health that has the same level of social welfare as the actual unequal distribution of health.

Atkinson SWI – Constant relative inequality aversion

The Atkinson SWI assumes constant relative inequality aversion and calculates the EDE health of a distribution based on the Atkinson inequality index:

$$h_{\text{ede}} = (1 - A_\varepsilon)\bar{h}$$

$$A_\varepsilon = 1 - \left[\frac{1}{n}\sum_{i=1}^{n}\left[\frac{h_i}{\bar{h}}\right]^{1-\varepsilon}\right]^{\frac{1}{1-\varepsilon}}$$

where the parameter ε, which can take any value from 0 to infinity, specifies the level of inequality aversion. The higher the ε, the further the index tilts towards concern for health improvement among less healthy individuals rather than more healthy individuals. A value of 0 represents a classic 'utilitarian' view that all that matters is sum total health and not inequality in the distribution of health. Whereas as the value approaches infinity the Atkinson index comes to represent the 'maximin' view that all that matters is improving the health of the least healthy individual, irrespective of the health of all other individuals.

Kolm SWI – Constant absolute inequality aversion

Like the Atkinson index the Kolm (1976a, 1976b) 'leftist' index is also based in the SWF framework but instead of constant relative risk aversion assumes constant absolute risk aversion. The Kolm SWI can be written as:

$$h_{\text{ede}} = \bar{h} - K_\alpha$$

$$K_\alpha = \left(\frac{1}{\alpha}\right)\log\left(\frac{1}{n}\sum_{i=1}^{n}e^{\alpha[\bar{h}-h_i]}\right)$$

where the parameter α specifies the level of inequality aversion.

Evaluating our fairness adjusted health distributions for their degree of unfair health inequality using the appropriately parameterised inequality measure and combining this with the estimated mean health for the unadjusted health distributions estimated for each of the interventions being compared gives us a measure of social welfare, the EDE level of health, that can be used to compare and rank the interventions. Further social value judgements need to be made about the appropriateness of relative versus absolute measures of inequality as well as about the degree of inequality aversion to use in these measures. These social value judgements are fully transparent in the evaluation process and should be provided by the decision maker. As with the fairness related social value judgements the sensitivity of conclusions of the analysis to these parameters should be explored.

Social welfare functions used in the health inequalities literature

The most commonly used SWF in the health inequalities literature is the iso-elastic form proposed by (Wagstaff, 1991) which in the simple case of two groups can be written as:

$$W = [\alpha h_a^{-r} + (1-\alpha) h_b^{-r}]^{-\frac{1}{r}}$$

where h_a and h_b are the respectively the health of group a and group b, α represents the relative weight attached to the health of the two groups (this parameter pivots the SWF around the 45 degree line of equal health) and the r parameter represents the degree of absolute inequality aversion (this parameter determines the degree of curvature of the SWF).

This SWF was empirically calibrated and used to calculate 'fair innings' equity weights by Alan Williams (1997). The α parameter is assumed to be 0.5 (i.e. groups have equal priority) across a range of inequality aversion values (values of r), these two parameters determine the shape of the SWF and an absolute EDE health of 70 QALYs (a fair innings) together with current health endowments determine the position of the SWF. The slope of the tangents to this calibrated SWF at the points describing the current health endowment give the equity weights for a particular value of r. These weights can then be utilised in a CEA to maximise weighted expected lifetime QALYs in a socially optimal manner.

This SWF has also been empirically calibrated by Dolan and Tsuchiya (2009) to estimate both individual responsibility as represented by α and inequality aversion as represented by r. Individual responsibility attempts to deal with equity relevant characteristics in an unadjusted health distribution to correct for fair differences in health and then any remaining unfair inequality is dealt with by the inequality aversion parameter.

These SWFs are useful in starting to think about how inequality aversion can be incorporated into CEA and in conceptually untangling fair and unfair inequalities — they are however not ideal for our purpose.

The equity weights derived from the fair inning construction need to be constantly updated as the distribution of health changes, while in the Dolan and Tsuchiya (2009) formulation the empirical values derived for the inequality aversion and responsibility parameters are notoriously difficult to uniquely identify and unpick. Given these limitations we prefer the two step process of fairness adjustment of our health distribution followed by the application of more conventional univariate social welfare indices.

STYLISED EXAMPLE

In this example we consider two health interventions A and B for which an extended CEA has been used to estimate the distributions of health – accounting for the baseline health distribution, the distribution of health gains, and the distribution of opportunity costs – associated with each of the health interventions. In this case we make the social value judgement that all inequality in the distribution should be regarded as unfair so no further adjustment is necessary. The resulting distributions of health are displayed in Fig. 2 in terms of health by population quintile, where the population is ordered from the least healthy to the healthiest with the quintiles showing the average level of health in each fifth of the population.

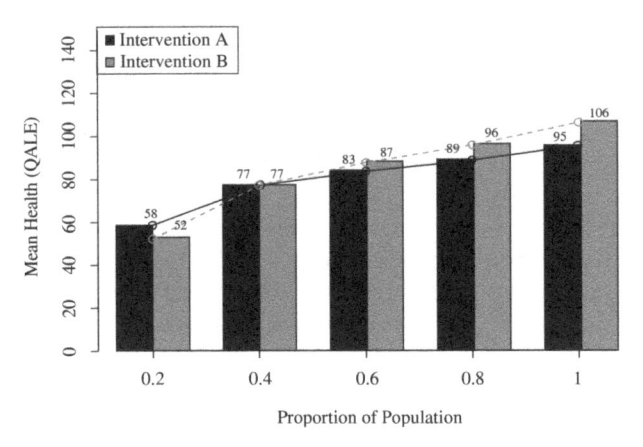

Fig. 2. Estimated Distributions of Health Associated with the Two Interventions Compared.

Mean health in the distribution resulting from intervention A is 80 QALYs per person, whereas in the distribution resulting from intervention B mean health is 84 QALYS per person. It is obvious from Fig. 2 that intervention A results in a more equal health distribution while intervention B results in a higher mean health. However, it is not obvious which distribution we should prefer.

Turning to our dominance rules, we can see that neither distribution Pareto dominates the other. Furthermore, Atkinson's theorem does not apply since the mean levels of health are different. This leaves us only to test for generalised Lorenz dominance, to see if Shorrocks' theorem can be used to unambiguously rank the distributions. The generalised Lorenz curves for the two estimated distributions are shown in Fig. 3 where we see that the curves cross hence Shorrocks theorem does not apply.

Given that we have been unable to rank the health distributions using our dominance rules, we next try to rank the distributions by calculating

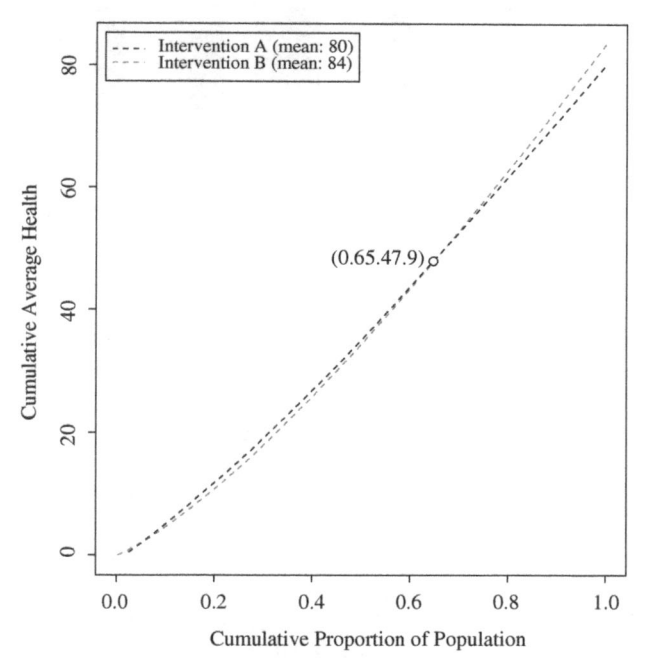

Fig. 3. Generalised Lorenz Curves for the Estimated Distributions of Health Associated with the Two Interventions Compared.

Table 1. Social Welfare Indices Comparing the Two Estimated Distributions of Health.

	Distribution A	Distribution B	Difference B−A
Mean Health	80.37	83.70	3.32
Atkinson SWI ($\varepsilon = 0.5$)	79.36	81.85	2.49
Atkinson SWI ($\varepsilon = 1.5$)	70.14	58.80	−11.34
Kolm SWI ($\alpha = 0.0125$)	78.89	80.84	1.95
Kolm SWI ($\alpha = 0.05$)	70.63	67.31	−3.32

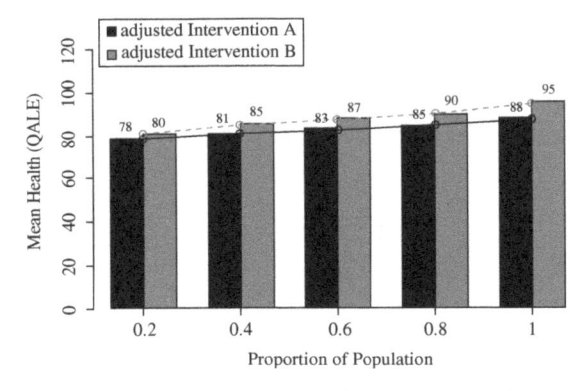

Fig. 4. Fairness Adjusted Distributions of Health Associated with the Two Interventions.

social welfare indices for the two distributions. Both Atkinson and Kolm indices have been calculated for the two distributions at both high and low levels of inequality aversion (see Table 1). We can see from the SWIs that at low levels of inequality aversion both the relative and absolute indices rank the more unequal but higher mean health distribution B above distribution A, however for both indices as inequality aversion increases the ranking is reversed.

We have seen that our ranking is sensitive to social welfare judgements around the type and level of inequality aversion expressed in our social welfare indices. We next explore the sensitivity of our rankings to alternative social welfare judgements about the fairness of the various dimensions of the health variation. Let us now assume that all health variation in the distribution is fair apart from the variation associated with income. We

Table 2. Social Welfare Indices Comparing the Adjusted Distributions of Health.

	Distribution A	Distribution B	Difference B−A
Mean Health	80.37	83.70	3.32
Atkinson SWI ($\varepsilon = 0.5$)	80.33	83.62	3.29
Atkinson SWI ($\varepsilon = 1.5$)	80.26	83.47	3.21
Kolm SWI ($\alpha = 0.0125$)	80.29	83.52	3.23
Kolm SWI ($\alpha = 0.05$)	80.06	82.99	2.93

standardise the health distributions for the other population characteristics captured in the analysis, in this case gender and ethnicity, leaving only variation associated with income as depicted in Fig. 4. We can now see from these adjusted distributions that not only is mean health higher in the distribution associated with intervention B but also that this distribution Pareto dominates the distribution associated with intervention A. Using these social value judgements regarding fairness, we could unambiguously rank intervention B as being better than intervention A. We can confirm this ranking by re-examining our SWIs for the adjusted distributions as shown in Table 2.

DISCUSSION

The income inequality literature provides a rich set of tools for incorporating distributional concerns into economic analysis. In this chapter we have explored ways in which these methods can be applied to assess the cost-effectiveness and health inequality impact of public health interventions.

We have seen that traditional bivariate health inequality analysis, while useful in exploring particular social determinants of health, can be limiting in the context of practical CEA when decision makers may be interested in multiple unfair sources of health inequality. Drawing from the wider literature on economic inequality, our methods allow us more fully to describe health distributions in a way that is more informative in the context of public health priority setting.

In order to use these methods we have seen that we need to extend CEA to calculate not only the distribution of health benefits due to particular interventions but also the distribution of health opportunity costs due to activities displaced by the interventions. We also need to calculate the baseline distribution of health levels and the final distribution of health levels associated with each intervention, in order set the health changes in context. Finally, we need to evaluate the final health distributions associated with each intervention by applying dominance rules and, where necessary, social welfare indices that explicitly characterise the nature of any trade-off between reducing health inequality and improving total population health.

We have also seen that a number of social value judgements need to be made to allow us to adjust and rank the resulting distributions of health. The methods we propose make these social value judgements transparent and expose them as parameters to the decision maker. Our stylised example has shown that it is essential to test the sensitivity of the rankings produced by such an analysis to alternate social value judgements to appreciate the robustness of any conclusions that can be drawn.

NOTE

1. This typifies the use of cost-effectiveness analysis by health technology assessment agencies such as NICE in the United Kingdom.

ACKNOWLEDGEMENT

The authors would like to thank Karl Claxton, Tony Culyer, Nigel Rice and Mark Sculpher for their role in steering the project work and to acknowledge the Public Health Research Consortium for funding the work.

REFERENCES

Atkinson, A. B. (1970). On the measurement of inequality. *Journal of economic theory*, *2*(3), 244–263.

Cowell, F. (2011). *Measuring inequality* (pp. 40–53). Oxford University Press.

Dalton, H. (1920). The measurement of the inequality of incomes. *The Economic Journal*, *30* (119), 348–361.

Dolan, P., & Tsuchiya, A. (2009). The social welfare function and individual responsibility: Some theoretical issues and empirical evidence. *Journal of health economics*, *28*(1), 210–220.

Fleurbaey, M., & Schokkaert, E. (2009). Unfair inequalities in health and health care. *Journal of health economics*, *28*(1), 73–90.

Hausman, D. (2007). What's wrong with health inequalities? *Journal of Political Philosophy*, *15*(1), 46–66.

Kolm, S.-C. (1976a). Unequal inequalities – I. *Journal of Economic Theory*, *12*(3), 416–442.

Kolm, S.-C. (1976b). Unequal inequalities – II. *Journal of Economic Theory*, *13*(1), 82–111. Elsevier.

Le Grand, J. (1987). Inequalities in health: Some international comparisons. *European economic review*, *31*, 182–191.

Mackenbach, J. P., & Kunst, A. E. (1997). Measuring the magnitude of socio-economic inequalities in health: An overview of available measures illustrated with two examples from Europe, *Social Science & Medicine 44*(6), 757–771. Elsevier.

Sen, A. K. (1973). *On economic inequality* (pp. 1–46). Norton.

Shorrocks, A. F. (1983). Ranking income distributions. *Economica*, *50*(197), 3.

Wagstaff, A. (1991). QALYs and the equity-efficiency trade-off. *Journal of Health Economics 10*(1), 21–41. Elsevier.

Wagstaff, A., Paci, P., & van Doorslaer, E. (1991). On the measurement of inequalities in health. *Social science & medicine (1982)*, *33*(5), 545–557.

Williams, A. (1997). Intergenerational equity: An exploration of the "fair innings" argument. *Health economics*, *6*(2), 117–132.